British Approved Names 2012

British Pharmacopoeia Commission

Published on the recommendation of the Commission on Human Medicines

Effective date: 1 January 2012

London: The Stationery Office

In respect of Great Britain:
THE DEPARTMENT OF HEALTH

In respect of Northern Ireland:
THE DEPARTMENT OF HEALTH, SOCIAL SERVICES AND PUBLIC
SAFETY

Published by The Stationery Office (TSO) on behalf of the Medicines and
Healthcare products Regulatory Agency (MHRA).

First published 2011

ISBN   9780113229222

Communications relating to British Approved Names should be sent to the
British Pharmacopoeia Commission Office:

MHRA
5th Floor, 151 Buckingham Palace Road
London SW1W 9SZ
Telephone: +00 44 (0)20 3080 6561
E-mail: bpcom@mhra.gsi.gov.uk
Website: www.mhra.gov.uk/pharmacopoeia

Contents

	Page
British Pharmacopoeia Commission	iv
British Pharmacopoeia Expert Advisory Group on Nomenclature	vi
Expert Advisory Groups, Panels of Experts and Working Parties	vii
Code of Practice	viii
Introduction	ix
General Notices	xi
Guiding Principles	xv
Key to Pronunciation	xviii
Symbols and Abbreviations	xviii
Guide to Using the BAN 2012	xx
British Approved Names	1
Names for Combinations of Substances	312
Names for Ions and Groups	314

Appendices

A. Structures	315
B. Guidelines for the Construction of Pharmaceutical Trademarks	321
C. Discontinued Substances and Products	322

Membership of the British Pharmacopoeia Commission

Membership of the British Pharmacopoeia Expert Advisory Group on Nomenclature

Chairman
Dr J K Aronson

Vice-Chairman
Dr L Tsang

Dr M Ahmed, Dr G Cook, Mr P W Golightly[1], Mr D Mehta, Dr G P Moss, Miss C Preston, Dr R Thorpe

[1] *Retired, 31 December 2010*

Corresponding members
Dr R G Balocco-Mattavelli, Dr A D McNaught, Mrs E M Cortés-Montjano, Dr J S Robertson

British Pharmacopoeia Commission Expert Advisory Group on Nomenclature Secretariat
Dr P Holland, Mr A Evans, Mrs L Schachar, Miss K Deats (July to September 2010)

Current members of staff of the Commission who have taken part in the production of this edition include:

Secretariat
Mrs M Vallender *(Editor-in-Chief)*
Mr S Young (*Head of Science*)
Mrs M Barrett, Ms J Francomb, Mr A Gibb, Dr R A Pask-Hughes, Mr J Pound, Dr F J Swanson, Mr R L Turner, Mr M Whaley

Administrative
Mrs M Cumberbatch, Mr B F Delahunty, Mr W Jeffries, Mrs D Myburgh, Miss J Paine

ISO 9001
FS 27268

Expert Advisory Groups, Panels of Experts and Working Parties

Members of Expert Advisory Groups, Panels of Experts and Working Parties are appointed by the British Pharmacopoeia Commission.

The duties of the members are as follows:

(a) To collaborate in the preparation and revision of Monographs, Appendices and Supplementary Chapters for inclusion in the British Pharmacopoeia and British Pharmacopoeia (Veterinary).

(b) To collaborate in the preparation and revision of Monographs, Methods and General Chapters of the European Pharmacopoeia.

(c) To collaborate in the preparation and revision of the list of names to be used as titles for monographs of the British Pharmacopoeia and British Pharmacopoeia (Veterinary).

Members of Expert Advisory Groups, Panels of Experts and Working Parties are usually appointed for a (renewable) term of 4 years.

Code of Practice

Members of the British Pharmacopoeia Commission and its supporting Expert Advisory Groups, Panels of Experts and Working Parties are required to comply with a Code of Practice on Declaration of Interests in the Pharmaceutical Industry.

British Pharmacopoeia Commission

Chairs and members of the British Pharmacopoeia Commission are required to make a full declaration of interests on appointment and annually thereafter. They must also inform the BP Secretariat promptly of any changes to these interests during the year. These interests are published in the Medicines Act 1968 Advisory Bodies Annual Reports which is available via the MHRA website (www.mhra.gov.uk).

Relevant interests must be declared at meetings and are recorded in the Minutes.

Expert Advisory Groups, Panels of Experts and Working Parties

Chairs and members are required to make a full declaration of interests on appointment and to update the Secretariat if these interests change during their term of office. A record is kept of those experts who have declared specific interests, but these are not published.

Relevant interests must be declared at meetings and are recorded in the Minutes.

Introduction

The British Approved Names book is a British Pharmacopoeia publication. This new edition consolidates the drug names in *British Approved Names 2007* with the 57 names published in its four Supplements. A further 70 recommended International Nonproprietary Names (rINNs) have been adopted as British Approved Names and are included in this edition. These new names have been included either because marketing authorisations have been granted for the UK or because they are the subjects of European Pharmacopoeia monographs that will be included in future editions of the British Pharmacopoeia. A list of names newly introduced in this edition follows this Introduction.

ADDITIONS

Spelling changes The spelling of the stem 'sulph' has been changed to 'sulf'. This change is harmonised with that adopted for European Pharmacopoeia monographs, which are reproduced in the British Pharmacopoeia for the convenience of the users.

Status Each entry is followed by the abbreviation '(BAN)', '(rINN)' or '(pINN)' to denote that the name is a British Approved Name, a recommended International Nonproprietary Name or a proposed International Nonproprietary Name.

GENERAL INFORMATION

Action and use statements The statements under 'Action and use' aim to achieve consistency within each class of substances based on the information available at the time of the publication of the name as a British Approved Name. The action and use statements in the British Approved Names book are intended only to provide information on the principal actions and/or clinical or pharmaceutical uses of the materials; they are not intended to be comprehensive. Action and use statements are intended neither to be binding on prescribers nor to limit their discretion on deciding which treatments best meet the clinical needs of a patient under their care.

Dual-labelling The two exceptions where dual-name entries are listed in this publication are adrenaline (rINN epinephrine) and noradrenaline (rINN norepinephrine). This is because the names Adrenaline and Noradrenaline are used in the titles of monographs in the European Pharmacopoeia; they are thus the official names in use in the 37 Member States that are party to the Convention on the Elaboration of a European Pharmacopoeia. They are also the names used for the associated formulation monographs published in the British Pharmacopoeia. For continuity, cross references of British Approved Names to the corresponding recommended International Nonproprietary Names have been retained in the main text of this edition.

BIOLOGICAL AND BIOTECHNOLOGICAL SUBSTANCES

There continues to be an increase in the number of new biological and biotechnological products being marketed for the treatment and/or the prevention of diseases. The World Health Organization has published a review of International Nonproprietary Names for biological and biotechnological substances (INN Working Document 05.179). This document provides extensive information on the established schemes for naming biological and biotechnological substances. Some fusion proteins have been named under the INN nomenclature system. Greek letters spelt in full have been used to denote differences in glycosylation patterns, as for instance epoetin alfa and epoetin beta. This document will be regularly updated to reflect new policies and include newly assigned International Nonproprietary Names.

Examples of stems for biological and biotechnological substances are included in the list of stems given under General Notices. The WHO Expert Committee on Biological Standardization (ECBS) is responsible for adopting names for natural human blood products or vaccines.

Appendix C: Discontinued Substances and Products The title of this Appendix has been changed from 'British Approved Names Assigned to Discontinued or Non-marketed Compounds' to 'British Approved Names Assigned to Discontinued Compounds or Compounds Not Actively Marketed'.

Cross-references to former BANs Cross-references within the specific BAN entries linking new BANs to former BANs have been removed. It is anticipated that stakeholders will now be familiar with the changes between the two types of names, for example alphaxalone and alfaxalone.

ACKNOWLEDGEMENTS

The British Pharmacopoeia Commission wishes to record its appreciation of the scientific advice received from members of its Expert Advisory Group on Nomenclature.

NEW ADDITIONS

Agomelatine
Alanine*
Alglucosidase Alfa
Aliskiren
Altizide *
Alvocidib
Amifampridine
Anidulafungin
Azacitidine
Bendamustine
Betacarotene*
Canakinumab
Cediranib
Ceftaroline Fosamil
Colesevelam
Corifollitropin Alfa
Dabigatran
Dabigatran Etexilate
Darunavir
Dasatinib
Degarelix
Denosumab
Desflurane*
Dronedarone
Eculizumab
Epinastine*
Eplerenone
Epoetin Delta
Epoetin Theta
Eptotermin Alfa
Erdosteine
Erlotinib

Eslicarbazepine
Etravirine
Everolimus
Febuxostat
Ferric Carboxymaltose
Fesoterodine
Fosaprepitant
Fulvestrant
Gadofosveset
Glutathione*
Golimumab
Histidine*
Icatibant
Indacaterol
Isoleucine*
Ivabradine
Lacosamide
Lapatinib
Laropiprant
Lasofoxifene
Leucine*
Linaprazan
Liraglutide
Lysine*
Maraviroc
Metacresol*
Methionine*
Methylnaltrexone Bromide
Micafungin
Mifamurtide
Mitotane
Natalizumab

Nepafenac
Nicotinamide*
Nicotine*
Nicotinic Acid*
Niflumic Acid*
Nifuroxazide*
Nilotinib
Ofatumumab
Olmesartan
Orbifloxacin*
Palifermin
Panitumumab
Paliperidone
Pazopanib
Pegvisomant
Perflutren
Phloroglucinol*
Plerixafor
Prasugrel
Proline*
Racecadotril*
Raltegravir
Ranolazine
Retapamulin
Rifaximin*
Rivaroxaban
Romiplostim
Rotigotine
Roxithromycin*
Sapropterin
Saxagliptin
Selamectin*

Serine*
Silodosin
Sitagliptin
Sorafenib
Sugammadex
Sulesomab
Sunitinib
Tafluprost
Taurine
Tedisamil
Teriparatide
Tetrabenazine
Threonine*
Ticagrelor
Tigecycline
Tocofersolan
Tolvaptan
Trabectedin
Trabedersen
Trehalose
Tryptophan*
Tyrosine*
Ulipristal
Ustekinumab
Valine*
Velaglucerase Alfa
Vernakalant
Vildagliptin
Vinflunine
Vinpocetine*
Yohimbine Hydrochloride

*associated with British or European Pharmacopoeia monographs

General Notices

British Approved Names

British Approved Names are devised or selected by the British Pharmacopoeia Commission and published by the Health Ministers on the recommendation of the Commission on Human Medicines to provide a list of names of substances or articles referred to in section 100 of the Medicines Act 1968. British Approved Names are short, distinctive names, selected in accordance with the Guiding Principles shown on page xv, for substances the systematic chemical or other scientific names of which are too complex for convenient general use.

If any substance or article to which section 99 of the Act applies becomes the subject of a monograph in the British Pharmacopoeia or other compendium prepared under that section, the British Approved Name (BAN) of that substance should be suitable for placing at the head of the monograph. The issue of a British Approved Name does not imply that the substance or article will necessarily be included in the British Pharmacopoeia or other compendium or that the British Pharmacopoeia Commission is prepared to recommend the use of the substance or article in medicine.

Recommended International Nonproprietary Names

Unless otherwise indicated each name defined in this edition is the English language form of a recommended International Nonproprietary Name (rINN). In cases where no rINN exists, '(BAN)' has been added to follow the name in question.

British Approved Names (Modified)

British Approved Names (Modified), developed as described below, have the same status under the Medicines Act 1968 as the British Approved Names from which they are derived.

Salts

When a British Approved Name exists for an acid or base, the name of the corresponding salt should be formed by following normal chemical practice whenever possible; the resulting name is known as a *British Approved Name (Modified)* (BANM).

When naming the salt of an acid, the British Approved Name of which ends in *-ic acid*, the name of the anion is formed by changing *-ic acid* to *-ate*; the name is preceded by that of the cation, eg *valproic acid* giving *sodium valproate*. When naming the salts of other acids, the name of the anion is identical to that of the acid and is followed by the name of the cation, eg *ampicillin* giving *ampicillin sodium*.

For the salts of bases, the British Approved Name of the base is followed by the conventional anion name, eg *acebutolol* giving *acebutolol hydrochloride*. The British Approved Name of a quaternary salt includes the anion and may be modified by substitution of a different anion.

Esters	Modification of names following normal chemical practice has traditionally been employed to provide names for esters of steroid alcohols, eg *betamethasone valerate*. In other esters, the names adopted will depend upon whether the biological activity lies in the acid or alcohol or within the ester itself and on whether a British Approved Name exists for the acid or alcohol in question. For further recommendations on the formation of *British Approved Names (Modified)*, see Guiding Principles B2 and B3.
Pronunciation	Each British Approved Name, except for abandoned or discontinued substances, is provided with an indication of its pronunciation given in phonetic terms defined below.
Nonproprietary Names of Medicinal Products	A nonproprietary name for a medicinal product combines the British Approved Name of the substance with an appropriate term drawn from the relevant general monograph of the British Pharmacopoeia and, in the majority of cases, are the Standard Terms as published by the Council of Europe (*see British Pharmacopoeia 2012, Supplementary Chapter II B*).
	Where the substance name is a British Approved Name (Modified), the modifying term is omitted from the nonproprietary name of the product unless two or more formulations containing different forms of the basic substance exist. In such cases the modifying term is retained. Tablets of trihexyphenidyl hydrochloride, for example, are known simply as *trihexyphenidyl tablets*, since tablets containing trihexyphenidyl are formulated only with its hydrochloride salt. Promethazine, however, is formulated as tablets containing either the hydrochloride or the teoclate salts and the nonproprietary names of the two tablet forms are *promethazine hydrochloride tablets* and *promethazine teoclate tablets* respectively.
Chemical Nomenclature	Each British Approved Name entry includes (1) a systematic chemical name in accordance with the rules of the International Union of Pure and Applied Chemistry (IUPAC) or (2) a brief statement of its biological, biotechnological or botanical source. However, certain concessions to long-established nomenclature terminology in pharmaceutical chemistry are made, details of which are in Appendix A.
	The structures of a large proportion of the substances defined contain one or more chiral centres. The British Approved Name applies only to the specific isomer or racemate indicated by the systematic chemical name, eg *laropiprant* refers only to the (*R*)-isomer of {4-[(4-chlorophenyl)methyl]-7-fluoro-5-(methanesulfonyl)-1,2,3,4-tetrahydrocyclopenta[*b*]indol-3-yl}acetic acid.

Structural Formulae and Stereochemistry	Many of the substances defined in this edition exist as a mixture of two enantiomeric forms or as a mixture of four or more stereoisomers. In drawing the structures of single chiral centre molecules, a convention has been adopted whereby the 'R' isomer has been drawn and the words *and enantiomer* added beneath. When a molecule contains two or more chiral centres, each centre has been identified by an asterisk (*) and the words, for example, *mixture of 4 stereoisomers* added beneath. In some cases a polychiral substance may exist as a pair of stereoisomers, in which case the site of epimerisation is marked with an asterisk (*) and the words *and epimer at C** added beneath.

To promote clarity in the structural formulae the following abbreviations are frequently used:

Me:	$-CH_3$	Bu^s:	$-CH(CH_3)CH_2CH_3$
Et:	$-CH_2CH_3$	Bu^n:	$-CH_2CH_2CH_2CH_3$
Pr^i:	$-CH(CH_3)_2$	Bu^t:	$-C(CH_3)_3$
Pr^n:	$-CH_2CH_2CH_3$	Ph:	$-C_6H_5$
Bu^i:	$-CH_2CH(CH_3)_2$	Ac:	$-COCH_3$

The 1-letter and 3-letter codes for amino acids that constitute peptide and polypeptide chains are defined in Appendix A, section F1.

Appendix A: Structures gives the basic skeletal structures of some important groups of substances of natural origin, such as steroids, cephalosporins, penicillins, prostaglandins and opioids, showing the numbering system and the normal stereochemistry of each group. It provides the systematic chemical names of certain key substances, such as penicillanic acid and prostanoic acid, which have been used as convenient and familiar bases of chemical definitions.

Chemical Abstracts Service Registry Numbers	Chemical Abstracts Service (CAS) Registry Numbers corresponding to almost every British Approved Name are included in order to provide easy access to scientific literature on any particular substance through computer databases. They are printed in *italic type*.

Code Designations	Laboratory codes are often used to identify substances during the period of investigation and may appear in the scientific literature. Such codes, when known, are included to facilitate relating a substance described by a code to a British Approved Name subsequently assigned to it.

Synonyms	Proposed International Nonproprietary Names and United States Adopted Names that differ significantly from the corresponding British Approved Name are included and are followed by '(pINN)' or '(USAN)', as appropriate. Additionally, other nonproprietary names by which a substance has previously been known may be given.

Discontinued Substances and Products   British Approved Names for substances that have either been abandoned during development or are no longer commercially available in the UK are listed in Appendix C.

Action and Use   The statements in italics indicating the action and/or use are based largely on information supplied by the manufacturer and are expressed, wherever possible, in terms of the therapeutic classification used in the *British National Formulary*. The British Pharmacopoeia Commission is not in a position to comment on the efficacy of the substance for the action claimed.

Guiding Principles

When a recommended International Nonproprietary Name is published, it will be adopted as the BAN. When no INN exists the guiding principles given below should be used in devising or selecting new BANs.

A1   Names should be distinctive in sound and spelling. They should not be inconveniently long and should not be liable to confusion with names in common use. They should be free from conflict with trade marks and from misleading connotations.

A2   The name for a substance belonging to a group of therapeutically or pharmacologically related substances should, when appropriate, show this relationship. Names that are likely to cause alarm or expectations in patients through an anatomical, physiological, pathological or therapeutic suggestion should be avoided.

These primary principles are implemented by using the following secondary principles:

B1   In devising the name of the first substance in a new pharmacological group, consideration should first be given to the opportunity for devising further suitable names for related substances belonging to the new group by means of a common stem *(see Guiding Principle B7)*.

B2   In devising names for therapeutically active acids, one-word names are preferred; their salts should be named without modifying the acid name, eg *fenoprofen* and *fenoprofen calcium*, *naproxen* and *naproxen sodium*.

B3   Names for substances that are used as salts should in general apply to the active base or the active acid. Names for different salts of the same active substance should differ only in respect of the name of the inactive counter-ion. For quaternary ammonium substances, the cation and anion should be named as separate components.

B4   The use of an isolated letter or number should be avoided; hyphenated construction is also undesirable, except in the prefix *co-* used in British Approved Names for combinations of substances (eg *co-trimoxazole*).

B5   To facilitate the acceptance and pronunciation of British Approved Names in other countries, *f* should normally be used instead of *ph*, *t* instead of *th*, *i* instead of *y;* names beginning with *h* and *k* should be avoided.

B6   Provided that the names suggested are in accordance with these principles, names proposed by the company discovering or first developing and marketing a pharmaceutical preparation should receive preferential consideration.

B7   Group relationships in British Approved Names *(see Guiding Principle A2)* should, if possible, be shown by using a common stem. The stem should only be used for substances of the appropriate group. The following list contains examples of stems for groups of substances. Where a stem is shown without any hyphens it may be used anywhere in the name.

A full list of common stems is contained in Document
WHO/EDM/QSM/2009 and addenda available from the the World Health Organization.

Examples:

-adol	analgesics
-antrone	antineoplastics; anthraquinone derivatives
-ast	antiasthmatics, antiallergics when not acting primarily as antihistamines
-astine	antihistamines, not otherwise classifiable
-azocine	narcotic antagonists/agonists related to 6,7-benzomorphan
-buzone	anti-inflammatory analgesics, phenylbutazone derivatives
-cain-	anti-arrhythmic agents with local anaesthetic activity
-caine	local anaesthetics
cef-	antibiotics, derivatives of cephalosporanic acid
-cillin	antibiotics, derivatives of 6-aminopenicillanic acid
-conazole	systemic antifungals of the miconazole group
-dipine	calcium channel blockers, nifedipine derivatives
-fylline	*N*-methylated xanthine derivatives
-floxacin	fluorine-containing antibacterial agents of the quinolone group
gest	steroids, progestogens
gli-	sulfonylurea hypoglycaemics
-grel	platelet aggregation inhibitors
io-	iodine-containing contrast media
-kalim	potassium channel openers
*-mab**	monoclonal antibodies:

	-amab	rat origin
	-emab	hamster origin
	-imab	primate origin
	-omab	mouse origin
	-umab	human origin
	-ximab	chimerical origin
	-zumab	humanized
	-xizumab	chimeric-humanized
substem for target class	*-b(a)-*	bacterial
	-c(i)-	cardiovascular
	-f(u)-	fungal
	-k(i)-	interleukin
	-l(i)-	immunomodulating
	-n(e)-	neural
	-s(o)-	bone
	-tox(a)-	toxin
	t(u)-	tumour
	-v(i)-	viral

-metacin	anti-inflammatory substances of the indometacin group
-mustine	antineoplastic, alkylating agents, (β-chloroethyl)amine derivative
-mycin	antibiotics produced by *Streptomyces* strains
-nercept	tumour necrosis factor antagonists
-nidazole	antiprotozoal substances of the metronidazole group
-olol	beta adrenoceptor antagonists
-oxacin	antibacterial agents of the quinolone group
-pafant	platelet-activating factor antagonists
-poetin	erythropoietin analogues
-pramine	substances of the imipramine group
-pride	substances of the sulpiride group
-pril	inhibitors of angiotensin-converting enzyme
-prilat	inhibitors of angiotensin-converting enzyme
-profen	anti-inflammatory substances of the ibuprofen group
prost	prostaglandins
-racetam	substances of the piracetam group
-relin	hypophyseal hormone release-stimulating peptides
-rsen	antisense oligonucleotide
-sartan	angiotensin II receptor antagonists, antihypertensive (non-petidic)
-setron	serotonin ($5HT_3$) receptor antagonists
-stat	enzyme inhibitors
-steine	substances of the acetylcysteine group
-tidine	histamine H_2 receptor antagonists of the cimetidine group
-triptan	serotonin ($5HT_{1D}$) receptor agonists
-vaptan	vasopressin receptor antagonists
-verine	spasmolytics with a papaverine-like action
-vastatin	HMG CoA reductase inhibitors
-vir	antivirals
-zotan	serotonin ($5HT_{1A}$) receptor agonists

* Products containing an immunoglobulin variable domain which binds to a defined target are named using the suffix *-mab*. In addition, both the name of the species on which the immunoglobulin sequence of the mAb is based and the target class are indicated in the name (for example, onartuzumab, *onar-tu-zumab*). For a fuller explanation see INN Working Document 05.179, updated December 2010.

Key to Pronunciation

1. Consonants are given their usual values with the following restrictions:

    g   as in *good*
    h   as in *hard* except in the following combinations:
                    ch as in *child*
                    th as in *thick*
    j   as in *job*

2. Vowels are given their usual short values with the exception of the following:

ä	as in *tame*	ö	as in *no*
á	as in *malt*	ôl	as in *hole*
ar	as in *far*	oo	as in *moon*
ë	as in *seen*	or	as in *more*
er	as in *herd*	ú	as in *full*
eer	as in *beer*	ü	as in *cute*
ï	as in *site*	ûr	as in *pure*
îr	as in *fire*		

3. Stressed syllables are in *italics*.

Symbols and Abbreviations

•	Subject of a monograph in the British or European Pharmacopoeias
♣	Subject of a monograph in the *British Pharmacopoeia (Veterinary)*
BAN	British Approved Name
BANM	British Approved Name (Modified)
BSI	British Standards Institution Common Name
ISO	International Standards Organization Common Name
pINN	Proposed International Nonproprietary Name
rINN	Recommended International Nonproprietary Name
INNM	International Nonproprietary Name (Modified)
USAN	United States Adopted Name

Guide to Using the BAN 2012

Systematic chemical name(s)

Subject of a British or European Pharmacopoeia monograph

● **Amikacin** (rINN) a·mi·*kä*·sin
6-*O*-(3-Amino-3-deoxy-α-D-glucopyranosyl)-4-*O*-(6-amino-6-deoxy-α-D-glucopyranosyl)-*N*¹-[(2*S*)-4-amino-2-hydroxybutyryl]-2-deoxy-D-streptamine; $C_{22}H_{43}N_5O_{13}$; *37517-28-5*

   ● **Amikacin Sulfate** *39831-55-5*
   Aminoglycoside antibacterial

Molecular formula

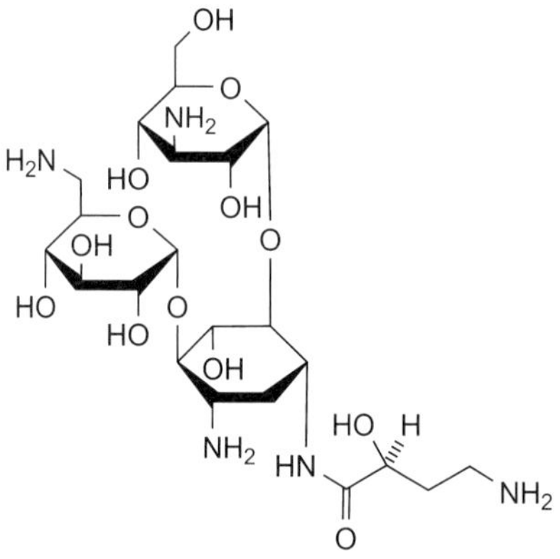

Both names are used for labelling of products in the UK

Modified BAN (BANM)

● **Adrenaline/Epinephrine** (BAN/rINN) a·*dre*·na·lën/e·pi·*ne*·frën
(*R*)-1-(3,4-Dihydroxyphenyl)-2-methylaminoethanol; $C_9H_{13}NO_3$; *51-43-4*

   ● **Adrenaline Acid Tartrate/Epinephrine Acid Tartrate**
   epinephrine bitartrate (USP); *51-42-3*
   Adrenoceptor agonist

Modified INN (rINNM)

Graphic formula

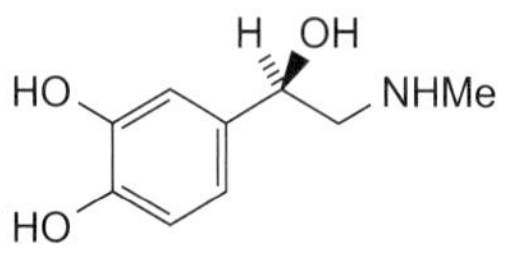

Apomorphine (BAN) ä·pö·*mor*·fën
6aβ-Aporphine-10,11-diol; $C_{17}H_{17}NO_2$; *58-00-4*
● **Apomorphine Hydrochloride**

314-19-2 (anhydrous); *41372-20-7 (hemihydrate)*
Dopamine receptor agonist; treatment of Parkinson's disease

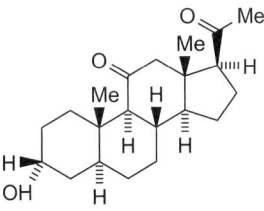

♣ **Alfaxalone** (rINN) al·*faks*·a·lön
3α-Hydroxy-5α-pregnane-11,20-dione; $C_{21}H_{32}O_3$; *23930-19-0*
Intravenous general anaesthetic (veterinary)

Alletorphine see Appendix C

Alphaxalone *see Alfaxolone*

British Approved Names

Abacavir (rINN) a·*ba*·ka·veer

{(1*S*,4*R*)-4-[2-Amino-6-(cyclopropylamino)-9*H*-purin-9-yl]cyclopent-2-enyl}methanol; $C_{14}H_{18}N_6O$; *168146-84-7*; 1592U89

Abacavir Sulfate

Nucleoside reverse transcriptase inhibitor; antiviral (HIV)

Abafungin (rINN) a·ba·*fun*·gin

Hexahydropyrimidin-2-ylidene{4-[2-(2,4-xylyloxy)phenyl]-1,3-thiazol-2-yl}amine; $C_{21}H_{22}N_4OS$; *129639-79-8*; Bay w 6341

Antifungal

Abanoquil (rINN) a·*ba*·nö·kwil

6,7-Dimethoxy-2-(1,2,3,4-tetrahydro-6,7-dimethoxyisoquinolin-2-yl)quinolin-4-ylamine; $C_{22}H_{25}N_3O_4$; *90402-40-7*

Abanoquil Mesilate *118931-00-3*; UK-52,046-27

Alpha₁-adrenoceptor antagonist

Abatacept (rINN) a·*ba*·tá·sept

1-25-Oncostatin M (human precursor) fusion protein with CTLA-4 (antigen) (human) fusion protein with immunoglobulin G1 (human heavy chain fragment), bimolecular (146→146')-disulfide; $C_{1875}H_{2945}O_{577}S_{19}$ (reduced protein); *332348-12-6*

Human tumour necrosis factor receptor

MGVLLTQRTL	LSLVLALLFP	SMASMAMHVA
QPAVVLASSR	GIASFVCEYA	SPGKATEVRV
TVLRQADSQV	TEVCAATYMM	GNELTFLDDS
ICTGTSSGNQ	VNLTIQGLRA*	MDTGLYICKV
ELMYPPPYYL	GIGNGTQIYV*	IDPEPCPDSD
QEPKSSDKTH	TSPPSPAPEL	LGGSSVFLFP
PKPKDTLMIS	RTPEVTCVVV	DVSHEDPEVK
FNWYVDGVEV	HNAKTKPREE	QYNSTYRVVS*
VLTVLHQDWL	NGKEYKCKVS	NKALPAPIEK
TISKAKGQPR	EPQVYTLPPS	RDELTKNQVS
LTCLVKGFYP	SDIAVEWESN	GQPENNYKTT
PPVLDSDGSF	FLYSKLTVDK	SRWQQGNVFS
CSVMHEALHN	HYTQKSLSLS	PGK

2

* glycosylation site

Abciximab (rINN) ab·*siks*·i·mab

Immunoglobulin G (human-mouse monoclonal c7E3 clone p7E3V$_H$hC$_g$4 Fab fragment anti-human platelet glycoprotein IIb/IIIa complex), disulfide with human-mouse monoclonal c7E3 clone p7E3V$_k$hC$_k$ light chain; *143653-53-6*; c7E3

Monoclonal antibody (platelet glycoprotein IIb/IIIa receptors); antithrombotic

Abiraterone (rINN) a·bi·*ra*·te·rön

17-(3-Pyridyl)androsta-5,16-dien-3β-ol; $C_{24}H_{31}NO$; *154229-19-3*; CB 7598

Abiraterone Acetate CB 7630

Inhibitor of the 17-hydroxylase/C17-20 lyase enzyme complex; treatment of prostate carcinoma

Acadesine (rINN) a·*ka*·de·sën

5-Amino-1-(β-D-ribofuranosyl)imidazole-4-carboxamide; $C_9H_{14}N_4O_5$; *2627-69-2*; GP-1-110-0

Purine nucleoside analogue; inhibitor of platelet aggregation

Acamprosate (rINN) a·*kam*·prö·sät
3-Acetamidopropane-1-sulfonic acid; $C_5H_{11}NO_4S$; *77337-76-9*
● **Acamprosate Calcium**
Treatment of alcoholism

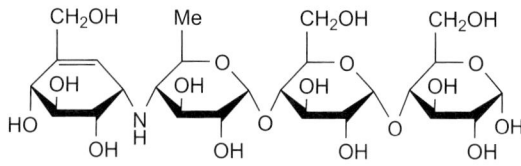

● **Acarbose** (rINN) *a*·kar·bös
O-{4-Amino-4,6-dideoxy-*N*-[(1*S*)-(1,4,6/5)-4,5,6-trihydroxy-3-hydroxymethylcyclohex-2-enyl]-α-D-glucopyranosyl}(1→4)-*O*-α-D-glucopyranosyl-(1→4)-D-glucopyranose; $C_{25}H_{43}NO_{18}$; *56180-94-0*
Alpha-glucosidase inhibitor; treatment of diabetes mellitus

and enantiomer

Acebutolol (rINN) a·së·*bü*·to·lol
(2*RS*)-3′-Acetyl-4′-(2-hydroxy-3-isopropylaminopropoxy)-butyranilide; $C_{18}H_{28}N_2O_4$; *37517-30-9*
● **Acebutolol Hydrochloride** *34381-68-5*
Beta-adrenoceptor antagonist

and enantiomer

● **Aceclofenac** (rINN) a·së·*klö*·fe·nak
[2-(2,6-Dichloroanilino)phenyl]acetoxyacetic acid; $C_{16}H_{13}Cl_2NO_4$; *89796-99-6*
Cyclo-oxygenase inhibitor; analgesic; anti-inflammatory

Acedapsone (rINN) a·së·*dap*·sön
Bis(4-acetamidophenyl)sulfone; $C_{16}H_{16}N_2O_4S$; *77-46-3*; CI 556
Folic acid synthetase inhibitor; treatment of leprosy

Acefluranol (rINN) a·së·*flûr*·ra·nol
(1) (1*RS*,2*SR*)-4,4′-Diacetoxy-5,5′-difluoro-(1-ethyl-2-methylethylene)di-*m*-phenylene diacetate; (2) (α*RS*,α′*SR*)-α-Ethyl-5,5′-difluoro-α′-methylbibenzyl-3,3′,4,4′-tetrayl tetra-acetate; $C_{25}H_{26}F_2O_8$; *80595-73-9*; BX 591
Antioestrogen

Acefylline Piperazine (rINN) a·*si*·fi·lën pi·*pe*·ra·zën
Piperazine bis(theophyllin-7-ylacetate); $(C_9H_{10}N_4O_4)_2$·$C_4H_{10}N_2$; *18428-63-2*
Non-selective phosphodiesterase inhibitor; treatment of reversible airways obstruction

● **Acemetacin** (rINN) a·së·*me*·ta·sin
O-(1-*p*-Chlorobenzoyl-5-methoxy-2-methylindol-3ylacetyl)¬glycollic acid; $C_{21}H_{18}ClNO_6$; *53164-05-9*
Cyclo-oxygenase inhibitor; analgesic; anti-inflammatory

● **Acenocoumarol** (rINN) a·së·nö·*koo*·ma·rol
(*RS*)-4-Hydroxy-3-(1-*p*-nitrophenyl-3-oxobutyl)coumarin; $C_{19}H_{15}NO_6$; *152-72-7*
Vitamin K epoxide reductase inhibitor; oral anticoagulant

and enantiomer

Acepifylline *see Acefylline Piperazine*

Acepromazine (rINN) a·së·*prö*·ma·zën
10-(3-Dimethylaminopropyl)phenothiazin-2-yl methyl ketone; $C_{19}H_{22}N_2OS$; *61-00-7*
✤ **Acepromazine Maleate** *3598-37-6*
Dopamine receptor antagonist; neuroleptic (veterinary)

The symbol '¬' in systematic chemical names signifies line continuation

Acesulfame (rINN) a·së·*sul*·fäm

6-Methyl-1,2,3-oxathiazin-4(3*H*)-one 2,2-dioxide; $C_4H_5NO_4S$; *33665-90-6*
- **Acesulfame Potassium** HOE 095K; H73 3293
Sweetening agent

Acetarsol (rINN) see Appendix C

- **Acetazolamide** (rINN) a·së·ta·*zo*·la·mïd

N-(5-Sulfamoyl-1,3,4-thiadiazol-2-yl)acetamide; $C_4H_6N_4O_3S_2$; *59-66-5*
Carbonic anhydrase inhibitor; diuretic; treatment of glaucoma, ocular hypertension, mountain sickness

Acetohexamide (rINN) a·së·tö·*heks*·a·mïd

1-(4-Acetylphenylsulfonyl)-3-cyclohexylurea; $C_{15}H_{20}N_2O_4S$; *968-81-0*
Inhibition of ATP-dependent potassium channels (sulfonylurea); treatment of diabetes mellitus

Acetomenaphthone (rINN) a·së·tö·me·*naf*·thön

2-Methyl-1,4-naphthylene diacetate; $C_{15}H_{14}O_4$; *573-20-6*
Vitamin K analogue

Acetorphine (rINN) see Appendix C

- **Acetylcholine Chloride** (rINN) a·së·tïl·*kö*·lën

2-Acetoxyethyltrimethylammonium chloride; $C_7H_{16}ClNO_2$; *60-31-1*
Cholinoceptor agonist

- **Acetylcysteine** (rINN) a·së·tïl·*sis*·tän

N-Acetyl-L-cysteine; $C_5H_9NO_3S$; *616-91-1*
Sulfydryl donor; antidote to paracetamol poisoning; mucolytic

Acetylmethadol (rINN) a·së·tïl·*me*·tha·dol

4-Dimethylamino-1-ethyl-2,2-diphenylpentyl acetate; $C_{23}H_{31}NO_2$; *509-74-0*
Opioid receptor agonist; analgesic

mixture of stereoisomers

Acexamic Acid (rINN) a·seks·*a*·mik *a*·sid

6-Acetamidohexanoic acid; $C_8H_{15}NO_3$; *57-08-9*
- **Zinc Acexamate** *70020-71-2*
Antifibrinolytic

- **Aciclovir** (rINN) ä·*sï*·klö·veer

(1) 2-Amino-9-(2-hydroxyethoxymethyl)-9*H*-purin-6(1*H*)-one;
(2) 9-(2-Hydroxyethoxymethyl)guanine; acyclovir; $C_8H_{11}N_5O_3$; *59277-89-3*
Purine nucleoside analogue; antiviral (herpesviruses)

Acinitrazole *see Aminitrozole*

- **Acipimox** (rINN) ä·*sï*·pi·moks

5-Methylpyrazine-2-carboxylic acid 4-oxide; $C_6H_6N_2O_3$; *51037-30-0*
Lipid-regulating drug

- **Acitretin** (rINN) ä·si·*tre*·tin

(1) (2*E*,4*E*,6*E*,8*E*)-9-(4-Methoxy-2,3,6-trimethylphenyl)-3,7-dimethylnona-2,4,6,8-tetraenoic acid; (2) 3-Methoxy-15-ϕ-caroten-15-oic acid; $C_{21}H_{26}O_3$; *55079-83-9*
Vitamin A analogue (retinoid); treatment of psoriasis, ichthyosis, Darier's disease

Aclarubicin (rINN) a·kla·*roo*·bi·sin
Methyl (1*R*,2*R*,4*S*)-4-(*O*-{2,6-dideoxy-4-*O*-[(2*R*,6*S*)-tetrahydro-6-methyl-5-oxopyran-2-yl}-α-L-*lyxo*-hexopyranosyl}(1→4)-2,3,6-trideoxy-3-dimethylamino-L-*lyxo*-hexopyranosyloxy)-2-ethyl-1,2,3,4,6,11-hexahydro-2,5,7-trihydroxy-6,11-dioxonaphthacene-1-carboxylate; C$_{42}$H$_{53}$NO$_{15}$; *57576-44-0*
Aclarubicin Hydrochloride
Cytotoxic; anthracycline antibacterial

Aclatonium Napadisilate (rINN) ak·la·*tö*·në·um na·pa·*di*·si·lät
Bis[2-(*O*-acetyllactoyloxy)ethyltrimethylammonium naphthalene-1,5-disulfonate; C$_{30}$H$_{46}$N$_2$O$_{14}$S$_2$; *55077-30-0*; SKF 100916-J
Cholinoceptor agonist

Acolbifene (rINN) a·*kol*·bi·fën
(2*S*)-3-(4-Hydroxyphenyl)-4-methyl-2-{4-[2-(piperidin-1-yl)ethoxy]phenyl}-2*H*-1-benzopyran-7-ol; C$_{29}$H$_{31}$NO$_4$; *182167-02-8*
Selective oestrogen receptor modulator

Acrivastine (rINN) a·kri·*vas*·tën
(*E*)-3-{6-[(*E*)-3-Pyrrolidin-1-yl-1-*p*-tolylprop-1-enyl]-2-pyridyl}acrylic acid; C$_{22}$H$_{24}$N$_2$O$_2$; *87848-99-5*
Histamine H$_1$ receptor antagonist; antihistamine

Acrosoxacin *see Rosoxacin*

Actaplanin (rINN) see Appendix C

Actinomycin (BAN) ak·ti·nö·*mī*·sin
Antimicrobial chromopeptolides with antitumour activity produced by *Streptomyces antibioticus* and *Streptomyces chrysomallus*; cactinomycin is actinomycin C; *8052-16-2*; dactinomycin is actinomycin D; *50-76-0*
Cytotoxic antibacterial

Activated Prothrombin Complex (BAN)
A preparation from human plasma containing factor VIII inhibitor by-passing activity
Activated prothrombin complex

Adalimumab (rINN) a·da·*li*·mü·mab
Immunoglobulin G 1 (human monoclonal D2E7 heavy chain anti-human tumour necrosis factor), disulfide with human monoclonal D2E7κ-chain, dimer
Immunomodulator

Adapalene (rINN) a·*da*·pa·lën
(1) 6-[4-Methoxy-3-(tricyclo[3.3.1.1^{3,7}]dec-1-yl)phenyl-2-naphthoic acid; (2) 6-[3-(1-Adamantyl)-4-methoxyphenyl]-2-naphthoic acid; C$_{28}$H$_{28}$O$_3$; *106685-40-9*
Vitamin A analogue (retinoid); treatment of acne

Adefovir (rINN) a·*de*·fö·veer
[2-(6-Amino-9*H*-purin-9-yl)ethoxymethyl]phosphonic acid; C$_8$H$_{12}$N$_5$O$_4$P; *106941-25-7*
Adefovir Dipivoxil *142340-99-6*
Nucleotide viral polymerase inhibitor; antiviral (hepatitis B)

● **Adenosine** (BAN) a·*den*·ö·sën
(*R*)-1-(6-Amino-9*H*-purin-9-yl)-1-deoxy-D-ribofuranose;
C$_{10}$H$_{13}$N$_5$O$_4$; *58-61-7*
Antiarrhythmic

Adenosine Phosphate (rINN) see Appendix C

Adicillin (rINN) see Appendix C

Adinazolam (rINN) a·di·*nä*·zö·lam
8-Chloro-6-phenyl-4*H*-[1,2,4]triazolo[4,3-][1,4]benzodiazepin-
1-ylmethyldimethylamine; C$_{19}$H$_{18}$ClN$_5$; *37115-32-5*; U-41123
Adinazolam Mesilate *57938-82-6*; U-41123F
Benzodiazepine

Adipiodone (iodipamide) a·di·*pï*·ö·dön
3,3′-Adipoyldiaminobis(2,4,6-tri-iodobenzoic acid);
C$_{20}$H$_{14}$I$_6$N$_2$O$_6$; *606-17-7*
Adipiodone Meglumine (rINN) *3521-84-4*
Iodinated contrast medium

● **Adrenaline/Epinephrine** (rINN) a·*dre*·na·lën/e·pi·*ne*·frën
(*R*)-1-(3,4-Dihydroxyphenyl)-2-methylaminoethanol;
C$_9$H$_{13}$NO$_3$; *51-43-4*
  ● **Adrenaline Acid Tartrate/Epinephrine Acid Tartrate**
  epinephrine bitartrate (USAN); *51-42-3*
Adrenoceptor agonist

Agalsidase Alfa (rINN) a·*gal*·si·däs al·fa
Human α-galactosidase isoenzyme A, isolated from human cell
line, clone RAG 001 glycoform α; *104138-64-9*

agalsidase alfa has the following amino acid sequence:

LDNGLARTPT	MGWLHWERFM	CNLDCQEEPD
SCISEKLFME	MAELMVSEGW	KDAGYEYCLI
DDCWMAPQRD	SEGRLQADPQ	RFPHGIRQLA
NYVHSKGLKL	GIYADVGN*KT	CAGFPGSFGY
YDIDAQTFAD	WGVDLLKFDG	CYCDSLENLA
DGYKHMSLAL	*NRTGRSIVYS	CEWPLYMWPF
QKP*NYTEIRQ	YCNHWRNFAD	IDDSWKSIKS
ILDWTSFNQE	RIVDVAGPGG	WNDPDMLVIG
NFGLSWNQQV	TQMALWAIMA	APLFMSNDLR
HISPQAKALL	QDKDVIAINQ	DPLGKQGYQL
RQGDNFEVWE	RPLSGLAWAV	AMINRQEIGG
PRSYTIAVAS	LGKGVACNPA	CFITQLLPVK
RKLGFYEWTS	RLRSHINPTG	TVLLQLENTM
QMSLKDLL		

*glycosylation site (asparagine)

Agomelatine (rINN) a·gö·mel·á·tën
N-[2-(7-Methoxynaphthalen-1-yl)ethyl]acetamide;
C$_{15}$H$_{17}$NO$_2$; *138112-76-2*;
*Melatonin receptor agonist; selective 5HT$_{2c}$ antagonist;
antidepressant*

Aklomide (rINN) ak·lö·mïd
2-Chloro-4-nitrobenzamide; C$_7$H$_5$ClN$_2$O$_3$; *3011-89-0*
Treatment of coccidiosis (veterinary)

Alafosfalin (rINN) a·la·*fos*·fa·lin
(1*R*)-L-(l-Alaninamido)ethylphosphonic acid; C$_5$H$_{13}$N$_2$O$_4$P;
60668-24-8; Ro 03-7008
Phosphonopeptide antibacterial

● **Alanine** (rINN) *al*·an·ïn
L-Alanine; (*S*)-2-Aminopropanoic acid; C$_3$H$_7$NO$_2$; *56-41-7*;
Amino acid

● **Albendazole** (rINN) al·*ben*·da·zôl

Methyl 5-propylthio-1*H*-benzimidazol-2-ylcarbamate; $C_{12}H_{15}N_3O_2S$; *54965-21-8*
Benzimidazole antihelminthic (veterinary)

Albendazole Oxide (rINN)

Methyl 5-(propylsulfinyl)benzimidazol-2-ylcarbamate; albendazole sulfoxide; $C_{12}H_{15}N_3O_3S$; *54029-12-8*
Benzimidazole antihelminthic (veterinary)

Alclofenac (rINN) al·*klö*·fe·nak

(4-Allyloxy-3-chlorophenyl)acetic acid; $C_{11}H_{11}ClO_3$; *22131-79-9*
Cyclo-oxygenase inhibitor; analgesic; anti-inflammatory

Alclometasone (rINN) al·klö·*me*·ta·sön

7α-Chloro-11β,17α,21-trihydroxy-16α-methylpregna-1,4-diene-3,20-dione; $C_{28}H_{37}ClO_7$; *67452-97-5*
Alclometasone Dipropionate *66734-13-2*
Glucocorticoid (veterinary)

● **Alcuronium Chloride** (rINN) al·kûr·*rö*·në·um

N,N-Diallyldinortoxiferinium dichloride; $C_{44}H_{50}Cl_2N_4O_2$; *15180-03-7*
Non-depolarizing neuromuscular blocker

Aldesleukin (rINN) al·des·*loo*·kin

Des-alanyl-1, serine-125 human interleukin-2; recombinant interleukin-2; *110942-02-4*
Recombinant interleukin-2

aldesleukin has the following amino acid sequence:

```
PTSSSTKKTG    LQLEHLLLDL    QMILNGINNY

KNPKLTRMLT    FKFYMPKKAT    ELKHLQCLEE

ELKPLEEVLN    LAQSKNFHLR    PRDLISNINV

IVLELKGSET    TFMCEYADET    ATIVEFLNRW

ITFSQSIIST    LT
```

Aldosterone (rINN) al·dö·*steer*·rön

11,18-Hemiacetal of 11β,21-dihydroxy-3,20-dioxopregn-4-en-18-al; $C_{21}H_{28}O_5$; *52-39-1*
Mineralocorticoid

Alefacept (rINN) a·*le*·fa·sept

1–92 Antigen LFA-3 (human) fusion protein with human immunoglobulin G1 (hinge-CH2-CH3 γ1-chain), dimer; *222535-22-0*
Human tumour necrosis factor receptor

Alemtuzumab (rINN) a·lem·*tü*·zü·mab

Immunoglobulin G1 (human-rat monoclonal CAMPATH-1H¬ γ1-chain anti-human antigen CD52), disulfide with human-rat monoclonal CAMPATH-1H light chain dimer; *216503-57-0*
Monoclonal antibody (lymphocyte CD52)

Alendronic Acid (rINN) a·len·*dro*·nik

4-Amino-1-hydroxybutane-1,1-diylbis(phosphonic acid); $C_4H_{13}NO_7P_2$; *66376-36-1*
● **Sodium Alendronate** *121268-17-5*
Bisphosphonate; treatment of osteoporosis

Alexitol Sodium (rINN) a·*leks*·i·tol

Sodium poly(hydroxyaluminium) carbonate—hexitol complex; *66813-51-2*
Antacid

The symbol '¬' in systematic chemical names signifies line continuation

● **Alfacalcidol** (rINN) al·fa·*kal*·si·dol
9,10-Secocholesta-5,7,10(19)-triene-1α,3β-diol;
1α-hydroxycholecalciferol; 1α-hydroxyvitamin D_3; 1α-OHD$_3$;
$C_{27}H_{44}O_2$; *41294-56-8*;
Vitamin D analogue

● **Alfadex** (rINN) *al*·fa·deks
Cyclomaltohexaose; alphacyclodextrin; $C_{36}H_{60}O_{30}$;
10016-20-3
Cyclodextran; carrier molecule for drug delivery systems

Alfadolone (rINN) al·*fa*·do·lön
3α,21-Dihydroxy-5α-pregnane-11,20-dione; $C_{21}H_{32}O_4$;
14107-37-0
♣ **Alfadolone Acetate** *23930-37-2*
Intravenous general anaesthetic (veterinary)

Alfaprostol (rINN) al·fa·*pros*·tol
Methyl (*Z*)-7-{(1*R*,2*S*,3*R*,5*S*)-2-[(3*S*)-5-cyclohexyl-3-
hydroxypent-1-ynyl]-3,5-dihydroxycyclopentyl}hept-5-
enoate; $C_{24}H_{38}O_5$; *74176-31-1*
Prostaglandin (PGF$_{2α}$) analogue

♣ **Alfaxalone** (rINN) al·*faks*·a·lön
3α-Hydroxy-5α-pregnane-11,20-dione; $C_{21}H_{32}O_3$; *23930-19-0*
Intravenous general anaesthetic (veterinary)

Alfentanil (rINN) al·*fen*·ta·nil
N-{1-[2-(4-Ethyl-5-oxo-2-tetrazolin-1-yl)ethyl]-4-
(methoxymethyl)-4-piperidyl}propionanilide; $C_{21}H_{32}N_6O_3$;
71195-58-9
● **Alfentanil Hydrochloride** *70879-28-6; 69049-06-5*
Opioid receptor agonist; analgesic

Alfimeprase (rINN) al·fi·*mep*·räs
[3-L-Serine]fibrolase-(3-203)-peptide (fibrolase: fibrinolytic
enzyme isolated from *Agkistrodon contrix* venom);
259074-76-5
Fibrinolytic metalloproteinase

alfimeprase has the following amino acid sequence:

```
SFPQRYVQ      LVIVADHRMN    TKYNGDSDKI

RQWVHQIVNT    INEIYRPLNI    QFTLVGLEIW

SNQDLITVTS    VSHDTLASFG    NWRETDLLRR

QRHDNAQLLT    AIDFDGDTVG    LAYVGGMCQL

KHSTGVIQDH    SAINLLVALT    MAHELGHNLG

MNHDGNQCHC    GANSCVMAAM    LSDQPSKLFS

DCSKKDYQTF    LTVNNPQCIL    NKP
```

Alfuzosin (rINN) al·*fü*·zö·sin
N-{3-[4-Amino-6,7-dimethoxyquinazolin-2-
yl(methyl)amino]propyl}tetrahydro-2-furamide; $C_{19}H_{27}N_5O_4$;
81403-80-7; SL 77 499-10
● **Alfuzosin Hydrochloride** *81403-68-1*
Alpha$_1$-adrenoceptor antagonist

Algestone Acetonide (INNM) al·jes·tön a·se·to·nïd

16α,17α-Isopropylidenedioxypregn-4-ene-3,20-dione;
$C_{24}H_{34}O_4$; 595-77-7
Progestogen

● Alginic Acid (rINN) al·ji·nik

A polyuronic acid composed of residues of D-mannuronic and L-guluronic acids obtained chiefly by extraction of algae belonging to the Phaeophyceae; mainly species of *Laminaria*; 9005-32-7
Treatment of gastro-oesophageal reflux disease, excipient, thickening agent

Alglucerase (rINN) al·gloo·se·räs

Macrophage-targeted β-glucocerebrosidase; monomeric glycoprotein of 497 amino acids with glycosylation making up about 6% of the molecule; 143003-46-7
Beta-glucocerebrosidase; treatment of Gaucher's disease

alglucerase has the following amino acid sequence:

ARPCIPKSFG	YSSVVCVCNA	TYCDSFDPPT
FPALGTFSRY	ESTRSGRRME	LSMGPIQANH
TGTGLLLTLQ	PEQKFQKVKG	FGGAMTDAAA
LNILALSPPA	QNLLLKSYFS	EEGIGYNIIR
VPMASCDFSI	RTYTYADTPD	DFQLHNFSLP
EEDTKLKIPL	IHRALQLAQR	PVSLLASPWT
SPTWLKTNGA	VNGKGSLKGQ	PGDIYHQTWA
RYFVKFLDAY	AEHKLQFWAV	TAENEPSAGL
LSGYPFQCLG	FTPEHQRDFI	ARDLGPTLAN
STHHNVRLLM	LDDQRLLLPH	WAKVVLTDPE
AAKYVHGIAV	HWYLDFLAPA	KATLGETHRL
FPNTMLFASE	ACVGSKFWEQ	SVRLGSWDRG
MQYSHSITTN	LLYHVVGWTD	WNLALNPEGG
PNWVRNFVDS	PIIVDITKDT	FYKQPNFYHL
GHFSKFIPEG	SGRVGLVASQ	KNDLDAVALM
HPDGSAVVVV	LNRSSKDVPL	TIKDPAVGFL
EYISPGYSIH	TYLWRRQ	

Alglucosidase Alfa (rINN) al·gloo·cö·si·däz

Human lysosomal prepro-α-glucosidase-(57-952)-peptide 199-arginine-223-histidine variant; 420784-05-0;
Enzyme replacement therapy; treatment of Pompe's disease

alglucosidase alfa has the following amino acid sequence:

QQGASRPGPR	DAQAHPGRPR	AVPTQCDVPP	NSRFDCAPDK
AITQEQCEAR	GCCYIPAKQG	LQGAQMGQPW	CFFPPSYPSY
KLENLSSSEM	GYTATLTRTT	PTFFPKDILT	LRLDVMMETE
NRLHFTIKDP	ANRRYEVPLE	TPRVHSRAPS	PLYSVEFSEE
PFGVIVHRQL	DGRVLLNTTV	APLFFADQFL	QLSTSLPSQY
ITGLAEHLSP	LMLSTSWTRI	TLWNRDLAPT	PGANLYGSHP
FYLALEDGGS	AHGVFLLNSN	AMDVVLQPSP	ALSWRSTGGI
LDVYIFLGPE	PKSVVQQYLD	VVGYPFMPPY	WGLGFHLCRW
GYSSTAITRQ	VVENMTRAHF	PLDVQWNDLD	YMDSRRDFTF
NKDGFRDFPA	MVQELHQGGR	RYMMIVDPAI	SSSGPAGSYR
PYDEGLRRGV	FITNETGQPL	IGKVWPGSTA	FPDFTNPTAL
AWWEDMVAEF	HDQVPFDGMW	IDMNEPSNFI	RGSEDGCPNN
ELENPPYVPG	VVGGTLQAAT	ICASSHQFLS	THYNLHNLYG
LTEAIASHRA	LVKARGTRPF	VISRSTFAGH	GRYAGHWTGD
VWSSWEQLAS	SVPEILQFNL	LGVPLVGADV	CGFLGNTSEE
LCVRWTQLGA	FYPFMRNHNS	LLSLPQEPYS	FSEPAQQAMR
KALTLRYALL	PHLYTLFHQA	HVAGETVARP	LFLEFPKDSS
TWTVDHQLLW	GEALLITPVL	QAGKAEVTGY	FPLGTWYDLQ
TVPIEALGSL	PPPPAAPREP	AIHSEGQWVT	LPAPLDTINV
HLRAGYIIPL	QGPGLTTTES	RQQPMALAVA	LTKGGEARGE
LFWDDGESLE	VLERGAYTQV	IFLARNNTIV	NELVRVTSEG
AGLQLQKVTV	LGVATAPQQV	LSNGVPVSNF	TYSPDTKVLD
ICVSLLMGEQ	FLVSWC		

* glycosylation sites

Alimemazine (rINN) a·li·mem·a·zën

Dimethyl(2-methyl-3-phenothiazin-10-ylpropyl)amine;
$(C_{18}H_{22}N_2S)_2$; 84-96-8
● Alimemazine Tartrate 4330-99-8
Histamine H$_1$ receptor antagonist; antihistamine

and enantiomer

The symbol '¬' in systematic chemical names signifies line continuation

Alinidine (rINN) a·*li*·ni·dën
N-Allyl-2,6-dichloro-*N*-(2-imidazolin-2-yl)aniline;
$C_{12}H_{13}Cl_2N_3$; *33178-86-8*
Alinidine Hydrobromide St-567-BR
Anion channel blocker; class V antiarrhythmic drug

Alipamide (rINN) a·*li*·pa·mïd
4-Chloro-*N′,N′*-dimethyl-3-sulfamoylbenzohydrazide;
$C_9H_{12}ClN_3O_3S$; *3184-59-6*; CI-546
Thiazide-like diuretic

Aliskiren (rINN) a·*lis*·ki·ren
(2*S*,4*S*,5*S*,7*S*)-5-Amino-*N*-(2-carbamoyl-2-methylpropyl)-4-hydroxy-7-{[4-methoxy-3-(3-methoxypropoxy)phenyl]¬methyl}-8-methyl-2-(propan-2-yl)nonanamide; $C_{30}H_{53}N_3O_6$;
173334-57-1
Renin inhibitor; antihypertensive

Alitretinoin (rINN) a·li·tre·ti·*nö*·in
(2*E*,4*E*,6*Z*,8*E*)-3,7-Dimethyl-9-(2,6,6-trimethylcyclohex-1-enyl)nona-2,4,6,8-tetraenoic acid; 9-*cis*-retinoic acid; $C_{20}H_{28}O_2$;
5300-03-8
Vitamin A analogue (retinoid); treatment of Kaposi's sarcoma

● **Allantoin** (BAN) a·*lan*·tö·in
2,5-Dioxoimidazolidin-4-ylurea; $C_4H_6N_4O_3$; *97-59-6*
Astringent; keratolytic

Alletorphine (rINN) see Appendix C

Allomethadione (rINN) a·*loks*·i·dön
(±)-3-Allyl-5-methyl-1,3-oxazolidine-2,4-dione; $C_7H_9NO_3$;
526-35-2
Antiepileptic; keratolyic

and enantiomer

● **Allopurinol** (rINN) a·lö·*pûr*·ri·nol
1*H*-Pyrazolo[3,4-*d*]pyrimidin-4-ol; $C_5H_4N_4O$; *315-30-0*
Xanthine oxidase inhibitor; treatment of gout and hyperuricaemia

Allylestrenol (rINN) see Appendix C

Allylprodine (rINN) see Appendix C

Almagate (rINN) *al*·ma·gät
Aluminium trimagnesium carbonate heptahydroxide dihydrate;
$AlMg_3(CO_3)(OH)_7,2H_2O$; *66827-12-1*
Antacid

Almasilate (rINN) see Appendix C

Almitrine (rINN) *al*·mi·trën
N,N′-Diallyl-6-[4-(4,4′-difluorobenzhydryl)piperazin-1-yl]-1,3,5-triazine-2,4-diyldiamine; $C_{26}H_{29}F_2N_7$; *27469-53-0*
Respiratory stimulant

10

Almotriptan (rINN) al·mo·*trip*·tan

Dimethyl{2-[5-(pyrrolidin-1-ylsulfonylmethyl)indol-3-yl]¬ethyl}amine; $C_{17}H_{25}N_3O_2S$; *154323-57-6*; LAS 31416

Almotriptan Maleate

Serotonin 5HT$_1$ receptor agonist; treatment of migraine

Almurtide (rINN) al·mür·tid

N^2-[(2-Acetamido-2-deoxy-D-glucopyranos-3-O-yl)acetyl-L-alanyl]-D-glutamic acid 1-amide; $C_{18}H_{30}N_4O_{11}$; NorMDP

Almurtide Sodium *60355-77-3*

Immunostimulant

Alniditan (rINN) al·*ni*·di·tan

(R)-N-Chroman-2-ylmethyl-N'-(1,4,5,6-tetrahydropyrimidin-2-yl)propane-1,3-diamine; $C_{17}H_{26}N_4O$; *152317-89-0*; R91274

Alniditan Dihydrochloride

Serotonin 5HT$_1$ receptor agonist; treatment of migraine

● **Aloin** (BAN) a·lö·in

10-β-D-Glucopyranosyl-1,8-dihydroxy-3-hydroxymethyl-9(10H)-anthrone; barbaloin; $C_{21}H_{22}O_9$; *5133-19-7*

Anthraquinone stimulant laxative

Alosetron (rINN) a·*lö*·se·tron

2,3,4,5-Tetrahydro-5-methyl-2-(5-methylimidazol-4-ylmethyl)-pyrido[4,3-b]indol-1-one; $C_{17}H_{18}N_4O$; *122852-42-0*

Alosetron Hydrochloride *122852-69-1*

Serotonin 5HT$_3$ receptor antagonist; treatment of irritable bowel syndrome

Aloxidone *see Allomethadione*

● **Aloxiprin** (rINN) a·*loks*·i·prin

Polymeric condensation product of aluminium oxide and O-acetylsalicylic acid; *9014-67-9*

Salicylate; antipyretic analgesic; anti-inflammatory

Alphacetylmethadol (rINN) al·fa·së·til·*me*·tha·dol

(1R,4R)-4-Dimethylamino-1-ethyl-2,2-diphenylpentyl acetate; $C_{23}H_{31}NO_2$; *17199-58-5*

Opioid receptor agonist

Alpha-Cypermethrin (BAN) al·fa·sï·per·*më*·thrin

(SR)-α-Cyano-3-phenoxybenzyl (1RS,3RS)-3-(2,2-dichloro¬vinyl)-2,2-dimethylcyclopropanecarboxylate; $C_{22}H_{19}Cl_2NO_3$; *67375-30-8*

Insecticide (veterinary)

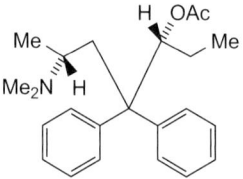

and enantiomer

Alphadolone *see Alfadolone*

Alphameprodine (rINN) al·fa·*me*·prö·dën

(3S,4R)-3-Ethyl-1-methyl-4-phenyl-4-piperidyl propionate; $C_{17}H_{25}NO_2$; *468-51-9*

Opioid receptor agonist; analgesic

The symbol '¬' in systematic chemical names signifies line continuation

Alphamethadol (rINN) al·fa·*me*·tha·dol

(3*R*,6*R*)-6-Dimethylamino-4,4-diphenylheptan-3-ol; $C_{21}H_{29}NO$; *17199-54-1*
Opioid receptor agonist

Alphaprodine (rINN) see Appendix C

Alphaxalone *see Alfaxalone*

Alpidem (rINN) see Appendix C

Alprazolam (rINN) al·*prä*·zö·lam

8-Chloro-1-methyl-6-phenyl-4*H*-[1,2,4]triazolo[4,3-*a*][1,4]-benzodiazepine; $C_{17}H_{13}ClN_4$; *28981-97-7*
Alprazolam Mesilate *57938-82-6*; U-41,123
Benzodiazepine

Alprenolol (rINN) al·*pre*·no·lol

1-(2-Allylphenoxy)-3-isopropylaminopropan-2-ol; $C_{15}H_{23}NO_2$; *13655-52-2*
Alprenolol Benzoate
●**Alprenolol Hydrochloride** *13707-88-5*
Beta-adrenoceptor antagonist

and enantiomer

●**Alprostadil** (rINN) al·*prost*·a·dil

(1) 7-{(1*R*,2*R*,3*R*)-3-Hydroxy-2-[(*E*)-(3*S*)-3-hydroxyoct-1-enyl]-5-oxocyclopentyl}heptanoic acid; (2) (13*E*)-(11*R*,15*S*)-11,15-Dihydroxy-9-oxoprost-13-enoic acid; $C_{20}H_{34}O_5$; *745-65-3*
Prostaglandin E₁ (PGE₁)

Alprostadil Alfadex (INNM) al·*prost*·a·dil *al*·fa·deks

(1) α-Cyclodextrin—7-{(1*R*,2*R*,3*R*)-3-hydroxy-2-[(*E*)-(3*S*)-3-hydroxyoct-1-enyl]-5-oxo-cyclopentyl}heptanoic acid;
(2) cyclomaltohexaose—(13*E*)-(11*R*,15*S*)-11,15-dihydroxy-9-oxoprost-13-enoic acid; $C_{20}H_{34}O_5 \cdot x[C_{36}H_{60}O_{30}]$; PGE₁ α-CD
Prostaglandin E₁ (PGE₁)

●**Alteplase** (rINN) *al*·te·pläs

Recombinant tissue-type plasminogen activator produced by a Chinese hamster ovary (CHO) cell line transformed with the human t-PA gene; a glycosylated protein of 527 residues having the amino acid sequence of human tissue plasminogen activator; *105857-23-6*
Tissue-type plasminogen activator; fibrinolytic

For labelling purposes the name carries an approved code, in parentheses and in lower case letters, indicative of the method of production.

The following code is approved:
(**rch**) produced from genetically engineered Chinese hamster ovary cells.

alteplase has the following amino acid sequence:

SYQVICRDEK	TQMIYQQHQS	WLRPVLRSNR
VEYCWCNSGR	AQCHSVPVKS	CSEPRCFNGG
TCQQALYFSD	FVCQCPEGFA	GKCCEIDTRA
TCYEDQGISY	RGTWSTAESG	AECTNWNSSA
LAQKPYSGRR	PDAIRLGLGN	HNYCRNPDRD
SKPWCYVFKA	GKYSSEFCST	PACSEGNSDC
YFGNGSAYRG	THSLTESGAS	CLPWNSMILI
GKVYTAQNPS	AQALGLGKHN	YCRNPDGDAK
PWCHVLKNRR	LTWEYCDVPS	CSTCGLRQYS
QPQFR		
IKGGLFADIA	SHPWQAAIFA	KHRRSPGERF
LCGGILISSC	WILSAAHCFQ	ERFPPHHLTV
ILGRTYRVVP	GEEEQKFEVE	KYIVHKEFDD
DTYDNDIALL	QLKSDSSRCA	QESSVVRTVC
LPPADLQLPD	WTECELSGYG	KHEALSPFYS
ERLKEAHVRL	YPSSRCTSQH	LLNRTVTDNM
LCAGDTRSGG	PQANLHDACQ	GDSGGPLVCL
NDGRMTLVGI	ISWGLGCGQK	DVPGVYTKVT
NYLDWIRDNM	RP	

● **Altizide** (rINN) al·*ti*·zïd

6-Chloro-1,1-dioxo-3-{[(prop-2-en-1-yl)sulfanyl]methyl}-3,4-dihydro-2*H*-1,2,4-benzothiadiazine-7-sulfonamide; althiazide (USAN) $C_{11}H_{14}ClN_3O_4S_3$; *5588-16-9*;
Thiazide diuretic

Altrenogest (rINN) al·*tre*·nö·jest

(1) 17α-Allyl-17β-hydroxy-19-norandrosta-4,9,11-trien-3-one;
(2) 17β-Hydroxy-19,21,24-trinorchola-4,9,11,22-tetraen-3-one;
$C_{21}H_{26}O_2$; *850-52-2*
Progestogen (veterinary)

Altretamine (rINN) al·*tre*·ta·mën

N^2,N^2,N^4,N^4,N^6,N^6-Hexamethyl-1,3,5-triazine-2,4,6-triamine;
$C_9H_{18}N_6$; *645-05-6*; NSC-13875
Cytotoxic

Aluminium Clofibrate (rINN) *klö*·fi·brät

Bis[2-(4-chlorophenoxy)-2-ethylpropionato]hydroxoaluminium;
$C_{20}H_{21}AlCl_2O_7$; *14613-01-5*
Fibrate; lipid-regulating drug

Alverine (rINN) *al*·ve·rën

Ethylbis(3-phenylpropyl)amine; $C_{20}H_{27}N$; *150-59-4*
● **Alverine Citrate** *5560-59-8*
Smooth muscle relaxant; antispasmodic

Alvimopan (rINN) al·*vim*·ö·pan

[(2*S*)-2-{[(3*R*,4*R*)-4-(3-Hydroxyphenyl)-3,4-dimethylpiperidin-1-yl]methyl}-3-phenylpropanamido]acetic acid; $C_{25}H_{32}N_2O_4$;
156053-89-3
Opioid receptor agonist; analgesic

Alvocidib (rINN) al·*vö*·*si*·dib

(-)-2-(2-Chlorophenyl)-5,7-dihydroxy-8-[(3*S*,4*R*)-3-hydroxy-1-methylpiperidin-4-yl]-4*H*-chromen-4-one;
$C_{21}H_{20}ClNO_5$; *146426-40-6*;
Alvocidib Hydrochloride *131740-09-5*
Cyclin-dependent kinase inhibitor; antineoplastic

Amafolone (rINN) a·*ma*·fo·lön

3α-Amino-2β-hydroxy-5α-androstan-17-one; $C_{19}H_{31}NO_2$;
50588-47-1
Amafolone Hydrochloride Org 6001
Antiarrhythmic

Amantadine (rINN) a·*man*·ta·dën

Tricyclo[3.3.1.1.^{3,7}]dec-1-ylamine; 1-adamantanamine;
$C_{10}H_{17}N$; *768-94-5*
● **Amantadine Hydrochloride** *665-66-7*;
Viral replication inhibitor (influenza A); dopamine receptor agonist; treatment of influenza and Parkinson's disease

Ambazone (rINN) *am*·ba·zön

6-Amidinohydrazonocyclohexa-1,4-dien-3-one thiosemicarbazone; $C_8H_{11}N_7S$; *6011-12-7*
Antiseptic

The symbol '¬' in systematic chemical names signifies line continuation

Ambenonium Chloride (rINN) am·be·*nö*·në·um

N,N'-Oxalylbis(*N*-2-aminoethyl-*N*-2-chlorobenzyldiethyl¬ ammonium) dichloride; $C_{28}H_{42}Cl_4N_4O_2$; *115-79-7*
Cholinesterase inhibitor

Ambenoxan (rINN) am·be·*noks*·an

2,3-Dihydro-1,4-benzodioxin-2-ylmethyl[2-(2-methoxyethoxy)ethyl]amine; $C_{14}H_{21}NO_4$; *2455-84-7*
Skeletal muscle relaxant

Ambicromil (rINN) am·*bï*·krö·mil

4,6-Dioxo-10-propyl-4*H*,6*H*-pyrano[3,2-*g*]chromene-2,8-dicarboxylic acid; $C_{17}H_{12}O_8$; *58805-38-2*
Ambicromil Calcium probicromil calcium (USAN); *71144-97-3*
Treatment of asthma, food allergy, allergic conjunctivitis and rhinitis

Ambrisentan (rINN) am·bri·*sen*·tan

(+)-(2*S*)-2-[(4,6-Dimethylpyrimidin-2-yl)oxy]-3-methoxy-3,3-diphenylpropanoic acid; $C_{22}H_{22}N_2O_4$; *177036-94-1*
Endothelin-A receptor antagonist

Ambroxol (rINN) am·*broks*·ol

trans-4-[(2-Amino-3,5-dibromobenzyl)amino]cyclohexanol; $C_{13}H_{18}Br_2N_2O$; *18683-91-5*
● **Ambroxol Hydrochloride** *23828-92-4*
Mucolytic expectorant

Ambucetamide (rINN) am·bü·*se*·ta·mïd

(±)-2-Dibutylamino-2-(4-methoxyphenyl)acetamide; $C_{17}H_{28}N_2O_2$; *519-88-0*
Smooth muscle relaxant; antispasmodic

and enantiomer

Ambuside (rINN) *am*·bü·sïd

5-Allylsulfamoyl-2-chloro-4-(3-hydroxybut-2-enylideneamino)benzenesulfonamide; $C_{13}H_{16}ClN_3O_5S$; *3754-19-6*
Thiazide-like diuretic

Ambutonium Bromide (BAN) am·bü·*tö*·në·um

(3-Carbamoyl-3,3-diphenylpropyl)ethyldimethylammonium bromide; $C_{20}H_{27}BrN_2O$; *115-51-5*
Choline antagonist

Amcinonide (rINN) am·*si*·no·nïd

16α,17α-Cyclopentylidenedioxy-9α-fluoro-11β-hydroxy-3,20-dioxopregna-1,4-dien-21-yl acetate; $C_{28}H_{35}FO_7$; *51022-69-6*; CL 34699
Corticosteroid

Ameltolide (rINN) a·*mel*·to·lïd

4-Aminobenzo-2′,6′-xylide; $C_{15}H_{16}N_2O$; *787-93-9*; LY201116
Antiepileptic

Ametazole (BAN) a·*me*·ta·zôl

2-(Pyrazol-3-yl)ethylamine; betazole (pINN); $C_5H_9N_3$; *105-20-4*
Ametazole Hydrochloride *138-92-1*
Stimulant of gastric secretion

Amethocaine *see Tetracaine*

Amfebutamone *see Bupropion*

Amfecloral (rINN) am·*fe*·klor·ral

α-Methylphenethyl(2,2,2-trichloroethylidene)amine;
$C_{11}H_{12}Cl_3N$; *5581-35-1*
Amfetamine analogue

and enantiomer

Amfenac (rINN) am·fe·nak

(2-Amino-3-benzoylphenyl)acetic acid; $C_{15}H_{13}NO_3$; *51579-82-9*
Amfenac Sodium *61618-27-7*
Cyclo-oxygenase inhibitor

Amfetamine (rINN) am·*fe*·ta·mën

(*RS*)-α-Methylphenethylamine; $C_9H_{13}N$; *300-62-9*
● **Amfetamine Sulfate** *60-13-9*
Releases dopamine; central nervous system stimulant

and enantiomer

Amfonelic Acid (rINN) am·fö·*ne*·lik

7-Benzyl-1-ethyl-1,4-dihydro-4-oxo-1,8-naphthyridine-3-
carboxylic acid; $C_{18}H_{16}N_2O_3$; *15180-02-6*
Dopamine reuptake inhibitor; central nervous system stimulant

Amicarbalide (rINN) a·mi·*kar*·ba·lïd

(1) 1,3-Bis(3-amidinophenyl)urea; (2) 3,3′-Diamidino¬
carbanilide; $C_{15}H_{16}N_6O$; *3459-96-9*
Amicarbalide Isetionate *3671-72-5*
Antiprotozoal

Amidantel (rINN) a·mi·*dan*·tel

4′-(1-Dimethylaminoethylideneamino)-2-methoxyacetanilide;
$C_{13}H_{19}N_3O_2$; *49745-00-8*
Amidantel Hydrochloride
Antihelminthic

Amidefrine (rINN) a·*mï*·de·frën

(±)-3′-(1-Hydroxy-2-methylaminoethyl)methanesulfonanilide;
$C_{10}H_{16}N_2O_3S$; *1421-68-7*
*Alpha-adrenoreceptor agonist; vasoconstrictor, nasal
decongestant*

and enantiomer

● **Amidotrizoic Acid** (rINN) a·*mï*·dö·tri·*zö*·ik

3,5-Diacetamido-2,4,6-tri-iodobenzoic acid; $C_{11}H_9I_3N_2O_4$;
117-96-4
Meglumine Amidotrizoate *131-49-7*
● **Sodium Amidotrizoate** *737-31-5*
Iodinated contrast medium

Amifampridine (rINN) a·mi·*fam*·pri·dën

Pyridine-3,4-diamine; $C_5H_7N_3$; *54-96-6*;
*Potassium-channel blocker; treatment of Lambert-Eaton
myasthenic syndrome*

Amifloxacin (rINN) a·mi·*floks*·a·sin
6-Fluoro-1,4-dihydro-1-methylamino-7-(4-methylpiperazin-1-yl)-4-oxoquinoline-3-carboxylic acid; $C_{16}H_{19}FN_4O_3$; *86393-37-5*

Amifloxacin Mesilate *88036-80-0*
Fluoroquinolone antibacterial

Amifostine (rINN) a·mi·*fos*·tën
S-[2-(3-Aminopropylamino)ethyl] dihydrogenphosphoro¬
thioate; $C_5H_{15}N_2O_3PS$; *20537-88-6*
Cytoprotective

● **Amikacin** (rINN) a·mi·*kä*·sin
6-*O*-(3-Amino-3-deoxy-α-D-glucopyranosyl)-4-*O*-(6-amino-6-deoxy-α-D-glucopyranosyl)-N^1-[(2*S*)-4-amino-2-hydroxy¬
butyryl]-2-deoxy-D-streptamine; $C_{22}H_{43}N_5O_{13}$;
37517-28-5

● **Amikacin Sulfate** *39831-55-5;*
Aminoglycoside antibacterial

Amiloride (rINN) a·*mi*·lor·rïd
N-Amidino-3,5-diamino-6-chloropyrazine-2-carboxamide;
$C_6H_8ClN_7O$; *2609-46-3*
● **Amiloride Hydrochloride** *17440-83-4 (dihydrate)*;
2016-88-8 (anhydrous)
Sodium channel blocker; potassium-sparing diuretic

Aminacrine *see Aminoacridine*

Aminitrozole (rINN) a·mi·*nï*·tra·zôl
N-(5-Nitro-1,3-thiazol-2-yl)acetamide; nithiamide (USAN);
$C_5H_5N_3O_3S$; *140-40-9*
Antiprotozoal; treatment of trichomoniasis

Aminoacridine (rINN) a·mï·nö·*a*·kri·dën
Acridin-9-ylamine; $C_{13}H_{10}N_2$; *90-45-9*
Aminoacridine Hydrochloride *134-50-9*
Antiseptic

Aminocaproic Acid (rINN) a·mï·nö·ka·*prö*·ik
6-Aminohexanoic acid; $C_6H_{13}NO_2$; *60-32-2*
Antifibrinolytic

● **Aminoglutethimide** (rINN) a·mï·nö·gloo·*te*·thi·mïd
2-(4-Aminophenyl)-2-ethylglutarimide; $C_{13}H_{16}N_2O_2$; *125-84-8*
Inhibitor of adrenal corticosteroid synthesis; used in chemical adrenalectomy

Aminometradine (rINN) a·mï·nö·*me*·tra·dën
1-Allyl-6-amino-3-ethylpyrimidine-2,4(1*H*,3*H*)-dione;
$C_9H_{13}N_3O_2$; *642-44-4*
Diuretic

● **Aminophylline** (rINN) a·mi·*no*·fi·lën
3,7-Dihydro-1,3-dimethylpurine-2,6(1*H*)-dione—ethylene
diamine(2:1); $C_{16}H_{24}N_{10}O_4$; *317-34-0*
Non-selective phosphodiesterase inhibitor; treatment of reversible airways obstruction

Aminopromazine (rINN) see Appendix C

Aminopterin Sodium (rINN) a·mi·nö·*te*·rin

Sodium 4-aminopteroylglutamate; $C_{19}H_{18}N_8Na_2O_5$; *58602-66-7*
Dihydrofolate reductase inhibitor; cytotoxic

Aminorex (rINN) a·*mi*·nor·reks

(±)-4,5-Dihydro-5-phenyl-1,3-oxazol-2-ylamine; $C_9H_{10}N_2O$; *2207-50-3*
Amfetamine analogue; appetite suppressant

and enantiomer

Amiodarone (rINN) a·mï·*ö*·da·rön

2-Butylbenzofuran-3-yl 4-(2-diethylaminoethoxy)-3,5-di-iodophenyl ketone; $C_{25}H_{29}I_2NO_3$; *1951-25-3*
● **Amiodarone Hydrochloride** *19774-82-4*
Potassium channel blocker; class III antiarrhythmic

Amiphenazole (rINN) a·mi·*fen*·a·zôl

5-Phenyl-1,3-thiazole-2,4-diyldiamine; $C_9H_9N_3S$; *490-55-1*
Respiratory stimulant

Amisometradine (rINN) a·mï·sö·*me*·tra·dën

6-Amino-3-methyl-1-(2-methylallyl)pyrimidine-2,4(1*H*,3*H*)-dione; $C_9H_{13}N_3O_2$; *550-28-7*
Diuretic

● **Amisulpride** (rINN) a·mi·*sul*·prïd

(*RS*)-4-Amino-*N*-[(1-ethylpyrrolidin-2-yl)methyl]-5-(ethylsulfonyl)-*o*-anisamide; $C_{17}H_{27}N_3O_4S$; *71675-85-9*; DAN-216
Dopamine receptor antagonist; neuroleptic

and enantiomer

♣ **Amitraz** (rINN) *a*·mi·traz

Methylbis(2,4-xylyliminomethyl)amine; $C_{19}H_{23}N_3$; *33089-61-1*
Topical parasiticide; acaricide (veterinary)

Amitriptyline (rINN) a·mi·*trip*·ti·lën

3-(10,11-Dihydro-5*H*-dibenzo[*a*,*d*]cyclohepten-5-ylidene)propyldimethylamine; $C_{20}H_{23}N$; *50-48-6*
● **Amitriptyline Embonate** *17086-03-2*
● **Amitriptyline Hydrochloride** *549-18-8*
Monoamine reuptake inhibitor; tricyclic antidepressant

Amlexanox (rINN) am·*leks*·a·noks

2-Amino-7-isopropyl-5-oxo-5*H*-[1]benzopyrano[2,3-*b*]¬pyridine-3-carboxylic acid; $C_{16}H_{14}N_2O_4$; *68302-57-8*
Mast cell stabilizer

Amlodipine (rINN) am·*lö*·di·pën

(±)-3-Ethyl 5-methyl 2-(2-aminoethoxymethyl)-4-(2-chlorophenyl)-1,4-dihydro-6-methylpyridine-3,5-dicarboxylate; $C_{20}H_{25}ClN_2O_5$; *88150-42-9*
Amlodipine Maleate *88150-47-4*; UK-48340-11
● **Amlodipine Besilate** *111470-99-6*
Calcium channel blocker

and enantiomer

● **Amobarbital** (rINN) a·mö·*bar*·bi·tal

5-Ethyl-5-isopentylbarbituric acid; $C_{11}H_{18}N_2O_3$; *57-43-2*
● **Amobarbital Sodium** *64-43-7*
Barbiturate

The symbol '¬' in systematic chemical names signifies line continuation

Amodiaquine (rINN) see Appendix C

Amorolfine (rINN) a·mo·*rol*·fën

cis-4-{(*RS*)-3-[4-(1,1-Dimethylpropyl)phenyl]-2-methyl¬
propyl}-2,6-dimethylmorpholine; $C_{21}H_{35}NO$; *78613-35-1*
Amorolfine Hydrochloride *78613-38-4*
Antifungal

and epimer at C*

Amoxapine (rINN) a·*moks*·a·pën
2-Chloro-11-(piperazin-1-yl)dibenz[*b,f*][1,4]oxazepine;
$C_{17}H_{16}ClN_3O$; *14028-44-5*
Monoamine reuptake inhibitor; tricyclic antidepressant

Amoxicillin (rINN) a·*moks*·i·*si*·lin
6-(α-D-*p*-Hydroxyphenylglycylamino)penicillanic acid;
$C_{16}H_{19}N_3O_5S$; *26787-78-0*
● **Amoxicillin Sodium** *34642-77-8*
● **Amoxicillin Trihydrate** *61336-70-7*
Penicillin antibacterial

Amperozide (rINN) am·*pe*·rö·zïd
4-[4,4-Bis(4-fluorophenyl)butyl]-*N*-ethylpiperazine-1-
carboxamide; $C_{23}H_{29}F_2N_3O$; *75558-90-6*
Amperozide Hydrochloride *75529-73-6*
Serotonin 5HT$_2$ receptor antagonist; neuroleptic (veterinary)

Amphetamine *see Amfetamine*

Amphomycin (rINN) see Appendix C

● **Amphotericin** (rINN) am·fö·*te*·ri·sin
A mixture of antifungal polyenes produced by certain strains of
Streptomyces nodosus
Amphotericin B: (3*R*,5*R*,8*R*,9*R*,11*S*,13*R*,15*S*,16*R*,17*S*,19*R*,34*S*,
35*R*, 36*R*,37*S*)-19-(3-amino-3,6-dideoxy-β-D-mannopyranosy-
loxy)-16-carboxy-3,5,8,9,11,13,15,35-octahydroxy-34,36-
dimethyl-13,17-epoxyoctatriaconta-20,22,24,26,28,30,32-
heptaen-37-olide; $C_{47}H_{73}NO_{17}$; *1397-89-3*
Antifungal

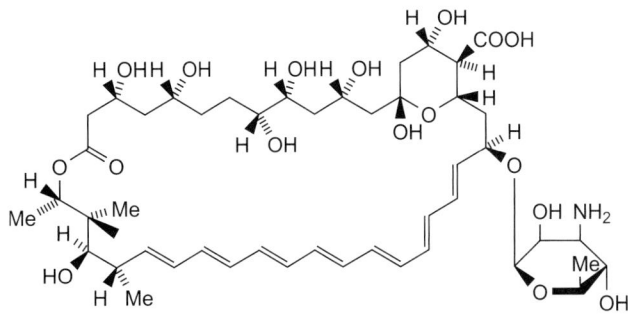

● **Ampicillin** (rINN) am·pi·*si*·lin
(6*R*)-6-(α-D-Phenylglycylamino)penicillanic acid; $C_{16}H_{19}N_3O_4S$;
69-53-4
● **Ampicillin Sodium** *69-52-3*
● **Ampicillin Trihydrate** *7177-48-2*
Penicillin antibacterial

Ampiroxicam (rINN) am·pi·*roks*·i·kam
4-[1-(Ethoxycarbonyloxy)ethoxy]-2-methyl-*N*-(2-pyridyl)-2*H*-
1,2-benzothiazine-3-carboxamide 1,1-dioxide; $C_{20}H_{21}N_3O_7S$;
99464-64-9; CP-65703
Cyclo-oxygenase inhibitor; analgesic; anti-inflammatory

and enantiomer

Amprenavir (rINN) am·*pren*·a·veer
(3*S*)-Tetrahydro-3-furyl [(1*S*,2*R*)-1-benzyl-2-hydroxy-3-
(*N*¹-isobutylsulfanilamido)propyl]carbamate; $C_{25}H_{35}N_3O_6S$;
161814-49-9
Protease inhibitor; antiviral (HIV)

Amprolium (rINN) am·*prö*·lë·um

1-(4-Amino-2-propylpyrimidin-5-ylmethyl)-2-methyl¬
pyridinium chloride; $C_{14}H_{19}ClN_4$; *121-25-5*
♣ **Amprolium Hydrochloride** *137-88-2*
Antiprotozoal; prevention and treatment of coccidiosis
(veterinary)

Amrinone (rINN) see Appendix C

Amsacrine (rINN) *am*·sa·krën

4′-(Acridin-9-ylamino)methanesulfon-*m*-anisidide;
$C_{21}H_{19}N_3O_3S$; *51264-14-3*
Amsacrine Lactate
Cytotoxic

● **Amylmetacresol** (rINN) ä·mïl·me·ta·*krë*·sol

6-Pentyl-*m*-cresol; $C_{12}H_{18}O$; *1300-94-3*
Antiseptic

Amylobarbitone *see Amobarbital*

Amylocaine (BAN) a·*mï*·lö·kän

(*RS*)-1-(Dimethylaminomethyl)-1-methylpropyl benzoate;
$C_{14}H_{21}NO_2$; *644-26-8*
Local anaesthetic

and enantiomer

Anagrelide (rINN) a·*na*·gre·lïd

6,7-Dichloro-1,5-dihydroimidazol[2,1-*b*]quinazolin-2(3*H*)-one;
$C_{10}H_7Cl_2N_3O$; *68475-42-3*
Cyclic nucleotide phosphodiesterase inhibitor; control of
thrombocythaemia

Anakinra (rINN) a·na·*kin*·ra

N^2-l-Methionylinterleukin 1 receptor antagonist (human isoform
x reduced); *143090-92-0;*
Interleukin-1 receptor antagonist

anakinra has the following amino acid sequence:

M	RPSGRKSSKM	QAFRIWDVNQ	KTFYLRNNQL
	VAGYLQGPNV	NLEEKIDVVP	IEPHALFLGI
	HGGKMCLSCV	KSGDLTRLQL	EAVNITDLSE
	NRKQDKRFAF	IRSDSGPTTS	FESAACPGWF
	LCTAMEADQP	VSLTNMPDEG	VMVTKFYFQE
	DE		

Anaritide (rINN) a·*na*·ri·tïd

N-L-Arginyl-[8-L-methionine-21α-L-phenylalanine-21β-L-
arginine-2lχ-L-tyrosine]-atriopeptin-21 (rat); $C_{112}H_{175}N_{39}O_{35}S_3$;
95896-08-5; Wy 47663
Anaritide Acetate *104595-79-1*
Natriuretic peptide type A; diuretic

```
Arg-Ser-Ser-Cys-Phe-Gly-Gly-Arg-
Met-Asp-Arg-Ile-Gly-AlaVGln-Ser-
Gly-Leu-Gly-Cys-Asn-Ser-Phe-Arg-
Tyr
```

Anastrozole (rINN) a·*nas*·tro·zôl

2,2′-Dimethyl-2,2′-[5-(1*H*-1,2,4-triazol-1-ylmethyl)-1,3-
phenylene]bis(propiononitrile); $C_{17}H_{19}N_5$; *120511-73-1*
Aromatase inhibitor; treatment of breast carcinoma

Ancrod (rINN) *an*·krod

An enzyme obtained from the venom of the Malayan pit-viper,
Calloselasma rhodostoma Boie, 1827, formerly *Agkistrodon*
rhodostoma, acting specifically on fibrinogen by the release of
fibrinopeptide A; *9046-56-4*
Anticoagulant enzyme; fibrin cleavage

Androstanolone (rINN) an·drö·*stan*·o·lön

17β-Hydroxy-5α-androstan-3-one; $C_{19}H_{30}O_2$; *521-18-6*
Anabolic steroid; androgen

Angiotensinamide (rINN) see Appendix C

Anidoxime (rINN) a·ni·*doks*·ëm

3-Diethylaminopropiophenone *O*-(*p*-methoxyphenyl¬
carbamoyl)oxime; $C_{21}H_{27}N_3O_3$; *34297-34-2*; BRL 11870;
E-142
Analgesic

Anidulafungin (rINN) a·ni·*dü*·lá·fun·gin

6,N^6.1-Anhydro-(4*R*,5*R*)-4,5-dihydroxy-N^2-{[3^4-(pentyloxy)-
1^1,2^1:2^4,3^1-terphenyl-1^4-yl]carbonyl}-L-ornithyl-L-threonyl-(4*R*)-
4-hydroxy-L-prolyl-(*S*)-4-hydroxy-4-(4-hydroxyphenyl)-
L-threonyl-L-threonyl-(3*S*,4*S*)-3-hydroxy-4-methyl-L-proline;
$C_{58}H_{73}N_7O_{17}$; *166663-25-8*;
Antifungal

Anileridine (rINN) a·ni·*le*·ri·dën

Ethyl 1-(4-aminophenethyl)-4-phenylpiperidine-4-
carboxylate; $C_{22}H_{28}N_2O_3$; *144-14-9*
Analgesic

Anisindione (rINN) see Appendix C

Anistreplase (rINN) see Appendix C

Antazoline (rINN) an·*tä*·zö·lën

N-Benzyl-*N*-(2-imidazolin-2-ylmethyl)aniline; $C_{17}H_{19}N_3$;
91-75-8
● **Antazoline Hydrochloride** *2508-72-7*
Antazoline Phosphate *154-68-7*
Antazoline Sulfate *24359-81-7*
Histamine H_1 receptor antagonist; antihistamine

Antilymphocyte Immunoglobulin (Horse) (BAN)
see Appendix C

Antithrombin III (rINN) an·ti·*throm*·bin

The glycoprotein antithrombin obtained from human plasma;
antithrombin III human; AT III; *52014-67-2*
Anticoagulant factor

Apaflurane (rINN) ä·pa·*flûr*·rän

1,1,1,2,3,3,3-Heptafluoropropane; C_3HF_7; *431-89-0*
Pharmaceutical propellant

Apolizumab (rINN) a·po·*li*·zü·mab

Immunoglobin G1, anti-(human histocompatibility antigen HLA-
DR) (human-mouse monoclonal Hu1D10a1-chain),
disulfide with human-mouse monoclonal Hu1D10 light chain,
dimer
Monoclonal antibody (lymphocyte HLA-DR)

Apomorphine (BAN) ä·pö·*mor*·fën

6aβ-Aporphine-10,11-diol; $C_{17}H_{17}NO_2$; *58-00-4*
● **Apomorphine Hydrochloride** *314-19-2 (anhydrous)*;
41372-20-7 (hemihydrate)
Dopamine receptor agonist; treatment of Parkinson's disease

Apraclonidine (rINN) a·pra·*klo*·ni·dën

2,6-Dichloro-N^1-imidazolidin-2-ylidene-*p*-phenylenediamine; $C_9H_{10}Cl_2N_4$; *66711-21-5*; AL02145

Apraclonidine Hydrochloride *73218-79-8*

Alpha$_2$-adrenoceptor agonist; control of intraocular pressure

Apramycin (rINN) ä·pra·*mï*·sin

An antimicrobial base produced by *Streptomyces tenebrarius*; 4-*O*-[(2*S*,3*R*,4a*S*,6*R*,7*S*,8*R*,8a*R*)-3-Amino-6-(4-amino-4-deoxy-α-D-glucopyranosyloxy)-8-hydroxy-7-methylaminoperhydro¬pyrano[3,2-*b*]pyran-2-yl]-2-deoxy-D-streptamine; $C_{21}H_{41}N_5O_{11}$; *37321-09-8*

♣ **Apramycin Sulfate**

Aminoglycoside antibacterial (veterinary)

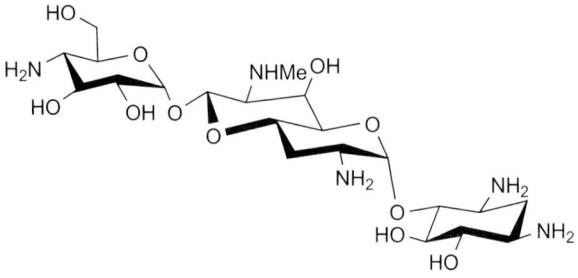

Aprindine (rINN) *a*·prin·dën

N-(3-Diethylaminopropyl)-*N*-indan-2-ylaniline; $C_{22}H_{30}N_2$; *37640-71-4*; 99170

Class I antiarrhythmic

● **Aprotinin** (rINN) a·prö·*tï*·nin

A polypeptide proteinase inhibitor; *9004-04-0*

Antifibrinolytic

```
RPDFCLEPPY    TGPCKARIIR    YFYNAKAGLC

QTFVYGGCRA    KRNNFKSAED    CMRTCGGA
```

Aptocaine (rINN) *ap*·tö·kän

2-Pyrrolidin-1-ylpropiono-*o*-toluidide; $C_{14}H_{20}N_2O$; *19281-29-9*

Local anaesthetic

and enantiomer

Arbutamine (rINN) ar·*bü*·ta·mën

(*R*)-4-(1-Hydroxy-2-[4-(4-hydroxyphenyl)butylamino]ethyl)¬pyrocatechol; $C_{18}H_{23}NO_4$

Arbutamine Hydrochloride *125251-66-3*

Beta-adrenoceptor agonist; cardiac stress testing

Ardacin (rINN) *ar*·da·sin

A mixture of aridicin A, aridicin B, aridicin C and aridicin C_2; glycopeptide antibiotics derived from the species *Kibdelosporangium aridium*, strain ATCC 39323; aridicin; $C_{81}H_{82}Cl_4N_8O_{30}$ (A); *117742-13-9*; AAD 216; SK&F 100814

Feed additive (veterinary)

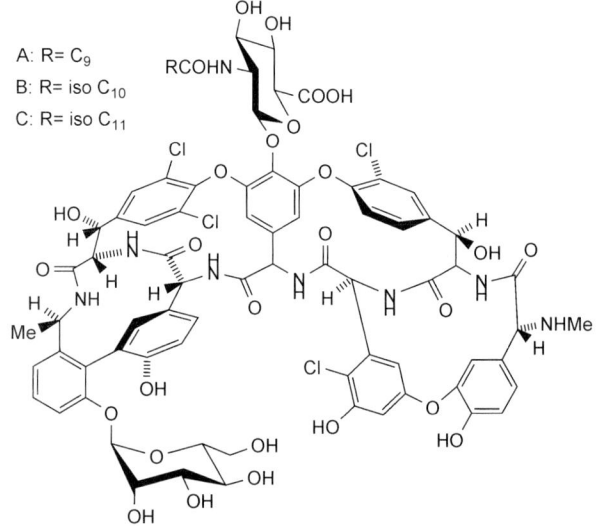

A: R= C_9
B: R= iso C_{10}
C: R= iso C_{11}

Argatroban (rINN) ar·*ga*·trö·ban

(2*R*,4*R*)-4-Methyl-1-{N^2-{[(3*RS*)-1,2,3,4-tetrahydro-3-methyl-8-quinolyl]sulfonyl}-L-arginyl}piperidine-2-carboxylic acid; $C_{23}H_{36}N_6O_5S$; *74863-84-6 (anhydrous)*; *141396-28-3 (monohydrate)*; MCI-9038; MD-805; DK-7419; GN1600

Direct thrombin inhibitor; oral anticoagulant

and epimer at C*

Arginine Glutamate (rINN) *ar*·ji·nën *gloo*·ta·mät

L-Arginine salt of L-glutamic acid; $C_6H_{14}N_4O_2·C_5H_9NO_4$; *74-79-3*

Amino acid; nutrient

The symbol '¬' in systematic chemical names signifies line continuation

Argipressin (rINN) ar·ji·*pres*·sin

[8-Arginine]vasopressin; $C_{46}H_{65}N_{15}O_{12}S_2$; *113-79-1*
Vasopressin analogue; treatment of diabetes insipidus,
bleeding from oesophageal varices

```
Cys-Tyr-Phe-Gln-Asn-Cys-Pro-
Arg-Gly-NH2
```

Aripiprazole (rINN) a·ri·*pi*·pra·zôl

7-{4-[4-(2,3-Dichlorophenyl)piperazin-1-yl]butoxy}-3,4-
dihydroquinolin-2(1*H*)-one; $C_{23}H_{27}Cl_2N_3O_2$; *129722-12-9*
Dopamine D_2 receptor antagonist; neuroleptic

Arofylline (rINN) a·*ro*·fi·lën

3-(4-Chlorophenyl)-1-propylxanthine; $C_{14}H_{13}ClN_4O_2$;
136145-07-8; LAS 31025
Phosphodiesterase IV inhibitor

Arprinocid (rINN) ar·*pri*·nö·sid

9-(2-Chloro-6-fluorobenzyl)adenine; $C_{12}H_9ClFN_5$; *55779-18-5*
Antihelminthic; treatment of coccidiosis

Arsanilic Acid (rINN) see Appendix C

Artemether (rINN) ar·te·*më*·ther

(3*R*,5a*S*,6*R*,8a*S*,9*R*,10*S*,12*R*,12a*R*)-Decahydro-10-methoxy-
3,6,9-trimethyl-3,12-epoxy-12*H*-pyrano[4,3-*j*][1,2]¬
benzodioxepin; $C_{16}H_{26}O_5$; *71963-77-4*
Anitprotozoal (malaria)

Artesunate (rINN) ar·të·*soo*·nät

(3*R*,5a*S*,6*R*,8a*S*,9*R*,10*S*,12*R*,12a*R*)-Decahydro-3,6,9-trimethyl-
3,12-epoxy-12*H*-pyrano[4,3-*j*]-[1,2]benzodioxepin-10-yl
hydrogen succinate; $C_{19}H_{28}O_8$; *182824-33-5*
Anitprotozoal (malaria)

Articaine (rINN) *ar*·ti·kän

Methyl 4-methyl-3-(2-propylaminopropionamido)thiophene-2-
carboxylate; $C_{13}H_{20}N_2O_3S$; *23964-58-1*
● **Articaine Hydrochloride** *23964-57-0*
Local anaesthetic

and enantiomer

● **Ascorbic Acid** (rINN) as·*kor*·bik

L-Ascorbic acid; vitamin C; $C_6H_8O_6$; *50-81-7*; component in
many proprietary preparations
Vitamin C

Ascorbyl Gamolenate (rINN) see Appendix C

Asenapine (rINN) a·*se*·na·pën

(3a*RS*,12b*RS*)-5-Chloro-2-methyl-2,3,3a,12b-tetrahydro-1*H*-
dibenzo[2,3:6,7]oxepino[4,5-*c*]pyrrole; $C_{17}H_{16}ClNO$;
85650-56-2
Mixed neurotransmitter receptor antagonist; neuroleptic

and enantiomer

Asobamast (rINN) a·só·ba·mast
2-Ethoxyethyl [4-(3-methyl-1,2-oxazol-5-yl)1,3-thiazol-2-yl]oxamate; $C_{13}H_{15}N_3O_5S$; *104777-03-9*
Histamine H_1 receptor antagonist; antihistamine

Asoprisnil (rINN) ä·sö·*pris*·nil
11β-[4-[(*E*)-(Hydroxyimino)methyl]phenyl]-17β-methoxy-17α-(methoxymethyl)estra-4,9-dien-3-one; $C_{28}H_{35}NO_4$; *163883-88-3*
Selective progesterone modulator

● **Aspartame** (rINN) *as*·par·täm
(1) (3*S*)-3-Amino-*N*-[(α*S*)-(α-methoxycarbonylphenethyl)]¬succinamic acid; (2) Methyl-L-aspartyl-L-phenylalaninate; $C_{14}H_{18}N_2O_5$; *53906-69-7*
Sweetening agent

● **Aspirin** (BAN) *as*·pi·rin
O-Acetylsalicylic acid; $C_9H_8O_4$; *50-78-2*; component in many proprietary preparations
Aspirin Lysine
Salicylate; non-selective cyclo-oxygenase inhibitor; antipyretic; analgesic; anti-inflammatory

● **Astemizole** (rINN) as·*te*·mi·zôl
1-(4-Fluorobenzyl)benzimidazol-2-yl[1-(4-methoxyphenethyl)-4-piperidyl]amine; $C_{28}H_{31}FN_4O$; *68844-77-9*
Histamine H_1 receptor antagonist; antihistamine

Asulacrine (BAN) a·*sü*·la·krën
9-[2-Methoxy-4-(methylsulfonylamino)anilino]-*N*,5-dimethylacridine-4-carboxamide; $C_{24}H_{24}N_4O_4S$; *80841-47-0*; CI-921; NSC 343499
Inhibitor of DNA topoisomerase II; cytotoxic

Atazanavir (rINN) a·ta·*za*·na·veer
Dimethyl (3*S*,8*S*,9*S*,12*S*)-9-benzyl-3,12-di-*tert*-butyl-8-hydroxy-4,11-dioxo-6-[4-(2-pyridyl)benzyl]-2,5,6,10,13-penta-azate-tradecanedioate; $C_{38}H_{52}N_6O_7$; *198904-31-3*;
Atazanavir Sulfate *229975-97-7*; BMS-232632-05
Antiviral (HIV)

● **Atenolol** (rINN) a·*ten*·o·lol
(*RS*)-4-(2-Hydroxy-3-isopropylaminopropoxy)phenyl¬acetamide; $C_{14}H_{22}N_2O_3$; *29122-68-7*
Beta-adrenoceptor antagonist

and enantiomer

Atipamezole (rINN) a·ti·*pa*·me·zôl
4-(2-Ethylindan-2-yl)imidazole; $C_{14}H_{16}N_2$; *104054-27-5*
Atipamezole Hydrochloride *104075-48-1*
Alpha$_2$-adrenoceptor antagonist; reversal of sedative effect of medetomidine (veterinary)

Atomoxetine (rINN) a·tö·*moks*·e·tën
(*R*)-*N*-Methyl-3-phenyl-3-(*o*-tolyloxy)propylamine; $C_{17}H_{21}NO$; *83105-26-3*
Noradrenaline reuptake inhibitor; treatment of attention deficit hyperactivity disorder (ADHD)

The symbol '¬' in systematic chemical names signifies line continuation

Atorvastatin (rINN) a·tor·va·*sta*·tin

(3*R*,5*R*)7-[2-(4-Fluorophenyl)-5-isopropyl-3-phenyl-4-(phenylcarbamoyl)pyrrol-1-yl]-3,5-dihydroxyheptanoic acid; $C_{33}H_{35}FN_2O_5$; *134523-00-5*
Atorvastatin Calcium *134523-03-8*
HMG Co-A reductase inhibitor; lipid-regulating drug

Atosiban (rINN) a·*tö*·si·ban

[1-(3-Sulfanylpropanoyl),2-(4-*O*-ethyltyrosine),4-L-threonine-8-L-ornithine]oxytocin; $C_{43}H_{67}N_{11}O_{12}S_2$; *90779-69-4*
Oxytocin antagonist; treatment of premature labour

Atovaquone (rINN) a·*tö*·va·kwön

2-[*trans*-4-(4-Chlorophenyl)cyclohexyl]-3-hydroxy-1,4-naphthoquinone; $C_{22}H_{19}ClO_3$; *95233-18-4*
Antiprotozoal (malaria)

● **Atracurium Besilate** (rINN) a·tra·*kûr*·rë·um be·si·lät

2,2′-(3,11-Dioxo-4,10-dioxatridecamethylene)bis(1,2,3,4-tetrahydro-6,7-dimethoxy-2-methyl-1-veratrylisoquinolinium) di(benzenesulfonate); $C_{65}H_{82}N_2O_{18}S_2$; *64228-81-5*; 33A74
Non-depolarizing neuromuscular blocker

mixture of stereoisomers

Atropine (BAN) a·trö·pën

(1*R*,3*r*,5*S*)-Tropan-3-yl (*RS*)-tropate; $C_{17}H_{23}NO_3$; *51-55-8*
● **Atropine Methobromide** *2870-71-5*
● **Atropine Methonitrate** *52-88-0*
● **Atropine Sulfate** *5908-99-6*
Anticholinergic

and enantiomer at C*

Auranofin (rINN) or·*ra*·nö·fin

S-(Triethylphosphoranediylaurio)-1-thio-β-D-glucopyranose 2,3,4,6-tetra-acetate; $C_{20}H_{34}AuO_9PS$; *34031-32-8*
Gold salt; treatment of rheumatoid arthritis

Avilamycin (rINN) a·vi·la·*mï*·sin

An antibacterial obtained from cultures of *Streptomyces viridochromogenes*, or the same substance produced by any other means; consists mainly of avilamycin A; *11051-71-1*;
Avilamycin A: *O*-(1*R*)-4-*C*-acetyl-6-deoxy-2,3-*O*-methylene-D-galactopyranosylidene-(1→3-4)-2-*O*-isobutyryl-α-L-lyxopyranosyl *O*-2,6-dideoxy-4-O-(3,5-dichloro-4-hydroxy-6-methyl-*o*-anisoyl)-β-D-*arabino*-hexopyranosyl-(1→4)-*O*-2,6-dideoxy-D-*arabino*-hexopyranosylidene-(1→3-4)-*O*-2,6-dideoxy-3-*C*-methyl-D-*arabino*-hexopyranosyl-(1→3)-*O*-6-deoxy-4-*O*-methyl-β-D-galactopyranosyl-(1→4)-2,6-di-*O*-methyl-β-D-mannopyranoside; $C_{61}H_{88}Cl_2O_{32}$; *69787-79-7*
Avilamycin C: *69787-80-0*
Antibacterial (veterinary)

	R	R₁ + R₂
Avilamycin A:	$-CO-CHMe_2$	$=O$
Avilamycin C:	$-CO-CHMe_2$	$-H + -OH$

Aviptadil (rINN) a·*vip*·ta·dil

Vasoactive intestinal polypeptide; *40077-57-4*
Analogue of vasoactive intestinal peptide
aviptadil has the following amino acid sequence:

```
H₂N-His-Ser-Asp-Ala-Val-Phe-
Tyr-Asp-Asn-Tyr-Thr-Arg-Leu-
Arg-Lys-Gln-Met-Ala-Val-Lys-
Lys-Tyr-Leu-Asn-Ser-Ile-Leu-
Asn-NH₂
```

Avizafone (rINN) a·*vï*·za·fön

L-Lysyl-(2′-benzoyl-4′-chloro-*N*′-methyl)glycinanilide;
$C_{22}H_{27}ClN_4O_3$; *65617-86-9*; Ro 03-7355/000
Avizafone Hydrochloride *60067-16-5*; Ro 03-7355/002
Benzodiazepine

Avoparcin (rINN) ä·vö·*par*·sin

A glycopeptide antibacterial obtained from cultures of
Streptomycescandidus or the same substance obtained by any
other means; *37332-99-3*
Glycopeptide antibacterial drug (veterinary)

Azacitidine (rINN) as·á·*sit*·i·dën

4-Amino-1-*β*-D-ribofuranosyl-1,3,5-triazin-2(1*H*)-one;
$C_8H_{12}N_4O_5$; *320-67-2*;
Cytidine analogue; antineoplastic

Azacyclonol (rINN) ä·za·*sï*·klö·nol

α-Phenyl-α-4-piperidylbenzyl alcohol; $C_{18}H_{21}NO$; *115-46-8*
Histamine H₁ receptor antagonist; antihistamine

Azalomycin (rINN) a·zä·lö·*mï*·sin

A mixture of related macrolide antibiotics produced by
Streptomyces hygroscopicus var· *azalomyceticus*; *54182-65-9*
Antibacterial

Azamethiphos (BAN) ä·za·*me*·thi·fos

S-[(6-Chloro-2,3-dihydro-2-oxo-[1,3]oxazolo[4,5-*b*]pyridin-3-
yl)methyl] *O*,*O*-dimethyl phosphorothioate; $C_9H_{10}ClN_2O_5PS$;
35575-96-3; CGA 18809; OMS No 1825
Organophosphorus insecticide

Azamethonium Bromide (rINN) ä·za·me·*thö*·në·um

2,2′-Methyliminobis(diethyldimethylammonium) dibromide;
$C_{13}H_{33}Br_2N_3$; *306-53-6*
Ganglion blocker

Azanidazole (rINN) ä·za·*nï*·da·zôl

4-[(*E*)-2-(1-Methyl-5-nitroimidazol-2-yl)vinyl]pyrimidin-2-
ylamine; $C_{10}H_{10}N_6O_2$; *62973-76-6*
Antiprotozoal

♣ **Azaperone** (rINN) ä·*za*·pe·rön

4′-Fluoro-4-[4-(2-pyridyl)piperazin-1-yl]butyrophenone;
$C_{19}H_{22}FN_3O$; *1649-18-9*
Dopamine receptor antagonist; neuroleptic (veterinary)

Azapetine (BAN) ä·*za*·pe·tën

6-Allyl-6,7-dihydro-5*H*-dibenz[*c*,*e*]azepine; $C_{17}H_{17}N$; *146-36-1*
Azapetine Phosphate *130-83-6*
Alpha-adrenoceptor agonist

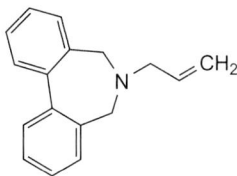

● **Azapropazone** (rINN) ä·za·*prö*·pa·zön

5-Dimethylamino-9-methyl-2-propylpyrazolo[1,2-*a*][1,2,4]¬
benzotriazine-1,3(2*H*)-dione; apazone (USAN); $C_{16}H_{20}N_4O_2$;
13539-59-8
Cyclo-oxygenase inhibitor; analgesic; anti-inflammatory

The symbol '¬' in systematic chemical names signifies line continuation

Azaribine (rINN) ä·za·ri·bën

(1) 2-β-D-Ribofuranosyl-1,2,4-triazine-3,5(2*H*,4*H*)-dione-2′,3′,5′-triacetate; (2) 6-Azauridine 2′,3′,5′-triacetate; $C_{14}H_{17}N_3O_9$; *2169-64-4*
Cytotoxic

Azatadine (rINN) ä·za·ta·dën

6,11-Dihydro-11-(1-methyl-4-piperidylidene)-5*H*-benzo[5,6]cyclohepta[1,2-*b*]pyridine; $C_{20}H_{22}N_2$; *3964-81-6*
Azatadine Maleate *3978-86-7*
Histamine H_1 receptor antagonist; antihistamine

Azatepa (rINN) ä·za·*të*·pa

P,*P*-Bis(aziridin-1-yl)-*N*-ethyl-*N*-1,3,4-thiadiazol-2-yl phosphinamide; $C_8H_{14}N_5OPS$; *125-45-1*
Cytotoxic

● **Azathioprine** (rINN) ä·za·*thï*·ö·prën

6-(1-Methyl-4-nitroimidazol-5-ylthio)purine; $C_9H_7N_7O_2S$; *446-86-6*
Immunosuppressant

Azelastine (rINN) ä·ze·*las*·tën

(*RS*)-4-(4-Chlorobenzyl)-2-(1-methylazepan-4-yl)phthalazin-1(2*H*)-one; $C_{22}H_{24}ClN_3O$; *58581-89-8*
Azelastine Hydrochloride *79307-93-0*
Histamine H_1 receptor antagonist; antihistamine

and enantiomer

Azepexole (rINN) ä·ze·*peks*·ôl

6-Ethyl-5,6,7,8-tetrahydro-4*H*-[1,3]oxazolo[4,5-*d*]azepin-2-ylamine; $C_9H_{15}N_3O$; *36067-73-9*
Azepexole Dihydrochloride BHT 933
Alpha-adrenoceptor agonist

Azetepa *see Azatepa*

Azidamfenicol (rINN) a·zï·dam·*fe*·ni·kol

2-Azido-*N*-[(α*R*,β*R*)-β-hydroxy-α-hydroxymethyl-4-nitrophenethyl]acetamide; $C_{11}H_{13}N_5O_5$; *13838-08-9*
Antibacterial

Azidocillin (rINN) a·zï·dö·*si*·lin

6-(D-2-Azido-2-phenylacetamido)penicillanic acid; $C_{16}H_{17}N_5O_4S$; *17243-38-8*; BRL 2534; SPC 297D
Penicillin antibacterial

Azimilide (rINN) a·*zim*·i·lïd

(*E*)-{1-{[5-(4-Chlorophenyl)furfurylidene]amino}-3-[4-(4-methylpiperazin-1-yl)butyl]imidazolidine-2,4-dione; $C_{23}H_{28}ClN_5O_3$; *149908-53-2*; NE-10064
Azimilide Hydrochloride (2HCl) *149888-94-8*
Potassium channel blocker; antiarrhythmic

Azithromycin (rINN) a·zi·thrö·*mï*·sin

(2*R*,3*S*,4*R*,5*R*,8*R*,10*R*,11*R*,12*S*,13*S*,14*R*)-13-(2,6-Dideoxy-3-*C*,3-*O*-dimethyl-α-L-*ribo*-hexopyranosyloxy)-2-ethyl-3,4,10-trihydroxy-3,5,6,8,10,12,14-heptamethyl-11-(3,4,6-trideoxy-3-dimethylamino-β-D-*xylo*-hexopyranosyloxy)-1-oxa-6-azacyclopentadecan-15-one; $C_{38}H_{72}N_2O_{12}$; *83905-01-5*
Macrolide antibacterial

Azlocillin (rINN) see Appendix C

Azovan Blue (BAN) *ä*·zö·van

Tetrasodium 1,1′-diamino-8,8′-dihydroxy-7,7′-(2,2′-dimethyl¬biphenyl-4,4′-diylbisdiazo)di(naphthalene-2,4-disulfonate); Evans Blue (USAN); $C_{34}H_{24}N_6Na_4O_{14}S_4$; *6968-33-8*
Dyestuff

Aztreonam (rINN) az·*trë*·ö·nam

(*Z*)-2-{2-Amino-1,3-thiazol-4-yl-[(2*S*,3*S*)-2-methyl-4-oxo-1-sulfoazetidin-3-ylcarbamoyl]methyleneamino-oxy}-2-methylpropionic acid; $C_{13}H_{17}N_5O_8S_2$; *78110-38-0*
Monobactam antibacterial

Azuresin (BAN) a·*zûr*·re·sin

7-Aminophenothiazin-3-ylidene(dimethyl)ammonium chloride; *8050-34-8*; $C_{14}H_{14}ClN_3S$
Dyestuff; diagnostic agent; cationic exchange resin

Bacampicillin (rINN) ba·kam·pi·*si*·lin

1-(Ethoxycarbonyloxy)ethyl 6-(α-D-phenylglycylamino)¬penicillanate; $C_{21}H_{27}N_3O_7S$; *50972-17-3*
● **Bacampicillin Hydrochloride** *37661-08-8*
Penicillin antibacterial

and enantiomer C*

● **Bacitracin** (rINN) ba·si·*trä*·sin

One or more antimicrobial polypeptides produced by certain strains of *Bacillus licheniformis* and *Bacillus subtilis* var· *Tracy*; *1405-87-4*
● **Bacitracin Zinc** *1405-89-6*
Polypeptide antibacterial

● **Baclofen** (rINN) *ba*·klö·fen

4-Amino-3-(4-chlorophenyl)butyric acid; $C_{10}H_{12}ClNO_2$; *1134-47-0*
Skeletal muscle relaxant

and enantiomer

Balipramine *see Depramine*

Balsalazide (rINN) bal·*sal*·a·zïd

(*E*)-5-[4-(2-Carboxyethylcarbamoyl)phenylazo]-2-hydroxy¬benzoic acid; $C_{17}H_{15}N_3O_6$; *80573-04-2*
Balsalazide Sodium *150399-21-6 (disodium, dihydrate)*
Aminosalicylate; treatment of ulcerative colitis

Bambermycin (rINN) bam·ber·*mï*·sin

An antibacterial complex containing mainly moenomycins A and C obtained from cultures of *Streptomyces bambergiensis* or the same substance obtained by any other means; bambermycins (USAN); *11015-37-5*
Antibacterial (veterinary)

Bambuterol (rINN) bam·*bü*·ter·ol

(*RS*)-5-(2-*tert*-Butylamino-l-hydroxyethyl)-*m*-phenylene bis(dimethylcarbamate); $C_{18}H_{29}N_3O_5$; *81732-65-2*
● **Bambuterol Hydrochloride**
Beta$_2$-adrenoceptor agonist; bronchodilator

The symbol '¬' in systematic chemical names signifies line continuation

Bamethan (rINN) *ba·me·than*
2-Butylamino-1-(4-hydroxyphenyl)ethanol; $C_{12}H_9NO_2$; *3703-79-5*
Bamethan Sulfate *5716-20-1*
Vasodilator; treatment of peripheral vascular disease

Bamifylline (rINN) *ba·mi·fi·lën*
8-Benzyl-7-[2-(N-ethyl-2-hydroxyethylamino)ethyl]¬
theophylline; $C_{20}H_{27}N_5O_3$; *2016-63-9*
Non-selective phosphodiesterase inhibitor (xanthine); treatment of reversible airways obstruction

Bamipine (rINN) *ba·mi·pën*
N-Benzyl-N-(1-methyl-4-piperidyl)aniline; $C_{19}H_{24}N_2$; *4945-47-5*
Histamine H_1 receptor antagonist; antihistamine

Banoxantrone (rINN) *ba·noks·an·trön*
1,4-Bis[2-(dimethylazinoyl)ethylamino]-5,8-dihydroxy-9,10-anthraquinone; $C_{22}H_{28}N_4O_6$; *136470-65-0*
Cytotoxic

Baquiloprim (rINN) *ba·kwi·lö·prim*
5-(8-Dimethylamino-7-methyl-5-quinolylmethyl)pyrimidin-2,4-diyldiamine; $C_{17}H_{20}N_6$; *102280-35-3*
Antibacterial (veterinary)

● **Barbital** (rINN) *bar·bi·tal*
5,5-Diethylbarbituric acid; $C_8H_{12}N_2O_3$; *57-44-3*
Barbital Sodium *144-02-5*
Barbiturate

Basiliximab (rINN) *ba·si·liks·i·mab*
Immunoglobulin G1 (human–mouse monoclonal CHI621 heavy chain anti-human interleukin 2 receptor), disulfide with human-mouse monoclonal CHI621 light chain, dimer; *179045-86-4*
Monoclonal antibody (CD-25 antigen of the interleukin receptor on T lymphocytes)

Batimastat (rINN) *ba·ti·ma·stat*
(2S,3R)-N^1-Hydroxy-3-isobutyl-N^4-[(S)-α-(methylcarbamoyl)¬phenethyl]-2-(2-thienylthiomethyl)succinamide; $C_{23}H_{31}N_3O_4S_2$; *130370-60-4*; BB-94
Matrix metalloproteinase inhibitor; cytotoxic

Becaplermin (rINN) be·ka·*pler*·min

Recombinant human platelet-derived growth factor B; a recombinant protein produced by genetically engineered *Saccharomyces cerevisiae* cells that is similar in amino acid composition and biological activity to the endogenous human PDGF-BB homodimer; RWJ 60235
Recombinant human platelet-derived growth factor B; treatment of diabetic skin ulcers

For labelling purposes the following three-letter code, to indicate the method of production is approved:
(rys) produced by fermentation using *Saccharomyces cerevisiae* containing a recombinant plasmid

becaplermin has the following glycosylated amino acid sequence:

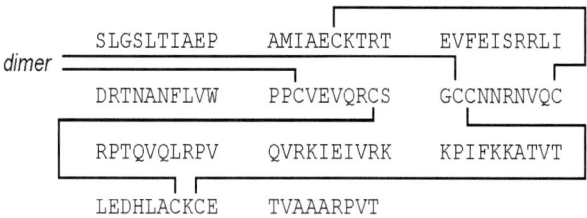

Beclamide (rINN) *be*·kla·mïd

N-Benzyl-3-chloropropionamide; $C_{10}H_{12}ClNO$; *501-68-8*
Antiepileptic

Beclobrate (rINN) be·klö·brät

Ethyl 2-(4-*p*-Chlorobenzylphenoxy)-2-methylbutyrate; $C_{20}H_{23}ClO_3$; *55937-99-0*
Fibrate; lipid-regulating drug

and enantiomer

Beclometasone (rINN) be·klö·*me*·ta·sön

9α-Chloro-11β,17α,21-trihydroxy-16β-methylpregna-1,4-diene-3,20-dione; $C_{28}H_{37}ClO_7$; *4419-39-0*
● **Beclometasone Dipropionate** *5534-09-8*
Glucocorticoid

Bemegride (rINN) *be*·me·grïd

3-Ethyl-3-methylglutarimide; $C_8H_{13}NO_2$; *64-65-3*
Respiratory stimulant

Bemetizide (rINN) be·*me*·ti·zïd

6-Chloro-3,4-dihydro-3-(1-phenylethyl)-2*H*-1,2,4-benzothiadazine-7-sulfonamide 1,1-dioxide; $C_{15}H_{16}ClN_3O_4S_2$; *1824-52-8*
Thiazide diuretic

and enantiomer

Bemiparin Sodium (rINN) be·*mi*·pa·rin *sö*·dë·um

Sodium salt of depolymerised heparin obtained by alkaline degradation of quaternary ammonium salt of heparin from pork intestinal mucosa: the majority of the components have a 2-*O*-sulfo-4-*erythro*-hex-enepyranosuronic acid at the non-reducing end and a 2-*N*,6-*O*-disulfo-D-glucosamine structure at the reducing end; the average molecular weight is 3600 (3000 to 4200); the degree of sulfatation is about 2 per disaccharidic unit; *9041-08-1*
Low molecular weight heparin

Benactyzine (rINN) be·nak·*tï*·zën

2-Diethylaminoethyl benzilate; $C_{20}H_{25}NO_3$; *302-40-9*
Anticholinergic

Benaprizine (rINN) see Appendix C

Benazepril (rINN) be·*nä*·ze·pril

{(3*S*)-3-[(1*S*)-1-Ethoxycarbonyl-3-phenylpropylamino]-2,3,4,5-tetrahydro-2-oxo-1*H*-1-benzazepin-1-yl}acetic acid; $C_{24}H_{28}N_2O_5$; *86541-75-5*
♣ **Benazepril Hydrochloride** *86541-74-4*
Angiotensin converting enzyme inhibitor (veterinary)

The symbol '¬' in systematic chemical names signifies line continuation

Bendamustine (rINN) ben·dá·*muss*·tën
4-{5-[Bis(2-chloroethyl)amino]-1-methylbenzimidazol-
2-yl}butanoic acid; $C_{16}H_{21}Cl_2N_3O_2$; *16506-27-7;*
Bendamustine Hydrochloride *3543-75-7*
*Cytotoxic alkylating agent; treatment of chronic lymphocytic
leukaemia*

Bendazac (rINN) *ben*·da·zak
(1-Benzylindazol-3-yloxy)acetic acid; $C_{16}H_{14}N_2O_3$; *20187-55-7*
Bendazac Lysine *81919-14-4;* AF 1934
Cyclo-oxygenase inhibitor; analgesic; anti-inflammatory

Bendrofluazide *see Bendroflumethiazide*

● **Bendroflumethiazide** (rINN) ben·drö·floo·me·*thï*·a·zïd
3-Benzyl-3,4-dihydro-6-trifluoromethyl-2*H*-1,2,4-
benzothiadiazine-7-sulfonamide 1,1-dioxide;
$C_{15}H_{14}F_3N_3O_4S_2$; *73-48-3*
Thiazide diuretic

● **Benethamine Penicillin** (rINN) be·*ne*·tha·mën
Benzyl(phenethyl)ammonium (6*R*)-6-(2-phenylacetamido)¬
penicillanate; $C_{16}H_{17}N_2O_4S.C_{15}H_{18}N$; *751-84-8*
Penicillin antibacterial

Benfluorex (rINN) ben·*floo*·or·reks
2-({(1*RS*)-1-Methyl-2-[3-(trifluoromethyl)phenyl]ethyl}¬
amino)ethyl benzoate; $C_{19}H_{20}F_3NO_2$; *23602-78-0*
● **Benfluorex Hydrochloride** *23642-66-2*
Lipid-regulating drug

and enantiomer

● **Benorilate** (rINN) be·*no*·ri·lät
4-Acetamidophenyl *O*-acetylsalicylate; $C_{17}H_{15}NO_5$; *5003-48-5*
*Salicylate-paracetamol derivative; antipyretic; analgesic;
anti-inflammatory*

Benoxaprofen (rINN) see Appendix C

Benperidol (rINN) ben·*pe*·ri·dol
1-{1-[3-(4-Fluorobenzoyl)propyl]-4-piperidyl}benzimidazolin-
2-one; $C_{22}H_{24}FN_3O_2$; *2062-84-2*
Dopamine receptor antagonist; neuroleptic

Benserazide (rINN) ben·*se*·ra·zïd
2-Amino-3-hydroxy-2′-(2,3,4-trihydroxybenzyl)¬
propionohydrazide; $C_{10}H_{15}N_3O_5$; *322-35-0*
Benserazide Hydrochloride *14919-77-8*
Dopa decarboxylase inhibitor

and enantiomer

Bensuldazic Acid (rINN) ben·sul·*dä*·zik
(5-Benzyl-6-thioxo-1,3,5-thiadiazin-3-yl)acetic acid;
$C_{12}H_{14}N_2O_2S_2$; *1219-77-8*
♣ **Sodium Bensuldazate** *1950-15-8*
Antifungal (veterinary)

Bentiromide (rINN) ben·*ti*·rö·mïd
4-(*N*-Benzoyl-L-tyrosylamino)benzoic acid; $C_{23}H_{20}N_2O_5$;
37106-97-1; Ro 11-7891
Diagnostic aid

● **Benzalkonium Chloride** (rINN) ben·zal·*kö*·në·um
Alkylbenzyldimethylammonium chlorides; *8001-54-5*
Antiseptic

● **Benzathine Benzylpenicillin** (rINN) *ben*·za·thën
N,N'-Dibenzylethylenediammonium bis[(6*R*)-6-(2-phenyl¬
acetamido)penicillanate]; penicillin G benzathine (USAN);
$(C_{16}H_{17}N_2O_4)_2.C_{16}H_{22}N_2$; *1538-09-6*
Penicillin antibacterial

Benzatropine (rINN) ben·za·*trö*·pën
(1*R*,3*r*,5*S*)-3-Benzhydryloxytropane; $C_{21}H_{25}NO$; *86-13-5*
● **Benzatropine Mesilate** *132-17-2*
Anticholinergic

● **Benzbromarone** (rINN) benz·*brö*·ma·rön
3,5-Dibromo-4-hydroxyphenyl 2-ethylbenzofuran-3-yl ketone;
$C_{17}H_{12}Br_2O_3$; *3562-84-3*
Uricosuric; treatment of hyperuricaemia

Benzestrol (rINN) benz·*ës*·trol
4,4'-(1,2-Diethyl-3-methyltrimethylene)diphenol; $C_{20}H_{26}O_2$;
85-95-0
Oestrogen

mixture of 8 stereoisomers

Benzethidine (rINN) see Appendix C

● **Benzethonium Chloride** (rINN) ben·ze·*thö*·në·um
Benzyldimethyl-2-{2-[4-(1,1,3,3-tetramethylbutyl)¬
phenoxy]ethoxy}ethylammonium chloride; $C_{27}H_{42}ClNO_2$;
121-54-0
Antiseptic

Benzfetamine (rINN) benz·*fet*·a·mën
(+)-*N*-Benzyl-*N*,α-dimethylphenethylamine; $C_{17}H_{21}N$; *156-08-1*
Amfetamine analogue

Benzhexol *see Trihexyphenidyl*

Benzilonium Bromide (rINN) ben·zi·*lö*·në·um
3-Benziloyloxy-1,1-diethylpyrrolidinium bromide;
$C_{22}H_{28}BrNO_3$; *1050-48-2*
Anticholinergic

Benziodarone (rINN) ben·zï·*ö*·da·rön
2-Ethylbenzofuran-3-yl 4-hydroxy-3,5-di-iodophenyl ketone;
$C_{17}H_{12}I_2O_3$; *68-90-6*
Uricosuric; treatment of hyperuricaemia

● **Benzocaine** (rINN) ben·zö·kän
Ethyl 4-aminobenzoate; $C_9H_{11}NO_2$; *94-09-7*; component in
many proprietary preparations
Local anaesthetic

Benzoctamine (rINN) see Appendix C

The symbol '¬' in systematic chemical names signifies line continuation

Benzonatate (rINN) ben·zö·na·tät

3,6,9,12,15,18,21,24,27-Nonaoxaoctacosyl 4-butylamino¬
benzoate; $C_{30}H_{53}NO_{11}$; *104-31-4*
Cough suppressant

Benzphetamine *see Benzfetamine*

Benzquinamide (rINN) benz·*kwi*·na·mïd

3-Diethylcarbamoyl-1,3,4,6,7,11b-hexahydro-9,10-dimethoxy-
2*H*-benzo[*a*]quinolizin-2-yl acetate; $C_{22}H_{32}N_2O_5$; *63-12-7*
Antiemetic

Benzthiazide (rINN) benz·*thï*·a·zïd

3-Benzylthiomethyl-6-chloro-1,2,4-benzothiadiazine-7-
sulfonamide 1,1-dioxide; $C_{15}H_{14}ClN_3O_4S_3$; *91-33-8*
Thiazide diuretic

Benztropine *see Benzatropine*

Benzydamine (rINN) ben·*zï*·da·mën

3-(1-Benzylindazol-3-yloxy)propyldimethylamine;
$C_{19}H_{23}N_3O$; *642-72-8*
Benzydamine Hydrochloride *132-69-4*
Cyclo-oxygenase inhibitor; analgesic; anti-inflammatory

Benzylpenicillin (rINN) ben·zïl·pe·ni·*si*·lin

6-(2-Phenylacetamido)penicillanic acid; $C_{16}H_{18}N_2O_4S$; *61-33-6*
● **Benzylpenicillin Potassium** *113-98-4*
● **Benzylpenicillin Sodium** *69-57-8*
Penicillin antibacterial

♣ **Bephenium Hydroxynaphthoate** (rINN) be·*fë*·në·um
hï·droks·ë·*naf*·thö·ät

Benzyldimethyl-2-phenoxyethylammonium 3-hydroxy-2-
naphthoate; $C_{28}H_{29}NO_4$; *3818-50-6*
Antihelminthic (veterinary)

Bepridil (rINN) be·pri·dil

N-Benzyl-*N*-(3-isobutoxy-2-pyrrolidin-1-ylpropyl)aniline;
$C_{24}H_{34}N_2O$; *64706-54-3*
Bepridil Hydrochloride *74764-40-2*; Org 5730
Calcium channel blocker

and enantiomer

Beractant (BAN) be·*rak*·tant

A modified bovine lung extract containing mostly
phospholipids, modified by the addition of dipalmitoyl¬
phosphatidyl choline (DPPC), palmitic acid and tripalmitin;
108778-82-1
Lung surfactant

Bertilimumab (rINN) ber·ti·*li*·mü·mab

Immunoglobulin G4, anti-(human eotaxin 1) (human
monoclonal CAT-213 γ4-chain), disulfide with human
monoclonal CAT 213 γ-chain, dimer; *375348-49-5*
Immunomodulator

Besilesomab (rINN) bessi·*le*·zö·mab

Immunoglobin G1, anti-(human CEA (carcinoembryonic
antigen)-related antigen) (mouse monoclonal BW 250/183
heavy chain), disulfide with mouse monoclonal
BW 250/183κ-chain, dimer; *537694-98-7*
Monoclonal antibody (CEA-related)

● **Betacarotene** (rINN) bë·ta·*ka*·rö·tën

(*all-E*)-β-β-carotene; $C_{40}H_{56}$; *7235-40-7*
*Precursor of vitamin A; treatment of vitamin A deficiency;
reduction in severity of photosensitivity reactions*

Betacetylmethadol (rINN) bë·*ta*·së·til·*meth*·a·dol
4-Dimethylamino-1-ethyl-2,2-diphenylpentyl acetate (β-form);
$C_{23}H_{31}NO_2$; *17199-59-6*
Opioid receptor agonist; analgesic

- **Betadex** (rINN) *bë*·ta·deks
(1) Cyclo-α-(1→4)-D-heptaglucopyranoside;
(2) Cycloheptakis(1→4)-α-D-glucosyl; $C_{42}H_{70}O_{35}$; *7585-39-9*
Carrier molecule for drug delivery systems

Betahistine (rINN) bë·ta·*his*·tën
Methyl-2-(2-pyridyl)ethylamine; $C_8H_{12}N_2$; *5638-76-6*
- **Betahistine Dihydrochloride** *5579-84-0*
- **Betahistine Mesilate** *54856-23-4*
Histamine H_1 receptor antagonist; antihistamine

Betameprodine (rINN) bë·ta·*me*·prö·dën
(3*S*,4*S*)-3-Ethyl-1-methyl-4-phenyl-4-piperidyl propionate;
$C_{17}H_{25}NO_2$; *468-50-8*
Opioid receptor agonist; analgesic

Betamethadol (rINN) bë·ta·*me*·tha·dol
6-Dimethylamino-4,4-diphenylheptan-3-ol (β-form); $C_{21}H_{29}NO$;
17199-55-2
Opioid receptor agonist; analgesic

- **Betamethasone** (rINN) bë·ta·*me*·tha·sön
9α-Fluoro-11β,17α,21-trihydroxy-16β-methylpregna-1,4-
diene-3,20-dione; $C_{22}H_{29}FO_5$; *378-44-9*
- **Betamethasone Acetate** *987-24-6*
Betamethasone Adamantoate *40242-27-1*
- **Betamethasone Dipropionate** *5593-20-4*
- **Betamethasone Sodium Phosphate** *151-73-5*
- **Betamethasone Valerate** *2152-44-5*
Glucocorticoid

Betamethasone Acibutate (rINN) bë·ta·*me*·tha·sön a·së·*bü*·tät
9α-Fluoro-11β-hydroxy-16β-methyl-3,20-dioxopregna-1,4-
diene-17,21-diyl 21-acetate 17-isobutyrate; $C_{28}H_{37}FO_7$;
5534-05-4
Glucocorticoid

Betanidine (rINN) be·*ta*·ni·dën
2-Benzyl-1,3-dimethylguanidine; $C_{10}H_{15}N_3$; *55-73-2*
Betanidine Sulfate *114-85-2*
Adrenergic neuron blocker

Betaprodine (rINN) bë·ta·*prö*·dën

(3*S*,4*S*)-1,3-Dimethyl-4-phenyl-4-piperidyl propionate;
C₁₆H₂₃NO₂; *468-59-7*
Opioid receptor agonist; analgesic

Betaxolol (rINN) bë·*taks*·o·lol

1-[4-(2-Cyclopropylmethoxyethyl)phenoxyl-3-isopropyl¬
aminopropan-2-ol; C₁₈H₂₉NO₃; *63659-18-7*
● **Betaxolol Hydrochloride** *63659-19-8*
Beta-adrenoceptor antagonist

and enantiomer

Bethanechol Chloride (BAN) be·*tha*·ne·kol

2-Carbamoyloxypropyltrimethylammonium chloride;
C₇H₁₇ClN₂O₂; *590-63-6*
Cholinoceptor agonist

and enantiomer

Bethanidine see *Betanidine*

Betiatide (rINN) bë·*ti*·a·tïd

[(Benzoylthio)acetyl]glycylglycylglycine; C₁₅H₁₇N₃O₆S;
103725-47-9
Radiocontrast medium

Bevantolol (rINN) be·*van*·to·lol

1-(3,4-Dimethoxyphenethylamino)-3-*m*-tolyloxypropan-2-ol;
C₂₀H₂₇NO₄; *59170-23-9*
Bevantolol Hydrochloride *42864-78-8*; CI 775
Beta-adrenoceptor antagonist

and enantiomer

Bevonium Metilsulfate (rINN) be·*vö*·në·um më·thïl·*sul*·fät

2-Benziloyloxymethyl-1,1-dimethylpiperidinium methylsulfate,
C₂₃H₃₁NO₇S; *5205-82-3*
Anticholinergic

Bexarotene (rINN) beks·*a*·rö·tën

4-[1-(5,6,7,8-Tetrahydro-3,5,5,8,8-pentamethyl-2-
naphthyl)vinyl]benzoic acid; C₂₄H₂₈O₂; *153559-49-0*
Retinoid receptor agonist; treatment of T cell lymphoma

● **Bezafibrate** (rINN) bë·za·*fï*·brät

2-[4-(2-*p*-Chlorobenzamidoethyl)phenoxy]-2-methylpropionic
acid; C₁₉H₂₀ClNO₄; *41859-67-0*
Fibrate; lipid-regulating drug

Bezitramide (rINN) be·*zi*·tra·mïd

4-[4-(2,3-Dihydro-2-oxo-3-propionyl-1*H*-benzimidazol-l-
yl)piperidino]-2,2-diphenylbutyronitrile; C₃₁H₃₂N₄O₂;
15301-48-1
Opioid receptor agonist; analgesic

Bialamicol (rINN) bï·a·*la*·mi·kol

3,3′-Diallyl-5,5′-bis(diethylaminomethyl)biphenyl-4,4′-diol;
C₂₈H₄₀N₂O₂; *493-75-4*
Antiprotozoal

Bibapcitide (rINN) bï·*bap*·si·tïd

$S^{13},S^{13'}$-[Oxybis(methylene)(2,5-dioxopyrrolidin-1,3-diyl)]bis[N^1,S^5-(1-oxoethano)-D-tyrosyl-S-(3-aminopropyl)-L-cysteinylglycyl-L-α-aspartyl-L-cysteinylglycylglycyl-S-(acetamidomethyl)-L-cysteinylglycyl-S-(acetamidomethyl)-L-cysteinylglycylglycyl-L-cysteinamide; $C_{112}H_{162}N_{36}O_{43}S_{10}$; *153507-46-1*
Radiopharmaceutical; diagnosis of deep vein thrombosis

Bibenzonium Bromide (rINN) bï·ben·*zö*·në·um

2-(1,2-Diphenylethoxy)ethyltrimethylammonium bromide; $C_{19}H_{26}BrNO$; *15585-70-3*
Cough suppressant

and enantiomer

Bicalutamide (rINN) bï·ka·*loo*·ta·mïd

(*RS*)-4'-Cyano-α',α',α'-trifluoro-3-(4-fluorophenylsulfonyl)-2-hydroxy-2-methylpropiono-*m*-toluidide; $C_{18}H_{14}F_4N_2O_4S$; *90357-06-5*
Antiandrogen; treatment of prostate cancer

and enantiomer

Biciromab (rINN) bï·*si*·rö·mab

Mouse T2Gls cell anti-human fibrin II β-chain monoclonal immunoglobulin G Fab' fragment;
Monoclonal antibody (fibrin antibody)

Bidimazium Iodide (rINN) bi·di·*mä*·zë·um

4-(Biphenyl-4-yl)-2-(4-dimethylaminostyryl)-3-methyl-1,3-thiazolium iodide; $C_{26}H_{25}IN_2S$; *21817-73-2*; 65-318
Antihelminthic

Bifluranol (rINN) bï·*flûr*·ra·nol

(1*R*,2*S*)-4,4'-(1-Methyl-2-ethylethylene)bis(3-fluorophenol); $C_{17}H_{18}F_2O_2$; *34633-34-6*; BX 341
Benign prostatic hyperplasia

● **Bifonazole** (rINN) bï·*fo*·na·zôl

1-(α-Biphenyl-4-ylbenzyl)imidazole; $C_{22}H_{18}N_2$; *60628-96-8*; BAY h 4502
Antifungal

and enantiomer

Bile Salts (rINN) see Appendix C

Bimatoprost (rINN) bï·*ma*·tö·prost

(*Z*)-7-{(1*R*,2*R*,3*R*,5*S*)-3,5-Dihydroxy-2-[(1*E*,3*S*)-3-hydroxy-5-phenylpent-1-enyl]cyclopentyl}-*N*-ethylhept-5-enamide; $C_{25}H_{37}NO_4$; *155206-00-1*
Prostaglandin (PGF$_{2\alpha}$) analogue

Binodenoson (rINN) bï·nö·*de*·nö·son

2-[(*E*)-2-(Cyclohexylmethylene)hydrazino]adenosine; $C_{17}H_{25}N_7O_4$; *144348-08-3*
Adenosine A$_{2A}$ receptor agonist; vasodilator

The symbol '¬' in systematic chemical names signifies line continuation

Bioallethrin (BAN) bï·ö·a·*lë*·thrin

(*RS*)-3-Allyl-2-methyl-4-oxocyclopent-2-enyl (1*R*,3*R*)-2,2-dimethyl-3-(2-methylprop-1-enyl)cyclopropanecarboxylate; $C_{19}H_{26}O_3$; *584-79-2*; *28434-00-6* (*S*-isomer)
Pyrethroid insecticide

and epimer at C*

Biperiden (rINN) bï·*pe*·ri·den

1-(Bicyclo[2.2.1]hept-2-en-5-yl)-1-phenyl-3-piperidinopropan-1-ol; $C_{21}H_{29}NO$; *514-65-8*
● **Biperiden Hydrochloride** *1235-82-1*
Biperiden Lactate *7085-45-2*
Anticholinergic

and enantiomer

● **Biphasic Insulin Injection** (BAN)

A sterile suspension of beef insulin in a solution of pork insulin; *8063-29-4*
Hormone; treatment of diabetes mellitus

● **Biphasic Isophane Insulin Injection** (BAN)

A sterile suspension of beef insulin complexed with protamine in a solution of pork insulin or a sterile suspension of human insulin complexed with protamine in a solution of human insulin; *8063-29-4*
Hormone; treatment of diabetes mellitus

● **Bisacodyl** (rINN) bi·sa·*kö*·dïl

4,4′-(2-Pyridylmethylene)di(phenyl acetate); $C_{22}H_{19}NO_4$; *603-50-9*
Stimulant laxative

Bismuth Glycollylarsanilate *see Glycobiarsol*

Bisoprolol (rINN) bï·*so*·pro·lol

1-[4-(2-Isopropoxyethoxymethyl)phenoxy]-3-isopropylamino¬propan-2-ol; $C_{18}H_{31}NO_4$; *66722-44-9*
● **Bisoprolol Fumarate** *66722-45-0*
Beta-adrenoceptor antagonist

and enantiomer

Bisoxatin (rINN) bi·*soks*·a·tin

2,2-Bis(4-hydroxyphenyl)-2*H*-1,4-benzoxazin-3(4*H*)-one; $C_{20}H_{15}NO_4$; *17692-24-9*
Stimulant laxative

Bithionol (rINN) bï·*thï*·o·nol

2,2′-Thiobis(4,6-dichlorophenol); $C_{12}H_6Cl_4O_2S$; *97-18-7*
Antihelminthic

Bitolterol (rINN) bï·*tol*·te·rol

4-[2-(*tert*-Butylamino)-1-hydroxyethyl]-*o*-phenylene¬di-*p*-toluate; $C_{28}H_{31}NO_5$; *30392-40-6*
Bitolterol Mesilate *30392-41-7*; WIN 32784
Beta$_2$-adrenoceptor agonist; bronchodilator

and enantiomer

Bivalirudin (rINN) bï·va·*li*·roo·din

$C_{98}H_{138}N_{24}O_{33}$; *128270-60-0*; BG8967
Direct thrombin inhibitor; anticoagulant

```
D-Phe-Pro-Arg-Pro-Gly-Gly-Gly-Gly-
Asn-Gly-Asp-Phe-Glu-Glu-Ile-Pro-
Glu-Glu-Tyr-Leu
```

Bleomycin (rINN) blë·ö·mï·sin

A mixture of glycopeptide antibiotics produced by *Streptomyces verticillus*; *11056-06-7*
● **Bleomycin Sulfate** *9041-93-4*
Cytotoxic antibacterial

A₂: $R = -NH[CH_2]_3\overset{+}{S}Me_2$
B₂: $R = -NH[CH_2]_4NH - \overset{\parallel}{\underset{NH}{C}} - NH_2$

Boldenone (rINN) see Appendix C

Bolmantalate (rINN) bol·*man*·ta·lät

3-Oxestr-4-en-17β-yl adamantane-1-carboxylate; $C_{29}H_{40}O_3$; *1491-81-2*
Androgen

Bornaprine (rINN) *bor*·na·prën

3-Diethylaminopropyl 2-phenylbicyclo[2.2.1]heptane-2-carboxylate; sormodren; $C_{21}H_{31}NO_2$; *20448-86-6*
Anticholinergic

Bortezomib (rINN) bor·*te*·zö·mib

{(1*R*)-3-Methyl-1-[(2*S*)-3-phenyl-2-(pyrazin-2-carboxamido)¬propanamido]butyl}boronic acid; $C_{19}H_{25}BN_4O_4$; *179324-69-7*
Proteasome inhibitor; cytotoxic

Bosentan (rINN) *bö*·sen·tan

4-*tert*-Butyl-*N*-[6-(2-hydroxyethoxy)-5-(2-methoxyphenoxy)-2,2´-bipyrimidin-4-yl]benzenesulfonamide; $C_{27}H_{29}N_5O_6S$; *147536-97-8*
Endothelin A receptor antagonist

Bovactant (BAN) bö·*vak*·tant

An extract of bovine lung containing about 92% of phospholipids, 3·2% of cholesterol, 0·6% of surfactant-associated hydrophobic proteins and 0·4% of free fatty acid; mean relative molecular mass of phospholipids, about 760; SF-Rl 1
Lung surfactant

Bovine Fibrin (BAN) see Appendix C

Bretylium Tosilate (rINN) bre·*ti*·lë·um

2-Bromobenzyl-*N*-ethyldimethylammonium *p*-toluenesulfonate; $C_{18}H_{24}BrNO_3S$; *61-75-6*
Antiarrhythmic

Brimonidine (rINN) brï·*mo*·ni·dën

5-Bromoquinoxalin-6-yl(2-imidazolin-2-yl)amine; $C_{11}H_{10}BrN_5$; *59803-98-4*; UK-14304-18
Brimonidine Tartrate *79570-19-7*
Alpha₂-adrenoceptor agonist; treatment of hypertension

Brinzolamide (rINN) brin·*zol*·a·mïd

(*R*)-4-(Ethylamino)-3,4-dihydro-2-(3-methoxypropyl)-2*H*-thieno[3,2-*e*][1,2]thiazine-6-sulfonamide 1,1-dioxide; $C_{12}H_{21}N_3O_5S_3$; *138890-62-7*
Carbonic anhydrase inhibitor; treatment of glaucoma and ocular hypertension

The symbol '¬' in systematic chemical names signifies line continuation

Brocresine (rINN) brö·*kre*·sën

α-Amino-oxy-6-bromo-*m*-cresol; $C_7H_8BrNO_2$; *555-65-7*
Histidine decarboxylase inhibitor

Brofezil (rINN) *brö*·fe·zil

2-(4-*p*-Bromophenyl-1,3-thiazol-2-yl)propionic acid;
$C_{12}H_{10}BrNO_2S$; *17969-45-8*
Brofezil Sodium ICI 54594
Analgesic; anti-inflammatory

and enantiomer

● **Bromazepam** (rINN) brö·*mä*·ze·pam

7-Bromo-1,3-dihydro-5-(2-pyridyl)-1,4-benzodiazepin-2-one;
$C_{14}H_{10}BrN_3O$; *1812-30-2*
Benzodiazepine

Bromazine (rINN) *brö*·ma·zën

2-(4-Bromobenzhydryloxy)ethyldimethylamine; $C_{17}H_{20}BrNO$;
118-23-0
Histamine H_1 receptor antagonist; antihistamine

and enantiomer

Bromebric Acid (rINN) brö·*me*·brik

(*E*)-3-*p*-Anisoyl-3-bromoacrylic acid; $C_{11}H_9BrO_4$; *5711-40-0*
Sodium Bromebrate
Cytotoxic

Bromelains (rINN) *brö*·me·läns

A concentrate of proteolytic enzymes derived from *Ananas
comosus* Merr·; *9001-00-7*
Proteolytic enzyme

Bromhexine (rINN) brom·*heks*·ën

2-Amino-3,5-dibromobenzyl(cyclohexyl)methylamine;
$C_{14}H_{20}Br_2N_2$; *3572-43-8*
● **Bromhexine Hydrochloride** *611-75-6*
Mucolytic

Bromindione (rINN) brö·min·*di*·ön

2-(4-Bromophenyl)indan-1,3-dione; $C_{15}H_9BrO_2$; *1146-98-1*
Anticoagulant (indanedione)

Bromociclen (rINN) see Appendix C

Bromocriptine (rINN) brö·mö·*krip*·tën

(1) (5′S)-2-Bromo-12′-hydroxy-2′-isopropyl-5′-isobutyl￢
ergotaman-3′,6′,18-trione; (2) 2-Bromo-α-ergocryptine;
$C_{32}H_{40}BrN_5O_5$; *25614-03-3*
● **Bromocriptine Mesilate** *22260-51-1*
Dopamine receptor agonist

Bromocyclen *see Bromociclen*

Bromodiphenhydramine *see Bromazine*

Bromperidol (rINN) brom·*pe*·ri·dol

4-(4-*p*-Bromophenyl-4-hydroxypiperidino)-4′-fluorobutyro￢
phenone; $C_{21}H_{23}BrFNO_2$; *10457-90-6*; R 11333
● **Bromperidol Decanoate** *75067-66-2*; R 46541
Dopamine receptor antagonist; neuroleptic

Brompheniramine (rINN) brom·fe·nï·ra·mën

3-(4-Bromophenyl)-3-(2-pyridyl)propyldimethylamine; $C_{16}H_{19}BrN_2$; 86-22-6

● **Brompheniramine Maleate** 980-71-2

Histamine H_1 receptor antagonist; antihistamine

and enantiomer

● **Bronopol** (rINN) brö·nö·pol

2-Bromo-2-nitropropane-1,3-diol; $C_3H_6BrNO_4$; 52-51-7

Antibacterial preservative

Bropirimine (rINN) brö·pi·ri·mën

2-Amino-5-bromo-6-phenylpyrimidin-4(3H)-one; $C_{10}H_8BrN_3O$; 056741-95-8; U54,461S; U-54,461

Immunomodulator

Brotianide (rINN) brö·ti·a·nïd

2-Bromo-6-(4-bromophenylthiocarbamoyl)-4-chlorophenyl acetate; $C_{15}H_{10}Br_2ClNO_2S$; 23233-88-7

Antihelminthic

Brotizolam (rINN) brö·ti·zö·lam

2-Bromo-4-(2-chlorophenyl)-9-methyl-6H-thieno[3,2-f][1,2,4]triazolo[4,3-a][1,4]diazepine; $C_{15}H_{10}BrClN_4S$; 57801-81-7; We 941-BS

Benzodiazepine

Bucetin (rINN) bü·së·tin

3-Hydroxybutyro-p-phenetidine; $C_{12}H_{17}NO_3$; 1083-57-4

Cyclo-oxygenase inhibitor; antipyretic; analgesic

and enantiomer

Bucindolol (rINN) bü·sin·do·lol

2-{2-Hydroxy-3-[2-(indol-3-yl)-1,1-dimethylethylamino]propoxy}benzonitrile; $C_{22}H_{25}N_3O_2$; 71119-11-4

Bucindolol Hydrochloride 70369-47-0; MJ 13105-1

Beta-adrenoceptor antagonist

and enantiomer

Buclizine (rINN) bü·kli·zën

(RS)-1-(4-tert-Butylbenzyl)-4-(4-chlorobenzhydryl)piperazine; $C_{28}H_{33}ClN_2$; 82-95-1

● **Buclizine Hydrochloride** 129-74-8

Histamine H_1 receptor antagonist; antiemetic

and enantiomer

Buclosamide (rINN) bü·klö·za·mïd

N-Butyl-4-chlorosalicylamide; $C_{11}H_{14}ClNO_2$; 575-74-6

Antifungal

● **Budesonide** (rINN) bü·de·so·nïd

16α,17α-Butylidenedioxy-11β,21-dihydroxypregna-1,4-diene-3,20-dione; $C_{25}H_{34}O_6$; 51333-22-3

Glucocorticoid

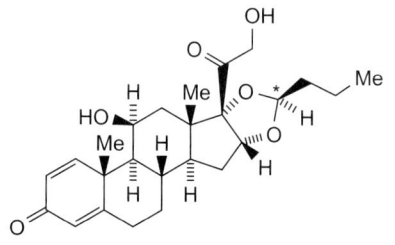

and epimer at C*

The symbol '¬' in systematic chemical names signifies line continuation

Bufexamac (rINN) bü·*feks*·a·mak
2-(4-Butoxyphenyl)acetohydroxamic acid; $C_{12}H_{17}NO_3$; *2438-72-4*
Cyclo-oxygenase inhibitor; analgesic; anti-inflammatory

Buflomedil (rINN) bü·*flö*·me·dil
2′,4′,6′-Trimethoxy-4-(pyrrolidin-1-yl)butyrophenone; $C_{17}H_{25}NO_4$; *55837-25-7*
● **Buflomedil Hydrochloride** *35543-24-9*
Vasodilator

Bufrolin (rINN) bü·fro·lin
6-Butyl-1,4,7,10-tetrahydro-4,10-dioxo-1,7-phenanthroline-2,8-dicarboxylic acid; $C_{18}H_{16}N_2O_6$; *54867-56-0*
Bufrolin Sodium ICI 74917
Mast cell stabilizer

Bufuralol (rINN) bü·*für*·ra·lol
2-*tert*-Butylamino-1-(7-ethylbenzofuran-2-yl)ethanol; $C_{16}H_{23}NO_2$; *54340-62-4*
Bufuralol Hydrochloride Ro 03-4787
Beta-adrenoceptor antagonist

and enantiomer

Bufylline (BAN) bü·fi·lën
Theophylline salt of 2-amino-2-methylpropan-1-ol (1:1); ambuphylline (USAN); $C_7H_8N_4O_2.C_4H_{11}NO$; *5634-34-4*
Non-selective phosphodiesterase inhibitor; treatment of reversible airways obstruction

Bumetanide (rINN) bü·*me*·ta·nïd
3-Butylamino-4-phenoxy-5-sulfamoylbenzoic acid; $C_{17}H_{20}N_2O_5S$; *28395-03-01*
Loop diuretic

Bunamidine (rINN) bü·*na*·mi·dën
N^1,N^1-Dibutyl-4-hexyloxy-1-naphthamidine; $C_{25}H_{38}N_2O$; *3748-77-4*
♣ **Bunamidine Hydrochloride** *1055-55-6*
Antihelminthic

Bunamiodyl (rINN) bü·na·*mï*·ö·dïl
3-Butyramido-α-ethyl-2,4,6-tri-iodocinnamic acid; $C_{15}H_{16}I_3NO_3$; *1233-53-0*
Iodinated contrast medium

Buniodyl *see Bunamiodyl*

Buparvaquone (rINN) bü·*par*·va·kwön
trans-2-(4-*tert*-Butylcyclohexylmethyl)-3-hydroxy-1,4-naphthoquinone; $C_{21}H_{26}O_3$; *88426-33-9*; BW 720C
Antiprotozoal

Buphenine (rINN) bü·fe·nën
1-(4-Hydroxyphenyl)-2-(1-methyl-3-phenylpropylamino)propan-1-ol; nylidrin (USAN); $C_{19}H_{25}NO_2$; *447-41-6*
Non-selective beta-adrenoceptor agonist

mixture of isomers

Bupivacaine (rINN) bü·*pi*·va·kän

1-Butyl-2-piperidylformo-2′,6′-xylidide; $C_{18}H_{28}N_2O$; *2180-92-9*
- **Bupivacaine Hydrochloride** *14252-80-3 (monohydrate)*; *18010-40-7 (anhydrous)*
Local anaesthetic

and enantiomer

- **Buprenorphine** (rINN) bü·pre·*nor*·fën

(1) (2*S*)-2-[(−)-(5*R*,6*R*,7*R*,14*S*)-17-Cyclopropylmethyl-4,5-epoxy-3-hydroxy-6-methoxy-6,14-ethanomorphinan-7-yl]-3,3-dimethylbutan-2-ol; (2) (6*R*,7*R*,14*S*)-17-Cyclopropylmethyl-7,8-dihydro-7-[(1*S*)-1-hydroxy-1,2,2-trimethylpropyl]-6-*O*-methyl-6,14-ethano-17-normorphine; $C_{29}H_{41}NO_4$; *52485-79-7*
- **Buprenorhine Hydrochloride** *53152-21-9*
Opioid receptor partial agonist; analgesic

Bupropion (rINN) bü·*prö*·pë·on

2-(*tert*-Butylamino)-3′-chloropropiophenone; $C_{13}H_{18}ClNO$; *34911-55-2*
Bupropion Hydrochloride *31677-93-7*
Antidepressant; smoking cessation

and enantiomer

Buquineran (rINN) bü·*kwi*·ner·ran

1-Butyl-3-[1-(6,7-dimethoxyquinazolin-4-yl)-4-piperidyl]urea; $C_{20}H_{29}N_5O_3$; *59184-78-0*; UK-14275
Positive inotrope

- **Buserelin** (rINN) bü·*se*·re·lin
$C_{60}H_{86}N_{16}O_{13}$; *57982-77-1*
Buserelin Acetate *68630-75-1*
Gonadotrophin releasing hormone (gonadorelin) analogue; treatment of prostate cancer

```
5-oxoPro-His-Trp-Ser-Tyr-D-Ser(tert-Bu)-
Leu-Arg-Pro-NHEt
```

Buspirone (rINN) *bü*·spi·rön

8-{4-[4-(Pyrimidin-2-yl)piperazin-1-yl]butyl}-8-azaspiro[4.5]decane-7,9-dione; $C_{21}H_{31}N_5O_2$; *36505-84-7*
- **Buspirone Hydrochloride** *33386-08-2*
Non-benzodiazepine hypnotic; treatment of anxiety

- **Busulfan** (rINN) bü·*sul*·fan

Tetramethylene di(methanesulfonate); $C_6H_{14}O_6S_2$; *55-98-1*
Cytotoxic alkylating agent

Butacaine (rINN) *bü*·ta·kän

3-(Dibutylamino)propyl 4-aminobenzoate; $C_{18}H_{30}N_2O_2$; *149-16-6*
Butacaine Sulfate *149-15-5*
Local anaesthetic

Butafosfan (rINN) bü·ta·*fos*·fan

1-Butylamino-1-methylethylphosphinic acid; $C_7H_{18}NO_2P$; *17316-67-5*
Source of phosphorus

Butalamine (rINN) bü·*ta*·la·mën

2-(3-Phenyl-1,2,4-oxadiazol-5-ylamino)ethyldibutylamine; $C_{18}H_{28}N_4O$; *22131-35-7*
Butalamine Hydrochloride LA 1221
Vasodilator

The symbol '¬' in systematic chemical names signifies line continuation

Butamirate (rINN) bü·*ta*·mi·rät

2-(2-Diethylaminoethoxy)ethyl 2-phenylbutyrate; $C_{18}H_{29}NO_3$; *18109-80-3*
Cough suppressant

Me, H, O, O, NEt₂

and enantiomer

Butanilicaine (rINN) bü·ta·*ni*·li·kän

2-Butylamino-6′-chloroaceto-*o*-toluidide; $C_{13}H_{19}ClN_2O$; *3785-21-5*
Butanilicaine Phosphate
Local anaesthetic

Me, H, N, NHBu^n, Cl, O

Butaprost (rINN) *bü*·ta·prost

(1) Methyl (*E*)-(11*R*,16*R*)-11,16-dihydroxy-9-oxo-16-(1-propylcyclobutyl)-17,18,19,20-tetranorprost-13-enoate;
(2) Methyl-7-{(1*R*,2*R*,3*R*)-3-hydroxy-2-[(1*E*,4*R*)-4-hydroxy-4-(1-propylcyclobutyl)but-1-enyl]-5-oxocyclopentyl}heptanoate; $C_{24}H_{40}O_5$; *69648-38-0*; BAY q 4218
Prostaglandin analogue

O, H, COOMe, HO, H, Me, HO, H

Butaxamine (rINN) bü·*taks*·a·mën

(±)-*erythro*-1-(2,5-Dimethoxyphenyl)-2-*tert*-butylamino¬propan-1-ol; $C_{15}H_{25}NO_3$; *2922-20-5*
Beta₂-adrenoceptor antagonist

MeO, H, OH, NHBu^t, H, Me, OMe

and enantiomer

Butenafine (rINN) bü·*ten*·a·fën

4-*tert*-Butylbenzyl(methyl)(1-naphthalenemethyl)amine;
$C_{23}H_{27}N$; *101828-21-1*
Butenafine Hydrochloride *101827-46-7*; KP-363
Antifungal

Me, N, Bu^t

Butetamate (rINN) bü·*te*·ta·mät

2-Diethylaminoethyl 2-phenylbutyrate; $C_{16}H_{25}NO_2$; *14007-64-8*
Butetamate Citrate
Relaxation of bronchial smooth muscle

Me, O, O, NEt₂, H

and enantiomer

Buthalital Sodium (rINN) see Appendix C

Butikacin (rINN) bü·tik·*kä*·sin

6-*O*-(3-Amino-3-deoxy-α-D-glucopyranosyl)-4-*O*-(6-amino-6-deoxy-α-D-glucopyranosyl)-*N*¹-[(2*S*)-4-amino-2-hydroxybutyl]-2-deoxy-D-streptamine; $C_{22}H_{45}N_5O_{12}$; *59733-86-7*
Aminoglycoside antibacterial

NH₂, O, OH, OH, HO, OH, O, NH₂, OH, O, OH, OH, H, OH, NH₂, H₂N, NH

Butirosin Sulfate (INNM) bü·*ti*·rö·sin

A mixture of the (1:2) sulfates of the A and B components of an antibacterial produced by *Bacillus circularis*;
$C_{21}H_{41}N_5O_{12},2H_2SO_4$; *12772-35-9*
Aminoglycoside antibacterial complex

Component A: 1-*N*-[(*S*)-4-Amino-2-hydroxybutyryl]-2-deoxy-4-*O*-(2,6-diamino-2,6-dideoxy-α-D-glucopyranosyl)-5-*O*-(β-D-xylofuranosyl)streptamine

Component B: 1-*N*-[(*S*)-4-Amino-2-hydroxybutyryl]-2-deoxy-4-*O*-(2,6-diamino-2,6-dideoxy-α-D-glucopyranosyl)-5-*O*-(β-D-ribofuranosyl)streptamine

NH₂, O, OH, HO, H₂N, O, HO, OR, NH₂, H, OH, H₂N, NH, O, R =, HO, O, OH, OH, *form A*, HO, O, OH, OH, *form B*

● **Butobarbital** (rINN) bü·tö·*bar*·bi·tal

5-Butyl-5-ethylbarbituric acid; $C_{10}H_{16}N_2O_3$; *77-28-1*
Barbiturate

Butoconazole (rINN) bü·tö·*kon*·a·zôl

1-[4-(4-Chlorophenyl)-2-(2,6-dichlorophenylthio) butyl]¬
imidazole; $C_{19}H_{17}Cl_3N_2S$; *64872-76-0*
Butoconazole Nitrate *64872-77-1*; RS-35887-00-10-3
Antifungal

and enantiomer

Butorphanol (rINN) bü·*tor*·fa·nol

(–)-17-(Cyclobutylmethyl)morphinan-3,14-diol; $C_{21}H_{29}NO_2$;
42408-82-2
Butorphanol Tartrate *58786-99-5*
Opioid receptor partial agonist; analgesic

Butoxamine *see Butaxamine*

Butriptyline (rINN) see Appendix C

● **Butylated Hydroxyanisole** (BAN) hï·droks·ë·*a*·ni·sôl

2-*tert*-Butyl-4-methoxyphenol; $C_{11}H_{16}O_2$; *25013-16-5*
Preservative

● **Butylated Hydroxytoluene** (BAN) hï·droks·ë·*tol*·ü·ën

2,6-Di-*tert*-butyl-*p*-cresol; $C_{15}H_{24}O$; *128-37-0*
Preservative

Cabergoline (rINN) ka·*ber*·gö·lën

(8*R*)-6-Allyl-*N*-[3-(dimethylamino)propyl]-*N*-(ethyl¬
carbamoyl) ergoline-8-carboxamide; $C_{26}H_{37}N_5O_2$; *81409-90-7*
Dopamine D_2 receptor agonist

Cadexomer–Iodine (INNM) ka·*deks*·o·mer

2-Hydroxytrimethylene cross-linked (1→4)-α-D-glucan
carboxymethylether containing iodine within the helix-structure
Disinfectant

Cadralazine (rINN) ka·*dra*·la·zën

Ethyl 3-{6-[ethyl(2-hydroxypropyl)amino]pyridazin-3-yl}¬
carbazate; $C_{12}H_{21}N_5O_3$; *64241-34-5*; CGP 18684/E; ISF 2469
Treatment of hypertension

and enantiomer

Cafedrine (rINN) *ka*·fe·drën

7-[2-(β-Hydroxy-α-methylphenethylamino)ethyl]theophylline;
$C_{18}H_{23}N_5O_3$; *58166-83-9*
Treatment of hypertension

mixture of 4 stereoisomers

● **Caffeine** (BAN) *ka*·fën

3,7-Dihydro-1,3,7-trimethylpurine-2,6(1*H*)-dione; $C_8H_{10}N_4O_2$;
58-08-2; component in many proprietary preparations
Central nervous system stimulant

● **Calcifediol** (rINN) kal·si·fe·*di*·ol

(5*Z*,7*E*)-(3*S*)-9,10-Secocholesta-5,7,10(19)-triene-3,25-diol;
calcidiol; $C_{27}H_{44}O_2$; *19356-17-3*
Vitamin D analogue

The symbol '¬' in systematic chemical names signifies line continuation

Calcipotriol (rINN) kal·si·pö·*trï*·ol

(5Z,7E,22E)-(lS,3R,24S)-26,27-Cyclo-9,10-secocholesta-5,7,10(19),22-tetraene-1,3,24-triol; calcipotriene (USAN); $C_{27}H_{40}O_3$; *112828-00-9*
Vitamin D analogue

Calcitonin (rINN) kal·si·*tö*·nin

A polypeptide hormone of ultimobranchial origin, extractable from the thyroid gland of mammalian species or the ultimobranchial gland of non-mammals, that lowers the calcium concentration in plasma of mammals; thyrocalcitonin; $C_{145}H_{240}N_{44}O_{48}S_2$; *9007-12-9*
Calcitonin (Pork)
● **Calcitonin (Salmon)** A component of natural salmon calcitonin produced synthetically; *47931-85-1*
Hormone

calcitonin (salmon) has the following amino acid sequence:

```
Cys-Ser-Asn-Leu-Ser-Thr-Cys-Val-

Leu-Gly-Lys-Leu-Ser-Gln-Glu-Leu-

His-Lys-Leu-Gln-Thr-Tyr-Pro-Arg-

Thr-Asn-Thr-Gly-Ser-Gly-Thr-Pro-NH₂
```

● **Calcitriol** (rINN) kal·si·*trï*·ol

(1) (5Z,7E)-9,10-Secocholesta-5,7,10(19)-triene-1α,3β,25-triol;
(2) 1α,25-Dihydroxycholecalciferol; $C_{27}H_{44}O_3$; *32222-06-3*
Vitamin D analogue

Calcium Benzamidosalicylate (rINN) see Appendix C

Calcium Folinate *see Folinic Acid*

● **Calcium Levofolinate** (rINN) *kal*·cë·um lë·vö·*fö*·li·nät

Calcium N-{4-[(6S)-2-amino-5-formyl-1,4,5,6,7,8-hexahydro-4-oxopteridin-6-ylmethyl)amino]benzoyl}-L-glutamate; levoleucovorin calcium (USAN); $C_{20}H_{21}CaN_7O_7$; *80433-71-2*
Antidote to folic acid antagonists

Calcium Levulinate (rINN) kal·së·um le·*vü*·li·nät

Calcium 4-oxopentanoate; $C_{10}H_{14}CaO_6$; *591-64-0; 5743-49-7 (dihydrate)*
Source of calcium

Calcium Trisodium Pentetate (rINN) *pen*·te·tät

Calcium trisodium nitrilodiethylenedinitrilopenta-acetate; $C_{14}H_{18}CaN_3Na_3O_{10}$; *1317-31-3*
Chelating agent; treatment of heavy metal poisoning

Caldiamide Sodium (INNM) kal·*dï*·a·mïd

Sodium [6-carboxylatomethyl-3,9-bis(methylcarbamoylmethyl)-3,6,9-triazaundecanedioato-κ³-N^3,N^6,N^9-κ³-O^1,O^6,O^{11}(3–)¬ calciate(II)]; $C_{16}H_{26}CaN_5NaO_8$,xH_2O; *122760-91-2*
MRI contrast medium

Calfactant (BAN) cal·*fak*·tant
An unmodified calf lung lavage extract mostly phospholipids and surfactant specific proteins (SP-B & SP-C)
Lung surfactant

Calteridol Calcium (INNM) kal·*te*·ri·dol
Calcium (*RS*)-bis{[10-(2-hydroxypropyl-κ*O*)-1,4,7,10-tetra-azacyclododecane-1,4,7-triyltriacetato-*O*^{1},*O*^{4},*O*^{7}, *N*^{1},¬
N^4, *N*^{7},*N*^{10}(3–)]calciate(II)}; $C_{34}H_{58}Ca_3N_8O_{14}$; *121915-83-1*
Contrast medium

and enantiomer

Cambendazole (rINN) kam·*ben*·da·zôl
Isopropyl [2-(1,3-thiazol-4-yl)benzimidazol-5-yl]carbamate; $C_{14}H_{14}N_4O_2S$; *26097-80-3*
Antihelminthic

Canakinumab (rINN) ka·ná·*kin*·ü·mab
Immunoglobulin G1, anti-[Homo sapiens interleukin 1, beta (IL1B)] human monoclonal ACZ885; gamma1 heavy chain (Homo sapiens VH-IGHG1*03) (221-214')-disulfide with kappa light chain (Homo sapiens V-KAPPA-IGKC*01); (227-227":230-230")-bisdisulfide dimer;
light chain *402710-27-4*
heavy chain *402710-25-2*;
Monoclonal antibody (interleukin-1β antibody); treatment of periodic syndromes

canakinumab has the following amino acid sequence:

Light chain

EIVLTQSPDF	QSVTPKEKVT	ITCRASQSIG	SSLHWYQQKP
DQSPKLLIKY	ASQSFSGVPS	RFSGSGSGTD	FTLTINSLEA
EDAAAYYCHQ	SSSLPFTFGP	GTKVDIKRTV	AAPSVFIFPP
SDEQLKSGTA	SVVCLLNNFY	PREAKVQWKV	DNALQSGNSQ
ESVTEQDSKD	STYSLSSTLT	LSKADYEKHK	VYACEVTHQG
LSSPVTKSFN	RGEC		

Heavy chain

PEVQLVESGGG	VVQPGRSLRL	SCAASGFTFS	VYGMNWVRQA
PGKGLEWVAI	IWYDGDNQYY	ADSVKGRFTI	SRDNSKNTLY
LQMNGLRAED	TAVYYCARDL	RTGPFDYWGQ	GTLVTVSSAS
TKGPSVFPLA	PSSKSTSGGT	AALGCLVKDY	FPEPVTVSWN
SGALTSGVHT	FPAVLQSSGL	YSLSSVVTVP	SSSLGTQTYI
CNVNHKPSNT	KVDKRVEPKS	CDKTHTCPPC	PAPELLGGPS
VFLFPPKPKD	TLMISRTPEV	TCVVVDVSHE	DPEVKFNWYV
DGVEVHNAKT	KPREEQYŇST	YRVVSVLTVL	HQDWLNGKEY
KCKVSNKALP	APIEKTISKA	KGQPREPQVY	TLPPSREEMT
KNQVSLTCLV	KGFYPSDIAV	EWESNGQPEN	NYKTTPPVLD
SDGSFFLYSK	LTVDKSRWQQ	GNVFSCSVMH	EALHNHYTQK
SLSLSPGK			

* glycosylation site

Candesartan (rINN) kan·des·*ar*·tan
2-Ethoxy-1-[2′-(1*H*-tetrazol-5-yl)biphenyl-4-ylmethyl]-1*H*-benzimidazole-7-carboxylic acid; $C_{24}H_{20}N_6O_3$; *139481-59-7*
Candesartan Cilexetil *145040-37-5*
Angiotensin II (AT₁) receptor antagonist

Candicidin (rINN) kan·di·*si*·din
A mixture of heptaenes produced by *Streptomyces griseus* and other species of *Streptomyces*; *1403-17-4*
Antifungal

Candoxatril (rINN) kan·*doks*·a·tril
cis-4-{1-[(*S*)-2-(Indan-5-yloxycarbonyl)-3-(2-methoxy¬
ethoxy)propyl] cyclopentylcarbonylamino}¬
cyclohexanecarboxylic acid; $C_{29}H_{41}NO_7$; *118785-03-8*;
UK-79,300
Endopeptidase inhibitor; treatment of hypertension

The symbol '¬' in systematic chemical names signifies line continuation

Candoxatrilat (rINN) kan·doxs·a·*tri*·lat

cis-4-{1-[(*S*)-2-Carboxy-3-(2-methoxyethoxy)propyl]¬
cyclopentylcarbonylamino}cyclohexane carboxylic acid;
$C_{20}H_{33}NO_7$; *118783-94-1*; UK-73,967
Endopeptidase inhibitor; treatment of hypertension

Canertinib (rINN) kan·*er*·tin·ib

N-{4-[(3-Chloro-4-fluorophenyl)amino]-7-[3-(morpholin-4yl)¬
propoxy]quinazolin-6-yl-prop-2-enamide; $C_{24}H_{25}ClFN_5O_3$;
267243-28-7
Cytotoxic

Cangrelor (rINN) *kan*·gre·lor

N-6-[2-(Methylsulfanyl)ethyl]-2-[(3,3,3-trifluoro) propyl¬
sulfanyl)]adenosine 5′-β,γ-μ-dichloromethylenetriphosphate;
$C_{17}H_{25}N_5Cl_2F_3O_{12}P_3S_2$; AR-C69931XX
*Purine (P2Y₁₂) receptor antagonist; inhibitor of platelet
aggregation*

Cannabinol (rINN) ka·*na*·bi·nol

6,6,9-Trimethyl-3-pentyl-6*H*-dibenzo[*b,d*]pyran-1-ol; $C_{21}H_{26}O_2$;
521-35-7
Cannabinoid

Canrenoic Acid (rINN) See Appendix C

Capecitabine (rINN) ka·pe·*si*·ta·bën

(1) Pentyl 1-[(5-deoxy-β-D-ribofuranosyl)-5-fluoro-2-oxo-1,2-
dihydropyrimidin-4-yl]carbamate; (2) 5-Fluoro-*N*⁴-(pentyloxy¬
carbonyl)-5′-deoxycytosine; $C_{15}H_{22}FNO_6$; *154361-50-9*
Pyrimidine analogue; cytotoxic; treatment of colorectal cancer

Capreomycin (rINN) kap·rë·ö·*mï*·sin

A mixture of antimicrobial peptides produced by *Streptomyces
capreolus*; *11003-38-6*
● **Capreomycin Sulfate** *1405-37-4*
Antituberculosis drug

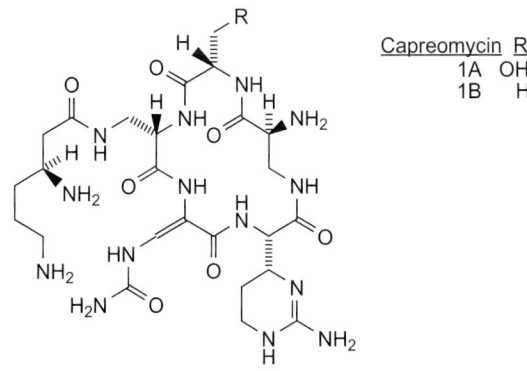

Capreomycin	R
1A	OH
1B	H

Capromab (rINN) *ka*·prö·mab

Immunoglobulin G1, anti-(human B lymphoma cell) (mouse
monoclonal 7E11-C5.3 γ1-chain), disulfide with mouse
monoclonal 7E11-C5.3 light chain, dimer; *151763-64-3*
Capromab Pendetide *145464-28-4*
Monoclonal antibody; imaging of prostate cancer

Caproxamine (rINN) See Appendix C

Captodiame (rINN) kap·tö·*dï*·äm

2-(4-Butylthiobenzhydrylthio)ethyldimethylamine; $C_{21}H_{29}NS_2$;
486-17-9
Anxiolytic

Captopril (rINN) *kap·tö·pril*

1-[(2*S*)-3-Mercapto-2-methylpropionyl]-L-proline; C$_9$H$_{15}$NO$_3$S; *62571-86-2*; SQ14225
Angiotensin converting enzyme inhibitor

Carabersat (rINN) ka·*ra*·ber·sat

N-[(3*R*,4*S*)-6-Acetyl-3-hydroxy-2,2-dimethylchroman-4-yl]-4-fluorobenzamide; C$_{20}$H$_{20}$FNO$_4$; *185122-82-1*; SB-204269-EO
Antiepileptic

Caramiphen (rINN) ka·*ra*·mi·fen

2-Diethylaminoethyl 1-phenylcyclopentane-1-carboxylate; C$_{18}$H$_{27}$NO$_2$; *77-22-5*
Anticholinergic

Carazolol (rINN) ka·*ra*·zo·lol

1-(Carbazol-4-yloxy)-3-isopropylaminopropan-2-ol; C$_{18}$H$_{22}$N$_2$O$_2$; *57775-29-8*; BM 51052
Beta-adrenoceptor antagonist

and enantiomer

Carbachol (rINN) *kar*·ba·kol

2-Carbamoyloxyethyltrimethylammonium chloride; C$_6$H$_{15}$ClN$_2$O$_2$; *51-83-2*
Cholinoceptor agonist

Carbadox (rINN) *kar*·ba·doks

Methyl 3-(quinoxalin-2-ylmethylene)carbazate 1,4-dioxide; C$_{11}$H$_{10}$N$_4$O$_4$; *6804-07-5*
Antibacterial (veterinary)

Carbamazepine (rINN) kar·ba·*mä*·ze·pën

5*H*-Dibenz[*b,f*]azepine-5-carboxamide; C$_{15}$H$_{12}$N$_2$O; *298-46-4*
Antiepileptic

Carbaryl (BAN) *kar*·ba·rïl

1-Naphthyl methylcarbamate; C$_{12}$H$_{11}$NO$_2$; *63-25-2*
Insecticide

Carbasalate Calcium (rINN) kar·*ba*·sa·lät *kal*·së·um

Calcium bis[2-(acetoxy)benzoate]-urea; carbaspirin calcium (USAN); C$_{19}$H$_{18}$CaN$_2$O$_9$; *5749-67-7*
Salicylate; non-selective cyclo-oxygenase inhibitor; antipyretic; analgesic; anti-inflammatory

Carbenicillin (rINN) kar·be·ni·*si*·lin

6-(2-Carboxy-2-phenylacetamido)penicillanic acid; C$_{17}$H$_{18}$N$_2$O$_6$S; *4697-36-3*
Carbenicillin Sodium *4800-94-6*
Penicillin antibacterial

The symbol '¬' in systematic chemical names signifies line continuation

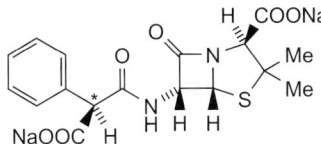

and enantiomer at C*

Carbenoxolone (rINN) kar·be·*noks*·o·lön

3β-(3-Carboxypropionyloxy)-11-oxo-olean-12-en-30-oic acid; $C_{34}H_{50}O_7$; *5697-56-3*
- **Carbenoxolone Sodium** *7421-40-1*
Treatment of peptic ulcer

Carbetocin (rINN) kar·*bë*·tö·sin

2,1-Desamino-4,1-desthio-$O^{4,2}$-methyl[1-homocysteine]⌐oxytocin ; $C_{45}H_{69}N_{11}O_{12}S$; *37025-55-1*
Oxytocin analogue

H₂C⎯⎯⎯⎯⎯⎯⎯
CH₂·CH₂·CO-Tyr(Me)-Ile-Gln-Asn-Cys-Pro-
Leu-Gly-NH₂

- **Carbidopa** (rINN) kar·bi·*dö*·pa

(S)-3-(3,4-Dihydroxyphenyl)-2-hydrazino-2-methylpropionic acid; $C_{10}H_{14}N_2O_4$; *28860-95-9*
Dopa decarboxylase inhibitor

Carbifene (rINN) *kar*·bi·fën

2-Ethoxy-N-methyl-N-[2-(N-methyl-N-phenethylamino)ethyl]-2,2-diphenylacetamide; $C_{18}H_{34}N_2O_2$; *15687-16-8*
Analgesic; anti-inflammatory

- **Carbimazole** (rINN) kar·*bi*·ma·zôl

Ethyl 3-methyl-2-thioxo-4-imidazoline-1-carboxylate; $C_7H_{10}N_2O_2S$; *22232-54-8*
Thionamide antithyroid drug

Carbinoxamine (rINN) see Appendix C

Carbiphene *see Carbifene*

- **Carbocisteine** (rINN) kar·bö·*sis*·tän

S-Carboxymethyl-L-cysteine; $C_5H_9NO_4S$; *2387-59-9*
Mucolytic

Carbocloral (rINN) kar·bö·*klor*·ral

Ethyl (2,2,2-trichloro-1-hydroxyethyl)carbamate; $C_5H_8Cl_3NO_3$; *541-79-7*
Cholinoceptor agonist

and enantiomer

Carbofenotion (rINN) kar·bö·fë·nö·*ti*·on

S-4-Chlorophenylthiomethyl O,O-diethyl phosphorodithioate; $C_{11}H_{16}ClO_2PS_3$; *786-19-6*
Insecticide

Carbolonium Bromide *see Hexcarbacholine*

- **Carbomer** (rINN) *kar*·bo·mer

A polymer of acrylic acid cross-linked with allyl sucrose; *54182-57-9*
Stabilizer in pharmaceutical products

Carbophenothion *see Carbofenotion*

- **Carboplatin** (rINN) kar·bö·*pla*·tin

cis-Diammine (cyclobutane-1,1-dicarboxylato)platinum; $C_6H_{12}N_2O_4Pt$; *41575-94-4*
Platinum-containing cytotoxic

Carboprost (rINN) *kar·bö·prost*

(1) (Z)-7-{(1R,2R,3R,5S)-3,5-Dihydroxy-2-[(E)-(3S)-3-hydroxy-3-methyloct-1-enyl]cyclopentyl}hept-5-enoic acid;

(2) (5Z,13E)-(9S,11R,15S)-9,11,15-Trihydroxy-15-methylprosta-5,13-dienoic acid; $C_{21}H_{36}O_5$; *35700-23-3*

Carboprost Trometamol *58551-69-2*

Prostaglandin (PGF$_{2\alpha}$) analogue

Carbromal (rINN) *kar·brö·mal*

(2-Bromo-2-ethylbutyryl)urea; $C_7H_{13}BrN_2O_2$; *77-65-6*

Hypnotic

Carbutamide (rINN) *kar·bü·ta·mïd*

1-Butyl-3-sulfanilylurea; $C_{11}H_{17}N_3O_3S$; *339-43-5*

Inhibition of ATP-dependent potassium channels (sulfonylurea); treatment of diabetes mellitus

Carbuterol (rINN) *kar·bü·te·rol*

[5-(2-*tert*-Butylamino-1-hydroxyethyl)-2-hydroxyphenyl]urea; $C_{13}H_{21}N_3O_3$; *34866-47-2*

Carbuterol Hydrochloride *34866-46-1*; SK&F 40383-A

Beta$_2$-adrenoceptor agonist; bronchodilator

and enantiomer

Carfecillin (rINN) see Appendix C

Carfenazine (rINN) *kar·fe·na·zën*

1-(10-{3-[4-(2-Hydroxyethyl)piperazin-1-yl]propyl}pheno¬thiazin-2-yl)propan-1-one; $C_{24}H_{31}N_3O_2S$; *2622-30-2*

Carfenazine Maleate *2975-34-0*

Dopamine receptor antagonist; neuroleptic

Carindacillin (rINN) *ka·rin·da·si·lin*

6-(2-Indan-5-yloxycarbonyl-2-phenylacetamido)penicillanic acid; $C_{26}H_{26}N_2O_6S$; *35531-88-5*

Carindacillin Sodium carbenicillin indanyl sodium (USAN); *26605-69-6*; CP-15464-2

Penicillin antibacterial

and enantiomer at C*

Carisoprodol (rINN) *ka·rï·sö·prö·dol*

2-Methyl-2-propyltrimethylene carbamate isopropylcarbamate; $C_{12}H_{24}N_2O_4$; *78-44-4*

Skeletal muscle relaxant

and enantiomer

Carmellose (rINN) *kar·me·lös*

A poly(carboxymethyl) ether of cellulose; carboxymethylcellulose; *9000-11-7*;

Carmellose Calcium *9050-04-8*

Carmellose Sodium *9004-32-4*

Excipient; bulk laxative

Carmustine (rINN) *kar·mus·tën*

1,3-Bis(2-chloroethyl)-1-nitrosourea; $C_5H_9Cl_2N_3O_2$; *154-93-8*

Cytotoxic alkylating agent

Carnidazole (rINN) *kar·nï·da·zôl*

O-Methyl [2-(2-methyl-5-nitroimidazol-1-yl)ethyl]thio¬carbamate; $C_8H_{12}N_4O_3S$; *42116-76-7*

Antiprotozoal (veterinary)

The symbol '¬' in systematic chemical names signifies line continuation

Carperidine (rINN) kar·*pe*·ri·dën
  Ethyl 1-(2-carbamoylethyl)-4-phenylpiperidine-4-carboxylate;
  $C_{17}H_{24}N_2O_3$; *7528-13-4*
  Cough suppressant

Carphenazine *see Carfenazine*

Carprofen (rINN) kar·prö·fen
  2-(6-Chlorocarbazol-2-yl)propionic acid; $C_{15}H_{12}ClNO_2$;
  53716-49-7
  Cyclo-oxygenase inhibitor; analgesic; anti-inflammatory

and enantiomer

Carsalam (rINN) kar·sa·lam
  (1) 1,3-Benzoxazine-2,4(3*H*)-dione;
  (2) *O*-Carbamoylsalicylic acid lactam;
  $C_8H_5NO_3$; *2037-95-8*
  Analgesic

● **Carteolol** (rINN) see Appendix C

Carticaine *see Articaine*

Carumonam (rINN) ka·*roo*·mo·nam
  (*Z*)-(2-Amino-1,3-thiazol-4-yl){[(2*S*,3*S*)-2-carbamoyl¬
  oxymethyl-4-oxo-1-sulfoazetidin-3-yl]carbamoyl}¬
  methyleneamino-oxyacetic acid; $C_{12}H_{14}N_6O_{10}S_2$; *87638-04-8*;
  AMA 1080
  Carumonam Sodium *86832-68-0*; AMA 1080(2Na)
  Monobactam antibacterial

● **Carvedilol** (rINN) kar·*ve*·di·lol
  1-Carbazol-4-yloxy-3-[2-(2-methoxyphenoxy)ethylamino]¬
  propan-2-ol; $C_{24}H_{26}N_2O_4$; *72956-09-3*
  Beta-adrenoceptor antagonist; arteriolar vasodilator

and enantiomer

Caspofungin (rINN) kas·pö·*fun*·gin
  5.1,6-Anhydro[(4*R*,5*S*)-5-(2-aminoethylamino)-*N*²-(10,12-
  dimethyltetradecanoyl)-4-hydroxy-L-ornithyl-L-threonyl-*trans*-
  4-hydroxy-L-prolyl-(*S*)-4-hydroxy-4-(*p*-hydroxyphenyl)-
  L-threonyl-*threo*-3-hydroxy-L-ornithyl-*trans*-3-hydroxy-
  L-proline]; $C_{52}H_{88}N_{10}O_{15}$; *162808-62-0*
  Caspofungin Acetate *179463-17-3*
  Antifungal

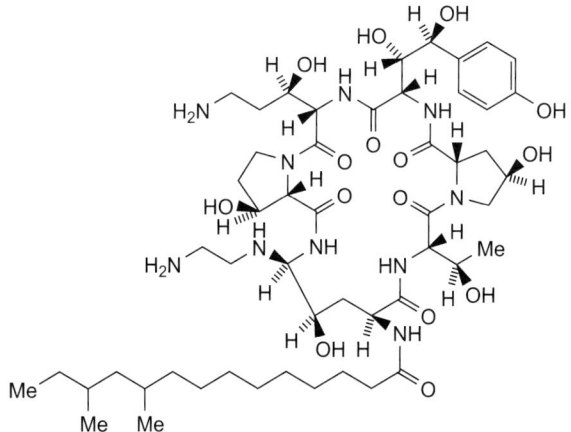

Cediranib (rINN) ke·*di*·rá·nib
  4-[(4-Fluoro-2-methyl-1*H*-indol-5-yl)oxy]-6-methoxy-7-[3-
  (pyrrolidin-1-yl)propoxy]quinazoline; $C_{25}H_{27}FN_4O_3$; AZD2171
  288383-20-0;
  Cediranib Maleate *857036-77-2*; AZD2171 maleate
  Vascular endothelial growth factor; tyrosine kinase inhibitor

Cefacetrile (rINN) ke·*fas*·e·trïl
  3-(Acetyloxy)methyl)-7-[(cyanoacetyl)amino]-8-oxo-5-thia-1-
  azabicyclo[4.2.0]oct-2-ene-2-carboxylic acid; $C_{13}H_{13}N_3O_6S$;
  10206-21-0
  Cefacetrile Sodium *23239-41-0*
  Antibacterial (veterinary)

● **Cefaclor** (pINN) *ke·fa·klor*

3-Chloro-7-(α-D-phenylglycylamino)-3-cephem-4-carboxylic acid; $C_{15}H_{14}ClN_3O_4S$; *53994-73-3*
Cephalosporin antibacterial

Cefaloram (pINN) see Appendix C

Cefaloridine (pINN) (cephaloridine) ke·fa·*lor*·ri·dën

3-(1-Pyridiniomethyl)-7-[(2-thienyl)acetamido]-3-cephem-4-carboxylate; $C_{19}H_{17}N_3O_4S_2$; *50-59-9*
Cephalosporin antibacterial

● **Cefadroxil** (pINN) ke·fa·*droks*·il

7-[α-D-(*p*-Hydroxyphenyl)glycylamino]-3-methyl-3-cephem-4-carboxylic acid; $C_{16}H_{17}N_3O_5S$; *50370-12-2*
Cephalosporin antibacterial

Cefalotin (pINN) *ke*·fa·lö·tin

7-[(2-Thienyl)acetamido]cephalosporanic acid; $C_{16}H_{15}N_2NaO_6S_2$; *153-61-7*
● **Cefalotin Sodium** *58-71-9*
Cephalosporin antibacterial

● **Cefalexin** (pINN) ke·fa·*leks*·in

3-Methyl-7-(α-D-phenylglycylamino)-3-cephem-4-carboxylic acid; $C_{16}H_{17}N_3O_4S$; *15686-71-2 (anhydrous)*; *23325-78-2 (monohydrate)*
Cephalosporin antibacterial

Cefamandole (pINN) ke·fa·*man*·dôl

7-D-Mandelamido-3-[(1-methyltetrazol-5-yl)thiomethyl]-3-cephem-4-carboxylic acid; $C_{18}H_{18}N_6O_5S_2$; *34444-01-4*
Cephalosporin antibacterial

Cefaloglycin (pINN) ke·fa·lö·*glï*·sin

7-(α-D-Phenylglycylamino)cephalosporanic acid; $C_{18}H_{19}N_3O_6S$; *3577-01-3*
Cephalosporin antibacterial

● **Cefamandole Nafate** (rINN) ke·fa·*man*·dôl *na*·fät

Sodium 7-[(αR)-α-formyloxy(phenyl)acetamido]-3-[(1-methyltetrazol-5-yl)thiomethyl]-3-cephem-4-carboxylate; $C_{19}H_{17}N_6NaO_6S_2$; *42540-40-9*
Cephalosporin antibacterial

♣ **Cefalonium** (pINN) ke·fa·*lö*·në·um

3-(4-Carbamoyl-1-pyridiniomethyl)-7-[(2-thienyl)acetamido]-3-cephem-4-carboxylate; $C_{20}H_{18}N_4O_5S_2$; *5575-21-3*
Cephalosporin antibacterial (veterinary)

Cefapirin (pINN) ke·fa·*pi*·rin

7-[2-(4-Pyridylthio)acetamido]cephalosporanic acid; $C_{17}H_{17}N_3O_6S_2$; *21593-23-7*
● **Cefapirin Sodium** *24356-60-3*; BL-P1322
Cephalosporin antibacterial

The symbol '¬' in systematic chemical names signifies line continuation

Cefatrizine (pINN) ke·fa·*tri*·zën

7-[α-D-(*p*-Hydroxyphenyl)glycylamino]-3-(1*H*-1,2,3-triazol-4-ylthiomethyl)-3-cephem-4-carboxylic acid; $C_{18}H_{18}N_6O_5S_2$; *51627-14-6*; BL-S640
● **Cefatrizine Propylene Glycol**
Cephalosporin antibacterial

Cefazedone (rINN) ke·*fä*·ze·dön

7-[2-(3,5-Dichloro-4-oxo-1-pyridyl)acetamido]-3-(5-methyl-1,3,4-thiadiazol-2-ylthiomethyl)-3-cephem-4-carboxylic acid; $C_{18}H_{15}Cl_2N_5O_5S_3$; *56187-47-4*
Cefazedone Sodium EMD 30087
Cephalosporin antibacterial

Cefazolin (pINN) (cephazolin) ke·*fä*·zö·lin

3-[(5-Methyl-1,3,4-thiadiazol-2-yl)thiomethyl]-7-(tetrazol-1-ylacetamido)-3-cephem-4-carboxylic acid; $C_{14}H_{14}N_8O_4S_3$; *25953-19-9*
● **Cefazolin Sodium** *27164-46-1*
Cephalosporin antibacterial

Cefdinir (rINN) *kef*·di·neer

7-{(2-Amino-1,3-thiazol-4-yl)-2-[(*Z*)-hydroxyimino]¬acetamido}-3-vinylcephem-4-carboxylic acid; $C_{14}H_{13}N_5O_5S_2$; *91832-40-5*; C1-983; FK 482
Cephalosporin antibacterial

Cefempidone (rINN) ke·*fem*·pi·dön

7-[2-(2-Amino-1,3-thiazol-5-yl)-2-[(*Z*)-2-oxopyrrolidin-3-yloxyimino)]acetamido]-3-pyridiniomethyl-3-cephem-4-carboxylate; $C_{22}H_{21}N_7O_6S_2$; *103238-57-9*; GR 50692; TA 5901
Cephalosporin antibacterial

Cefepime (rINN) *kef*·e·pëm

7-{(2-Amino-1,3-thiazol-4-yl)-2-[(*Z*)-methoxyimino]¬acetamido}-3-(1-methylpyrrolidiniomethyl)-3-cephem-4-carboxylate; $C_{19}H_{24}N_6O_5S_2$; *88040-23-7*; BMY-28142
● **Cefepime Hydrochloride** (1:1); *123171-59-5 (monohydrate)*; BMY-28142 (2HCl.H₂O)
Cephalosporin antibacterial

Cefetecol (rINN) see Appendix C

● **Cefixime** (rINN) *ke*·fiks·ëm

7-{2-(2-Amino-1,3-thiazol-4-yl)-2-[(*Z*)-carboxymethoxy¬imino)]acetamido}-3-vinyl-3-cephem-4-carboxylic acid; $C_{16}H_{15}N_5O_7S_2$; *79350-37-1*
Cephalosporin antibacterial

Cefodizime (rINN) see Appendix C

Cefonicid (rINN) ke·*fo*·ni·sid

7-[(*R*)-Mandelamido]-3-(1-sulfomethyl-1*H*-tetrazol-5-ylthiomethyl)-3-cephem-4-carboxylic acid; $C_{18}H_{18}N_6O_8S_3$; *61270-58-4*
Cefonicid Sodium *61270-78-8*; SK&F D-75073-Z₂
Cephalosporin antibacterial

Cefoperazone (rINN) ke·fö·*pe*·ra·zön

7-[*N*-(4-Ethyl-2,3-dioxopiperazin-1-ylcarbonyl)-L-2-(4-
hydroxyphenyl)glycylamino]-3-(1-methyl-1*H*-
tetrazol-5-ylthiomethyl)-3-cephem-4-carboxylic acid;
$C_{25}H_{27}N_9O_8S_2$; *62893-19-0*; T-15 51; CP-52640 (*anhydrous*);
CP-52640-3 (*dihydrate*)
● **Cefoperazone Sodium** *62893-20-3*
Cephalosporin antibacterial

Cefotiam (rINN) ke·fö·*ti*·am

7-[2-(2-Amino-1,3-thiazol-4-yl)acetamido]-3-[1-(2-
dimethylaminoethyl)-1*H*-tetrazol-5-ylthiomethyl]-3-cephem-4-
carboxylic acid; $C_{18}H_{23}N_9O_4S_3$; *61622-34-2*; CGP 14221E
Cefotiam Hydrochloride *66309-69-1*; SCE 963
Cephalosporin antibacterial

Ceforanide (rINN) ke·*for*·ra·nïd

7-[2-(α-Amino-*o*-tolyl)acetamido]-3-(1-carboxymethyl-1*H*-
tetrazol-5-ylthiomethyl)-3-cephem-4-carboxylic acid;
$C_{20}H_{21}N_7O_6S_2$; *60925-61-3*; BL-S786
Cephalosporin antibacterial

Cefoxazole (rINN) ke·*foks*·a·zôl

7-(3-*o*-Chlorophenyl-5-methyl-1,2-oxazol-4-ylcarboxamido)¬
cephalosporanic acid; $C_{21}H_{18}ClN_3O_7S$; *36920-48-6*
Cephalosporin antibacterial

Cefotaxime (rINN) ke·fö·*taks*·ëm

(*Z*)-7-[2-(2-Amino-1,3-thiazol-4-yl)-2-(methoxyimino)¬
acetamido]cephalosporanic acid; $C_{16}H_{17}N_5O_7S_2$; *60846-21-1*
● **Cefotaxime Sodium** *64485-93-4*
Cephalosporin antibacterial

Cefoxitin (rINN) ke·*foks*·i·tin

3-Carbamoyloxymethyl-7-methoxy-7-[2-(2-thienyl)acetamido]-
3-cephem-4-carboxylic acid; $C_{16}H_{17}N_3O_7S_2$; *35607-66-0*
● **Cefoxitin Sodium** *33564-30-6*
Cephalosporin antibacterial

Cefotetan (rINN) ke·fö·*të*·tan

2-{4-[4-Carboxy-7-methoxy-3-(1-methyl-1*H*-
tetrazol-5-ylthiomethyl)-3-cephem-7-ylcarbamoyl]-1,3-
dithietan-2-ylidene}malonamic acid; $C_{17}H_{17}N_7O_8S_4$;
69712-56-7; YM 09330; ICI 156,834
Cephalosporin antibacterial

Cefpirome (rINN) *kef*·pi·röm

(*Z*)-7-[2-(2-Amino-1,3-thiazol-4-yl)-2-(methoxyimino)¬
acetamido]-3-(6,7-dihydro-5*H*-cyclopenta[*b*]pyridiniomethyl)-
3-cephem-4-carboxylate; $C_{22}H_{22}N_6O_5S_2$; *84957-29-9*
Cefpirome Sulfate *98753-19-6*
Cephalosporin antibacterial

The symbol '¬' in systematic chemical names signifies line continuation

Cefpodoxime (rINN) kef·pö·*doks*·ëm
7-[(*Z*)-2-(2-Amino-1,3-thiazol-4-yl)-2-(methoxyimino)¬
acetamido]-3-methoxymethyl-3-cephem-4-carboxylic acid;
C$_{15}$H$_{17}$N$_5$O$_6$S$_2$; *80210-62-4*
● **Cefpodoxime Proxetil** *87239-81-4*
Cephalosporin antibacterial

● **Cefprozil** (rINN) *kef*·prö·zil
7-(D-4-Hydroxyphenylglycylamino)-3-(prop-1-enyl)cephem-4-
carboxylic acid; C$_{18}$H$_{19}$N$_3$O$_5$S; *121123-17-9*;
BMY-28100-03-800
Cephalosporin antibacterial

Cefquinome (rINN) *kef*·kwi·nöm
7-[(*Z*)-2-(2-Amino-1,3-thiazol-4-yl)-2-(methoxyimino)¬
acetamido]-3-(5,6,7,8-tetrahydroquinoliniomethyl)-3-cephem-4-
carboxylate; C$_{23}$H$_{24}$N$_6$O$_5$S$_2$; *84957-30-2*
Cefquinome Sulfate *123766-80-3*
Cephalosporin antibacterial

● **Cefradine** (rINN) *kef*·ra·dën
7-(α-D-Cyclohexa-1,4-dienylglycylamino)-3-methyl-3-cephem-
4-carboxylic acid; C$_{16}$H$_{19}$N$_3$O$_4$S; *38821-53-3*
Cephalosporin antibacterial

Cefsulodin (rINN) see Appendix C

Ceftaroline Fosamil (rINN) kef·*ta*·ro·lën *fo*·sa·mil
(6*R*,7*R*)-7-{(2*Z*)-2-(Ethoxyimino)-2-[5-(phosphonoamino)-
1,2,4-thiadiazol-3-yl]acetamido}-3-{[4-(1-methylpyridin-1-
ium-4-yl)-1,3-thiazol-2-yl]sulfanyl}-8-oxo-5-thia-1-
azabicyclo[4.2.0]oct-2-ene-2-carboxylate; C$_{22}$H$_{21}$N$_8$O$_8$PS$_4$;
229016-73-3;
Antibacterial; antihelminthic

Ceftazidime (rINN) kef·*ta*·zi·dëm
7-[(*Z*)-2-(2-Amino-1,3-thiazol-4-yl)-2-(1-carboxy-1-
methylethoxyimino)acetamido]-3-(1-pyridiniomethyl)-3-
cephem-4-carboxylate; C$_{22}$H$_{22}$N$_6$O$_7$S$_2$; *72558-82-8*; GR 20263
Cephalosporin antibacterial

Ceftibuten (rINN) kef·ti·*bü*·ten
7-[2-(2-Amino-1,3-thiazol-4-yl)-4-carboxyisocrotonamido]-3-
cephem-4-carboxylic acid; C$_{15}$H$_{14}$N$_4$O$_6$S$_2$; *97519-39-6*
Cephalosporin antibacterial

Ceftiofur (rINN) kef·*ti*·ö·fûr
7-[(*Z*)-2-(2-Amino-1,3-thiazol-4-yl)-2-(methoxyimino)¬
acetamido]-3-(2-furoylthiomethyl)-3-cephem-4-carboxylic acid;
C$_{19}$H$_{17}$N$_5$O$_7$S$_3$; *80370-57-6*; CM 31,916
Ceftiofur Hydrochloride *103980-44-5*; U-64279A
Ceftiofur Sodium *104010-37-9*; U-64279E
Cephalosporin antibacterial

Ceftizoxime (rINN) see Appendix C

Ceftriaxone (rINN) kef·trī·*aks*·ön

7-[(*Z*)-2-(2-Amino-1,3-thiazol-4-yl)-2-(methoxyimino)¬
acetamido]-3-[(2,5-dihydro-6-hydroxy-2-methyl-5-oxo-1,2,4-
triazin-3-yl)thiomethyl]-3-cephem-4-carboxylic acid;
$C_{18}H_{18}N_8O_7S_3$; *73384-59-5*

● **Ceftriaxone Sodium** *104376-79-6*
Cephalosporin antibacterial

Cefuracetime (rINN) ke·fûr·*ra*·se·tëm

7-[(*Z*)-2-(2-Furyl)-2-(methoxyimino)acetamido]cephalosporanic
acid; $C_{17}H_{17}N_3O_8S$; *39685-31-9*; *640/1*
Cephalosporin antibacterial

Cefuroxime (rINN) ke·fûr·*roks*·ëm

3-Carbamoyloxymethyl-7-[(*Z*)-2-(2-furyl)-2-(methoxyimino)¬
acetamido]-3-cephem-4-carboxylic acid; $C_{16}H_{16}N_4O_8S$;
55268-75-2

● **Cefuroxime Axetil** *64544-07-6*
Cefuroxime Pivoxetil *100680-33-9*
● **Cefuroxime Sodium** *56238-63-2*
Cephalosporin antibacterial

Celecoxib (rINN) se·lë·*koks*·ib

4-[5-*p*-Tolyl-3-(trifluoromethyl)pyrazol-1-yl]benzene¬
sulfonamide; $C_{17}H_{14}F_3N_3O_2S$; *169590-42-5*
*Cyclo-oxygenase (COX-2) inhibitor; analgesic;
anti-inflammatory*

Celiprolol (rINN) se·*li*·pro·lol

(*RS*)-3-{3-Acetyl-4-[3-(*tert*-butylamino)-2-hydroxypropoxy]¬
phenyl}-1,1-diethylurea; $C_{20}H_{33}N_3O_4$; *56980-93-9*

● **Celiprolol Hydrochloride** *57470-78-7*
Beta-adrenoceptor antagonist

and enantiomer

● **Cellacefate** (rINN) se·*la*·së·fät

An approximately 75% esterified cellulose containing acetate
and hydrogen phthalate groups in the ratio of 2:1; cellulose
acetate phthalate (USAN); *9004-38-0*
Enteric coating in pharmaceutical products

● **Celucloral** (rINN) se·lü·*klor*·ral

Hydroxyethylcellulose reaction product with chloral; ML 1034
Hypnotic (veterinary)

Cephalexin *see Cefalexin*

Cephaloglycin *see Cefaloglycin*

Cephalonium *see Cefalonium*

Cephaloram *see Cefaloram*

Cephaloridine *see Cefaloridine*

Cephalosporin C (rINN) see Appendix C

Cephalothin *see Cefalothin*

Cephamandole *see Cefamandole*

Cephamandole Nafate *see Cefamandole Nafate*

Cephazolin *see Cefazolin*

Cephoxazole *see Cefoxazole*

Cephradine *see Cefradine*

Cerivastatin (rINN) se·ri·va·*sta*·tin

(*E*)-(3*R*,5*S*)-7-[4-(4-Fluorophenyl)-2,6-di-isopropyl-5-
methoxymethyl-3-pyridyl]-3,5-dihydroxyhept-6-enoic acid;
$C_{26}H_{34}FNO_5$
Cerivastatin Sodium *143201-11-0*
HMG-CoA reductase inhibitor; lipid-regulating drug

Certolizumab Pegol (rINN) ser·to·li·zü·mab pe·gol
Immunoglobulin, anti-(human tumour necrosis factor a) Fab′
fragment (human-mouse monoclonal CDP870 heavy chain),
disulfide with human-mouse monoclonal CDP870 light chain,
pegylated at Cys-221; *428863-50-7*
Monoclonal antibody (TNF alfa)

certolizumab has the following pegylated amino acid sequence:

```
DIQMTQSPSS    LSASVGDRVT    ITCKASQNVG

TNVAWYQQKP    GKAPKALIYS    ASFLYSGVPY

RFSGSGSGTD    FTLTISSLQP    EDFATYYCQQ

YNIYPLTFGQ    GTKVEIKRTV    AAPSVFIFPP

SDEQLKSGTA    SVVCLLNNFY    PREAKVQWKV

DNALQSGNSQ    ESVTEQDSKD    STYSLSSTLT

LSKADYEKHK    VYACEVTHQG    LSSPVTKSFN

RGEC


EVQLVESGGG    LVQPGGSLRL    SCAASGYVFT

DYGMNWVRQA    PGKGLEWMGW    INTYIGEPIY

ADSVKGRFTF    SLDTSKSTAY    LQMNSLRAED

TAVYYCARGY    RSYAMDYWGQ    GTLVTVSSAS

TKGPSVFPLA    PSSKSTSGGT    AALGCLVKDY

FPEPVTVSWN    SGALTSGVHT    FPAVLQSSGL

YSLSSVVTVP    SSSLGTQTYI    CNVNHKPSNT
                *
KVDKKVEPKS    CDKTHTCAA
```

*pegylation site

Certoparin Sodium (rINN) ser·to·pa·rin
Sodium salt of depolymerised heparin obtained by isoamyl
nitrite-degradation of heparin from pork intestinal mucosa;
the majority of the components have a 2-*O*-sulfo-α-
L-idopyranosuronic acid structure at the non-reducing end and
a 6-*O*-sulfo-2,5-anhydro-D-mannose moiety at the reducing end
of their chain; the molecular weight of 70% of the components
is less than 10,000 and the average molecular weight is about
6000; the degree of sulfation is about 2 to 2·5 per disaccharide
unit
Low molecular weight heparin

Ceruletide (rINN) se·roo·le·tïd
$C_{58}H_{73}N_{13}O_{21}S_2$; *17650-98-5*
Ceruletide Diethylamine *71247-25-1*
Cholecystokinin analogue; aid in radiodiagnostic imagery

```
              SO3H
               |
5-oxoPro-Gln-Asp-Tyr-Thr-Gly-Trp-

Met-Asp-Phe-NH2
```

Cetalkonium Chloride (rINN) së·tal·kö·në·um
Benzyl(hexadecyl)dimethylammonium chloride; $C_{25}H_{46}ClN$;
122-18-9
Antiseptic

Cetilistat (rINN) se·ti·li·stat
2-(Hexadecyloxy)-6-methyl-4*H*-3,1-benzoxazin-4-one;
$C_{25}H_{39}NO_3$; *282526-98-1*
Gastrointestinal lipase inhibitor; treatment of obesity

Cetirizine (rINN) se·ti·ri·zën
(*RS*)-2-[4-(4-Chlorobenzhydryl)piperazine-1-yl]ethoxyacetic
acid; $C_{21}H_{25}ClN_2O_3$; *83881-51-0*
● **Cetirizine Hydrochloride** (2HCl); *83881-52-1*
Histamine H_1 receptor antagonist; antihistamine

and enantiomer

Cetomacrogol 1000 (rINN) së·tö·ma·krö·gol
Polyethylene glycol 1000 monocetyl ether; polyoxyethylene
glycol 1000 monocetyl ether; *9004-95-9*
Emulsifying agent

Cetoxime (rINN) së·toks·ëm
2-(*N*-Benzylanilino)acetamide oxime; $C_{15}H_{17}N_3O$; *25394-78-9*
Histamine H_1 receptor antagonist; antihistamine

● **Cetrimide** (rINN) se·tri·mïd
Trimethyl(tetradecyl)ammonium bromide together with smaller
amounts of dodecyl- and hexadecyl-trimethylammonium
bromides; *8044-71-1*; component in many other proprietary
preparations
Antiseptic

Cetrimonium Bromide (INNM) se·tri·*mö*·në·um

Hexadecyltrimethylammonium bromide; $C_{19}H_{42}BrN$; *57-09-0*
Antiseptic

$$Me-[CH_2]_{15}-\overset{+}{N}Me_3 \quad Br^-$$

Cetrorelix (rINN) së·trö·*rë*·liks

[*N*-Acetyl-3-(2-naphthyl)]-D-alanyl-4-chloro-D-phenylalanyl-3-
(3-pyridyl)-D-alanyl-L-seryl-L-tyrosyl-N^5-carbamoyl-D-ornithyl-
L-leucyl-L-arginyl-L-prolyl-D-alaninamide; $C_{70}H_{92}ClN_{17}O_{14}$;
120287-85-6
Luteinizing hormone releasing hormone (LHRH) inhibitor

● **Cetylpyridinium Chloride** (rINN) së·til·pi·ri·*di*·në·um

1-Hexadecylpyridinium chloride; $C_{21}H_{38}ClN$;
123-03-5 (anhydrous); 6004-24-6 (monohydrate)
Antiseptic

● **Chenodeoxycholic Acid** (rINN) kë·nö·dë·oks·ë·*kö*·lik

3α,7α-Dihydroxy-5β-cholan-24-oic acid; chenodiol (USAN);
$C_{24}H_{40}O_4$; *474-25-9*
Bile acid; treatment of gallstones

Chlophedianol *see Clofedanol*

Chloral Betaine *see Cloral Betaine*

● **Chloral Hydrate** (BAN) *klor*·ral

2,2,2-Trichloroethane-1,1-diol; $C_2H_3Cl_3O_2$; *302-17-0*
Hypnotic

Chloralodol (rINN) See Appendix C

● **Chlorambucil** (rINN) klor·*ram*·bü·sil

4-{4-Bis(2-chloroethyl)amino]phenyl}butyric acid;
$C_{14}H_{19}Cl_2NO_2$; *305-03-3*
Cytotoxic alkylating agent

Chloramine *see Tosylchloramide Sodium*

● **Chloramphenicol** (rINN) klor·ram·*fe*·ni·kol

2,2-Dichloro-*N*-[(*aR,βR*)-β-hydroxy-α-hydroxymethyl-4-
nitrophenethyl]acetamide; $C_{11}H_{12}Cl_2N_2O_5$; *56-75-7*
● **Chloramphenicol Palmitate** *530-43-8*; present as a
component in many veterinary anti-infective preparations
● **Chloramphenicol Sodium Succinate** *982-57-0*
Antibacterial

Chlorbetamide (rINN) klor·*bë*·ta·mïd

2,2-Dichloro-*N*-(2,4-dichlorobenzyl)-*N*-(2-
hydroxyethyl)acetamide; $C_{11}H_{11}Cl_4NO_2$; *97-27-8*
Antiprotozoal (veterinary)

Chlorbutol *see Chlorobutanol*

Chlorcyclizine (rINN) klor·*sï*·kli·zën

(*RS*)-1-(4-Chlorobenzhydryl)-4-methylpiperazine; $C_{18}H_{21}ClN_2$;
82-93-9
● **Chlorcyclizine Hydrochloride** *1620-21-9*
Histamine H_1 receptor antagonist; antihistamine

and enantiomer

Chlordantoin *see Clordantoin*

The symbol '¬' in systematic chemical names signifies line continuation

• **Chlordiazepoxide** (rINN) klor·dï·ä·ze·poks·ïd
7-Chloro-2-methylamino-5-phenyl-3H-1,4-benzodiazepine¬
4-oxide; $C_{16}H_{14}ClN_3O$; *58-25-3*
  • **Chlordiazepoxide Hydrochloride** *438-41-5*
Benzodiazepine

Chlorfenvinphos *see Clorfenvinfos*

Chlorhexadol *see Chloralodol*

Chlorhexidine (rINN) klor·*heks*·i·dën
5,5′-Bis(4-chlorophenyl)-1,1′-hexamethylenebiguanide;
$C_{22}H_{30}Cl_2N_{10}$; *55-56-1*; salts of chlorhexidine are components of a
large number of proprietary preparations
  • **Chlorhexidine Acetate** *56-95-1*
  • **Chlorhexidine Gluconate** *18472-51-0*
  • **Chlorhexidine Hydrochloride** *3697-42-5*
Antiseptic

Chlorisondamine Chloride (rINN) klor·ï·*son*·da·mën
4,5,6,7-Tetrachloro-2-methyl-2-(2-trimethylammonioethyl)¬
isoindolinium dichloride; $C_{14}H_{20}Cl_6N_2$; *69-27-2*
Anticholinergic (nicotinic)

Chlormadinone (rINN) klor·*mad*·i·nön
6-Chloro-17α-hydroxypregna-4,6-diene-3,20-dione;
$C_{23}H_{29}ClO_4$; *1961-77-9*
Chlormadinone Acetate
Progestogen

Chlormerodrin (rINN) klor·*me*·rö·drin
(*RS*)-Chloro(2-methoxy-3-ureidopropyl)mercury;
$C_5H_{11}ClHgN_2O_2$; *10375-56-1*
Mercurial diuretic

and enantiomer

Chlormethiazole *see Clomethiazole*

Chlormethine (rINN) *klor*·me·thën
Bis(2-chloroethyl)methylamine; mechlorethamine (USAN);
$C_5H_{11}Cl_2N$; *51-75-2*
  • **Chlormethine Hydrochloride** *55-86-7*
Cytotoxic alkylating agent

Chlormezanone (rINN) see Appendix C

Chlormidazole (rINN) see Appendix C

• **Chlorobutanol** (rINN) klor·rö·*bü*·ta·nol
1,1,1-Trichloro-2-methylpropan-2-ol; $C_4H_7Cl_3O$; *57-15-8*
(*anhydrous); 6001-64-5 (hemihydrate)*
Disinfectant preservative

Chloropyramine (rINN) klor·rö·*pi*·ra·mën
2-[4-Chlorobenzyl(2-pyridyl)amino]ethyldimethylamine;
$C_{16}H_{26}ClN_3$; *59-32-5*
Histamine H_1 receptor antagonist; antihistamine

Chloropyrilene (rINN) klor·rö·*pi*·ri·lën
2-[(5-Chloro-2-thenyl)(2-pyridyl)amino]ethyldimethylamine;
$C_{14}H_{18}ClN_3S$; *148-65-2*
Histamine H_1 receptor antagonist; antihistamine

Chloroquine (rINN) *klor·rö·kwën*

(*RS*)-4-(7-Chloro-4-quinolylamino)pentyldiethylamine; $C_{18}H_{26}ClN_3$; *54-05-7*
- ●**Chloroquine Phosphate** *50-63-5*
- ●**Chloroquine Sulfate** *132-73-0*

Antiprotozoal (malaria)

and enantiomer

●**Chlorothiazide** (rINN) *klor·rö·thï·a·zïd*

6-Chloro-2*H*-1,2,4-benzothiadiazine-7-sulfonamide 1,1-dioxide; $C_7H_6ClN_3O_4S_2$; *58-94-6*
Diuretic

Chlorotrianisene (rINN) *klor·rö·trï·a·ni·sën*

Chlorotris(4-methoxyphenyl)ethylene; $C_{23}H_{21}ClO_3$; *569-57-3*
Oestrogen

●**Chloroxylenol** (rINN) *klor·ro·zï·le·nol*

4-Chloro-3,5-xylenol; C_8H_9ClO; *88-04-0*
Antiseptic

Chlorphenesin (rINN) *klor·fen·ë·sin*

(*RS*)-3-(4-Chlorophenoxy)propane-1,2-diol; $C_{10}H_{12}ClNO_4$; *104-29-0*
Antifungal

and enantiomer

Chlorphenamine (rINN) *klor·fen·a·mën*

(*RS*)-3-(4-Chlorophenyl)-3-(2-pyridyl)propyldimethylamine; $C_{16}H_{19}ClN_2$; *132-22-9*
- ●**Chlorphenamine Maleate** *113-92-8*
Histamine H_1 receptor antagonist; antihistamine

and enantiomer

Chlorpheniramine *see Chlorphenamine*

Chlorphenoctium Amsonate (rINN) *klor·fe·nok·të·um*

Bis[2,4-dichlorophenoxymethyldimethyl(octyl)ammonium] 4,4´-diaminostilbene-2,2´-disulfonate; $C_{31}H_{41}Cl_2N_3O_5S_2$; *7168-18-5*
Antifungal

Chlorphenoxamine (rINN) *klor·fe·noks·a·mën*

(*RS*)-2-[1-(4-Chlorophenyl)-1-phenylethoxy]ethyl dimethyl¬amine; $C_{18}H_{22}ClNO$; *77-38-3*
Anticholinergic

and enantiomer

Chlorphentermine (rINN) *klor·fen·ter·mën*

4-Chloro-α,α-dimethylphenethylamine; $C_{10}H_{14}ClN$; *461-78-9*
Appetite suppressant

Chlorproguanil (rINN) *klor·prö·gwa·nil*

1-(3,4-Dichlorophenyl)-5-isopropylbiguanide; $C_{11}H_{15}Cl_2N_5$; *537-21-3*
Antiprotozoal (malaria)

The symbol '¬' in systematic chemical names signifies line continuation

Chlorpromazine (rINN) klor·*prö*·ma·zën
3-(2-Chlorophenothiazin-10-yl)propyldimethylamine;
$C_{17}H_{19}ClN_2S$; *50-53-3*
Chlorpromazine Hydrochloride *69-09-0*
Dopamine receptor antagonist; neuroleptic

Chlorpropamide (rINN) klor·*prö*·pa·mïd
1-(4-Chlorophenylsulfonyl)-3-propylurea; $C_{10}H_{13}ClN_2O_3S$;
94-20-2
*Inhibition of ATP-dependent potassium channels (sulfonylurea);
treatment of diabetes mellitus*

Chlorprothixene (rINN) klor·prö·*thiks*·ën
(Z)-3-[2-Chloro(thioxanthen-9-ylidene)]propyldimethylamine;
$C_{18}H_{18}ClNS$; *113-59-7*
Chlorprothixene Hydrochloride *6469-93-8*
Dopamine receptor antagonist; neuroleptic

Chlorpyrifos (BAN) klor·*pi*·ri·fos
O,O-Diethyl O-3,5,6-trichloro-2-pyridyl phosphorothioate;
$C_9H_{11}Cl_3NO_3PS$; *2921-88-2*
Organophosphorus insecticide

Chlorquinaldol (rINN) klor·kwi·*nal*·dol
5,7-Dichloro-2-methylquinolin-8-ol; $C_{10}H_7Cl_2NO$; *72-80-0*
Disinfectant

Chlortalidone (rINN) klor·*ta*·li·dön
(RS)-2-Chloro-5-(1-hydroxy-3-oxoisoindolin-1-yl)benzene-
sulfonamide; $C_{14}H_{11}ClN_2O_4S$; *77-36-1*
Thiazide-like diuretic

and enantiomer

Chlortetracycline (rINN) klor·te·tra·*si*·klën
(4S,4aS,5aS,6S,12aS)-7-Chloro-4-dimethylamino-
1,4,4a,5,5a,6,11,12a-octahydro-3,6,10,12,12a-pentahydroxy-6-
methyl-1,11-dioxonaphthacene-2-carboxamide;
7-chlorotetracycline; $C_{22}H_{23}ClN_2O_8$; *57-62-5*
Chlortetracycline Hydrochloride *64-72-2*
Tetracycline antibacterial

Chlorthalidone *see Chlortalidone*

Chlorthenoxazine (rINN) klor·the·*noks*·a·zën
2-(2-Chloroethyl)-2,3-dihydro-1,3-benzoxazin-4-one;
$C_{10}H_{10}ClNO_2$; *132-89-8*
Cyclo-oxygenase inhibitor; analgesic; anti-inflammatory

Chlorzoxazone (rINN) klor·*zoks*·a·zön
5-Chloro-1,3-benzoxazol-2(3H)-one; $C_7H_4ClNO_2$; *95-25-0*
Skeletal muscle relaxant

Cholecalciferol *see Colecalciferol*

Cholesterol (BAN) kö·*le*·ste·rol
Cholest-5-en-3β-ol; $C_{27}H_{46}O$; *57-88-5*
Excipient

Cholestyramine *see Colestyramine*

● **Choline Salicylate** (rINN) kö·lën sa·*li*·si·lät
Choline salt of salicylic acid; $C_{12}H_{19}NO_4$; *2016-36-6*
Salicylate; non-selective cyclo-oxygenase inhibitor; analgesic; anti-inflammatory

● **Choline Theophyllinate** (rINN) kö·lën thë·o·*fi*·li·nät
Choline 1,2,3,6-tetrahydro-1,3-dimethyl-2,6-dioxo-7*H*-purin-7-ide; oxtriphylline (USAN); $C_{12}H_{21}N_5O_3$; *4499-40-5*
Non-selective phosphodiesterase inhibitor (xanthine); treatment of reversible airways obstruction

● **Chondroitin Sulfate Sodium** (rINN) kon·*drö*·it·in
[4)-(β-D-Glucopyranosyluronic acid)-(1→3)-[2-(acetylamino)-2-deoxy-β-D-alactopyranosyl 4-sulfate]-(1→] and [4)-(β-D-glucopyranosyluronic acid)-(1→3)-[2-(acetylamino)-2-deoxy-β-D-galactopyranosyl 6-sulfate]-(1→], sodium salt;
$H_2O(C_{14}H_{19}NNa_2O_{14}S)_x$; *9082-07-9*
Acid mucopolysaccharide; treatment of osteoarthritis

R=SO₃Na and R'=H
or
R=H and R'=SO₃Na

Choriogonadotropin Alfa (rINN) ko·rë·ö·go·na·dö·*trö*·pin al·fa
Human chorionic gonadotropin (protein moiety reduced), glycoform α; *177073-44-8*

α-*subunit*: chorionic gonadotropin (human α-subunit protein moiety reduced); *56832-30-5*

β-*subunit*: chorionic gonadotropin (human β-subunit protein moiety reduced); *56832-34-9*
Gonadotropic hormone

choriogonadotropin alfa has the following amino acid sequence:

α–*subunit*

APDVQDCPEC	TLQENPFFSQ	PGAPILQCMG
CCFSRAYPTP	LRSKKTMLVQ	KNVTSESTCC
VAKSYNRVTV	MGGFKVENHT	ACHCSTCYYH
KS		

β–*subunit*

SKEPLRPRCR	PINATLAVEK	EGCPVCITVN
TTICAGYCPT	MTRVLQGVLP	ALPQVVCNYR
DVRFESIRLP	GCPRGVNPVV	SYAVALSCQC
ALCRRSTTDC	GGPKDHPLTC	DDPRFQDSSS
SKAPPPSLPS	PSRLPGPSDT	PLIPQ

● **Chorionic Gonadotrophin** (rINN) ko·ri·*o*·nik gon·a·dö·*trö*·fin
A preparation of a glycoprotein fraction secreted by the placenta and obtained from the urine of pregnant women, having the action of the pituitary luteinising hormone; *9002-61-3*
Gonadotropic hormone

Chymopapain (rINN) *kï*·mö·pa·pän
A proteolytic enzyme isolated from papaya latex, differing from papainin electrophoretic mobility, solubility and substrate specificity; the approximate molecular weight is 27,000; *9001-09-6*
Proteolytic enzyme

● **Chymotrypsin** (rINN) kï·mö·*trip*·sin
An enzyme obtained from chymotrypsinogen by activation with trypsin; α-chymotrypsin; *9004-07-3*
Proteolytic enzyme

Ciamexon (rINN) sï·a·*meks*·on
(*RS*)-1-(2-Methoxy-6-methyl-3-pyridylmethyl)aziridine-2-carbonitrile; $C_{11}H_{13}N_3O$; *75985-31-8*; BM 41·332
Immunoregulator

and enantiomer

Cibenzoline (rINN) sï·*ben*·zö·lën
2-(2,2-Diphenylcyclopropyl)-2-imidazoline; cifenline (USAN); $C_{18}H_{18}N_2$; *53267-01-9*
Cibenzoline Succinate cifenline succinate (USAN); *100678-32-8*
Class I antiarrhythmic

The symbol '¬' in systematic chemical names signifies line continuation

Ciclacillin (rINN) see Appendix C

Ciclazindol (rINN) sï·*kla*·zin·dol

(*RS*)-10-(*m*-Chlorophenyl)-2,3,4,10-tetrahydropyrimido⌐
[1,2-*a*]indol-10-ol; $C_{17}H_{15}ClN_2O$; *37751-39-6*
Ciclazindol Hydrochloride *37647-52-2*; Wy 23409
Tetracyclic antidepressant

and enantiomer

Cicletanine (rINN) sï·*kle*·ta·nën

(*RS*)-3-*p*-Chlorophenyl-1,3-dihydro-6-methylfuro[3,4-*c*]⌐
pyridin-7-ol; $C_{14}H_{12}ClNO_2$; *89943-82-8*
Cicletanine Hydrochloride *82747-56-6*
Thiazide-like diuretic

and enantiomer

Ciclobendazole (rINN) sï·klö·*ben*·da·zôl

Methyl 5-(cyclopropylcarbonyl)benzimidazol-2-ylcarbamate;
$C_{13}H_{13}N_3O_3$; *31431-43-3*
Antihelminthic

●**Ciclopirox** (rINN) sï·klö·*pï*·roks
6-Cyclohexyl-1-hydroxy-4-methyl-2-pyridone; $C_{12}H_{17}NO_2$;
29342-05-0
●**Ciclopirox Olamine** *41621-49-2*
Antifungal

Cicloprofen (rINN) sï·klö·*prö*·fen
(*RS*)-2-(Fluoren-2-yl)propionic acid; $C_{16}H_{14}O_2$; *36950-96-6*;
SQ 20824
Cyclo-oxygenase inhibitor; analgesic; anti-inflammatory

and enantiomer

Cicloprolol (rINN) see Appendix C

Ciclosidomine (rINN) sï·klö·*si*·do·mën
N-Cyclohexylcarbonyl-3-morpholinosydnone imine;
$C_{13}H_{20}N_4O_3$; *66564-16-7*
Ciclosidomine Hydrochloride PR-G 138-CL
Nitric oxide analogue; treatment of hypertension

●**Ciclosporin** (rINN) sï·klö·*spor*·rin
Cyclo-[-[(*R*)-4-(*E*)-but-2-enyl-*N*,4-dimethyl-L-threonyl]-
L-homoalanyl-(*N*-methylglycyl)-(*N*-methyl-L-leucyl)-L-valyl-
(*N*-methyl-L-leucyl)-L-alanyl-D-alanyl-(*N*-methyl-L-leucyl)-
(*N*-methyl-L-leucyl)-(*N*-methyl-L-valyl)-]; cyclosporin A;
$C_{62}H_{111}N_{11}O_{12}$; *59865-13-3*
Calcineurin inhibitor; immunosuppressant

Ciclotizolam (rINN) sï·klö·*ti*·zö·lam
2-Bromo-4-(2-chlorophenyl)-9-cyclohexyl-6*H*-
[3,2-*f*][1,2,4]triazolo[4,3-*a*][1,4]diazepine; $C_{20}H_{18}BrClN_4S$;
58765-21-2; We 973-BS
Benzodiazepine

Cicloxolone (rINN) sï·*kloks*·o·lön
3β-(*cis*-2-Carboxycyclohexylcarbonyloxy)-11-oxo-18β-olean-12-
en-30-oic acid; $C_{38}H_{56}O_7$; *52247-86-6*
Treatment of gastric ulcers

and epimer at C*

Cidofovir (rINN) sï·*dö*·fo·veer

1-[(*S*)-3-Hydroxy-2-(phosphonomethoxy)propyl]cytosine;
C₈H₁₄N₃O₆P; *149394-66-1*
Antiviral

Ciladopa (rINN) sï·la·*dö*·pa

(*S*)-2-[4-(β-Hydroxy-3,4-dimethoxyphenethyl)piperazin-l-yl]¬
cycloheptatrienone; C₂₁H₂₆N₂O₄; *80109-27-9*
Ciladopa Hydrochloride *83529-09-3*; AY-27110
Nucleoside analogue

Cilastatin (rINN) sï·la·*sta*·tin

S-{(*Z*)-6-Carboxy-6-[(*S*)-2,2-dimethylcyclopropane¬
carboxamido]hex-5-enyl}-ʟ-cysteine; C₁₆H₂₆N₂O₅S; *82009-34-5*
●**Cilastatin Sodium** *81129-83-1*
Dehydropeptidase-I inhibitor; inhibition of the renal metabolism of imipenem

●**Cilazapril** (rINN) sï·*lä*·za·pril

(1*S*,9*S*)-9-[(*S*)-1-Ethoxycarbonyl-3-phenylpropylamino]-10-
oxoperhydropyridazino[1,2-*a*][1,2]diazepine-1-carboxylic acid;
C₂₂H₃₁N₃O₅; *88768-40-5*
Angiotensin converting enzyme inhibitor

Cilazaprilat (rINN) sï·*lä*·za·pri·lat

N-[1*S*,9*S*)-1-Carboxy-10-oxoperhydropyridazino¬
[1,2-*a*][1,2]diazepin-9-yl]-4-phenyl-ʟ-homoalanine;
C₂₀H₂₇N₃O₅; *90139-06-3*
Angiotensin converting enzyme inhibitor

Cilostazol (rINN) sï·*lo*·sta·zôl

6-[4-(1-Cyclohexyl-1*H*-tetrazol-5-yl)butoxy]-3,4-
dihydroquinolin-2(1*H*)-one; C₂₀H₂₇N₅O₂; *73963-72-1*
Antiplatelet drug

●**Cimetidine** (rINN) sï·*me*·ti·dën

2-Cyano-1-methyl-3-[2-(5-methylimidazol-4-
ylmethylthio)ethyl]guanidine; C₁₀H₁₆N₆S; *51481-61-9*
●**Cimetidine Hydrochloride** *70059-30-2*
Histamine H₂ receptor antagonist; treatment of peptic ulceration

Cinacalcet (rINN) si·na·*kal*·set

N-[(1*R*)-1-(1-Naphthyl)ethyl]-3-[3-(trifluoromethyl)phenyl]¬
propan-1-amine; C₂₂H₂₂F₃N; *226256-56-0*
Calcimetic; increasing sensitivity of calcium-sensing receptors in the parathyroid gland; treatment of secondary hyperparathyroidism and hypercalcaemia in parathyroid carcinoma

Cinchocaine (rINN) *sin·kö·kän*

2-Butoxy-*N*-(2-diethylaminoethyl)quinoline-4-carboxamide; $C_{20}H_{29}N_3O_2$; *85-79-0*
● **Cinchocaine Hydrochloride** *61-12-1*
Local anaesthetic

Cinchophen (rINN) *sin·kö·fen*

2-Phenylquinoline-4-carboxylic acid; $C_{16}H_{11}NO_2$; *132-60-5*
Uricosuric; treatment of gout

Cinepazet (rINN) *sï·ne·pä·zet*

Ethyl 4-(3,4,5-trimethoxycinnamoyl)piperazin-1-ylacetate;
$C_{20}H_{28}N_2O_6$; *23887-41-4*
Cinepazet Maleate *50679-07-7*
Vasodilator; treatment of angina pectoris

Cinepazide (rINN) *sï·ne·pä·zïd*

1-(Pyrrolidin-1-ylcarbonylmethyl)-4-(3,4,5-trimethoxy¬
cinnamoyl)piperazine; $C_{22}H_{31}N_3O_5$; *23887-46-9*
Vasodilator; treatment of peripheral vascular disorders

Cinfenoac (rINN) *sin·fe·nö·ak*

4-[2-(4-Carboxymethoxybenzoyl)vinyl]benzoic acid; $C_{18}H_{14}O_6$;
66984-59-6
Cinfenoac Sodium BX 568A
Cyclo-oxygenase inhibitor; analgesic; anti-inflammatory

● **Cinnarizine** (rINN) *si·na·ri·zën*

1-Benzhydryl-4-cinnamylpiperazine; $C_{26}H_{28}N_2$; *298-57-7*
Histamine H_1 receptor antagonist; antihistamine

Cinoxacin (rINN) see Appendix C

Cinoxolone (rINN) *si·noks·o·lön*

Cinnamyl 3β-acetoxy-11-oxo-18β-olean-12-en-30-oate;
$C_{41}H_{56}O_5$; *31581-02-9*; BX 311
Treatment of gastric ulcers

● **Ciprofibrate** (rINN) *sï·prö·fi·brät*

2-[4-(2,2-Dichlorocyclopropyl)phenoxy]-2-methylpropionic
acid; $C_{13}H_{14}Cl_2O_3$; *52214-84-3*
Fibrate; lipid-regulating drug

● **Ciprofloxacin** (rINN) *sï·prö·floks·a·sin*

1-Cyclopropyl-6-fluoro-1,4-dihydro-4-oxo-7-piperazin-1-yl¬
quinoline-3-carboxylic acid; $C_{17}H_{18}FN_3O_3$; *85721-33-1*
● **Ciprofloxacin Hydrochloride** *86483-48-9*
Ciprofloxacin Lactate
Fluoroquinolone antibacterial

● **Cisapride** (rINN) *sis*·a·prïd
cis-4-Amino-5-chloro-*N*-{1-[3-(4-fluorophenoxy)propyl]-3-methoxy-4-piperidyl}2-methoxybenzamide; C₂₃H₂₉ClFN₃O₄; *81098-60-4*

  ● **Cisapride Tartrate**
  Enterokinetic agent

and enantiomer

Cisatracurium Besilate (rINN) sis·a·tra·*kür*·rë·um
(1*R*,1′*R*,2*R*,2′*R*)-2,2′-(3,11-Dioxo-4,10-dioxatrideca¬
methylene) bis(1,2,3,4-tetrahydro-6,7-dimethoxy-2-methyl-1-veratrylisoquinolinium) dibenzenesulfonate; C₆₅H₈₂N₂O₁₈S₂; *96946-42-8*
Non-depolarizing neuromuscular blocker

● **Cisplatin** (rINN) sis·*pla*·tin
cis-Diamminedichloroplatinum; Cl₂H₆N₂Pt; *15663-27-1*
Platinum-containing cytotoxic

Citalopram (rINN) sï·*ta*·lö·pram
1-(3-Dimethylaminopropyl)-1-(4-fluorophenyl)-1,3-dihydroisobenzofuran-5-carbonitrile; C₂₀H₂₁FN₂O; *59729-33-8*

  ● **Citalopram Hydrobromide** *59729-32-7*
  ● **Citalopram Hydrochloride** *85118-27-0*
  Selective serotonin reuptake inhibitor; antidepressant

and enantiomer

● **Cladribine** (rINN) *kla*·dri·bën
2-Chloro-2′-deoxyadenosine; C₁₀H₁₂ClN₅O₃; *4291-63-8*
Purine analogue; cytotoxic

Clamidoxic Acid (rINN) See Appendix C

Clamoxyquine (rINN) kla·*moks*·ë·kwën
5-Chloro-7-(3-diethylaminopropylaminomethyl)quinolin-8-ol; C₁₇H₂₄ClN₃O; *2545-39-3*
Clamoxyquine Hydrochloride *4724-59-8*; CI 443
Antiprotozoal

● **Clarithromycin** (rINN) kla·ri·thrö·*mï*·sin
(2*R*,3*S*,4*S*,5*R*,6*R*,8*R*,10*R*,11*R*,12*S*,13*R*)-3-(2,6-Dideoxy-3-*C*,3-*O*-dimethyl-α-L-*ribo*-hexopyranosyloxy)-11,12-dihydroxy-6-methoxy-2,4,6,8,10,12-hexamethyl-9-oxo-5-(3,4,6-trideoxy-3-dimethylamino-β-D-*xylo*-hexopyranosyl¬oxy)pentadecan-13-olide; C₃₈H₆₉NO₁₃; *81103-11-9*
Macrolide antibacterial

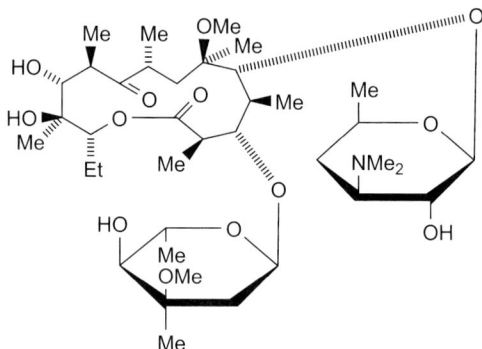

Clavulanic Acid (rINN) *kla*·vü·la·nik
(*Z*)-(2*R*,5*R*)-3-(2-Hydroxyethylidene)-7-oxo-4-oxa-1-aza¬bicyclo [3.2.0]heptane-2-carboxylic acid; C₈H₉NO₅; *58001-44-8*
● **Potassium Clavulanate**
Beta-lactamase inhibitor; potentiation of the action of amoxicillin and ticarcillin

♣ **Clazuril** (rINN) *kla·zûr·ril*

(*RS*)-4-Chlorophenyl[2-chloro-4-(2,3,4,5-tetrahydro-3,5-dioxo-1,2,4-triazin-2-yl)phenyl]acetonitrile; $C_{17}H_{10}Cl_2N_4O_2$;
101831-36-1
Treatment of coccidiosis; antiprotozoal (veterinary)

and enantiomer

Clebopride (rINN) *kle·bö·prïd*

4-Amino-*N*-(1-benzylpiperidin-4-yl)-5-chloro-2-methoxy¬
benzamide; $C_{20}H_{24}ClN_3O_2$; *55905-53-8*
● **Clebopride Malate** *57645-91-7*
Dopamine receptor antagonist; antiprotozoal (veterinary)

Clefamide (rINN) *kle·fa·mïd*

2,2-Dichloro-*N*-(2-hydroxyethyl)-*N*-[4-(4-nitrophenoxy)¬
benzyl]acetamide; $C_{17}H_{16}Cl_2N_2O_5$; *3576-64-5*
Antiprotozoal

Clemastine (rINN) *kle·mas·tën*

(2*R*)-2-{2-[(*R*)-4-Chloro-α-methylbenzhydryloxy]ethyl}
1-methylpyrrolidine; $C_{21}H_{26}ClNO$; *15686-51-8*
● **Clemastine Fumarate** *14976-57-9*
Histamine H_1 receptor antagonist; antihistamine

Clemeprol (rINN) see Appendix C

Clemizole (rINN) see Appendix C

Clemizole Penicillin (rINN) see Appendix C

Clenbuterol (rINN) *klen·bü·te·rol*

1-(4-Amino-3,5-dichlorophenyl)-2-*tert*-butylaminoethanol;
$C_{12}H_{18}Cl_2N_2O$; *37148-27-9*
● **Clenbuterol Hydrochloride** *21898-19-1*
Beta$_2$-adrenoceptor agonist; bronchodilator

and enantiomer

Clenpyrin (BAN) klen·*pï*·rin

N-(1-Butylpyrrolidin-2-ylidene)-3,4-dichloroaniline;
$C_{14}H_{18}Cl_2N_2$; *27050-41-5*
Insecticide

Cletoquine (rINN) *kle·tö·kwën*

2-{*N*-[4-(7-Chloro-4-quinolylamino)pentyl]amino}ethanol;
$C_{16}H_{22}ClN_3O$; *4298-15-1*
Analgesic; anti-inflammatory

and enantiomer

Clidinium Bromide (rINN) klï·*di*·në·um

3-Benziloyloxy-1-methylquinuclidinium bromide;
$C_{22}H_{26}BrNO_3$; *3485-62-9*
Anticholinergic

Climbazole (rINN) *klim*·ba·zôl

1-(4-Chlorophenoxy)-1-(imidazol-1-yl)-3,3-dimethylbutan-2-
one; $C_{15}H_{17}ClN_2O_2$; *38083-17-9*; BAY e 6975; MEB 6401
Antifungal

and enantiomer

Clindamycin (rINN) klin·da·*mï*·sin

Methyl 7-chloro-6,7,8-trideoxy-6-[(2S,4R)-1-methyl-4-propylprolylamino]-1-thio-L-*threo*-D-*galacto*-octopyranoside; (7S)-chloro-7-deoxylincomycin; $C_{18}H_{33}ClN_2O_5S$

- **Clindamycin Hydrochloride** *21462-39-5*
- **Clindamycin Palmitate Hydrochloride** *25507-04-4*
- **Clindamycin Phosphate** *24729-96-2*

Lincosamide antibacterial

- **Clioquinol** (rINN) klï·ö·*kwi*·nol

5-Chloro-7-iodoquinolin-8-ol; iodochlorhydroxyquin; C_9H_5ClINO; *130-26-7*
Antibacterial; antiprotozoal

Clioxanide (rINN) klï·*oks*·a·nïd

2-(4-Chlorophenylcarbamoyl)-4,6-di-iodophenyl acetate; $C_{15}H_{10}ClI_2NO_3$; *14437-41-3*
Antihelminthic

- **Clobazam** (rINN) *klö*·ba·zam

7-Chloro-1,5-dihydro-1-methyl-5-phenyl-1,5-benzodiazepine-2,4(3H)-dione; $C_{16}H_{13}ClN_2O_2$; *22316-47-8*
Benzodiazepine

Clobetasol (rINN) klö·*bë*·ta·sol

21-Chloro-9α-fluoro-11β,17α-dihydroxy-16β-methylpregna-1,4-diene-3,20-dione; $C_{22}H_{28}ClFO_4$; *25122-41-2*
- **Clobetasol Propionate** *25122-46-7*
Glucocorticoid

Clobetasone (rINN) klö·*bë*·ta·sön

21-Chloro-9α-fluoro-17α-hydroxy-16β-methylpregna-1,4-diene-3,11,20-trione; $C_{22}H_{26}ClFO_4$; *54063-32-0*
- **Clobetasone Butyrate** *25122-57-0*
Glucocorticoid

Clobuzarit (rINN) klö·*bü*·za·rit

2-(4′-Chlorobiphenyl-4-ylmethoxy)-2-methylpropionic acid; $C_{17}H_{17}ClO_3$; *22494-47-9*; ICI 55897
Cyclo-oxygenase inhibitor; analgesic; anti-inflammatory

Clociguanil (rINN) klö·*si*·gwa·nil

1-(3,4-Dichlorobenzyloxy)-1,2-dihydro-2,2-dimethyl-1,3,5-triazine-4,6-diyldiamine; $C_{12}H_{15}Cl_2N_5O$; *3378-93-6*
Antiprotozoal (malaria)

Clodantoin (rINN) klö·*dan*·tö·in

5-(1-Ethylpentyl)-3-(trichloromethylthio)hydantoin; $C_{11}H_{17}Cl_3N_2O_2S$; *5588-20-5*
Antifungal

mixture of 4 stereoisomers

Clodronic Acid (rINN) klö·*dro*·nik

(Dichloromethylene)bisphosphonic acid; $CH_4Cl_2O_6P_2$; *10596-23-3*
Sodium Clodronate (2Na) *22560-50-5*
Bisphosphonate; treatment of osteolytic lesions and hypercalcaemia

The symbol '¬' in systematic chemical names signifies line continuation

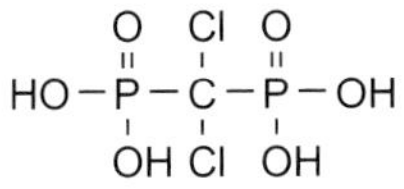

Clofarabine (rINN) klö·*fa*·rá·bën
2-Chloro-9-(2-deoxy-2-fluoro-β-D-arabinofuranosyl)-9*H*-purine-6-amine; $C_{10}H_{11}ClFN_5O_3$; *123318-82-1*
Nucleoside analogue; cytotoxic

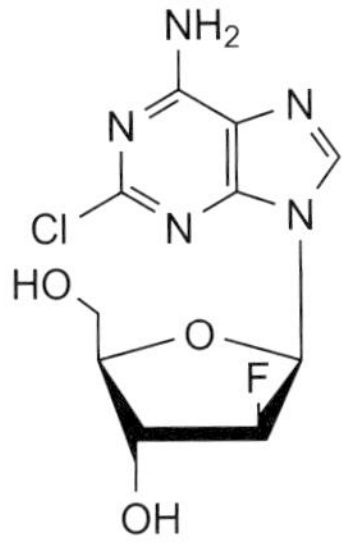

● **Clofazimine** (rINN) klö·*fa*·zi·mën
3-(4-Chloroanilino)-10-(4-chlorophenyl)-2,10-dihydrophenazin-2-ylideneisopropylamine; $C_{27}H_{22}Cl_2N_4$; *2030-63-9*
Antileprosy drug

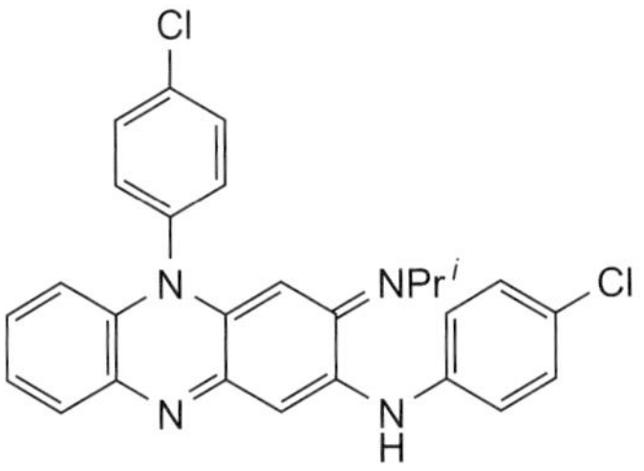

Clofedanol (rINN) klö·*fe*·da·nol
α-Chlorophenyl-α-(2-dimethylaminoethyl)benzyl alcohol; $C_{17}H_{20}ClNO$; *791-35-5*
Clofedanol Hydrochloride
Cough suppressant

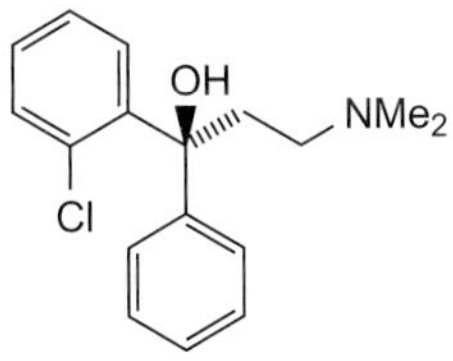

and enantiomer

Clofenvinfos (rINN) klö·fen·*vin*·fos
2-Chloro-1-(2,4-dichlorophenyl)vinyl diethyl phosphate; $C_{12}H_{14}Cl_3O_4P$; *470-90-6*
Insecticide (veterinary)

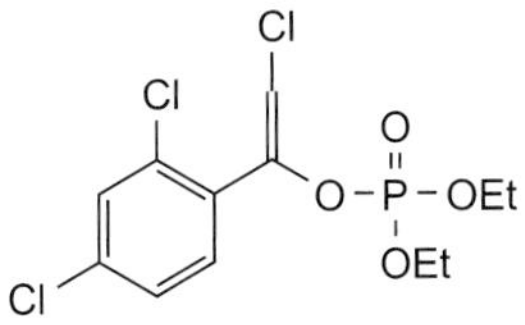

● **Clofibrate** (rINN) klö·fib·rät
Ethyl 2-(4-chlorophenoxy)-2-methylpropionate; $C_{12}H_{15}ClO_3$; *637-07-0*
Fibrate; lipid-regulating drug

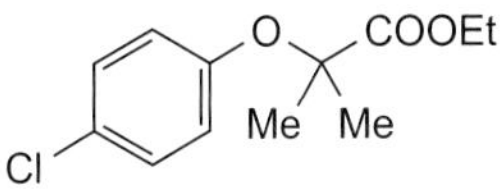

Clofluperol (rINN) klö·*floo*·pe·rol
4-[4-(4-Chloro-3-trifluoromethylphenyl)-4-hydroxypiperidino)]-4′-fluorobutyrophenone; seperidol (USAN); $C_{22}H_{22}ClF_4NO_2$; *10457-91-7*
Dopamine receptor antagonist; neuroleptic

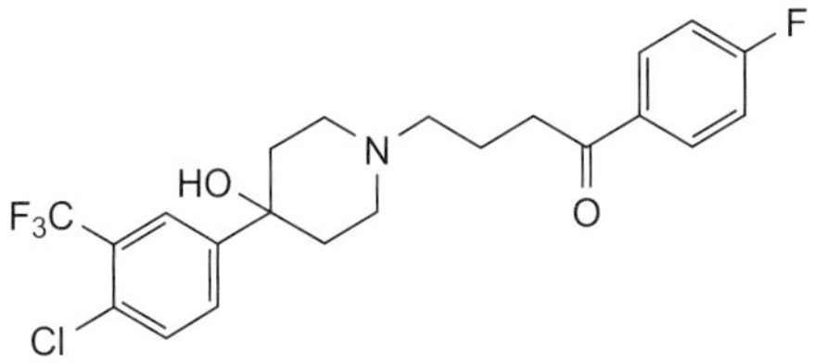

Clogestone (rINN) klö·jes·tön
6-Chloro-3β,17α-dihydroxypregna-4,6-diene-20-one; $C_{25}H_{33}ClO_5$; *20047-75-0*
Progestogen

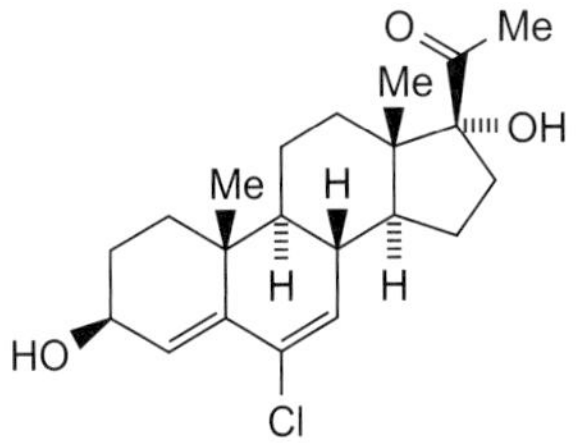

Cloguanamil (rINN) klö·*gwa*·na·mil
1-Amidino-3-(3-chloro-4-cyanophenyl)urea; $C_9H_8ClN_5O$; *21702-93-2*
Antiprotozoal (malaria)

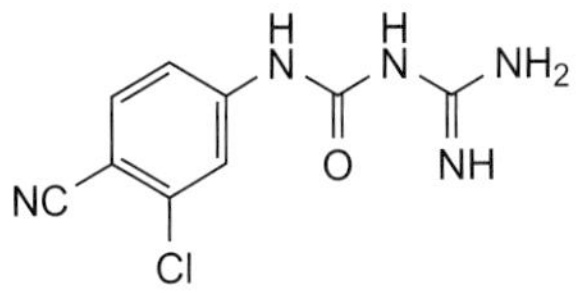

Clomacran (rINN) klö·ma·kran
3-(2-Chloro-9,10-dihydroacridin-9-yl)propyldimethylamine; $C_{18}H_{21}ClN_2$; *5310-55-4*
Dopamine receptor antagonist; neuroleptic

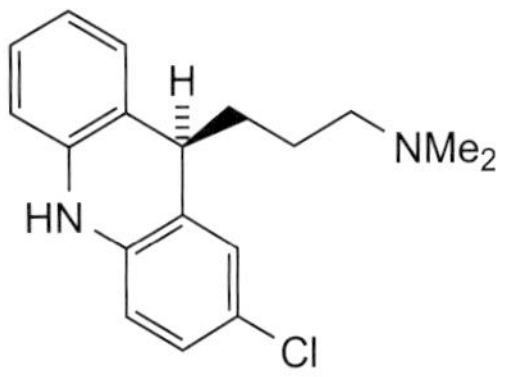

and enantiomer

68

● **Clomethiazole** (rINN) klö·me-*thï*·a·zôl

5-(2-Chloroethyl)-4-methyl-1,3-thiazole; C_6H_8ClNS; *533-45-9*;
  ● **Clomethiazole Edisilate** *1867-58-9*
Hypnotic

● **Clomifene** (rINN) *klö*·mi·fën

2-[*p*-(2-Chloro-1,2-diphenylvinyl)phenoxy]diethylamine;
$C_{26}H_{28}ClNO$; *911-45-5*
  ● **Clomifene Citrate** *50-41-9*
Estrogen receptor modulator

● **Clomipramine** (rINN) klö·*mi*·pra·mën

3-(3-Chloro-10,11-dihydro-5*H*-dibenz[*b,f*]azepin-5-yl)propyl¬
dimethylamine; $C_{19}H_{23}ClN_2$; *303-49-1*
  ● **Clomipramine Hydrochloride** *17321-77-6*
Monoamine reuptake inhibitor; tricyclic antidepressant

● **Clomocycline** (rINN) see Appendix C

● **Clonazepam** (rINN) klö·*nä*·ze·pam

5-(2-Chlorophenyl)-1,3-dihydro-7-nitro-1,4-benzodiazepin-
2-one; $C_{15}H_{10}ClN_3O_3$; *1622-61-3*
Benzodiazepine

● **Clonidine** (rINN) *klo*·ni·dën

2,6-Dichloro-*N*-imidazolidin-2-ylideneaniline; $C_9H_9Cl_2N_3$;
4205-90-7
  ● **Clonidine Hydrochloride** *4205-91-8*
Alpha₂-adrenoceptor agonist; treatment of hypertension

Clonitazene (rINN) klö·*nï*·ta·zën

2-(2-*p*-Chlorobenzyl-5-nitrobenzimidazol-1-yl)ethyldiethyl¬
amine; $C_{20}H_{23}ClN_4O_2$; *3861-76-5*
Opioid receptor agonist; analgesic

Clopamide (rINN) *klö*·pa·mïd

4-Chloro-*N*-(*cis*-2,6-dimethylpiperidino)-3-sulfamoyl¬
benzamide; $C_{14}H_{20}ClN_3O_3S$; *636-54-5*
Thiazide-like diuretic

Clopenthixol (rINN) klö·pen·*thiks*·ol

2-{4-[3-(2-Chloro-10*H*-dibenzo[*b,e*]thiin-10-ylidene)propyl]¬
piperazin-1-yl}ethanol; $C_{22}H_{25}ClN_2OS$; *982-24-1*
Dopamine receptor antagonist; neuroleptic

Clopidogrel (rINN) klö·*pi*·dö·grel

Methyl (*S*)-2-chlorophenyl(4,5,6,7-tetrahydrothieno¬
[3,2-*c*]pyridin-5-yl)acetate; $C_{16}H_{16}ClNO_2S$; *94188-84-8*;
SR 25990 C
Clopidogrel Besilate
Clopidogrel Sulfate
Inhibitor of ADP-mediated platelet aggregation

Clopidol (rINN) *klö*·pi·dol

3,5-Dichloro-2,6-dimethylpyridin-4-ol; $C_7H_7Cl_2NO$;
2971-90-6
Antiprotozoal

Clopirac (rINN) *klö*·pi·rak

(1-*p*-Chlorophenyl-2,5-dimethylpyrrol-3-yl)acetic acid;
$C_{14}H_{14}ClNO_2$; *42779-82-8*
Cyclo-oxygenase inhibitor; analgesic; anti-inflammatory

The symbol '¬' in systematic chemical names signifies line continuation

Cloponone (rINN) *klö*·po·nön

(*RS*)-2,2-Dichloro-*N*-[4-chloro-α-(chloromethyl)phenacyl]¬
acetamide; $C_{11}H_9Cl_4NO_2$; *15301-50-5*
Antiseptic

and enantiomer

Cloprednol (rINN) klö·*pred*·nol

6-Chloro-11β,17α,21-trihydroxypregna-1,4,6-triene-3,20-dione;
$C_{21}H_{25}ClO_5$; *5251-34-3*; RS 4691
Glucocorticoid

Cloprostenol (rINN) klö·*prost*·e·nol

(1) (±)-(*Z*)-7-{(1*R*,2*R*,3*R*,5*S*)-2-[(*E*)-(3*R*)-4-(3-Chlorophenoxy)-
3-hydroxybut-1-enyl]-3,5-dihydroxycyclopentyl}hept-5-enoic
acid; (2) (±)-(5*Z*,13*E*)-(9*S*,11*R*,15*R*)-16-(3-Chlorophenoxy)-
9,11,15-trihydroxy-ω-tetranorprosta-5,13-dienoic acid;
$C_{22}H_{29}ClO_6$; *40665-92-7*
♣ **Cloprostenol Sodium** *55028-72-3*
Prostaglandin (PGF$_{2α}$) analogue (veterinary)

and enantiomer

Cloquinate (rINN) *klö*·kwi·nät

Chloroquine bis(8-hydroxy-7-iodoquinoline-5-sulfonate);
$C_{18}H_{26}ClN_3·(C_9H_6INO_4S)_2$; *7270-12-4*
Antiprotozoal

and enantiomer

Cloral Betaine (rINN) *klor*·ral *bë*·tän

Chloral hydrate–betaine adduct; $C_7H_{14}Cl_3NO_4$; *2218-68-0*
Hypnotic

Clorazepic Acid (BAN) klor·ra·*zë*·pik

7-Chloro-2,3-dihydro-2-oxo-5-phenyl-1*H*-1,4-benzodiazepine-
3-carboxylic acid; $C_{16}H_{11}ClN_2O_3$; *20432-69-3*
● **Dipotassium Clorazepate** (potassium clorazepate)
7109-90-7
Benzodiazepine

and enantiomer

Clorexolone (rINN) see Appendix C

Clorgiline (rINN) klor·*ji*·lën

3-(2,4-Dichlorophenoxy)propyl(methyl)(prop-2-ynyl)amine;
$C_{13}H_{15}Cl_2NO$; *17780-72-2*
Inhibitor of monoamine oxidase type A; antidepressant

Clorindione (rINN) klor·in·*di*·ön

2-(4-Chlorophenyl)indan-1,3-dione; $C_{15}H_9ClO_2$; *1146-99-2*
Anticoagulant

Clorprenaline (rINN) klor·*pren*·a·lën

1-(2-Chlorophenyl)-2-isopropylaminoethanol; $C_{11}H_{16}ClNO$;
3811-25-4
Beta-adrenoceptor agonist

and enantiomer

Clorsulon (rINN) *klor·sü·lon*
4-Amino-6-(trichlorovinyl)benzene-1,3-disulfonamide;
$C_8H_8Cl_3N_3O_4S_2$; *60200-06-8*
Antihelminthic (veterinary)

Closantel (rINN) *klö·san·tel*
5′-Chloro-4′-(4-chloro-α-cyanobenzyl)-3,5-di-iodosalicyl-*o*-toluidide; $C_{22}H_{14}Cl_2I_2N_2O_2$; *57808-65-8*
♣ **Closantel Sodium** *61438-64-0*
Antihelminthic (veterinary)

and enantiomer

Clostebol Acetate (INNM) *klo·ste·bol a·së·tät*
4-Chloro-3-oxoandrost-4-en-17β-yl acetate; $C_{19}H_{27}ClO_2$;
1093-58-9
Androgen

Clotiapine (rINN) *klö·ti·a·pën*
2-Chloro-11-(4-methylpiperazin-1-yl)dibenzo[*b,f*][1,4]¬
thiazepine; $C_{18}H_{18}ClN_3S$; *2058-52-8*
Dopamine receptor antagonist; neuroleptic

Cloticasone (rINN) see Appendix C

● **Clotrimazole** (rINN) *klö·tri·ma·zôl*
1-(2-Chlorotrityl)imidazole; $C_{22}H_{17}ClN_2$; *23593-75-1*
Antifungal

Cloxacillin (rINN) *kloks·a·si·lin*
6-(3-*o*-Chlorophenyl-5-methyl-1,2-oxazole-4-carboxamido)-penicillanic acid; $C_{19}H_{18}ClN_3O_5S$; *61-72-3*
♣ **Cloxacillin Benzathine** *32222-55-2*
● **Cloxacillin Sodium** *7081-44-9*
Penicillin antibacterial

Clozapine (rINN) *klö·za·pën*
8-Chloro-11-(4-methylpiperazin-1-yl)-5*H*-dibenzo¬
[*b,e*][1,4]diazepine; $C_{18}H_{19}ClN_4$; *5786-21-0*
Dopamine D_4 receptor antagonist; neuroleptic

● **Co-amilofruse** (BAN) *see Names for Combinations of Substances*

● **Co-amilozide** (BAN) *see Names for Combinations of Substances*

● **Co-amoxiclav** (BAN) *see Names for Combinations of Substances*

● **Co-beneldopa** (BAN) *see Names for Combinations of Substances*

● **Cocaine** (BAN) *kö·kän*
(1*R*,2*R*,3*S*,5*S*)-2-(Methoxycarbonyl)tropan-3-yl benzoate;
$C_{17}H_{21}NO_4$; *50-36-2*
● **Cocaine Hydrochloride** *53-21-4*
Local anaesthetic

Cocarboxylase (rINN) *kö·kar·boks·i·läz*
3-(4-Amino-2-methylpyrimidin-5-ylmethyl)-5-{2-
[dihydroxyphosphinyloxy(hydroxy)phosphinyloxy]ethyl}-4-
methyl-1,3-thiazolium hydroxide; diphosphothiamine;
$C_{12}H_{20}N_4O_8P_2S$; *154-87-0*
Co-enzyme

The symbol '¬' in systematic chemical names signifies line continuation

● **Co-careldopa**(BAN) *see Names for Combinations of Substances*

● **Co-codamol** (BAN) *see Names for Combinations of Substances*

● **Co-codaprin** (BAN) *see Names for Combinations of Substances*

Co-cyprindiol (BAN) *see Names for Combinations of Substances*

● **Cod-liver Oil**
The oil obtained from the fresh liver of the cod *Gadus callarius* L· and other species of Gadus refined and clarified by filtration at about 0°
Source of vitamins A and D

Codactide (rINN) kö·*dak*·tïd
[1-D-Serine,17,18-lysine]corticotrophin-(1-18)-octadecapeptide amide
Corticotrophin analogue

```
D-Ser-Tyr-Ser-Met-Glu-His-Phe-Arg-
   Try-Gly-Lys-Pro-Val-Gly-Lys-Lys-
      Lys-Lys-NH₂
```

● **Co-danthramer** (BAN) *see Names for Combinations of Substances*

● **Co-danthrusate** (BAN) *see Names for Combinations of Substances*

● **Codeine** (BAN) *kö*·dën
7,8-Didehydro-4,5-epoxy-3-methoxy-17-methylmorphinan-6-ol; $C_{18}H_{21}NO_3$; *76-57-3*
● **Codeine Hydrochloride** *1422-07-7*
● **Codeine Phosphate** *52-28-8* (*anhydrous*); *41444-62-6* (*hemihydrate*); component in many proprietary preparations
Opioid receptor agonist; analgesic

● **Codergocrine Mesilate** (rINN) kö-*der*·gö·krën *me*·si·lät
Equal mass proportions of the methanesulfonates of
(a) dihydroergocornine, (b) dihydroergocristine and
(c) α- and β-dihydroergocriptine in the ratio
2:1; dihydroergotoxine mesilate; ergoloid mesilates (USAN)
Vasodilator

● **Co-dydramol** (BAN) *see Names for Combinations of Substances*

● **Co-fluampicil** (BAN) *see Names for Combinations of Substances*

Co-flumactone (BAN) *see Names for Combinations of Substances*

Colaspase (BAN) see Appendix C

● **Colecalciferol** (rINN) kö·lë·kal·*si*·fe·rol
(5Z,7E)-(3S)-9,10-Secocholesta-5,7,10(19)-trien-3-ol; vitamin D₃; $C_{27}H_{44}O$; *67-97-0*
Vitamin D analogue (vitamin D3)

Colesevelam (rINN) kö·lë·se·*vel*·am
Poly([1-(aminomethyl)ethane-1,2-diyl]-*co*-[1-[(decylamino)methyl]ethane-1,2-diyl]-*co*-(5-hydroxy-3,7-diazanonane-1,1,9,9-tetrayl)-*co*-{1-[(trimethylazaniumyl)methyl]ethane-1,2-diyl}) chloride; $(C_3H_7N)_7(C_3H_5ClO)_6(C_{12}H_{27}ClN_2)_{17}(C_{13}H_{27}N)_{20}$; *182815-43-6*;
Colesevelam Hydrochloride *182815-44-7*
Bile acid sequestrant; lipid-regulating drug

The ratio of w:x:y:z is approximately 7:6:17:20.

Colestipol (rINN) kö·*lest*·i·pol
Co-polymer of diethylenetriamine and 1-chloro-2,3-epoxypropane; *50925-79-6*
Colestipol Hydrochloride *37296-80-3*
Lipid-regulating drug

● **Colestyramine** (rINN) kö·lë·*stï*·ra·mën
A styryl–divinylbenzene copolymer (about 2% divinylbenzene) containing quaternary ammonium groups; *11041-12-6*
Colestyramine Chloride
Lipid-regulating drug

Colfosceril Palmitate (rINN) kol·*fo*·ser·ril *parl*·mi·tät
1,2-Dipalmitoyl-*sn*-glycero(3)phosphocholine; $C_{40}H_{80}NO_8P$; *63-89-8*
Lung surfactant

Colistimethate (rINN) ko·li·sti·*me*·thät

An antibiotic obtained from colistin sulfate by sulfomethylation with formaldehyde and sodium bisulfite; *30387-39-4*

● **Colistimethate Sodium** *8068-28-8*
Antibacterial

Colistin (rINN) *ko*·lis·tin

A mixture of antimicrobial peptides produced by a strain of *Bacillus polymyxa var· colistinus*; *1066-17-7*

● **Colistin Sulfate** *1264-7-8*
Antibacterial

Colistin Sulfomethate *see Colistimethate*

Co-magaldrox (BAN) *see Names for Combinations of Substances*

Co-methiamol (BAN) *see Names for Combinations of Substances*

Co-phenotrope (BAN) *see Names for Combinations of Substances*

● **Copovidone** (BAN) kö·*po*·vi·dön

A co-polymer of 1-vinylpyrrolidone and vinyl acetate in the mass proportions 3:2
Excipient

Copovithane (BAN) kö·*po*·vi·thän

Copolymer of 2-methylenetrimethylene bis(methylcarbamate) and 1-vinyl-2-pyrrolidone in the approximate ratio of 1 part to 4 parts respectively; *68045-74-9*; BAY i 7433
Immunomodulator

Copper Tetramibi Tetrafluoroborate (BAN)

Tetrakis(2-methoxy-2-methylpropyl isocyanide-*kN*-copper(I) tetrafluoroborate; $C_{24}H_{44}BCuF_4N_4O_4$
Radiocontrast medium

Co-prenozide (BAN) *see Names for Combinations of Substances*

● **Co-proxamol** (BAN) *see Names for Combinations of Substances*

Corifollitropin Alfa (rINN) ko·ri·*fo*·li·trö·pin

Follicle stimulating hormone (human α-subunit reduced), complex with follicle stimulating hormone (human β-subunit reduced) fusion protein with 118-145-chorionic gonadotropin (human β-subunit); *195962-23-3*
Recombinant human follicle stimulating hormone; treatment of female infertility

corifollitropin alfa has the following amino acid sequence:

```
APDVQDCPEC   TLQENPFFSQ   PGAPILQCMG   CCFSRAYPTP
                   *
LRSKKTMLVQ   KNVTSESTCC   VAKSYNRVTV   MGGFKVENHT
                                                  *
ACHCSTCYYH   KS
              *

      *                         *
NSCELTNITI   AIEKEECRFC   ISINTTWCAG   YCYTRDLVYK

DPARPKIQKT   CTFKELVYET   VRVPGCAHHA   DSLYTYPVAT
                                           *
QCHCGKCDSD   STDCTVRGLG   PSYCSFGEMK   ESSSSKAPPP
  *     *         *      *
SLPSPSRLPG   PSDTPILPQ
```

* glycosylation   sites

Corticotropin (rINN) kor·ti·kö·*tro*·pin

The peptide hormone from the anterior lobe of the pituitary which increases the rate at which corticoid hormones are secreted by the adrenal gland; adrenocorticotrophin; ACTH; *9002-60-2*
Adrenocorticotrophic steroid

Cortisone (rINN) *kor*·ti·sön

17α,21-Dihydroxypregn-4-ene-3,11,20-trione; $C_{23}H_{30}O_6$; *53-06-5*

● **Cortisone Acetate** *50-04-4*
Corticosteroid

Cortodoxone (rINN) kor·tö·*doks*·ön

17α,21-Dihydroxypregn-4-ene-3,20-dione; $C_{21}H_{30}O_4$; *152-58-9*
Glucocorticoid

Co-simalcite (BAN) *see Names for Combinations of Substances*

● **Co-tenidone** (BAN) *see Names for Combinations of Substances*

Co-tetroxazine (BAN) *see Names for Combinations of Substances*

● **Co-triamterzide** (BAN) *see Names for Combinations of Substances*

Co-trifamole (BAN) *see Names for Combinations of Substances*

♣ **Co-trimazine** (BAN) *see Names for Combinations of Substances*

● **Co-trimoxazole** (BAN) *see Names for Combinations of Substances*

Coumafos (rINN) *kü*·ma·fos

O-3-Chloro-4-methylcoumarin-7-yl *O,O*-diethyl phosphoro¬thioate; $C_{14}H_{16}ClO_5PS$; *56-72-4*
Insecticide

Coumetarol (rINN) see Appendix C

Co-zidocapt (BAN) *see Names for Combinations of Substances*

Crisantaspase (BAN) kri·*san*·ta·späz

L-Asparagine amidohydrolase obtained from cultures of *Erwinia chrysanthemi* (syn· *E· carotovora*); *9015-68-3*
Asparaginase; cytotoxic

The symbol '¬' in systematic chemical names signifies line continuation

Cromakalim (rINN) krö·*ma*·ka·lim

(±)-*trans*-3-Hydroxy-2,2-dimethyl-4-(2-oxopyrrolidin-1-yl)chroman-6-carbonitrile; $C_{16}H_{18}N_2O_3$; *94470-67-4*;
BRL 34915
Potassium channel opener

and enantiomer

Cromoglicic Acid (rINN) krö·mö·*glï*·sik

4,4′-Dioxo-5,5′-(2-hydroxytrimethylenedioxy)di(4*H*-chromene-2-carboxylic acid); $C_{23}H_{16}O_{11}$; *16110-51-3*
● **Sodium Cromoglicate** cromolyn sodium (USAN);
15826-37-6
Cromone; treatment of asthma, food allergy, allergic
conjunctivitis, rhinitis

Cropropamide (rINN) krö·*prö*·pa·mïd

N-[1-(Dimethylcarbamoyl)propyl]-*N*-propylcrotonamide;
$C_{13}H_{24}N_2O_2$; *633-47-6*
Respiratory stimulant

and enantiomer

Croscarmellose (rINN) kros·*kar*·me·lös

A cross-linked, partly *O*-carboxymethylated cellulose
● **Croscarmellose Sodium**
Excipient

● **Crospovidone** (rINN) kros·*po*·vi·dön

A cross-linked homopolymer of 1-vinyl-2-pyrrolidone;
9003-39-8
Excipient

● **Crotamiton** (rINN) krö·*ta*·mi·ton

N-Ethylcrotono-*o*-toluidide; $C_{13}H_{17}NO$; *483-63-6*
Acaricide

Crotetamide (rINN) krö·*te*·ta·mïd

N-[1-(Dimethylcarbamoyl)propyl]-*N*-ethylcrotonamide;
$C_{12}H_{22}N_2O_2$; *6168-76-9*
Central nervous system stimulant

and enantiomer

Crotoxyfos (BAN) krö·*toks*·i·fos

1-Phenylethyl-3-(dimethoxyphosphinyloxy)isocrotonate;
$C_{14}H_{19}O_6P$; *7700-17-6*
Insecticide

and enantiomer

Crufomate (rINN) *kroo*·fö·mät

4-*tert*-Butyl-2-chlorophenyl methyl methylphosphoramidate;
$C_{12}H_{19}ClNO_3P$; *299-86-5*
Insecticide; antihelminthic

Cumetharol *see Coumetarol*

Cuproxoline (rINN) kü·*proks*·o·lën

Copper(II)bis(5,7-disulfo-8-quinolyl oxide)—diethylamine
(1:4); $C_{18}H_{12}CuN_2O_{14}S_4$; *13007-93-7*
Treatment of copper deficiency

Cyacetacide (rINN) sï·a·*se*·ta·sïd

2-Cyanoacetohydrazide; $C_3H_5N_3O$; *140-87-4*
Antihelminthic

● **Cyanocobalamin** (rINN) sï·a·nö·kö·*ba*·la·min

*Co*α-[(5,6-Dimethylbenzimidazolyl]-*Co*β-cyanocobamide;
vitamin B12; $C_{63}H_{88}CoN_{14}O_{14}P$; *68-19-9*
Vitamin B_{12} analogue

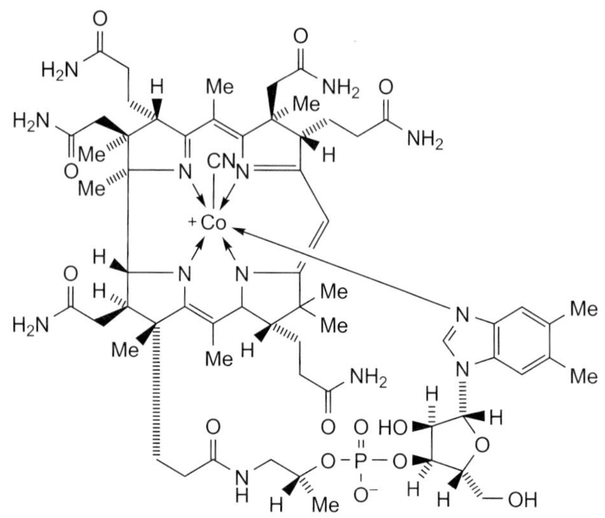

Cyclamic Acid (BAN) sï·*kla*·mik

N-Cyclohexylsulfamic acid; hexamic acid; $C_6H_{13}NO_3S$; *100-88-9*
Sweetening agent

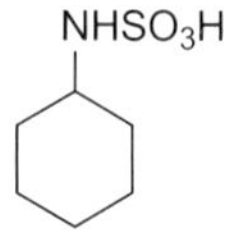

Cyclandelate (rINN) see Appendix C

Cyclarbamate (rINN) see Appendix C

● **Cyclizine** *sï*·kli·zën

1-Benzhydryl-4-methylpiperazine; $C_{18}H_{22}N_2$; *82-92-8*
● **Cyclizine Hydrochloride** *303-25-3*
Cyclizine Lactate *5897-19-8*
Cyclizine Tartrate
Histamine H_1 receptor antagonist; antihistamine

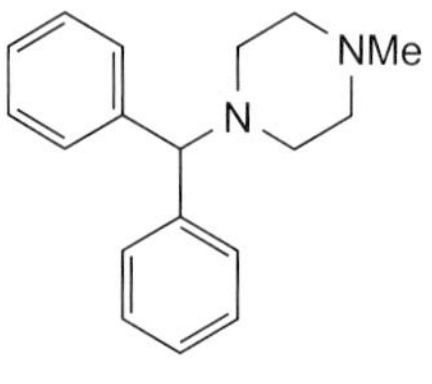

Cyclobarbital (rINN) sï·klö·*bar*·bi·tal

5-(Cyclohex-1-enyl)-5-ethylbarbituric acid; $C_{12}H_{16}N_2O_3$;
52-31-3
● **Cyclobarbital Calcium** *5897-20-1*
Barbiturate

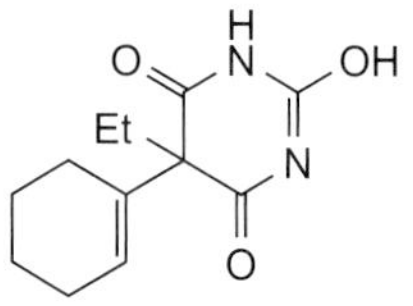

Cyclocoumarol (rINN) sï·klö·*kü*·ma·rol

3,4-Dihydro-2-methoxy-2-methyl-4-phenyl-2*H*-pyrano¬
[3,2-*c*]chromen-5-one; $C_{20}H_{18}O_4$; *518-20-7*
*Vitamin K epoxide reductase inhibitor; oral anticoagulant
(coumarin)*

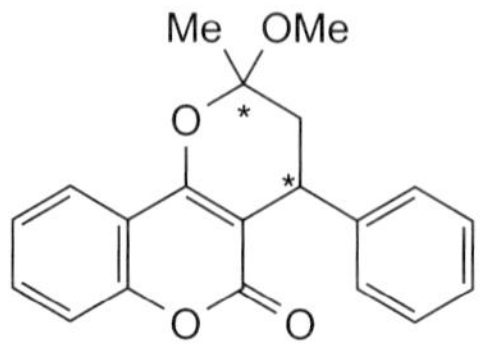

mixture of 4 stereoisomers

Cyclofenil (rINN) sï·*klö*·fe·nil

4,4′-Cyclohexylidenemethanediyldi(phenyl acetate); $C_{23}H_{24}O_4$;
2624-43-3
Antioestrogen

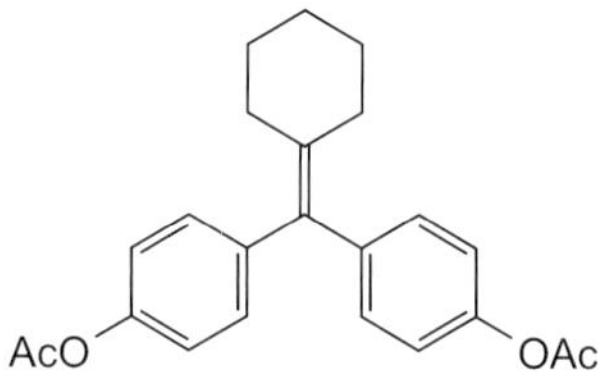

Cycloguanil Embonate (rINN) sï·*klö*·gwa·nil *em*·bo·nät
Bis(6-amino-1-*p*-chlorophenyl-1,2-dihydro-2,2-dimethyl-1,3,5-
triazin-4-ylammonium) 3,3′-dihydroxy-4,4′-methylenedi-
(2-naphthoate); $(C_{11}H_{15}ClN_5)_2.C_{23}H_{14}O_6$; *609-78-9*
Antiprotozoal (malaria)

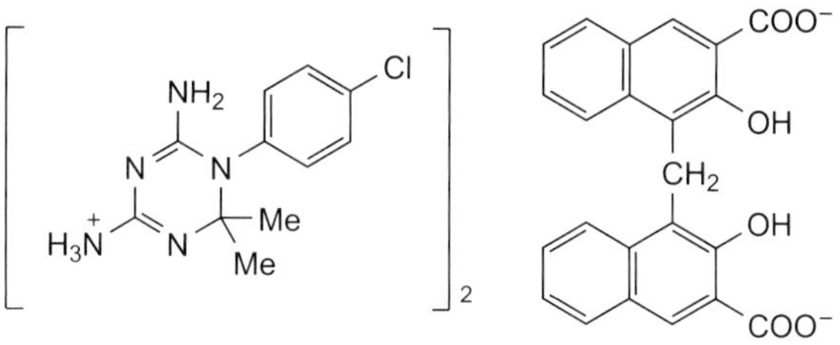

Cyclomethycaine (rINN) sï·klö·*meth*·ë·kän

3-(2-Methylpiperidino)propyl 4-cyclohexyloxybenzoate;
$C_{22}H_{33}NO_3$; *139-62-8*
Cyclomethycaine Sulfate *50978-10-4*
Local anaesthetic

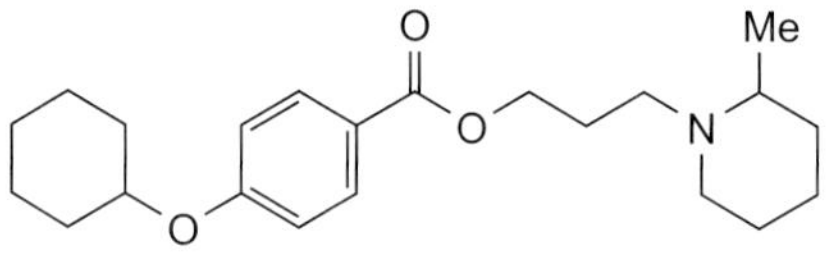

The symbol '¬' in systematic chemical names signifies line continuation

Cyclopentamine (rINN) sï·klö·*pen*·ta·mën

2-Cyclopentyl-1-methylethyl(methyl)amine; $C_9H_{19}N$; *102-45-4*
Cyclopentamine Hydrochloride
Nasal decongestant

and enantiomer

● **Cyclopenthiazide** (rINN) sï·klö·pen·*thï*·a·zïd

(RS)-6-Chloro-3-cyclopentylmethyl-3,4-dihydro-2H-1,2,4-
benzothiadiazine-7-sulfonamide 1,1-dioxide; $C_{13}H_{18}ClN_3O_4S_2$;
742-20-1
Thiazide-like diuretic

and enantiomer

Cyclopentolate (rINN) sï·klö·*pen*·to·lät

2-Dimethylaminoethyl 2-(1-hydroxycyclopentyl)-2-phenyl¬
acetate; $C_{17}H_{25}NO_3$; *512-15-2*
● **Cyclopentolate Hydrochloride** *5870-29-1*
Anticholinergic

● **Cyclophosphamide** (rINN) sï·klö·*fos*·fa·mïd

2-Bis(2-chloroethyl)aminoperhydro-1,3,2-oxazaphosphorinane
2-oxide; $C_7H_{15}Cl_2N_2O_2P$; *50-18-0 (anhydrous)*; *6055-19-2*
(monohydrate)
Cytotoxic alkylating agent

Cycloprolol *see Cicloprolol*

Cycloserine (rINN) see Appendix C

Cyclosporin *see Ciclosporin*

Cyclothiazide (rINN) sï·klö·*thï*·a·zïd

6-Chloro-3,4-dihydro-3-(norborn-5-en-2-yl)-2H-1,2,4-
benzothiadiazine-7-sulfonamide 1,1-dioxide; $C_{14}H_{16}ClN_3O_4S_2$;
2259-96-3
Thiazide diuretic

mixture of stereoisomers

Cycrimine (rINN) See Appendix C

Cyfluthrin (BAN) sï·*floo*·thrin

(RS)-α-Cyano-4-fluoro-3-phenoxybenzyl (1RS,3RS; 1RS,3SR)-
3-(2,2-dichlorovinyl)-2,2-dimethylcyclopropanecarboxylate;
$C_{22}H_{18}Cl_2FNO_3$; *68359-37-5*; Bay Vl 1704
Insecticide (veterinary)

1S,3S-isomer

Cyhalothrin (BAN) sï·*hä*·lö·thrin

(RS)-α-Cyano-3-phenoxybenzyl (Z)-(1RS,3RS)-3-(2-chloro-
3,3,3-trifluoropropenyl)-2,2-dimethylcyclopropanecarboxylate;
$C_{23}H_{19}ClF_3NO_3$; *68085-85-8*; PP 563
Insecticide (veterinary)

and enantiomer plus epimer at C*

Cypenamine (rINN) see Appendix C

Cypermethrin (BAN) sï·per·*më*·thrin

(RS)-α-Cyano-3-phenoxybenzyl (1RS,3RS)-3-(2,2-
dichlorovinyl)-2,2-dimethylcyclopropanecarboxylate;
$C_{21}H_{19}Cl_2NO_3$; *52315-07-8*
Insecticide (veterinary)

and enantiomer plus epimer at C*

Cyprenorphine (rINN) see Appendix C

Cyproheptadine (rINN) sï·prö·*hep*·ta·dën

5-(1-Methylpiperidin-4-ylidene)-5*H*-dibenzo[*a,d*]cycloheptene; C$_{21}$H$_{21}$N; *129-03-3*
● **Cyproheptadine Hydrochloride** *969-33-5*
Histamine H$_1$ receptor antagonist; antihistamine

Cyproterone (rINN) sï·*prö*·te·rön

6-Chloro-1β,2β-dihydro-17α-hydroxy-3*H*-cyclopropa[1,2]¬
pregna-4,6-diene-3,20-dione; C$_{22}$H$_{27}$ClO$_3$; *2098-66-0*
● **Cyproterone Acetate** *427-51-0*
Antiandrogen

Cyromazine (rINN) sï·*rö*·ma·zën

N-Cyclopropyl-1,3,5-triazine-2,4,6-triamine; C$_6$H$_{10}$N$_6$; *66215-27-8*
Insecticide (veterinary)

Cysteamine *see Mercaptamine*

● **Cytarabine** (rINN) sï·*ta*·ra·bën

1-β-D-Arabinofuranosylcytosine; C$_9$H$_{13}$N$_3$O$_5$; *147-94-4*
Pyrimidine analogue; cytotoxic

Cythioate (BAN) sï·*thï*·ö·ät

O,O-Dimethyl *O*-(4-sulfamoylphenyl) phosphorothioate; C$_8$H$_{12}$NO$_5$PS$_2$; *115-93-5*
Insecticide (veterinary)

Dabigatran (rINN) da·bi·*gat*·ran

3-[[2-{[(4-(Aminoiminomethyl)phenyl]amino}methyl)-1-
methyl-1*H*-benzimidazol-5-yl]carbonyl](pyridin-2-yl)amino-
propanoic acid; C$_{25}$H$_{25}$N$_7$O$_3$; *211914-51-1*
Direct thrombin inhibitor; oral anticoagulant

Dabigatran Etexilate (rINN) da·bi·*gat*·ran ë·*teks*·il·ät

Ethyl [[[2-[[[4-[[[(hexyloxy)carbonyl]amino]iminomethyl]¬
phenyl]amino]methyl]-1-methyl-1*H*-benzimidazol-5-yl]¬
carbonyl}(pyridin-2-yl)amino]propanoate; C$_{25}$H$_{25}$N$_7$O$_3$;
211915-06-9
Direct thrombin inhibitor; oral anticoagulant

● **Dacarbazine** (rINN) da·*kar*·ba·zën

5-(3,3-Dimethyltriazeno)imidazole-4-carboxamide; C$_6$H$_{10}$N$_6$O;
4342-03-4
Cytotoxic alkylating agent

Daclizumab (rINN) da·*kli*·zü·mab

Immunogloblin G1 (human-mouse monoclonal clone 1H4-
gamma-chain anti-human interleukin 2 receptor), disulphide
with human-mouse monoclonal clone 1H4 light chain, dimer;
152923-56-3
*Monoclonal antibody (CD-25 antigen of interleukin receptors
on T lymphocytes)*

Dactinomycin (rINN) dak·ti·nö·*mï*·sin

N$^{2·1}$*N*$^{2'·1'}$-(2-Amino-4,6-dimethyl-3-oxo-3*H*-phenoxazine-1,9-
diyldicarbonyl)bis[threonyl-D-valylprolyl(*N*-methylglycyl)(*N*-
methylvaline)-1.5-3.1-lactone]; actinomycin D; C$_{62}$H$_{86}$N$_{12}$O$_{16}$;
50-76-0
Cytostatic antibacterial

The symbol '¬' in systematic chemical names signifies line continuation

Dacuronium Bromide (rINN) da·kûr·*rö*·në·um
1,1′-(3α-Acetoxy-17β-hydroxy-5α-androstan-2β,16β-diyl)bis(1-methylpiperidinium) dibromide; $C_{33}H_{58}Br_2N_2O_3$; *27115-86-2*
Non-depolarizing neuromuscular blocker

Dalbavancin (rINN) dal·bá·*van*·sin
5,31-Dichloro-38-de(methoxycarbonyl)-7-demethyl-19-deoxy-56-O-[2-deoxy-2-[(10-methylundecanoyl)amino]-α-D-glucopyranuronosyl]-38-[[3-(dimethylamino)propyl] carbamoyl]-42-O-α-D-mannopyranosyl-15-N-methyl (ristomycin A aglycone) (main component); $C_{88}H_{100}Cl_2N_{10}O_{28}$; *171500-79-1*
Glycopeptide antibacterial

Dalfopristin (rINN) dal·fö·*pris*·tin
(5E,10E,12E,)-(3R,4R,14S,26R,26aS)-26-{[2-(Diethylamino)ethyl]sulfonyl}-8,9,14,15,24,25,26,26a-octahydro-14-hydroxy-3-isopropyl-4,12-dimethyl-3H-21,18-azeno-1H,22H-pyrrolo[2,1-c][1,8,4,19]dioxadiazacyclotetracosene-1,7,16,22(4H,17H)-tetrone; $C_{34}H_{50}N_4O_9S$; *112362-50-2*
Dalfopristin Mesilate
Streptogramin antibacterial

Dalteparin Sodium (rINN) dal·*te*·pa·rin
Sodium salt of depolymerised heparin obtained by nitrous acid degradation of heparin from pork intestinal mucosa; the majority of the components have a 6-O-sulfo-2,5-anhydro-D-mannitol structure at the reducing end of their chain; the molecular weight of 90% of the components is between 2000 and 9000 and the average molecular weight is about 5000; the sulfur content is about 11%
Low molecular weight heparin

Danaparoid Sodium (rINN) da·*na*·pa·roid
A low-molecular-weight heparinoid consisting of a mixture of the sodium salts of heparan sulfate (approximately 84%), dermatan sulfate (approximately 12%), and chondroitin-4-and 6-sulfates (approximately 4%); it is derived from pig intestinal mucosa; average molecular weight about 5500; *83513-48-8*
Heparinoid; prevention of deep vein thrombosis

Danazol (rINN) *da*·na·zol
[1,2]Oxazolo[4′,5′:2,3]-17α-pregn-4-en-20-yn-17β-ol; $C_{22}H_{27}NO_2$; *17230-88-5*
Inhibitor of gonadotrophin secretion; androgen; antioestrogen

Daniquidone (rINN) da·*ni*·kwi·dön
8-Aminoisoindolo[1,2-b]quinazolin-12(10H)-one; $C_{15}H_{11}N_3O$; *67199-66-0*
Cytotoxic

Danofloxacin (rINN) da·nö·*floks*·a·sin
1-Cyclopropyl-6-fluoro-1,4-dihydro-7-{(1S,4S)-5-methyl-2,5-diazabicyclo[2.2.1]hept-2-yl}-4-oxoquinoline-3-carboxylic acid; $C_{19}H_{20}FN_3O_3$; *112398-08-0*
Danofloxacin Mesilate *119478-55-6*
Fluoroquinolone antibacterial

78

Danthron *see Dantron*

● **Dantrolene** (rINN) *dan·trö·lën*
1-(5-*p*-Nitrophenylfurfurylideneamino)hydantoin; $C_{14}H_{10}N_4O_5$;
7261-97-4

● **Dantrolene Sodium** *14663-23-1*
Skeletal muscle relaxant

● **Dantron** (rINN) *dan·tron*
1,8-Dihydroxyanthraquinone; $C_{14}H_8O_4$; *117-10-2*
Anthraquinone stimulant laxative

● **Dapsone** (rINN) *dap·sön*
Bis(4-aminophenyl) sulfone; $C_{12}H_{12}N_2O_2S$; *80-08-0*
Folic acid synthesis inhibitor; treatment of leprosy

Daptomycin (rINN) *dap·tö·mï·sin*
N-Decanoyl-L-tryptophyl-L-asparaginyl-L-aspartyl-
L-threonylglycyl-L-ornithyl-L-aspartyl-D-alanyl-L-aspartylglycyl-
D-seryl-*threo*-3-methyl-L-glutamyl-3-anthraniloyl-L-alanine
1.13-3.4-lactone; *103060-53-3*
Lipopeptide antibacterial

```
CH3·[CH2]8·CO-Trp-ASn-Asp-Thr-Gly-Orn-Asp-
D-Ala-Asp-Gly-D-Ser-threo(3-Me)Glu-Kyn
```

Kyn = Kynurenine = 3-anthraniloylalanine

Darbepoetin Alfa (rINN) *dar·be·pö·e·tin al·fa*
[30-L-Asparagine, 32-L-threonine, 87-L-valine, 88-L-asparagine,
90-L-threonine]erythropoietin (human); *209810-58-2*
Erythropoietin analogue

darbepoetin alfa has the following amino acid sequence:

```
APPRLICDSR   VLERYLLEAK   EAENITTGCN
ETCSLNENIT   VPDTKVNFYA   WKRMEVGQQA
VEVWQGLALL   SEAVLRGQAL   LVNSSQVNET
LQLHVDKAVS   GLRSLTTLLR   ALGAQKEAIS
PPDAASAAPL   RTITADTFRK   LFRVYSNFLR
GKLKLYTGEA   CRTGD
```

● **Darifenacin** (rINN) *da·ri·fe·na·sin*
(*S*)-2-{1-[2-(2,3-Dihydrobenzo[*b*]furan-5-yl)ethyl]pyrrolidin-3-
yl}-2,2-diphenylacetamide; $C_{28}H_{30}N_2O_2$; *133099-04-4*
Darifenacin Hydrobromide *133099-07-7*
M_3 *muscarinic receptor antagonist; anticholinergic*

Darunavir (rINN) *da·roo·na·veer*
(3*R*,3a*S*,6a*R*)-Hexahydrofuro[2,3-*b*]furan-3-yl *N*-{(1*S*,2*R*)-1-
benzyl-2-hydroxy-3-[4-amino-*N*-(2-methylpropyl)¬
benzenesulfonamido]propyl}carbamate; $C_{27}H_{37}N_3O_7S$;
206361-99-1
Protease inhibitor; antiviral (HIV)

Dasatinib (rINN) *dá·sat·in·ib*
N-(2-Chloro-6-methylphenyl)-2-({6-[4-(2-hydroxyethyl)¬
piperazin-1-yl]-2-methylpyrimidin-4-yl}amino)-1,3-thiazole-
5-carboxamide; $C_{22}H_{26}ClN_7O_2S$; *302962-49-8*
Tyrosine kinase inhibitor; antineoplastic

Daunorubicin (rINN) *dor·nö·roo·bi·sin*
An anthracycline antibacterial produced by *Streptomyces
peuceticus* and *Streptomyces coeruleorubidus*; (1*S*,3*S*)-3-acetyl-
1,2,3,4,6,11-hexahydro-3,5,12-trihydroxy-10-methoxy-6,11-
dioxonaphthacen-1-yl 3-amino-2,3,6-trideoxy-α-L-*lyxo*-
hexopyranoside; $C_{27}H_{29}NO_{10}$; *20830-81-3*
● **Daunorubicin Hydrochloride** *23541-50-6*
Cytostatic; anthracycline antibacterial

78

The symbol '¬' in systematic chemical names signifies line continuation

Dazmegrel (rINN) *daz·me·grel*
3-(3-Imidazol-l-ylmethyl-2-methylindol-l-yl)propionic acid; C$_{16}$H$_{17}$N$_3$O$_2$; *76894-77-4*
Thromboxane synthetase inhibitor

Dazoxiben (rINN) *da·zoks·i·ben*
4-(2-Imidazol-l-ylethoxy)benzoic acid; C$_{12}$H$_{12}$N$_2$O$_3$; *78218-09-4*
Dazoxiben Hydrochloride *74226-22-5*
Thromboxane synthetase inhibitor

Deanol (rINN) *dë·a·nol*
2-Dimethylaminoethanol; C$_4$H$_{11}$NO; *3342-61-8*
Cholinoceptor agonist

Debrisoquine (rINN) *de·brï·sö·kwën*
1,2,3,4-Tetrahydroisoquinoline-2-carboxamidine; C$_{10}$H$_{13}$N$_3$; *1131-64-2*
● **Debrisoquine Sulfate** *581-88-4*
Adrenergic neuron blocker

Debropol (rINN) *de·brö·pol*
(*RS*)-2-Bromo-2-nitropropan-l-ol; C$_3$H$_6$BrNO$_3$; *24403-04-1*
Antiseptic; preservative

Decamethonium Iodide (rINN) see Appendix C

Decitabine (rINN) *dë·sï·ta·bën*
4-Amino-1-(2-deoxy-β-D-*erythro*-pentofuranosyl)-1,3,5-triazin-2(1*H*)-one; C$_8$H$_{12}$N$_4$O$_4$; *2353-33-5*
Pyrimidine analogue; cytotoxic

♣ **Decoquinate** (rINN) *de·kö·kwi·nät*
Ethyl 6-decyloxy-7-ethoxy-4-hydroxyquinoline-3-carboxylate; C$_{24}$H$_{35}$NO$_5$; *18507-89-6*
Antiprotozoal (veterinary)

Deferiprone (rINN) *de·fe·ri·prön*
3-Hydroxy-1,2-dimethyl-4-pyridone; C$_7$H$_9$NO$_2$; *30652-11-0*
Chelating agent (iron)

Defibrotide (rINN) *dë·fi·brö·tïd*
Polydeoxyribonucleotides from bovine lung; the molecular weights range between 45,000 and 55,000
Antithrombotic; fibrinolytic

Deflazacort (rINN) *dë·flä·za·kort*
11β-Hydroxy-2′-methyl-3,20-dioxo[1,3]oxazolo[5′,4′:16,17]¬pregn-4-en-21-yl acetate; C$_{25}$H$_{31}$NO$_6$; *14484-47-0*
Glucocorticoid

Degarelix (rINN) *de·gá·re·liks*
N-Acetyl-3-(naphthalen-2-yl)-D-alanyl-4-chloro-D-phenylalanyl-3-(pyridin-3-yl)-D-alanyl-L-seryl-4-({[(4S)-2,6-dioxohexahydropyrimidin-4-yl]carbonyl}amino)-L-phenylalanyl-4-(carbamoylamino)-D-phenylalanyl-L-leucyl-*N*^{6}-(propan-2-yl)-L-lysyl-L-prolyl-D-alaninamide; C$_{82}$H$_{103}$ClN$_{18}$O$_{16}$; *214766-78-6*;
Gonadotrophin-releasing hormone analogue; treatment of prostate cancer

Dehydrocholic Acid (rINN) see Appendix C

Dehydroemetine (rINN) dë·hĭ·drö·*e*·me·tën
(*S*)-3-Ethyl-1,6,7,11b-tetrahydro-9,10-dimethoxy-2-[(*R*)-
(1,2,3,4-tetrahydro-6,7-dimethoxy-1-isoquinolylmethyl)]-4*H*-
benzo[*a*]quinolizine; 2,3-dehydroemetine; $C_{29}H_{38}N_2O_4$;
4914-30-1
Antiprotozoal; amoebiasis

Delmadinone (rINN) del·*ma*·di·nön
6-Chloro-17α-hydroxypregna-1,4,6-triene-3,20-dione;
$C_{21}H_{25}ClO_3$;*15262-77-8*
Delmadinone Acetate *13698-49-2*
Progestogen

Delprostenate (rINN) del·*pros*·te·nät
(1) Methyl (2*E*,5*Z*)-7-{(1*R*,2*R*,3*R*,5*S*)-2-[(*E*)-(3*R*)-4-(3-
chlorophenoxy)-3-hydroxybut-1-enyl]-3,5-dihydroxy
cyclopentyl}hepta-2,5-dienoate; (2) Methyl (2*E*,5*Z*,13*E*)-
(9*S*,11*R*,15*R*)-16-(3-chlorophenoxy)-9,11,15-trihydroxy-ω-
tetranorprosta-2,5,13-trienoate; $C_{23}H_{29}ClO_6$; *62524-99-6*
Prostanoid (veterinary)

♣ **Deltamethrin** (BAN) del·ta·*më*·thrin
(*S*)-α-Cyano-3-phenoxybenzyl (1*R*,3*S*)-3-(2,2-dibromovinyl)-
2,2-dimethylcyclopropanecarboxylate; $C_{22}H_{19}Br_2NO_3$;
52918-63-5
Insecticide (veterinary)

Dembrexine (rINN) dem·*breks*·ën
trans-4-(3,5-Dibromo-2-hydroxybenzylamino)cyclohexanol;
$C_{13}H_{17}Br_2NO_2$; *83200-09-3*
♣ **Dembrexine Hydrochloride** *52702-51-9*
Mucolytic (veterinary use)

Demecarium Bromide (rINN) see Appendix C

Demeclocycline (rINN) de·më·klö·*sĭ*·klën
(1) (4*S*,4a*S*,5a*S*,6*S*,12a*S*)-7-Chloro-4-dimethylamino-1,4,4a,5,¬
5a, 6,11,12a-octahydro-3,6,10,12,12a-pentahydroxy-
1,11-dioxonaphthacene-2-carboxamide; (2) 7-Chloro-6-
demethyl-tetracycline; $C_{21}H_{21}ClN_2O_8$; *127-33-3*
● **Demeclocycline Hydrochloride** *64-73-3*
Tetracycline antibacterial

Demecolcine (rINN) de·më·*kol*·sën
(*RS*)-6,7-Dihydro-1,2,3,10-tetramethoxy-7-methylamino-5*H*-
benzo[*a*]heptalen-9-one; $C_{21}H_{25}NO_5$; *477-30-5*
Antimitotic agent (veterinary)

and enantiomer

Denatonium Benzoate (rINN) de·na·*tö*·në·um
Benzyldiethyl(2,6-xylylcarbamoylmethyl)ammonium benzoate;
$C_{28}H_{34}N_2O_3$; *3734-33-6*
Denaturant for alcohol in toiletries

Denbufylline (rINN) den·*bü*·fi·lën
1,3-Dibutyl-3,7-dihydro-7-acetonylpurine-2,6(1*H*)-dione;
$C_{16}H_{24}N_4O_3$; *57076-71-8*
*Non-selective phosphodiesterase inhibitor (xanthine);
treatment of reversible airways obstruction*

The symbol '¬' in systematic chemical names signifies line continuation

Denileukin Difitox (rINN) de·ni·lü·kin *di*·fi·toks
N-L-Methionyl-387-L-histidine-388-L-alanine-1–388-toxin
(*Corynebacterium diphtheriae* strain C7) (388–2′)-protein with
2–133-interleukin 2 (human clone pTIL2-21a); *173146-27-5*
Cytotoxic

denileukin difitox has the following amino acid sequence:

```
MGADDVVDSS    KSFVMENFSS    YHGTKPGYVD

SIQKGIQKPK    SGTQGNYDDD    WKGFYSTDNK

YDAAGYSVDN    ENPLSGKAGG    VVKVTYPGLT

KVLALKVDNA    ETIKKELGLS    LTEPLMEQVG

TEEFIKRFGD    GASRVVLSLP    FAEGSSSVEY

INNWEQAKAL    SVELEINFET    RGKRGQDAMY

EYMAQACAGN    RVRRSVGSSL    SCINLDWDVI

RDKTKTKIES    LKEHGPIKNK    MSESPNKTVS

EEKAKQYLEE    FHQTALEHPE    LSELKTVTGT

NPVFAGANYA    AWAVNVAQVI    DSETADNLEK

TTAALSILPG    IGSVMGIADG    AVHHNTEEIV

AQSIALSSLM    VAQAIPLVGE    LVDIGFAAYN

FVESIINLFQ    VVHNSYNRPA    YSPGHKTHAP

TSSSTKKTQL    QLEHLLLDLQ    MILNGINNYK

NPKLTRMLTF    KFYMPKKATE    LKHLQCLEEE

LKPLEEVLNL    AQSKNFHLRP    RDLISNINVI

VLELKGSETT    FMCEYADETA    TIVEFLNRWI

TFCQSIISTL    T
```

Denosumab (rINN) de·*nös*·ü·mab

Immunoglobulin G2, anti-(human tumor necrosis factor ligand
superfamily member 11 (human osteoclast differentiation
factor)) (human monoclonal AMG162 heavy chain), disulfide
with human monoclonal AMG162 light chain, dimer;
615258-40-7;
*Monoclonal antibody (receptor activator of nuclear factor
kappa B ligand); treatment of osteoporosis*

denosumab has the following amino acid sequence:

Heavy chain

```
EVQLLESGGG    LVQPGGSLRL    SCAASGFTFS    SYAMSWVRQA

PGKGLEWVSG    ITGSGGSTYY    ADSVKGRFTI    SRDNSKNTLY

LQMNSLRAED    TAVYYCAKDP    GTTVIMSWFD    PWGQGTLVTV

SSASTKGPSV    FPLAPCSRST    SESTAALGCL    VKDYFPEPVT

VSWNSGALTS    GVHTFPAVLQ    SSGLYSLSSV    VTVPSSNFGT

QTYTCNVDHK    PSNTKVDKTV    ERKCCVECPP    CPAPPVAGPS

VFLFPPKPKD    TLMISRTPEV    TCVVVDVSHE    DPEVQFNWYV

DGVEVHNAKT    KPREEQFNST    FRVVSVLTVV    HQDWLNGKEY

KCKVSNKGLP    APIEKTISKT    KGQPREPQVY    TLPPSREEMT

KNQVSLTCLV    KGFYPSDIAV    EWESNGQPEN    NYKTTPPMLD

SDGSFFLYSK    LTVDKSRWQQ    GNVFSCSVMH    EALHNHYTQK

SLSLSPGK
```

Light chain

```
EIVLTQSPGT    LSLSPGERAT    LSCRASQSVR    GRYLAWYQQK

PGQAPRLLIY    GASSRATGIP    DRFSGSGSGT    DFTLTISRLE

PEDFAVFYCQ    QYGSSPRTFG    QGTKVEIKRT    VAAPSVFIFP

PSDEQLKSGT    ASVVCLLNNF    YPREAKVQWK    VDNALQSGNS

QESVTEQDSK    DSTYSLSSTL    TLSKADYEKH    KVYACEVTHQ
```

Deoxycortone *see Desoxycortone*

Depramine (rINN) see Appendix C

Deprodone *de*·prö·dön
11β,17α-Dihydroxypregna-1,4-diene-3,20-dione; $C_{21}H_{28}O_4$;
20423-99-8
Deprodone Propionate *20424-00-4*
Glucocorticoid

Deptropine (rINN) *dep*·trö·pën
(1*R*,3*r*,5*S*)-3-(10,11-Dihydrodibenzo[*a,d*]cycloheptadien-5-
yloxy)tropane; $C_{23}H_{27}NO$; *604-51-3*
● **Deptropine Citrate** *2169-75-7*
Histamine H_1 receptor antagonist; anticholinergic

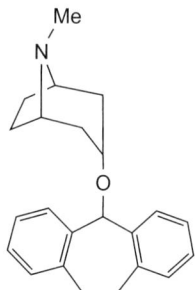

● **Dequalinium Chloride** (rINN) de·kwa·*li*·në·um
N,N-Decamethylenebis(4-amino-2-methylquinolinium chloride);
$C_{30}H_{40}Cl_2N_4$; *522-51-0*
Antiseptic

Deserpidine (rINN) dë·*ser*·pi·dën
Methyl 11-demethoxy-*O*-(3,4,5-trimethoxybenzoyl)reserpate;
$C_{32}H_{38}N_2O_8$; *131-01-1*
Rauwolfia alkaloid; treatment of hypertension

Desferrioxamine (BAN) *dez*·fe·rë·*oks*·a·mën
30-Amino-3,14,25-trihydroxy-3,9,14,20,25-penta-azatria¬
contane-2,10,13,21,24-pentaone; deferoxamine (pINN);
$C_{25}H_{48}N_6O_8$; *70-51-9*
● **Desferrioxamine Mesilate** *138-14-7*
Chelating agent (iron)

● **Desflurane** (rINN) dez·*floo*·rän
(2*RS*)-2-(Difluoromethoxy)-1,1,1,2-tetrafluoroethane;
$C_3H_2F_6O$; *57041-67-5*
General anaesthetic

and enantiomer

Desipramine (rINN) de·*zi*·pra·mën
3-(10,11-Dihydro-5*H*-dibenz[*b,f*]azepin-5-yl)propyl(methyl)¬
amine; $C_{18}H_{22}N_2$; *50-47-5*
● **Desipramine Hydrochloride** *58-28-6*
Monoamine reuptake inhibitor; tricyclic antidepressant

Desirudin (rINN) de·si·*roo*·din
63-Desulfohirudin (hirudin isoform HV2); *120993-53-5*
Direct thrombin inhibitor; anticoagulant

```
VVYTDCTESG    QNLCLCEGSN    VCGQGNKCIL

GSDGEKNQCV    TGEGTPKPQS    HNDGDFEEIP

EEYLQ
```

● **Deslanoside** (rINN) dez·*lan*·o·sïd
3β-[(*O*-β-D-Glucopyranosyl-(1→4)-*O*-2,6-dideoxy-β-D-*ribo*-
hexopyranosyl-(1→4)-*O*-2,6-dideoxy-β-D-*ribo*-hexopyranosyl-
(1→4)-*O*-2,6-dideoxy-β-D-*ribo*-hexopyranosyl)oxy]-12,14-
dihydroxy-5β,12β-card-20(22)-enolide; deacetyl-lanatoside C;
$C_{47}H_{74}O_{19}$; *17598-65-1*
Na / K-ATPase inhibitor; cardiac glycoside

Desloratadine (rINN) des·lor·*ra*·ta·dën
8-Chloro-6,11-dihydro-11-(4-piperidylidene)-5*H*-benzo[5,6]¬
cyclohepta[1,2-*b*]pyridine; $C_{19}H_{19}ClN_2$; *100643-71-8*;
SCH 34117
Histamine H_1 receptor antagonist; antihistamine

Deslorelin (rINN) see Appendix C

● **Desmopressin** (rINN) des·mö·*pres*·sin
[1-Deamino,8-ᴅ-arginine]vasopressin; $C_{46}H_{64}N_{14}O_{12}S_2$;
16679-58-6
Desmopressin Acetate (rINN) *62288-83-9;*
62357-86-2 (trihydrate)
Vasopressin analogue; treatment of diabetes insipidus;
nocturnal enuresis; haemophilia; von Willebrand's disease

```
┌─────────────────────────────────────────┐
S·CH₂·CH₂·CO-Tyr-Phe-Gln-Asn-Cys-Pro-

ᴅ-Arg-Gly-NH₂
```

● **Desogestrel** (rINN) de·zö·*jes*·trel
13β-Ethyl-11-methylene-18,19-dinor-17α-pregn-4-en-20-yn-
17β-ol; $C_{22}H_{30}O$; *54024-22-5*
Progestogen

Desomorphine (rINN) de·zö·*mor*·fën
(1) (−)-(5*S*)-4,5-Epoxy-17-methylmorphinan-3-ol;
(2) 6-Deoxy-7,8-dihydromorphine; $C_{17}H_{21}NO_2$; *427-00-9*
Opioid receptor agonist; analgesic

Desonide (rINN) see Appendix C

Desoximetasone (rINN) de·zoks·ë·*me*·ta·sön
9α-Fluoro-11β,21-dihydroxy-16α-methylpregna-1,4-diene-3,20-
dione; $C_{22}H_{29}FO_4$; *382-67-2*
Glucocorticoid

Desoxycortone (rINN) dëz·oks·ë·*kor*·tön
21-Hydroxypregn-4-ene-3,20-dione; (rINN); $C_{21}H_{30}O_2$; *64-85-7*
● **Desoxycortone Acetate** desoxycorticosterone acetate
(USAN); *56-47-3*
Desoxycortone Pivalate *808-48-0*
Mineralocorticoid

Desoxymethasone *see Desoximetasone*

Desvenlafaxine (rINN) dez·*ven*·la·*faks*·ën
4-[(*RS*)-2-(Dimethylamino)-1-(1-hydroxycyclohexyl)ethyl]¬
phenol; $C_{16}H_{25}NO_2$; *93413-62-8*
Inhibition of 5HT and noradrenaline reuptake; antidepressant

and enantiomer

Detomidine (rINN) de·*to*·mi·dën
4-(2,3-Dimethylbenzyl)imidazole; $C_{12}H_{14}N_2$; *76631-46-4*
♣ **Detomidine Hydrochloride** *90038-01-0*
Alpha₂-adrenoceptor agonist (veterinary)

● **Dexamethasone** (rINN) deks·a·*me*·tha·sön
9α-Fluoro-11β,17α,21-trihydroxy-16α-methylpregna-1,4-diene-
3,20-dione; $C_{22}H_{29}FO_5$; *50-02-2*
● **Dexamethasone Acetate** *55812-90-3*
● **Dexamethasone Isonicotinate** *2265-67-7*
Dexamethasone Phenylpropionate *1879-72-7*
Dexamethasone Phosphate *312-93-6*
Dexamethasone Pivalate *1926-94-9*
● **Dexamethasone Sodium Phosphate** *2392-39-4*
Glucocorticoid

Dexamfetamine (rINN) deks·am·*fe*·ta·mën
(*S*)-α-Methylphenethylamine; (+)-amphetamine;
dextroamphetamine (USAN); $C_9H_{13}N$; *51-64-9*
● **Dexamfetamine Sulfate** *51-63-8*
Amfetamine

Dexbrompheniramine (rINN) deks·brom·fen·ï·ra·mën
(*R*)-3-(4-Bromophenyl)-3-(2-pyridyl)propyldimethylamine;
$C_{16}H_{19}BrN_2$; *132-21-8*
Dexbrompheniramine Maleate *2391-03-9*
Histamine H_1 receptor antagonist; antihistamine

Dexchlorpheniramine (rINN) deks·klor·fen·ï·ra·mën
(*S*)-[3-(4-Chlorophenyl)-3-(2-pyridyl)propyl]dimethylamine;
$C_{16}H_{19}ClN_2$; *25523-97-1*
●**Dexchlorpheniramine Maleate** *2438-32-6*
Histamine H_1 receptor antagonist; antihistamine

Dexetimide (rINN) deks·e·ti·mïd
(*S*)-2-(1-Benzyl-4-piperidyl)-2-phenylglutarimide; $C_{23}H_{26}N_2O_2$;
21888-98-2
Anticholinergic

Dexfenfluramine (rINN) deks·fen·*flûr*·ra·mën
(*S*)-*N*-Ethyl-α-methyl-3-trifluoromethylphenethylamine;
$C_{12}H_{16}F_3N$; *3239-44-9*
Appetite suppressant

Dexibuprofen (rINN) deks·ï·bü·*prö*·fen
(*S*)-2-(4-Isobutylphenyl)propionic acid; $C_{13}H_{18}O_2$; *51146-56-6*
Cyclo-oxygenase inhibitor; analgesic; anti-inflammatory

Dexketoprofen (rINN) deks·kë·tö·*prö*·fen
(*S*)-2-(3-Benzoylphenyl)propionic acid; $C_{16}H_{14}O_3$; *22161-81-5*
Dexketoprofen Trometamol
Cyclo-oxygenase inhibitor; analgesic; anti-inflammatory

Dexmedetomidine (rINN) deks·me·de·*to*·mi·dën
(*S*)-4-[1-(2,3-Xylyl)ethyl]imidazole; $C_{13}H_{16}N_2$; *113775-47-6*
Alpha$_2$-adrenoceptor antagonist

Dexpanthenol (rINN) deks·*pan*·the·nol
(*R*)-2,4-Dihydroxy-*N*-(3-hydroxypropyl)-3,3-dimethyl¬
butyramide; $C_9H_{19}NO_4$; *81-13-0*
Vitamin B$_5$ analogue

Dexpropranolol (rINN) deks·prö·*pra*·no·lol
(*R*)-1-Isopropylamino-3-(1-naphthyloxy)propan-2-ol;
$C_{16}H_{21}NO_2$; *5051-22-9*
Beta-adrenoceptor antagonist

Dexrazoxane (rINN) deks·ra·*zoks*·än
(*S*)-4,4′-Propylenedi(piperazine-2,6-dione); $C_{11}H_{16}N_4O_4$;
24584-09-6
Dexrazoxane Hydrochloride
Protection against anthracycline-induced cardiotoxicity

●**Dextran** (rINN) *deks*·tran
Polyanhydroglucose produced by the action of *Leuconostoc
mesenteroides* on sucrose and subsequent controlled hydrolysis
and fractionation of the high molecular weight dextran thus
formed, or the same substance obtained by any other means.
The weight-average molecular weight is referred to by a
specifying number: *eg* dextran 40, 45, 70, 110, 150. The number
multiplied by 1000 corresponds to the approximate weight-
average molecular weight, *eg* dextran 40 has a weight-average
molecular weight of about 40,000; *9004-54-0*
Plasma substitute

●**Dextranomer** (rINN) deks·*tra*·no·mer
Dextran cross-linked with 1-chloro-2,3-epoxypropane;
56087-11-7
*Fluid absorber; treatment of burns, wounds, and skin ulcers;
preparation for skin grafting*

The symbol '¬' in systematic chemical names signifies line continuation

Dextriferron (rINN) deks·tri·*fe*·ron
A colloidal solution of iron(III) hydroxide in complex with partially hydrolysed dextrin; *8063-26-1*
Treatment of iron deficiency

● **Dextrin** (BAN) *deks*·trin
Maize or potato starch partially hydrolysed by heat with or without the aid of suitable acids or buffers; *9004-53-9*
Excipient

Dextromethorphan (rINN) deks·trö·me·*thor*·fan
(1) (+)-3-Methoxy-17-methylmorphinan; (2) (9*S*,13*S*,14*S*)-6,18-Dideoxy-7,8-dihydro-3-*O*-methylmorphine; $C_{18}H_{25}NO$; *125-71-3*
● **Dextromethorphan Hydrobromide**
6700-34-1 (monohydrate); *125-69-9 (anhydrous)*
Opioid receptor agonist; cough suppressant

Dextromoramide (rINN) deks·trö·*mo*·ra·mïd
(*S*)-1-(3-Methyl-4-morpholino-2,2-diphenylbutyryl) pyrrolidine; $C_{25}H_{32}N_2O_2$; *357-56-2*
● **Dextromoramide Tartrate** *2922-44-3*
Opioid receptor agonist; analgesic

Dextropropoxyphene (pINN) deks·trö·prö·*poks*·ë·fën
(1*S*,2*R*)-1-Benzyl-3-dimethylamino-2-methyl-1-phenylpropyl propionate; $C_{22}H_{29}NO_2$; *469-62-5*
● **Dextropropoxyphene Hydrochloride** propoxyphene hydrochloride (USAN); *1639-60-7*
● **Dextropropoxyphene Napsilate** (rINN) *26570-10-5*
Opioid receptor agonist; analgesic

Dextrorphan (rINN) deks·*tror*·fan
(+)-17-Methylmorphinan-3-ol; $C_{17}H_{23}NO$; *125-73-5*
N-methyl-D-aspartate (NMDA) receptor antagonist; cough suppressant

Dextrothyroxine (rINN) see Appendix C

Diacetamate (rINN) see Appendix C

Diacetolol (rINN) dï·a·*se*·to·lol
3′-Acetyl-4′-(2-hydroxy-3-isopropylaminopropoxy)acetanilide; $C_{16}H_{24}N_2O_4$; *28197-69-5*
Diacetolol Hydrochloride *69796-04-9*
Beta-adrenoceptor antagonist

and enantiomer

Diacetylnalorphine (BAN) dï·*a*·së·til·na·*lor*·fën
(1) (−)-(5*R*,6*S*)-17-Allyl-4,5-epoxymorphin-7-en-3,6-diyl diacetate; (2) 3,6-Di-*O*-acetyl-17-allyl-17-normorphine; $C_{23}H_{27}NO_5$; *2748-74-5*
Opioid receptor agonist

Diamocaine (rINN) dï·*a*·mö·kän
2-[1-(2-Anilinoethyl)-4-phenyl-4-piperidyloxy]ethyl¬diethylamine; $C_{25}H_{37}N_3O$; *27112-37-4*
Local anaesthetic

Diamorphine (BAN) dï·a·*mor*·fën
4,5-Epoxy-17-methylmorphinan-3,6-diyl diacetate; $C_{21}H_{23}NO_5$; *561-27-3*
● **Diamorphine Hydrochloride** *1502-95-0*
Opioid receptor agonist; analgesic

Diamfenetide (rINN) dï·am·*fe*·ne·tïd
β,β′-Oxydi(aceto-*p*-phenetidide); $C_{20}H_{24}N_2O_5$; *36141-82-9*
Antihelminthic (veterinary)

Diampromide (rINN) see Appendix C

Diamthazole (rINN) see Appendix C

Diatrizoic Acid *see Amidotrizoic Acid*

Diaveridine (rINN) dï·a·*ve*·ri·dën
5-Veratrylpyrimidine-2,4-diyldiamine; $C_{13}H_{16}N_4O_2$; *5355-16-8*;
Antiprotozoal

● **Diazepam** (rINN) dï·*ä*·ze·pam
7-Chloro-1,3-dihydro-1-methyl-5-phenyl-1,4-benzodiazepin-2-
one; $C_{16}H_{13}ClN_2O$; *439-14-5*
Benzodiazepine

Diazinon *see Dimpylate*

● **Diazoxide** (rINN) dï·a·*zoks*·ïd
7-Chloro-3-methyl-2*H*-1,2,4-benzothiadiazine 1,1-dioxide;
$C_8H_7ClN_2O_2S$; *364-98-7*
Vasodilator; treatment of hypertension

Dibekacin (rINN) dï·*be*·ka·sin
6-*O*-(3-Amino-3-deoxy-α-D-glucopyranosyl)-2-deoxy-4-*O*-
(2,6-diamino-2,3,4,6-tetradeoxy-α-D-*erythro*-hexopyranosyl)-
D-streptamine; 3′,4′-dideoxykanamycin B; $C_{18}H_{37}N_5O_8$;
34493-98-6
Dibekacin Sulfate *58580-55-5*
Aminoglycoside antibacterial

Dibenzepin (rINN) see Appendix C

Dibotermin Alfa (rINN) dï·bö·*ter*·min
Human recombinant bone morphogenic protein-2 (hrBMP-2);
246539-15-1
*Bone morphogenetic protein (growth factor); orthopaedic
surgery*

dibotermin alfa has the following amino acid sequence:

QAKHKQRKRL	KSSCKRHPLY	VDFSDVGWND
WIVAPPGYHA	FYCHGECPFP	LADHLNSTNH
AIVQTLVNSV	NSKIPKACCV	PTELSAISML
YLDENEKVVL	KNYQDMVVEG	CGCR

Dibrompropamidine (rINN) dï·brom·prö·*pa*·mi·dën
3,3′-Dibromo-4,4′-trimethylenedioxydibenzamidine;
$C_{17}H_{18}Br_2N_4O_2$; *496-00-4*
● **Dibrompropamidine Isetionate** *614-87-9*
Antiseptic

Dibupyrone (rINN) see Appendix C

Dichlofenthion (BAN) dï·klö·fen·*thï*·on
O-2,4-Dichlorophenyl *O,O*-diethyl phosphorothioate;
$C_{10}H_{13}Cl_2O_3PS$; *97-17-6*
Organophosphorus insecticide

Dichloralphenazone (rINN) see Appendix C

● **Dichlorophen** (rINN) dï·*klor*·rö·fen
2,2′-Methylenebis(4-chlorophenol); $C_{13}H_{10}Cl_2O_2$; *97-23-4*
Antihelminthic

The symbol '¬' in systematic chemical names signifies line continuation

Dichlorophenarsine (rINN) dï·klor·rö·fe·*nar*·sën
3-Amino-4-hydroxyphenyldichloroarsine; C₆H₆AsCl₂NO;
455-83-4
Antifungal

Dichloroxylenol (rINN) dï·klor·rö·*zï*·le·nol
2,4-Dichloro-3,5-xylenol; C₈H₈Cl₂O; *133-53-9*
Antiseptic

Dichlorphenamide *see Diclofenamide*

Dichlorvos (rINN) *dï*·klor·vos
2,2-Dichlorovinyl dimethyl phosphate; C₄H₇Cl₂O₄P; *62-73-7*
Antihelminthic; insecticide (veterinary)

Dichromium Trioxide (BAN) dï·*krö*·më·um trï·*oks*·ïd
Chromium(III) sesquioxide; Cr₂O₃; *1308-38-9*
Diagnostic agent

♣ **Diclazuril** (rINN) dï·*klaz*·ûr·ril
(±)-4-Chlorophenyl[2,6-dichloro-4-(2,3,4,5-tetrahydro-3,5-
dioxo-1,2,4-triazin-2-yl)phenyl]acetonitrile; C₁₇H₉Cl₃N₄O₂;
101831-37-2
Antiprotozoal (veterinary); coccidiosis

Diclofenac (rINN) dï·*klö*·fe·nak
[2-(2,6-Dichloroanilino)phenyl]acetic acid; C₁₄H₁₁Cl₂NO₂;
15307-86-5
● **Diclofenac Diethylamine**
● **Diclofenac Potassium** *15307-81-0*
● **Diclofenac Sodium** *15307-79-6*
Cyclo-oxygenase inhibitor; analgesic; anti-inflammatory

Diclofenamide (rINN) see Appendix C

Dicloxacillin (rINN) dï·kloks·a·*si*·lin
6-[3-(2,6-Dichlorophenyl)-5-methyl-1,2-oxazole-4-
carboxamido]penicillanic acid; C₁₉H₁₇Cl₂N₃O₅S; *3116-76-5*
● **Dicloxacillin Sodium** *13412-64-1 (monohydrate)*;
343-55-5 (anhydrous)
Penicillin antibacterial

Dicobalt Edetate (rINN)
Cobalt [ethylenediaminetetra-acetato(4-)-*N,N′,O,O′*]cobalt(II);
C₁₀H₁₂Co₂N₂O₈; *36499-65-7*
Treatment of cyanide poisoning

Dicyclomine *see Dicycloverine*

Dicycloverine (rINN) dï·*sï*·klö·ver·rën
2-Diethylaminoethyl bicyclohexyl-1-carboxylate; C₁₉H₃₅NO₂;
77-19-0
● **Dicycloverine Hydrochloride** *67-92-5*
Anticholinergic

● **Didanosine** (rINN) dï·*da*·nö·sën
2′,3′-Dideoxy-1,9-dihydro-9-β-D-ribofuranosyl-6*H*-purine-6-
one; 2′,3′-dideoxyinosine; DDI; C₁₀H₁₂N₄O₃
Nucleoside reverse transcriptase inhibitor; antiviral (HIV)

Dieldrin (rINN) see Appendix C

● **Dienestrol** (dienoestrol) dï·ën·*ë*·strol
4,4′-{Bis[(*E*)-ethylidene]ethylene}diphenol; C₁₈H₁₈O₂; *84-17-3*
Oestrogen

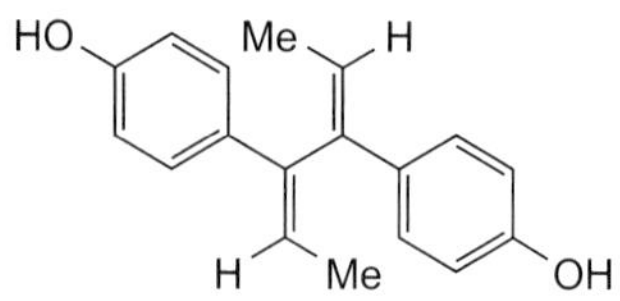

Dienogest (rINN) dï·*ë*·nö·gest
17β-Hydroxy-3-oxo-19-nor-17α-pregna-4,9-diene-21-nitrile;
$C_{20}H_{25}NO_2$; *65928-58-7*
Progestogen

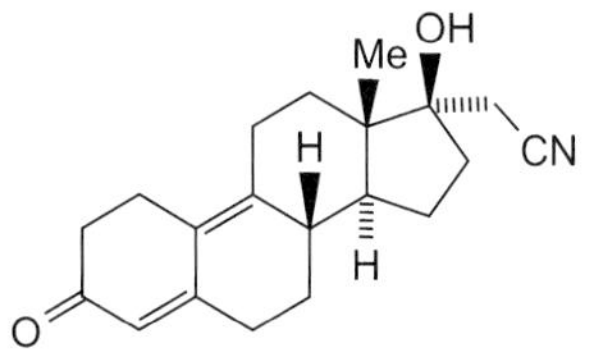

Diethadione (rINN) see Appendix C

Diethazine (rINN) dï·*eth*·a·zën
2-(Phenothiazin-10-yl)ethyldiethylamine; $C_{18}H_{22}N_2S$; *60-91-3*
Anticholinergic

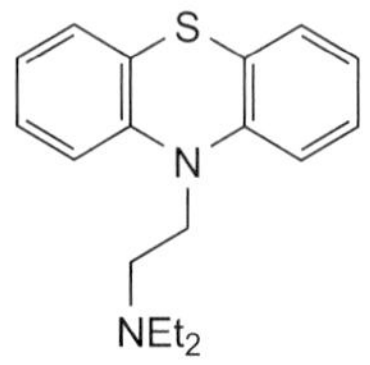

Diethylcarbamazine (rINN) dï·ë·thïl·kar·*ba*·ma·zën
N,N-Diethyl-4-methylpiperazine-1-carboxamide; $C_{10}H_{21}N_3O$;
90-89-1
● **Diethylcarbamazine Citrate** *1642-54-2*
Antihelminthic

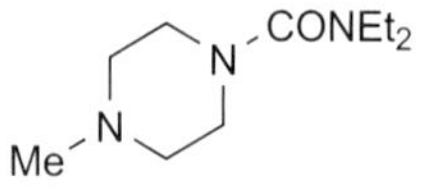

Diethylpropion (rINN) dï·ë·thïl·*prö*·pë·on
α-Diethylaminopropiophenone; amfepramone (pINN);
$C_{13}H_{19}NO$; *90-84-6*
● **Diethylpropion Hydrochloride** *134-80-5*
Appetite suppressant

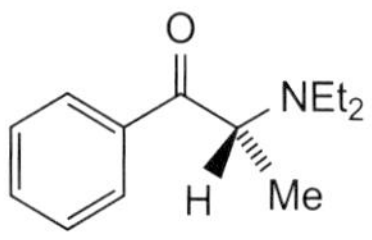

and enantiomer

● **Diethylstilbestrol** (rINN) dï·ëthïl·stil·*bë*·strol
(E)-4,4′-(1,2-Diethylvinylene)diphenol; $C_{18}H_{20}O_2$; *56-53-1*
Oestrogen

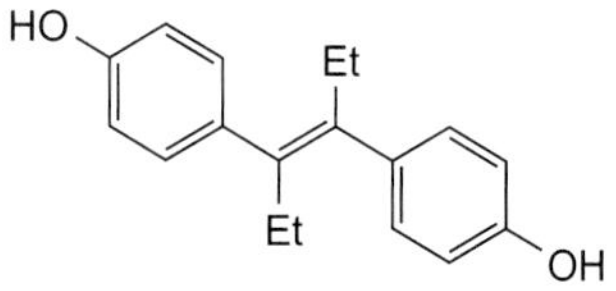

Diethylthiambutene (rINN) dï·ë·thïl·thï·am·*bú*·tën
Diethyl[3,3-di-(2-thienyl)-1-methylprop-2-enyl]amine;
$C_{16}H_{21}NS_2$; *86-14-6*
Diethylthiambutene Hydrochloride
Opioid receptor agonist

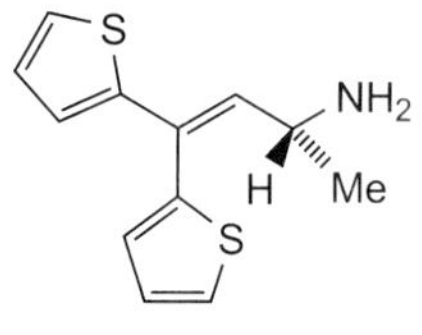

and enantiomer

Diethyltoluamide (rINN) dï·ë·thïl·tol·*ü*·a·mïd
N,N-Diethyl-m-toluamide; $C_{12}H_{17}NO$; *134-62-3*
Insecticide

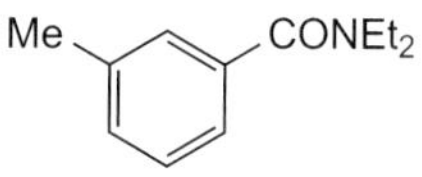

Difenidol (rINN) dï·*fe*·ni·dol
1,1-Diphenyl-4-piperidinobutan-1-ol; $C_{21}H_{27}NO$; *972-02-1*
Antiemetic

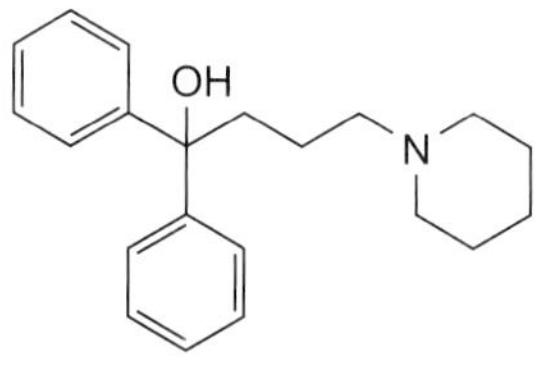

Difenoxin (rINN) dï·fen·*oks*·in
1-(3-Cyano-3,3-diphenylpropyl)-4-phenylpiperidine-4-
carboxylic acid; $C_{28}H_{28}N_2O_2$; *28782-42-5*
Opioid receptor agonist

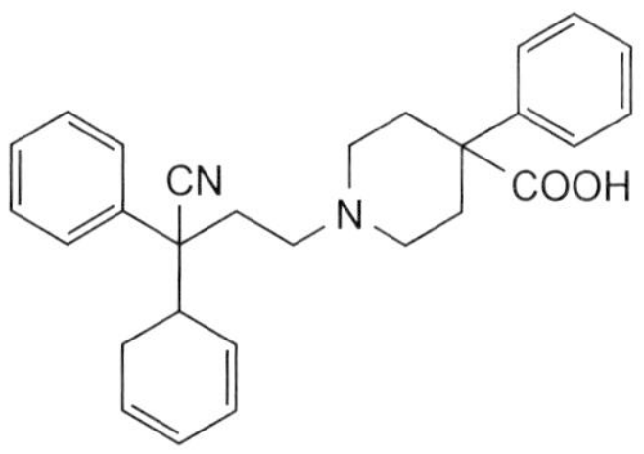

Difetarsone (rINN) dï·fe·*tar*·sön
N,N′-Ethylenebis(4-aminophenylarsonic acid); $C_{14}H_{18}As_2N_2O_6$;
3639-19-18
Antiprotozoal

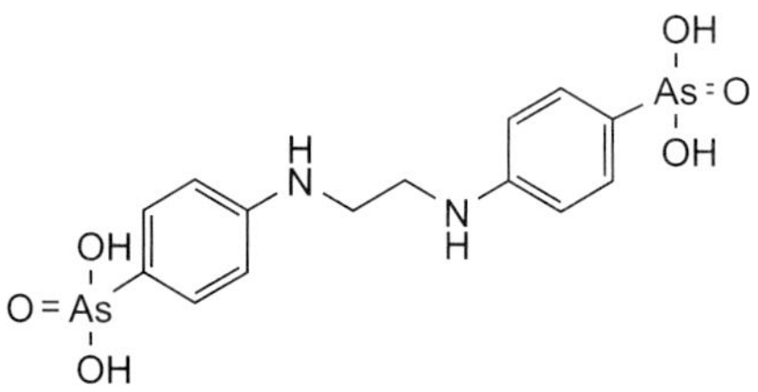

The symbol '¬' in systematic chemical names signifies line continuation

89

Diflorasone (rINN) dï·*flo*·ra·sön
6α,9α-Difluoro-11β,17α,21-trihydroxy-16β-methylpregna-1,4-diene-3,20-dione; $C_{22}H_{28}F_2O_5$; *2557-49-5*
Diflorasone Diacetate *33564-31-7*
Glucocorticoid

Diflucortolone (rINN) dï·floo·*kor*·to·lön
6α,9α-Difluoro-11β,21-dihydroxy-16α-methylpregna-1,4-diene-3,20-dione; $C_{22}H_{28}F_2O_4$; *2607-06-9*
● **Diflucortolone Valerate** *59198-70-8*
Glucocorticoid

Diflumidone (rINN) dï·*floo*·mi·dön
3′-Benzoyldifluoromethanesulfonanilide; $C_{14}H_{11}F_2NO_3S$; *22736-85-2*
Cyclo-oxygenase inhibitor; analgesic; anti-inflammatory

● **Diflunisal** (rINN) dï·*floo*·ni·sal
5-(2,4-Difluorophenyl)salicylic acid; $C_{13}H_8F_2O_3$; *22494-42-4*
Salicylate; non-selective cyclo-oxygenase inhibitor; antipyretic; analgesic; anti-inflammatory

● **Digitoxin** (rINN) di·ji·*toks*·in
3β-[(O-2,6-Dideoxy-β-D-*ribo*-hexopyranosyl-(1→4)-O-2,6-dideoxy-β-D-*ribo*-hexopyranosyl-(1→4)-2,6-dideoxy-β-D-*ribo*-hexopyranosyl)oxy]-14β-hydroxy-5β-card-20(22)-enolide; $C_{41}H_{64}O_{13}$; *71-63-6*
Na /K-ATPase inhibitor; cardiac glycoside

● **Digoxin** (rINN) di·*joks*·in
3β-[O-2,6-Dideoxy-β-D-*ribo*-hexopyranosyl-(1→4)-O-2,6-dideoxy-β-D-*ribo*-hexopyranosyl-(1→4)-2,6-dideoxy-β-D-*ribo*-hexopyranosyl)oxy]-12β,14β-dihydroxy-5β-card-20(22)-enolide; $C_{41}H_{64}O_{14}$; *20830-75-5*
Na /K-ATPase inhibitor; cardiac glycoside

Dihydralazine (rINN) dï·hï·*dra*·la·zën
Phthalazine-1,4-diyldihydrazine; $C_8H_{10}N_6$; *484-23-1*
● **Dihydralazine Sulfate** *7327-87-9*
Vasodilator

Dihydrocodeine (rINN) dï·hï·drö·*kö*·dën
4,5-Epoxy-3-methoxy-17-methylmorphinan-6-ol; $C_{18}H_{23}NO_3$; *125-28-0*
● **Dihydrocodeine Tartrate** *5965-13-9*
Opioid receptor agonist; analgesic

Dihydroergocristine (rINN) dï·hï·drö·er·gö·*kris*·tën
(1) (2′*R*,5′*S*)-5′-Benzyl-9,10-dihydro-12′-hydroxy-
2′-isopropyl-18-oxoergotaman-3′,6′-dione;
(2) (6a*R*,9*R*,10a*R*)-*N*-[(2*R*,5*S*,10a*S*,10b*S*)-5-Benzyl-10b-
hydroxy-2-isopropyl-3,6-dioxooctahydro-8*H*-[1,3]oxazolo[3,2-
a]pyrrolo[2,1-*c*]pyrazin-2-yl]-7-methyl-4,6,6a,7,8,9,10,10a-
octahydroindolo[4,3-*fg*]quinoline-9-carboxamide; $C_{35}H_{34}N_5O_5$;
17479-19-5
● **Dihydroergocristine Mesilate** *24730-10-7*
Vasodilator

Dihydroergotamine (rINN) see Appendix C

Dihydrostreptomycin (rINN) dï·hï·drö·strep·tö·*mï*·sin
O-2-Deoxy-2-methylamino-α-L-glucopyranosyl-(1→2)-*O*-5-
deoxy-3-*C*-hydroxymethyl-α-L-lyxofuranosyl-(1→4)-N^1,N^3-
diamidino-D-streptamine; $C_{21}H_{41}N_7O_{12}$; *128-46-1*
♣ **Dihydrostreptomycin Sulfate** *5490-27-7*
Aminoglycoside antibacterial

● **Dihydrotachysterol** (rINN) dï·hï·drö·ta·*kis*·ste·rol
(5*Z*,7*E*)-(3*S*,10*S*)-9,10-Secoergosta-5,7,22-trien-3-ol; $C_{28}H_{46}O$;
67-96-9
Vitamin D analogue

Di-iodohydroxyquinoline (rINN) see Appendix C

Dilevalol dï·*le*·va·lol
5-{(*R*)-1-Hydroxy-2-[(*R*)-1-methyl-3-
phenylpropylamino]ethyl}salicylamide; $C_{19}H_{24}N_2O_3$;
75659-07-3
Dilevalol Hydrochloride *75659-08-4*
Beta-adrenoceptor antagonist

Diloxanide (rINN) dï·*loks*·a·nïd
2,2-Dichloro-4′-hydroxy-*N*-methylacetanilide; $C_9H_9Cl_2NO_2$;
579-38-4
● **Diloxanide Furoate** *3736-81-0*
Antiprotozoal

Diltiazem (rINN) dil·*tï*·a·zem
(2*S*,3*S*)-5-(2-Dimethylaminoethyl)-2,3,4,5-tetrahydro-2-(4-
methoxyphenyl)-4-oxo-1,5-benzothiazepin-3-yl acetate;
$C_{22}H_{26}N_2O_4S$; *42399-41-7*
● **Diltiazem Hydrochloride** *33286-22-5*
Calcium channel blocker

Dimefline (rINN) see Appendix C

● **Dimenhydrinate** (rINN) dï·men·*hï*·dri·nät
2-Benzhydryloxyethyldimethylammonium 8-chloro-1,2,3,6-
tetrahydro-1,3-dimethyl-2,6-dioxo-7*H*-purin-7-ide;
$C_{17}H_{21}NO.C_7H_7ClN_4O_2$; *523-87-5*
Histamine H₁ receptor antagonist; antihistamine

Dimenoxadol (rINN) dï·men·*oks*·a·dol
2-Dimethylaminoethyl 2-ethoxy-2,2-diphenylacetate;
$C_{20}H_{25}NO_3$; *509-78-4*
Opioid receptor agonist

Dimepheptanol (rINN) dï·me·*fep*·ta·nol
6-Dimethylamino-4,4-diphenylheptan-3-ol; $C_{21}H_{29}NO$;
545-90-4
Opioid receptor agonist

The symbol '¬' in systematic chemical names signifies line continuation

mixture of isomers

Dimepregnen (rINN) dï·me·*preg*·nen
3β-Hydroxy-6α,16α-dimethylpregn-4-en-20-one; $C_{23}H_{36}O_2$;
21208-26-4
Antiestrogen

Dimepropion *see Metamfepramone*

● **Dimercaprol** (rINN) dï·mer·*ka*·prol
2,3-Dimercaptopropan-1-ol; BAL; $C_3H_8OS_2$; *59-52-9*
Chelating agent for use in heavy metal poisoning

and enantiomer

Dimesone (rINN) *dï*·me·sön
9α-Fluoro-11β,21-dihydroxy-16α,17α-dimethylpregna-1,4-
diene-3,20-dione; $C_{23}H_{31}FO_4$; *25092-07-3*
Cyclo-oxygenase inhibitor; analgesic; anti-inflammatory

Dimethisoquin *see Quinisocaine*

Dimethisterone (rINN) dï·me·*thi*·ste·rön
17β-Hydroxy-6α,21-dimethyl-17α-pregn-4-en-20-yn-3-one;
$C_{17}H_{24}N_2O$; *79-64-1*
Progestogen

Dimethothiazine *see Dimetotiazine*

Dimethoxanate (rINN) dï·me·*thoks*·a·nät
2-(2-Dimethylaminoethoxy)ethyl phenothiazine-10-carboxylate;
$C_{19}H_{22}N_2O_3S$; *477-93-0*
Cough suppressant

● **Dimethyl Sulfoxide** (rINN) dï·me·thïl sul·*foks*·ïd
Dimethyl sulfoxide; DMSO; C_2H_6OS; *67-68-5*
Pharmaceutical solvent; excipient

Dimethylthiambutene (rINN) dï·me·thïl·thï·am·*bú*·tën
Dimethyl[3,3-di-(2-thienyl)-1-methylprop-2-enyl]amine;
$C_{14}H_{17}NS_2$; *524-84-5*
Opioid receptor agonist

and enantiomer

Dimethyltubocurarine (rINN) dï·me·thïl·tü·bö·kûr·*rar*·rën
Dimethyl ether of (+)-tubocurarine; $C_{39}H_{46}N_2O_6$; *33335-58-9*
Opioid receptor agonist

(cation)

● **Dimeticone** (rINN) dï·*me*·ti·kön
Poly(dimethylsiloxane); each dimeticone name is followed
by a number referring to the viscosity of the substance:
eg dimeticone 20 (viscosity of 17·0 to 23·0 centistokes)
dimeticone 200 (viscosity of 190 to 210 centistokes); *9006-65-9*
Antifoaming agent; water repellent

Dimetindene (rINN) dï·*me*·tin·dën
Dimethyl(2-{3-[1-(2-pyridyl)ethyl]-1*H*-inden-2-yl}ethyl)¬
amine; $C_{20}H_{24}N_2$; *5636-83-9*
● **Dimetindine Maleate** *3614-69-5*
Histamine H_1 receptor antagonist; antihistamine

and enantiomer

Dimetotiazine (rINN) see Appendix C

♣ **Dimetridazole** (rINN) dï·me·*tri*·da·zôl
1,2-Dimethyl-5-nitroimidazole; $C_5H_7N_3O_2$; *551-92-8*
Antiprotozoal (veterinary)

Diminazene (rINN) dï·*mi*·na·zën
1,3-Bis(4-amidinophenyl)triazene; $C_{14}H_{15}N_7$; *536-71-0*
Diminazene Aceturate *908-53-4*
Antiprotozoal (veterinary)

♣ **Dimpylate** (rINN) *dim*·pi·lät
O,O-Diethyl *O*-(2-isopropyl-6-methylpyrimidin-4-yl) phosphorothioate; $C_{12}H_{21}N_2O_3PS$; *333-41-5*
Insecticide (veterinary)

♣ **Dinitolmide** (rINN) dï·*ni*·tol·mïd
3,5-Dinitro-*o*-toluamide; $C_8H_7N_3O_5$; *148-01-6*
Antiprotozoal (veterinary)

Dinoprost (rINN) *di*·nö·prost
(1) (*Z*)-7-{1*R*,2*R*,3*R*,5*S*)-3,5-Dihydroxy-2-[(*E*)-(3*S*)-3-hydroxyoct-1-enyl]cyclopentyl}hept-5-enoic acid;
(2) (5*Z*,13*E*)-(9*S*,11*R*,15*S*)-9,11,15-Trihydroxyprosta-5,13-dienoic acid; prostaglandin $F_{2\alpha}$; $C_{20}H_{34}O_5$; *537-11-1*
● **Dinoprost Trometamol** *38562-01-5*
Prostaglandin $F_{2\alpha}$ ($PGF_{2\alpha}$); inducer of uterine muscle contraction

● **Dinoprostone** (rINN) dï·nö·*pros*·tön
(1) (*Z*)-7-{(1*R*,2*R*,3*R*)-3-Hydroxy-2-[(*E*)-(3*S*)-3-hydroxyoct-1-enyl]-5-oxocyclopentyl}hept-5-enoic acid;
(2) (5*Z*,13*E*)-11*R*,15*S*-Dihydroxy-9-oxoprosta-5,13-dienoic acid; prostaglandin E_2; $C_{20}H_{32}O_5$; *363-24-6*
Prostaglandin E_2 (PGE_2); inducer of uterine muscle contraction

● **Diosmin** (rINN) dï·*os*·min
7-[[6-O-(6-Deoxy-α-L-mannopyranosyl)-β-D-glucopyranosyl]oxy]-5-hydroxy-2-(3-hydroxy-4-methoxy¬phenyl)-4*H*-1-benzopyran-4-one; $C_{28}H_{32}O_{15}$; *520-27-4*
Chronic venous insufficiency (flavonoid)

● **Dioxamate** (rINN) dï·*oks*·a·mät
2-Methyl-2-nonyl-1,3-dioxolan-4-ylmethyl carbamate; $C_{15}H_{29}NO_4$; *3567-40-6*
Treatment of Parkinson's disease

mixture of 4 isomers

Dioxaphetyl Butyrate (rINN) dï·oks·*a*·fë·tïl *bú*·ti·rät
Ethyl 4-morpholino-2,2-diphenylbutyrate; $C_{22}H_{27}NO_3$; *467-86-7*
Opioid receptor agonist

Dioxation (rINN) dï·oks·a·*ti*·on
A mixture consisting essentially of *cis*-and *trans-S,S'*-1,4-dioxan-2,3-diyl bis(*O,O*-diethyl phosphorodithioate); $C_{12}H_{26}O_6P_2S_4$; *78-34-2*
Organophosphorus insecticide

mixture of 4 stereoisomers

The symbol '¬' in systematic chemical names signifies line continuation

Dipenine Bromide *see Diponium Bromide*

Diperodon (rINN) dï·*pe*·rö·don
3-Piperidinopropylene bis(phenylcarbamate); $C_{22}H_{27}N_3O_4$; *101-08-6*
Local anaesthetic

and enantiomer

Diphemanil Metilsulfate (rINN) dï·*fe*·ma·nil
4-Benzhydrylidene-1,1-dimethylpiperidinium methylsulfate; $C_{21}H_{27}NO_4S$; *62-97-5*
Anticholinergic

Diphenadione (rINN) dï·fe·na·*di*·ön
2-Diphenylacetylindan-1,3-dione; $C_{23}H_{16}O_3$; *82-66-6*
Oral anticoagulant (indanedione)

Diphenhydramine (rINN) dï·fen·*hï*·dra·mën
2-Benzhydryloxyethyldimethylamine; $C_{17}H_{21}NO$; *58-73-1*
● **Diphenhydramine Hydrochloride** *147-24-0*
Histamine H_1 receptor antagonist; antihistamine

Diphenidol *see Difenidol*

Diphenoxylate (rINN) dï·fe·*noks*·i·lät
Ethyl 1-(3-cyano-3,3-diphenylpropyl)-4-phenylpiperidine-4-carboxylate; $C_{30}H_{32}N_2O_2$; *915-30-0*
● **Diphenoxylate Hydrochloride** *3810-80-8*
Opioid receptor agonist; treatment of diarrhoea

Diphenylpyraline (rINN) dï·fë·nïl·*pi*·ra·lën
4-Benzhydryloxy-1-methylpiperidine; $C_{19}H_{23}NO$; *147-20-6*
● **Diphenylpyraline Hydrochloride** *132-18-3*
Histamine H_1 receptor antagonist; antihistamine

Dipipanone (rINN) dï·*pi*·pa·nön
4,4-Diphenyl-6-piperidinoheptan-3-one; $C_{24}H_{31}NO$; *467-83-4*
● **Dipipanone Hydrochloride** *856-87-1*
Opioid receptor agonist

and enantiomer

Dipivefrine (rINN) dï·*pi*·ve·frën
(*RS*)-4-[1-Hydroxy-2-(methylamino)ethyl]-*o*-phenylene dipivalate; dipivefrin; $C_{19}H_{29}NO_5$; *52365-63-6*
● **Dipivefrine Hydrochloride** *64019-93-8*
Adrenaline prodrug; treatment of glaucoma

and enantiomer

Diponium Bromide (rINN) dï·*pö*·në·um brö·mïd
2-(Dicyclopentylacetoxy)ethyltriethylammonium bromide; $C_{20}H_{38}BrNO_2$; *2001-81-2*
Anticholinergic

Diprenorphine (rINN) dï·pre·*nor*·fën
(1) 2-[(−)-(5*R*,6*R*,7*R*,14*S*)-17-Cyclopropylmethyl-4,5-epoxy-3-hydroxy-6-methoxy-6,14-ethanomorphinan-7-yl]propan-2-ol;
(2) (6*R*,7*R*,14*S*)-17-Cyclopropylmethyl-7,8-dihydro-7-(1-hydroxy-1-methylethyl)-6-*O*-methyl-6,14-ethano-17-normorphine; $C_{26}H_{35}NO_4$; *14357-78-9*
♣ **Diprenorphine Hydrochloride** *16808-86-9*
Opioid receptor antagonist (veterinary)

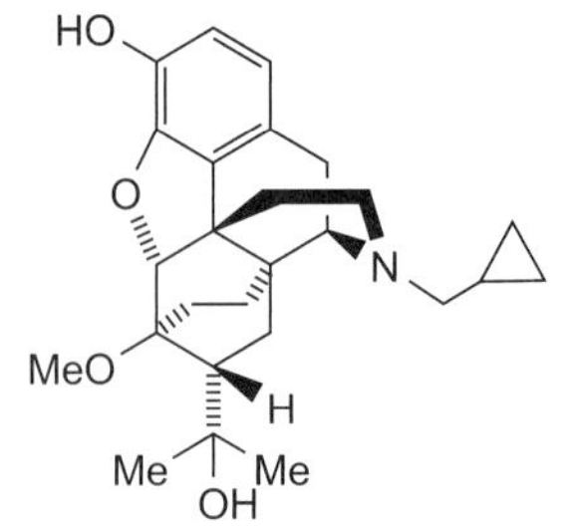

Diprobutine (rINN) see Appendix C

● **Diprophylline** (rINN) dï·*prö*·fi·lën
7-(2,3-Dihydroxypropyl)theophylline; $C_{10}H_{14}N_4O_4$; *479-18-5*
Non-selective phosphodiesterase inhibitor (xanthine);
treatment of reversible airways obstruction

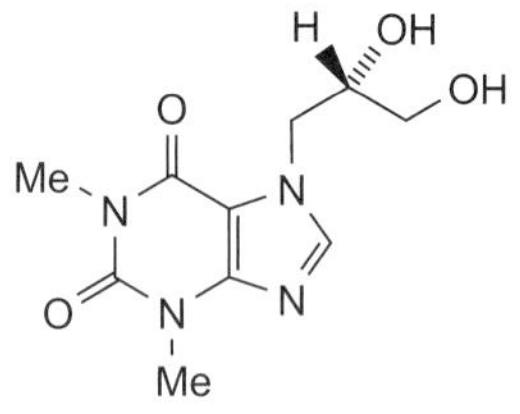

and enantiomer

Diproteverine (rINN) dï·prö·*te*·ver·rën
1-(3,4-Diethoxybenzyl)-3,4-dihydro-6,7-di-isopropoxy¬
isoquinoline; $C_{26}H_{35}NO_4$; *69373-95-1*
Diproteverine Hydrochloride *69373-88-2*
Calcium channel blocker; treatment of angina pectoris

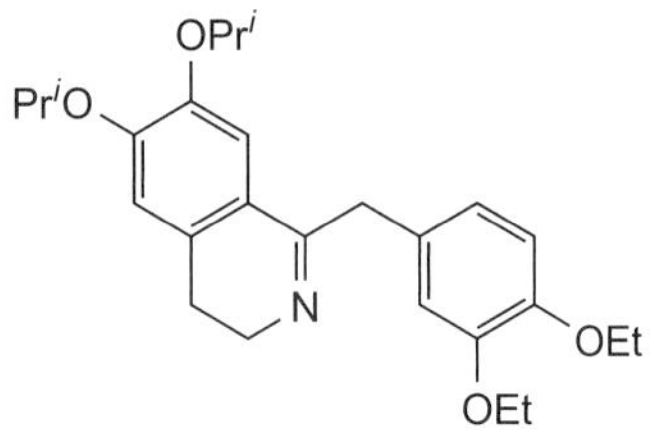

● **Dipyridamole** (rINN) dï·pi·*ri*·da·môl
2,2′,2″,2‴-{[4,8-Dipiperidinopyrimido[5,4-*d*]pyrimidine-2,6-
diyl]dinitrilo}tetraethanol; $C_{24}H_{40}N_8O_4$; *58-32-2*
Adenosine reuptake inhibitor; inhibitor of platelet aggregation

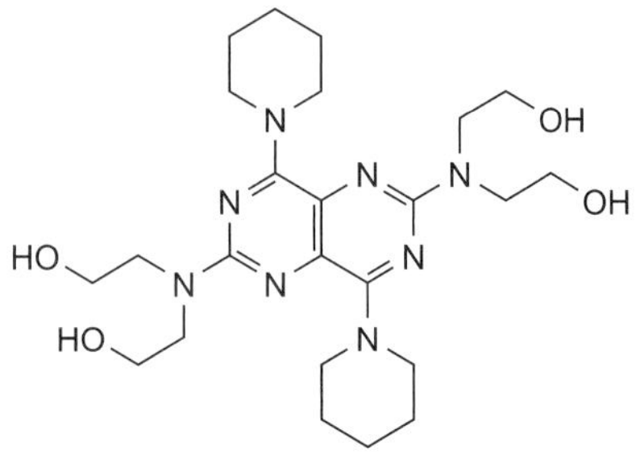

Dipyrone (BAN) dï·*pi*·rön
Sodium (2,3-dimethyl-5-oxo-1-phenyl-3-pyrazolin-4-yl)¬
(methyl)aminomethanesulfonate; noramidopyrine
methanesulfonate sodium (pINN); methampyrone;
metamizole sodium; $C_{13}H_{16}N_3NaO_4S$; *68-89-3*
Analgesic

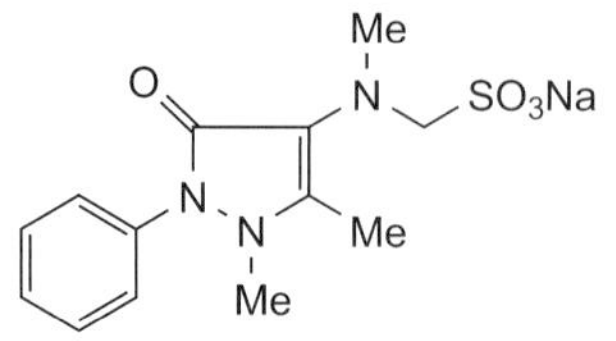

● **Diquafosol** (rINN) dï·*kwa*·fö·sol
P^1,P^4-bis(5^1-Uridyl) tetrahydrogen tetraphosphate;
$C_{18}H_{26}N_4O_{23}P_4$; *59985-21-6*
P2Y$_2$ receptor agonist; treatment of dry eyes

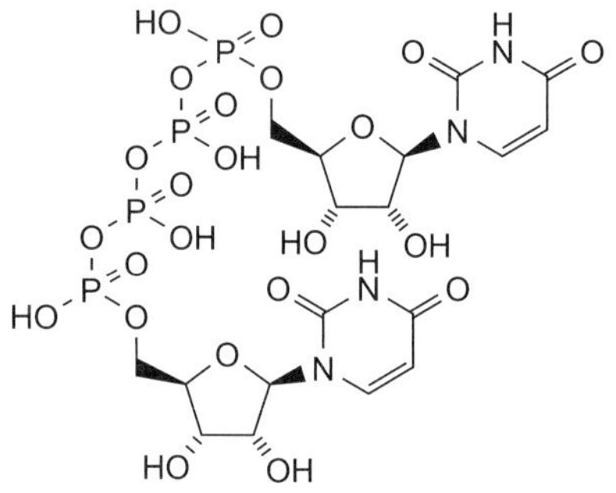

● **Dirithromycin** (rINN)di·ri·thrö·*mï*·cin
(1*R*,2*R*,3*R*,6*R*,7*S*,8*S*,9*R*,10*R*,12*R*,13*S*,15*R*,17*S*)-7-(2,6-Dideoxy-
3-*C*,3-*O*-dimethyl-α-L-*ribo*-hexopyranosyloxy)-3-ethyl-2,10-
dihydroxy-15-(2-methoxyethoxymethyl)-2,6,8,10,12,17-
hexamethyl-9-(3,4,6-trideoxy-3-dimethylamino-β-L-*xylo*-hex-
opyranosyloxy)-4,16-dioxa-14-azabicyclo[11.3.1]hepta¬
decan-5-one; $C_{42}H_{78}N_2O_{14}$; *62013-04-1*
Macrolide antibacterial

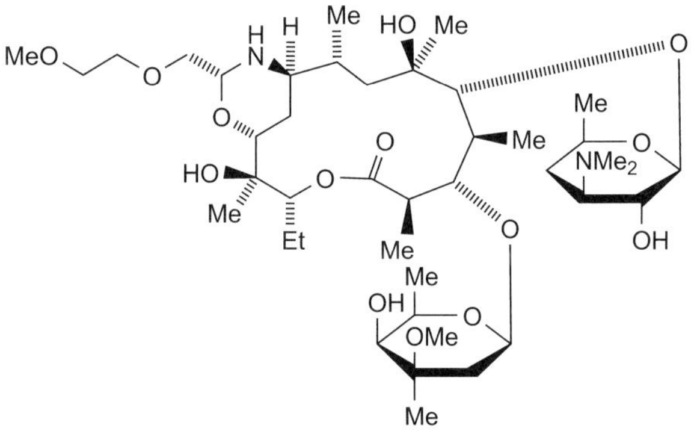

Disodium Edetate *see Edetic Acid*

Disofenin (rINN) see Appendix C

The symbol '¬' in systematic chemical names signifies line continuation

- **Disopyramide** (rINN) dï·sö·*pi*·ra·mïd
  4-Di-isopropylamino-2-phenyl-2-(2-pyridyl)butyramide;
  $C_{21}H_{29}N_3O$; *3737-09-5*
  - **Disopyramide Phosphate** *22059-60-5*
  Class I antiarrhythmic

and enantiomer

- **Dispersible Cellulose** (BAN)
  Microcrystalline cellulose containing about 10% of carmellose sodium
  Excipient

Distigmine Bromide (rINN) dï·*stig*·mën
3,3′-[*N*,*N*′-Hexamethylenebis(methylcarbamoyloxy)]bis(1-methylpyridinium bromide); $C_{22}H_{32}Br_2N_4O_4$; *15876-67-2*
Cholinesterase inhibitor

$2Br^-$

Disulfamide see Appendix C

- **Disulfiram** (rINN) dï·*sul*·fi·ram
  Tetraethylthiuram disulfide; $C_{10}H_{20}N_2S_4$; *97-77-8*
  Aldehyde dehyrogenase inhibitor; treatment of alcoholism

Disulphamide *see Disulfamide*

Dithiazanine (rINN) dï·thï·*a*·za·nën
3-Ethyl-2-[5-(3-ethyl-1,3-benzothiazol-2-ylidene)penta-1,3-dienyl]-1,3-benzothiazolium *(cation)*; $C_{23}H_{23}N_2S_2$; *514-73-8*
Antihelminthic

(cation)

- **Dithranol** (rINN) *di*·thra·nol
  1,8-Dihydroxyanthrone; dioxyanthranol; anthralin (USAN);
  $C_{14}H_{10}O_3$; *1143-38-0*; *480-22-8*
  Dithranol Triacetate *16203-97-7*
  Coal tar extract; treatment of psoriasis

Ditophal (rINN) *di*·tö·fal
S,*S*′-Diethyl dithioisophthalate; $C_{12}H_{14}O_2S_2$; *584-69-0*
Antileprosy drug

- **Dobutamine** (rINN) dö·*bú*·ta·mën
  (±)-4-[2-(3-*p*-Hydroxyphenyl-1-methylpropylamino)ethyl]pyrocatechol; $C_{18}H_{23}NO_3$; *34368-04-2*
  - **Dobutamine Hydrochloride** *49745-95-1*
  Beta₁-adrenoceptor agonist

and enantiomer

- **Docetaxel** (rINN) dö·së·*taks*·el
  tert-Butyl {(1*S*,2*R*)-2-[(2*S*,5*R*,7*S*,10*R*,13*S*)-4-acetoxy-2-benzoyloxy-1,7,10-trihydroxy-9-oxo-5,20-epoxytax-11-en-13-yloxycarbonyl]-2-hydroxy-1-phenylethyl}carbamate;
  $C_{43}H_{53}NO_{14}$; *114977-28-5*
  Taxane cytotoxic

- **Docusate Sodium** (rINN) *do*·kü·sät *sö*·dë·um
  Sodium 1,4-bis(2-ethylhexyloxycarbonyl)ethanesulfonate;
  dioctyl sodium sulfosuccinate; $C_{20}H_{37}NaO_7S$; *577-11-7*
  Stimulant laxative; faecal softener

mixture of stereoisomers

Dodicin (BAN) *dö·di·sin*
3,6,9-Triazahenicosanoic acid; $C_{18}H_{39}N_3O_2$; *6843-97-6*
Surface disinfectant

$Me-[CH_2]_{11}-\overset{H}{N}\frown\overset{H}{N}\frown\overset{H}{N}-COOH$

Dofamium Chloride (rINN) see Appendix C

Dofetilide (rINN) *dö·fe·ti·lïd*
4′-(2-{Methyl[4-(methylsulfonylamino)phenethyl] amino}¬
ethoxy)methanesulfonanilide; $C_{19}H_{27}N_3O_5S_2$; *115256-11-6*
Class III antiarrhythmic

Dolasetron (rINN) *do·la·së·tron*
(6R,8r,9aS)-3-Oxoperhydro-2H-2,6-methanoquinolizin-8-yl
indole-3-carboxylate; $C_{19}H_{20}N_2O_3$; *115956-12-2*
Dolasetron Mesilate *115956-13-3 (monohydrate)*
*Serotonin 5HT$_3$ receptor antagonist; treatment of nausea and
vomiting*

● **Domiphen Bromide** (rINN) *dö·mi·fen*
Dodecyldimethyl-2-phenoxyethylammonium bromide;
$C_{22}H_{40}BrNO$; *538-71-6*
Antiseptic

● **Domperidone** (rINN) *dom·pe·ri·dön*
5-Chloro-1-{1-[3-(2,3-dihydro-2-oxobenzimidazol-1-yl)propyl]-
4-piperidyl}-1,3-dihydrobenzimidazol-2-one; $C_{22}H_{24}ClN_5O_2$;
57808-66-9
● **Domperidone Maleate**
Peripheral dopamine receptor antagonist; antiemetic

Donepezil (rINN) *dö·ne·pe·zil*
(RS)-2-[(1-Benzyl-4-piperidyl)methyl]-5,6-dimethoxyindan-1-
one; $C_{24}H_{29}NO_3$; *142057-79-2*
Donepezil Hydrochloride *142057-77-0*
*Acetylcholinesterase inhibitor; treatment of dementia in
Alzheimer's disease*

and enantiomer

Donetidine (rINN) *do·ne·ti·dën*
5-(1,2-Dihydro-2-oxo-4-pyridylmethyl)-2-{2-[5-(dimethyl¬
aminomethyl)furfurylthio]ethylamino}pyrimidin-4(1H)-one;
$C_{20}H_{25}N_5O_3S$; *99248-32-5*
Histamine H$_1$ receptor antagonist

Dopamine (rINN) *dö·pa·mën*
4-(2-Aminoethyl)pyrocatechol; $C_8H_{11}NO_2$; *51-61-6*
● **Dopamine Hydrochloride** *62-31-7*
*Dopamine receptor antagonist; beta$_1$-adrenoceptor agonist;
alpha-adrenoceptor agonist*

Dopexamine (rINN) *dö·peks·a·mën*
4-{2-[6-(Phenethylamino)hexylamino]ethyl}pyrocatechol;
$C_{22}H_{32}N_2O_2$; *86197-47-9*
● **Dopexamine Hydrochloride** *86484-91-5*
Beta$_2$-adrenoceptor agonist; bronchodilator

The symbol '¬' in systematic chemical names signifies line continuation

Doramectin (rINN) dor·ra·*mek*·tin
(l0*E*,14*E*,16*E*)-(l*R*,4*S*,5′*S*,6*S*,6′*R*,8*R*,12*S*,13*S*,20*R*,21*R*,24*S*)-6′-
Cyclohexyl-5′,6′-dihydro-21,24-dihydroxy-5′,11,13,22-
tetramethyl-2-oxo-3,7,19-trioxatetracyclo[15.6.1.1^{4,8}.0^{20,24}]¬
pentacosa-10,14,16,22-tetraene-6-spiro-2′(2*H*-pyran)-12-yl 2,6-
dideoxy-4-*O*-(2,6-dideoxy-3-*O*-methyl-α-L-*arabino*-
hexopyranosyl)-3-*O*-methyl-α-L-*arabino*-hexopyranoside;
C$_{50}$H$_{74}$O$_{14}$; *117704-25-3*
Antihelminthic (veterinary)

Dornase Alfa (rINN) dor·näs al·fa
Recombinant human deoxyribonuclease I, derived from cloned
human pancreatic deoxyribonuclease I and having the same
amino acid sequence and glycosylation pattern as human
deoxyribonuclease I. It is capable of enzymatic digestion of
high molecular weight, leukocyte-derived, extracellular DNA;
143831-71-4
Mucolytic, DNA hydrolysis; treatment of cystic fibrosis

For labelling purposes, the following three letter code, to
indicate the method of production, is approved:
(rch) produced from genetically engineered Chinese hamster
ovary cells.

dornase alfa has the following amino acid sequence:

LKIAAFNIQT	FGETKMSNAT	LVSYIVQILS
RYDIALVQEV	RDSHLTAVGK	LLDNLNQDAP
DTYHYVVSEP	LGRNSYKERY	LFVYRPDQVS
AVDSYYYDDG	CEPCGNDTFN	REPAIVRFFS
RFTEVREFAI	VPLHAAPGDA	VAEIDALYDV
YLDVQEKWGL	EDVMLMGDFN	AGCSYVRPSQ
WSSIRLWTSP	TFQWLIPDSA	DTTATPTHCA
YDRIVVAGML	LRGAVVPDSA	LPFNFQAAYG
LSDQLAQAIS	DHYPVEVMLK	

Dorzolamide (rINN) dor·*zol*·a·mïd
(4*S*,6*S*)-4-Ethylamino-5,6-dihydro-6-methyl-4*H*-thieno[2,3-*b*]¬
thiopyran-2-sulfonamide 7,7-dioxide; C$_{10}$H$_{16}$N$_2$O$_4$S$_3$;
120279-96-1
● **Dorzolamide Hydrochloride** *130693-82-2*
*Carbonic anhydrase inhibitor; treatment of glaucoma and
ocular hypertension*

Dosulepin (rINN) dö·*sü*·le·pin
(*E*)-3-(Dibenzo[*b*,*e*]thiepin-11-ylidene)propyldimethylamine;
C$_{19}$H$_{21}$NS; *113-53-1*
● **Dosulepin Hydrochloride** *897-15-4 (monohydrate)*
Monoamine reuptake inhibitor; tricyclic antidepressant

Dothiepin *see Dosulepin*

Doxacurium Chloride (rINN) doks·a·*kur*′·rë·um
A mixture of the (1*R*,1′*S*,2*S*,2′*R*), (1*R*,1′*R*,2*S*,2′*S*) and
(1*S*,1′*S*,2*R*,2′*R*) stereoisomers (a *meso* isomer and two
enantiomers respectively) of 1,1′,2,2′, 3,3′,4,4′-octahydro-
6,6′,7,7′,8,8′-hexamethoxy-2,2′-dimethyl-1,1′-bis(3,4,5-
trimethoxybenzyl)-2,2′-[butanedioylbis(oxytrimethylene)]di-
isoquinolinium dichloride, each isomer being in a *trans*
configuration at the 1 and 2 positions of the isoquinolinium
rings; C$_{56}$H$_{78}$Cl$_2$N$_2$O$_{16}$;
83348-52-1 (total racemate); *106819-53-8 (meso-isomer)*
Non-depolarizing neuromuscular blocker

mixture of stereoisomers

Doxapram (rINN) *doks·a·pram*
(*RS*)-1-Ethyl-4-(2-morpholinoethyl)-3,3-diphenyl-2-pyrrolidone;
$C_{24}H_{30}N_2O_2$; *309-29-5*
● **Doxapram Hydrochloride** *7081-53-0; 113-07-5 (anhydrous)*
Respiratory stimulant

and enantiomer

Doxazosin (rINN) *doks·a·zö·sin*
2-[4-(2,3-Dihydro-1,4-benzodioxin-2-ylcarbonyl)piperazin-l-yl]-
6,7-dimethoxyquinazolin-4-ylamine; $C_{23}H_{25}N_5O_5$;
74191-85-8
● **Doxazosin Mesilate** *77883-43-3*
Alpha$_1$-adrenoceptor antagonist

Doxepin (rINN) *doks·ë·pin*
(*E*)-3-(Dibenz[*b,e*]oxepin-11-ylidene)propyldimethylamine;
$C_{19}H_{21}NO$; *1668-19-5*
● **Doxepin Hydrochloride** *1229-29-4*
Monoamine reuptake inhibitor; tricyclic antidepressant

Doxibetasol (rINN) *doks·ë·bë·ta·sol*
9α-Fluoro-11β,17α-dihydroxy-16β-methylpregna-1,4-
diene-3,20-dione; $C_{22}H_{29}FO_4$; *1879-77-2*
Glucocorticoid

Doxorubicin (rINN) *doks·ö·roo·bi·sin*
An anthracycline antibacterial produced by *Streptomyces*
coeruleorubidus or *S. peucetius* var. *coesius*; (8*S*,10*S*)-10-
[(3-amino-2,3,6-trideoxy-α-L-*lyxo*-hexopyranosyl)oxy]-8-
hydroxyacetyl-6,8,11-trihydroxy-1-methoxy-7,8,9,10-
tetrahydronaphthacene-5,12-dione; 3-hydroxyacetyl¬
daunorubicin; $C_{27}H_{29}NO_{11}$; *23214-92-8*
● **Doxorubicin Hydrochloride** *25316-40-9*
Anthracycline antibacterial; cytotoxic

Doxybetasol *see Doxibetasol*

● **Doxycycline** (rINN) *doks·ë·si·klën*
(1) (4*S*,4a*R*,5*S*,5a*R*,6*R*,12a*S*)-4-Dimethylamino-1,4,4a,5,5a,6,¬
11,12a-octahydro-3,5,10,12,12a-pentahydroxy-6-methyl-
1,11-dioxonaphthacene-2-carboxamide; (2) 6-Deoxy-5β-
hydroxytetracycline; $C_{22}H_{24}N_2O_8$; *564-25-0*
● **Doxycycline Hyclate** Doxycycline hydrochloride
hemiethanolate hemihydrate; *24390-14-5*
Tetracycline antibacterial

Doxycycline Fosfatex (BAN) *doks·ë·si·klën fos·fa·teks*
6-Deoxy-5β-hydroxytetracycline—metaphosphoric
acid—sodium metaphosphate in the ratio 3:3:1;
$(C_{22}H_{24}N_2O_8)_3 \cdot NaPO_3 \cdot (HPO_3)_3$; *83038-87-3*
Tetracycline antibacterial

Doxylamine (rINN) *doks·il·a·mën*
Dimethyl-2-[α-methyl-α-(2-pyridyl)benzyloxy]ethylamine;
$C_{17}H_{22}N_2O$; *469-21-6*
● **Doxylamine Succinate** *562-10-7*
Histamine H$_1$ receptor antagonist; antihistamine

and enantiomer

Draflazine (rINN) *dra·fla·zën*
(+)-1-(4-Amino-2,6-dichlorocarbaniloylmethyl)-4-
[5,5-bis(4-fluorophenyl)pentyl]piperazine-2-carboxamide;
$C_{30}H_{33}Cl_2F_2N_5O_2$; *120770-34-5*
*Nucleoside transport inhibitor; treatment of angina pectoris
(vasodilator)*

The symbol '¬' in systematic chemical names signifies line continuation

Dronedarone (rINN) drö·*ne*·dá·rön
N-[2-Butyl-3-{4-[3-(dibutylamino)propoxy]benzoyl}-5-benzofuranyl]methanesulfonamide;
$C_{31}H_{44}N_2O_5S$; *141626-36-0*;
Dronedarone Hydrochloride *141625-93-6*
Antiarrhythmic

● **Droperidol** (rINN) drö·*pe*·ri·dol
1-{1-[3-(4-Fluorobenzoyl)propyl]-1,2,3,6-tetrahydro-4-pyridyl}benzimidazolin-2-one; $C_{22}H_{22}FN_3O_2$; *548-73-2*
Dopamine receptor antagonist; Beta₁-adrenoceptor agonist; alpha-adrenoceptor agonist; neuroleptic

Dropropizine (rINN) drö·*prö*·pi·zën
3-(4-Phenylpiperazin-1-yl)propane-1,2-diol; $C_{13}H_{20}N_2O_2$;
17692-31-8
Cough suppressant

and enantiomer

● **Drospirenone** (rINN) drö·*spi*·re·nön
6β,7β:15β,16β-dimethylene-3-oxo-17α-pregn-4-ene-21-carbolactone; $C_{24}H_{30}O_3$; *67392-87-4*
Aldosterone receptor antagonist

Drostanolone (rINN) drö·*sta*·no·lön
17β-Hydroxy-2α-methyl-5α-androstan-3-one; dromostanolone;
$C_{20}H_{32}O_2$; *58-19-5*
Drostanolone Propionate *521-12-0*
Androgen

Drotebanol (rINN) drö·*te*·ba·nol
3,4-Dimethoxy-17-methylmorphinan-6,14-diol; $C_{19}H_{27}NO_4$;
3176-03-2
Opioid receptor agonist; cough suppressant

Drotrecogin Alfa (activated) (rINN) drö·tre·*ko*·jin
Blood coagulation factor XIV (human); *98530-76-8*
Antithrombotic

drotrecogin alfa (activated) has the following amino acid sequence:

ANSFLJJJRH	SSLJRJCIJJ	ICDFJJAKJI
FQNVDDTLAF	WSKHVDGDQC	LVLPLEHPCA
SLCCGHGTCI	BGIGSFSCDC	RSGWEGRFCQ
REVSFLNCSL	DNGGCTHYCL	EEVGWRRCSC
APGYKLGDDL	LKCHPAVKFP	CGRPWKRMEK
KRSHL		
		DTE
DQEDQVDPRL	IDGKMTRRGD	SWPQVVLLDS
KKKLACGAVL	IHPSWVLTAA	HCMDESKKLL
VRLGEYDLRR	WEKWELDLDI	KEVFVHPNYS
KSTTDNDIAL	LHLAQPATLS	QTIVPICLPD
SGLAERELNQ	AGQETLVTGW	GYHSSREKEA
KRNRTFVLNF	IKIPVVPHNE	CSEVMSNMVS
ENMLCAGILG	DRQDACEGDS	GGPMVASFHG
TWFLVGLVSW	GEGCGLLHNY	GVYTKVSRYL
DWIHGHIRDK	EAPQKSWAP	

* glycosylation sites

$$B = -NH{-}$$
$$J = -NH{-}$$

Droxypropine (rINN) see Appendix C

Duloxetine (rINN) dü·*loks*·e·tën
(*S*)-*N*-Methyl-3-(1-naphthyloxy)-3-(2-thienyl)propan-1-amine;
$C_{18}H_{19}NOS$; *116539-59-4*
Duloxetine Hydrochloride *136434-34-9*
Inhibition of 5HT and noradrenaline uptake; antidepressant

Dutasteride (rINN) dü·*ta*·ster·rïd
(1) 3-Oxo-2′,5′-bis(trifluoromethyl)-4-aza-5α-androst-1-ene-
17β-carboxanilide; (2) α,α,α,α′,α′,α′-Hexafluoro-3-oxo-4-aza-
5α-androst-1-ene-17β-carboxy-2′,5′-xylidide; $C_{27}H_{30}F_6N_2O_2$;
164656-23-9
*5-Alpha reductase inhibitor; treatment of benign prostatic
hyperplasia*

Dyclonine (rINN) dï·klö·nën
4′-Butoxy-3-piperidinopropiophenone; $C_{18}H_{27}NO_2$; *586-60-7*
Dyclonine Hydrochloride *536-43-6*
Local anaesthetic

● **Dydrogesterone** (rINN) dï·drö·*jes*·te·rön
9β,10α-Pregna-4,6-diene-3,20-dione; $C_{21}H_{28}O_2$; *152-62-5*
Progestogen

Dyflos (BAN) dï·flos
Di-isopropyl phosphorofluoridate; $C_6H_{14}FO_3P$; *55-91-4*
Acetylcholinesterase inhibitor

● **Ebastine** (rINN) *e*·ba·stën
4′-*tert*-Butyl-4-[4-(benzhydryloxy)piperidino]butyrophenone;
$C_{32}H_{39}NO_2$; *90729-43-4*
Histamine H_1 receptor antagonist; antihistamine

Ecogramostim (rINN) e·kö·gra·*mos*·tim
Recombinant methionyl human granulocyte macrophage
colony-stimulating factor; *123120-99-0*
*Recombinant methionyl human granulocyte macrophage
colony-stimulating factor*

ecogramostim has the following amino acid sequence:

```
MAPARSPSPS    TQPWEHVNAI    QEARRLLNLS

RDTAAEMNET    VEVISEMFDL    QEPTCLQTRL

ELYKQGLRGS    LTKLKGPLTM    IASHYKQHCP

PTPETSCATQ    IITFESFKEN    LKDFLLVIPF

DCWEPVQE
```

● **Econazole** (rINN) ë·*ko*·na·zôl
1-[2,4-Dichloro-β-(*p*-chlorobenzyloxy)phenethyl]imidazole;
$C_{18}H_{15}Cl_3N_2O$; *27220-47-9*
● **Econazole Nitrate** *68797-31-9*
Antifungal

and enantiomer

Ecothiopate Iodide (rINN) e·kö·*thï*·ö·pät
(2-Diethoxyphosphinylthioethyl)trimethylammonium iodide;
$C_9H_{23}INO_3PS$; *513-10-0*
Cholinesterase inhibitor; cholinergic

Ectylurea (rINN) ek·tïl·ûr·*rë*·a
(2-Ethylcrotonoyl)urea; $C_7H_{12}N_2O_2$; *95-04-5*
Hypnotic; anxiolytic

The symbol '¬' in systematic chemical names signifies line continuation

Eculizumab (rINN) e·*koo*·li·zü·mab
Immunoglobulin, anti-(human complement C5 α-chain)
(human-mouse monoclonal 5G1.1 heavy chain), disulfide with
human-mouse monoclonal 5G1.1 light chain, dimer;
219685-50-4
*Monoclonal antibody; treatment of paroxysmal nocturnal
haemoglobinuria*

eculizumab has the following amino acid sequence:

Heavy chain sequence:

QVQLVQSGAE	VKKPGASVKV	SCKASGYIFS
NYWIQWVRQA	PGQGLEWMGE	ILPGSGSTEY
TENFKDRVTM	TRDTSTSTVY	MELSSLRSED
TAVYYCARYF	FGSSPNWYFD	VWGQGTLVTV
SSASTKGPSV	FPLAPCSRST	SESTAALGCL
VKDYFPEPVT	VSWNSGALTS	GVHTFPAVLQ
SSGLYSLSSV	VTVPSSNFGT	QTYTCNVDHK
PSNTKVDKTV	ERKCCVECPP	CPAPPVAGPS
VFLFPPKPKD	TLMISRTPEV	TCVVVDVSQE
DPEVQFNWYV	GDVEVHNAKT	KPREEQFNST
YRVVSVLTVL	HQDWLNGKEY	KCKVSNKGLP
SSIEKTISKA	KGQPREPQVY	TLPPSQEEMT
KNQVSLTCLV	KGFYPSDIAV	EWESNGQPEN
NYKTTPPVLD	SDGSFFLYSR	LTVDKSRWQE
GNVFSCSVMH	EALHNHYTQK	SLSLSLGK

Light chain sequence:

DIQMTQSPSS	LSASVGDRVT	ITCGASENIY
GALNWYQQKP	GKAPKLLIYG	ATNLADGVPS
RFSGSGSGTD	FTLTISSLQP	EDFATYYCQN
VLNTPLTFGQ	GTKVEIKRTV	AAPSVFIFPP
SDEQLKSGTA	SVVCLLNNFY	PREAKVQWKV
DNALQSGNSQ	ESVTEQDSKD	STYSLSSTLT
LSKADYEKHK	VYACEVTHQG	LSSPVTKSFN
RGEC		

● **Edetic Acid** (rINN) e·*dë*·tik
Ethylenediaminetetra-acetic acid; $C_{10}H_{16}N_2O_8$; *60-00-4*
● **Disodium Edetate** *139-33-3*
Chelating agent

Edogestrone (rINN) e·dö·*jes*·trön
3,3-Ethylenedioxy-6-methyl-20-oxopregn-5-en-17α-yl acetate;
$C_{26}H_{38}O_5$; *809-01-8*
Progestogen

Edratide (rINN) ed·ra·tïd
glycyl-L-tyrosyl-L-tyrosyl-L-tryptophyl-L-seryl-L-tryptophyl-L-
isoleucyl-L-arginyl-L-glutaminyl-L-prolyl-L-prolylglycyl-L-
lysylglycyl-L-glutamyl-L-glutamyl-L-tryptophyl-L-isoleucyl⌐
glycine; $C_{111}H_{149}N_{27}O_{28}$; *433922-67-9*
Immunomodulator

```
H-Gly-Tyr-Tyr-Trp-Ser-Trp-Ile-Arg-Gin-Pro-
                                          10
   Pro-Gly-Lys-Gly-Glu-Glu-Trp-Ile-Gly-OH
                                        19
```

● **Edrophonium Chloride** (rINN) e·drö·*fö*·në·um
Ethyl(3-hydroxyphenyl)dimethylammonium chloride;
$C_{10}H_{16}ClNO$; *116-38-1*
Cholinesterase inhibitor

Efaroxan (rINN) e·fa·*roks*·an
(±)-2-(2-Ethyl-2,3-dihydrobenzo[*b*]furan-2-yl)-2-imidazoline;
$C_{13}H_{16}N_2O$; *89197-32-0*
Efaroxan Hydrochloride *89197-00-2*
Alpha₂-adrenoceptor antagonist

and enantiomer

Efavirenz (rINN) e·fa·*vîr*·renz
(*S*)-6-Chloro-4-(cyclopropylethynyl)-1,4-dihydro-4-
(trifluoromethyl)-3,1-benzoxazin-2-one; $C_{14}H_9ClF_3NO_2$;
154598-52-4
Non-nucleoside reverse transcriptase inhibitor; antiviral (HIV)

Eflornithine (rINN) ë·*flor*·ni·thën
2-Difluoromethyl-DL-ornithine; $C_6H_{12}F_2N_2O_2$; *67037-37-0*
Antiprotozoal

and enantiomer

Eformoterol *see Formoterol*

Efrotomycin (rINN) ë·frö·tö·*mï*·sin

An antibacterial produced by *Streptomyces lactamdurans* and comprising three components: efrotomycin A$_1$, efrotomycin A$_2$ (an isomer of A$_1$) and efrotomycin B; C$_{59}$H$_{88}$N$_2$O$_{20}$; *56592-32-6*

Efrotomycin A$_1$: (*R*)-2-{(2*R*,3*R*,4*R*,6*S*)-4-[6-Deoxy-4-*O*-(6-deoxy-2,4-di-*O*-methyl-α-L-*manno*-hexopyranosyl)-3-*O*-methyl-β-D-*allo*-hexopyranosyloxy]-2,3-dihydroxy-5,5-dimethyl-6-[(1*E*,3*Z*)-penta-1,3-dienyl]perhydropyran-2-yl}*N*-[(2*Z*,4*E*)-(6*S*,7*R*)-7-{(2*S*,3*S*,4*R*,5*R*)-5-[(1*E*,3*E*,5*E*)-7-(1,2-dihydro-4-hydroxy-1-methyl-2-oxo-3-pyridyl)-6-methyl-7-oxohepta-1,3,5-trienyl]tetrahydro-3,4-dihydroxy-2-furyl}6-methoxy-5-methylocta-2,4-dienyl]butyramide

Efrotomycin A$_2$: As for efrotomycin A$_1$, except that for '(1*E*,3*E*,5*E*)' read '(1*E*,3*E*,5*Z*)'

Efrotomycin B: (*R*)-2-{(2*R*,3*R*,4*R*,6*S*)-4-[6-Deoxy-4-*O*-(6-deoxy-2,4-di-*O*-methyl-α-L-*manno*hexopyranosyl)-3-*O*-methyl-β-D-*allo*-hexopyranosyloxy]-2,3-dihydroxy-5,5-dimethyl-6-[(1*E*,3*Z*)-penta-1,3-dienyl]perhydropyran-2-yl}*N*-[(2*Z*,4*E*)-(6*S*,7*R*)-7-{(2*S*,3*S*,4*R*,5*R*)-5-[(1*E*,3*E*)-4-(3,4,5,6-tetrahydro-3,6-dimethyl-4,5-dioxo-2*H*-pyrano[3,2-*c*]pyridin-2-yl)buta-1,3-dienyl]tetrahydro-3,4-dihydroxy-2-furyl}6-methoxy-5-methylocta-2,4-dienyl]butyramide

Antibacterial (veterinary)

Eletriptan (rINN) e·lë·*trip*·tan

(*R*)-2-[3-(1-Methylpyrrolidin-2-ylmethyl)indol-5-yl]ethyl phenyl sulfone; C$_{22}$H$_{26}$N$_2$O$_2$S; *143322-58-1*

Eletriptan Hydrobromide

Serotonin 5HT$_1$ receptor agonist; treatment of migraine

Elliptinium Acetate (rINN) e·lip·*ti*·në·um

9-Hydroxy-2,5,11-trimethyl-6*H*-pyrido[4,3-*b*]carbazolium acetate; C$_{20}$H$_{20}$N$_2$O$_3$; *58337-35-2*

Cytotoxic

Embramine (rINN) *em*·bra·mën

2-(4-Bromo-α-methylbenzhydryloxy)ethyldimethylamine; C$_{18}$H$_{22}$BrNO; *3565-72-8*

Histamine H$_1$ receptor antagonist; antihistamine

and enantiomer

Embutramide (rINN) em·*bú*·tra·mïd

N-(β,β-Diethyl-*m*-methoxyphenethyl)-4-hydroxybutyramide; C$_{17}$H$_{27}$NO$_3$; *15687-14-6*

Opioid receptor agonist; analgesic

Emedastine (rINN) e·me·*das*·tën

1-(2-Ethoxyethyl)-2-(4-methyl-1*H*-1,4-diazepan-1-yl)-benzimidazole; C$_{17}$H$_{26}$N$_4$O; *87233-61-2*

●**Emedastine Fumarate** (1:2) *87233-62-3*

Histamine H$_1$ receptor antagonist; antihistamine

Emepronium Bromide (rINN) e·me·*prö*·në·um

Ethyldimethyl(1-methyl-3,3-diphenylpropyl)ammonium bromide; C$_{20}$H$_{28}$BrN; *3614-30-0*

Anticholinergic

and enantiomer

Emepronium Carrageenate (BAN) e·me·*prö*·në·um ka·ra·*gë*·nät

The ethyldimethyl(1-methyl-3,3-diphenylpropyl)ammonium salt of carrageenan, a linear polysaccharide of sulfated galactose and 3,6-anhydrogalactose residues existing in two principal fractions (κ-and λ-carrageenan)

Anticholinergic

Emetine (BAN) *e*·me·tën

6′,7′,10,11-Tetramethyoxyemetan; C$_{29}$H$_{40}$N$_2$O$_4$; *483-18-1*

●**Emetine Hydrochloride** *316-42-7*

Antiprotozoal

Emiglitate (rINN) ë·*mig*·li·tät
Ethyl 4-{2-[(2*R*,3*R*,4*R*,5*S*)-3,4,5-trihydroxy-2-(hydroxymethyl)piperidino]ethoxy}benzoate; $C_{17}H_{25}NO_7$; *80879-63-6*
Alpha-glucosidase inhibitor; treatment of diabetes mellitus

Emylcamate (rINN) see Appendix C

Enalapril (rINN) ë·*na*·la·pril
N-{*N*-[(*S*)-1-Ethoxycarbonyl-3-phenylpropyl]-L-alanyl}-L-proline; $C_{20}H_{28}N_2O_5$; *75847-73-3*
● **Enalapril Maleate** *76095-16-4*
Angiotensin converting enzyme inhibitor

● **Enalaprilat** (rINN) ë·na·la·pri·*lat*
N-{*N*-[(*S*)-1-Carboxy-3-phenylpropyl]-L-alanyl}-L-proline; $C_{18}H_{24}N_2O_5$; *76420-72-9*
Angiotensin converting enzyme inhibitor

Enbucrilate (rINN) see Appendix C

Encainide (rINN) *en*·kā·nïd
2′-[2-(1-Methyl-2-piperidyl)ethyl]-*p*-anisanilide; $C_{22}H_{28}N_2O_2$; *37612-13-8*
Class I antiarrhythmic

Enciprazine (rINN) en·*si*·pra·zën
1-(4-*o*-Methoxyphenylpiperazin-1-yl)-3-(3,4,5-trimethoxyphenoxy)propan-2-ol; $C_{23}H_{32}N_2O_6$; *68576-86-3*
Enciprazine Hydrochloride *68576-88-5*
Anxiolytic

and enantiomer

Endralazine (rINN) en·*dra*·la·zën
6-Benzoyl-5,6,7,8-tetrahydropyrido[4,3-*c*]pyridazin-3-yl-hydrazine; $C_{14}H_{15}N_5O$; *39715-02-1*
Vasodilator; treatment of hypertension

Enflurane (rINN) en·flûr·rän
2-Chloro-1,1,2-trifluoroethyl difluoromethyl ether; $C_3H_2ClF_5O$; *13838-16-9*
General anaesthetic

and enantiomer

Enfuvirtide (rINN) en·*fü*·veer·tïd
159519-65-0
Antiviral (HIV)

enfuvirtide has the following amino acid sequence:

```
H3C-CO-Tyr-Thr-Ser-Leu-Ile-His-Ser-

Leu-Ile-Glu-Glu-Ser-Gln-Asn-Gln-

Gln-Glu-Leu-Leu-Glu-Leu-Asp-Lys-

Trp-Ala-Ser-Leu-Trp-Asn-Trp-Phe-NH2
```

♣ **Enilconazole** (rINN) e·nil·*ko*·na·zôl
(*RS*)-Allyl 1-(2,4-dichlorophenyl)-2-(imidazol-1-yl)ethyl ether; imazalil (BSI/ISO); $C_{14}H_{14}Cl_2N_2O$; *73790-28-0; 35554-44-0*
Antifungal (veterinary)

and enantiomer

Eniluracil (rINN) e·nil·*ûr*·ra·sil
5-Ethynylpyrimidine-2,4(1*H*,3*H*)-dione; $C_6H_4N_2O_2$; *59989-18-3*
Dihydropyrimidine dehydrogenase inhibitor; cytotoxic

Enoxacin (rINN) e·*noks*·a·sin
1-Ethyl-6-fluoro-1,4-dihydro-4-oxo-7-(piperazin-1-yl)-1,8-naphthyridine-3-carboxylic acid; $C_{15}H_{17}FN_4O_3$; *74011-58-8*
Fluoroquinolone antibacterial

Enoxaparin Sodium (rINN) ë·noks·*a*·pa·rin
A low-molecular-weight heparin, bearing at the non-reducing
end of its chain a (3*R*,4*S*)-3,4-dihydro-4-hydroxy-6-(sodio-
oxycarbonyl)-3-(sodio-oxysulfonyloxy)-2*H*-pyran-2-yl group
Low molecular weight heparin

Enoximone (rINN) e·*noks*·i·mön
4-Methyl-5-[4-(methylthio)benzoyl]-4-imidazolin-2-one;
$C_{12}H_{12}N_2O_2S$; *77671-31-9*
Inhibitor of phosphodiesterase type III; positive inotrope

Enoxolone (rINN) e·*noks*·o·lön
3β-Hydroxy-11-oxo-olean-12-en-30-oic acid; $C_{30}H_{46}O_4$;
471-53-4
Treatment of benign peptic ulcer disease

Enpiprazole (rINN) see Appendix C

Enprostil (rINN) en·*pros*·til
(1) Methyl (*E*)-(11*R*,15*R*)-11,15-dihydroxy-9-oxo-16-phenoxy-
17,18,19,20-tetranorprosta-4,5,13-trienoate; (2) Methyl 7-{(*E*)-
(1*R**,2*R**,3*R**)-3-hydroxy-2-[(3*R**)-3-hydroxy-4-phenoxybut-1-
enyl]-5-oxocyclopentyl}hepta-4,5-dienoate; $C_{23}H_{28}O_6$;
73121-56-9
Prostaglandin (PGF$_{2\alpha}$) analogue

and enantiomer

♣ **Enrofloxacin** (rINN) en·ro·*floks*·a·sin
1-Cyclopropyl-7-(4-ethylpiperazin-1-yl)-6-fluoro-1,4-dihydro-
4-oxoquinoline-3-carboxylic acid; $C_{19}H_{22}FN_3O_3$; *93106-60-6*
Fluoroquinolone antibacterial (veterinary)

Entacapone (rINN) en·*ta*·ka·pön
(*E*)-2-Cyano-3-(3,4-dihydroxy-5-nitrophenyl)-*N*,*N*-diethyl¬
acrylamide; $C_{14}H_{15}N_3O_5$; *130929-57-6*
*Catechol-O-methyl transferase inhibitor; treatment of
Parkinson's disease*

Epanolol (rINN) e·*pa*·no·lol
(*RS*)-*N*-[2-(3-*o*-Cyanophenoxy-2-hydroxypropylamino)ethyl]-
2-(4-ydroxyphenyl)acetamide; $C_{20}H_{23}N_3O_4$; *86880-51-5*
Beta-adrenoceptor antagonist

and enantiomer

Ephedrine (BAN) *e*·fe·drën
(1*R*,2*S*)-2-Methylamino-1-phenylpropan-1-ol; $C_{10}H_{15}NO$;
299-42-3 (anhydrous); *50906-05-3 (hemihydrate)*

Ephedrine Hydrochloride *50-98-6*
Ephedrine Sulfate *134-72-5*
Adrenoceptor agonist

Epicillin (rINN) e·pi·*si*·lin
(6*R*)-6-(α-D-Cyclohexa-1,4-dienylglycylamino)penicillanic acid;
$C_{16}H_{21}N_3O_4S$; *26674-90-3*
Penicillin antibacterial

Epiestriol (rINN) e·pë·*ës*·trë·ol
Estra-1,3,5(10)-triene-3,16β,17β-triol; $C_{18}H_{24}O_3$; *547-81-9*
Oestrogen

Epimestrol (rINN) e·pi·*mës*·trol
3-Methoxyestra-1,3,5(10)-triene-16α,17α-diol; $C_{19}H_{26}O_3$; *7004-98-0*
Oestrogen

Epinastine (rINN) e·pi·*na*·stën
(13b*RS*)-9,13b-Dihydro-1*H*-dibenzo[*c,f*]imidazo[1,5-*a*]¬ azepin-3-amine; $C_{16}H_{15}N_3$; *80012-43-7*;
•**Epinastine Hydrochloride**
Antihistamine

and enantiomer

Epioestriol *see Epiestriol*

Epirubicin (rINN) e·pi·*roo*·bi·sin
(8*S*,10*S*)-10-(3-Amino-2,3,6-trideoxy-α-L-*arabino*-hexopyranosyloxy)-8-glycolloyl-7,8,9,10-tetrahydro-6,8,11-trihydroxy-1-methoxynaphthacene-5,12-dione; $C_{27}H_{29}NO_{11}$; *56420-45-2*
• **Epirubicin Hydrochloride** *56390-09-1*
Anthracycline antibacterial; cytostatic

Epitizide (rINN) e·*pi*·tï·zïd
6-Chloro-3,4-dihydro-3-(2,2,2-trifluoroethylthiomethyl)-2*H*-1,2,4-benzothiadiazine-7-sulfonamide 1,1-dioxide; $C_{10}H_{11}ClF_3N_3O_4S_3$; *1764-85-8*
Thiazide diuretic

and enantiomer

Epitumomab (rINN) e·pi·*tü*·mö·mab
Mouse IgG 1 monoclonal antibody (HMFG1) that binds the human muc-1 gene product; *263547-71-3*
Monoclonal antibody (human episialin)

Epitumomab Cituxetan (rINN) e·pi·*tü*·mö·mab sï·*tuks*·e·tan
N-({4-[2-[*N,N*-bis(carboxymethyl)amino]-3-(*N*-{2-[*N,N*-bis(carboxymethyl)amino]ethyl}-*N*-[carboxymethyl]amino)¬ propyl]anilino}thiocarbonyl); (mouse IgG1 monoclonal antibody (HMFG1) that binds the human muc-1 gene product); *263547-71-3*
Monoclonal antibody (human episialin)

Ig-NH₂=Epitumomab

Eplerenone (rINN) e·*ple*·re·nön
9,11α-Epoxy-7α-(methoxycarbonyl)-3-oxo-17α-pregn-4-ene-21,17β-carbolactone; $C_{24}H_{30}O_6$; *107724-20-9*
Aldosterone receptor antagonist; antihypertensive

Eplivanserin (rINN) e·pli·*van*·ser·rin
(*E*)-1-(2-Fluorophenyl)-3-(4-hydroxyphenyl)prop-2-enone (*Z*)-*O*-[2-(dimethylamino)ethyl]oxime; $C_{19}H_{21}FN_2O_2$; *130579-75-8*
Serotonin 5HT$_{2a}$ receptor antagonist; treatment of sleep disorders

Epoetin Alfa (rINN) e·*pö*·e·tin al·fa
Recombinant human erythropoietin derived from a cloned human erythropoietin gene; *113427-24-0*
Erythropoietin analogue
For labelling purposes, the following three letter code, to indicate the method of production, is approved:
(rch) produced from genetically engineered Chinese hamster ovary cells

epoetin alfa has the following glycosylated amino acid sequence:

APPRLICDSR	VLERYLLEAK	EAENITTGCA
EHCSLNENIT	VPDTKVNFYA	WKRMEVGQQA
VEVWQGLALL	SEAVLRGQAL	LVNSSQPWEP
LQLHVDKAVS	GLRSLTTLLR	ALGAQKEAIS
PPDAASAAPL	RTITADTFRK	LFRVYSNFLR
GKLKLYTGEA	CRTGD	

Epoetin Beta (rINN) e·*pö*·e·tin *bë*·ta
Recombinant human erythropoietin, derived from a cloned human erythropoietin gene, having the same amino acid sequence as epoetin alfa but differing in the glycosylation pattern; *122312-54-3*
Erythropoietin analogue
For labelling purposes, the following three letter code, to indicate the method of production, is approved:
(rch) produced from genetically engineered Chinese hamster ovary cells

Epoetin Gamma (rINN) e·*pö*·e·tin ga·ma
Recombinant human erythropoietin derived from a cloned human erythropoetin gene and having the same amino acid sequence as epoetin alfa but differing in the glycosylation pattern; *130455-76-4*
Erythropoietin analogue
For labelling purposes, the following three letter code, to indicate the method of production, is approved:
(rch) produced from genetically engineered Chinese hamster ovary cells

Epoetin Delta (rINN) e·*pö*·e·tin del·ta
Recombinant human erythropoietin derived from a human erythropoetin gene and having the same amino acid sequence as epoetin alfa but differing in glycosylation pattern; *261256-80-3*
Erythropoietin analogue

Epoetin Theta (rINN) e·*pö*·e·tin *thë*·ta
Recombinant human erythropoietin, derived from a cloned human erythropoietin gene, having the same amino acid sequence as epoetin alfa but differing in the glycosylation pattern; *762263-14-9*
Erythropoietin analogue
For labelling purposes, the following three letter code, to indicate the method of production, is approved:
(rch) produced from genetically engineered Chinese hamster ovary cells

Epoprostenol Sodium (INNM) e·pö·*pros*·te·nol
(1) Sodium (*Z*)-5-{(3a*R*,4*R*,5*R*,6a*S*)-5-hydroxy-4-[(*E*)-(3*S*)-3-hydroxyoct-1-enyl]perhydrocyclopenta[*b*]furan-2-ylidene}¬ valerate; (2) Sodium (5*Z*,13*E*)-(9*S*,11*R*,15*S*)-6,9-epoxy-11,15-dihydroxyprosta-5,13-dienoate; prostacyclin sodium; $C_{20}H_{31}NaO_5$; *61849-14-7*
Prostaglandin I$_2$ (PGI$_2$)

Epostane (rINN) e·pö·stän
4α,5α-Epoxy-3,17β-dihydroxy-4β,17α-dimethyl-5α-androst-2-ene-2-carbonitrile; $C_{22}H_{31}NO_3$; *80471-63-2*
Antiprogestogenic; oxytocic

Epristeride (rINN) ë·*pris*·te·rïd
17β-(*tert*-Butylcarbamoyl)androsta-3,5-diene-3-carboxylic acid; $C_{25}H_{37}NO_3$; *119169-78-7*
5-Alpha-reductase inhibitor; treatment and control of benign prostatic hyperplasia

Eprosartan (rINN) e·prö·*sar*·tan
(*E*)-α-{2-Butyl-5-[2-carboxy-3-(2-thienyl)prop-1-enyl]-1*H*-imidazol-1-yl}-*p*-toluic acid; $C_{23}H_{24}N_2O_4S$; *133040-01-4*
Eprosartan Mesilate *133040-01-4*
Angiotensin II (AT$_1$) receptor antagonist

Epsiprantel (rINN) ep·si·*pran*·tel
2-Cyclohexylcarbonyl-1,2,3,4,6,7,8,12b-octahydropyrazino-[2,1-*a*][2]benzazepin-4-one; $C_{20}H_{26}N_2O_2$; *98123-83-2*
Antihelminthic

and enantiomer

The symbol '¬' in systematic chemical names signifies line continuation

Eptacog Alfa (Activated) (rINN) *ep·ta·kog al·fa*
Blood-coagulation factor VII (human clone λHVII2463 protein moiety); *102786-52-7*
Recombinant factor VIIa

eptacog alfa has the following amino acid sequence:

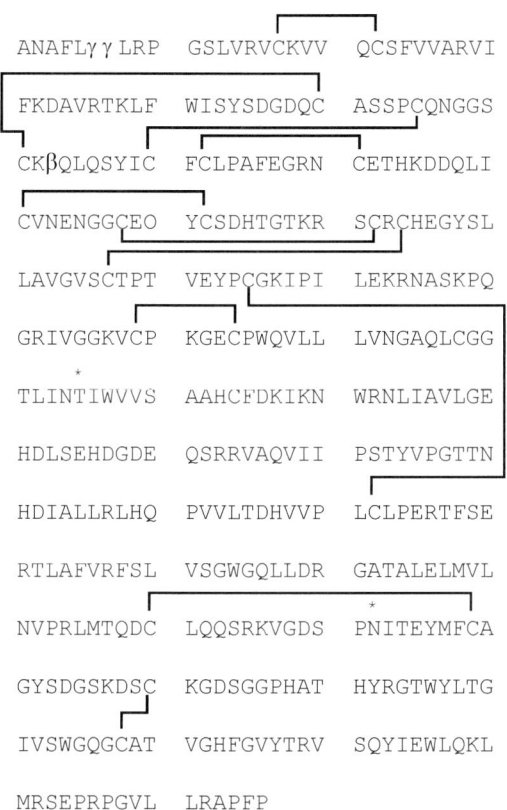

ANAFLγγLRP GSLVRVCKVV QCSFVVARVI

FKDAVRTKLF WISYSDGDQC ASSPCQNGGS

CKβQLQSYIC FCLPAFEGRN CETHKDDQLI

CVNENGGCEO YCSDHTGTKR SCRCHEGYSL

LAVGVSCTPT VEYPCGKIPI LEKRNASKPQ

GRIVGGKVCP KGECPWQVLL LVNGAQLCGG

TLINTIWVVS AAHCFDKIKN WRNLIAVLGE

HDLSEHDGDE QSRRVAQVII PSTYVPGTTN

HDIALLRLHQ PVVLTDHVVP LCLPERTFSE

RTLAFVRFSL VSGWGQLLDR GATALELMVL

NVPRLMTQDC LQQSRKVGDS PNITEYMFCA

GYSDGSKDSC KGDSGGPHAT HYRGTWYLTG

IVSWGQGCAT VGHFGVYTRV SQYIEWLQKL

MRSEPRPGVL LRAPFP

★ = glycosylation sites
β = β-hydroxyaspartic acid
γ = γ-carboxyglutamic acid

Eptifibatide (rINN) *ep·ti·fi·ba·tïd*
S^1,S^6-Cyclo[N^6-carbamimidoyl-N^2-(3-sulfanylpropanoyl)-L-lysylglycyl-L-α-aspartyl-L-tryptophyl-L-prolyl-L-cysteinamide]; $C_{35}H_{49}N_{11}O_9S_2$; *148031-34-9*
Glycoprotein IIb/IIIa receptor inhibitor; antiplatelet drug

```
     S ───────────────────────────────┐
     |                                 |
        HN    NH₂                      |
          \ //                         |
           N⁶                          |
     CH₂·CH₂·CO-Lys-Gly-Asp-Trp-Pro-Cys-NH₂
```

Eptotermin alfa (rINN) *ep·tö·ter·min al·fa*
Human recombinant bone morphogenetic protein 7 (hrBMP-7) or osteogenic protein-1 (OP-1); *129805-33-0*
Bone morphogenetic protein (growth factor); orthopaedic surgery

eptotermin has the following amino acid sequence:

STGSKQRSQN RSKTPKNQEA LRMANVAENS SSDQRQACKK

HELYVSFRDL GWQDWIIAPE GYAAYYCEGE CAFPLNSYMN

ATNHAIVQTL VHFINPETVP KPCCAPTQLN AISVLYFDDS

SNVILKKYRN MVVRACGCH

Erbulozole (rINN) *er·bü·lo·zôl*
Ethyl(2RS, 4RS)-4-[2-(imidazol-1-ylmethyl)-2-(4-methoxy¬phenyl)-1,3-dioxolan-4-ylmethylthio]carbanilate; $C_{24}H_{27}N_3O_5S$; *124784-31-2*
Microtubulin inhibitor; cytotoxic

and enantiomer

Erdosteine (rINN) *er·do·stën*
({2-Oxo-2-[(2-oxothiolan-3-yl)amino]ethyl}sulfanyl)acetic acid; $C_8H_{11}NO_4S_2$; *84611-23-4*
Mucolytic

● **Ergocalciferol** (rINN) *er·gö·kal·si·fe·rol*
(5Z,7E)-(3S)-9,10-Secoergosta-5,7,10(19),22-tetraen-3-ol; vitamin D_2; calciferol; $C_{28}H_{44}O$; *50-14-6*
Vitamin D analogue (vitamin D_2)

Ergometrine (rINN) *er·gö·me·trën*
(1) 9,10-Didehydro-N-[(S)-2-hydroxy-1-methylethyl]-6-methyl-ergoline-8β-carboxamide; (2) N^8-(2-Hydroxy-1-methylethyl)-D-lysergamide; $C_{19}H_{23}N_3O_2$; *60-79-7*
● **Ergometrine Maleate** ergonovine maleate (USAN); *129-51-1*
Oxytocic

Ergotamine (rINN) *er·go·ta·mën*
(5′S)-5′-Benzyl-9,10-dihydro-12′-hydroxy-2′-methyl-3′,6′,18-trioxoergotaman; $C_{33}H_{35}N_5O_5$; *113-15-5*
● **Ergotamine Tartrate** *379-79-3*
Oxytocic

Erlotinib (rINN) er·*lot*·in·ib

N-(3-Ethynylphenyl)-6,7-bis(2-methoxyethoxy)quinazolin-4-amine; $C_{22}H_{23}N_3O_4$; *183321-74-6*

Erlotininb Hydrochloride *183319-69-9*

Tyrosine kinase inhibitor acting on epidermal growth factor receptors; treatment of cancer

Ertapenem (rINN) er·ta·*pen*·em

(4R,5S,6S)-3-{[(3S,5S)-5-[(3-Carboxyphenylcarbamoyl)¬pyrrolidin-3-ylthio]}-6-[(R)-1-hydroxyethyl]-4-methyl-7-oxo-1-azabicyclo[3.2.0]hept-2-ene-2-carboxylic acid; $C_{22}H_{25}N_3O_7S$; *153832-46-3*

Carbapenem antibacterial

● **Erythromycin** (rINN) e·ri·thrö·*mï*·sin

A mixture of macrolide antibiotics produced by a strain of *Streptomyces erythreus*. The major component is erythromycin A.

Erythromycine A: (2R,3S,4S,5R,6R,8R,10R,11R,12S,13R)-5-(3-Amino-3,4,6-trideoxy-N,N-dimethyl-β-D-*xylo*-hexopyranosyl¬oxy)-3-(2,6-dideoxy-3-C,3-O-dimethyl-α-L-*ribo*-hexopyranosyloxy)-13-ethyl-6,11,12-trihydroxy-2,4,6,8,10,12-hexamethyl-9-oxotridecan-13-olide; $C_{37}H_{67}NO_{13}$; *114-07-8*

● **Erythromycin Ethyl Succinate** *41342-53-4*

● **Erythromycin Lactobionate** *3847-29-8*

● **Erythromycin Stearate** *643-22-1*

Erythromycin Thiocyanate *7704-67-8*

Macrolide antibacterial

● **Erythromycin Estolate** (INNM)

Erythromycin 2′-propionate dodecyl sulfate; $C_{40}H_{71}NO_{14}\cdot C_{12}H_{26}O_4S$; *3521-62-8*

Macrolide antibacterial

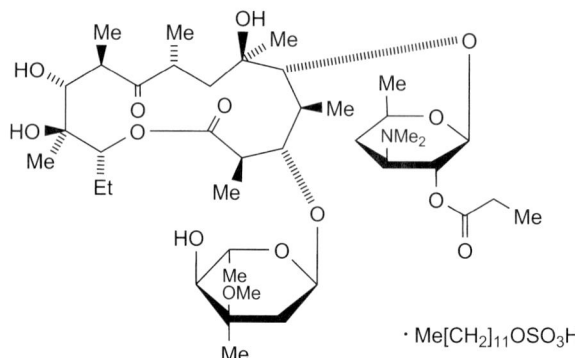

● Erythropoetin *see Epoetin Alfa, Epoetin Beta, Epoetin Gamma, Epoetin Delta and Epoetin Theta*

Escitalopram (rINN) e·sï·*ta*·lö·pram

(S)-1-(3-Dimethylaminopropyl)-1-(4-fluorophenyl)-1,3-dihydroisobenzofuran-5-carbonitrile; $C_{20}H_{21}FN_2O$; *128196-01-0*

Escitalopram Oxalate *219861-08-2*

Selective serotonin reuptake inhibitor; antidepressant

Esflurbiprofen (rINN) es·flûr·*bï*·prö·fen

(S)-2-(2-Fluorobiphenyl-4-yl)propionic acid; $C_{15}H_{13}FO_2$; *51543-39-6*

Cyclo-oxygenase inhibitor; analgesic; anti-inflammatory

Esketamine (rINN) es·*ke*·ta·mën

(S)-2-(2-Chlorophenyl)-2-(methylamino)cyclohexanone; $C_{13}H_{16}ClNO$; *33643-46-8*

● **Esketamine Hydrochloride** *33795-24-3*

General anaesthetic

Eslicarbazepine (rINN) es·li·*kar*·ba·ze·pën

(10S)-10-Hydroxy-10,11-dihydro-5H-dibenzo[b,f]azepin-5-carboxamide; $C_{15}H_{14}N_2O_2$; *104746-04-5*

Eslicarbazepine Acetate *236395-14-5*

Antiepileptic

Esmolol (rINN) *es·mo·lol*
Methyl 3-[4-(2-hydroxy-3-isopropylaminopropoxy)phenyl]¬
propionate; $C_{16}H_{25}NO_4$; *84057-94-3*
Esmolol Hydrochloride *81161-17-3*
Beta-adrenoceptor antagonist

and enantiomer

Esomeprazole (rINN) e·sö·*me*·pra·zôl
(*S*)-5-Methoxy-2-[(4-methoxy-3,5-dimethyl-2-pyridyl)methyl¬
sulfinyl]benzimidazole; $C_{17}H_{19}N_3O_3S$
●**Esomeprazole Magnesium**
Proton pump inhibitor; treatment of peptic ulcer disease

Espatropate (rINN) es·*pa*·trö·pät
(*R*)-Quinuclidin-3-yl (*R*)-3-hydroxy-2-1*H*-(imidazol-1-yl)-2-
phenylpropionate; $C_{19}H_{23}N_3O_3$; *132829-83-5*
Anticholinergic

●**Estradiol** (rINN) ë·stra·*di*·ol
Estra-1,3,5(10)-triene-3,17β-diol; $C_{18}H_{24}O_2$; *50-28-2*
●**Estradiol Benzoate** *50-50-0*
●**Estradiol Valerate** *979-32-8*
Oestrogen

Estramustine (rINN) ës·tra·*mus*·tën
17β-Hydroxyestra-1,3,5(10)-trien-3-yl 3-bis(2-chloroethyl)¬
carbamate; $C_{23}H_{31}Cl_2NO_3$; *2998-57-4*
●**Estramustine Sodium Phosphate** *52205-73-9*
Cytotoxic alkylating agent

●**Estriol** (rINN) *ës*·trë·ol
Estra-1,3,5(10)-triene-3,16α,17β-triol; $C_{18}H_{24}O_3$; *50-27-1*
Oestrogen

Estriol Sodium Succinate (rINN)
Disodium 3-hydroxy-estra-1,3,5(10)-triene-16α,17β-diyl
disuccinate; $C_{26}H_{30}Na_2O_9$; *113-22-4*
Oestrogen

Estriol Succinate (rINN)
3-Hydroxy-estra-1,3,5(10)-triene-16α,17β-diyl di(hydrogen
succinate); $C_{26}H_{32}O_9$; *514-68-1*
Oestrogen

Estrone (rINN) *ës*·trön
3β-Hydroxyestra-1,3,5(10)-trien-17-one; $C_{18}H_{22}O_2$; *53-16-7*
Oestrogen

●**Estropipate** (rINN) ës·*trö*·pi·pät
17-Oxestra-1,3,5-(10)-trien-3-yl hydrogen sulfate—piperazine
(1:1); piperazine estrone sulfate; $C_{18}H_{22}O_5S \cdot C_4H_{10}N_2$; *7280-37-7*
Oestrogen

110

● **Etacrynic Acid** (rINN) e·ta·*krï*·nik
[2,3-Dichloro-4-(2-ethylacryloyl)phenoxy]acetic acid;
$C_{13}H_{12}Cl_2O_4$; *58-54-8*
Loop diuretic

Etafedrine (rINN) see Appendix C

Etamiphylline (rINN) e·ta·*mi*·fi·lën
7-(2-Diethylaminoethyl)theophylline; $C_{13}H_{21}N_5O_2$; *314-35-2*
♣ **Etamiphylline Camsilate** *19326-29-5*
Non-selective phosphodiesterase inhibitor (xanthine); treatment of reversible airways obstruction

Etamivan (rINN) e·*ta*·mi·van
N,N-Diethylvanillamide; $C_{12}H_{17}NO_3$; *304-84-7*
Respiratory stimulant

● **Etamsylate** (rINN) e·*tam*·si·lät
Diethylammonium 2,5-dihydroxybenzenesulfonate;
$C_6H_6O_5S·C_4H_{11}N$; *2624-44-4*
Antifibrinolytic

Etanercept (rINN) e·*tan*·er·sept
1–235-Tumour necrosis factor receptor (human) fusion protein with 236–467-immunoglobulin G1 (human) γ1-chain Fc fragment, dimer; *185243-69-0*
Human tumour necrosis factor receptor

etanercept has the following amino acid sequence:

LPAQVAFTPY	APEPGSTCRL	REYYDQTAQM
CCSKCSPGQH	AKVFCTKTSD	TVCDSCEDST
YTQLWNWVPE	CLSCGSRCSS	DQVETQACTR
EQNRICTCRP	GWYCALSKQE	GCRLCAPLRK
CRPGFGVARP	GTETSDVVCK	PCAPGTFSNT
TSSTDICRPH	QICNVVAIPG	NASMDAVCTS
TSPTRSMAPG	AVHLPQPVST	RSQHTQPTPE
PSTAPSTSFL	LPMGPSPPAE	GSTGDEPKSC
DKTHTCPPCP	APELLGGPSV	FLFPPKPKDT
LMISRTPEVT	CVVVDVSHED	PEVKFNWYVD
GVEVHNAKTK	PREEQYNSTY	RVVSVLTVLH
QDWLNGKEYK	CKVSNKALPA	PIEKTISKAK
GQPREPQVYT	LPPSREEMTK	NQVSLTCLVK
GFYPSDIAVE	WESNGQPENN	YKTTPPVLDS
DGSFFLYSKL	TVDKSRWQQG	NVFSCSVMHE
ALHNHYTQKS	LSLSPGK	

2

Etebenecid (rINN) et·ë·*be*·ne·sid
4-Diethylsulfamoylbenzoic acid; $C_{11}H_{15}NO_4S$; *1213-06-5*
Uricosuric

Etenzamide *see Ethenzamide*

Eterobarb (rINN) e·*te*·rö·barb
5-Ethyl-1,3-bis(methoxymethyl)-5-phenylperhydropyrimidine-2,4,6-trione; $C_{16}H_{20}N_2O_5$; *27511-99-5*
Anticonvulsant

Ethacridine (rINN) e·*tha*·kri·dën
7-Ethoxyacridine-3,9-diamine; $C_{15}H_{15}N_3O$; *442-16-0*
● **Ethacridine Lactate** *1837-57-6; 6402-23-9 (monohydrate)*
Antiseptic

Ethacrynic Acid *see Etacrynic Acid*

Ethambutol (rINN) e·*tham*·bü·tol
(*S*,*S*)-*N*,*N'*-Ethylenebis(2-aminobutan-1-ol); $C_{10}H_{24}N_2O_2$;
74-55-5
● **Ethambutol Hydrochloride** *1070-11-7*
Antituberculosis drug

Ethamivan *see Etamivan*

Ethamsylate *see Etamsylate*

Ethchlorvynol (rINN) eth·klor·*vï*·nol
1-Chloro-3-ethylpent-1-en-4-yn-3-ol; C_7H_9ClO; *118-18-8*
Hypnotic

and enantiomer

Ethebenecid *see Etebenecid*

Ethenzamide (rINN) e·*then*·za·mïd
2-Ethoxybenzamide; $C_9H_{11}NO_2$; *938-73-8*
Salicylate; non-selective cyclo-oxygenase inhibitor; antipyretic;
analgesic; anti-inflammatory

Ethiazide (rINN) e·*thï*·a·zïd
(*RS*)-6-Chloro-3-ethyl-3,4-dihydro-2*H*-1,2,4-benzothiadiazine-
7-sulfonamide 1,1-dioxide; $C_9H_{12}ClN_3O_4S_2$; *1824-58-4*
Thiazide diuretic

and enantiomer

Ethinamate (rINN) e·*thi*·na·mät
1-Ethynylcyclohexyl carbamate; $C_9H_{13}NO_2$; *126-52-3*
Thiazide diuretic

● **Ethinylestradiol** (rINN) e·thi·nïl·ë·stra·*di*·ol
19-Nor-17α-pregna-1,3,5(10)-trien-20-yne-3,17β-diol;
$C_{20}H_{24}O_2$; *57-63-6*
Oestrogen

● **Ethionamide** (rINN) e·*thï*·on·a·mïd
2-Ethylpyridine-4-carbothioamide; $C_8H_{10}N_2S$; *536-33-4*
Antituberculosis drug

Ethisterone (rINN) e·*thi*·ste·rön
17β-Hydroxy-17α-pregn-4-en-20-yn-3-one; $C_{21}H_{28}O_2$;
434-03-7
Oestrogen

Ethoglucid *see Etoglucid*

Ethoheptazine (rINN) e·thö·*hep*·ta·zën
Ethyl 1-methyl-4-phenylperhydroazepine-4-carboxylate;
$C_{16}H_{23}NO_2$; *77-15-6*
Ethoheptazine Citrate *2085-42-9*
Opioid analgesic

Ethomoxane (rINN) e·thö·*moks*·än
(*RS*)-Butyl(8-ethoxy-1,4-benzodioxan-2-ylmethyl)amine;
$C_{15}H_{23}NO_3$; *16509-23-2*
Alpha-adrenoceptor antagonist

and enantiomer

♣ **Ethopabate** (BAN) e·thö·pa·bät
Methyl 4-acetamido-2-ethoxybenzoate; $C_{12}H_{15}NO_4$; *59-06-3*
Antiprotozoal

Ethopropazine *see Profenamine*

Ethosalamide *see Etosalamide*

● **Ethosuximide** (rINN) e·thö·*suk*·si·mïd
(*RS*)-2-Ethyl-2-methylsuccinimide; $C_7H_{11}NO_2$; *77-67-8*
Antiepileptic

Ethotoin (rINN) see Appendix C

Ethybenztropine *see Etybenzatropine*

Ethyl Biscoumacetate (rINN) bis·koo·*ma*·së·tät
Ethyl bis(4-hydroxy-2-oxo-2*H*-chromen-3-yl)acetate; $C_{22}H_{16}O_8$; *548-00-5*
Vitamin K epoxide reductase inhibitor; oral anticoagulant (coumarin)

Ethyl Dibunate (rINN) see Appendix C

Ethyl Pyrophosphate (rINN) pï·rö·*fos*·fät
Tetraethyl pyrophosphate; $C_8H_{20}O_7P_2$
Cholinesterase inhibitor

Ethylestrenol (rINN) ë·thïl·*ës*·tre·nol
19-Nor-17α-pregn-4-en-17β-ol; $C_{20}H_{32}O$; *965-90-2*
Anabolic steroid; androgen

Ethylmethylthiambutene (rINN) ë·thïl·më·thïl·thï·am·*bü*·tën
[3,3-Di-(2-thienyl)-1-methylprop-2-enyl]ethylmethylamine; $C_{15}H_{19}NS_2$; *441-61-2*
Opioid receptor agonist; analgesic

and enantiomer

Ethylmorphine (BAN) ë·thïl·*mor*·fën
7,8-Didehydro-4,5-epoxy-3-ethoxy-17-methylmorphinan-6-ol; $C_{19}H_{23}NO_3$; *76-58-4*
● **Ethylmorphine Hydrochloride** *125-30-4*
Opioid receptor agonist; analgesic

Ethyloestrenol *see Ethylestrenol*

Ethynodiol *see Etynodiol*

Etidocaine (rINN) see Appendix C

Etidronic Acid (rINN) e·ti·*dron*·ik
1-Hydroxyethylidenedi(phosphonic acid); $C_2H_8N_7P_2$; *2809-21-4*
● **Etidronate Disodium** *7414-83-7*
Bisphosphonate; treatment of osteoporosis; Paget's disease

Etifenin (rINN) e·ti·*fen*·in
2,6-Diethylphenylcarbamoylmethyliminodi(acetic acid); $C_{16}H_{22}N_2O_5$; *63245-28-3*
Investigation of the hepatobiliary system

Etifoxine (rINN) see Appendix C

Etilefrine (rINN) e·til·*e*·frën
(*RS*)-2-Ethylamino-1-(3-hydroxyphenyl)ethanol; $C_{10}H_{15}NO_2$; *709-55-7*
● **Etilefrine Hydrochloride** *943-17-9*
Adrenoceptor agonist

and enantiomer

Etiprednol Dicloacetate (rINN) e·ti·*pred*·nol di·clö·*a*·së·tät
Ethyl 17α-(dichloroacetoxy)-11β-hydroxy-3-oxoandrosta-1,4-diene-17β-carboxylate; $C_{24}H_{30}Cl_2O_6$; *199331-40-3*
Glucocorticoid

Etisazole (rINN) e·*ti*·sa·zôl
1,2-Benzothiazol-3-yl(ethyl)amine; $C_9H_{10}N_2S$; *7716-60-1*
Antifungal

Etisomicin (rINN) e·ti·sö·*mi*·sin
(1) 4-*O*-[(2*S*,3*R*)-*cis*-3-Amino-6-aminomethyl-3,4-dihydro-2*H*-pyran-2-yl]-2-deoxy-6-*O*-(3-deoxy-4-*C*-methyl-3-ethylamino-β-L-arabinopyranosyl)-D-streptamine; (2) 2-Deoxy-6-*O*-(3-deoxy-4-*C*-methyl-3-ethylamino-β-L-arabinopyranosyl)-4-*O*-(2,6-diamino-2,3,4,6-tetradeoxy-α-D-*glycero*-hex-4-enopyranosyl)-D-streptamine; $C_{20}H_{39}N_5O_7$; *70639-484*
Antituberculosis drug

The symbol '¬' in systematic chemical names signifies line continuation

Etodolac (rINN) e·*tö*·dö·lak
1,8-Diethyl-1,3,4,9-tetrahydropyrano[3,4-*b*]indol-1-ylacetic
acid; $C_{17}H_{21}NO_3$; *41340-25-4*
Cyclo-oxygenase inhibitor; analgesic; anti-inflammatory

Etofenamate (rINN) e·tö·*fe*·na·mät
2-(2-Hydroxyethoxy)ethyl *N*-(α,α,α-trifluoro-*m*-tolyl)¬
anthranilate; $C_{18}H_{18}F_3NO_4$; *30544-47-9*
Cyclo-oxygenase inhibitor; analgesic; anti-inflammatory

Etofylline (rINN) e·*to*·fi·lën
3,7-Dihydro-7-(2-hydroxyethyl)-1,3-dimethyl-1*H*-purine-2,6-
dione; $C_9H_{12}N_4O_3$; *519-37-9*
*Non-selective phosphodiesterase inhibitor (xanthine); treatment
of reversible airways obstruction*

Etoglucid (rINN) see Appendix C

Etomidate (rINN) e·*to*·mi·dät
(*R*)-Ethyl-1-(α-methylbenzyl)imidazole-5-carboxylate;
$C_{14}H_{16}N_2O_2$; *33125-97-2*
Intravenous general anaesthetic

Etonitazene (rINN) e·tö·*ni*·ta·zën
2-[2-(4-Ethoxybenzyl)-5-nitrobenzimidazol-1-yl]ethyl diethyl¬
amine; $C_{22}H_{28}N_4O_3$; *911-65-9*
Opioid receptor agonist; analgesic

Etonogestrel (rINN) e·tö·nö·*ges*·trel
17β-Hydroxy-11-methylene-18-homo-19-nor-17α-pregn-
4-en-20-yn-3-one; $C_{22}H_{28}O_2$; *54048-10-1*
Progestogen

Etoposide (rINN) e·*to*·pö·sïd
(5*S*,5a*R*,8a*S*,9*S*)-9-(4,6-*O*-Ethylidene-β-D-glucopyranosyloxy)-
5,8,8a,9-tetrahydro-5-(4-hydroxy-3,5-dimethoxyphenyl)¬
isobenzofuro[5,6-*f*][1,3]benzodioxol-6(5a*H*)-one; $C_{29}H_{32}O_{13}$;
33419-42-0
Inhibitor of DNA topoisomerase type II; cytotoxic

Etoricoxib (rINN) e·to·ri·*coks*·ib
5-Chloro-6′-methyl-3-[4-(methylsulfonyl)phenyl]-2,3′-
bipyridine; $C_{18}H_{15}ClN_2O_2S$; *202409-33-4*
*Cyclo-oxygenase (COX-2) inhibitor; analgesic;
anti-inflammatory*

Etorphine (rINN) e·*tor*·fën
(1) (2*R*)-2-[(5*R*,6*R*,7*R*,14*R*)-4,5-Epoxy-3-hydroxy-6-methoxy-
17-methyl-6,14-ethenomorphinan-7-yl]pentan-2-ol; (2)
(6*R*,7*R*,14*R*)-7,8-Dihydro-7-[(1*R*)-1-hydroxy-1-methylbutyl]-6-
O-methyl-6,14-ethenomorphine; $C_{25}H_{33}NO_4$; *14521-96-1*
♣ **Etorphine Hydrochloride** *13764-49-3*
Opioid receptor agonist; analgesic

Etosalamide (rINN) see Appendix C

Etoxeridine (rINN) e·toks·*e*·ri·dën
Ethyl 1-[2-(2-hydroxyethoxy)ethyl]-4-phenylpiperidine-4-
carboxylate; $C_{18}H_{27}NO_4$; *469-82-9*
Opioid receptor agonist; analgesic

Etravirine (rINN) et·rá·*vi*·rën
4-[6-Amino-5-bromo-2-(4-cyanoanilino)pyrimidin-4-yloxy]-
3,5-dimethylbenzonitrile; $C_{20}H_{15}BrN_6O$; *269055-15-4*
Non-nucleoside reverse transcriptase inhibitor; antiviral (HIV)

Etretinate (rINN) see Appendix C

Etryptamine (rINN) ë·*trip*·ta·mën
1-(Indol-3-ylmethyl)propylamine; α-ethyltryptamine; $C_{12}H_{16}N_2$;
2235-90-7
Antidepressant

and enantiomer

Etybenzatropine (rINN) e·të·ben·za·*trö*·pën
(1*R*,3*r*,5*S*)-3-Benzhydryloxy-8-ethylnortropane; $C_{22}H_{27}NO$;
524-83-4
Anticholinergic

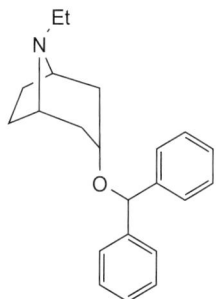

Etynodiol (rINN) ë·ti·nö·*di*·ol
19-Nor-17α-pregn-4-en-20-yne-3β,17β-diol; $C_{20}H_{28}O_2$;
1231-93-2
● **Etynodiol Diacetate** *297-76-7*
Progestogen

Eucatropine (rINN) ü·ka·*trö*·pën
1,2,2,6-Tetramethyl-4-piperidyl mandelate; $C_{17}H_{25}NO_3$;
100-91-4
Anticholinergic

mixture of 8 stereoisomers

Eufauserase (rINN) ü·*for*·se·räs
A broad-spectrum, monocomponent serine-protease enzyme,
extracted and purified from *Euphausia superba* (Antarctic krill)
Enzyme; debridement of necrotic tissue

eufauserase has the following amino acid sequence:

```
                        Chain A

    AVENCGPVAP      RNK

    IVGGMEVTPH      AYPWQVGLFI      DDMYFCGGSI

    ISDEWVLTAH      CMDGAGFVEV      VMGAHSIHDE

    TEATQVRATS      TDFFTHENWN      SFTLSNDLAL

    IKMPAPIEFN      DVIOPVCLPT      YTDASDDFVG

    ESVTLTGWGK      PSDSAFGIAE      QLREVDVTTI

    TTADCQAYYG      IVTDKILCID      SEGGHGSCNG

    DSGGPMNYVT      GGVTQTRGIT      SFGSSTGCET

    GYPDGYTRVT      SYLDWIESNT      GIAIDP

                        Chain B
```

Euphausia Extract (rINN) ü·*for*·së·a
A purified extract from *Euphausia superba* (Antarctic krill)
containing water-extractable macromolecules, mainly proteins
in the molecular weight range 10-60 kDa; the main action is due
to the serine-proteases present with a molecular weight range of
20-40 kDa.
Enzyme; debridement of necrotic tissue

Everolimus (rINN) ev·er·*ol*·im·us
(3S,6R,7E,9R,10R,12R,14S,15E,17E,19E,21S,23S,26R,27R,¬
34aS)-9,27-Dihydroxy-3-{(2R)-1-[(1S,3R,4R)-4-(2-
hydroxyethoxy)-3-methoxycyclohexyl]propan-2-yl}-10,21-
dimethoxy-6,8,12,14,20,26-hexamethyl-
9,10,12,13,14,21,22,23,24,25,26,27,32,33,34,34a-
hexadecahydro-23,27-epoxy-3H-pyrido[2,1-c][1,4]¬
oxaazacyclohentriacontine-1,5,11,28,29(4H,6H,31H)-pentone;
$C_{53}H_{83}NO_{14}$;*159351-69-6*
Calcineurin inhibitor; immunosuppressant

Evicromil (BAN) ë·*vi*·krö·mil
8-Ethyl-5-hydroxy-4-oxo-6-vinyl-4H-chromene-2-carboxylic
acid; $C_{14}H_{12}O_5$; *62571-88-4*
*Cromone; treatment of asthma, food allergy, allergic
conjunctivitis, rhinitis*

Exametazime (rINN) eks·a·*me*·ta·zëm
(RS,RS)-3,3′-(2,2-Dimethyltrimethylenedi-imino)di(butan-2-one
oxime); $C_{13}H_{28}N_4O_2$; *100551-63-1*
Brain imaging

Exemestane (rINN) eks·ë·*mes*·tän
6-Methyleneandrosta-1,4-diene-3,17-dione; $C_{20}H_{24}O_2$;
107868-30-4
Aromatase inhibitor; treatment of breast carcinoma

Exenatide (rINN) eks·*en*·a·tïd
L-Histidylglycyl-L-glutamylglycyl-L-threonyl-L-phenylalanyl-L-
threonyl-L-seryl-L-aspartyl-L-leucyl-L-seryl-L-lysyl-L-gluta-
minyl-L-methionyl-L-glutamyl-L-glutamyl-L-glutamyl-L-alanyl-
L-valyl-L-arginyl-L-leucyl-L-phenylalanyl-L-isoleucyl-L-glu-
tamyl-L-tryptophyl-L-leucyl-L-lysyl-L-asparaginylglycyl¬
glycyl-L-prolyl-L-seryl-L-serylglycyl-L-alanyl-L-prolyl-L-prolyl-
L-prolyl-L-serinamide; *141758-74-9*
Incretin mimetic; treatment of type II diabetes mellitus

```
H-His-Gly-Glu-Gly-Thr-Phe-Thr-Ser-Asp-Leu-
                                        10
  Ser-Lys-Gin-Met-Glu-Glu-Glu-Ala-Val-Arg-
                                        20
  Leu-Phe-Ile-Glu-Trp-Leu-Lys-Asn-Gly-Gly-
                                        30
  Pro-Ser-Ser-Gly-Ala-Pro-Pro-Pro-Ser-NH2
                                        39
```

Ezetimibe (rINN) e·*ze*·ti·mïb
(3R,4S)-1-(4-Fluorophenyl)-3-[(3S)-3-(4-fluorophenyl)-3-
hydroxypropyl]-4-(4-hydroxyphenyl) azetidin-2-one;
$C_{24}H_{21}F_2NO_3$; *163222-33-1*
Inhibition of intestinal lipid absorption; lipid-regulating drug

Factor VIII (rDNA) *see Octacog Alfa*

Factor IX Fraction (BAN)
A preparation of human blood containing coagulating factors II,
IX and X
Factor IX substitute

Famciclovir (rINN) fam·*si*·klö·veer
2-[2-(2-Amino-9H-purin-9-yl)ethyl]trimethylene diacetate;
$C_{14}H_{19}N_5O_4$; *104227-87-4*
Purine nucleoside analogue; antiviral (herpes viruses)

●**Famotidine** (rINN) fa·*mö*·ti·dën
3-[2-(Diaminomethyleneamino)-1,3-thiazol-4-ylmethylthio]-N-
sulfamoylpropionamidine; $C_8H_{15}N_7O_2S_3$; *76824-35-6*
Histamine H_2 receptor antagonist;treatment of peptic ulceration

Famprofazone (rINN) see Appendix C

Fanetizole (rINN) fa·*ne*·ti·zôl
Phenethyl(4-phenyl-1,3-thiazol-2-yl)amine; $C_{17}H_{16}N_2S$;
79069-94-6
Fanetizole Mesilate *79069-95-7*
Immunomodulator

Fanthridone *see Fantridone*

Fantofarone (rINN) fan·*to*·fa·rön
3,4-Dimethoxyphenethyl{3-[4-(2-isopropylindolizin-1-
ylsulfonyl)phenoxy]propyl}(methyl)amine; $C_{31}H_{38}N_2O_5S$;
114432-13-2
Calcium channel blocker

Fantridone (rINN) see Appendix C

Fazadinium Bromide (rINN) see Appendix C

♣ **Febantel** (rINN) *fe*·ban·tel
2′-[2,3-Bis(methoxycarbonyl)guanidino]-5′-phenylthio-2-
methoxyacetanilide; $C_{20}H_{22}N_4O_6S$; *58306-30-2*
Antihelminthic (veterinary)

Febuxostat (rINN) fe·*buks*·ö·stat
2-[3-Cyano-4-(2-methylpropoxy)phenyl]-4-methylthiazole-
5-carboxylic acid; $C_{16}H_{16}N_2O_3S$; *144060-53-7*;
Xanthine oxidase inhibitor; treatment of gout

● **Felbinac** (rINN) *fel*·bi·nak
Biphenyl-4-ylacetic acid; $C_{14}H_{12}O_2$; *5728-52-9*
Cyclo-oxygenase inhibitor; analgesic; anti-inflammatory

● **Felodipine** (rINN) fe·*lö*·di·pën
Ethyl methyl 4-(2,3-dichlorophenyl)-1,4-dihydro-2,6-
dimethylpyridine-3,5-dicarboxylate; $C_{18}H_{19}Cl_2NO_4$; *72509-76-3*
Calcium channel blocker

● **Felypressin** (rINN) fe·lë·*pres*·sin
2-L-Phenylalanine-8-L-lysine-vasopressin; $C_{46}H_{65}N_{13}O_{11}S_2$;
56-59-7
Vasopressin analogue; vasoconstrictor in local anaesthesia

```
Cys-Phe-Phe-Gln-Asn-Cys-Pro-Lys-Gly-NH₂
```

Fenamisal (rINN) fe·*nam*·i·sal
Phenyl 4-aminosalicylate; $C_{13}H_{11}NO_3$; *133-11-9*
Antituberculosis drug

♣ **Fenbendazole** (rINN) fen·*ben*·da·zôl
Methyl 5-(phenylthio)-1*H*-benzimidazol-2-ylcarbamate;
$C_{15}H_{13}N_3O_2S$; *43210-67-9*
Antihelminthic (veterinary)

Fenbenicillin (rINN) fen·be·ni·*si*·lin
6-(2-Phenoxy-2-phenylacetamido)penicillanic acid;
α-phenoxybenzylpenicillin; $C_{22}H_{22}N_2O_5S$; *1926-48-3*
Penicillin antibacterial

and enantiomer at C*

● **Fenbufen** (rINN) *fen*·bü·fen
4-(Biphenyl-4-yl)-4-oxobutyric acid; $C_{16}H_{14}O_3$; *36330-85-5*
Cyclo-oxygenase inhibitor; analgesic; anti-inflammatory

Fenbutrazate (rINN) fen·bü·tra·zät
2-(3-Methyl-2-phenylmorpholino)ethyl 2-phenylbutyrate;
$C_{23}H_{29}NO_3$; *4378-36-3*
Fenbutrazate Hydrochloride *8004-38-4*
Appetite suppressant

Fencamfamin (rINN) see Appendix C

Fenclofos (rINN) fen·klö·fos
O,O-Dimethyl *O*-(2,4,5-trichlorophenyl) phosphorothioate;
$C_8H_8Cl_3O_3PS$; *299-84-3*
Organophosphorus insecticide

Fenclofenac (rINN) fen·klö·fe·nak
[2-(2,4-Dichlorophenoxy)phenyl]acetic acid; $C_{14}H_{10}Cl_2O_3$;
34645-84-6
Cyclo-oxygenase inhibitor; analgesic; anti-inflammatory

Fenclozic Acid (rINN) see Appendix C

Fendosal (rINN) fen·dö·sal
5-(4,5-Dihydro-2-phenyl-3*H*-benz[*e*]indol-3-yl)salicylic acid;
$C_{25}H_{19}NO_3$; *53597-27-6*
Cyclo-oxygenase inhibitor; analgesic; anti-inflammatory

Fenetylline (rINN) see Appendix C

Fenfluramine (rINN) fen·flûr·ra·mën
Ethyl(α-methyl-3-trifluoromethylphenethyl)amine; $C_{12}H_{16}F_3N$;
458-24-2
● **Fenfluramine Hydrochloride** *404-82-0*
Amfetamine analogue; appetite suppressant

Fenfluthrin (rINN) fen·*floo*·thrin
2,3,4,5,6-Pentafluorobenzyl (1*R*,3*S*)-3-(2,2-dichlorovinyl)-2,2-
dimethylcyclopropanecarboxylate; $C_{15}H_{11}Cl_2F_5O_2$; *75867-00-4*
Parasiticide

Fengabine (rINN) *fen*·ga·bën
(*Z*)-α-Butylimino-4-chloro-α-(2-chlorophenyl)-*o*-cresol;
$C_{17}H_{17}Cl_2NO$; *80018-06-0*
Antidepressant

Fenimide (rINN) see Appendix C

Fenisorex (rINN) fe·nï·sö·reks
(*RS*)-*cis*-7-Fluoro-1-phenylisochroman-3-ylmethylamine;
$C_{16}H_{16}FNO$; *34887-52-0*
Appetite suppressant

Fenitrothion (BAN) fe·nï·trö·*thï*·on
O,O-Dimethyl *O*-4-nitro-*m*-tolyl phosphorothioate;
$C_9H_{12}NO_5PS$; *122-14-5*
Organophosphorus insecticide

Fenmetramide (rINN) see Appendix C

● **Fenofibrate** (rINN) fë·*no*·fi·brät
Isopropyl 2-(4-*p*-chlorobenzoylphenoxy)-2-methylpropionate;
$C_{20}H_{21}ClO_4$; *49562-28-9*
Fibrate; lipid-regulating drug

Fenoldopam (rINN) fĕ·*nol*·dö·pam
6-Chloro-2,3,4,5-tetrahydro-l-*p*-hydroxyphenyl-l*H*-3-
benzazepine-7,8-diol; $C_{16}H_{16}ClNO_3$; *67227-56-9*
Fenoldopam Mesilate *67227-57-0*
Dopamine D_1 receptor agonist; vasodilator

and enantiomer

Fenoprofen (rINN) fĕ·nö·*prö*·fen
2-(3-Phenoxyphenyl)propionic acid; $C_{15}H_{14}O_3$; *31879-05-7*
● **Fenoprofen Calcium** *34957-40-5*

Cyclo-oxygenase inhibitor; analgesic; anti-inflammatory

and enantiomer

Fenoterol (rINN) fe·*nö*·te·rol
1-(3,5-Dihydroxyphenyl)-2-(4-hydroxy-α-methylphen¬
ethylamino)ethanol; $C_{17}H_{21}NO_4$; *13392-18-2*
● **Fenoterol Hydrobromide** *1944-12-3*
Beta$_2$-adrenoceptor agonist; bronchodilator

mixture of 4 stereoisomers

Fenoxypropazine (rINN) see Appendix C

Fenpipramide (rINN) see Appendix C

Fenpiprane (rINN) see Appendix C

Fenprostalene (rINN) fen·*pros*·ta·lën
(1) Methyl (±)-7-{(1*R*,2*R*,3*R*,5*S*)-3,5-dihydroxy-2-[(*E*)-(3*R*)-3-
hydroxy-4-phenoxybut-1-enyl]cyclopentyl}hepta-4,5-dienoate;
(2) Methyl (13*E*)-(9*S**,11*R**,15*R**)-16-phenoxy-9,11,15-
trihydroxytetranorprosta-4,5,13-trienoate; $C_{23}H_{30}O_6$;
69381-94-8
Prostaglandin (PGF$_{2\alpha}$) analogue (veterinary)

and enantiomer

● **Fentanyl** (rINN) *fen*·ta·nïl
N-(1-Phenethyl-4-piperidyl)propionanilide; $C_{22}H_{28}N_2O$;
437-38-7
● **Fentanyl Citrate** *990-73-8*
Opioid receptor agonist; analgesic

♣ **Fenthion** (rINN) fen·*thï*·on
O,O-Dimethyl *O*-4-methylthio-*m*-tolyl phosphorothioate;
$C_{10}H_{15}O_3PS_2$; *55-38-9*
Insecticide (veterinary)

Fentiazac (rINN) fen·*tï*·a·zak
4-(4-Chlorophenyl)-2-phenyl-1,3-thiazol-5-ylacetic acid;
$C_{17}H_{12}ClNO_2S$; *18046-21-4*
Cyclo-oxygenase inhibitor; analgesic; anti-inflammatory

Fenticlor (rINN) *fen*·ti·klor
2,2′-Thiobis(4-chlorophenol); $C_{12}H_8Cl_2O_2S$; *97-24-5*
Antifungal

Fenticonazole (rINN) fen·ti·*ko*·na·zôl
1-(2,4-Dichlorophenyl)-2-(imidazol-1-yl)ethyl 4-(phenylthio)¬
benzyl ether; $C_{24}H_{20}Cl_2N_2OS$; *72479-26-6*
● **Fenticonazole Nitrate** *73151-29-8*
Antifungal

The symbol '¬' in systematic chemical names signifies line continuation

and enantiomer

Fenvalerate (rINN) fen·*val*·er·rät
(*RS*)-α-Cyano-3-phenoxybenzyl (*RS*)-2-(4-chlorophenyl)-3-methylbutyrate; $C_{25}H_{22}ClNO_3$; *51630-58-1*
Ectoparasiticide and insecticide (veterinary)

mixture of 4 stereoisomers

Fenyramidol (rINN) fen·i·*ra*·mi·dol
1-Phenyl-2-(2-pyridylamino)ethanol; $C_{13}H_{14}N_2O$; *553-69-5*
Analgesic

and enantiomer

Feprazone (rINN) *fe*·pra·zön
4-(3-Methylbut-2-enyl)-1,2-diphenylpyrazolidine-3,5-dione; $C_{20}H_{20}N_2O_2$; *30748-29-9*
Analgesic; anti-inflammatory

Ferric Carboxymaltose (rINN) fe·*rik* car·*boks*·ë·*mal*·tös
Poly[D-glucopyranosyl(1→4)]-D-gluconic acid complex of hydrated iron(III) oxide; *9007-72-1*;
Used in prevention and treatment of anaemia

Ferristene (rINN) *fe*·ris·tën
Iron ferrite with carrier particles of mono-sized spheres of cross-linked poly(ammonium styrenesulfonate); iron ferrite with carrier particles; *155773-56-1*
Contrast enhancement in magnetic resonance imaging

Fertirelin (rINN) fer·*ti*·re·lin

<Glu-His-Trp-Ser-Tyr-Gly-Leu-Arg-Pro(Et)

$C_{55}H_{76}N_{16}O_{12}$; *38234-21-8*
Fertirelin Acetate *106756-71-2*
Gonadotrophin-releasing hormone analogue

Ferucarbotran (BAN) fe·roo·*kar*·bö·tran
A non-stoichiometric polycrystalline mixture of iron(II) and iron(III) oxides (magnetite Fe_3O_4 and maghemite-γ Fe_2O_3) in which iron(II) oxide is specified to be less than 5%. It is a colloidal aqueous suspension of superparamagnetic iron oxide particles coated with carboxydextran. By transmittance electron microscopy (TEM) the iron oxide core has a diameter of 3 to 5 nm. The hydrodynamic diameter of the coated particles measured by photon correlation spectroscopy (PCS) is 45 to 65 nm. In the colloidal aqueous suspension, the carboxydextran coat has a thickness of about 25 nm (calculated from PCS measurement).
Contrast enhancement in magnetic resonance imaging

Ferumoxides (BAN) fe·roo·*moks*·ïds
Colloidal particles of non-stoichiometric magnetite; $(Fe_2O_3)_m$ $(FeO)_n$; *119683-68-0*
Contrast enhancement in magnetic resonance imaging

Ferumoxsil (BAN) fe·roo·*moks*·il
Colloidal particles of non-stoichiometric magnetite with a silicone polymer bonded to iron oxide.
Contrast enhancement in magnetic resonance imaging

Fesoterodine (rINN) fez·ö·ter·ö·dën
2-[(1*R*)-3-(Diisopropylamino)-1-phenylpropyl]-4-(hydroxymethyl)phenyl isobutyrate;
$C_{26}H_{37}NO_3$; *286930-02-7*
Fesoterodine Fumarate *286930-03-8*
Antimuscarinic; overactive bladder syndrome

Fetoxilate (rINN) see Appendix C

Fexofenadine (rINN) feks·ö·*fen*·a·dën
(*RS*)-2-(4-{1-Hydroxy-4-[4-(α-hydroxybenzhydryl)piperidino]butyl}phenyl)-2-methylpropionic acid;
$C_{32}H_{39}NO_4$
● **Fexofenadine Hydrochloride** *138452-21-8*
Histamine H_1 receptor antagonist; antihistamine

and enantiomer

Fibrinolysin (Human) (rINN) fi·brin·ö·*li*·sin
The proteolytic enzyme derived from the activation of plasminogen which converts fibrin into soluble products; plasmin; fibrinase; *9004-09-5*
Fibrinolytic enzyme

● **Filgrastim** (rINN) fil·gras·tim
Recombinant methionyl human granulocyte colony stimulating factor expressed by *E·coli; 121181-53-1*
Recombinant methionyl human granulocyte colony-stimulating factor

filgrastim has the following amino acid sequence:

MTPLGPASSL	PQSFLLKCLE	QVRKIQGDGA
ALQEKLCATY	KLCHPEELVL	LGHSLGIPWA
PLSSCPSQAL	QLAGCLSQLH	SGLFLYQGLL
QALEGISPEL	GPTLDTLQLD	VADFATTIWQ
QMEELGMAPA	LQPTQGAMPA	FASAFQRRAG
GVLVASHLQS	FLEVSYRVLR	HLAQP

● **Finasteride** (rINN) fi·*na*·ster·rïd
N^{17}-*tert*-Butyl-3-oxo-4-aza-5α-androst-1-ene-17β-carboxamide; $C_{23}H_{36}N_2O_2$; *98319-26-7*
5-Alpha reductase inhibitor; treatment of benign prostatic hyperplasia

Fipronil (rINN) *fi*·prö·nil
(*RS*)-5-Amino-1-(2,6-dichloro-4-trifluoromethylphenyl)-4-(trifluoromethylsulfinyl)pyrazole-3-carbonitrile; $C_{12}H_4Cl_2F_6N_4OS$; *120068-37-3*
Acaricide and insecticide (veterinary)

and enantiomer

Flavoxate (rINN) fla·*voks*·ät
2-Piperidinoethyl 3-methyl-4-oxo-2-phenyl-4*H*-chromene-8-carboxylate; $C_{24}H_{25}NO_4$; *15301-69-6*
● **Flavoxate Hydrochloride** *3717-88-2*
Anticholinergic

Flazalone (rINN) see Appendix C

Flecainide (rINN) *fle*·kä·nïd
N-(2-Piperidylmethyl)-2,5-bis(2,2,2-trifluoroethoxy)benzamide; $C_{17}H_{20}F_6N_2O_3$; *54143-55-4*
● **Flecainide Acetate** *54143-55-4*
Class I antiarrhythmic

and enantiomer

Fleroxacin (rINN) fle·*roks*·a·sin
6,8-Difluoro-1-(2-fluoroethyl)-1,4-dihydro-7-(4-methyl¬piperazin-1-yl)-4-oxoquinoline-3-carboxylic acid; $C_{17}H_{18}F_3N_3O_3$; *79660-72-3*
Fluoroquinolone antibacterial

Fletazepam (rINN) fle·*tä*·ze·pam
7-Chloro-5-(2-fluorophenyl)-2,3-dihydro-1-(2,2,2-trifluoro¬ethyl)-1*H*-1,4-benzodiazepine; $C_{17}H_{13}ClF_4N_2$; *34482-99-0*
Benzodiazepine

Floctafenine (rINN) flok·*ta*·fe·nën
2,3-Dihydroxypropyl *N*-(8-trifluoromethyl-4-quinolyl)¬anthranilate; $C_{20}H_{17}F_3N_2O_4$; *23779-99-9*
Cyclo-oxygenase inhibitor; analgesic; anti-inflammatory

The symbol '¬' in systematic chemical names signifies line continuation

and enantiomer

Florantyrone (rINN) flor·ran·*ti*·rön
4-(Fluoranthen-8-yl)-4-oxobutyric acid; $C_{20}H_{14}O_3$; *519-95-9*
Choleretic

Florfenicol (rINN) flor·*fe*·ni·kol
2,2-Dichloro-*N*-[(α*S*,β*R*)-α-(fluoromethyl)-β-hydroxy-4-
methanesulfonylphenethyl]acetamide; $C_{12}H_{14}Cl_2FNO_4S$;
76639-94-6
Antibacterial (veterinary)

Flosequinan (rINN) see Appendix C

♣ **Fluanisone** (rINN) floo·*a*·ni·sön
4′-Fluoro-4-[4-(2-methoxyphenyl)piperazin-l-yl]butyro-
phenone; $C_{21}H_{25}FN_2O_2$; *1480-19-9*
Dopamine receptor antagonist; neuroleptic (veterinary)

● **Flubendazole** (rINN) floo·*ben*·da·zôl
Methyl 5-(4-fluorobenzoyl)-1*H*-benzimidazol-2-ylcarbamate;
$C_{16}H_{12}FN_3O_3$; *31430-15-6*
Benzimidazole antihelminthic

Fluclorolone Acetonide (rINN) see Appendix C

Flucloxacillin (rINN) floo·kloks·a·*si*·lin
6-[3-(2-Chloro-6-fluorophenyl)-5-methyl-1,2-oxazole-4-
carboxamido]penicillanic acid; $C_{19}H_{17}ClFN_3O_5S$; *5250-39-5*
  ● **Flucloxacillin Magnesium** *58486-36-5*
  ● **Flucloxacillin Sodium** *1847-24-1*
Penicillin antibacterial

● **Fluconazole** (rINN) floo·*ko*·na·zôl
2-(2,4-Difluorophenyl)-1,3-bis(1*H*-1,2,4-triazol-l-yl)propan-2-
ol; $C_{13}H_{12}F_2N_6O$; *86386-73-4*
Antifungal

● **Flucytosine** (rINN) floo·*si*·tö·sën
4-Amino-5-fluoropyrimidin-2(1*H*)-one; 5-fluorocytosine;
$C_4H_4FN_3O$; *2022-85-7*
Antifungal

● **Fludarabine Phosphate** (INNM) floo·*da*·ra·bën fos·fät
9-β-D-Arabinofuranosyl-2-fluoroadenine 5′-(dihydrogen
phosphate); $C_{10}H_{13}FN_5O_7P$; *75607-67-9*;
21679-14-1 (fludarabine)
Purine analogue; cytotoxic

Fludrocortisone (rINN) floo·drö·*kor*·ti·sön
9α-Fluoro-11β,17α,21-trihydroxypregn-4-ene-3,20-dione;
$C_{21}H_{29}FO_5$; *127-31-1*
  ● **Fludrocortisone Acetate** *514-36-3*
Mineralocorticoid

Fludroxycortide (rINN) floo·droks·ë·*kor*·tïd
6α-Fluoro-11β,21-dihydroxy-16α,17α-isopropylidenedioxy-
pregn-4-ene-3,20-dione; flurandrenolide (USAN); $C_{24}H_{33}FO_6$;
1524-88-5
Mineralocorticoid

Flufenamic Acid (rINN) floo·fe·*na*·mik
N-(α,α,α-Trifluoro-*m*-tolyl)anthranilic acid; $C_{14}H_{10}F_3NO_2$;
530-78-9
Cyclo-oxygenase inhibitor; analgesic; anti-inflammatory

Flugestone (rINN) *floo*·jes·tön
9α-Fluoro-11β,17α-dihydroxypregn-4-ene-3,20-dione;
$C_{23}H_{31}FO_5$; *337-03-1*
Flugestone Acetate Fluorogestone acetate (USAN); *2529-45-5*
Progestogen

● **Flumazenil** (rINN) floo·*ma*·ze·nil
Ethyl 8-fluoro-5,6-dihydro-5-methyl-6-oxo-4*H*-imidazo[1,5-
a][1,4]benzodiazepine-3-carboxylate; $C_{15}H_{14}FN_3O_3$;
78755-81-4
Benzodiazepine receptor antagonist

Flumedroxone (rINN) see Appendix C

● **Flumequine** (rINN) *floo*·me·kwën
(*RS*)-9-Fluoro-6,7-dihydro-5-methyl-1-oxo-1*H*,5*H*-pyrido¬
[3,2,1-*ij*]quinoline-2-carboxylic acid; $C_{14}H_{12}FNO_3$; *42835-25-6*
Antibacterial

and enantiomer

Flumeridone (rINN) floo·*me*·ri·dön
5-Chloro-1-{4-[3-(5-fluoro-2,3-dihydro-2-oxobenzimidazol-1-
yl)propyl]piperidino}-1,3-dihydrobenzimidazol-2-one;
$C_{22}H_{23}ClFN_5O_2$; *75444-64-3*
Dopamine receptor antagonist; antiemetic

Flumetasone (rINN) floo·*me*·ta·sön
6α,9α-Difluoro-11β,17α,21-trihydroxy-16α-methylpregna-1,4-
diene-3,20-dione; $C_{22}H_{28}F_2O_5$; *2135-17-3*
● **Flumetasone Pivalate** *2002-29-1*
Glucocorticoid

Flumethiazide (rINN) see Appendix C

Flumethrin (BAN) floo·më·thrin
α-Cyano-4-fluoro-3-phenoxybenzyl 3-(β,4-dichlorostyryl)-2,2-
dimethylcyclopropanecarboxylate; $C_{28}H_{22}Cl_2FNO_3$; *69770-45-2*
Insecticide (veterinary)

Flumezapine (rINN) floo·*me*·za·pën
7-Fluoro-2-methyl-4-(4-methylpiperazin-1-yl)-10*H*-thieno[2,3-
b][1,5]benzodiazepine; $C_{17}H_{19}FN_4S$; *61325-80-2*
Antipsychotic

Flunarizine (rINN) floo·*na*·ri·zën
trans-1-Cinnamyl-4-(4,4′-difluorobenzhydryl)piperazine;
$C_{26}H_{26}F_2N_2$; *52468-60-7*
● **Flunarizine Hydrochloride** *30484-77-6*
Calcium channel blocker

The symbol '¬' in systematic chemical names signifies line continuation

123

Flunisolide (rINN) floo·ni·so·lïd
6α-Fluoro-11β,21-dihydroxy-16α,17α-isopropylidene¬
dioxypregna-1,4-diene-3,20-dione; $C_{24}H_{31}FO_6$; *3385-03-3*
Glucocorticoid

● **Flunitrazepam** (rINN) floo·ni·*trä*·ze·pam
5-(2-Fluorophenyl)-1,3-dihydro-1-methyl-7-nitro-1,4-benzo¬
diazepin-2-one; $C_{16}H_{12}FN_3O_3$; *1622-62-4*
Benzodiazepine

Flunixin (rINN) floo·*niks*·in
2-(α³,α³,α³-Trifluoro-2,3-xylidino)nicotinic acid;
$C_{14}H_{11}F_3N_2O_2$; *38677-85-9*
♣ **Flunixin Meglumine** *42461-84-7*
Cyclo-oxygenase inhibitor; analgesic; anti-inflammatory

Fluocinolone (rINN) floo·ö·*si*·no·lön
6α,9α-Difluoro-11β,16α,17α,21-tetrahydroxypregna-1,4-
diene-3,20-dione; $C_{21}H_{26}F_2O_4$; *807-38-5*
● **Fluocinolone Acetonide** *67-73-2*
Glucocorticoid

● **Fluocinonide** (rINN) floo·ö·*si*·no·nïd
6α,9α-Difluoro-11β-hydroxy-16α,17α-isopropylidenedioxy-
3,20-dioxopregna-1,4-diene-21-yl acetate; $C_{26}H_{32}F_2O_7$; *356-12-7*
Glucocorticoid

Fluocortin Butyl (INNM) floo·ö·*kor*·tin
Butyl 6α-fluoro-11β-hydroxy-16α-methyl-3,20-dioxopregna-
1,4-dien-21-oate; $C_{26}H_{35}FO_5$; *33124-50-4*
Glucocorticoid

Fluocortolone (rINN) floo·ö·*kor*·to·lön
6α-Fluoro-11β,21-dihydroxy-16α-methylpregna-1,4-diene-3,20-
dione; $C_{22}H_{29}FO_4$; *152-97-6*
● **Fluocortolone Hexanoate** *303-40-2*
● **Fluocortolone Pivalate** *29205-06-9*
Glucocorticoid

Fluopromazine *see Triflupromazine*

Fluorescein (BAN) *flûr*·re·sën
3′6′-Dihydroxyspiro[isobenzofuran-1(3H),9′(9H)-xanthen]-3-
one; $C_{20}H_{12}O_5$; *2321-07-5*
● **Fluorescein Sodium** *518-47-8*
Fluorescein Dilaurate
*Detection of corneal lesions, retinal angiography and
pancreatic function testing*

● **Fluorometholone** (rINN) flûr·rö·*me*·tho·lön
9α-Fluoro-11β,17α-dihydroxy-6α-methylpregna-1,4-diene-
3,20-dione; $C_{22}H_{29}FO_4$; *426-13-1*
Glucocorticoid

● **Fluorouracil** (rINN) flûr·rö·*ûr*·ra·sil
(*1*) 5-Fluoropyrimidine-2,4(1H,3H)-dione;
(*2*) 5-Fluorouracil; $C_4H_3FN_2O_2$; *51-21-8*
Pyrimidine analogue; cytotoxic

Fluoxetine (rINN) floo·*oks*·e·tën
N-Methyl-3-phenyl-3-(α,α,α-trifluoro-*p*-tolyloxy)¬
propylamine; $C_{17}H_{18}F_3NO$; *54910-89-3*
● **Fluoxetine Hydrochloride** *59333-67-4*
Selective serotonin reuptake inhibitor; antidepressant

and enantiomer

Fluoxymesterone (rINN) floo·oks·ë·*mes*·te·rön
9α-Fluoro-11β,17β-dihydroxy-17α-methylandrost-4-en-3-one;
$C_{20}H_{29}FO_3$; *76-43-7*
Anabolic steroid; androgen

Fluparoxan (rINN) floo·pa·*roks*·an
(3a*S*,9a*S*)-5-Fluoro-2,3,3a,9a-tetrahydro-1*H*-[1,4]benzo¬
dioxino[2,3-*c*]pyrrole; $C_{10}H_{10}FNO_2$; *101389-86-0*
Fluparoxan Hydrochloride *101389-87-1*
Alpha₂-adrenoceptor antagonist; antidepressant

Flupentixol (rINN) floo·pen·*tiks*·ol
(*Z*)-2-{4-[3-(2-Trifluoromethylthioxanthen-9-ylidene)¬
propyl]piperazin-1-yl}ethanol; $C_{23}H_{25}F_3N_2OS$; *2709-56-0*
● **Flupentixol Decanoate** *30909-51-4*
● **Flupentixol Hydrochloride** *2413-38-9*
Dopamine receptor antagonist; neuroleptic

Fluperolone (rINN) floo·*pe*·ro·lön
(21*S*)-9α-Fluoro-11β,17α,21-trihydroxy-21-methylpregna-1,4-
diene-3,20-dione; $C_{22}H_{29}FO_6$; *3841-11-0*
Glucocorticoid

Fluphenazine (rINN) floo·*fe*·na·zën
2-{4-[3-(2-Trifluoromethylphenothiazin-10-yl)propyl]¬
piperazin-1-yl}ethanol; $C_{22}H_{26}F_3N_3OS$; *69-23-8*
● **Fluphenazine Decanoate** *5002-47-1*
● **Fluphenazine Enantate** *2746-81-8*
● **Fluphenazine Hydrochloride** *146-56-5*
Dopamine receptor antagonist; neuroleptic

Flupirtine (rINN) *floo*·per·tën
Ethyl 2-amino-6-(4-fluorobenzylamino)-3-pyridylcarbamate;
$C_{15}H_{17}FN_4O_2$; *56995-20-1*
Flupirtine Maleate *75507-68-5*; D 9998
Analgesic

Fluprednidene (rINN) floo·*pred*·ni·dën
9α-Fluoro-11β,17α,21-trihydroxy-16-methylenepregna-1,4-
diene-3,20-dione; $C_{22}H_{27}FO_5$; *2193-87-5*
Glucocorticoid

Fluprednisolone (rINN) floo·pred·*ni*·so·lön
6α-Fluoro-11β,17α,21-trihydroxypregna-1,4-diene-3,20-dione;
$C_{21}H_{27}FO_5$; *53-34-9*
Glucocorticoid

Fluprofen (rINN) *floo*·prö·fen
2-(3´-Fluorobiphenyl-4-yl)propionic acid; $C_{15}H_{13}FO_2$;
17692-38-5
Cyclo-oxygenase inhibitor; analgesic; anti-inflammatory

and enantiomer

and enantiomer

Fluproquazone (rINN) floo·*prö*·kwa·zön
4-(4-Fluorophenyl)-1-isopropyl-7-methylquinazolin-2(1*H*)-one;
C$_{18}$H$_{17}$FN$_2$O; *40507-23-1*
Analgesic; anti-inflammatory

Fluprostenol (rINN) floo·*pros*·te·nol
(1) (*Z*)-7-{(1*R*,2*R*,3*R*,5*S*)-2-[(*E*)-(3*R*)-3-Hydroxy-4-(3-tri-
fluoromethylphenoxy)-but-1-enyl]-3,5-dihydroxycyclo-
pentyl}hept-5-enoic acid; (2) *ent*-(5*Z*,13*E*)-(9*S*,11*R*,15*R*)-
9,11,15-Trihydroxy-16-(3-trifluoromethylphenoxy)-ω-
tetranorprosta-5,13-dienoic acid; C$_{23}$H$_{28}$F$_3$O$_6$; *40666-16-8*
Fluprostenol Sodium *55028-71-2*
Prostanoid leuteolytic

and enantiomer

Flurandrenolone *see Fludroxycortide*

Flurazepam (rINN) flûr·*rä*·ze·pam
7-Chloro-1-(2-diethylaminoethyl)-5-(2-fluorophenyl)-1,3-
dihydro-1,4-benzodiazepin-2-one; C$_{21}$H$_{23}$ClFN$_3$O; *17617-23-1*
Flurazepam Dihydrochloride *1172-18-5*
● **Flurazepam Monohydrochloride** *36105-20-1*
Benzodiazepine

● **Flurbiprofen** (rINN) flûr·*bï*·prö·fen
2-(2-Fluorobiphenyl-4-yl)propionic acid; C$_{15}$H$_{13}$FO$_2$; *5104-49-4*
● **Flurbiprofen Sodium** *56767-76-1*
Cyclo-oxygenase inhibitor; analgesic; anti-inflammatory

Flurotyl (rINN) *flûr*·rö·tïl
Bis(2,2,2-trifluoroethyl) ether; C$_4$H$_4$F$_6$O; *333-36-8*
Central nervous system stimulant

Flusoxolol (rINN) floo·*sok*·so·lol
(*S*)-1-{4-[2-(*p*-Fluorophenethyloxy)ethoxy]phenoxy}-3-
isopropylaminopropan-2-ol; C$_{22}$H$_{30}$FNO$_4$; *84057-96-5*
Beta-adrenoceptor antagonist

● **Fluspirilene** (rINN) floo·*spi*·ri·lën
8-[4,4-Bis(4-fluorophenyl)butyl]-1-phenyl-1,3,8-triazaspiro-
[4.5]decan-4-one; C$_{29}$H$_{31}$F$_2$N$_3$O; *1841-19-6*
Antipsychotic

● **Flutamide** (rINN) *floo*·ta·mïd
α′,α′,α′-Trifluoro-4′-nitroisobutyro-*m*-toluidide; C$_{11}$H$_{11}$F$_3$N$_2$O$_3$;
13311-84-7
Antiandrogen

Fluticasone (rINN) floo·*tï*·ka·sön
S-Fluoromethyl 6α,9α-difluoro-11β,17α-dihydroxy-
16α-methyl-3-oxoandrosta-1,4-diene-17β-carbothioate;
C$_{22}$H$_{27}$F$_3$O$_5$S; *90566-53-3*
● **Fluticasone Propionate** *80474-14-2*
Glucocorticoid

● **Flutrimazole** (rINN) floo·*trim*·a·zôl
(*RS*)-1-(2,4′-difluorotrityl)imidazole; C₂₂H₁₆F₂N₂; *119006-77-8*
Antifungal

and enantiomer

Fluvastatin (rINN) floo·va·*sta*·tin
(*E*)-(3*RS*,5*SR*)-7-[3-(4-Fluorophenyl)-1-isopropylindol-2-yl]-3,5-dihydroxyhept-6-enoic acid; C₂₄H₂₆FNO₄; *93957-54-1*
  ● **Fluvastatin Sodium** *93957-55-2*
HMG Co-A reductase inhibitor; lipid-regulating drug

and anantiomer

Fluvoxamine (rINN) floo·*voks*·a·mën
(*E*)-5-Methoxy-4′-trifluoromethylvalerophenone *O*-2-aminoethyloxime; C₁₅H₂₁F₃N₂O₂; *54739-18-3*
  ● **Fluvoxamine Maleate** *61718-82-9*
Selective serotonin reuptake inhibitor; antidepressant

● **Folic Acid** (rINN) fö·lik
N-[4-(2-Amino-1,4-hydro-4-oxopteridin-6-ylmethylamino)¬benzoyl]-ʟ-glutamic acid; C₁₉H₁₉N₇O₆; *59-30-3*
Vitamin B component

Folinic Acid (rINN) fö·*lin*·ik
5-Formyltetrahydropteroylglutamic acid; leucovorin;
C₂₀H₂₃N₇O₇
  ● **Calcium Folinate** leucovorin calcium (USAN); *1492-18-8*
Disodium Folinate
Vitamin B component

Follitropin Alfa (rINN) fo·li·*trö*·pin al·fa
Recombinant human follicle-stimulating hormone, alpha-glycoform; it consists of two subunits: human gonadotrophin α-subunit protein moiety reduced and human follicle-stimulating hormone clone λ 15B β-subunit protein moiety reduced; *146479-72-3*
Recombinant human follicle stimulating hormone; treatment of female infertility

the two subunits have the following amino acid sequences:

α-subunit:

```
APDVQDCPEC    TLQENPFFSQ    PGAPILQCMG

CCFSRAYPTP    LRSKKTMLVQ    KNVTSESTCC
                              *
VAKSYNRVTV    MGGFKVENHT    ACHCSTCYYH

KS
```

β-subunit:

```
           *                           *
NSCELTNITI    AIEKEECRFC    ISINTTWCAG

YCYTRDLVYK    DPARPKIQKT    CTFKELVYET

VRVPGCAHHA    DSLYTYPVAT    QCHCGKCDSD

STDCTVRGLG    PSYCSFGEMK    E
```

*glycosylation sites
α-subunit: C₄₃₇H₆₈₂N₁₂₂O₁₃₄S₁₃
β-subunit: C₅₃₈H₈₃₃N₁₄₅O₁₇₁S₁₃

Follitropin Beta (rINN) fo·li·*trö*·pin bë·ta
Recombinant human follicle-stimulating hormone, beta-glycoform; it consists of two subunits: human gonadotrophin α-subunit protein moiety and human follicle-stimulating hormone β-subunit; the two subunits have the same amino acid sequences and molecular formulae as follitropin alfa; *169108-34-3*
Recombinant human follicle stimulating hormone; treatment of female infertility

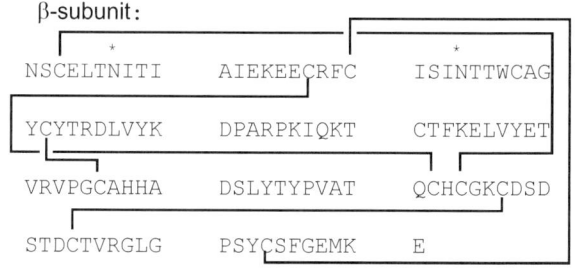

The symbol '¬' in systematic chemical names signifies line continuation

Fomepizole (rINN) fö·*me*·pi·zôl
4-Methylpyrazole; $C_4H_6N_2$; *7554-65-6*
Alcohol dehydrogenase inhibitor; treatment of alcoholism

Fomidacillin (rINN) fo·mï·da·*si*·lin
6-[D-2-(3,4-Dihydroxyphenyl)-N^2-(4-ethyl-2,3-dioxopiperazin-1-ylcarbonyl)glycylamino]-N'-formylpenicillanic acid;
$C_{24}H_{28}N_6O_{10}S$; *98048-07-8*
Fomidacillin Sodium *86117-56-8*
Penicillin antibacterial

Fomivirsen (rINN) fö·mi·*veer*·sen
dGuoP(S)dCydP(S)dGuoP(S)dThdP(S)dThdP(S)dThdP(S)⌐
dGuoP(S)dCydP(S)dThdP(S)dCydP(S)dThdP(S)dThdP(S)⌐
dCydP(S)dThdP(S)dThdP(S)dCydP(S)dThdP(S)dThdP(S)⌐
dGuoP(S)dCydP(S)dGuo; $C_{204}H_{263}N_{63}O_{114}P_{20}S_{20}$; *144245-52-3*
Antiviral (cytomegalovirus)

Fomocaine (rINN) *fö*·mö·kän
4-[3-(α-Phenoxy-*p*-tolyl)propyl]morpholine; $C_{20}H_{25}NO_2$;
17692-39-6
Local anaesthetic

Fondaparinux Sodium (rINN) fon·*da*·pa·rin·uks *so*·dë·um
Decasodium methyl *O*-2-deoxy-6-*O*-sulfo-2-(sulfoamino)-
α-D-glucopyranosyl-(1→4)-*O*-β-D-glucopyranosyl-(1→4)-*O*-2-
deoxy-3,6-di-*O*-sulfo-2-(sulfoamino)-β-D-glucopyranosyl-
(1→4)-2-*O*-sulfo-β-L-idopyranosyl-2-deoxy-6-*O*-sulfo-2-
(sulfoamino)-β-D-glucopyranoside;
$C_{31}H_{43}N_3Na_{10}O_{49}S_8$; *114870-03-0*
Inhibitor of activated factor X; anticoagulant

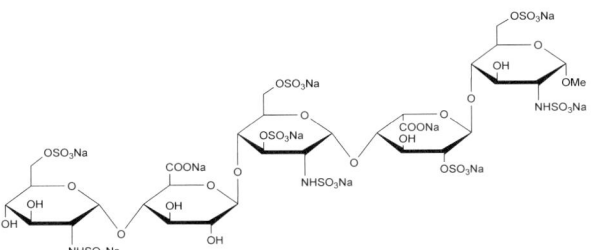

Fontolizumab (rINN) fon·*to*·li·zü·mab
Immunoglobulin G1, anti(human interferon α) (human-mouse
monoclonal HuZAF α1-chain), disulfide with human-mouse
monoclonal HuZAF light chain, dimer; *326859-36-3*;
Monoclonal antibody (interferon gamma)

Formebolone (rINN) for·*me*·bo·lön
11α,17β-Dihydroxy-17α-methyl-3-oxoandrosta-1,4-diene-2-
carbaldehyde; $C_{21}H_{28}O_4$;
2454-11-7
Androgen; anabolic steroid

Formestane (rINN) *for*·me·stän
4-Hydroxyandrost-4-ene-3,17-dione; $C_{19}H_{26}O_3$; *566-48-3*
Aromatase inhibitor; treatment of breast cancer

Forminitrazole (rINN) for·mi·*ni*·tra·zôl
N-(5-Nitro-1,3-thiazol-2-yl)formamide; $C_4H_3N_3O_3S$; *500-08-3*
Antiprotozoal

Formocortal (rINN) for·mö·*kor*·tal
3-(2-Chloroethoxy)-6-formyl-9α-fluoro-11β-hydroxy-16α,17α-
isopropylidenedioxy-20-oxopregna-3,5-dien-21-yl acetate;
$C_{29}H_{38}ClFO_8$; *2825-60-7*
Glucocorticoid

Formoterol (rINN) for·*mö*·te·rol
2′-Hydroxy-5′-{(*RS*)-1-hydroxy-2[(*RS*)-4-methoxy-α-
methylphenethylamino]ethyl}formanilide; $C_{19}H_{24}N_2O_4$;
73573-87-2

●**Formoterol Fumarate** *43229-80-7*
Beta₂-adrenoceptor agonist; bronchodilator

and enantiomer

Fosaprepitant (rINN) fos·á·*pre*·pi·tant
(3-{[(2*R*,3*S*)-2-{(1*R*)-1-[3,5-Bis(trifluoromethyl)phenyl]¬
ethoxy}-3-(4-fluorophenyl)morpholin-4-yl]methyl}-5-oxo-
4,5-dihydro-1*H*-1,2,4-triazol-1-yl)phosphonic acid;
$C_{23}H_{22}F_7N_4O_6P$; *172673-20-0*;
Fosaprepitant Dimeglumide *265121-04-8*
Neurokinin-1 (NK₁) receptor antagonist; treatment of nausea
and vomiting

Fosazepam (rINN) see Appendix C

● **Foscarnet Sodium** (rINN) fos·*kar*·net
Trisodium phosphonatoformate; CNa_3O_5P; *63585-09-1*
Antiviral (cytomegalovirus)

Fosfestrol (rINN) fos·*fës*·trol
(*E*)-4,4′-(1,2-Diethylvinylene)bis(phenyl dihydrogen
orthophosphate); $C_{18}H_{22}O_8P_2$; *522-40-7*
● **Fosfestrol Sodium** *23519-26-8*
Oestrogen

Fosfluconazole (rINN) fos·flü·*kon*·a·zôl
1-(2,4-Difluorophenyl)-2-(1*H*-1,2,4-triazol-1-yl)-1-[(1*H*-1,2,4-
triazol-1-yl)methyl]ethyl dihydrogen phosphate; $C_{13}H_{13}F_2N_6O_4P$
Antifungal

Fosfomycin (rINN) fos·fö·*mï*·sin
(1*R*,2*S*)-1,2-Epoxypropylphosphonic acid; $C_3H_7O_4P$;
23155-02-4

● **Fosfomycin Calcium** *23155-02-4*
● **Fosfomycin Sodium** *26016-99-9*
● **Fosfomycin Trometamol** fosfomycin tromethamine (USAN);
78964-85-9
Phosphonic acid derivative; antibacterial

Fosinopril (rINN) fo·*si*·nö·pril
(4*S*)-4-Cyclohexyl-1-{[(*RS*)-2-methyl-1-(propionyloxy)¬
propoxy]-(4-phenylbutyl)phosphinylacetyl}-L-proline;
$C_{30}H_{46}NO_7P$; *97825-24-6*
● **Fosinopril Sodium** *88889-14-9*
Angiotensin converting enzyme inhibitor

Fosphenytoin (rINN) fos·fen·ë·*tö*·in
2,5-Dioxo-4,4-diphenylimidazolidin-1-ylmethyl dihydrogen
phosphate; $C_{16}H_{15}N_2O_6P$; *93390-81-9*
Fosphenytoin Sodium (1:2) *92134-98-0 (heptahydrate)*
Antiepileptic

Fosquidone (rINN) see Appendix C

Fotemustine (rINN) fö·të·*mus*·tën
(±)-Diethyl {1-[3-(2-chloroethyl)-3-nitrosoureido]ethyl}¬
phosphonate; $C_9H_{19}ClN_3O_5P$; *92118-27-9*
Cytotoxic

and enantiomer

Framycetin (rINN) fra·mi·*së*·tin
An antimicrobial base produced by certain strains of
Streptomyces fradiae or *Streptomyces decaris*; 2-deoxy-4-*O*-(2,6-
diamino-2,6-dideoxy-α-D-glucopyranosyl)-5-*O*-[3-*O*-(2,6-
diamino-2,6-dideoxy-β-L-idopyranosyl)-β-D-ribofuranosyl]-D-
streptamine; neomycin B; $C_{23}H_{46}N_6O_{13}$; *119-04-0*
● **Framycetin Sulfate** *4146-30-9*
Antibacterial

The symbol '¬' in systematic chemical names signifies line continuation

Frentizole (rINN) *fren·ti·zôl*
1-(6-Methoxy-1,3-benzothiazol-2-yl)-3-phenylurea;
$C_{15}H_{13}N_3O_2S$; *26130-02-9*
Immunomodulator

Frovatriptan (rINN) *frö·va·trip·tan*
(6*R*)-5,6,7,8-Tetrahydro-6-methylaminocarbazole-3-
carboxamide; $C_{14}H_{17}N_3O$; *158747-02-5*
Frovatriptan Succinate *158930-17-7 (monohydrate)*
Serotonin 5HT$_1$ receptor agonist; treatment of migraine

Frusemide *see Furosemide*

Fulvestrant (rINN) *fúl·vës·trant*
7α-{9-[(4,4,5,5,5-Pentafluoropentyl)sulfinyl]nonyl}estra-
1,3,5(10)-triene-3,17β-diol; $C_{32}H_{47}F_5O_3S$; *129453-61-8*
Oestrogen receptor antagonist; treatment of breast cancer

Fumagillin (rINN) *fü·ma·ji·lin*
An alicyclic antibiotic produced by certain strains of *Aspergillus
fumigatis*; 4-(1,2-epoxy-1,5-dimethylhex-4-enyl)-5-methoxy-1-
oxaspiro[2.5]oct-6-yl hydrogen deca-2,4,6,8-tetraenedioate;
$C_{26}H_{34}O_7$; *23110-15-8*
Antibacterial

Furacrinic Acid (rINN) *fûr·ra·krï·nik*
6-Methyl-5-(2-ethylacryloyl)benzofuran-2-carboxylic acid;
$C_{15}H_{14}O_4$; *23580-33-8*
Loop diuretic

Furaltadone (rINN) see Appendix C

● **Furazolidone** (rINN) *fûr·ra·zo·li·dön*
3-(5-Nitrofurfurylideneamino)-2-oxazolidone; $C_8H_7N_3O_5$;
67-45-8
Antiprotozoal; antibacterial

Furethidine (rINN) see Appendix C

Furomine (rINN) see Appendix C

● **Furosemide** (rINN) *fûr·rö·se·mïd*
4-Chloro-*N*-furfuryl-5-sulfamoylanthranilic acid;
$C_{12}H_{11}ClN_2O_5S$; *54-31-9*
Loop diuretic

Fusafungine (rINN) *fü·sa·fun·jën*
A depsipeptide antibiotic produced by *Fusarium lateritium
437*; *1393-87-9*
Antibacterial

● **Fusidic Acid** (rINN) *fü·si·dik*
An antibiotic produced by a strain of *Fusidium*; (17*Z*)-ent-16α-
acetoxy-3β,11β-dihydroxy-4β,8β,14α-trimethyl-18-nor-5β,10α-
cholesta-17(20),24-dien-21-oic acid; $C_{31}H_{48}O_6$;
6990-06-3
● **Sodium Fusidate** *751-94-0*
Antibacterial

Fuzlocillin (rINN) füz·lö·*si*·lin

6-{[(*E*)-*N*-(3-Furfurylideneamino-2-oxoimidazolidin-l-ylcarbonyl)-D-2-(4-hydroxyphenyl)glycyl]amino}penicillanic acid; $C_{25}H_{26}N_6O_8S$; *66327-51-3*
Penicillin antibacterial

• **Gabapentin** (rINN) ga·ba·*pen*·tin

[1-(Aminomethyl)cyclohexyl]acetic acid; $C_9H_{17}NO_2$; *60142-96-3*
Antiepileptic

Gadobenic Acid (rINN) ga·dö·*bë*·nik

[2-(Benzyloxymethyl)-6-(carboxylatomethyl-κ*O*)-3,9-bis¬(carboxymethyl-κ*O*)-3,6,9-triazaundecanedioato-κ³-*N³,N⁶,N⁹*-κ²*O*¹·¹¹] gadolinium(III); $C_{22}H_{28}GdN_3O_{11}$; *113662-23-0*
Contrast agent for magnetic resonance imaging

Gadodiamide (rINN) ga·dö·*di*·a·mïd

Aqua[6-carboxylatomethyl-3,9-bis(methylcarbamoylmethyl-κ-*O*)-3,6,9-triazaundecanedioato-κ³-*N³,N⁶,N⁹*-κ³-*O¹,O⁶,O¹¹*¬(3−)gadolinium(III)]; $C_{16}H_{28}GdN_5O_9$, xH_2O; *122795-43-1*
Contrast agent for magnetic resonance imaging

Gadofosveset (rINN) ga·dö·*fos*·ve·set

Trihydrogen {*N*-[(2*R*)-2-[bis(carboxylato-κ*O*-methyl)amino-κ*N*]-3-({[(4,4-diphenylcyclohexyl)oxy]phosphoryl}oxy)propyl]-*N'*-(carboxylato-κ*O*-methyl)-*N,N'*-ethane-1,2-diyldiglycinato-κ*O*,κ*N*}gadolinate(3−);
$C_{33}H_{41}GdN_3O_{14}P$; *201688-00-8*;
Gadofosveset Trisodium *193901-90-5*
MRI contrast medium

Gadopentetic Acid (rINN) ga·dö·pen·*te*·tik

{*N',N'*-Bis(carboxymethyl)-*N',N'*-[(acetato)iminodiethylene]¬diglycinato-*O,O',O',N,N'N'*}gadolinium(3+); $C_{14}H_{20}GdN_3O_{10}$; *80529-93-7*
Meglumine Gadopentetate *86050-77-3*
Contrast agent for magnetic resonance imaging

Gadoteric Acid (rINN) ga·do·*te*·rik

Hydrogen [1,4,7,10-tetrakis(carboxylatomethyl)-1,4,7,10-tetra-azacyclododecane-κ⁴*N*]gadolinate(1−); $C_{16}H_{25}GdN_4O_8$; *72573-82-1*
Contrast agent for magnetic resonance imaging

Gadoteridol (rINN) ga·dö·*te*·ri·dol

[10-(2-Hydroxypropyl-κ*O*)-1,4,7,10-tetra-azacyclododecane-1,4,7-triyltriacetato-*O¹,O⁴,O⁷,N¹,N⁴,N⁷,N¹⁰*(3−)]gadolinium(III); $C_{17}H_{29}GdN_4O_7$; *120066-54-8*
Contrast agent for magnetic resonance imaging

The symbol '¬' in systematic chemical names signifies line continuation

Gadoversetamide (rINN) ga·dö·ver·*se*·ta·mïd
[*N,N*-Bis(2-{[(carboxymethyl)][(2-methoxyethyl)-
carbamoyl]methyl}aminoethyl)glycinato(3–)]gadolinium;
$C_{20}H_{34}GdN_5O_{10}$; *131069-91-5*
Contrast agent for magnetic resonance imaging

Galantamine (rINN) ga·*lan*·ta·mën
(4a*S*,6*R*,8a*S*)-5,6,9,10,11,12-Hexahydro-3-methoxy-11-methyl-
4a*H*-[1]benzofurano[3a,3,2-*ef*][2]benzazepin-6-ol; $C_{17}H_{21}NO_3$;
357-70-0
● **Galantamine Hydrobromide** *1953-04-4*
Cholinesterase inhibitor; treatment of Alzheimer's disease

Galdansetron (rINN) gal·*dan*·se·tron
(3*R*)-1,2,3,9-Tetrahydro-9-methyl-3-(5-methyl-1*H*-imidazol-4-
ylmethyl)carbazol-4-one; $C_{18}H_{19}N_3O$; *116684-92-5*
Galdansetron Hydrochloride
*Serotonin 5HT₃ receptor antagonist; treatment of nausea and
vomiting*

Gallamine (rINN) ga·la·mën
2,2′,2′-(Benzene-1,2,3-triyltrioxy)tris(triethylamine);
$C_{12}H_{21}N_3O_3$; *153-76-4*
● **Gallamine Triethiodide** *65-29-2*
Non-depolarizing neuromuscular blocker

Gallopamil (rINN) ga·*lo*·pa·mil
5-(3,4-Dimethoxyphenethyl-*N*-methylamino)-2-isopropyl-2-
(3,4,5-trimethoxyphenyl)valeronitrile; $C_{28}H_{40}N_2O_5$; *16662-47-8*
Calcium channel blocker

and enantiomer

Galsulfase (rINN) gal·*sul*·fäs
N-Acetylgalactosamine 4-sulfatase (hamster CSL-4S-342 cell);
$C_{2529}H_{3843}N_{689}O_{716}S_{16}$; *552858-79-4*
Recombinant human arylsulfatase B; mucopolysaccharidosis

galsulfase has the following amino acid sequence:

AGASRPPHLV	FLLADDLGWN	DVGFHGSRIR
TPHLDALAAG	GVLLDNYYTQ	PLCTPSRSQL
LTGRYQIRTG	LQHQIIWPCQ	PSCVPLDEKL
LPQLLKEAGY	TTHMVGKWHL	GMYRKECLPT
RRGFDTYFGY	LLGSEDYYSH	ERCTLIDALN
VTRCALDFRD	GEEVATGYKN	MYSTNIFTKR
AIALITNHPP	EKPLFLYLAL	QSVHEPLQVP
EEYLKPYDFI	QDKNRHHYAG	MVSLMDEAVG
NVTAALKSSG	LWNNTVFIFS	TDNGGQTLAG
GNNWPLRGRK	WSLWEGGVRG	VGFVASPLLK
QKGVKNRELI	HISDWLPTLV	KLARGHTNGT
KPLDGFDVWK	TISEGSPSPR	IELLHNIDPN
FVDSSPCPRN	SMAPAKDDSS	LPEYSAFNTS
VHAAIRHGNW	KLLTGYPGCG	YWFPPPSQYN
VSEIPSSDPP	TKTLWLFDID	RDPEERHDLS
REYPHIVTKL	LSRLQFYHKH	SVPVYFPAQD
PRCDPKATGV	WGPWM	

Gamolenic Acid (rINN) see Appendix C

● **Ganciclovir** (rINN) gan·*sï*·klö·veer
9-{[2-Hydroxy-1-(hydroxymethyl)ethoxy]methyl}guanine;
$C_9H_{13}N_5O_4$; *82410-32-0*
Antiviral (cytomegalovirus)

Ganirelix (rINN) ga·*ni*·re·liks
N-Acetyl-3-(2-naphthyl)-D-alanyl-*p*-chloro-D-phenylalanyl-3-
(3-pyridyl)-D-alanyl-L-seryl-L-tyrosyl-*N*⁶-(*N,N*′-diethyl¬
carbamimidoyl)-D-lysyl-L-leucyl-*N*⁶-(*N,N*′-diethylcarb¬
amimidoyl)-L-lysyl-L-prolyl-D-alaninamide; $C_{80}H_{113}ClN_{18}O_{13}$;
124904-93-4
Ganirelix Acetate *129311-55-3 (1:2)*
*Luteinizing-hormone-releasing-hormone antagonist;
treatment of female infertility*

Gantacurium Chloride (rINN) gan·tá·*cü*·rë·um
(1*R*,2*S*)-2-(3-{[(2*Z*)-2-Chloro-4-{3-[(1*S*,2*R*)-6,7-dimethoxy-2-
methyl-1-(3,4,5-trimethoxyphenyl)-1,2,3,4-tetrahydro¬
isoquinolinium-2-yl]propoxy}-4-oxobut-2-enoyl]oxy}propyl)-
6,7-dimethoxy-2-methyl-1-[(3,4,5-trimethoxyphenyl)methyl]-
1,2,3,4-tetrahydroisoquinolinium dichloride; $C_{53}H_{69}Cl_3N_2O_{14}$;
213998-46-0
Non-depolarizing neuromuscular blocker

Garenoxacin (rINN) *ga*·ren·*oks*·a·sin
1-Cyclopropyl-8-(difluoromethoxy)-7-[(1*R*)-1-methyl-2,3-
dihydro-1*H*-isoindol-5-yl]-4-oxo-1,4-dihydroquinoline-3-
carboxylic acid; $C_{23}H_{20}F_2N_2O_4$; *194804-75-6*
Fluoroquinolone antibacterial

Gastric Mucin (BAN) gas·trik mü·sin
High molecular weight glycoprotein precipitated by ethanol
(60%) after pepsin/hydrochloric acid digestion of hogs' stomach
linings
Artificial saliva; dry mouth

Gavestinel (rINN) ga·*ves*·ti·nel
4,6-Dichloro-3-[2-(phenylcarbamoyl)vinyl]indole-2-carboxylic
acid; $C_{18}H_{12}Cl_2N_2O_3$; *153436-22-7*; GV 150526X
NMDA (glycine) receptor antagonist

(*E*-isomer)

Gefarnate (rINN) *je*·fa·nät
A mixture of stereoisomers of 3,7-dimethylocta-2,6-dienyl
5,9,13-trimethyltetradeca-4,8,12-trienoate; geranyl farnesyl¬
acetate; $C_{27}H_{44}O_2$; *51-77-4*
Treatment of peptic ulcer disease, gastritis

mixture of isomers

Gefitinib (rINN) ge·*fi*·ti·nib
N-[(3-Chloro-4-fluorophenyl)-7-methoxy-6-(3-morpholino¬
propoxy)]quinazolin-4-amine; $C_{22}H_{24}ClFN_4O_3$; *184475-35-2*
Cytotoxic

Gemcitabine (rINN) gem·*sï*·ta·bën
(1) 4-Amino-1-(2-deoxy-2,2-difluoro-β-D-ribofuranosyl)¬
pyrimidin-2(1*H*)-one; *(2)* 2′-Deoxy-2′,2′-difluoro cytidine;
$C_9H_{11}F_2N_3O_4$; *95058-81-4*

● **Gemcitabine Hydrochloride** *122111-03-9*
Pyrimidine analogue; cytotoxic

Gemeprost (rINN) *je*·me·prost
(1) Methyl (*E*)-7-{(1*R*,2*R*,3*R*)-3-hydroxy-2-[(*E*)-(3*R*)-3-hydroxy-
4,4-dimethyloct-1-enyl]-5-oxocyclopentyl}hept-2-enoate; *(2)*
Methyl (2*E*,13*E*)-(11*R*,15*R*)-11,15-dihydroxy-16,16-dimethyl-9-
oxoprosta-2,13-dienoate; $C_{23}H_{38}O_5$; *64318-79-2*
Prostaglandin ($PGF_{2\alpha}$) analogue

● **Gemfibrozil** (rINN) jem·*fi*·brö·zil
2,2-Dimethyl-5-(2,5-xylyloxy)valeric acid; $C_{15}H_{22}O_3$;
25812-30-0
Fibrate; lipid-regulating drug

The symbol '¬' in systematic chemical names signifies line continuation

Gentamicin (rINN) jen·ta·*mï*·sin
A mixture of aminoglycoside antibiotics produced by
Micromonospora purpurea; *1403-66-3*
● **Gentamicin Sulfate** *1405-41-0*
Aminoglycoside antibacterial

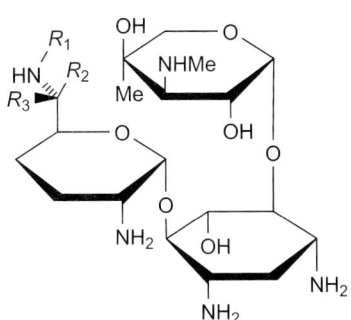

Gentamicin	R_1	R_2	R_3
C_1	Me	Me	H
C_2	H	H	H
C_{1a}	H	Me	H
C_{2a}	H	H	Me
C_{2b}	Me	H	H

● **Gestodene** (rINN) *jes*·tö·dën
13β-Ethyl-17β-hydroxy-18,19-dinor-17α-pregna-4,15-dien-
20-yn-3-one; $C_{21}H_{26}O_2$;*60282-87-3*
Progestogen

Gestonorone (rINN) jes·*ton*·or·rön
17α-Hydroxy-19-norpregn-4-ene-3,20-dione; $C_{20}H_{28}O_2$
Gestonorone Caproate *1253-28-7*
Progestogen

Gestrinone (rINN) *je*·stri·nön
13β-Ethyl-17α-ethynyl-17β-hydroxygona-4,9,11-trien-3-one;
$C_{21}H_{24}O_2$; *16320-04-0*
Progestogen

Glaspimod (rINN) *gla*·spi·mod
(2*S*,7*S*)-N^2,$N^{2'}$-[2,7-bis(L-5-Oxoprolyl-L-glutamyl-L-aspartyl‐
amino)octanedioyl]di-L-lysine; $C_{48}H_{74}N_{12}O_{22}$; *134143-28-5*
Immunomodulator

Glatiramer Acetate (BAN) gla·*ti*·ra·mer *a*·se·tät
Acetate salt of synthetic polypeptides prepared by chemically
reacting the protected and activated derivatives of four amino
acids: L-glutamic acid (L-Glu), L-alanine (L-Ala), L-tyrosine
(L-Tyr) and L-lysine (L-Lys) in a specific ratio. The molar
fraction of each amino acid residue ranges as follows:

L-Glu 0.129-0.153, L-Ala 0.329-0.462, L-Tyr 0.086-0.100 and
L-Lys 0.300-0.374. The average molecular weight is between
4700 and 11,000 daltons with at least 68% of the material within
the range of 2,500 to 28,000 daltons; *147245-92-9*
Immunomodulator

Gleptoferron (rINN) glep·tö·*fe*·ron
Macromolecular complex of iron (III) hydroxide and
dextranglucoheptonic acid; *57680-55-4*
Iron salt

● **Glibenclamide** (rINN) glï·*ben*·kla·mïd
1-{4-[2-(5-Chloro-2-methoxybenzamido)ethyl]benzene‐
sulfonyl}-3-cyclohexylurea; glyburide (USAN); $C_{23}H_{28}ClN_3O_5S$;
10238-21-8
Inhibition of ATP-dependent potassium channels (sulfonylurea);
treatment of diabetes mellitus

Glibornuride (rINN) glï·*bor*·nûr·rïd
1-[(2*S*,3*R*)-2-Hydroxyborn-3-yl]-3-tosylurea; $C_{18}H_{26}N_2O_4S$;
26944-48-9
Inhibition of ATP-dependent potassium channels (sulfonylurea);
treatment of diabetes mellitus

● **Gliclazide** (rINN) *glï·*kla·zïd
1-(3-Azabicyclo[3.3.0]oct-3-yl)-3-*p*-tolylsulfonylurea;
$C_{15}H_{21}N_3O_3S$; *21187-98-4*
Inhibition of ATP-dependent potassium channels (sulfonylurea);
treatment of diabetes mellitus

● **Glimepiride** (rINN) gli·*me*·pi·rïd
trans-1-{4-[2-(3-Ethyl-4-methyl-2-oxo-3-pyrroline-1-
carboxamido)ethyl]phenylsulfonyl}-3-(4-methyl cyclo¬
hexyl)urea; $C_{24}H_{34}N_4O_5S$; *93479-97-1*
Inhibition of ATP-dependent potassium channels (sulfonylurea);
treatment of diabetes mellitus

● **Glipizide** (rINN) *glï·*pi·zïd
1-Cyclohexyl-3-{4-[2-(5-methylpyrazine-2-carboxamido)¬
ethyl]phenylsulfonyl}urea; $C_{21}H_{27}N_5O_4S$; *29064-61-9*
Inhibition of ATP-dependent potassium channels (sulfonylurea);
treatment of diabetes mellitus

● **Gliquidone** (rINN) *glï·*kwi·dön
1-Cyclohexyl-3-{*p*-[2-(3,4-dihydro-7-methoxy-4,4-dimethyl-
1,3-dioxo-2(1*H*)-isoquinolyl)ethyl]phenylsulfonyl}urea;
$C_{27}H_{33}N_3O_6S$; *33342-05-1*
Inhibition of ATP-dependent potassium channels (sulfonylurea);
treatment of diabetes mellitus

Glisoxepide (rINN) glï·*soks*·ë·pïd
1-Azepan-1-yl-3-{4-[2-(5-methyl-1,2-oxazole-3-
carboxamido)ethyl]phenylsulfonyl}urea; $C_{20}H_{27}N_5O_5S$;
25046-79-1
Inhibition of ATP-dependent potassium channels (sulfonylurea);
treatment of diabetes mellitus

Gloxazone (rINN) *gloks*·a·zön
3-Ethoxy-2-oxobutyraldehyde bis(thiosemicarbazone);
$C_8H_{16}N_6OS_2$; *2507-91-7*
Antiprotozoal

and enantiomer

● **Glucagon** (rINN) *gloo*·ka·gon
A peptide hormone produced by the α-cells of the Islets of
Langerhans; *16941-32-5*
Hormone; treatment of hypoglycaemia

For labelling purposes, the following three-letter code, to
indicate the method of production, is approved:

(rys) produced by fermentation using Saccharomyces cerevisiae
containing a recombinant plasmid

glucagon has the following amino acid sequence:

```
His-Ser-Gln-Gly-Thr-Phe-Thr-Ser-Asp-Tyr-

Ser-Lys-Tyr-Leu-Asp-Ser-Arg-Arg-Ala-Gln-

Asp-Phe-Val-Gln-Trp-Leu-Met-Asn-Thr
```

Glucalox (rINN) see Appendix C

Glucuronamide (rINN) see Appendix C

● **Glutathione** (BAN) gloo·*tá*·thï·ôn
L-γ-Glutamyl-L-cysteinylglycine; $C_{10}H_{17}N_3O_6S$; *70-18-8*
Prevention of neurotoxicity induced by cisplatin therapy

● **Glutethimide** (rINN) gloo·*te*·thi·mïd
(*RS*)-2-Ethyl-2-phenylglutarimide; $C_{13}H_{15}NO_2$; *77-21-4*
Hypnotic

and enantiomer

Glycalox see Glucalox

Glycobiarsol (rINN) *glï·*kö·bï·*ar*·sol
[4-Glycolamidophenylarsonato(1−)]oxobismuth; $C_8H_9AsBiNO_6$;
116-49-4
Antiprotozoal

The symbol '¬' in systematic chemical names signifies line continuation

[structure diagram]

Glycopyrronium Bromide (rINN) glï·kö·pi·*rö*·në·um
3-(α-Cyclopentylmandeloyloxy)-1,1-dimethylpyrrolidinium bromide; glycopyrrolate (USAN); $C_{19}H_{28}BrNO_3$; *596-51-0*
Anticholinergic

[structure diagram]

and enantiomer

Glymidine Sodium (rINN) *glï*·mi·dën
Sodium salt of *N*-[5-(2-methoxyethoxy)pyrimidin-2-yl]¬benzenesulfonamide; $C_{13}H_{15}N_3O_4S$; *3459-20-9*
Inhibition of ATP-dependent potassium channels (sulfonylurea); treatment of diabetes mellitus

[structure diagram]

Glysobuzole (rINN) see Appendix C

Golimumab (rINN) go·li·*mü*·mab
Immunoglobulin G1, anti-(human tumor necrosis factor α) (human monoclonal CNTO 148 γ1-chain), disulfide with human monoclonal CNTO 148 κ-chain, dimer; *476181-74-5*;
Monoclonal antibody (TNFα); treatment of arthritis

Gonadorelin (rINN) go·na·dö·*rë*·lin
Luteinising hormone-and follicle stimulating hormone-releasing factor; $C_{55}H_{75}N_{17}O_{13}$; *33515-09-2*

Gonadorelin Acetate *52699-48-6*
Gonadorelin Hydrochloride *51952-41-1*
Gonadotrophin-releasing hormone; treatment of prostate cancer

```
5-oxoPro-His-Trp-Ser-Tyr-Gly-Leu-Arg-Pro-Gly-NH2
```

Gonadotrophin *see Chorionic Gonadotrophin and Serum Gonadotrophin*

Goserelin (rINN) gö·*se*·re·lin
$C_{59}H_{84}N_{18}O_{14}$; *65807-02-5*
Goserelin Acetate
Gonadotrophin-releasing hormone, gonadorelin analogue; treatment of prostate cancer

```
5-oxoPro-His-Trp-Ser-Tyr-D-Ser(tert-Bu)-Leu-Arg-
Pro-NH·NH·CONH2
```

Gramicidin (rINN) gra·mi·*sï*·din
An antimicrobial cyclic polypeptide produced by the growth of *Bacillus brevis* Dubos
Polypeptide antibacterial

Granisetron (rINN) gra·*ni*·se·tron
1-Methyl-*N*-[(3*r*)-9-methyl-9-azabicyclo[3.3.1]non-3-yl]-1*H*-indazole-3-carboxamide; $C_{18}H_{24}N_4O$
Granisetron Hydrochloride *107007-99-8*
Serotonin 5HT$_3$ receptor antagonist; treatment of nausea and vomiting

[structure diagram]

Grepafloxacin (rINN) see Appendix C

Griseofulvin (rINN) gri·zë·ö·*ful*·vin
(1′*S*,6′*R*)-7-Chloro-2′,4,6-trimethoxy-6′-methyl-3*H*-spiro¬[benzo[*b*]furan-2,1′-cyclohex[2]ene]-3,4′-dione; $C_{17}H_{17}ClO_6$; *126-07-8*
Antibacterial

[structure diagram]

Growth Hormone (rINN) see Appendix C

Guaifenesin (rINN) gwï·fen·*ë*·sin
3-(2-Methoxyphenoxy)propane-1,2-diol; $C_{10}H_{14}O_4$; *93-14-1*; present in many antitussive preparations
Expectorant

[structure diagram]

and enantiomer

Guamecycline (rINN) gwa·më·*sï*·klën
*N*²-(4-Guanidinoformimidoylpiperazin-1-ylmethyl)tetracycline; $C_{29}H_{38}N_8O_8$; *16545-11-2*
Antibacterial

[structure diagram]

Guanacline (rINN) see Appendix C

Guanethidine (rINN) gwa·*ne*·thi·dën
1-[2-(Perhydroazocin-1-yl)ethyl]guanidine; $C_{10}H_{22}N_4$; *55-65-2*
Guanethidine Monosulfate *645-43-2*
Adrenergic neuron blocker

Guanfacine (rINN) *gwan·*fa·sën
N-Amidino-2-(2,6-dichlorophenyl)acetamide; $C_9H_9Cl_2N_3O$;
29110-47-2
    Guanfacine Hydrochloride *29110-48-3*
Alpha₂-adrenoceptor agonist; treatment of hypertension

Guanoclor (rINN) *gwa·*nö·klor
1-[2-(2,6-Dichlorophenoxy)ethylamino]guanidine;
$C_9H_{12}Cl_2N_4O$; *5001-32-1*
    Guanoclor Sulfate *551-48-4*
Alpha₂-adrenoceptor agonist; treatment of hypertension

Guanoxan (rINN) *gwa·noks·*an
(*RS*)-1-(2,3-Dihydro-1,4-benzodioxin-2-ylmethyl)guanidine;
$C_{10}H_{13}N_3O_2$; *2165-19-7*
    Guanoxan Sulfate *5714-04-5*
Alpha₂-adrenoceptor agonist; treatment of hypertension

and enantiomer

Hachimycin (rINN) *ha·*chi·*mï·*sin
A mixture of heptaenes with antifungal activity produced by
Streptomyces hachijoensis; trichomycin; *1394-02-1*
Antifungal

Halazepam (rINN) *ha·lä·*ze·pam
7-Chloro-1,3-dihydro-5-phenyl-1-(2,2,2-trifluoroethyl)-1,4-
benzodiazepin-2-one; $C_{17}H_{12}ClF_3N_2O$; *23092-17-3*
Benzodiazepine

Halcinonide (rINN) hal·*si·*no·nïd
21-Chloro-9α-fluoro-11β-hydroxy-16α,17α-isopropyl¬
idenedioxypregn-4-ene-3,20-dione; $C_{24}H_{32}ClFO_5$; *3093-35-4*
Glucocorticoid

Haletazole (rINN) ha·*le·*ta·zôl
2-[4-(5-Chloro-1,3-benzothiazol-2-yl)phenoxy]ethyldiethy-
lamine; $C_{19}H_{21}ClN_2OS$; *15599-36-7*
Antifungal

Halofantrine (rINN) hä·lö·*fan·*trën
(*RS*)-3-Dibutylamino-1-(1,3-dichloro-6-trifluoromethyl-9-
phenanthryl)propan-1-ol; $C_{26}H_{30}Cl_2F_3NO$; *69756-53-2*
  ● **Halofantrine Hydrochloride**
Antiprotozoal (malaria)

and enantiomer

Halofenate (rINN) ha·*lo·*fe·nät
2-Acetamidoethyl 4-chlorophenyl(α,α,α-trifluoro-*m*-tolyl¬
oxy) acetate; $C_{19}H_{17}ClF_3NO_4$; *26718-25-2*
Lipid-regulating drug

and enantiomer

Halofuginone (rINN) hä·lö·*fü·*ji·nön
(*RS*)-*trans*-7-Bromo-6-chloro-3-[3-(3-hydroxy-2-piperidyl)¬
acetonyl]quinazolin-4(3*H*)-one; $C_{16}H_{17}BrClN_3O_3$; *55837-20-2*
    Halofuginone Hydrobromide *64924-67-0*
Antiprotozoal

and enantiomer

The symbol '¬' in systematic chemical names signifies line continuation

Halopenium Chloride (rINN) hä·lö·pë·në·um
(4-Bromobenzyl)[3-(4-chloro-2-isopropyl-5-methylphenoxy)propyl]dimethylammonium chloride; $C_{22}H_{30}BrCl_2NO$; *7008-13-1*
Antiseptic

● **Haloperidol** (rINN) hä·lö·*pe*·ri·dol
4-[4-(4-Chlorophenyl)-4-hydroxypiperidino]-4′-fluorobutyrophenone; $C_{21}H_{23}ClFNO_2$; *52-86-8*
● **Haloperidol Decanoate** *74050-97-8*
Dopamine receptor antagonist; neuroleptic

Halopyramine *see Chloropyramine*

● **Halothane** (rINN) *hä*·lö·thän
1-Bromo-1-chloro-2,2,2-trifluoroethane; $C_2HBrClF_3$; *151-67-7*
General anaesthetic

♣ **Haloxon** (rINN) ha·*loks*·on
Bis(2-chloroethyl) 3-chloro-4-methylcoumarin-7-yl phosphate; $C_{14}H_{14}Cl_3O_6P$; *321-55-1*
Antihelminthic (veterinary)

Halquinol (BAN) *hal*·kwi·nol
A mixture of chlorinated products of quinolin-8-ol containing about 65 per cent of 5,7-dichloroquinolin-8-ol; *8067-69-4*
Antiseptic

Hedaquinium Chloride (rINN) see Appendix C

Hemoglobin Raffimer (rINN) hë·mö·*glö*·bin *raf*· ï m·er
The polyaldehyde [(2R,4S,6R,8R,11S,13R)-1,14-dihydroxy-4-hydroxymethyl-3,5,7,10,12-pentaoxatetradecane-2,4,6,8,11,13-hexacarbaldehyde]derived from raffinose α-D-fructofuranosyl α-D-galactopyranosyl-(1→6)-α-D-glucopyranoside] by treatment with sodium periodate is reacted with human haemoglobin A_0 at the 2,3-DPG binding pocket. Both intermolecular and intramolecular crosslinking occurs. This product is reduced to generate covalent amine bonds with >95% crosslinked haemoglobin of which about 55% is polymerised; *197462-97-8*
Haemoglobin substitute

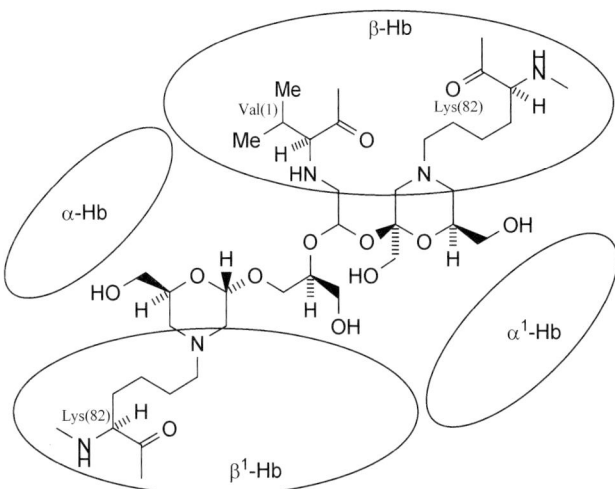

Heparin (BAN) *he*·pa·rin
An anionic polysaccharide of mammalian origin, with irregular sequence, consisting principally of alternating iduronate and glucosamine residues, most of which are sulfated; *9005-49-6*
● **Heparin Calcium** *3727-0-89-6*
● **Heparin Sodium** *9041-08-1*
Anticoagulant

Heptabarb (rINN) see Appendix C

Heptaminol (rINN) hep·*ta*·mi·nol
6-Amino-2-methylheptan-2-ol; $C_8H_{19}NO$; *372-66-7*
● **Heptaminol Hydrochloride** *543-15-7*
Non-selective phosphodiesterase inhibitor; treatment of reversible airways obstruction

and enantiomer

Hetacillin (rINN) he·ta·*si*·lin
6-[(4R)-2,2-Dimethyl-5-oxo-4-phenylimidazolidin-1-yl]penicillanic acid; $C_{19}H_{23}N_3O_4S$; *3511-16-8*
Penicillin antibacterial

Hetaflur (rINN) *he·ta·flûr*
Hexadecylamine hydrofluoride; $C_{16}H_{36}FN$; *3151-59-5; 143-27-1 (base)*
Fluoride analogue

$$Me \rightthreetimes CH_2 \rightthreetimes_{14}CH_2\overset{+}{N}H_3 \quad F^-$$

Hetastarch (BAN) *he·ta·starch*
A starch consisting of more than 90% of amylopectin and partially etherified with hydroxyethyl groups; hydroxyethyl-starch; *9005-27-0*
Plasma volume expander

Heteronium Bromide (rINN) *he·ter·rö·në·um*
(*RS*)-1,1-Dimethyl-3-(α-2-thienylmandeloyloxy)pyrrolidinium bromide; $C_{18}H_{22}BrNO_3S$; *7247-57-6*
Anticholinergic

and enantiomer

● **Hexachlorophene** (rINN) *heks·a·klor·rö·fën*
2,2′-Methylenebis(3,4,6-trichlorophenol); $C_{13}H_6Cl_6O_2$; *70-30-4*
Antiseptic

Hexadimethrine Bromide (rINN) *heks·a·dï·me·thrën*
Poly(4,4-dimethyl-4-ammoniodecyldimethylammonium dibromide); $[C_{13}H_{30}Br_2N_2]_n$; *9011-04-5*
Heparin neutralizer

Hexamethonium Bromide (rINN) *heks·a·me·thö·në·um*
N,N-Hexamethylenebis(trimethylammonium) dibromide; $C_{12}H_{30}Br_2N_2$; *55-97-0*
Ganglion blocker

Hexamethonium Iodide (INNM)
N,N-Hexamethylenebis(trimethylammonium) di-iodide; $C_{12}H_{30}I_2N_2$; *870-62-2*
Ganglion blocker

Hexamethonium Tartrate (INNM)
N,N-Hexamethylenebis(trimethylammonium) di(hydrogen tartrate); $C_{12}H_{30}N_2,2(C_4H_6O_6)$; *2079-78-9*
Ganglion blocker

Hexamidine (rINN) *heks·a·mi·dën*
4,4′-(Hexane-1,6-diyldioxy)dibenzamidamide; $C_{20}H_{26}N_4O_2$; *3811-75-4*
● **Hexamidine Isetionate** *659-40-5*
Antiprotozoal

Hexamine Hippurate *see Methenamine*

Hexaprofen (rINN) *heks·a·prö·fen*
2-(4-Cyclohexylphenyl)propionic acid; $C_{15}H_{20}O_2$; *24645-20-3*
Cyclo-oxygenase inhibitor; analgesic; anti-inflammatory

and enantiomer

Hexapropymate (rINN) *heks·a·prö·pi·mät*
1-(Prop-2-ynyl)cyclohexyl carbamate; $C_{10}H_{15}NO_2$; *358-52-1*
Hypnotic

Hexazole (BAN) *heks·a·zôl*
4-Cyclohexyl-3-ethyl-1,2,4-triazole; $C_{10}H_{17}N_3$; *4671-03-8*
Respiratory stimulant

Hexcarbacholine (rINN) *heks·kar·ba·kö·lën*
N,N′-Hexamethylenebis(2-carbamoyloxyethyltrimethyl¬ammonium) dibromide; $C_{18}H_{40}Br_2N_4O_4$; *306-41-2*
Neuromuscular blocker

The symbol '¬' in systematic chemical names signifies line continuation

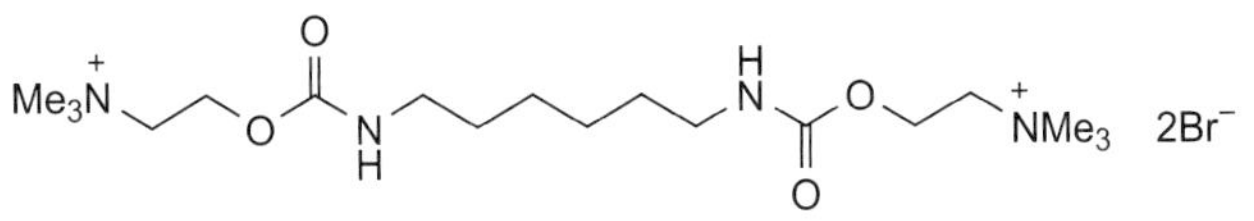

● **Hexetidine** (rINN) heks·*e*·ti·dën
1,3-Bis(2-ethylhexyl)perhydro-5-methylpyrimidin-5-ylamine;
$C_{21}H_{45}N_3$; *141-94-6*
Antiseptic

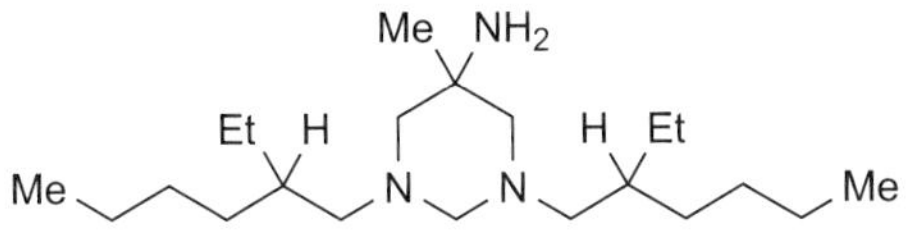

mixture of isomers

● **Hexobarbital** (rINN) heks·ö·*bar*·bi·tal
5-(Cyclohex-1-enyl)-1,5-dimethylbarbituric acid; $C_{12}H_{16}N_2O_3$;
56-29-1
Hexobarbital Sodium *50-09-9*
Barbiturate

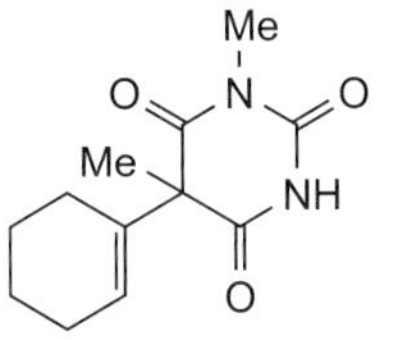

Hexobendine (rINN) heks·ö·*ben*·dën
Ethylenebis[(methyl)iminopropane-3,1-diyl] bis(3,4,5-
trimethoxybenzoate); $C_{30}H_{44}N_2O_{10}$; *54-03-5*
Vasodilator

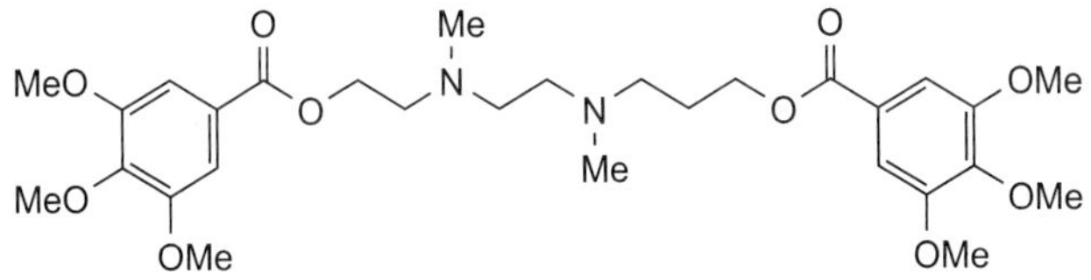

Hexocyclium Metilsufate (rINN) heks·ö·*si*·klë·um
4-(β-Cyclohexyl-β-hydroxyphenethyl)-1,1-dimethyl￢
piperazinium methylsulfate; $C_{21}H_{36}N_2O_5S$; *115-63-9*
Anticholinergic

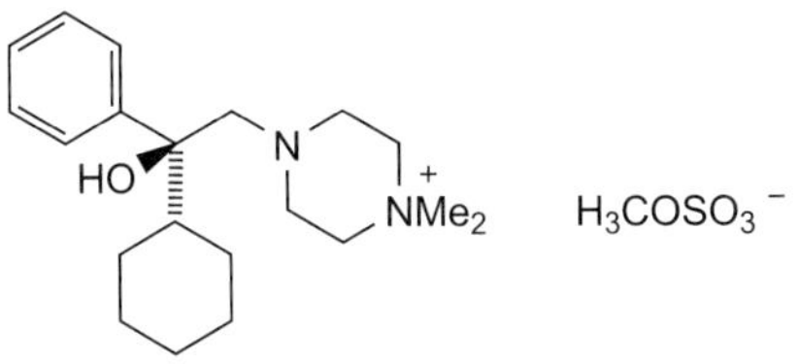

and enantiomer

Hexoprenaline (rINN) see Appendix C

● **Hexylresorcinol** (rINN) heks·ïl·re·*sor*·si·nol
4-Hexylbenzene-1,3-diol; $C_{12}H_{18}O_2$; *136-77-6*
Antihelminthic

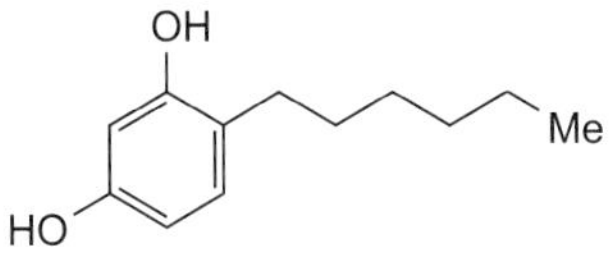

● **Histidine** (rINN) hiss·*ti*·dën
L-Histidine; (*S*)-2-Amino-3-(imidazol-4-yl)propanoic acid;
$C_6H_9N_3O_2$; *71-00-1*;
● **Histidine Hydrochloride** *645-32-2*
Amino acid

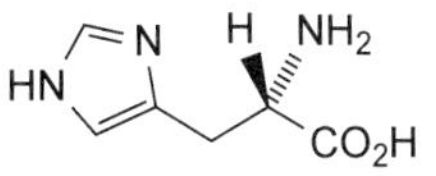

Homatropine (rINN) ho·*ma*·trö·pën
(1*R*,3*r*,5*S*)-Tropan-3-yl (*RS*)-mandelate; $C_{16}H_{21}NO_3$; *87-00-3*
● **Homatropine Hydrobromide** *51-56-9*
● **Homatropine Methylbromide** *80-49-9*
Anticholinergic

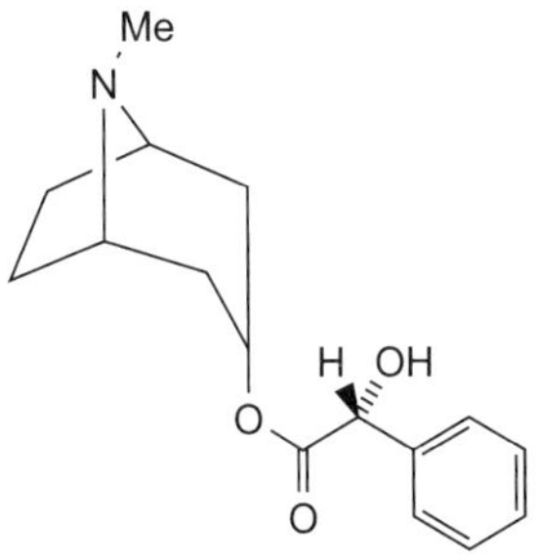

and enantiomer

♣ **Homidium Bromide** (rINN) ho·*mi*·dë·um
3,8-Diamino-5-ethyl-6-phenylphenanthridinium bromide;
$C_{21}H_{20}BrN_3$; *1239-45-8*
Antiprotozoal

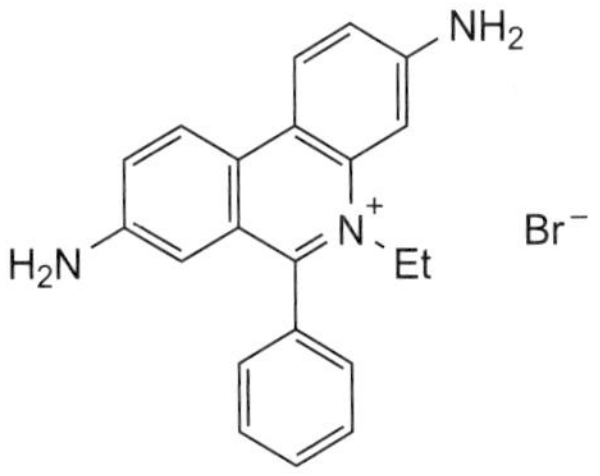

Homochlorcyclizine (rINN) hö·mö·klor·*si*·kli·zën
1-(4-Chlorobenzhydryl)perhydro-4-methyl-1,4-diazepine;
$C_{19}H_{23}ClN_2$; *848-53-3*
Histamine H₁ receptor antagonist; antihistamine

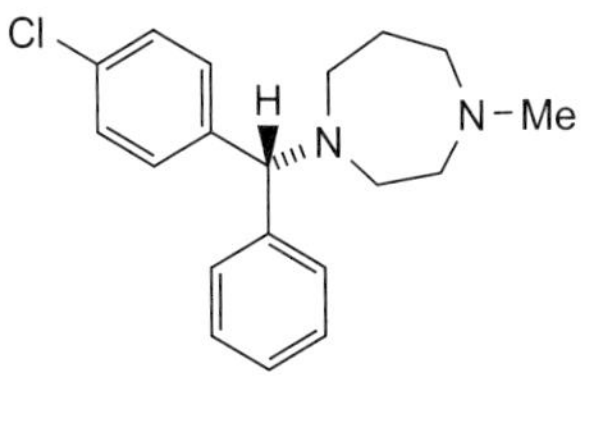

and enantiomer

Homprenorphine (rINN) hom·pre·*nor*·fĕn
(1) (2*R*)-2-[(-)-(5*R*,6*R*,7*R*,14*R*)-17-Cyclopropylmethyl-4,5-
epoxy-3,6-dimethoxy-6,14-ethenomorphinan-7-yl]butan-2-ol;
(2) 17-Cyclopropylmethyl-7,8-dihydro-7-[(1*R*)-1-hydroxy-1-
methylpropyl]-3,6-di-*O*-methyl-6,14-etheno-17-normorphine;
C₂₈H₃₇NO₄; *16549-56-7*
Opioid receptor agonist; analgesic

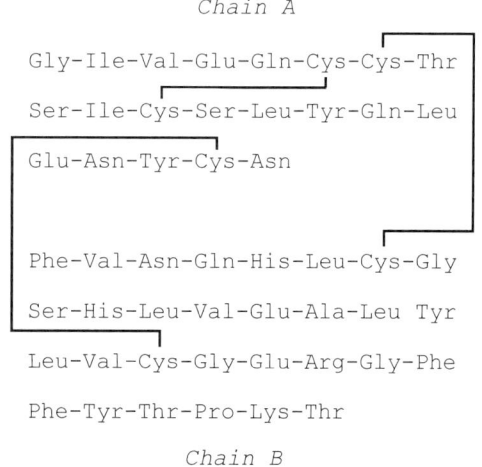

● **Human Insulin** (rINN)

A protein having the normal structure of the natural antidiabetic
principle produced by the human pancreas. When produced by
synthesis, semi-synthesis or other artificial means, the name, for
labelling purposes, carries in parentheses an approved code in
lower case letters indicative of the method of production;
C₂₅₇H₃₈₃N₆₅O₇₇S₆; *11061-68-0*; for trade names see *Biphasic
Insulin Injection*; *Biphasic Isophane Insulin Injection*; *Insulin
Injection*; *Insulin Zinc Suspension*; *Insulin Zinc Suspension
(Amorphous)*; *Insulin Zinc Suspension (Crystalline)and Isophane
Insulin Injection*
Hypoglycaemic

The following codes are approved and others will be made
available as the need arises:

(emp) produced by the enzymatic modification of insulin
obtained from the pancreas of the pig

(crb) produced by the chemical combination of the A and B
chains of the protein, each chain having been obtained
from bacteria genetically-modified by recombinant
DNA technology

(prb) produced from proinsulin obtained from bacteria
genetically-modified by recombinant DNA technology.
Hormone; treatment of diabetes mellitus

human insulin has the following amino acid sequence:

```
                  Chain A

      Gly-Ile-Val-Glu-Gln-Cys-Cys-Thr

      Ser-Ile-Cys-Ser-Leu-Tyr-Gln-Leu

      Glu-Asn-Tyr-Cys-Asn



      Phe-Val-Asn-Gln-His-Leu-Cys-Gly

      Ser-His-Leu-Val-Glu-Ala-Leu Tyr

      Leu-Val-Cys-Gly-Glu-Arg-Gly-Phe

      Phe-Tyr-Thr-Pro-Lys-Thr

                  Chain B
```

Human Menopausal Gonadotrophins (BAN)
Purified extract of human post-menopausal urine containing
follicle-stimulating hormone (FSH) and luteinising hormone
(LH); the relative *in-vivo* activity is designated as a ratio
*The following forms of Human Menopausal Gonadotrophins
are recognised:*
Human Menopausal Gonadotrophins (FSH:LH, 3:1)
Human Menopausal Gonadotrophins (FSH:LH, 2:1)
NB Human Menopausal Gonadotrophins (FSH:LH, 1:1) is
known as **menotrophin·**
Hormone; treatment of female infertility

see also Follitropin Alfa, Follitropin Beta and Menotrophin

Hyalosidase (rINN) hï·a·*lö*·si·däz
An enzyme catalysing the random hydrolysis of 1→4-linkages
between 2-acetamido-2-deoxy-β-D-glucose and β-D-glucuronate
residues in hyaluronic acid; hyaluronoglucosaminidase
(EC 3.2.1.35)
Purified form of hyaluronidase

Hyaluronic Acid (BAN) hï·a·lûr·*ro*·nik
(1→3)-*O*-(2-Acetamido-2-deoxy-β-D-glucopyranosyl)-(1→4)-
O-β-D-glucopyranosiduronan; *9004-61-9*
● **Sodium Hyaluronate** *9004-32-7*
*Natural component of the ground substance surrounding cells
(veterinary)*

● **Hyaluronidase** (rINN) hï·a·lûr·*ro*·ni·däz
Enzymes that depolymerise hyaluronic acid; *9001-54-1*
Used to promote absorption of fluid into tissues

Hydralazine (rINN) hï·*dra*·la·zën
Phthalazin-1-ylhydrazine; C₈H₈N₄; *86-54-4*
● **Hydralazine Hydrochloride** *304-20-1*
Vasodilator; treatment of hypertension

Hydrargaphen (rINN) see Appendix C

● **Hydrochlorothiazide** (rINN) hï·drö·klor·rö·*thï*·a·zïd
6-Chloro-3,4-dihydro-2*H*-1,2,4-benzothiadiazine-7-sulfonamide
1,1-dioxide; C₇H₈ClN₃O₄S₂; *58-93-5*
Thiazide diuretic

Hydrocodone (rINN) hï·drö·*kö*·dön
(1) (−)-(5*R*)-4,5-Epoxy-3-methoxy-17-methylmorphinan-6-one;
(2) 6-Deoxy-3-*O*-methyl-6-oxomorphine; C₁₈H₂₁NO₃; *125-29-1*

● **Hydrocodone Hydrogen Tartrate** *34195-34-1*
Opioid receptor agonist; cough suppressant

The symbol '¬' in systematic chemical names signifies line continuation

Hydrocortisone (rINN) hï·drö·*kor*·ti·sön
11β,17α,21-Trihydroxypregn-4-ene-3,20-dione; $C_{21}H_{30}O_5$;
50-23-7
● **Hydrocortisone Acetate** *50-03-3*
Hydrocortisone Butyrate *13609-67-1*
● **Hydrocortisone Hydrogen Succinate** *2203-97-6*
● **Hydrocortisone Sodium Phosphate** *6000-74-4*
● **Hydrocortisone Sodium Succinate** *125-04-2*
Corticosteroid

Hydroflumethiazide (rINN) hï·drö·floo·me·*thï*·a·zïd
3,4-Dihydro-6-trifluoromethyl-2*H*-1,2,4-benzothiadiazine-7-
sulfonamide 1,1-dioxide; $C_8H_8F_3N_3O_4S_2$; *135-09-1*
Thiazide diuretic

Hydromorphinol (rINN) hï·drö·*mor*·fi·nol
(1) (5*R*,6*S*)-4,5-Epoxy-17-methylmorphinan-3,6,14-triol;
(2) 7,8-Dihydro-14-hydroxymorphine; $C_{17}H_{21}NO_4$; *2183-56-4*
Opioid receptor agonist; analgesic

Hydromorphone (rINN) hï·drö·*mor*·fön
(1) (-)-(5*R*)-4,5-Epoxy-3-hydroxy-17-methylmorphinan-6-one;
(2) 6-Deoxy-7,8-dihydro-6-oxomorphine; $C_{17}H_{19}NO_3$; *466-99-9*
● **Hydromorphone Hydrochloride** *71-68-1*
Opioid receptor agonist; analgesic

● **Hydrotalcite** (rINN) hï·drö·*tal*·sït
Aluminium dimagnesium carbonate hexahydroxide tetrahydrate;
$Mg_6Al_2(OH)_{16}CO_3·4H_2O$; *12304-65-3*
Antacid

Hydroxamethocaine *see Hydroxytetracaine*

● **Hydroxocobalamin** (rINN) hï·droks·ö·kö·*ba*·la·min
*Co*α-[α-(5,6-Dimethylbenzimidazol-1-yl)]-*Co*β-
hydroxocobamide; $C_{62}H_{89}CoN_{13}O_{15}P$; *13422-51-0*
● **Hydroxocobalamin Acetate** *22465-48-1*
● **Hydroxocobalamin Chloride** *58288-50-9*
● **Hydroxocobalamin Sulphate**
Vitamin B$_{12}$ analogue

Hydroxyamfetamine (rINN) hï·droks·ë·am·*fe*·ta·mën
4-(2-Aminopropyl)phenol; $C_9H_{13}NO$; *103-86-6*
Adrenoceptor agonist

and enantiomer

Hydroxyapatite (BAN) hï·droks·ë·*a*·pa·tït
Decacalcium dihydroxide hexakis(orthophosphate);
$3Ca_3(PO_4)_2·Ca(OH)_2$; $Ca_5(OH)(PO_4)_3$; *1306-06-5*
Calcium salt

● **Hydroxycarbamide** (rINN) hï·droks·ë·*kar*·ba·mïd
$CH_4N_2O_2$; *127-07-1*
Cytotoxic alkylating drug

Hydroxychloroquine (rINN) hï·droks·ë·*klor*·rö·kwën
(*RS*)-2-[4-(7-Chloro-4-quinolylamino)pentyl(ethyl)amino]¬
ethanol; $C_{18}H_{26}ClN_3O$; *118-42-3*
● **Hydroxychloroquine Sulfate** *747-36-4*
Antiprotozoal (malaria)

Hydroxydione Sodium Succinate (rINN) hï·droks·ë·dï·ön
Sodium 3,20-dioxo-5α-pregnan-21-yl succinate; $C_{25}H_{35}NaO_6$; *53-10-1*
General anaesthetic

Hydroxypethidine (rINN) hï·droks·ë·*pe*·thi·dën
Ethyl 4-(3-hydroxyphenyl)-1-methylpiperidine-4-carboxylate; $C_{15}H_{21}NO_3$; *468-56-4*
Opioid receptor agonist

Hydroxyprocaine (rINN) hï·droks·ë·*prö*·kän
2-Diethylaminoethyl 4-aminosalicylate; $C_{13}H_{20}N_2O_3$; *487-53-6*
Local anaesthetic

Hydroxyprogesterone (rINN) hï·droks·ë·prö·*jes*·te·rön
17α-Hydroxypregn-4-ene-3,20-dione; $C_{21}H_{30}O_3$; *68-96-2*
● **Hydroxyprogesterone Caproate** (hydroxyprogesterone hexanoate) *630-56-8*
Progestogen

Hydroxystilbamidine (rINN) hï·droks·ë·stil·*ba*·mi·dën
2-Hydroxystilbene-4,4′-dicarboxamidine; $C_{16}H_{16}N_4O$; *495-99-8*
Antifungal; antiprotozoal

Hydroxytetracaine (rINN) see Appendix C

Hydroxytoluic Acid (rINN) hï·droks·ë·to·*lü*·ik
2-Hydroxy-*m*-toluic acid; $C_8H_8O_3$; *83-40-9*
Analgesic

Hydroxyurea *see Hydroxycarbamide*

Hydroxyzine (rINN) hï·droks·i·zën
(*RS*)-2-{2-[4-(*p*-Chloro-α-phenylbenzyl)piperazin-1-yl]¬ethoxy}ethanol; $C_{21}H_{27}ClN_2O_2$; *68-88-2*
● **Hydroxyzine Hydrochloride** *2192-20-3*
Histamine H_1 receptor antagonist

● **Hymecromone** (rINN) hï·*me*·krö·mön
7-Hydroxy-4-methyl-2*H*-1-benzopyran-2-one; $C_{10}H_8O_3$; *90-33-5*
Choleretic; antispasmodic

● **Hyoscine** (BAN) *hï*·ö·sën
(1*S*,3*s*,5*R*,6*R*,7*S*,8*s*)-6,7-Epoxy-3-[(*S*)-tropoyloxy]tropane; $C_{17}H_{21}NO_4$; *51-34-3*
● **Hyoscine Hydrobromide** Scopolamine hydrobromide (USAN); *114-49-8*
● **Hyoscine Butylbromide** *149-64-4*
Hyoscine Methobromide methscopolamine bromide (USAN); *155-41-9*
Hyoscine Methonitrate *6106-46-3*
Anticholinergic

Hyoscyamine (BAN) hï·ö·*sï*·a·mën
(1*R*,3*r*,5*S*)-Tropan-3-yl (*S*)-tropate; $C_{17}H_{23}NO_3$; *101-31-5*
● **Hyoscyamine Sulfate** *620-61-1*
Anticholinergic

• **Hypromellose** (rINN) hï·*prö*·me·lös
A mixed ether of cellulose containing, by weight, 27 to 30% of methoxyl groups and 4 to 7·5% of hydroxypropyl groups; *8063-82-9*

  • **Hypromellose Phthalate**
Artificial tears

Ibafloxacin (rINN) ï·ba·*floks*·a·sin
(*RS*)-9-Fluoro-6,7-dihydro-5,8-dimethyl-1-oxo-1*H*,5*H*-pyrido¬[3,2,1-*ij*]quinoline-2-carboxylic acid; $C_{15}H_{14}FNO_3$; *91618-36-9*
Fluoroquinolone antibacterial

Ibandronic Acid (rINN) ï·ban·*dro*·nik a·sid
1-Hydroxy-3-[methyl(pentyl)amino)propane-1,1-diylbis¬(phosphonic acid); $C_9H_{22}NO_7P_2$; *114084-78-5*
Sodium Ibandronate
Bisphosphonate; treatment of osteolytic lesions; osteoporosis; hypercalcaemia in malignancy

Ibopamine (rINN) ï·*bö*·pa·mën
4-(2-Methylaminoethyl)-*o*-phenylene di-isobutyrate; $C_{17}H_{25}NO_4$; *66195-31-1*
Dopamine receptor agonist

Ibritumomab Tiuxetan (rINN) i·bri·*tü*·mö·mab tï·*uks*·e·tan
Immunoglobulin G1, anti-(human CD20 (antigen) (mouse monoclonal IDEC-Y2B8 γ1-chain) disulfide, with mouse monoclonal IDEC-Y2B8 κ-chain, dimer 3-(4-{2-([{(S)-2-[bis(carboxymethyl)amino]propyl}(carboxymethyl)amino]¬methyl)-4-carboxy-3-(carboxymethyl)butyl}phenyl)thioureido conjugate; *206181-63-7*
Monoclonal antibody (CD-20 receptors on tumour cells)

Ibufenac (rINN) ï·*bú*·fe·nak
(4-Isobutylphenyl)acetic acid; $C_{12}H_{16}O_2$; *1553-60-2*
Cyclo-oxygenase inhibitor; analgesic; anti-inflammatory

• **Ibuprofen** (rINN) ï·bü·*prö*·fen
(*RS*)-2-(4-Isobutylphenyl)propionic acid; $C_{13}H_{18}O_2$; *15687-27-1*
Cyclo-oxygenase inhibitor; analgesic; anti-inflammatory

and enantiomer

Ibutilide (rINN) ï·*bü*·ti·lïd
(*RS*)-4′-{4-[Ethyl(heptyl)amino]-1-hydroxybutyl}¬methanesulfonanilide; $C_{20}H_{36}N_2O_3S$; *122647-31-8*
Ibutilide Fumarate *122647-32-9*
Class 1 antiarrhythmic

and enantiomer

Icatibant (rINN) ï·*kat*·ib·ant
N^2-{2-[D-Arginyl-L-arginyl-L-prolyl-(4*R*)-4-hydroxy-L-prolyl¬glycyl-3-(thiophen-2-yl)-L-alanyl-L-seryl]-({1-[(3*R*)-1,2,3,4-tetrahydroisoquinol-3-yl]carbonyl}-(2*S*,3a*S*,7a*S*)-hexahydro¬indolin-2-yl}carbonyl)}-L-arginine; $C_{59}H_{89}N_{19}O_{13}S$; *130308-48-4*;
Icatibant Acetate *138614-30-9*
Selective bradykinin B_2 antagonist; treatment of hereditary angioedema

• **Ichthammol** (BAN) *ik*·tha·mol
Ammonium salts of the sulfonic acids of an oily substance prepared from a bituminous schist or shale, together with ammonium sulfate and water; *8029-68-3*
Chronic lichenified eczema

Icodextrin (rINN) ï·*kö*·deks·trin
(1→4)-α-D-Glucan having more than 85% of its molecules
with molecular weights between 1640 and 45,000 with a
weight-average molecular weight of approximately 20,000;
[C₆H₁₀O₅]ₙ; *9004-53-9*
Glucose polymer; peritoneal dialysis

Icometasone Enbutate (rINN) ï·kö·*me*·ta·sön *en*·bü·tät
9α-Chloro-11β-hydroxy-16α-methyl-3,20-dioxopregna-1,4-
diene-17,21-diyl 17-butyrate 21-acetate; C₂₈H₃₇ClO₇;
103466-73-5
Glucocorticoid

Idarubicin (rINN) ï·da·*roo*·bi·sin
(7*S*,9*S*)-9-Acetyl-7-(3-amino-2,3,6-trideoxy-α-L-*lyxo*-hexo¬
pyranosyloxy)-7,8,9,10-tetrahydro-6,9,11-trihydroxy¬
naphthacene-5,12-dione; C₂₆H₂₇NO₉; *58957-92-9*
Idarubicin Hydrochloride *57852-57-0*
Anthracycline antibacterial; cytotoxic

Idazoxan (rINN) ï·da·*zoks*·an
(*RS*)-2-(2,3-Dihydro-1,4-benzodioxin-2-yl)-2-imidazoline;
C₁₁H₁₂N₂O₂; *79944-58-4*
Idazoxan Hydrochloride *79944-56-2*
Alpha₂-adrenoceptor antagonist

and enantiomer

Idoxifene (rINN) ï·*doks*·i·fën
(*E*)-1-{2-[4-(1-*p*-Iodophenyl-2-phenylbut-1-
enyl)phenoxy]ethyl}pyrrolidine; C₂₈H₃₀INO; *116057-75-1*
Selective oestrogen receptor modulator

● **Idoxuridine** (rINN) ï·doks·*ûr*·ri·dën
5-Iodo-1-(2-deoxy-β-D-*erythro*-pentofuranosylpyrimidine-
2,4(1*H*,3*H*)-dione; C₉H₁₁N₂O₅; *54-42-2*
Pyrimidine nucleoside analogue; antiviral (herpesviruses)

Idursulfase (rINN) ï·dur·*sul*·fäs
μ-L-Iduronate sulfate sulfatase; C₂₆₈₉H₄₀₅₇N₆₉₉O₇₉₂S₁₄
(subunit protein moiety reduced); *50936-59-9*
Iduronate-2-sulfatase;mucopolysaccharidosis type II

idursulfase has the following amino acid sequence:

```
SETQANSTTD    ALNVLLIIVD    DLRPSLGCYG

DKLVRSPNID    QLASNSLLFQ    NAFAQQAVCA

PSRVSFLTGR    RPDTTRLYDF    NSYWRVNAGN

FSTIPQYFKE    NGYVTMSVGK    VFNPGISSNN

TDDSPYSWSF    PPYNPSSEKY    ENTKTCRGPD

GELHANLLCP    VDVLDVPEGT    LPDKQSTEQA

IQLLEKMKTS    ASPFFLAVGY    HKPHIPFRYP

KEFQKLYPLE    NITLAPDPEV    PDGLPPVAYN

PWMDIRQRED    VQALNISVPY    GPIPVDFQRK

IRQSYFASVS    YLDTQVGRLL    SALDDLQLAN

STIIAFTSDH    GWALGEHGEW    AKYSNFDVAT

HVPLIFYVPG    RTASLPEAGE    KLFPYLDPFD

SASQLMEPGR    QSMDLVELVS    LFPTLAGLAG

LQVPPRCPVP    SFHVELCREG    KNLLKHFRFR

DLEEDPYLPG    NPRELIAYSQ    YPRPSDIPQW

HSDKPSLKDI    KIMGYSIRTI    DYRYTVWVGF

HPDEFLAHFS    DIHAGELYFV    DSDPLQDHNM

YNDSOGGDLF    QLLMP
```

●Ifosfamide (rINN) ï·*fos*·fa·mïd
3-(2-Chloroethyl)-2-(2-chloroethylamino)-1,3,2-oxaza-
phosphorinane 2-oxide; $C_7H_{15}Cl_2N_2O_2P$; *3778-73-2*
Cytotoxic alkylating agent

Iloperidone (rINN) ï·lö·*pe*·ri·dön
1-(4-{3-{4-(6-Fluoro-1,2-benzoxazol-3-yl)piperidino]propoxy}-
3-methoxyphenyl)ethanone; $C_{24}H_{27}FN_2O_4$;
133454-47-4
Dopamine receptor antagonist; neuroleptic

Iloprost (rINN) ï·lö·prost
(*E*)-5-{(3a*S*,4*R*,5*R*,6a*S*)-5-Hydroxy-4-[(*E*)-(3*S*,4*RS*)-3-hydroxy-
4-methyloct-1-en-6-ynyl]perhydropentalen-2-ylidene}¬
pentanoic acid; $C_{22}H_{32}O_4$; *73873-87-7*
Prostaglandin (PGI₂) analogue

and epimer at C*

Imatinib (rINN) i·*ma*·ti·nib
4′-Methyl-4-[(4-methylpiperazin-1-yl)methyl]-3′-{[4-(3-
pyridyl)pyrimidin-2-yl]amino}benzanilide; $C_{29}H_{31}N_7O$;
152459-95-5
Imatinib Mesilate
Cytotoxic

Imciromab Pentetate (INNM) im·*sï*·rö·mab *pen*·te·tät
An IgG2a antibody derived from the cell line R11D10
and directed to the heavy chain of human cardiac myosin;
126132-83-0
Monoclonal antibody (myosin)

Imidapril (rINN) i·*mï*·da·pril
(*S*)-3-{*N*-[(*S*)-1-Ethoxycarbonyl-3-phenylpropyl]-L-alanyl}-1-
methyl-2-oxoimidazolidine-4-carboxylic acid; $C_{20}H_{27}N_3O_6$;
89371-37-9
Imidapril Hydrochloride *89396-94-1*
Angiotensin converting enzyme inhibitor

Imidaprilat (rINN) i·mï·da·*pri*·lat
(4*S*)-3-{(2*S*)-2-[(1*S*)-1-Carboxy-3-phenylpropylamino]¬
propionyl}-1-methyl-2-oxoimidazolidine-4-carboxylic acid;
$C_{18}H_{23}N_3O_6$; *89371-44-8*
Angiotensin converting enzyme inhibitor

Imidocarb (rINN) i·*mï*·dö·karb
1,3-Bis[3-(2-imidazolin-2-yl)phenyl]urea; $C_{19}H_{20}N_6O$;
27885-92-3
Imidocarb Dipropionate
Antiprotozoal

Imiglucerase (rINN) i·mi·*gloo*·se·räs
Recombinant, human-derived, macrophage-targeted β-gluco¬
cerebrosidase (r-GCR); a monomeric glycoprotein of 497 amino
acids glycosylated at asparagine residues 19, 59, 146 and 270;
$C_{2532}H_{3843}N_{671}O_{711}S_{16}$; *154248-97-2*
Enzyme (β-glucocerebrosidase); treatment of Gaucher's disease

For labelling purposes, the following three-letter code, to
indicate the method of production, is approved:

(rch)   produced from genetically engineered chinese hamster
ovary cells

imiglucerase has the following amino acid sequence:

```
ARPCIPKSFG        YSSVVCVCNA        TYCDSFDPPT

FPALGTFSRY        ESTRSGRRME        LSMGPIQANH

TGTGLLLTLQ        PEQKFQKVKG        FGGAMTDAAA

LNILALSPPA        QNLLLKSYFS        EEGIGYNIIR

VPMASCDFSI        RTYTYADTPD        DFQLHNFSLP

EEDTKLKIPL        IHRALQLAQR        PVSLLASPWT

SPTWLKTNGA        VNGKGSLKGQ        PGDIYHQTWA

RYFVKFLDAY        AEHKLQFWAV        TAENEPSAGL

LSGYPFQCLG        FTPEHQRDFI        ARDLGPTLAN

STHHNVRLLM        LDDQRLLLPH        WAKVVLTDPE

AAKYVHGIAV        HWYLDFLAPA        KATLGETHRL

FPNTMLFASE        ACVGSKFWEQ        SVRLGSWDRG

MQYSHSIITN        LLYHVVGWTD        WNLALNPEGG

PNWVRNFVDS        PIIVDITKDT        FYKQPMFYHL

GHFSKFIPEG        SQRVGLVASQ        KNDLDAVALM

HPDGSAVVVV        LNRSSKDVPP        TIKDPAVGFL

ETISPGYSIH        TYLWHRQ
```

* glycosylation site

● **Imipenem** (rINN) i·*mi*·pe·nem
(5R,6S)-6-[(R)-1-Hydroxyethyl]-3-[2-(iminomethylamino)¬
ethylthio]-7-oxo-1-azabicyclo[3.2.0]hept-2-ene-2-carboxylic
acid; $C_{12}H_{17}N_3O_4S$; *64221-86-9*
Carbapenem antibacterial

Imipramine (rINN) i·*mi*·pra·mën
3-(10,11-Dihydro-5H-dibenz[b,f]azepin-5-yl)propyldimethyl¬
amine; $C_{19}H_{24}N_2$; *50-49-7*
● **Imipramine Hydrochloride** *113-52-0*
Monoamine reuptake inhibitor; tricyclic antidepressant

Imiquimod (rINN) i·*mi*·kwi·mod
1-Isobutyl-1H-imidazo[4,5-c]quinolin-4-ylamine; $C_{14}H_{16}N_4$;
99011-02-6
Immunomodulator; treatment of perianal and genital warts

Imolamine (rINN) i·*mo*·la·mën
Diethyl[2-(5-imino-3-phenyl-1,2,4-oxadiazolin-4-yl)ethyl]¬
amine; $C_{14}H_{20}N_4O$; *318-23-0*
Vasodilator

Impromidine (rINN) im·*prö*·mi·dën
1-(3-Imidazol-4-ylpropyl)-3-[2-(5-methylimidazol-4-
ylmethylthio)ethyl]guanidine; $C_{14}H_{23}N_7S$; *55273-05-7*
Impromidine Hydrochloride *65573-02-6*
Histamine H_2 receptor agonist

Indacaterol (rINN) in·dá·*kat*·er·ol
5-{(1R)-2-[(5,6-Diethyl-2,3-dihydro-1H-inden-2-yl)amino]-
1-hydroxyethyl}-8-hydroxyquinolin-2(1H)-one;
$C_{24}H_{28}N_2O_3$; *312753-06-3*
Indacaterol Maleate *753498-25-8*
*Beta$_2$-adrenoceptor agonist; treatment of chronic obstructive
pulmonary disease*

Indalpine (rINN) in·dal·pën
3-[2-(4-Piperidyl)ethyl]indole; $C_{15}H_{20}N_2$; *63758-79-2*
Monoamine reuptake inhibitor; antidepressant

● **Indapamide** (rINN) in·*da*·pa·mïd
(RS)-4-Chloro-N-(2-methylindolin-1-yl)-3-sulfamoylbenzamide;
$C_{16}H_{16}ClN_3O_3S$; *26807-65-8*
Thiazide-like diuretic

The symbol '¬' in systematic chemical names signifies line continuation

and enantiomer

Indenolol (rINN) in·*dë*·no·lol
1*H*-Inden-4(*or* 7)-yloxy-3-isopropylaminopropan-2-ol;
$C_{15}H_{21}NO_2$; *60607-68-3*
Beta-adrenoceptor antagonist

and enantiomer

Indinavir (rINN) in·*din*·a·veer
(2*R*,4*S*)-2-Benzyl-5-[(2*S*)-2-*tert*-butylcarbamoyl)-4-(3-pyridyl-
methyl)piperazin-1-yl]-4-hydroxy-*N*-[(1*S*,2*R*)-2-hydroxyindan-
1-yl]pentanamide; $C_{36}H_{47}N_5O_4$; *150378-17-9*
● **Indinavir Sulfate** *157810-81-6*
Protease inhibitor; antiviral (HIV)

Indisulam (rINN) in·*di*·sü·lam
N-(3-Chloroindol-7-yl)benzene-1,4-disulfonamide;
$C_{14}H_{12}ClN_3O_4S_2$; *165668-41-7*
Cytotoxic

Indolidan (rINN) in·*do*·li·dan
3,3-Dimethyl-5-(1,4,5,6-tetrahydro-6-oxopyridazin-3-yl)-
indolin-2-one; $C_{14}H_{15}N_3O_2$; *100643-96-7*
Inhibitor of phosphodiesterase type III; positive inotrope

● **Indometacin** (rINN) in·dö·*me*·ta·sin
1-(4-Chlorobenzoyl)-5-methoxy-2-methylindol-3-ylacetic acid;
$C_{19}H_{16}ClNO_4$; *53-86-1*
Cyclo-oxygenase inhibitor; analgesic; anti-inflammatory

Indoprofen (rINN) in·dö·*prö*·fen
(*RS*)-*p*-(1-Oxoisoindolin-2-yl)hydratropic acid; $C_{17}H_{15}NO_3$;
31842-01-0
Cyclo-oxygenase inhibitor; analgesic; anti-inflammatory

and enantiomer

Indoramin (rINN) in·*dor*·ra·min
N-[1-(2*H*-Indol-3-ylethyl)-4-piperidyl]benzamide; $C_{22}H_{25}N_3O$;
26844-12-2
● **Indoramin Hydrochloride** *33124-53-7*
Alpha$_1$-adrenoceptor antagonist

Infliximab (rINN) in·*fliks*·i·mab
Immunoglobulin G (human-mouse monoclonal cA2 heavy chain
anti-human tumour necrosis factor), disulfide with human
mouse monoclonal cA2 light chain, dimer; *170277-31-3*
Monoclonal antibody (TNF alfa)

Inosine Pranobex (INNM) *ï*·nö·sën *pra*·nö·beks
Inosine–2-hydroxypropyldimethylammonium 4-acetamido-
benzoate (1:3) $C_{10}H_{12}N_4O_5$·$C_{14}H_{22}N_2O_4$; *36703-88-5*
Antiviral (herpesviruses)

● **Inositol Nicotinate** (rINN) i·*nö*·si·tol
myo-Inositol hexanicotinate; inositol niacinate (USAN);
$C_{42}H_{30}N_6O_{12}$; *6556-11-2*
Vasodilator

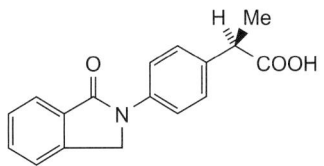

Inproquone (rINN) see Appendix C

Insulin (BAN) *see Biphasic Insulin Injection, Human Insulin, Insulin Zinc Suspension, Insulin Zinc Suspension (Amorphous), Insulin Zinc Suspension (Crystalline), Isophane Insulin and Neutral Insulin Injection*

● **Insulin Aspart** (rINN) in·sü·lin *as*·part
[28^B-L-aspartic acid]insulin (human); *116094-23-6*
Hormone; treatment of diabetes mellitus

insulin aspart has the following amino acid sequence:

Chain A

```
Gly-Ile-Val-Glu-Gln-Cys-Cys-Thr-
Ser-Ile-Cys-Ser-Leu-Tyr-Gln-Leu-
Glu-Asn-Tyr-Cys-Asn

Phe-Val-Asn-Gln-His-Leu-Cys-Gly-
Ser-His-Leu-Val-Glu-Ala-Leu-Tyr-
Leu-Val-Cys-Gly-Glu-Arg-Gly-Phe-
Phe-Tyr-Thr-Asp-Lys-Thr
```

Chain B

Insulin Detemir (rINN) *in·sü·lin de*·te·meer
Des-30^B-L-threonine-29^B-(N^6-myristoyl-L-lysine human insulin; *169148-63-4*
Hormone; treatment of diabetes mellitus

insulin detemir has the following amino acid sequence:

Chain A

```
Gly-Ile-Val-Glu-Gln-Cys-Cys-Thr-
Ser-Ile-Cys-Ser-Leu-Tyr-Gln-Leu-
Glu-Asn-Tyr-Cys-Asn

Phe-Val-Asn-Gln-His-Leu-Cys-Gly-
Ser-His-Leu-Val-Glu-Ala-Leu-Tyr-
Leu-Val-Cys-Gly-Glu-Arg-Gly-Phe-
Phe-Tyr-Thr-Pro-Lys
```

Me ～～～～～～～ $\overset{N^6}{\underset{O}{}}$

Chain B

Insulin Glargine (rINN) in·sü·lin glar·jën
21^A-Glycine-30^{B}a-L-arginine-30^{B}b-L-arginineinsulin (human); *160337-95-1*
Hormone; treatment of diabetes mellitus

insulin glargine has the following amino acid sequence:

Chain A

```
Gly-Ile-Val-Glu-Gln-Cys-Cys-Thr-
Ser-Ile-Cys-Ser-Leu-Tyr-Gln-Leu-
Glu-Asn-Tyr-Cys-Gly

Phe-Val-Asn-Gln-His-Leu-Cys-Gly-
Ser-His-Leu-Val-Glu-Ala-Leu-Tyr-
Leu-Val-Cys-Gly-Glu-Arg-Gly-Phe-
Phe-Tyr-Thr-Pro-Lys-Thr-Arg-Arg
```

Chain B

● **Insulin Injection** (BAN)
A neutral, sterile solution of insulin or of human insulin; neutral insulin; neutral insulin injection; soluble insulin
Hormone; treatment of diabetes mellitus

● **Insulin Lispro** (rINN) in·sü·lin lis·prö
28^B-L-Lysine-29^B-L-proline human insulin ; *133107-64-9*
Hormone; treatment of diabetes mellitus

insulin lispro has the following amino acid sequence:

Chain A

```
Gly-Ile-Val-Glu-Gln-Cys-Cys-Thr-
Ser-Ile-Cys-Ser-Leu-Tyr-Gln-Leu-
Glu-Asn-Tyr-Cys-Asn

Phe-Val-Asn-Gln-His-Leu-Cys-Gly-
Ser-His-Leu-Val-Glu-Ala-Leu-Tyr-
Leu-Val-Cys-Gly-Glu-Arg-Gly-Phe-
Phe-Tyr-Thr-Lys-Pro-Thr
```

Chain B

● **Insulin Zinc Suspension (Mixed)** (rINN)
A sterile, neutral suspension of beef or pork insulin (or a mixture of beef and pork insulin) or of human insulin complexed with a suitable zinc salt
Hormone; treatment of diabetes mellitus

● **Insulin Zinc Suspension (Amorphous)** (rINN)
A sterile, neutral suspension of beef or pork insulin (or a mixture of beef and pork insulin) complexed with a suitable zinc salt; the insulin is in a form insoluble in water
Hormone; treatment of diabetes mellitus

The symbol '¬' in systematic chemical names signifies line continuation

● **Insulin Zinc Suspension (Crystalline)** (rINN)
A sterile, neutral suspension of beef or pork insulin (or a mixture of beef and pork insulin) complexed with a suitable zinc salt; the insulin is in the form of crystals insoluble in water
Hormone; treatment of diabetes mellitus

Interferon (BAN) in·ter·*feer*·ron
Proteins formed by the interaction of animal cells with viruses, capable of conferring on animal cells resistance to virus infection; *9008-11-1*
Cytokine

● **Interferon Alfa** (rINN)
A family of secreted proteins, known previously as leucocyte interferon or lymphoblastoid interferon, that is produced according to the information coded by multiple interferon alfa genes.

Sub-species of the human alfa gene produce protein variants designated by the hyphenated addition of a number, *eg* interferon alfa-2, or in the case of a mixture of proteins, by an alphanumeric designation eg n1, n2 etc. The numbers conform with the recommendations of the Interferon Nomenclature Committee; the alphanumeric designations will be assigned by the World Health Organization on request. In the case of interferon alfa-2 the number is qualified according to the amino-acid residues X and Y at positions 23 and 34 in the chain by an arbitrary letter.

For labelling purposes, the name carries, in parenthesis, an approved code, in lower case letters, indicative of the method of production. The following codes are approved, and others will be made available on request:

(rbe) produced from bacteria (*E. coli*) genetically modified by recombinant DNA technology.

(lns) produced from cultured lymphoblasts from the Namalwa cell line that have been stimulated by a Sendai virus.

(bls) produced from leucocytes from human blood that have been stimulated by a Sendai virus.
Cytokine

interferon alfa has the following amino acid sequence:

```
(M)  CDLPQTHSLG    SRRTLMLLAQ    MRXISLFSCL

     KDRHDFGFPQ    EEFGNQFQKA    ETIPVLHEMI

     QQIFNLFSTK    DSSAAWDETL    LDKFYTELYQ

     QLNDLEACVI    QGVGVTETPL    MKEDSILAVR

     KYFQRITLYL    KEKKYSPCAW    EVVRAEIMRS

     FSLSTNLQES    LRSKE
```

The following examples of interferon alfa are recognised:

	Residue at position			
	23	**24**	**Code**	**CAS No:**
Alfa-2a	Lys (K)	His (H)	rbe	*76543-85-9*
Alfa-2b	Arg (R)	His (H)	rbe	*99210-65-8*
Alfa-2c	Arg (R)	Arg (R)	rbe	
Alfa-n1			lns	
Alfa-n2			bls	

Interferon Alfacon-1 (rINN) in·ter·*feer*·ron *al*·fa·kon
N-L-Methionyl-22-L-arginine-76-L-alanine-78-L-aspartic acid-79-L-glutamic acid-86-L-tyrosine-90-L-tyrosine-156-L-threonine-157-L-asparagine-158-L-leucineinterferon α1 (human lymphoblast reduced); $C_{870}H_{1366}N_{236}O_{259}S_9$; *118390-30-0*
Cytokine

interferon alfacon-1 has the following amino acid sequence:

```
(M)  CDLPQTHSLG    NRRALILLAQ    MRRISPFSCL

     KDRHDFGFPQ    EEFGNQFQKA    QAISVLHEMI

     QQTFNLFSTK    DSSAAWDESL    LEKFYTELYQ

     QLNDLEACVI    QEVGVEETPL    MNVDSILAVK

     KYFQRITLYL    TEKKYSPCAW    EVVRAEIMRS

     FSLSTNLQER    LRRKE
```


Interferon Beta (rINN)
A secreted protein, known previously as fibroblast interferon, that is produced according to the information coded by multiple interferon alfa genes.

Sub-species of the human beta gene produce protein variants designated by the hyphenated addition of a number, *eg* interferon beta-1. The numbers conform with the recommendations of the Interferon Nomenclature Committee; the alphanumeric designations will be assigned by the World Health Organization on request. In the case of interferon beta-1 the number is qualified by an arbitary letter according to the amino-acid residues at positions 1 and 17 in the chain and to whether or not glycosylation is present.

For labelling purposes, the following three-letter code, to indicate the method of production is approved:

(rch) produced from genetically engineered Chinese hamster ovary cells
Cytokine

interferon beta has the following amino acid sequence:

```
(M)  SYNLLGFLQR    SSNFQCQKLL    WQLNGRLEYC

     LKDRMNFDIP    EEIKQLQQFQ    KEDAALTIYE

     MLQNIFAIFR    QDSSSTGWNE*   TIVENLLANV

     YHQINHLKTV    LEEKLEKEDF    TRGKLMSSHL

     KRYYGRILHY    LKAKEYSHCA    WTIVRVEILR

     NFYFINRLTG    YLR
```

* glycosylation site

The following examples of inteferon beta are recognised:

	Interferon Beta-1a	Interferon Beta-1b
Residue at position 1	Met (M)	-
Residue at position 17	Cys (C)	Ser (S)
Glycosylation	yes (position 80)	no
Molecular formula	$C_{908}H_{1406}N_{246}O_{252}S_7$	$C_{903}H_{1397}N_{246}O_{252}S_5$
CAS Registry Number	145258-61-3	90598-63-3
Manufacturing code	rch	rbe

Iobitridol (rINN) ï·ö·*bi*·tri·dol
N,*N*′-Bis(2,3-dihydroxypropyl)-5-(3-hydroxy-2-hydroxy¬
methylpropionamido)-2,4,6-tri-iodo-*N*,*N*′-dimethyl iso¬
phthalamide; $C_{20}H_{28}I_3N_3O_9$; *136949-58-1*
Iodinated contrast medium

● **Interferon Gamma** (rINN)
A secreted protein, known previously as immune interferon, that is produced according to the information coded by a species of interferon gene. As with interferon alfa, protein variants of interferon gamma have been produced and are differentiated by alphanumeric suffixes. The qualifying terms are designated according to the nature of the termini X and Y at positions 1 and 139 in the chain (see below).

For labelling purposes, the name carries, in parenthesis an approved code, in lower case letters, indicative of the method of production (see under Interferon alfa).
Cytokine

interferon gamma has the following amino acid sequence:

```
X-QDPYVKEAEN    LKKYFNAGHS    DVADNGTLFL

 GILKNWKEES    DRKIMQSQIV    SFYFKLFKNF

 KDDQSIQKSV    ETIKEDMNVK    FFNSNKKKRD

 DFEKLTNYSV    TDLNVQRKAI    HELIQVMAEL

 SPAAKTGKRK    RSQMLFRGR-Y
```

mixture of stereoisomers

Iocarmic Acid (rINN) ï·ö·*kar*·mik
5,5′-(Adipoyldiamino)bis(2,4,6-tri-iodo-*N*-methylisophthalamic acid); $C_{24}H_{20}I_6N_4O_8$; *10397-75-8*
Meglumine Iocarmate *54605-45-7*
Iodinated contrast medium

The following examples of interferon gamma are recognised.

	Interferon Gamma-1a	Interferon Gamma-1b
Terminus X	Cys-Tyr-Cys (CTC)	Met (M)
Terminus Y	Arg-Ala-Ser-Gln (RASQ)	-OH
CAS Registry No:	98059-18-8	98059-61-1
Manufacturing code	Rbe	

Iocetamic Acid (rINN) ï·ö·se·*ta*·mik
(*RS*)-2-[*N*-(3-Amino-2,4,6-tri-iodophenyl)acetamidomethyl]propionic acid; $C_{12}H_{13}I_3N_2O_3$; *16034-77-8*
Iodinated contrast medium

and enantiomer

● **Inulin** (BAN)
Polysaccharide granules obtained from the tubers of *Dahlia variabelis, Helvanthus tuberosus* and other genera of the family Compositae
Diagnostic agent used in the determination of renal function (glomerular filtration rate)

Iodamide (rINN) ï·ö·da·mïd
α,5-Diacetamido-2,4,6-tri-iodo-*m*-toluic acid; $C_{12}H_{11}I_3N_2O_4$; *440-58-4*
Iodinated contrast medium

Iobenzamic Acid (rINN) ï·ö·ben·*za*·mik
N-(3-Amino-2,4,6-tri-iodobenzoyl)-*N*-phenyl-β-alanine; $C_{16}H_{13}N_2O_3$; *3115-05-7*
Iodinated contrast medium

Iodinated Glycerol (BAN)
A mixture of iodinated dimers of glycerol
Expectorant

The symbol '¬' in systematic chemical names signifies line continuation

Iodipamide *see Adipiodone*

● **Iodixanol** (rINN) ï·ö·*diks*·a·nol
rac-N,N′,N′′,N′′′-Tetrakis(2,3-dihydroxypropyl)-2,2′,4,4′,6,6′-hexaiodo-5,5′-[2-hydroxytrimethylenebis(acetylimino)]di-isohthalamide; $C_{35}H_{44}I_6N_6O_{15}$; *92339-11-2*
Iodinated contrast medium

mixture of isomers

Iodofenphos (BAN) ï·ö·dö·*fen*·fos
O-(2,5-Dichloro-4-iodophenyl) *O,O*-dimethylphosphoro¬thioate; $C_8H_8Cl_2O_3PS$; *18181-70-9*
Acaricide; insecticide

Iodothiouracil (rINN) ï·ö·dö·thï·ö·*ûr*·ra·sil
(1) 2,3-Dihydro-5-iodo-2-thioxopyrimidin-4(1*H*)-one;
(2) 5-Iodo-2-thiouracil; $C_4H_3IN_2OS$; *5984-97-4*
Antithyroid drug

Iodoxamic Acid (rINN) ï·ö·doks·*a*·mik
3,3′-(4,7,10,13-Tetraoxahexadecanedioyldiamino)bis(2,4,6-tri-iodobenzoic acid); $C_{26}H_{26}I_6N_2O_{10}$; *31127-82-9*
Meglumine Iodoxamate *51764-33-1*
Iodinated contrast medium

Iofendylate (rINN) ï·ö·*fen*·di·lät
Ethyl (*RS*)-10-(4-iodophenyl)undecanoate; $C_{19}H_{29}IO_2$; *99-79-6*
Iodinated contrast medium

and enantiomer

Ioflupane[123I] (rINN) ï·ö·*floo*·pän
Methyl (1*R*,2*R*,3*R*,5*S*)-8-(3-fluoropropyl)-3-([123I]-4-iodophenyl)-8-azabicyclo[3.2.1]octane-2-carboxylate;
$C_{18}H_{23}F^{123}INO_2$; *155798-07-5*
Iodinated contrast medium

Ioglicic Acid (rINN) ï·ö·*glï*·sik
5-Acetamido-2,4,6-tri-iodo-*N*-[(methylcarbamoyl)methyl]isophthalamic acid; $C_{13}H_{12}I_3N_3O_5$; *49755-67-1*
Iodinated contrast medium

Ioglycamic Acid (rINN) ï·ö·glï·*ka*·mik
3,3′-[Oxybis(methylenecarbonylimino)]bis(2,4,6-tri-iodo¬benzoic acid); $C_{18}H_{10}I_6N_2O_7$; *2618-25-9*
Meglumine Ioglycamate *14317-18-1*
Iodinated contrast medium

● **Iohexol** (rINN) ï·ö·heks·ol
N,N′-Bis(2,3-dihydroxypropyl)-5-[*N*-(2,3-dihydroxypropyl)¬acetamido]-2,4,6-tri-iodoisophthalamide; $C_{19}H_{26}IN_3O_9$;
66108-95-0
Iodinated contrast medium

mixture of isomers

Iomeprol (rINN) ï·ö·*me*·prol
N,N′-Bis(2,3-dihydroxypropyl)-2,4,6-tri-iodo-5-(*N*-methyl¬glycollamido)isophthalamide; $C_{17}H_{22}I_3N_3O_8$; *78649-41-9*
Iodinated contrast medium

mixture of isomers

mixture of isomers

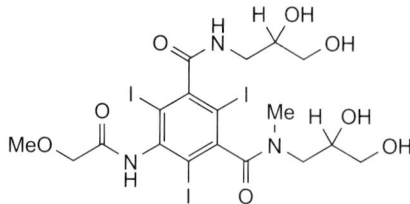

● **Iopamidol** (rINN) ï·ö·*pa*·mi·dol
(S)-N,N'-[Bis[2-hydroxy-1-(hydroxymethyl)ethyl]-2,4,6-tri-
iodo-5-lactamidoisophthalamide; $C_{17}H_{22}I_3N_3O_8$; *60166-93-0*
Iodinated contrast medium

● **Iopronic Acid** (rINN) ï·ö·*pro*·nik
2-[2-(3-Acetamido-2,4,6-tri-iodophenoxy)ethoxymethyl]butyric
acid; $C_{15}H_{18}I_3NO_5$; *37723-78-7*
Iodinated contrast medium

and enantiomer

● **Iopanoic Acid** (rINN) ï·ö·pa·*nö*·ik
(RS)-2-(3-Amino-2,4,6-tri-iodobenzyl)butyric acid;
$C_{11}H_{12}I_3NO_2$; *96-83-3*
Iodinated contrast medium

Iopydol (rINN) ï·ö·*pï*·dol
(RS)-1-(2,3-Dihydroxypropyl)-3,5-di-iodo-4-pyridone;
$C_8H_9I_2NO_3$; *5579-92-0*
Iodinated contrast medium

and enantiomer

and enantiomer

Iopentol (rINN) ï·ö·*pen*·tol
N,N'-Bis(2,3-dihydroxypropyl)-5-[*N*-(2-hydroxy-3-methoxy¬
propyl)acetamido]-2,4,6-tri-iodoisophthalamide; $C_{20}H_{28}I_3N_3O_9$;
89797-00-2
Iodinated contrast medium

Iopydone (rINN) ï·ö·*pï*·dön
3,5-Di-iodo-4-pyridone; $C_5H_3I_2NO$; *5579-93-1*
Iodinated contrast medium

mixture of isomers

Iophendylate *see Iofendylate*

● **Iopromide** (rINN) ï·ö·prö·mïd
N,N'-Bis(2,3-dihydroxypropyl)-2,4,6-tri-iodo-5-(2-
methoxyacetamido)-*N*-methylisophthalamide; $C_{18}H_{24}I_3N_3O_8$;
73334-07-3
Iodinated contrast medium

● **Iotalamic Acid** (rINN) ï·ö·ta·*la*·mik
5-Acetamido-2,4,6-tri-iodo-*N*-methylisophthalamic acid;
$C_{11}H_9I_3N_2O_4$; *2276-90-6*
Meglumine Iotalamate *13087-53-1*
Sodium Iotalamate *17692-74-9*
Iodinated contrast medium

The symbol '¬' in systematic chemical names signifies line continuation

• **Iotrolan** (rINN) ï·ö·*trö*·lan
N,N',N'',N'''-Tetrakis(2,3-dihydroxy-1-hydroxymethylpropyl)-
2,2′,4,4′,6,6′-hexaiodo-5,5′-(N,N'-dimethylmalonyldi-imino)di-
isophthalamide; $C_{37}H_{48}I_6N_6O_{18}$; *79770-24-4*
Iodinated contrast medium

mixture of isomers

Iotroxic Acid (rINN) ï·ö·*troks*·ik
3,3′-(3,6,9-Trioxaundecanedioyldi-iminobis(2,4,6-tri-iodo¬
benzoic acid); $C_{22}H_{18}I_6N_2O_9$;
51022-74-3
Meglumine Iotroxate
Iodinated contrast medium

Ioversol (rINN) ï·ö·*ver*·sol
N,N'-Bis(2,3-dihydroxypropyl)-5-[N-(2-hydroxyethyl)¬
glycollamido]-2,4,6-tri-iodoisophthalamide; $C_{18}H_{24}I_3N_3O_9$;
87771-40-2
Iodinated contrast medium

mixture of isomers

• **Ioxaglic Acid** (rINN) ï·oks·*a*·glik
N-(2-Hydroxyethyl)-2,4,6-tri-iodo-5-[2′,4′,6′-tri-iodo-3′-
(N-methylacetamido)-5′-methylcarbamoylhippuramido]iso¬
phthalamic acid; $C_{24}H_{21}I_6N_5O_8$; *59017-64-0*
Meglumine Ioxaglate *59018-13-2*
Sodium Ioxaglate *67992-58-9*
Iodinated contrast medium

• **Ipratropium Bromide** (rINN) ï·pra·*trö*·pë·um
(1R,3r,5S,8r)-8-Isopropyl-3-(±)-tropoyloxytropanium bromide;
$C_{20}H_{30}BrNO_3$; *22254-24-6*
Anticholinergic (antimuscarinic) bronchodilator

and enantiomer

Iprindole (rINN) ï·prin·dôl
5-(3-Dimethylaminopropyl)-6,7,8,9,10,11-
hexahydrocyclo-oct[b]indole; $C_{19}H_{28}N_2$; *5560-72-5*
Iprindole Hydrochloride *20432-64-8*
Monoamine reuptake inhibitor; tricyclic antidepressant

Iproclozide (rINN) i·prö·*klö*·zïd
2-(4-Chlorophenoxy)-2′-isopropylacetohydrazide;
$C_{11}H_{15}ClN_2O_2$; *3544-35-2*
Monoamine oxidase inhibitor; antidepressant

Iproniazid (rINN) i·prö·*nï*·a·zid
2′-Isopropylisonicotinohydrazide; $C_9H_{13}N_3O$; *54-92-2*
Iproniazid Phosphate *305-33-9*
Monoamine oxidase inhibitor; antidepressant

Ipronidazole (rINN) i·prö·*nï*·da·zôl
2-Isopropyl-1-methyl-5-nitroimidazole; $C_7H_{11}N_3O_2$;
14885-29-1
Antiprotozoal

Iproplatin (rINN) i·prö·*pla*·tin
(OC-6-33)-Dichlorodihydroxybis(isopropylamine)platinum;
$C_6H_{20}Cl_2N_2O_2Pt$; *62928-11-4*
Platinum-containing cytotoxic

154

Ipsalazide (rINN) ip·*sa*·la·zïd
4′-(3-Carboxy-4-hydroxyphenylazo)hippuric acid; $C_{16}H_{13}N_3O_6$;
80573-03-1
Ipsalazide Sodium
Aminosalicylate; treatment of ulcerative colitis

Ipsapirone (rINN) ip·sa·*pîr*·rön
2-{4-[4-(Pyrimidin-2-yl)piperazin-1-yl]butyl}-1,2-benzo¬
thiazol-3(2H)-one 1,1-dioxide; $C_{19}H_{23}N_5O_3S$; *95847-70-4*
Ipsapirone Hydrochloride *92589-98-5*
Anxiolytic

• **Irbesartan** (rINN) er·be·*sar*·tan
2-Butyl-3-{4-[2-(1H-tetrazol-5-yl)phenyl]benzyl}-1,3-
diazaspiro[4.4]non-1-en-4-one; $C_{25}H_{28}N_6O$; *138402-11-6*
Angiotensin II (AT₁) receptor antagonist

Irinotecan (rINN) i·ri·nö·*të*·kan
(S)-4,11-Diethyl-3,4,12,14-tetrahydro-4-hydroxy-3,14-
dioxo-1H-pyrano[3′,4′:6,7]indolizino[1,2-b]quinolin-9-yl [1,4′-
bipiperidine]-1′-carboxylate; $C_{33}H_{38}N_4O_6$; *97682-44-5*
Irinotecan Hydrochloride *136572-09-3 (trihydrate)*
Inhibitor of DNA topoisomerase type I; cytotoxic

Iron Sucrose (BAN) îr·on *sü*·krös
A complex of iron(III) hydroxide with sucrose containing traces
of sodium chloride and sodium hydroxide corresponding
approximately to the formula:
$[\{Na_{0.46}[FeO_{1.6}(OH)_{0.26}(H_2O)_{0.54}][C_{12}H_{22}O_{11}]_{2.61}\} + 0.18NaOH + 0.02NaCl]_n$ ($n = 43$) (mol. wt., 43,200 approx); iron(III)
hydroxide–sucrose complex; saccharated iron oxide; *8047-67-4*
Iron salt

Irtemazole (rINN) er·*te*·ma·zôl
(RS)-5-(α-Imidazol-1-ylbenzyl)-2-methylbenzimidazole;
$C_{18}H_{16}N_4$; *115574-30-6*
Uricosuric agent

and enantiomer

Isamoxole (rINN) see Appendix C

Isatoribine (rINN) ï·sa·*tor*·ri·bën
5-Amino-3-(β-D-ribofuranosyl)[1,3]thiazolo[4,5-d]pyrimidine-
2,7(3H,6H)-dione; $C_{10}H_{12}N_4O_6S$; *122970-40-5*
Immunomodulator

Isepamicin (rINN) ï·se·pa·*mï*·sin
4-O-(6-Amino-6-deoxy-α-D-glucopyranosyl)-1-N-(3-amino-
L-lactoyl)-2-deoxy-6-O-(3-deoxy-4-C-methyl-3-methylamino-
β-L-arabinopyranosyl)-D-streptamine; $C_{22}H_{43}N_5O_{12}$; *58152-03-7*
Aminoglycoside antibacterial

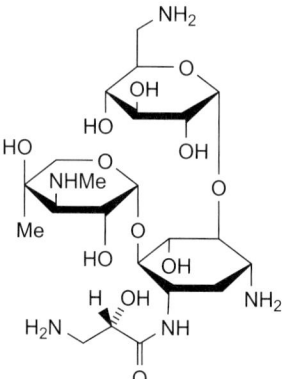

• **Isoaminile** (rINN) ï·sö·*am*·i·nïl
4-Dimethylamino-2-isopropyl-2-phenylpentanonitrile;
$C_{16}H_{24}N_2$; *77-51-0*
Isoaminile Citrate *126-10-3*
Cough suppressant

mixture of 4 stereoisomers

Isobuzole *see Glysobuzole*

The symbol '¬' in systematic chemical names signifies line continuation

Isocarboxazid (rINN) ï·sö·kar·*boks*·a·zid
2′-Benzyl-5-methyl-1,2-oxazole-3-carbohydrazide; $C_{12}H_{13}N_3O_2$; *59-63-2*
Monoamine oxidase inhibitor; antidepressant

● **Isoconazole** (rINN) ï·sö·*ko*·na·zôl
(RS)-1-[2,4-Dichloro-β-(2,6-dichlorobenzyloxy)phenethyl]¬imidazole; $C_{18}H_{14}Cl_4N_2O$;
27523-40-6
● **Isoconazole Nitrate** *40036-10-0*; R 15454
Antifungal

and enantiomer

Isoetarine (rINN) see Appendix C

Isoflupredone (rINN) ï·sö·*floo*·pre·dön
(1) 9α-Fluoro-11β,17α,21-trihydroxypregna-1,4-diene-3,20-dione; (2) 9α-Fluoroprednisolone; $C_{21}H_{27}FO_5$; *338-95-4*
Isoflupredone Acetate *338-98-7*
Glucocorticoid

● **Isoflurane** (rINN) ï·sö·*flûr*·rän
2-Chloro-2-difluoromethoxy-1,1,1-trifluoroethane; $C_3H_2ClF_5O$;
26675-46-7
General anaesthetic

and enantiomer

● **Isoleucine** (rINN) ï·sö·*loo*·sën
L-Isoleucine; (2S,3S)-2-Amino-3-methylpentanoic acid;
$C_6H_{13}NO_2$; *73-32-5*;
Amino acid

● **Isomalt** (BAN) *i*·sö·malt
A mixture of equal parts of 6-O-(α-D-glucopyranosyl)-D-glucitol and 1-O-(α-D-glucopyranosyl)-D-mannitol
Sweetening agent

Isometamidium Chloride (rINN) ï·sö·me·ta·*mi*·dë·um
8-(3-*m*-Amidinophenyl-1-triazeno)-3-amino-5-ethyl-6-phenyl phenanthridinium chloride; $C_{28}H_{26}ClN_7$; *34301-55-8*
Antiprotozoal

Isomethadone (rINN) ï·sö·*me*·tha·dön
(RS)-6-Dimethylamino-5-methyl-4,4-diphenylhexan-3-one;
$C_{21}H_{27}NO$; *466-40-0*
Opioid receptor agonist

and enantiomer

Isometheptene (rINN) ï·sö·me·*thep*·tën
(RS)-1,5-Dimethylhex-4-enyl(methyl)amine; $C_9H_{19}N$; *503-01-5*
● **Isometheptene Mucate**
Adrenoceptor agonist

and enantiomer

● **Isoniazid** (rINN) ï·sö·*ni*·a·zid
Isonicotinohydrazide; $C_6H_7N_3O$; *54-85-3*
Antituberculosis drug

● **Isophane Insulin** (rINN)
A buffered suspension of insulin with the isophanic equivalent of protamine and zinc chloride; isophane insulin (NPH)
Hormone; treatment of diabetes mellitus

Isoprazone (rINN) see Appendix C

Isoprednidene (rINN) ïˑsöˑ*pred*ˑniˑdën

11β,17α,21-Trihydroxy-16-methylenepregna-4,6-diene-3,20-dione; $C_{22}H_{28}O_5$; *17332-61-5*
Corticotropin inhibitor

Isoprenaline (rINN) ïˑsöˑ*pre*ˑnaˑlën

(*RS*)-1-(3,4-Dihydroxyphenyl)-2-isopropylaminoethanol; $C_{11}H_{17}NO_3$; *7683-59-2*
 ● **Isoprenaline Hydrochloride** isoproterenol hydrochloride (USAN); *51-30-9*
 ● **Isoprenaline Sulfate** *6700-39-6; (dihydrate); 299-95-6 (anhydrous)*
Adrenoceptor agonist

and enantiomer

Isopropamide Iodide (rINN) ïˑsöˑ*prö*ˑpaˑmïd

(3-Carbamoyl-3,3-diphenylpropyl)di-isopropylmethyl¬ammonium iodide; $C_{23}H_{33}IN_2O$; *71-81-8*
Anticholinergic

Isosorbide (rINN) ïˑsöˑ*sor*ˑbïd

1,4:3,6-Dianhydro-D-glucitol; $C_6H_{10}O_4$; *652-67-5*
Nitric oxide analogue; treatment of angina pectoris

● **Isosorbide Dinitrate** (rINN) ïˑsöˑ*sor*ˑbïd dïˑ*ni*ˑträt

1,4:3,6-Dianhydro-D-glucitol 2,5-dinitrate; sorbide nitrate; $C_6H_8N_2O_8$; *87-33-2*
Nitric oxide analogue; treatment of angina pectoris

● **Isosorbide Mononitrate** (rINN) ïˑsöˑ*sor*ˑbïd moˑnöˑ*ni*ˑträt

1,4:3,6-Dianhydro-D-glucitol 5-nitrate; $C_6H_9NO_6$; *16051-77-7*
Nitric oxide analogue; treatment of angina pectoris

Isothipendyl (rINN) see Appendix C

Isotiquimide (rINN) see Appendix C

● **Isotretinoin** (rINN) ïˑsöˑtreˑtiˑ*nö*ˑin

(1) (13*Z*)-15-Apo-β-caroten-15-oic acid; (2) (2*Z*,4*E*,6*E*,8*E*)-3,7-dimethyl-9-(2,6,6-trimethylcyclohex-1-enyl)nona-2,4,6,8-tetraenoic acid; (3) 13-*cis*-Retinoic acid; $C_{20}H_{28}O_2$; *4759-48-2*
Vitamin A analogue (retinoid); treatment of acne

Isoxepac (rINN) *ï*ˑsoksˑëˑpak

6,11-Dihydro-11-oxodibenz[*b,e*]oxepin-2-ylacetic acid; $C_{16}H_{12}O_4$; *55453-82-7*
Cyclo-oxygenase inhibitor; analgesic; anti-inflammatory

Isoxicam (rINN) *ï*ˑ*soks*ˑiˑkam

4-Hydroxy-2-methyl-*N*-(5-methyl-1,2-oxazol-3-yl)-2*H*-1,2-benzothiazine-3-carboxamide 1,1-dioxide; $C_{14}H_{13}N_3O_5S$; *34552-84-6*
Cyclo-oxygenase inhibitor; analgesic; anti-inflammatory

Isoxsuprine (rINN) *ï*ˑ*sok*ˑsüˑprën

(1*RS*,2*SR*)-1-(4-Hydroxyphenyl)-2-[(1*SR*)-1-methyl-2-phenoxy ethylamino]propan-1-ol; $C_{18}H_{23}NO_3$; *395-28-8*
 ● **Isoxsuprine Hydrochloride** *579-56-6*
Beta₂-adrenoceptor agonist

and enantiomer

● **Isradipine** (rINN) is·*ra*·di·pën
(*RS*)-Isopropyl methyl 4-(2,1,3-benzoxadiazol-4-yl)-1,4-dihydro-2,6-dimethylpyridine-3,5-dicarboxylate; $C_{19}H_{21}N_3O_5$; *75695-93-1*
Calcium channel blocker

and enantiomer

● **Itraconazole** (rINN) i·tra·*ko*·na·zôl
(±)-2-*sec*-Butyl-4-[4-(4-{4-[(2*R**,4*S**)-2-(2,4-dichlorophenyl)-2-(1*H*-1,2,4-triazol-1-ylmethyl)-1,3-dioxolan-4-yl methoxy]phenyl}piperazin-1-yl)phenyl]-2,4-dihydro-1,2,4-triazol-3-one; $C_{35}H_{38}Cl_2N_8O_4$; *84625-61-6*
Antifungal

and enantiomer

Itramin Tosilate (rINN) *i*·tra·min *tö*·s·ilät
2-Nitratoethylammonium *p*-toluenesulfonate; $C_2H_6N_2O_3.C_7H_8N_3S$; *13445-63-1*
Nitric oxide analogue; treatment of angina pectoris

Ivabradine (rINN) i·*va*·bra·dën
3-[3-({[(7*S*)-3,4-Dimethoxybicyclo[4.2.0]octa-1,3,5-trien-7-yl]methyl}methylamino)propyl]-7,8-dimethoxy-1,3,4,5-tetrahydro-2*H*-3-benzazepin-2-one; $C_{27}H_{36}N_2O_5$; *155974-00-8*;
Ivabradine Hydrochloride *148849-67-6*
Inhibitor of cardiac I$_f$ channels; treatment of angina pectoris

● **Ivermectin** (rINN) ï·ver·*mek*·tin
A mixture of ivermectin components B$_{1a}$ and B$_{1b}$; *70288-86-7*
Component B$_{1a}$: (10*E*,14*E*,16*E*,22*Z*)-(1*R*,4*S*,5′*S*,6*R*,6′*R*,8*R*,¬12*S*,13*S*, 20*R*,21*R*,24*S*)-6′-[(*S*)-*sec*-Butyl]-21,24-dihydroxy-5′,11,13,22-tetramethyl-2-oxo-(3,7,19-trioxatetracyclo [15.6.¬1. 1^{4,8}.0^{20,24}]pentcosa-10,14,16,22-tetraene)-6-spiro-2′-(perhydropyran)-12-yl 2,6-dideoxy-4-*O*-(2,6-dideoxy-3-*O*-methyl-α-L-*arabino*-hexopyranosyl)-3-*O*-methyl-α-L-*arabino*-hexopyranoside; *70161-11-4*
Component B$_{1b}$: as described above replacing '6′-[(*S*)-sec-Butyl]-' by '6′-isopropyl-' inserted after '21,24-dihydroxy-'; *70209-81-3*
Antihelminthic (veterinary)

B$_{1a}$, R = Et

B$_{1b}$, R = Me

● **Josamycin** (rINN) jö·sa·*mï*·sin
(4*R*,5*S*,6*S*,7*R*,9*R*,10*R*,11*E*,13*E*,16*R*)-4-(Acetoxy)-6-({3,6-dideoxy-4-*O*-[2,6-dideoxy-3-*C*-methyl-4-*O*-(3-methyl¬butanoyl)-α-L-*ribo*-hexopyranosyl]-3-(dimethylamino)-β-D-glucopyranosyl}oxy)-10-hydroxy-5-methoxy-9,16-dimethyl-7-(2-oxoethyl)oxacyclohexadeca-11,13-dien-2-one; $C_{42}H_{69}NO_{15}$; *56689-45-3*
● **Josamycin Propionate** *40922-77-8*
Antibacterial

Kallidinogenase (rINN) ka·li·di·*no*·je·näz
An enzyme that splits the kinin, kallidin, from kininogen; *9001-01-8*
Kininogen converting enzyme

158

Kanamycin (rINN) kä·na·*mï*·sin
An antimicrobial base produced by *Streptomyces kanamyceticus*; 6-*O*-D-(3-amino-3-deoxy-α-glucopyranosyl)-4-*O*-(6-amino-6-deoxy-α-D-glucopyranosyl)-2-deoxy-D-streptamine; kanamycin A; $C_{18}H_{36}N_4O_{11}$; *59-01-8*;

● **Kanamycin Sulfate** *25389-94-0*

● **Kanamycin Acid Sulfate**
Aminoglycoside antibacterial

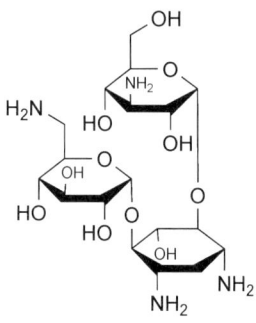

Ketamine (rINN) *kë*·ta·mën
2-(2-Chlorophenyl)-2-methylaminocyclohexanone; $C_{13}H_{16}ClNO$; *4740-88-1*

● **Ketamine Hydrochloride** *1867-66-9*
Intravenous general anaesthetic

and enantiomer

Ketanserin (rINN) kë·*tan*·se·rin
3-{2-[4-(4-Fluorobenzoyl)piperidino]ethyl}quinazoline-2,4(1*H*,3*H*)dione; $C_{22}H_{22}FN_3O_3$; *74050-98-9*; R41468
Ketanserin Tartrate R49945
Serotonin $5HT_{2a}$ receptor antagonist

Ketazolam (rINN) see Appendix C

● **Ketobemidone** (rINN) kë·tö·*be*·mi·dön
1-(4-*m*-Hydroxyphenyl-1-methyl-4-piperidyl)propan-1-one; cetobemidone (rINN); $C_{15}H_{21}NO_2$; *469-79-4*

● **Ketobemidone Hydrochloride**
Opioid receptor agonist; analgesic

● **Ketoconazole** (rINN) kë·tö·*kon*·a·zôl
1-Acetyl-4-{4-[2-(2,4-dichlorophenyl)-*r*-2-(1*H*-imidazol-1-ylmethyl)-1,3-dioxolan-*c*-4-ylmethoxy]phenyl}piperazine; $C_{26}H_{28}Cl_2N_4O_4$; *65277-42-1*
Antifungal

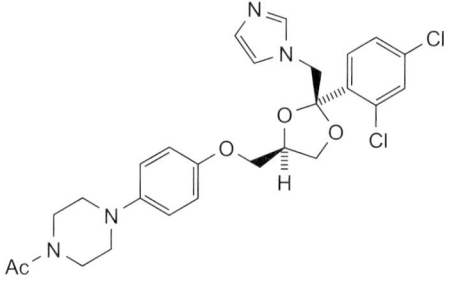

and enantiomer

● **Ketoprofen** (rINN) kë·tö·*prö*·fen
2-(3-Benzoylphenyl)propionic acid; $C_{16}H_{14}O_3$; *22071-15-4*
Cyclo-oxygenase inhibitor; analgesic; anti-inflammatory

and enantiomer

Ketorolac (rINN) kë·*to*·rö·lak
(*RS*)-5-Benzoyl-2,3-dihydro-1*H*-pyrrolizine-1-carboxylic acid; $C_{15}H_{13}NO_3$; *74103-06-3*
● **Ketorolac Trometamol** ketorolac tromethamine (USAN); *74103-07-4*
Cyclo-oxygenase inhibitor; analgesic; anti-inflammatory

and enantiomer

Ketotifen (rINN) kë·*tot*·i·fen
4-(1-Methylpiperidin-4-ylidene)-4*H*-benzo[4,5]cyclohepta[1,2-*b*]thiophen-10(9*H*)-one; $C_{19}H_{19}NOS$; *34580-13-7*

● **Ketotifen Fumarate** *34580-14-8*
Histamine H_1 receptor antagonist

Kitasamycin (rINN) ki·tä·sa·*mï*·sin

An antibiotic produced by *Streptomyces kitasatoensis*; it consists mainly of kitasamycins A₄ and A₅; leucomycin; *1392-21-8*

Kitasamycin A₄: (10*E*,12*E*)-(3*R*,4*R*,5*S*,6*R*,8*R*,9*R*,15*R*)-3-Acetoxy-5-[4-*O*-(4-*O*-butyryl-2,6-dideoxy-3-*C*-methyl-α-L-*ribo*-hexopyranosyl)-3,6-dideoxy-3-dimethylamino-β-D-*gluco*-hexopyranosyloxy]-6-formylmethyl-9-hydroxy-4-methoxy-8-methylhexadeca-10,12-dien-15-olide; $C_{41}H_{67}NO_{15}$

Kitasamycin A₅: (10*E*,12*E*)-(3*R*,4*R*,5*S*,6*R*,8*R*,9*R*,15*R*)-5-[4-*O*-(4-*O*-butyryl-2,6-dideoxy-3-*C*-methyl-α-L-*ribo*-hexo¬ pyranosyl)-3,6-dideoxy-3-dimethylamino-β-D-*gluco*-hexo¬ pyranosyloxy]-6-formylmethyl-3,9-dihydroxy-4-methoxy-8-methylhexadeca-10,12-dien-15-olide; $C_{39}H_{65}NO_{14}$; *18361-45-0*
Antibacterial (veterinary)

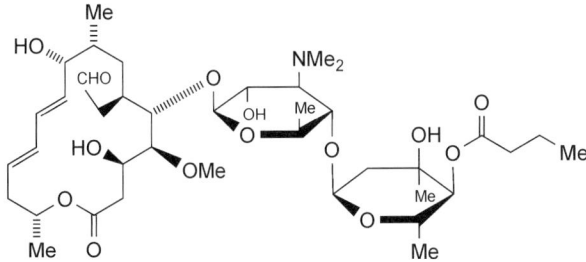

Kitasamycin A₅

Labetalol (rINN) la·*bë*·ta·lol

2-Hydroxy-5-[1-hydroxy-2-(1-methyl-3-phenylpropylamino)¬ ethyl]benzamide; $C_{19}H_{24}N_2O_3$; *36894-69-6*
● **Labetalol Hydrochloride** *32780-64-6*
Alpha- and beta-adrenoceptor antagonist

mixture of 4 isomers

Lachesine Chloride (rINN) see Appendix C

● **Lacidipine** (rINN) la·*si*·di·pën

Diethyl (*E*)-4-{2-[((*tert*-butoxycarbonyl)vinyl]phenyl}-1,4-dihydro-2,6-dimethylpyridine-3,5-dicarboxylate; $C_{26}H_{33}NO_6$; *103890-78-4*
Calcium channel blocker

● **Lactitol** (rINN) *lak*·ti·tol

4-*O*-(β-D-Galactopyranosyl)-D-glucitol; $C_{12}H_{24}O_{11}$; *585-86-4*
Osmotic laxative

Lacosamide (rINN) la·kö·*sa*·mïd

(2*R*)-2-(Acetamido)-*N*-benzyl-3-methoxypropanamide; $C_{13}H_{18}N_2O_3$; *175481-36-4*;
Antiepileptic

● **Lactulose** (rINN) *lak*·tü·lös

4-*O*-(b-D-Galactopyranosyl)-D-fructose; $C_{12}H_{22}O_{11}$; *4618-18-2*
Osmotic laxative

Laidlomycin (rINN) läd·lö·*mï*·sin

(2*S*,3*R*,4*R*)-4-[(2*S*,5*R*,7*S*,8*R*,9*S*)-9-Hydroxy-2,8-dimethyl-2-{(2*S*,2'*R*,3'*S*,5*R*,5'*R*)-octahydro2,3'-dimethyl-5'-[(2*S*,3*S*,¬ 5*R*,6*R*)-tetrahydro-6-hydroxy-6-hydroxymethyl-3,5-dimethyl-2*H*-pyran2-yl]-2,2'-bifuran-5-yl}-1,6-dioxaspiro[4.5]dec-7-yl]-2-methyl-3-propionyloxypentanoic acid; $C_{37}H_{62}O_{12}$; *56283-74-0*
Laidlomycin Propionate Potassium *84799-02-0*
Antiprotozoal (veterinary)

● **Lamivudine** (rINN) la·*miv*·ü·dën

(1) 4-Amino-1-[(2*R*,5*S*)-2-hydroxymethyl-1,3-oxathiazolan-5-yl]pyrimidin-2(1*H*)-one; (2) 1-[(2*R*,5*S*)-2-Hydroxymethyl-1,3-oxathiazolan-5-yl]cytosine; $C_8H_{11}N_3O_3S$; *134678-17-4*
Nucleoside reverse transcriptase inhibitor; antiviral (HIV)

Lamotrigine (rINN) la·*mo*·tri·jën
6-(2,3-Dichlorophenyl)-1,2,4-triazine-3,5-diyldiamine;
$C_9H_7ClN_5$; *84057-84-1*
Antiepileptic

Lamtidine (rINN) *lam*·ti·dën
3-Amino-1-methyl-1*H*-1,2,4-triazol-5-yl[3-(α-piperidino-*m*-tolyloxy)propyl]amine; $C_{18}H_{28}N_6O$; *73278-54-3*
Histamine H_2 receptor antagonist

Lanatoside C (rINN) see Appendix C

Lanproston (rINN) see Appendix C

Lanreotide (rINN) lan·*rë*·ö·tïd
S^2,S^7-Cyclo[3-(2-naphthyl)-D-alanyl-L-cysteinyl-L-tyrosyl-D-tryptophyl-L-lysyl-L-valyl-L-cysteinyl-L-threoninamide];
$C_{54}H_{69}N_{11}O_{10}S_2$; *108736-35-2*; *27984-74-1*
Somatostatin analogue; treatment of neuroendocrine tumours and acromegaly

Cys-Tyr-D-Trp-Lys-Val-Cys-Thr-NH₂

Lansoprazole (rINN) lan·*so*·pra·zôl
2-({3-Methyl-4-(2,2,2-trifluoroethoxy)-2-pyridyl)methyl}sulfinylbenzimidazole; $C_{16}H_{14}F_3N_3O_2S$;
103577-45-3
Proton pump inhibitor; treatment of peptic ulcer disease

Lapatinib (rINN) la·*pa*·tin·ib
N-{3-Chloro-4-[(3-fluorophenyl)methoxy]phenyl}-6-[5-({[2-(methylsulfonyl)ethyl]amino}methyl)furan-2-yl]quinazolin-4-amine; $C_{29}H_{26}ClFN_4O_4S$; *231277-92-2*;
Tyrosine kinase inhibitor acting on HER2 growth receptors; treatment of breast cancer

Lapisteride (rINN) la·*pis*·ter·rïd
N-[1-(4-Methoxyphenyl)-1-methylethyl]-3-oxo-4-aza-5α-androst-1-ene-17β-carboxamide; $C_{29}H_{40}N_2O_3$; *142139-60-4*
5-Alpha reductase inhibitor; treatment of benign prostatic hyperplasia

Laropiprant (rINN) la·*rö*·pip·rant
{(3*R*)-4-[(4-Chlorophenyl)methyl]-7-fluoro-5-(methanesulfonyl)-1,2,3,4-tetrahydrocyclopenta[*b*]indol-3-yl}acetic acid; $C_{21}H_{19}ClFNO_4S$; *571170-77-9*
Prostaglandin D_2 receptor DP_1 antagonist; reduction of niacin-induced adverse effects in the management of hyperlipidaemias

Lasalocid (rINN) la·*sal*·ö·sid
6-[(3*R*,4*S*,5*S*,7*R*)-7-{(2*S*,3*S*,5*S*)-5-Ethyl-5-[(2*R*,5*R*,6*S*)-5-ethyltetrahydro-5-hydroxy-6-methyl-2*H*-pyran-2-yl]tetra¬hydro-3-methyl-2-furyl}4-hydroxy-3,5-dimethyl-6-oxononyl]-2-hydroxy-*m*-toluic acid; $C_{34}H_{54}O_8$; *25999-31-9*
Lasalocid Sodium
Antiprotozoal

Lasofoxifene (rINN) la·sö·*foks*·if·ën
(5*R*,6*S*)-6-Phenyl-5-{4-[2-(pyrrolidin-1-yl)ethoxy]phenyl}-5,6,7,8-tetrahydronaphthalen-2-ol; $C_{28}H_{31}NO_2$; *180916-16-9*;
Lasofoxifene Tartrate *190791-29-8*
Selective oestrogen receptor modulator; treatment of osteoporosis

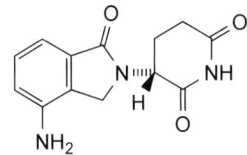

or enantiomer

and enantiomer

Latamoxef (rINN) see Appendix C

Latanoprost (rINN) la·*ta*·nö·prost
Isopropyl (*Z*)-(9*S*,11*R*,15*R*)-9,11,15-trihydroxy-17-phenyl-
18,19,20-trinorprost-5-enoate; $C_{26}H_{40}O_5$; *130209-82-4*
Prostaglandin (PGF$_{2\alpha}$) analogue

COOPr^i

Laudexium Metilsulfate (rINN) see Appendix C

Laurolinium Acetate (rINN) see Appendix C

● **Lauromacrogol** (rINN) lor·ro·*ma*·krö·gol
A mixture of monolauryl ethers of polyoxyethylene glycols
having a statistical average of 8 ethylene oxide groups per
molecule; *9015-55-8*
Non-ionic surfactant

Lavoltidine (rINN) see Appendix C

Lazabemide (rINN) la·*za*·be·mïd
N-(2-Aminoethyl)-5-chloropyridine-2-carboxamide;
$C_8H_{10}ClN_3O$; *103878-84-8*
*Monoamine oxidase type B inhibitor; treatment of Parkinson's
disease*

● **Leflunomide** (rINN) le·*floo*·nö·mïd
α,α,α-Trifluoro-5-methyl-1,2-isoxazol-4-ylcarboxo-*p*-toluidide;
$C_{12}H_9F_3N_2O_2$; *75706-12-6*
Immunomodulator

Lenalidomide (rINN) le·na·*lid*·ö·mïd
(3*RS*)-3-(4-Amino-1-oxo-1,3-dihydro-2*H*-isoindol-2-yl)¬
piperindine-2,6-dione; $C_{13}H_{13}N_3O_3$; *191732-72-6*
Cytotoxic; treatment of myloproliferative disorders

Lenercept (rINN) *len*·er·sept
1—182-tumour necrosis factor receptor (human reduced),
(182—104')-protein with 104-330-immunoglobulin G 1 (human
clone pTJ5 cγ 1 reduced); *156679-34-4*
Tumour necrosis factor receptor

*lenercept has the following amino acid sequence
(Cys—Cys bridges in the range 1-182 shown):*

LVPHLGDREK	RDSVCPQGKY	IHPQNNSICC
TKCHKGTYLY	NDCPGPGQDT	DCRECESGSF
TASENHLRHC	LSCSKCRKEM	GQVEISSCTV
DRDTVCGCRK	NQYRHYWSEN	LFQCFNCSLC
LNGTVHLSCQ	EKQNTVCTCH	AGFFLRENEC
VSCSNCKKSL	ECTKLCLPQI	ENVKGTEDSG
TTDKTHTCPP	CPAPELLGGP	SVFLFPPKPK
DTLMISRTPE	VTCVVVDVSH	EDPEVKFNWY
VDGVEVHNAK	TKPREEQYNS	TYRVVSVLTV
LHQDWLNGKE	YKCKVSNKAL	PAPIEKTISK
AKGQPREPQV	YTLPPSREEM	TKNQVSLTCL
VKGFYPSDIA	VEWESNGQPE	NNYKTTPPVL
DSDGSFFLYS	KLTVDKSRWQ	QGNVFSCSVM
HEALHNHYTQ	KSLSLSPGK	

Lenograstim (rINN) le·nö·*gra*·stim
Recombinant human granulocyte colony stimulating factor
(glycosylated) expressed by a transformed Chinese hamster
ovary cell line; (non-glycosylated protein); *62683-29-8*
Recombinant human granulocyte colony-stimulating factor

For labelling purposes, the following three-letter code, to
indicate the method of production, is approved:
(**rch**) produced from genetically engineered Chinese hamster
ovary cells

lenograstim has the following amino acid sequence:

TPLGPASSLP	QSFLLKCLEQ	VRKIQGDGAA
LQEKLCATYK	LCHPEELVLL	GHSLGIPWAP
LSSCPSQALQ	LAGCLSQLHS	GLFLYQGLLQ
ALEGISPELG	PTLDTLQLDV	ADFATTIWQQ
MEELGMAPAL	QPTQGAMPAF	ASAFQRRAGG
VLVASHLQSF	LEVSYRVLRH	LAQP

* glycosylation site

162

Lepirudin (rINN) le·*pi*·roo·din
1-L-Leucine-2-L-threonine-63-desulfohirudin (*Hirudo medicinalis* isoform HV1); *138068-37-8*
Direct thrombin inhibitor; anticoagulant

lepirudin has the following amino acid sequence:

```
LTYTDCTESG    QNLCLCEGSN    VCGQGNKCIL

GSDGEKNQCV    TGEGTPKPQS    HNDGDFEEIP

EEYLQ
```

Lercanidipine (rINN) ler·ka·*ni*·di·pën
(*RS*)-2-[3,3-Diphenylpropyl(methyl)amino]-1,1-dimethylethyl methyl 1,4-dihydro-2,6-dimethyl-4-(3-nitrophenyl)pyridine-3,5-dicarboxylate; $C_{36}H_{41}N_3O_6$; *100427-26-7*
Lercanidipine Hydrochloride *132866-11-6*
Calcium channel blocker

and enantiomer

● **Letrozole** (rINN) *le*·trö·zôl
4,4′-(1*H*-1,2,4-Triazol-1-ylmethylene)dibenzonitrile; $C_{17}H_{11}N_5$; *112809-51-5*
Aromatase inhibitor; treatment of breast carcinoma

● **Leucine** (rINN) *loo*·sën
L-Leucine; (*S*)-2-Amino-4-methylpentanoic acid; $C_6H_{13}NO_2$; *61-90-5*;
Amino acid

● **Leuprorelin** (rINN) loo·prö·*rë*·lin
$C_{59}H_{84}N_{16}O_{12}$; *53714-56-0*
Leuprorelin Acetate leuprolide acetate (USAN); *74381-53-6*
Gonadotropin releasing hormone (gonadorelin) analogue; treatment of prostate cancer

Levallorphan (rINN) lëv·a·*lor*·fan
(−)-17-Allylmorphinan-3-ol; $C_{19}H_{25}NO$; *152-02-3*
Levallorphan Tartrate *71-82-9*
Opioid receptor agonist

Levamfetamine (rINN) see Appendix C

♣ **Levamisole** (rINN) le·*vam*·i·sôl
(*S*)-2,3,5,6-Tetrahydro-6-phenylimidazo[2,1-*b*][1,3]thiazole; $C_{11}H_{12}N_2S$; *14769-73-4*
● **Levamisole Hydrochloride** *16595-80-5*
Immunostimulant; antihelminthic

Levcromakalim (rINN) lev·kro·*ma*·ka·lim
(1) *N*-[(3*S*,4*R*)-6-Cyano-3-hydroxy-2,2-dimethylchroman-4-yl]butane-4-lactam; (2) (3*S*,4*R*)-3-Hydroxy-2,2-dimethyl-4-(2-oxopyrrolidin-1-yl)chroman-6-carbonitrile; $C_{16}H_{18}N_2O_3$; *94535-50-9*
Potassium channel opener

● **Levetiracetam** (rINN) lev·e·ti·*ra*·së·tam
(*S*)-2-(2-Oxopyrrolidin-1-yl)butanamide; $C_8H_{14}N_2O_2$; *102767-28-2*
Antiepileptic

Levobunolol (rINN) lë·vö·*bu*·no·lol
(*S*)-5-(3-*tert*-Butylamino-2-hydroxypropoxy)-1,2,3,4-tetra¬hydro naphthalen-1-one; $C_{17}H_{25}NO_3$; *47141-42-4*
● **Levobunolol Hydrochloride** *27912-14-7*
Beta-adrenoceptor antagonist

His-Trp-Ser-Tyr-D-Leu-Leu-Arg-Pro-NHEt

Levobupivacaine (rINN) lë·vo·bü·*pi*·va·kän
(*S*)-1-Butyl-2-piperidylformo-2′,6′-xylidide; $C_{18}H_{28}N_2O$;
27262-47-1
Levobupivacaine Hydrochloride *27262-48-2*
Local anaesthetic

Levocabastine (rINN) lë·vö·*ka*·ba·stën
(3*S*,4*R*)-1-(*cis*-4-Cyano-4-*p*-fluorophenylcyclohexyl)-3-methyl-
4-phenylpiperidine-4-carboxylic acid; $C_{26}H_{29}FN_2O_2$;
79516-68-0
● **Levocabastine Hydrochloride** *79547-78-7*
Histamine H_1 receptor antagonist; antihistamine

● **Levocarnitine** (rINN) lë·vö·*kar*·ni·tën
(*R*)-3-Hydroxy-4-trimethylammoniobutyrate; $C_7H_{15}NO_3$;
541-15-1
Carnitine substitute

Levocetirizine (rINN) lë·vö·se·*ti*·ri·zën
(*R*)-2-[4-(4-Chlorobenzhydryl)piperazin-1-yl]ethoxyacetic acid;
$C_{21}H_{25}ClN_2O_3$; *130018-77-8*
Levocetirizine Hydrochloride (2HCl)
Histamine H_1 receptor antagonist; antihistamine

● **Levodopa** (rINN) lë·vö·*dö*·pa
3-(3,4-Dihydroxyphenyl)-L-alanine; L-dopa; $C_9H_{11}NO_4$;
59-92-7
Dopamine precursor; treatment of Parkinson's disease

● **Levodropropizine** (rINN) lë·vö·drö·*prö*·pi·zën
(*S*)-3-(4-Phenylpiperazin-1-yl)propane-1,2-diol; $C_{13}H_{20}N_2O_2$;
99291-25-5
Cough suppressant

Levofloxacin (rINN) lë·vö·*floks*·a·sin
(*S*)-9-Fluoro-2,3-dihydro-3-methyl-10-(4-methylpiperazin-1-yl)-
7-oxo-7*H*-pyrido[1,2,3-*de*][1,4]benzoxazine-6-carboxylic acid;
$C_{18}H_{20}FN_3O_4$; *100986-85-4*
Fluoroquinolone antibacterial

● **Levomenthol** (rINN) lë·vö·*men*·thol
(l*R*,2*S*,5*R*)-2-isopropyl-5-methylcyclohexanol; $C_{10}H_{20}O$;
2216-51-5
Decongestant

♣ **Levomepromazine** (rINN) lë·vö·me·*prö*·ma·zën
(*R*)-3-(2-Methoxyphenothiazin-10-yl)-2-methylpropyl¬
dimethylamine; ; $C_{19}H_{24}N_2OS$; *60-99-1*
● **Levomepromazine Hydrochloride** *4185-80-2*
● **Levomepromazine Maleate** *7104-38-3*
Dopamine receptor antagonist; neuroleptic

Levomethorphan (rINN) lë·vö·me·*thor*·fan
(−)-3-Methoxy-9α-methylmorphinan; $C_{18}H_{25}NO$; *125-70-2*
Cough suppressant

Levomoramide (rINN) lë·vö·*mo*·ra·mïd
(*R*)-1-(3-Methyl-4-morpholino-2,2-diphenylbutyryl) pyrrolidine;
$C_{25}H_{32}N_2O_2$; *5666-11-5*
Opioid receptor agonist

164

Levonantradol (rINN) lë·vö·*nan*·tra·dol
(6S,6aR,9R,10aR)-5,6,6a,7,8,9,10,10a-Octahydro-9-hydroxy-6-methyl-3-[(1R)-1-methyl-4-phenylbutoxy]phenanthridin-1-yl acetate; $C_{27}H_{35}NO_4$; 71048-87-8
Levonantradol Hydrochloride 70222-86-5; CP-50556-1
Cannabinoid; antiemetic

● **Levonorgestrel** (rINN) lë·vö·nor·*jes*·trel
(−)-13β-Ethyl-17β-hydroxy-18,19-dinor-17α-pregn-4-en-20-yn-3-one; D-norgestrel; $C_{21}H_{28}O_2$; 797-63-7
Progestogen

Levophenacylmorphan (rINN) lë·vö·fe·nä·sil·*mor*·fan
2-[(−)-3-Hydroxymorphinan-17-yl]acetophenone; $C_{24}H_{27}NO_2$; 10061-32-2
Opioid receptor agonist

Levopropoxyphene (rINN) lë·vö·prö·*poks*·ë·fën
(1R,2S)-1-Benzyl-3-dimethylamino-2-methyl-1-phenylpropyl propionate; $C_{22}H_{29}NO_2$; 2338-37-6
Cough suppressant

Levorphanol (rINN) le·*vor*·fa·nol
(−)-17-Methylmorphinan-3-ol; $C_{17}H_{23}NO$; 77-07-6
Levorphanol Tartrate 125-72-4 (anhydrous);
5985-38-6 (dihydrate)
Opioid receptor agonist

Levothyroxine (rINN) lë·vö·thï·*roks*·ën
O^4-(4-Hydroxy-3,5-di-iodophenyl)-3,5-di-iodo-L-tyrosine; $C_{15}H_{11}I_4NO_4$; 51-48-9

● **Levothyroxine Sodium** 55-03-8
Thyroid hormone replacement

Lexipafant (rINN) leks·*i*·pa·fant
Ethyl N-methyl-N-[α-(2-methylimidazo[4,5-c]pyridin-1-yl)tosyl]-L-leucinate; $C_{23}H_{30}N_4O_4S$; 139133-26-9
Platelet aggregating factor antagonist

Liarozole (rINN) lï·*a*·rö·zôl
(±)-5-(3-Chloro-α-imidazol-1-ylbenzyl)benzimidazole; $C_{17}H_{13}ClN_4$; 115575-11-6
Liarozole Hydrochloride
Testosterone aromatase inhibitor

and enantiomer

● **Lidocaine** (rINN) *li*·do·kän
2-Diethylaminoaceto-2′,6′-xylidide; $C_{14}H_{22}N_2O$; 137-58-6
● **Lidocaine Hydrochloride** 73-78-9 (anhydrous); 6108-05-0 (monohydrate)
Local anaesthetic; Class I antiarrhythmic

The symbol '¬' in systematic chemical names signifies line continuation

Lidoflazine (rINN) lï·dö·*flä*·zën
4-[3-(4,4′-Difluorobenzhydryl)propyl]piperazin-1-ylaceto-2′,6′-xylidide; $C_{30}H_{35}F_2N_3O$; *3416-26-0*
Calcium channel blocker

Lifarizine (rINN) lï·*fa*·ri·zën
1-Benzhydryl-4-(5-methyl-2-*p*-tolylimidazol-4-ylmethyl)¬piperazine; $C_{29}H_{32}N_4$; *119514-66-8*
Sodium channel blocker

Lignocaine *see Lidocaine*

Linaprazan (rINN) li·ná·*praz*·an
8-{[(2,6-dimethylphenyl)methyl]amino}-*N*-(2-hydroxyethyl)-2,3-dimethylimidazo[1,2-*a*]pyridine-6-carboxamide; $C_{21}H_{26}N_4O_2$; *248919-64-4*;
Proton pump inhibitor

Lincomycin (rINN) lin·kö·*mi*·sin
An antibiotic produced by *Streptomyces lincolnensis* var. *lincolnensis*; methyl 6-amino-6,8-dideoxy-*N*-[(2*S*,4*R*)-1-methyl-4-propylprolyl]-1-thio-α-D-*erythro*-D-*galacto*-octopyranoside; $C_{18}H_{34}N_2O_6S$; *154-21-2*
● **Lincomycin Hydrochloride** *859-18-7 (anhydrous)*;
7179-49-9 (hydrate)
Lincosamide antibacterial

● **Lindane** (rINN) *lin*·dän
1α,2α,3β,4α,5α,6β-Hexachlorocyclohexane; gamma benzene hexachloride; $C_6H_6Cl_6$; *58-89-9*
Insecticide

Linezolid (rINN) li·*nez*·o·lid
N-{[(*S*)-3-(3-Fluoro-4-morpholinophenyl)-2-oxo-1,3-oxazolidin-5-yl]methyl}acetamide; $C_{16}H_{20}FN_3O_4$; *165800-03-3*
Oxazolidinone antibacterial

Liothyronine (rINN) lï·ö·*thï*·rö·nën
4-*O*-(4-Hydroxy-3-iodophenyl)-3,5-di-iodo-L-tyrosine; (−)-tri-iodothyronine; $C_{15}H_{12}I_3NO_4$; *6893-02-3*
● **Liothyronine Sodium** *55-06-1*
Thyroid hormone replacement

Liraglutide (rINN) li·rá·*gloo*·tïd
N^{26}-(Hexadecanoyl-γ-L-glutamyl)-[34-L-arginine]GLP-1-(7-37)peptide; *204656-20-2*;
Incretin mimetic; treatment of type 2 diabetes mellitus

liraglutide has the following amino acid sequence:

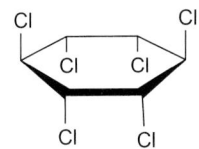

H–His-Ala-Glu-Gly-Thr-Phe-Thr-Ser-Asp-Val-Ser-

-Ser-Tyr-Leu-Glu-Gly-Gln-Ala-Ala-Lys-Glu-Phe

-Ile-Ala-Trp-Leu-Val-Arg-Gly-Arg-Gly- OH

● **Lisinopril** (rINN) lï·*si*·nö·pril
N-{*N*-[(*S*)-1-Carboxy-3-phenylpropyl]-L-lysyl}L-proline; $C_{21}H_{31}N_3O_5$; *76547-98-3*
Angiotensin converting enzyme inhibitor

Lisuride (rINN) *li·sûr·rïd*
8-Decarboxamido-8-(3,3-diethylureido)-D-lysergamide;
$C_{20}H_{26}N_4O$; *18016-80-3*
Lisuride Maleate
Dopamine receptor agonist

Liver Extract (BAN)
Extract of mammalian (usually pig) liver containing small
amounts of cyanocobalamin, folic acid and, possibly, other
haemopoietic factors; present in many preparations

Lobeline (rINN) *lö·be·lën*
2-{(2R,6S)-6-[(2S)-2-Hydroxy-2-phenylethyl]-1-
methylpiperidin-2-yl}-1-phenylethanone; $C_{22}H_{27}NO_2$; *90-69-7*
●**Lobeline Hydrochloride** *134-63-4*
Respiratory stimulant

Lodoxamide (rINN) *lö·doks·a·mïd*
N,N'-(2-Chloro-5-cyano-*m*-phenylene)dioxamic acid;
$C_{11}H_{16}ClN_3O_6$; *53882-12-5*
Lodoxamide Trometamol lodoxamide tromethamine (USAN);
63610-09-3
Cromone; prophylaxis of allergic conjuctivitis

Lofendazam (rINN) *lö·fen·da·zam*
8-Chloro-1,3,4,5-tetrahydro-1-phenyl-1,5-benzodiazepin-2-one;
$C_{15}H_{13}ClN_2O$; *29176-29-2*
Benzodiazepine

Lofentanil (rINN) *lö·fen·ta·nil*
Methyl (3R,4S)-3-methyl-1-phenethyl-4-(*N*-phenylpropion¬
amido)piperidine-4-carboxylate; $C_{25}H_{32}N_2O_3$; *61380-40-3*
Lofentanil Oxalate *61380-41-4*
Opioid receptor agonist

Lofepramine (rINN) *lö·fe·pra·mën*
5-{3-[*N*-(4-Chlorophenacyl)-*N*-methylamino]propyl}-10,11-
dihydro-5*H*-dibenz[*b,f*]azepine; $C_{26}H_{27}ClN_2O$; *23047-25-8*
●**Lofepramine Hydrochloride**
Monoamine reuptake inhibitor; tricyclic antidepressant

Lofexidine (rINN) *lö·feks·i·dën*
2-[1-(2,6-Dichlorophenoxy)ethyl]-2-imidazoline; $C_{11}H_{12}Cl_2N_2O$;
31036-80-3
Lofexidine Hydrochloride
Alpha$_2$-adrenoceptor agonist

and enantiomer

Lombazole (rINN) *lom·ba·zôl*
1-(α-Biphenyl-4-yl-2-chlorobenzyl)imidazole; $C_{22}H_{17}ClN_2$;
60628-98-0
Antimicrobial preservative

and enantiomer

Lomefloxacin (rINN) *lö·me·floks·a·sin*
(*RS*)-1-Ethyl-6,8-difluoro-1,4-dihydro-7-(3-methylpiperazin-1-
yl)-4-oxoquinoline-3-carboxylic acid; $C_{17}H_{19}F_2N_3O_3$;
98079-51-7
Lomefloxacin Hydrochloride *98079-52-8*
Fluoroquinolone antibacterial

and enantiomer

The symbol '¬' in systematic chemical names signifies line continuation

Lomeguatrib (rINN) lö·*me*·gwa·trib
6-[(4-Bromo-2-thienyl)methoxy]purin-2-amine; $C_{10}H_8N_5OS$; *192441-08-0*
O-6-alkylguanine-DNA-alkyltransferase inhibitor; cytotoxic

Lometrexol (rINN) lö·me·*treks*·ol
(*R*)-*N*-{4-[2-(2-Amino-3,4,5,6,7,8-hexahydro-4-oxopyrido[2,3-*d*]pyrimidin-6-yl)ethyl]benzoyl}-L-glutamic acid; $C_{21}H_{25}N_5O_6$; *106400-81-1*
Lometrexol Sodium *120408-07-3* (2Na)
Glycinnamide ribonucleotide formyltransferase inhibitor; cytotoxic

● **Lomustine** (rINN) *lö*·mus·tën
1-(2-Chloroethyl)-3-cyclohexyl-l-nitrosourea; $C_9H_{16}ClN_3O_2$; *13010-47-4*
Cytotoxic alkylating agent

Lonidamine (rINN) lo·*ni*·da·mën
1-(2,4-Dichlorobenzyl)indazole-3-carboxylic acid; $C_{15}H_{10}Cl_2N_2O_2$; *50264-69-2*
Antineoplastic

Loperamide (rINN) lö·*pe*·ra·mïd
4-(4-*p*-Chlorophenyl-4-hydroxypiperidino)-*N*,*N*-dimethyl-2,2-diphenylbutyramide; $C_{29}H_{33}ClN_2O_2$; *53179-11-6*
● **Loperamide Hydrochloride** *34552-83-5*
Inhibitor of mitochondrial function; cytotoxic

● **Loperamide Oxide** (rINN) lö·*pe*·ra·mïd
trans-4-(4-*p*-Chlorophenyl-4-hydroxypiperidino)-*N*,*N*-dimethyl-2,2-diphenylbutyramide N^4-oxide; $C_{29}H_{33}ClN_2O_3$; *106900-12-3*
Opioid receptor agonist; antidiarrhoeal

Lopinavir (rINN) lö·*pin*·a·veer
(*S*)-*N*-{(1*S*,3*S*,4*S*)-1-Benzyl-4-[2-(2,6-dimethylphenoxy)¬acetamido]-3-hydroxy-5-phenylpentyl}-3-methyl-2-(2-oxohexahydro-(2*H*)pyrimidin-1-yl)butanamide; $C_{37}H_{48}N_4O_5$; *192725-17-0*
Protease inhibitor; antiviral (HIV)

Loprazolam (rINN) lö·*prä*·zö·lam
(*Z*)-6-(2-Chlorophenyl)-2,4-dihydro-2-(4-methylpiperazin-1-ylmethylene)-8-nitroimidazo[1,2-*a*][1,4]benzodiazepin-1-one; $C_{23}H_{21}ClN_6O_3$; *61197-73-7*
● **Loprazolam Mesilate** *70111-54-5*
Benzodiazepine

Loracarbef (rINN) lor·ra·*kar*·bef
(6*R*,7*S*)-3-Chloro-8-oxo-7-D-phenylglycylamino-1-azabicyclo[4.2.0]oct-2-ene-2-carboxylic acid; $C_{16}H_{16}ClN_3O_4$; *76470-66-1*
Beta-lactam antibacterial

● **Loratadine** (rINN) lor·*rat*·a·dën
Ethyl 4-(8-chloro-5,6-dihydro-11*H*-benzo[5,6]cyclohepta[1,2-*b*]pyridin-11-ylidene)piperidine-1-carboxylate; $C_{22}H_{23}ClN_2O_2$; *79794-75-5*
Histamine H_1 receptor antagonist; antihistamine

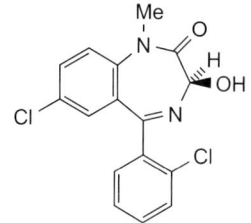

and enantiomer

● **Lorazepam** (rINN) lor·*rä*·ze·pam
7-Chloro-5-(2-chlorophenyl)-1,3-dihydro-3-hydroxy-1,4-benzodiazepin-2-one; $C_{15}H_{10}Cl_2N_2O_2$; *846-49-1*
Benzodiazepine

and enantiomer

Lorcainide (rINN) lor·kä·nïd
4′-Chloro-*N*-(1-isopropyl-4-piperidyl)-2-phenylacetanilide; $C_{22}H_{27}ClN_2O$; *59729-31-6*
Lorcainide Hydrochloride *58934-46-6*
Class I antiarrhythmic

Lorcinadol (rINN) see Appendix C

Loreclezole (rINN) lor·*re*·kle·zôl
(*Z*)-1-(β,2,4-Trichlorostyryl)-1*H*-1,2,4-triazole; $C_{10}H_6Cl_3N_3$; *117857-45-1*
Antiepileptic

● **Lormetazepam** (rINN) lor·me·*tä*·ze·pam
7-Chloro-5-(2-chlorophenyl)-1,3-dihydro-3-hydroxy-l-methyl-1,4-benzodiazepin-2-one; $C_{16}H_{12}Cl_2N_2O_2$; *848-75-9*
Benzodiazepine

Lornoxicam (rINN) lor·*noks*·i·kam
6-Chloro-4-hydroxy-2-methyl-*N*-2-pyridyl-2*H*-thieno[2,3-*e*]¬[1,2]thiazine-3-carboxamide 1,1-dioxide; $C_{13}H_{10}ClN_3O_4S_2$; *70374-39-9*; Ro-13-9297
Cyclo-oxygenase inhibitor; analgesic; anti-inflammatory

Losartan (rINN) lö·*sar*·tan
(2-Butyl-4-chloro-1-{4-[2-(2*H*-tetrazol-5-yl)phenyl]benzyl}-1*H*-imidazol-5-yl)methanol; $C_{22}H_{23}ClN_6O$; *114798-26-4*
Losartan Potassium *124750-99-8*
Angiotensin II (AT₁) receptor antagonist

Losoxantrone (rINN) lö·soks·*an*·trön
7-Hydroxy-2-[2-(2-hydroxyethylamino)ethyl]-5-[2-(2-hydroxyethylamino)ethylamino]naphtho[1,2,3-*cd*]indazol-6(2*H*)-one; $C_{22}H_{27}N_5O_4$; *88303-61-1*
Topoisomerase II inhibitor; cytotoxic

Loteprednol (rINN) lö·të·*pred*·nol
Chloromethyl 11β,17α-dihydroxy-3-oxoandrosta-1,4-diene-17β-carboxylate; $C_{21}H_{27}ClO_5$; *129260-79-3*
Loteprednol Etabonate (ester at O^{17}); *82034-46-6*
Glucocorticoid

The symbol '¬' in systematic chemical names signifies line continuation

● **Lovastatin** (rINN) lo·va·*sta*·tin
(3*R*,5*R*)-7-{(1*S*,2*S*,6*R*,8*S*,8a*R*)-{1,2,6,7,8,8a-Hexahydro-2,6-
dimethyl-8-[(*S*)-2-methylbutyryloxy]-1-naphthyl}3-
hydroxyheptan-5-olide; mevinolin; $C_{24}H_{36}O_5$; *75330-75-5*
HMG Co-A reductase inhibitor; lipid-regulating drug

Loviride (rINN) lö·vi·rïd
N^2-(6-acetyl-*m*-tolyl)-DL-2-(2,6-dichlorophenyl)glycinamide;
$C_{17}H_{16}Cl_2N_2O_2$; *147362-57-0*
Antiviral (HIV)

and enantiomer

Loxapine (rINN) *loks*·a·pën
2-Chloro-11-(4-methylpiperazin-1-yl)dibenz[*b,f*][1,4]oxazepine;
$C_{18}H_{18}ClN_3O$; *1977-10-2*
Dopamine receptor antagonist; neuroleptic

Lubeluzole (rINN) loo·*be*·lü·zô
(*S*)-1-{4-[1,3-benzothiazol-2-yl(methyl)amino]piperidino}-
3-(3,4-difluorophenoxy)propan-2-ol; $C_{22}H_{25}F_2N_3O_2S$;
144665-07-6
Neuroprotectant in stroke

Lucanthone (rINN) loo·*kan*·thön
1-(2-Diethylaminoethylamino)-4-methylthioxanthen-9-one;
$C_{20}H_{24}N_2OS$; *479-50-5*
Lucanthone Hydrochloride *548-57-2*
Antihelminthic

♣ **Lufenuron** (rINN) loo·*fen*·ûr·ron
(*RS*)-*N*-[2,5-Dichloro-4-(1,1,2,3,3,3-hexafluoropropoxy)phenyl-
carbamoyl]-2,6-difluorobenzamide; $C_{17}H_8Cl_2F_8N_2O_3$;
103055-07-8
Ectoparasiticide

and enantiomer

Lumefantrine (rINN) loo·me·*fan*·trën
(1*RS*)-2-(Dibutylamino)-1-{2,7-dichloro-9-[(*Z*)-4-
chlorobenzylidene]fluoren-4-yl}ethanol; $C_{30}H_{32}Cl_3NO$;
82186-77-4
Antiprotozoal (malaria)

Lumiracoxib (rINN) loo·*mï*·ra·*coks*·ib
{2-[(2-Chloro-6-fluorophenyl)amino]-5-methylphenyl}acetic
acid; $C_{15}H_{13}ClFNO_2$; *220991-20-8*
Cyclo-oxygenase inhibitor; analgesic; anti-inflammatory

Luprostiol (rINN) loo·*prost*·ë·ol
(1) (±)-(*Z*)-7-{(1*S*,2*R*,3*R*,5*S*)-2-[(2*S*)-3-(3-Chlorophenoxy)-2-
hydroxypropylthio]-3,5-dihydroxycyclopentyl}hept-5-enoic
acid; (2) (±)-(5*Z*)-(9*S*,11*R*,15*S*)-16-(3-Chlorophenoxy-9,11,15-
trihydroxy-ω-tetranor-13-thiaprost-5-enoic acid; $C_{21}H_{29}ClO_6S$;
67110-79-6
Prostaglandin (PGF$_{2\alpha}$) analogue (veterinary)

and enantiomer

170

Lurosetron (rINN) lûr·*rö*·së·tron
6-Fluoro-2,3,4,5-tetrahydro-5-methyl-2-(5-methylimidazol-4-ylmethyl)pyrido[4,3-*b*]indol-1-one; $C_{17}H_{17}FN_4O$; *128486-54-4*
Lurosetron Mesilate *143486-90-2*
Serotonin 5HT$_3$ receptor antagonist

Lutropin Alfa (rINN) *loo*·trö·pin al·fa
Luteinising hormone (human α-subunit reduced complex human α-subunit reduced), glycoform α;
α-subunit: $C_{437}H_{682}N_{122}O_{134}S_{13}$;
β-subunit: $C_{577}H_{929}N_{165}O_{161}S_{14}$; *56832-30-5*
Recombinant human luteinizing hormone; treatment of female infertility

Luxabendazole (rINN) luks·a·*ben*·da·zôl
Methyl 5-(4-fluorophenylsulfonyloxy)benzimidazol-2-ylcarbamate; $C_{15}H_{12}FN_3O_5S$; *90509-02-7*
Antihelminthic

● **Lymecycline** (rINN) lï·më·*sï*·klën
A water-soluble combination of tetracycline, lysine and formaldehyde; $C_{29}H_{38}N_4O_{10}$; *992-21-2*
Tetracycline antibacterial

● **Lynestrenol** (rINN) lï·*nës*·tre·nol
19-Nor-17α-pregn-4-en-20-yn-17β-ol; $C_{20}H_{28}O$; *52-76-6*
Progestogen

Lypressin (rINN) see Appendix C

Lysergide (rINN) see Appendix C

● **Lysine** (rINN) *lï*·sën
L-Lysine; (*S*)-2,6-Diaminohexanoic acid; $C_6H_{14}N_2O_2$; *56-87-1*;
● **Lysine Acetate** *57282-49-2*
● **Lysine Hydrochloride** *57282-49-2*
Amino acid

Lysuride *see Lisuride*

● **Macrogol** (rINN) *ma*·krö·gol
Polyethylene glycol of general formula H-(OCH$_2$CH$_2$)$_n$-OH where *n* varies from 3 to 225 approximately. Each macrogol name is followed by a number corresponding approximately to its average molecular weight, *eg* macrogol 300, 400, 1000, 4000; *9002-90-8*
Non-ionic surfactant

Macrogol 8 Stearate (polyoxyl 8 stearate)
Polyoxyethylene 8 stearate
Non-ionic surfactant

Macrogol 40 Stearate (rINN)
Polyoxyethylene 40 stearate
Non-ionic surfactant

Macrosalb(^{131}I) (rINN) *ma*·krö·salb
Macroaggregated iodinated (^{131}I) human albumin; *54182-63-7*
Human albumin macroaggregates; lung surfactant

Macrosalb(^{99m}Tc) (rINN) *ma*·krö·salb
Technetium(^{99m}Tc)-labelled macroaggregated human albumin; *54277-47-3*
Human albumin macroaggregates; lung surfactant

Maduramicin (rINN) ma·dûr·ra·*mï*·sin
Ammonium (2*R*,3*S*,4*S*,5*R*,6*S*)-tetrahydro-2-hydroxy-6-{(*R*)-1-[(2*S*,5*R*,7*S*,8*R*,9*S*)-9-hydroxy-2,8-dimethyl-2-{(2*S*,2′*R*,3′*S*,¬5*R*,5′*R*)-octahydro-2-methyl-3′-[(2*R*,4*S*,5*S*,6*S*)-tetrahydro-4,5-dimethoxy-6-methyl-2*H*-pyran-2-yloxy]-5′-[(2*S*,3*S*,5*R*,6*S*)-tetrahydro-6-hydroxy-3,5,6-trimethyl-2*H*-pyran-2-yl]2,2′-bifuran-5-yl}-1,6-dioxaspiro[4,5]dec-7-yl]ethyl}-4,5-dimethoxy-3-methyl-2*H*-pyran-2-acetate; $C_{47}H_{83}NO_{17}$; *84878-61-5*
Antibacterial (veterinary)

Mafenide (rINN) *ma*·fen·ïd
α-Aminotoluene-*p*-sulfonamide; $C_7H_{10}N_2O_2S$; *138-39-6*
Mafenide Acetate *13009-99-9*
Antibacterial

● Magaldrate (rINN) *mag*·al·drät
A synthetic combination of aluminium and magnesium
hydroxides and sulfuric acid corresponding approximately to
the formula $Al_5Mg_{10}(OH)_{31}(SO_4)_2,xH_2O$; *74978-16-8*
Antacid

● Malathion (BAN) mal·a·*thï*·on
Diethyl 2-(dimethoxyphosphinothioylthio)succinate;
$C_{10}H_{19}O_6PS_2$; *121-75-5*
Organophosphorus insecticide

and enantiomer

Maletamer (rINN) see Appendix C

● Maltitol (BAN) *mál*·ti·tol
D-Glucopyranosyl-D-glucitol; $C_{12}H_{24}O_{11}$; *585-88-6*
Sweetening agent

Mangafodipir (rINN) man·ga·*fö*·di·peer
Hexahydrogen (*OC*-6-13)-*N*,*N*′-ethane-1,2-diylbis{N-[2-methyl-
3-oxido-κ*O*-5-(phosphonatooxymethyl)-4-pyridylmethyl]¬
glycinato(*O*,*N*)}manganate(II); $C_{22}H_{30}MnN_4O_{14}P_2$; *155319-91-8*;
WIN 59010-2; S-095; MnDPDP
Mangafodipir Trisodium (rINN) *140678-14-4*
Contrast agent for magnetic resonance imaging

Manifaxine (rINN) ma·ni·*faks*·ën
(2*S*,3*S*,5*R*)-2-(3,5-Difluorophenyl)-3,5-dimethylmorpholin-2-ol;
$C_{12}H_{15}F_2NO_2$; *135306-42-2*
Manifaxine Hydrochloride *135306-42-2*
Treatment of attention deficit hyperactivity disorder

Mannomustine (rINN) man·ö·*mus*·tën
1,6-Bis(2-chloroethylamino)-1,6-dideoxy-D-mannitol;
$C_{10}H_{22}Cl_2N_2O_4$; *576-68-1*
Cytotoxic alkylating agent

Maprotiline (rINN) ma·*prö*·ti·lën
3-(9,10-Dihydro-9,10-ethanoanthracen-9-yl)propyl (methyl)¬
amine; $C_{20}H_{23}N$; *10262-69-8*
● Maprotiline Hydrochloride *10347-81-6*
Antidepressant

Maraviroc (rINN) ma·*ra*·veer·ök
4,4-Difluoro-*N*-[(1*S*)-3-{(1*R*,3*s*,5*S*)-3-[3-methyl-5-(propan-2-
yl)-4*H*-1,2,4-triazol-4-yl]-8-azabicyclo[3.2.1]octan-8-yl}-1-
phenylpropyl]cyclohexanecarboxamide; $C_{29}H_{41}F_2N_5O$;
376348-65-1
CCR5 receptor antagonist; antiviral (HIV)

♣ Marbofloxacin (rINN) mar·bö·*floks*·a·sin
9-Fluoro-2,3-dihydro-3-methyl-10-(4-methylpiperazin-1-yl)-7-
oxo-7*H*-pyrido[3,2,1-*ij*][4,1,2]benzoxadiazine-6-carboxylic acid;
$C_{17}H_{19}FN_4O_4$; *115550-35-1*
Fluroquinolone antibacterial

172

Maribavir (rINN) ma·*rib*·a·veer
5,6-Dichloro-2-(isopropylamino)-1-(β-L-ribofuranosyl)benz¬
imidazole; $C_{15}H_{19}Cl_2N_3O_4$; *176161-24-3*
Antiviral (cytomegalovirus)

Marimastat (rINN) ma·*ri*·ma·stat
(2S,3R)-3-{(S)-[2,2-Dimethyl-1-(methylcarbamoyl)propyl]¬
carbamoyl}-2-hydroxy-5-methylhexanohydroxamic acid;
$C_{15}H_{29}N_3O_5$; *154039-60-8*
Matrix metalloproteinase inhibitor

Mazindol (rINN) see Appendix C

Mazokalim (rINN) ma·*zo*·ka·lim
Ethyl (3S,4R)-4-{5-[3-hydroxy-2,2,3-trimethyl-4-(1,6-dihydro-
6-oxopyridazin-3-yloxy)chroman-6-yl]tetrazol-1-yl}butyrate;
$C_{23}H_{28}N_6O_6$; *164178-54-5*
Potassium channel opener; bronchodilator

Mebanazine (rINN) me·*ban*·a·zën
α-Methylbenzylhydrazine; $C_8H_{12}N_2$; *65-64-5*
Antidepressant

and enantiomer

● **Mebendazole** (rINN) me·*ben*·da·zôl
Methyl 5-benzoylbenzimidazol-2-ylcarbamate; $C_{16}H_{13}N_3O_3$;
31431-39-7
Benzimadazole antihelminthic

Mebeverine (rINN) me·*bev*·er·rën
(RS)-4-[Ethyl(4-methoxy-α-methylphenethyl)amino]butyl
veratrate; $C_{25}H_{35}NO_5$; *3625-06-7*
● **Mebeverine Hydrochloride** *2753-45-9*
Mebeverine Pamoate
Smooth muscle relaxant; antispasmodic

and enantiomer

Mebezonium Iodide (rINN) see Appendix C

Mebhydrolin (rINN) see Appendix C

Mebrofenin (rINN) me·*brö*·fe·nin
({[(3-Bromomesityl)carbamoyl]methyl}imino)diacetic acid;
$C_{15}H_{19}BrN_2O_5$; *78266-06-5*
Investigation of the hepatobiliary system

Mebutamate (rINN) me·*bü*·ta·mät
2-*sec*-Butyl-2-methyltrimethylene dicarbamate; $C_{10}H_{20}N_2O_4$;
64-55-1
Hypnotic

mixture of stereoisomers

Mecamylamine (rINN) me·ka·*mil*·a·men
(1R,2R,4S)-Methyl(2,3,3-trimethylbicyclo[2.2.1]hept-2-
yl)amine; $C_{11}H_{21}N$; *60-40-2*
Mecamylamine Hydrochloride *826-39-1*
Ganglion blocker

The symbol '¬' in systematic chemical names signifies line continuation

Mecasermin (rINN) me·ka·*ser*·min
Insulin like growth factor I (human);
68562-41-4
Recombinant insulin like growth factor 1 (human)

mecasermin has the following amino acid sequence:

```
  GPETLCGAEL    VDALQFVCGD    RGFYFNKPTG

  YGSSSRRAPQ    TGIVDECCFR    SCDLRRLEMY

  CAPLKPAKSA
```

Mecetronium Etilsulfate (rINN) me·se·*trö*·në·um
Ethyl(hexadecyl)dimethylammonium ethyl sulfate;
$C_{22}H_{49}NO_4S$; *3006-10-8*
Antiseptic

$$Me[CH_2]_{14}CH_2 \overset{Et}{\underset{+}{\overset{|}{-}N}}Me_2 \quad EtSO_4^-$$

Mecillinam (rINN) me·*si*·li·nam
6-(Perhydroazepin-1-ylmethyleneamino)penicillanic acid;
$C_{15}H_{23}N_3O_3S$; *32887-01-7*
Beta-lactam antibacterial

Meclocycline (rINN) me·klö·*si*·klën
(1) (4S,4aR,5S,5aR,12aS)-7-Chloro-4-dimethylamino-1,4,4a,5,¬
5a,6,11,12a-octahydro-3,5,10,12,12a-pentahydroxy-6-methyl-
ene-1,11-dioxonaphthacene-2-carboxamide; (2) 7-Chloro-6-
demethyl-6-deoxy-5β-hydroxy-6-methylenetetracycline;
$C_{22}H_{21}ClN_2O_8$; *2013-58-3*
Tetracycline antibacterial

♣ **Meclofenamic Acid** (rINN) me·klö·fe·*nam*·ik
N-(2,6-Dichloro-m-tolyl)anthranilic acid; $C_{14}H_{11}Cl_2NO_2$;
644-62-2
Cyclo-oxygenase inhibitor; analgesic; anti-inflammatory

Meclofenoxate (rINN) see Appendix C

Meclorisone (rINN) me·*klor*·i·sön
9,11β-Dichloro-17α,21-dihydroxy-16α-methylpregna-1,4-
diene-3,20-dione; $C_{22}H_{28}Cl_2O_4$; *4732-48-3*
Meclorisone Butyrate *10549-91-4*
Glucocorticoid

Meclozine (rINN) *me*·klö·zën
(RS)-1-(4-Chlorobenzhydryl)-4-(3-methylbenzyl)piperazine;
$C_{25}H_{27}ClN_2$; *569-65-3*
● **Meclozine Hydrochloride** meclizine hydrochloride (USAN);
1104-22-9 (anhydrous)
31884-77-2 (hydrate)
Histamine H_1 receptor antagonist; antihistamine

and enantiomer

Mecobalamin (rINN) me·kö·*ba*·la·min
*Co*α-[α-(5,6-Dimethylbenzimidazolyl)-*Co*β-methylcobamide;
$C_{63}H_{91}CoN_{13}O_{14}P$; *13422-55-4*
Vitamin B_{12} analogue

Mecysteine (rINN) *me*·sis·tän
L-Cysteine methyl ester; $C_4H_9NO_2S$; *2485-62-3*
Mecysteine Hydrochloride *5714-80-7*
Mucolytic

Medazepam (rINN) me·*dä*·ze·pam
7-Chloro-2,3-dihydro-1-methyl-5-phenyl-1*H*-1,4-benzo¬
diazepine; $C_{16}H_{15}ClN_2$; *2898-12-6*
Benzodiazepine

Medetomidine (rINN) me·de·*to*·mi·dën
(±)-4-[1-(2,3-Xylyl)ethyl]imidazole; $C_{13}H_{16}N_2$; *86347-14-0*
Alpha₂-adrenoceptor agonist (veterinary)

and enantiomer

Medigoxin *see Metildigoxin*

Medrogestone (rINN) me·drö·*jes*·tön
6,17α-Dimethylpregna-4,6-diene-3,20-dione; $C_{23}H_{32}O_2$;
977-79-7
Progestogen

Medronic Acid (rINN) me·*dron*·ik
Methylenebis(phosphonic acid); $CH_6O_6P_2$; *1984-15-2*
Disodium Medronate *25681-89-4*
Bisphosphonate; used for bone scanning

Medroxalol (rINN) me·*droks*·a·lol
5-{2-[3-(1,3-Benzodioxol-5-yl)-1-methylpropylamino]-1-
hydroxyethyl}salicylamide; $C_{20}H_{24}N_2O_5$; *56290-94-9*
Medroxalol Hydrochloride *70161-10-3*
Non-selective adrenoceptor agonist

mixture of stereoisomers

Medroxyprogesterone (rINN) me·droks·ë·prö·*jes*·te·rön
17α-Hydroxy-6α-methylpregn-4-ene-3,20-dione; $C_{22}H_{32}O_3$;
520-85-4
● **Medroxyprogesterone Acetate** *71-58-9*
Progestogen

● **Mefenamic Acid** (rINN) me·*fen*·a·mik
N-2,3-Xylylanthranilic acid; $C_{15}H_{15}NO_2$; *61-68-7*
Cyclo-oxygenase inhibitor; analgesic; anti-inflammatory

Mefloquine (rINN) me·flö·kwën
(*RS*)-2,8-Bis(trifluoromethyl)-4-quinolyl[(*SR*)-2-piperidyl]¬
methanol; $C_{17}H_{16}F_6N_2O$; *53230-10-7*
● **Mefloquine Hydrochloride** *51773-92-3*
Antiprotozoal (malaria)

and enantiomer

Mefruside (rINN) me·froo·sïd
4-Chloro-*N¹*-methyl-*N¹*-(2-methyltetrahydrofurfuryl)benzene-
1,3-disulfonamide; $C_{13}H_{19}ClN_2O_5S_2$; *7195-27-9*
Thiazide-like diuretic

and enantiomer

Megestrol (rINN) me·*jes*·trol
17α-Hydroxy-6-methylpregna-4,6-diene-3,20-dione; $C_{22}H_{30}O_3$;
3562-63-8
● **Megestrol Acetate** *595-33-5*
Progestogen

The symbol '¬' in systematic chemical names signifies line continuation

Meglumine (rINN) *meg*·loo·mën
1-Methylamino-1-deoxy-D-glucitol; $C_7H_{17}NO_5$; *6284-40-8*
Organic base used in the preparation of organic acids

Meladrazine (rINN) me·*la*·dra·zën
Tetraethyl(6-hydrazinotriazin-2,4-diyl)diamine; $C_{11}H_{23}N_7$;
13957-36-3
Smooth muscle relaxant; treatment of detrusor instability

Melarsonyl Potassium (rINN) me·*lar*·sö·nil
Dipotassium 2-[4-(4,6-diamino-1,3,5-triazin-2-ylamino)¬
phenyl]-1,3,2-dithiarsolan-4,5-dicarboxylate;
$C_{13}H_{11}AsK_2N_6O_4S_2$; *13355-55-0*
Antiprotozoal

Melarsoprol (rINN) me·*lar*·sö·prol
2-[4-(4,6-Diamino-1,3,5-triazin-2-ylamino)phenyl]-1,3,2-
dithiarsolan-4-ylmethanol; $C_{12}H_{15}AsN_6OS_2$; *494-79-1*
Antiprotozoal

Melengestrol (rINN) me·len·*jes*·trol
17α-Hydroxy-6-methyl-16-methylenepregna-4,6-diene-3,20-
dione; $C_{23}H_{30}O_3$; *5633-18-1*
Progestogen

Meloxicam (rINN) mc·*loks*·i·kam
4-Hydroxy-2-methyl-*N*-(5-methyl-1,3-thiazol-2-yl)-2*H*-1,2-
benzothiazine-3-carboxamide 1,1-dioxide; $C_{14}H_{13}N_3O_4S_2$;
71125-38-7
Cyclo-oxygenase inhibitor; analgesic; anti-inflammatory

Melperone (rINN) *mel*·pe·rön
4′-Fluoro-4-(4-methylpiperidino)butyrophenone; $C_{16}H_{22}FNO$;
3575-80-2
Melperone Hydrochloride *1622-79-3*
Dopamine receptor antagonist; neuroleptic

Melphalan (rINN) *mel*·fa·lan
4-Bis(2-chloroethyl)amino-L-phenylalanine; $C_{13}H_{18}Cl_2N_2O_2$;
148-82-3
Cytotoxic alkylating agent

Memantine (rINN) me·*man*·tën
3,5-Dimethyladamantan-1-amine; $C_{12}H_{21}N$; *1982-08-2*
Memantine Hydrochloride
Cholinesterase inhibitor; treatment of Alzheimer's disease

Menadiol (BAN) me·na·*di*·ol
2-Methylnaphthalene-1,4-diol; $C_{11}H_{10}O_2$; *481-85-6*

Menadiol Sodium Phosphate *6700-42-1*
Vitamin K analogue

Menadiol Potassium Sulfate (rINN) me·na·*di*·ol
Dipotassium 2-methylnaphthalene-1,4-disulfonate;
$C_{11}H_8K_2O_8S_2$; *1612-30-2*
Vitamin K analogue

● **Menadione** (BAN) me·na·*di*·ön
2-Methyl-1,4-naphthoquinone; $C_{11}H_8O_2$; *58-27-5*
Vitamin K analogue

Menadoxime (BAN) me·na·*doks*·ëm
Ammonium salt of 2-methylnaphthoquinone 4-oxime
O-carboxymethyl ether; $C_{13}H_{14}N_2O_4$; *6146-99-2*
Vitamin K analogue

Menbutone (rINN) *men*·bü·tön
4-(4-Methoxy-1-naphthyl)-4-oxobutyric acid; $C_{15}H_{14}O_4$;
3562-99-0
Menbutone Diethanolamine
Choleretic

● **Menotrophin** (BAN) men·ö·*trö*·fin
A dry preparation containing glycoprotein gonadotrophins
possessing follicle-stimulating and luteinising activities. It
contains not less than 40 units of follicle-stimulating hormone
activity per mg. The ratio of Units of luteinising hormone (LH)
activity to Units of follicle-stimulating hormone (FSH) activity
is approximately 1. The preparation is exclusively or
predominantly of pituitary origin and is obtained from the urine
of post-menopausal women but, where necessary, chorionic
gonadotrophin obtained from the urine of pregnant women may
be added to achieve the above ratio; menotropins (USAN);
9002-68-0
Gonadotrophin; treatmant of infertility

*See also Human Menopausal Gonadotrophin, Follitropin Alfa
and Follitropin Beta*

Mepacrine (rINN) *me*·pa·krën
6-Chloro-9-(4-diethylamino-1-methylbutylamino)-2-
methoxyacridine; $C_{23}H_{30}ClN_3O$; *83-89-6*
Mepacrine Hydrochloride *69-05-6* (2HCl);
6151-30-0 (2HCl, 2H$_2$O)
Antiprotozoal (malaria)

Mepartricin (rINN) me·*par*·tri·sin
A mixture of the methyl esters of two related polyene macrolide
antibiotics obtained from a strain of *Streptomyces aurofaciens* or
by any other means; *11121-32-70*
Antifungal

mepartricin A

Mepenzolate Bromide (rINN) see Appendix C

Mephenesin (rINN) me·fen·*ë*·sin
(*RS*)-3-*o*-Tolyloxypropane-1,2-diol; $C_{10}H_{14}O_3$; *59-47-2*
Skeletal muscle relaxant

and enantiomer

Mephenytoin (rINN) see Appendix C

Mephentermine (rINN) me·*fen*·ter·mën
N,α,α-Trimethylphenethylamine; $C_{11}H_{17}N$; *100-92-5*
Mephentermine Sulfate *1212-72-2*
Adrenoceptor agonist

Mepindolol (rINN) me·*pin*·do·lol
(*RS*)-1-Isopropylamino-3-(2-methylindol-4-yloxy)propan-2-ol;
$C_{15}H_{22}N_2O_2$; *23694-81-7*
Beta-adrenoceptor antagonist

and enantiomer

Mepiprazole (rINN) me·*pip*·ra·zôl
1-(3-Chlorophenyl)-4-[2-(5-methyl-1*H*-pyrazol-3-yl)ethyl]¬
piperazine; $C_{16}H_{21}ClN_4$; *20326-12-9*
Monoamine reuptake inhibitor

Mepivacaine (rINN) me·*pi*·va·kän
1-Methyl-2-piperidylformo-2′,6′-xylidide; $C_{15}H_{22}N_2O$; *96-88-8*
● **Mepivacaine Hydrochloride** *1722-62-9*
Local anaesthetic

and enantiomer

● **Meprobamate** (rINN) me·*prö*·ba·mät
2-Methyl-2-propyltrimethylene dicarbamate; $C_9H_{18}N_2O_4$;
57-53-4
Hypnotic

Meprochol (BAN) *me*·prö·kol
(2-Methoxyprop-2-enyl)trimethylammonium bromide;
$C_7H_{16}BrNO$; *590-31-8*
Cholinoceptor agonist

Meproscillarin (rINN) me·prö·*sil*·a·rin
14-Hydroxy-3β-(4-*O*-methyl-α-L-rhamnopyranosyloxy)-14β-
bufa-4,20,22-trienolide; $C_{31}H_{44}O_8$; *33396-37-1*
Na/K-ATPase inhibitor; cardiac glycoside

Meprotixol (rINN) see Appendix C

Meptazinol (rINN) mep·*ta*·zi·nol
3-(3-Ethyl-1-methylperhydroazepin-3-yl)phenol;
$C_{15}H_{23}NO$; *54340-58-8*
● **Meptazinol Hydrochloride** *34154-59-1*
Opioid receptor partial agonist; analgesic

Mepyramine (rINN) me·*pï*·ra·mën
2-(*N*-*p*-Anisyl-*N*-2-pyridylamino)ethyldimethylamine;
pyrilamine (USAN); $C_{17}H_{23}N_3O$; *91-84-9*
● **Mepyramine Maleate** *59-33-6*
Histamine H_1 receptor antagonist; antihistamine

Mequitazine (rINN) me·*kwi*·ta·zën
3-(Phenothiazin-10-ylmethyl)quinuclidine; $C_{20}H_{22}N_2S$;
29216-28-2
Histamine H_1 receptor antagonist; antihistamine

Meralluride (rINN) mer·*ral*·lûr·rïd
A mixture of (*RS*)-3-[3-(3-carboxypropionyl)ureido]-2-
methoxypropylhydroxomercury and theophylline; *8069-64-5*
Mercurial diuretic

and enantiomer

Mercaptamine (rINN) mer·kap·ta·mën
2-Aminoethanethiol; C_2H_7NS;
60-23-1
Aminothiol; treatment of cystinosis

Mercaptomerin (rINN) mer·kap·tö·*me*·rin
Disodium salt of carboxymethylthio[3-(3-carboxy-2,2,3-
trimethylcyclopentanecarboxamido)-2-methoxypropyl]mercury;
$C_{16}H_{25}HgNNa_2O_6S$; 20223-84-1
Mercurial diuretic

mixture of stereoisomers

●**Mercaptopurine** (rINN) mer·kap·tö·*pûr*·rën
Purine-6-thiol; $C_5H_4N_4S$; 50-44-2 (anhydrous);
6112-76-1 (monohydrate)
Thiopurine cytotoxic

Mercurophylline (rINN) mer·*kûr*·ro·fi·lën
A mixture of theophylline and the sodium salt of [3-(3-carboxy-
2,2,3-tri-methylcyclopentanecarboxamido)-2-methoxypropyl]¬
hydroxomercury; 8012-34-8
Mercurial diuretic

●**Meropenem** (rINN) me·*rö*·pe·nem
(4R,5S,6S)-3-[(3S,5S)-5-Dimethylcarbamoylpyrrolidin-3-ylthio]-
6-[(R)-1-hydroxyethyl]-4-methyl-7-oxo-1-
azabicyclo[3.2.0]hept-2-ene-2-carboxylic acid; $C_{17}H_{25}N_3O_5S$;
96036-03-2
Carbapenem antibacterial

●**Mesalazine** (rINN) me·*sal*·a·zën
5-Aminosalicylic acid; 5-ASA; $C_7H_7NO_3$; 89-57-6
Aminosalicylate; treatment of ulcerative colitis

●**Mesna** (rINN)
Sodium 2-mercaptoethanesulfonate; $C_2H_5NaO_3S_2$; 19767-45-4
Preventing adverse effects of cyclophosphamide and ifosfamide

Mesoridazine (rINN) mez·ö·*ri*·da·zën
(RS)-10-[2-(1-Methyl-2-piperidyl)ethyl]-2-(methylsulfinyl)¬
phenothiazine; $C_{21}H_{26}N_2OS_2$; 5588-33-0
Dopamine receptor antagonist; neuroleptic

and enantiomer

Mestanolone (rINN) see Appendix C

●**Mesterolone** (rINN) me·*ste*·ro·lön
17β-Hydroxy-1α-methyl-5α-androstan-3-one; $C_{20}H_{32}O_2$;
1424-00-6
Androgen

●**Mestranol** (rINN) *mes*·tra·nol
(1) 3-Methoxy-19-nor-17α-pregna-1,3,5(10)-trien-20-yn-
17β-ol; (2) Ethinylestradiol 3-methyl ether; $C_{21}H_{26}O_2$;
72-33-3
Oestrogen

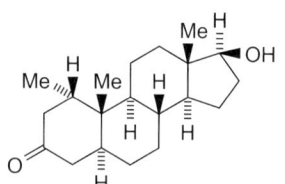

Mesulfen (rINN) *më*·sul·fen
2,7-Dimethylthianthrene; mesulfen (pINN); $C_{14}H_{12}S_2$; 135-58-0
Dopamine receptor agonist

The symbol '¬' in systematic chemical names signifies line continuation

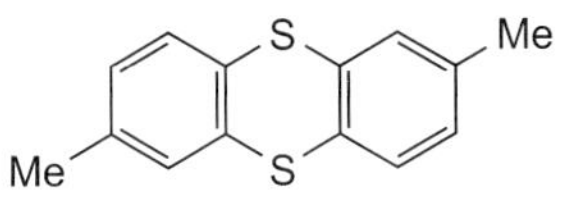

Mesuximide (rINN) me·*suks*·i·mïd
(*RS*)-*N*,2-Dimethyl-2-phenylsuccinimide; $C_{12}H_{13}NO_2$; *77-41-8*
Antiepileptic

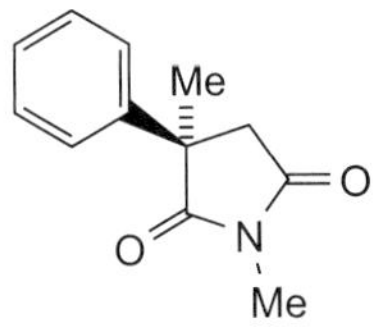

and enantiomer

Metacetamol (rINN) see Appendix C

● **Metacresol** (BAN) met·a·*krë*·sol
3-Methylphenol; C_7H_8O; *108-39-4*
Antiseptic; antimicrobial preservative

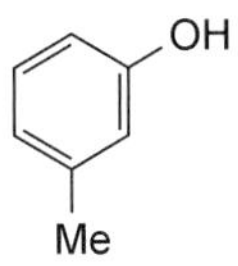

Metahexamide (rINN) met·a·*heks*·a·mïd
1-(3-Amino-*p*-tolylsulfonyl)-3-cyclohexylurea; $C_{14}H_{21}N_3O_3S$;
565-33-3
*Inhibitor of ATP-dependent potassium channels (sulfonylurea);
treatment of diabetes mellitus*

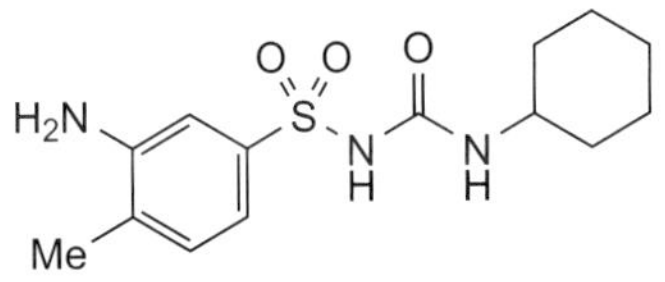

Metallibure (rINN) see Appendix C

Metamelfalan (rINN) me·ta·*mel*·fa·lan
3-[Bis(2-choroethyl)amino]-L-phenylalanine; $C_{13}H_{18}ClN_2O_2$;
1088-80-8
Cytotoxic alkylating agent

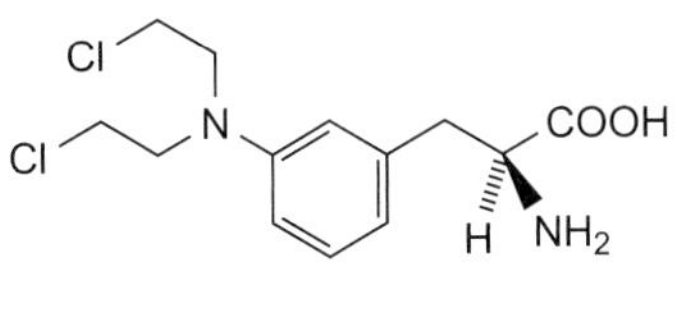

Metamfazone (rINN) see Appendix C

Metamfepramone (rINN) met·am·*fe*·pra·mön
α-Dimethylaminopropiophenone; $C_{11}H_{15}NO$; *15351-09-4*
Appetite suppressant

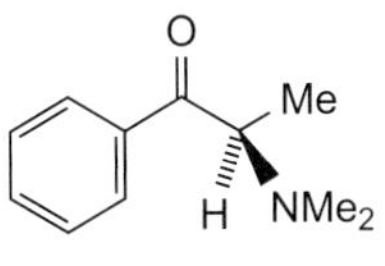

and enantiomer

Metaraminol (rINN) met·a·*ram*·i·nol
(1*R*,2*S*)-2-Amino-1-(3-hydroxyphenyl)propan-1-ol; $C_9H_{13}NO_2$;
54-49-9
● **Metaraminol Tartrate** *17171-57-2*
Adrenoceptor agonist

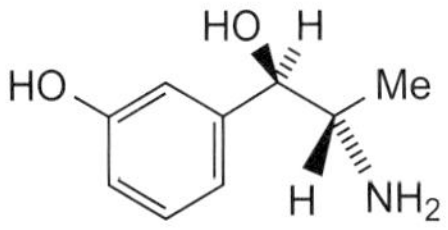

Metaxalone (rINN) me·*taks*·a·lön
(*RS*)-5-(3,5-Xylyloxymethyl)-2-oxazolidone; $C_{12}H_{15}NO_3$;
1665-48-1
Skeletal muscle relaxant

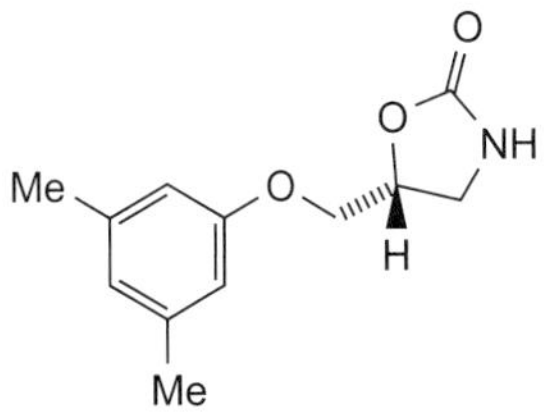

and enantiomer

Metazocine (rINN) me·*tä*·zö·sën
(2*R*,6*R*,11*R*)-1,2,3,4,5,6-Hexahydro-3,6,11-trimethyl-2,6-
methano-3-benzazocin-8-ol; $C_{15}H_{21}NO$; *3734-52-9*
Opioid receptor agonist

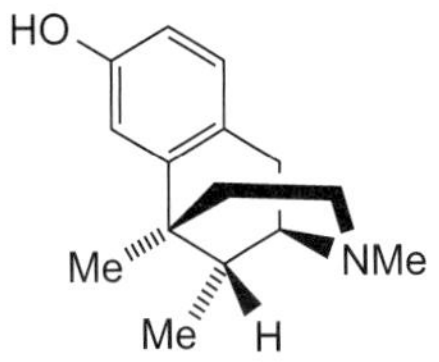

Metenolone (rINN) me·*ten*·o·lön
17β-Hydroxy-1-methyl-5α-androst-1-en-3-one; $C_{20}H_{30}O_2$;
153-00-4
Metenolone Acetate *434-05-9*
Opioid receptor agonist

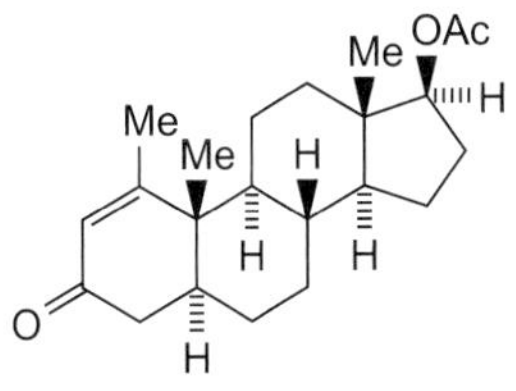

Metergoline (rINN) me·*ter*·gö·lën
Benzyl (8*S*,10*R*)-(1,6-dimethylergolin-8-ylmethyl)carbamate;
$C_{25}H_{29}N_3O_2$; *17692-51-2*
Serotonin 5HT receptor antagonist

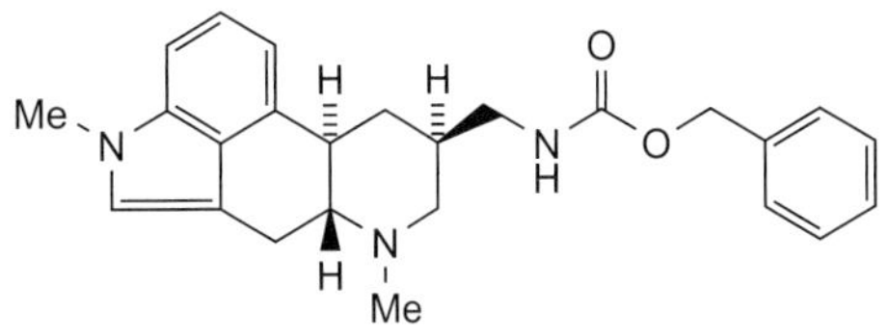

Metetoin (rINN) see Appendix C

Metformin (rINN) met·*for*·min
1,1-Dimethylbiguanide; $C_4H_{11}N_5$; *657-24-9*
● **Metformin Hydrochloride** *1115-70-4*
Biguanide; treatment of diabetes mellitus

Methacholine Chloride (rINN) me·tha·*kö*·lën
(1) Acetyl-β-methylcholine chloride; (2) (2-Acetoxypropyl)-
trimethylammonium chloride; $C_8H_{18}ClNO_2$; *62-51-1*
Cholinesterase inhibitor

and enantiomer

Methacycline (rINN) me·tha·*si*·klen
(1) 4S,4aR,5S,5aR,12aS)-4-Dimethylamino-1,4,4a,5,5a,6,¬
11,12a-octahydro-3,5,10,12,12a-pentahydroxy-6-methylene-
1,11-dioxonaphthacene-2-carboxamide; (2) 6-Demethyl-6-
deoxy-5β-hydroxy-6-methylenetetracycline; metacycline
(pINN); $C_{22}H_{22}N_2O_8$; *914-00-1*
Methacycline Hydrochloride *3963-95-9*
Tetracycline antibacterial

Methadone (rINN) *me*·tha·dön
6-Dimethylamino-4,4-diphenylheptan-3-one; amidine;
$C_{21}H_{27}NO$; *76-99-3*
● **Methadone Hydrochloride** *1095-90-5*
Opioid receptor agonist; analgesic

and enantiomer

Methadyl Acetate *see Acetylmethadol*

Methallenestril (rINN) see Appendix C

Methallibure *see Metallibure*

Methamphazone *see Metamphazone*

Methandienone (BAN) see Appendix C

Methanthelinium Bromide (rINN) me·than·the·*li*·në·um
Diethyl(methyl)[2-(xanthen-9-ylcarbonyloxy)ethyl]ammonium
bromide; $C_{21}H_{26}BrNO_3$; *53-46-3*
Anticholinergic

Methaphenilene (rINN) me·tha·*fe*·ni·lën
N-(2-Dimethylaminoethyl)-N-thenylaniline; $C_{15}H_{20}N_2S$;
493-78-7
Histamine H_1 receptor antagonist; antihistamine

Methapyrilene (rINN) me·tha·*pi*·ri·lën
2-(N-2-Pyridyl-N-2-thenylamino)ethyldimethylamine;
$C_{14}H_{19}N_3S$; *91-80-5*
Histamine H_1 receptor antagonist; antihistamine

◉ **Methaqualone** (rINN) me·*tha*·kwa·lön
2-Methyl-3-o-tolylquinazolin-4-(3H)-one; $C_{16}H_{14}N_2O$; *72-44-6*
Hypnotic

Metharbital (rINN) me·*thar*·bi·tal
5,5-Diethyl-1-methylbarbituric acid; $C_9H_{14}N_2O_3$; *50-11-3*
Barbiturate; antiepileptic

Methazolamide (rINN) me·tha·*zol*·a·mïd
N-(4-Methyl-2-sulfamoyl-Δ²-1,3,4-thiadiazolin-5-ylidene)¬
acetamide; $C_5H_8N_4O_3S_2$; *554-57-4*
*Carbonic anhydrase inhibitor; treatment of glaucoma and
ocular hypertension*

The symbol '¬' in systematic chemical names signifies line continuation

Methdilazine (rINN) meth·*dil*·a·zën
10-(1-Methylpyrrolidin-3-ylmethyl)phenothiazine; $C_{18}H_{20}N_2S$;
1982-37-2
Histamine H_1 receptor antagonist; antihistamine

Methenamine Hippurate (rINN) me·*then*·a·mën *hi*·pûr·rät
A 1:1 complex of hexamine and hippuric acid;
$C_6H_{12}N_4.C_9H_9NO_3$; *5714-73-8*
Antiseptic

Methenolone *see Metenolone*

Methestrol (rINN) me·*thës*·trol
4,4′-(1,2-Diethylethylene)di(*o*-cresol); $C_{20}H_{26}O_2$; *130-73-4*
Oestrogen

mixture of stereoisomers

Methetoin *see Metetoin*

Methicillin *see Meticillin*

Methimazole *see Thiamazole*

Methindizate *see Metindizate*

Methiodal Sodium (rINN) me·*thï*·ö·dal
Sodium iodomethanesulfonate; CH_2INaO_3S; *126-31-8*
Iodinated contrast medium

I CH$_2$SO$_3$Na

● **Methionine** (rINN) me·*thï*·ö·nïn
L-Methionine; (2*S*)-2-Amino-4-(methanesulfanyl)butanoic acid;
$C_5H_{13}NO_2$; *63-68-3*;
Amino acid

Methisazone *see Metisazone*

Methixene *see Metixene*

Methocarbamol (rINN) me·thö·*kar*·ba·mol
2-Hydroxy-3-(2-methoxyphenoxy)propyl carbamate;
$C_{11}H_{15}NO_5$; *532-03-6*
Skeletal muscle relaxant

and enantiomer

Methohexital (rINN) me·thö·*heks*·i·tal
5-Allyl-1-methyl-5-(1-methylpent-2-ynyl)barbituric acid;
$C_{14}H_{18}N_2O_3$; *18652-93-2*
● **Methohexital Sodium** *22151-68-4*
Intravenous barbiturate; general anaesthetic

mixture of 4 stereoisomers

Methoin *see Mephenytoin*

Methoserpidine (rINN) see Appendix C

● **Methotrexate** (rINN) me·thö·*treks*·ät
4-Amino-4-deoxy-10-methylpteroyl-L-glutamic acid;
amethopterin; $C_{20}H_{22}N_8O_5$; *59-05-2*
Methotrexate Sodium
Dihydrofolate reductase inhibitor; cytostatic

Methotrimeprazine *see Levomepromazine*

Methoxamine (rINN) me·*thoks*·a·mën
2-Amino-1-(2,5-dimethoxyphenyl)propan-1-ol; $C_{11}H_{17}NO_3$;
390-28-3
● **Methoxamine Hydrochloride** *61-16-5*
Adrenoceptor agonist

mixture of stereoisomers

Methoxsalen (BAN) me·*thoks*·a·len
9-Methoxyfuro[3,2-*g*]chromen-7-one; $C_{12}H_8O_4$; *298-81-7*
Aid to dermal pigmentation

Methoxyflurane (rINN) me·thoks·ë·*flûr*·rän
2,2-Dichloro-1,1-difluoroethyl methyl ether; $C_3H_4Cl_2F_2O$;
76-38-0
General anaesthetic

Methoxyphenamine (rINN) me·thoks·ë·*fen*·a·mën
2-Methoxy-α-methylphenethyl(methyl)amine; $C_{11}H_{17}NO$;
93-30-1
Adrenoceptor agonist

and enantiomer

Methsuximide *see Mesuximide*

Methyclothiazide (rINN) see Appendix C

Methyl Benzoquate (rINN) më·thïl *ben*·zö·kwät
Methyl 7-benzyloxy-6-butyl-1,4-dihydro-4-oxoquinoline-3-
carboxylate; nequinate (pINN); $C_{22}H_{23}NO_4$; *13997-19-8*
Antiprotozoal

Methyl Cysteine *see Mecysteine*

Methylbenzethonium Chloride (rINN) më·thïl·ben·ze·*thö*·në·um
Benzyldimethyl-2-{2-[4-(1,1,3,3-tetramethylbutyl)-*o*-
tolyloxy]ethoxy}ethylammonium chloride; $C_{28}H_{44}ClNO_2$;
25155-18-4
Antiseptic

Methylchromone (rINN) see Appendix C

Methyldesorphine (rINN) më·thïl·dez·*or*·fën
(1) (–)-(5*S*)-4,5-Epoxy-6,17-dimethylmorphin-6-en-3-ol;
(2) 7,8-Dihydro-6-deoxy-6,7-didehydromorphine; $C_{18}H_{21}NO_2$;
16008-36-9
Opioid receptor agonist

● **Methyldopa** (rINN) më·thïl·*dö*·pa
3-(3,4-Dihydroxyphenyl)-2-methyl-L-alanine; $C_{10}H_{13}NO_4$;
555-30-6 (anhydrous); *41372-08-1 (sesquihydrate)*
Alpha₂-adrenoceptor agonist; treatment of hypertension

Methyldopate (BAN) më·thïl·*dö*·pät
(1) Ethyl 3-(3,4-dihydroxyphenyl)-2-methyl-L-alaninate;
(2) Ethyl (–)-2-amino-2-(3,4-dihydroxybenzyl)propionate;
$C_{12}H_{17}NO_4$; *2544-09-4*
● **Methyldopate Hydrochloride** *2508-79-4*
Alpha₂-adrenoceptor agonist; treatment of hypertension

Methylene Blue *see Methylthioninium Chloride*

Methylephedrine (rINN) see Appendix C

Methylergometrine (rINN) më·thïl·er·gö·*me*·trën
(8*R*)-*N*-(1*S*)-1-(Hydroxymethyl)propyllysergamide;
methylergonovine; $C_{20}H_{25}N_3O_2$; *113-42-8*
● **Methylergometrine Maleate** *7054-07-1*
Oxytocic

Methylnaltrexone bromide (rINN) *më*·thïl·nal·*trex*·ön
(17*RS*)-17-(Cyclopropylmethyl)-4,5α-epoxy-3,14-
dihydroxy-17-methyl-6-oxomorphinan-17-ium bromide;
$C_{21}H_{26}BrNO_4$; *73232-52-7*;
Opioid receptor antagonist; treatment of opioid-induced
constipation

Methylpentynol (rINN) më·thïl·*pen*·tin·ol
3-Methylpent-1-yn-3-ol; $C_6H_{10}O$; *477-75-8*
Hypnotic; anxiolytic

and enantiomer

Methylphenidate (rINN) më·thïl·*fe*·ni·dät
Methyl 2-phenyl-2-piperidylacetate; $C_{14}H_{19}NO_2$; *113-45-1*
Methylphenidate Hydrochloride *298-59-9*
Narcolepsy; hyperactivity disorders in children

mixture of 4 stereoisomers

● **Methylphenobarbital** (rINN) më·thïl·fë·nö·*bar*·bi·tal
(*RS*)-5-Ethyl-1-methyl-5-phenylbarbituric acid; mephobarbital
(USAN); $C_{13}H_{14}N_2O_3$; *115-38-8*
Barbiturate

and enantiomer

● **Methylprednisolone** (rINN) më·thïl·pred·*ni*·so·lön
(1) 11β,17α,21-Trihydroxy-6α-methylpregna-1,4-diene-3,20-
dione; (2) 6α-Methylprednisolone; $C_{22}H_{30}O_5$; *83-43-2*
● **Methylprednisolone Acetate** *53-36-1*
● **Methylprednisolone Hydrogen Succinate** *2921-57-5*
Methylprednisolone Sodium Succinate *2375-03-3*
Methylprednisolone Suleptonate *90350-40-6*
Glucocorticoid

● **Methylrosanilinium Chloride** (rINN) *me*·thïl·*rös*·ani·li·në·um
N-(4-{bis[4-(Dimethylamino)phenyl]methylene}cyclohexa-2,5-
dienylidene)-*N*-methylmethanaminium; $C_{25}H_{30}ClN_3$; *548-62-9*
Antiseptic dye (gentian violet)

and epimer at N^+

● **Methyltestosterone** (rINN) më·thïl·tes·*tos*·ter·rön
17β-Hydroxy-17α-methylandrost-4-en-3-one; $C_{20}H_{30}O_2$;
58-18-4
Anabolic steroid

● **Methylthioninium Chloride** (rINN) më·thïl·thï·ö·*nin*·ë·um
3,7-Bis(dimethylamino)phenothiazin-5-ium chloride trihydrate;
CI basic blue 9 trihydrate; $C_{16}H_{18}ClN_3S,3H_2O$; *7220-79-3*
Reducing agent; antidote to methaemoglobinaemia

Methyprylon (rINN) me·thë·*pri*·lon
(*RS*)-3,3-Diethyl-5-methylpiperidine-2,4-dione; $C_{10}H_{17}NO_2$;
125-64-4
Hypnotic

and enantiomer

Methyridine (BAN) me·*thir*·ri·dën
2-(2-Methoxyethyl)pyridine; $C_8H_{11}NO$; *114-91-0*
Antihelminthic

Methysergide (rINN) me·thë·*ser*·jïd
(8*R*)-*N*-(1*S*)-(1-Hydroxymethyl)propyl-1-methyllysergamide;
$C_{21}H_{27}N_3O_2$; *361-37-5*
● **Methysergide Maleate** *129-49-7*
Non-selective 5HT receptor antagonist

Metiamide (rINN) me·*ti*·a·mïd
1-Methyl-3-[2-(5-methylimidazol-4-ylmethylthio)¬
ethyl]thiourea; $C_9H_{16}N_4S_2$; *34839-70-8*
Histamine H_2 receptor antagonist

Meticillin (rINN) me·thi·*si*·lin
6-(2,6-Dimethoxybenzamido)penicillanic acid;
$C_{17}H_{20}N_2O_6S$; *61-32-5*
Methicillin Sodium *7246-14-2*
Antibacterial

Metildigoxin (rINN) me·til·di·*joks*·in
3β-[*O*-(2,6-Dideoxy-4-*O*-methyl-D-*ribo*-hexopyranosyl)-(1→4)-
O-(2,6-dideoxy-D-*ribo*-hexopyranosyl)-(1→4)-2,6-dideoxy-D-
ribo-hexopyranosyloxy]-12β,14-dihydroxy-5β,14β-card-20(22)-
enolide; $C_{42}H_{66}O_{14}$; *30685-43-9*
Na/K-ATPase inhibitor; cardiac glycoside

Metindizate (rINN) me·*tin*·di·zät
2-(1-Methylperhydroindol-3-yl)ethyl benzilate; $C_{25}H_{31}NO_3$;
15687-33-9
Metindizate Hydrochloride
Antispasmodic

mixture of 8 stereoisomers

Metioprim (rINN) see Appendix C

● **Metipranolol** (rINN) me·ti·*pra*·no·lol
4-(2-Hydroxy-3-isopropylaminopropoxy)-2,3,6-trimethyl¬
phenyl acetate; $C_{17}H_{27}NO_4$; *22664-55-7*
Beta-adrenoceptor antagonist

and enantiomer

Metirosine (rINN) me·*tir*·rö·sën
(-)-α-Methyl-L-tyrosine; $C_{10}H_{13}NO_3$; *672-87-7*
Alpha-methyl-para-tyrosine; tyrosine hydroxylase inhibitor

Metisazone (rINN) see Appendix C

Metixene (rINN) me·*tiks*·ën
(*RS*)-9-(1-Methyl-3-piperidylmethyl)thioxanthene; $C_{20}H_{23}NS$;
4969-02-2
● **Metixene Hydrochloride** *7081-40-5*
Anticholinergic

and enantiomer

Metizoline (rINN) me·*ti*·zo·lën
2-(2-Methylbenzo[*b*]thienylmethyl)-2-imidazoline; $C_{13}H_{14}N_2S$;
17692-22-7
Vasoconstrictor; nasal congestion

● **Metoclopramide** (rINN) me·tö·*klö*·pra·mïd
4-Amino-5-chloro-*N*-(2-diethylaminoethyl)-2-methoxy¬
benzamide; $C_{14}H_{22}ClN_3O_2$; *364-62-5*
● **Metoclopramide Hydrochloride** *7232-21-5 (anhydrous)*;
54143-57-6 (hydrate)
Dopamine receptor antagonist; antiemetic

Metofoline (rINN) see Appendix C

● **Metolazone** (rINN) me·*to*·la·zön
(*RS*)-7-Chloro-1,2-dihydro-2-methyl-4-oxo-3-*o*-tolyl¬
quinazoline-6-sulfonamide; $C_{16}H_{16}ClN_3O_3S$; *17560-51-9*
Thiazide-like diuretic

The symbol '¬' in systematic chemical names signifies line continuation

and enantiomer

Metomidate (rINN) see Appendix C

Metopimazine (rINN) me·tö·*pi*·ma·zën
1-[3-(2-Methylsulfonylphenothiazin-10-yl)propyl]piperidine-4-carboxamide; $C_{22}H_{27}N_3O_3S_2$; *14008-44-7*
Dopamine receptor antagonist; antiemetic

Metopon (rINN) *me*·tö·pon
(1) (−)-(5R)-4,5-Epoxy-3-hydroxy-5,17-dimethylmorphinan-6-one; (2) 6-Deoxy-7,8-dihydro-5-methyl-6-oxomorphine; $C_{18}H_{21}NO_3$; *143-52-2*
Opioid receptor agonist

Metoprolol (rINN) me·*to*·pro·lol
1-Isopropylamino-3-*p*-(2-methoxyethyl)phenoxypropan-2-ol; $C_{15}H_{25}NO_3$; *54163-88-1*
● **Metoprolol Succinate** *98418-47-4*
● **Metoprolol Tartrate** *56392-17-7*
Beta-adrenoceptor antagonist

and enantiomer

Metoserpate (rINN) see Appendix C

Metrenperone (rINN) me·*tren*·pe·rön
3-[2-(4-*p*-Fluorobenzoylpiperidino)ethyl]-2,7-dimethyl⌐pyrido[1,2-*a*]pyrimidin-4-one; $C_{24}H_{26}FN_3O_2$; *81043-56-3*; R50970
Serotonin 5HT$_2$ receptor antagonist (veterinary)

● **Metrifonate** (rINN) me·*tri*·fo·nät
(*RS*)-Dimethyl 2,2,2-trichloro-1-hydroxyethylphosphonate; trichlorfon (USAN); $C_4H_8Cl_3O_4P$; *52-68-6*
Antihelminthic

and enantiomer

Metrizamide (rINN) me·*tri*·za·mïd
2-[3-Acetamido-2,4,6-tri-iodo-5-(*N*-methylacetamido)⌐benzamido]-2-deoxy-D-glucose; $C_{18}H_{22}I_3N_3O_8$; *55134-11-7*
Iodinated contrast medium

● **Metronidazole** (rINN) me·trö·*ni*·da·zôl
2-(2-Methyl-5-nitroimidazol-1-yl)ethanol; $C_6H_9N_3O_3$; *443-48-1*
Imidazole antibacterial

● **Metronidazole Benzoate** (BAN)
2-(2-Methyl-5-nitroimidazol-1-yl)ethyl benzoate; $C_{13}H_{13}N_3O_4$; *13182-89-3*
Imidazole antibacterial

● **Metyrapone** (rINN) me·*ti*·ra·pön
2-Methyl-1,2-di-(3-pyridyl)propan-1-one; $C_{14}H_{14}N_2O$; *54-36-4*
11-Beta-hydroxylase inhibitor; inhibition of the formation of corticosteroids

Metyzoline *see Metizoline*

- **Mexenone** (rINN) *meks·e·nön*
  2-Hydroxy-4-methoxy-4′-methylbenzophenone; $C_{15}H_{14}O_3$;
  1641-17-4
  Sunscreen

Mexiletine (rINN) meks·*il*·e·tën
  1-Methyl-2-(2,6-xylyloxy)ethylamine; $C_{11}H_{17}NO$; *31828-71-4*
  - **Mexiletine Hydrochloride** *5370-01-4*
  Class I antiarrhythmic

and enantiomer

Mezlocillin (rINN) see Appendix C

Mianserin (rINN) mï·*an*·se·rin
  (*RS*)-1,2,3,4,10,14b-Hexahydro-2-methyldibenzo[*c*,*f*]pyrazino¬
  [1,2-*a*]azepine; $C_{18}H_{20}N_2$; *24219-97-4*
  - **Mianserin Hydrochloride** *21535-47-7*
  Monoamine reuptake inhibitor; tetracyclic antidepressant

and enantiomer

Mibefradil (rINN) see Appendix C

Mibolerone (rINN) mï·*bol*·e·rön
  17β-Hydroxy-7α,17-dimethylestr-4-en-3-one; $C_{20}H_{30}O_2$;
  3704-09-4
  Anabolic steroid; androgen

Micafungin (rINN) mï·ká·*fun*·gin
  6,N^6.1-anhydro-(4*R*,5*R*)-4,5-Dihydroxy-N^2-(4-{5-[4-¬
  (pentyloxy)phenyl]-1,2-oxazol-3-yl}benzoyl)-L-ornithyl-
  L-threonyl-(4*R*)-4-hydroxy-L-prolyl-(4*S*)-4-hydroxy-4-[4-
  hydroxy-3-(sulfooxy)phenyl]-L-threonyl-(3*R*)-3-hydroxy-
  L-glutaminyl-(3*S*,4*S*)-3-hydroxy-4-methyl-L-proline;
  $C_{56}H_{71}N_9O_{23}S$; *235114-32-6*;
  Micafungin Sodium *208538-73-2*
  Antifungal

- **Miconazole** (rINN) mï·*kon*·a·zôl
  (*RS*)-1-[2,4-Dichloro-β-(2,4-dichlorobenzyloxy)phenethyl]¬
  imidazole; $C_{18}H_{14}Cl_4N_2O$; *22916-47-8*
  - **Miconazole Nitrate** *22832-87-7*
  Antifungal azole

and enantiomer

- **Midazolam** (rINN) mï·*däz*·ö·lam
  8-Chloro-6-(2-fluorophenyl)-1-methyl-4*H*-imidazo[1,5-*a*][1,4]¬
  benzodiazepine; $C_{18}H_{13}ClFN_3$; *59467-70-8*
  Midazolam Hydrochloride *59467-96-8*
  Benzodiazepine

Midodrine (rINN) mï·dö·drën
  (*RS*)-N^1-(β-Hydroxy-2,5-dimethoxyphenethyl)glycinamide;
  $C_{12}H_{18}N_2O_4$; *42794-76-3*
  Midodrine Hydrochloride *3092-17-9*
  Alpha₁-adrenoceptor agonist

and enantiomer

The symbol '¬' in systematic chemical names signifies line continuation

Mifamurtide (rINN) mi·*fam*·er·tïd

2-(*N*-{[(2*R*)-2-(2-Acetamido-2,3-dideoxy-D-glucopyranos-3-*O*-yl)propanoyl]-L-alanyl-D-γ–glutamyl-L-alanyl}amino)ethyl (2*R*)-2,3-bis(hexadecanoyloxy)propyl hydrogen phosphate; $C_{59}H_{109}N_6O_{19}P$; *83461-56-7*;
Immunomodulator; treatment of cancer

Mifepristone (rINN) mi·fe·*pris*·tön

11β-(4-Dimethylaminophenyl)-17β-hydroxy-17α-prop-1-ynylestra-4,9-dien-3-one; $C_{29}H_{35}NO_2$; *84371-65-3*
Progesterone antagonist

Miglitol (rINN) *mi*·gli·tol

(2*R*,3*R*,4*R*,5*S*)-1-(2-Hydroxyethyl)-2-(hydroxymethyl)-piperidine-3,4,5-triol; $C_8H_{17}NO_5$; *72432-03-2*
Alpha-glucosidase inhibitor; treatment of diabetes mellitus

Miglustat (rINN) *mi*·gloo·stat

1,5-(Butylimino)-1,5-dideoxy-D-glucitol; $C_{10}H_{21}NO_4$; *72599-27-0*
Alpha-glucosidase inhibitor; treatment of diabetes mellitus

Mikamycin (rINN) mi·ka·*mï*·sin

Antimicrobial substances produced by *Streptomyces mitakaensis*; certain components are identical with some constituents of ostreogrycin, pristinamycin and virginiamycin; *11006-76-10*
Aminoglycoside antibacterial

Milenperone (rINN) see Appendix C

Milnacipran (rINN) mil·*na*·si·pran

(±)-*cis*-2-Aminomethyl-*N*,*N*-diethyl-1-phenylcyclopropane-carboxamide; $C_{15}H_{22}N_2O$; *92623-85-3*
Milnacipran Hydrochloride *101152-94-7*
Inhibitor of 5HT and noradrenaline reuptake; antidepressant

and enantiomer

Milrinone (rINN) *mil*·ri·nön

1,6-Dihydro-2-methyl-6-oxo-[3,4′-bipyridine]-5-carbonitrile; $C_{12}H_9N_3O$; *78415-72-2*
Inhibitor of phosphodiesterase type III; positive inotrope

Miltefosine (rINN) mil·*tef*·o·sën

[2-(Trimethylammonio)ethyl][hexadecyloxyphosphonate]; $C_{21}H_{46}NO_4P$; *58066-85-6*
Progesterone antagonist

Minaprine (rINN) see Appendix C

Minaxolone (rINN) mi·*naks*·o·lön

11α-Dimethylamino-2β-ethoxy-3α-hydroxy-5α-pregnan-20-one; $C_{25}H_{43}NO_3$; *62571-87-3*
Minaxolone Citrate
General anaesthetic

Minepentate (rINN) see Appendix C

Minocromil (rINN) mï·*no*·krö·mil

6-Methylamino-4-oxo-10-propyl-4*H*-pyrano[3,2-*g*]quinoline-2,8-dicarboxylic acid; $C_{18}H_{16}N_2O_6$; *85118-44-1*
Minocromil Sodium *75452-62-9*
Cromone

Minocycline (rINN) mĭ·nö·sĭ·klën
(1) (4S,4aS,5aR,12aS)-4,7-Bis(dimethylamino)-
1,4,4a,5,5a,6,11,12a-octahydro-3,10,12,12a-tetrahydroxy-1,11-
dioxonaphthacene-2-carboxamide; (2) 6-Demethyl-6-deoxy-7-
dimethylaminotetracycline; $C_{23}H_{27}N_3O_7$; *11008-90-8*
● **Minocycline Hydrochloride** *13614-98-7*
Tetracycline antibacterial

Minoxidil (rINN) min·oks·i·dil
2,6-Diamino-4-piperidinopyrimidine 1-oxide; $C_9H_{15}N_5O$;
38304-91-5
Vasodilator; treatment of hypertension; male pattern baldness

Mioflazine (rINN) see Appendix C

Miristalkonium Chloride (rINN) mi·ri·stal·kö·në·um
Benzyldimethyl(tetradecyl)ammonium chloride; $C_{23}H_{42}ClN$;
139-08-2
Disinfectant

Mirococept (rINN) mi·ro·kö·sept
Myristoylated-peptidyl recombinant SCR1-3 of human
complement receptor type 1;
507453-82-9
Soluble complement receptor

mirococept has the following amino acid sequence:

```
MQCNAPEWLP    FARPTNLTDE    FEFPIGTYLN

YECRPGYSGR    PFSIICLKNS    VWTGAKDRCR

RKSCRNPPDP    VNGMVHVIKG    IQFGSQIKYS

CTKGYRLIGS    SSATCISSGD    TVIWDNETPI

CDRIPCGLPP    TITNGDFIST    NRENFHYGSV

VTYRCNPGSG    GRKVFELVGE    PSIYCTSNDD

QVGIWSGPAP    QCIIPNKC-OH
```

N-(myristoyl)GSSKSPSKKK

KKKPGD-(*S*-2-thiopyridyl)C-NH₂

Mirtazapine (rINN) mer·tä·za·pën
(RS)-1,2,3,4,10,14b-Hexahydro-2-methylpyrazino[2,1-a]¬
pyrido[2,3-c][2]benzazepine; $C_{17}H_{19}N_3$; *61337-67-5*
Inhibitor of 5HT and noradrenaline reuptake; antidepressant

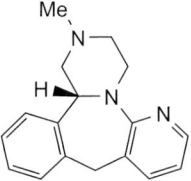

and enantiomer

Misonidazole (rINN) mĭ·sö·nĭd·a·zôl
(RS)-3-Methoxy-1-(2-nitroimidazol-1-yl)propan-2-ol;
$C_7H_{11}N_3O_4$; *13551-87-6*
Antiprotozoal

and enantiomer

● **Misoprostol** (rINN) mĭ·sö·pros·tol
(1) (±)-Methyl 7-[1R,2R,3R)-3-hydroxy-2-[(E)-(4RS)-4-
hydroxy-4-methyloct-1-enyl]-5-oxocyclopentyl]heptanoate;
(2) (±)-Methyl (13E)-11,16-dihydroxy-16-methyl-9-
oxoprost-13-enoate; $C_{22}H_{38}O_5$; *59122-46-2*
Prostaglandin (PGE₁) analogue

and enantiomer at C*

● **Mitobronitol** (rINN) mĭ·tö·bro·ni·tol
1,6-Dibromo-1,6-dideoxy-D-mannitol; $C_6H_{12}Br_2O_4$; *488-41-5*
Cytotoxic

Mitoclomine (rINN) see Appendix C

Mitoenamine (rINN) see Appendix C

● **Mitomycin** (rINN) mĭ·tö·mi·sin
(1S,2S,9S,9aR)-7-Amino-2,3,5,8,9,9a-hexahydro-9a-methoxy-6-
methyl-5,8-dioxo-1,2-epimino-1H-pyrrolo[1,2-a]indol-9-
ylmethyl carbamate; mitomycin C; $C_{15}H_{18}N_4O_5$; *50-07-7*
Antibacterial; cytotoxic

The symbol '¬' in systematic chemical names signifies line continuation

Mitopodozide (rINN) mï·tö·*pö*·dö·zïd
2′-Ethylpodophyllohydrazide; $C_{24}H_{30}N_2O_8$; *1505-45-8*
Cytotoxic

Mitoquidone (rINN) mï·*to*·kwi·dön
5,14-Dihydrobenz[5,6]isoindolo[2,1-*b*]isoquinoline-8,13-dione;
$C_{20}H_{13}NO_2$; *91753-07-0*; GR 30921
Cytotoxic

Mitotane (rINN) *mï*·tö·tän
1,1-Dichloro-2-(2-chlorophenyl)-2-(4-chlorophenyl)ethane;
$C_{14}H_{10}Cl_4$; *53-19-0*;
Adrenal cortex suppressant; treatment of adrenocortical cancer

Mitotenamine (rINN) see Appendix C

Mitoxantrone (rINN) mï·toks·*an*·trön
1,4-Dihydroxy-5,8-bis[2-(2-hydroxyethylamino)ethylamino]¬
anthraquinone; $C_{22}H_{28}N_4O_6$; *65271-80-9*
● **Mitoxantrone Hydrochloride** *70476-82-3*
Cytotoxic

Mitozantrone *see Mitoxantrone*

Mitozolomide (rINN) mï·tö·*zo*·lö·mïd
3-(2-Chloroethyl)-3,4-dihydro-4-oxoimidazo[5,1-*d*]-1,2,3,5-
tetrazine-8-carboxamide; $C_7H_7ClN_6O_2$; *85622-95-3*
Topoisomerase II inhibitor; cytotoxic

Mivacurium Chloride (rINN) mi·va·*kûr*·rë·um
A mixture of the (1*R*,1′*R*,2*S*,2′*S*), (1*R*,1′*R*,2*S*,2′*R*) and
(1*R*,1′*R*,2*R*,2′*R*) stereoisomers (the *trans-trans, trans-cis* and
cis-cis isomers respectively) of (*E*)-1,1′,2,2′,3,3′,4,4′-
octahydro-6,6′,7,7′-tetramethoxy-2,2′-dimethyl-1,1′-
bis(3,4,5-trimethoxybenzyl)-2,2′-[oct-4-enedioylbis
(oxytrimethylene)] di-isoquinolinium dichloride;
$C_{58}H_{80}Cl_2N_2O_{14}$; *106861-44-3 (total racemate)*
Non-depolarizing neuromuscular blocker

Mizolastine (rINN) mï·zö·*las*·tën
2-{1-[1-(4-Fluorobenzyl)-1*H*-benzimidazol-2-yl]-4-
piperidyl(methyl)amino}pyrimidin-4(1*H*)-one; $C_{24}H_{25}FN_6O$;
108612-45-9
Histamine H_1 receptor antagonist; antihistamine

Moclobemide (rINN) mö·*klö*·be·mïd
4-Chloro-*N*-(2-morpholinoethyl)benzamide; $C_{13}H_{17}ClN_2O_2$;
71320-77-9
Monoamine oxidase type A inhibitor; antidepressant

● **Modafinil** (rINN) mö·*da*·fi·nil
2-(Benzhydrylsulfinyl)acetamide; $C_{15}H_{15}NO_2S$; *68693-11-8*
Narcolepsy and sleep disorders

Modipafant (rINN) mö·*di*·pa·fant
Ethyl (*R*)-4-(2-chlorophenyl)-1,4-dihydro-6-methyl-2-[4-(2-
methyl-1*H*-imidazo[4,5-*c*]pyridin-1-yl)phenyl]-5-(2-pyridyl¬
carbamoyl)pyridine-3-carboxylate; $C_{34}H_{29}ClN_6O_3$;
122957-06-6; 122956-68-7 (racemate)
Platelet activating factor antagonist

Moexipril (rINN) mö·*eks*·i·pril
(3*S*)-2[(2*S*)-2{[(1*S*)-(1-Ethoxycarbonyl)-3-phenylpropyl]¬
amino}propanoyl]-1,2,3,4-tetrahydro-6,7-dimethoxyquinoline-3-
carboxylic acid; $C_{27}H_{34}N_2O_7$; *82586-52-5*
Moexipril Hydrochloride *82586-52-5*
Angiotensin converting enzyme inhibitor

Molgramostim (rINN) mol·gra·*mos*·tim
Recombinant granulocyte macrophage colony stimulating factor
expressed by *E. coli*; *99283-10-0*
Recombinant granulocyte macrophage colony-stimulating factor

molgramostim has the following amino acid sequence:

```
APARSPSPS      TQPWEHVNAI      QEARRLLNLS

RDTAAEMNET     VEVISEMFDL      QEPTCLQTRL

ELYKQGLRGS     LTKLKGPLTM      MASHYKQHCP

PTPETSCATQ     IITFESFKEN      LKDFLLVIPF

DCWEPVQE
```

Molindone (rINN) *mol*·in·dön
(*RS*)-3-Ethyl-1,5,6,7-tetrahydro-2-methyl-5-
(morpholinomethyl)indol-4-one; $C_{16}H_{24}N_2O_2$; *7416-34-4*
Molindone Hydrochloride *15622-65-8*
Dopamine receptor antagonist; neuroleptic

Molsidomine (rINN) mol·*si*·dö·mën
N-Ethoxycarbonyl-3-morpholinosydnonimine; $C_9H_{14}N_4O_4$;
25717-80-0
Nitric oxide donor; treatment of angina pectoris

Mometasone (rINN) mö·*me*·ta·sön
9α,21-Dichloro-11β,17-dihydroxy-16α-methylpregna-1,4-
diene-3,20-dione; $C_{22}H_{28}Cl_2O_4$; *105102-22-5*
● **Mometasone Furoate** *83919-23-7*
Glucocorticoid

Monensin (rINN) mo·*nen*·sin
An antibacterial substance produced by *Streptomyces
cinnamonensis*; 4-{2-[2-ethyl-3′-methyl-5′-(tetrahydro-6-
hydroxy-6-hydroxymethyl-3,5-dimethylpyran-2-yl)perhydro-
2,2′-bifuran-5-yl]-9-hydroxy-2,8-dimethyl-1,6-
dioxaspiro[4.5]dec-7-yl}3-methoxy-2-methylpentanoic acid;
$C_{36}H_{62}O_{11}$; *17090-79-8*

Monensin Sodium *22373-78-0*
Ionophore antimicrobial agent

Monoctanoin (BAN) mo·nok·*ta*·nö·in
A mixture of 1-*O*-decanoyl-*sn*-glycerol-3,1,2-*O*-dioctanoyl-
sn-glycerol-3 and 1-*O*-octanoyl-*sn*-glycerol-3 in which the
molecular ratio-range of the mono-octyl ester to the sum of
the monodecanoyl and dioctanoyl esters is 80 to 85:15 to 10
Dissolving cholesterol gallstones

Monosulfiram *see Sulfiram*

Montelukast (rINN) mon·të·*lü*·kast
(*R*)-[1-(1-{3-[2-(7-Chloro-2-quinolyl)vinyl]phenyl}-3-[2-(1-
hydroxy-1-methylethyl)phenyl]propylthiomethyl)cyclo¬
propyl]acetic acid; $C_{35}H_{36}ClNO_3S$; *158966-92-8*; MK-0476
Montelukast Sodium *151767-02-1*
Leukotriene CysLT$_1$ receptor antagonist; treatment of asthma

---

The symbol '¬' in systematic chemical names signifies line continuation

Mopidamol (rINN) mö·*pi*·da·mol
2,2′,2″,2‴-(4-Piperidinopyrimido[5,4-*d*]pyrimidine-2,6-diyldinitrilo)tetraethanol; $C_{19}H_{31}N_7O_4$; *13665-88-8*
Cytotoxic

Moracizine (rINN) mor·*ra*·si·zën
Ethyl 10-(3-morpholinopropionyl)phenothiazin-2-ylcarbamate; $C_{22}H_{25}N_3O_4S$; *31883-05-3*; moricizine (USAN)
Moracizine Hydrochloride *29560-58-8*
Class I antiarrhythmic

Morantel (rINN) *mo*·ran·tel
(*E*)-1,4,5,6-Tetrahydro-1-methyl-2-[2-(3-methyl-2-thienyl)vinyl]pyrimidine; $C_{12}H_{16}N_2S$; *20574-50-9*
Morantel Tartrate *26155-31-7*
Morantel Citrate
Antihelminthic

Morazone (rINN) see Appendix C

Moroctocog Alfa (rINN) mo·*rok*·to·cog al·fa
(1—742)–(1637—1648)-Blood-coagulation factor VIII (human reduced) complex with 1649—2332–blood-coagulation factor VIII (human reduced);
Blood coagulation factor VIII

Moroxydine (rINN) mo·*roks*·ë·dën
1-(Morpholinoformimidoyl)guanidine; $C_6H_{13}N_5O$; *3731-59-7*
Antiviral (herpesviruses)

Morpheridine (rINN) mor·*fe*·ri·dën
Ethyl 1-(2-morpholinoethyl)-4-phenylpiperidine-4-carboxylate; morpholinoethylnorpethidine; $C_{20}H_{30}N_2O_3$; *469-81-8*
Opioid receptor agonist

Morphine (BAN) mor·fën
(5*R*,6*S*)-7,8-Didehydro-4,5-epoxy-17-methylmorphinan-3,6-diol; $C_{17}H_{19}NO_3$; *57-27-2*
● **Morphine Hydrochloride** *52-26-6*
● **Morphine Sulfate** *64-31-3*
Morphine Tartrate *302-31-8*
Opioid receptor agonist; analgesic

Moxaverine (rINN) moks·*a*·ver·rën
1-Benzyl-3-ethyl-6,7-dimethoxyisoquinoline; $C_{20}H_{21}NO_2$; *10539-19-2*
Moxaverine Hydrochloride *1163-37-7*
Smooth muscle relaxant

♣ **Moxidectin** (rINN) moks·i·*dek*·tin
(6*R*,15*S*)-5-*O*-Demethyl-28-deoxy-25-[(*E*)-1,3-dimethylbut-1-enyl]-6,28-epoxy-23-oxomilbemycin B (*E*)-23-*O*-methyloxime; $C_{37}H_{53}NO_8$; *113507-06-5*
Antihelminthic; ectoparasiticide

Moxifloxacin (rINN) moks·i·*floks*·a·sin
1-Cyclopropyl-6-fluoro-8-methoxy-7-[(4a*S*,7a*S*)-octahydro-
6*H*-pyrrolo[3,4-*b*]pyridin-6-yl]-4-oxo-1,4-dihydroquinoline-3-
carboxylic acid; $C_{21}H_{24}FN_3O_4$; *151096-09-2*

● **Moxifloxacin Hydrochloride** *186826-86-8*
Fluoroquinolone antibacterial

Moxipraquine (rINN) moks·*i*·pra·kwën
4-{4-[6-(6-Methoxy-8-quinolylamino)hexyl]piperazin-1-
yl}butan-2-ol; $C_{24}H_{38}N_4O_2$; *23790-08-1*
Antiprotozoal

and enantiomer

Moxisylyte (rINN) moks·*is*·i·lït
4-(2-Dimethylaminoethoxy)-5-isopropyl-2-methylphenyl
acetate; $C_{16}H_{25}NO_3$; *54-32-0*
● **Moxisylyte Hydrochloride** *964-52-3*
Alpha-adrenoceptor antagonist

● **Moxonidine** (rINN) moks·*o*·ni·dën
4-Chloro-6-methoxy-2-methylpyrimidine-5-yl(2-imidazolin-2-
yl)amine; $C_9H_{12}ClN_5O$; *75438-57-2*
Imidazoline I_1 receptor agonist; treatment of hypertension

Mucin, Gastric *see Gastric Mucin*

● **Mupirocin** (rINN) mü·*pi*·rö·sin
9-[(2*E*)-4-[(2*S*,3*R*,4*R*,5*S*)-5-[(2*S*,3*S*,4*S*,5*S*)-2,3-Epoxy-5-
hydroxy-4-methylhexyl]tetrahydro-3,4-dihydroxypyran-2-yl]-3-
methylbut-2-enoyloxy]nonanoic acid; $C_{26}H_{44}O_9$; *12650-69-0*
● **Mupirocin Calcium** *11504-43-6*
Antibacterial

Mustine *see Chlormethine*

Muzolimine (rINN) *see Appendix C*

Mycophenolic Acid (rINN) mï·kö·fe·*no*·lik
(*E*)-6-(1,3-Dihydro-4-hydroxy-6-methoxy-7-methyl-3-
oxoisobenzofuran-5-yl)-4-methylhex-4-enoic acid; $C_{17}H_{20}O_6$;
24280-93-1
● **Mycophenolate Mofetil** *115007-34-6*
Inhibitor of nucleic acid synthesis; immunomodulator

Myralact (rINN) mï·ra·lakt
(2-Hydroxyethyl)tetradecylammonium lactate; $C_{19}H_{41}NO_4$;
15518-87-3
Antiseptic

Myrophine (rINN) mï·ro·fën
(1) (−)-(5*R*,6*S*)-3-Benzyloxy-4,5-epoxy-17-methylmorphin-7-
en-6-yl myristate; (2) 3-*O*-Benzyl-6-*O*-myristoylmorphine;
$C_{38}H_{51}NO_4$; *467-18-5*
Opioid receptor agonist

Nabilone (rINN) *na*·bi·lön
(±)-(6a*R*,10a*R*)-3-(1,1-Dimethylheptyl)-6a,7,8,9,10,10a-
hexahydro-1-hydroxy-6,6-dimethyl-6*H*-benzo[c]chromen-9-one;
$C_{24}H_{36}O_3$; *51022-71-0*
Cannabinoid

and enantiomer

The symbol '¬' in systematic chemical names signifies line continuation

Nabumetone (rINN) na·*bü*·me·tön
4-(6-Methoxy-2-naphthyl)butan-2-one; $C_{15}H_{16}O_2$; *42924-53-8*
Cyclo-oxygenase inhibitor; analgesic; anti-inflammatory

Nadide (rINN) nä·dïd
1-(3-Carbamoylpyridinio)-β-D-ribofuranoside 5-(adenosine-5′-diphosphate); $C_{21}H_{27}N_7O_{14}P_2$; *53-84-9*
Naturally occurring co-enzyme (nicotinimide adenine dinucleotide); treatment of alcohol and opioid addiction

Nadifloxacin (rINN) na·di·*floks*·a·sin
(*RS*)-9-Fluoro-6,7-dihydro-8-(4-hydroxypiperidino)-5-methyl-1-oxo-1*H*,5*H*-benzo[*ij*]quinolizine-2-carboxylic acid; $C_{19}H_{21}FN_2O_4$; *124858-35-1*
Fluoroquinolone antibacterial

and enantiomer

Nadolol (rINN) *na*·do·lol
(2*R*,3*S*)-5-(3-*tert*-Butylamino-2-hydroxypropoxy)-1,2,3,4-tetrahydronaphthalene-2,3-diol; $C_{17}H_{27}NO_4$; *42200-33-9*
Beta-adrenoceptor antagonist

and enantiomer at C*

Nadroparin Calcium (rINN) na·drö·*pa*·rin

Calcium salt of depolymerised heparin obtained by nitrous acid degradation of heparin from pork intestinal mucosa; the majority of the components have a 2-*O*-sulfo-α-L-idopyranosuronic acid structure at the non-reducing end and a 6-*O*-sulfo-2,5-anhydro-D-mannitol structure at the reducing end of their chain; the average molecular weight is about 4500; the degree of sulfation is about 2.1 per disaccharide unit
Low molecular weight heparin

Nafarelin (rINN) na·fa·*rë*·lin
5-oxo-L-prolyl-L-histidyl-L-tryptophyl-L-seryl-L-tyrosyl-3-(2-naphthyl)-D-alanyl-L-leucyl-L-arginyl-L-prolyglycinamide; *76932-56-4*
Nafarelin Acetate *86220-42-0*
Gonadotropin releasing hormone (gonadorelin) analogue; treatment of prostate cancer

nafarelin has the following amino acid sequence:

```
<Glu-His-Trp-Ser-Tyr-3-(naphthyl)-
D-Ala-Leu-Arg-Pro-Gly-NH₂
```

Nafazatrom (rINN) na·*fä*·za·trom
3-Methyl-1-[2-(2-naphthyloxy)ethyl]-5-pyrazolone; $C_{16}H_{16}N_2O_2$; *59040-30-1*
Lipoxygenase inhibitor; antithrombic

Nafcillin (rINN) naf·*si*·lin
6-(2-Ethoxy-1-naphthamido)penicillanic acid; $C_{21}H_{22}N_2O_5S$; *147-52-4*
Nafcillin Sodium *7717-50-6 (hydrate)*; *985-16-0 (anhydrous)*
Penicillin antibacterial

Nafenopin (rINN) see Appendix C

Naftalofos (rINN) naf·*ta*·lö·fos
Diethyl naphthalimido-oxyphosphonate; $C_{16}H_{16}NO_6P$; *1491-41-4*
Antihelminthic

Naftazone (rINN) *naf*·ta·zön
1,2-Naphthoquinone 2-semicarbazone; $C_{11}H_9N_3O_2$; *15687-37-3*
Inhibitor of platelet aggregation

Naftidrofuryl (rINN) naf·tï·drö·*für*·ïl
all rac-2-Diethylaminoethyl 3-(1-naphthyl)-2-tetrahydro¬
furfurylpropionate; $C_{24}H_{33}NO_3$; *31329-57-4*
● **Naftidrofuryl Oxalate** nafronyl oxalate (USAN); *3200-06-4*
Vasodilator

mixture of stereoisomers

Naftifine (rINN) *naf*·ti·fën
(*E*)-Cinnamyl(methyl)(1-naphthylmethyl)amine; $C_{21}H_{21}N$;
65472-88-0
Antifungal

Nagrestipen (rINN) na·*gres*·ti·pen
A genetically-engineered variant of a naturally occurring stem
cell inhibiting protein; macrophage inflammatory protein-1α;
150387-18-1
Protection of bone marrow stem cells

nagrestipen has the following amino acid sequence:

```
SLAADTPTAC    CFSYTSRQIP    QNFIAAYFET

SSQCSKPGVI    FLTKRSRQVC    ADPSEEWVQK

YVSDLELSA
```

Nalbuphine (rINN) *nal*·bü·fën
(1) (−)-(5*R*,6*S*,14*S*)-17-Cyclobutylmethyl-4,5-epoxy¬
morphinan-3,6,14-triol; (2) 17-Cyclobutylmethyl-7,8-
dihydro-14-hydroxy-17-normorphine; $C_{21}H_{27}NO_4$; *20594-83-6*
Nalbuphine Hydrochloride *23277-43-2*
Opioid receptor partial agonist; analgesic

● **Nalidixic Acid** (rINN) na·li·*diks*·ik
1-Ethyl-1,4-dihydro-7-methyl-4-oxo-1,8-naphthyridine-3-
carboxylic acid; $C_{12}H_{12}N_2O_3$; *389-08-2*
Quinolone antibacterial

Nalmefene (rINN) *nal*·me·fën
(5*S*)-17-Cyclopropylmethyl-4,5-epoxy-6-methylene¬
morphinan-3,14-diol; nalmetrene; $C_{21}H_{25}NO_3$; *55096-26-9*
Nalmefene Hydrochloride *58895-64-0*
Opioid receptor antagonist

Nalorphine (rINN) na·*lor*·fën
(1) (−)-(5*R*,6*S*)-17-Allyl-4,5-epoxymorphin-7-en-3,6-diol;
(2) 17-Allyl-17-normorphine; $C_{19}H_{21}NO_3$; *62-67-9*
Nalorphine Hydrobromide *1041-90-3*
Opioid receptor antagonist

Naloxone (rINN) na·*loks*·ön
(1) (−)-(5*R*,14*S*)-17-Allyl-4,5-epoxy-3,14-dihydroxy¬
morphinan-6-one;
(2) 17-Allyl-6-deoxy-7,8-dihydro-14-hydroxy-6-oxo-17-
normorphine; $C_{19}H_{21}NO_4$; *465-65-6*
● **Naloxone Hydrochloride** *51481-60-8*
Opioid receptor antagonist

Naltrexone (rINN) nal·*treks*·ön
(5*R*)-17-Cyclopropylmethyl-3,14-dihydroxy-4,5-epoxy¬
morphinan-6-one; $C_{20}H_{23}NO_4$; *16590-41-3*
● **Naltrexone Hydrochloride** *16676-29-2*
Opioid receptor antagonist

The symbol '¬' in systematic chemical names signifies line continuation

Nandrolone (rINN) *nan·dro·lön*
17β-Hydroxyestr-4-en-3-one; $C_{18}H_{26}O_2$; *434-22-0*
Nandrolone Cyclohexylpropionate *912-57-2*
● **Nandrolone Decanoate** *360-70-3*
♣ **Nandrolone Laurate** *26490-31-3*
● **Nandrolone Phenylpropionate** *62-90-8*
Anabolic steroid; androgen

Nanterinone (rINN) see Appendix C

● **Naphazoline** (rINN) *na·fä·zö·lën*
2-(1-Naphthylmethyl)-2-imidazoline; $C_{14}H_{14}N_2$; *835-31-4*
● **Naphazoline Hydrochloride** *550-99-2*
● **Naphazoline Nitrate** *5144-52-5*
Alpha-adrenoceptor agonist

Naphthalophos *see Naftalofos*

● **Naproxen** (rINN) *na·proks·en*
(*S*)-2-(6-Methoxy-2-naphthyl)propionic acid; $C_{14}H_{14}O_3$; *22204-53-1*
● **Naproxen Sodium** *26159-34-2*
Cyclo-oxygenase inhibitor; analgesic; anti-inflammatory

Narasin (rINN) *na·ra·sin*
2-[6-[5-(5-Ethyltetrahydro-5-hydroxy-6-methylpyran-2-yl)-15-hydroxy-2,10,12-trimethyl-1,6,8-trioxadispiro[4.1.5.3]¬
pentadec-13-en-9-yl]-2-hydroxy-1,3-dimethyl-4-oxoheptyl]¬
tetrahydro-3,5-dimethylpyran-2-yl]butyric acid;
$C_{43}H_{72}O_{11}$; *55134-13-9*
Antiprotozoal (veterinary)

Naratriptan (rINN) *na·ra·trip·tan*
N-Methyl-2-[3-(1-methylpiperidin-4-yl)indol-5-yl]ethane¬
sulfonamide; $C_{17}H_{25}N_3O_2S$; *121679-13-8*
Naratriptan Hydrochloride *121679-19-4*
Serotonin 5HT$_1$ receptor agonist; treatment of migraine

Natalizumab (rINN) *na·ta·li·zü·mab*
Immunoglobulin G 4 (human-mouse monoclonal AN100226 4-chain antihuman integrin 4), disulfide with human-mouse monoclonal AN100226 light chain, dimer; *189261-10-7*;
Immunomodulator

Natamycin (rINN) *na·ta·mï·sin*
A polyene antibiotic produced by *Streptomyces natalensis*; pimaricin; $C_{33}H_{47}NO_{13}$; *7681-93-8*
Antifungal

Nateglinide (rINN) *na·te·gli·nïd*
N-(*trans*-4-Isopropylcyclohexanecarbonyl-D-phenylalanine; $C_{19}H_{27}NO_3$; *105816-04-4*;
Stimulates insulin release; treatment of diabetes mellitus

Nealbarbital (rINN) *në·al·bar·bi·tal*
5-Allyl-5-neopentylbarbituric acid; $C_{12}H_{18}N_2O_3$; *561-83-1*
Barbiturate

Nebacumab (rINN) *ne·ba·kü·mab*
Immunoglobulin M (human monoclonal HA-lA anti-endotoxin), disulfide with human monoclonal HA-lA κ-chain, pentameric dimer; *138661-01-5*
Monoclonal antibody (bacterial endotoxin)

Nebivolol (rINN) ne·*bi*·vo·lol
(l*RS*,1′*RS*)-1,1′-[(2*RS*,2′*SR*)-Bis(6-fluorochroman-2-yl)]-
2,2′-iminodiethanol; $C_{22}H_{25}F_2NO_4$; *99200-09-6*
Nebivolol Hydrochloride
Beta-adrenoceptor antagonist

and enantiomer

Nedocromil (rINN) ne·*do*·krö·mil
9-Ethyl-6,9-dihydro-4,6-dioxo-10-propyl-4*H*-pyrano[3,2-g]¬
quinoline-2,8-dicarboxylic acid; $C_{19}H_{17}NO_7$; *69049-73-6*
Nedocromil Calcium *101626-68-0*
Nedocromil Sodium *69049-74-7*
Cromone; treatment of asthma; food allergy;
allergic conjunctivitis; rhinitis

Nefazodone (rINN) ne·*fä*·zö·dön
2-{3-[4-(3-Chlorophenyl)piperazin-1-yl]propyl)-5-ethyl-2,4-
dihydro-4-(2-phenoxyethyl)-1,2,4-triazol-3-one; $C_{25}H_{32}ClN_5O_2$;
83366-66-9
Nefazodone Hydrochloride *82752-99-6*
Monoamine reuptake inhibitor; antidepressant

Nefopam (rINN) *ne*·fö·pam
(*RS*)-3,4,5,6-Tetrahydro-5-methyl-1-phenyl-1*H*-2,5-
benzoxazocine; $C_{17}H_{19}NO$; *13669-70-0*
Nefopam Hydrochloride *23327-57-3*
Non-opioid analgesic

and enantiomer

Nelarabine (rINN) ne·*la*·ra·bën
2-Amino-9-(β-D-arabinofuranosyl)-6-methoxy-9*H*-purine;
$C_{11}H_{15}N_5O_5$; *121032-29-9*
Cytotoxic; antimetabolite

Nelfinavir (rINN) nel·*fin*·a·veer
(3*S*,4a*S*,8a*S*)-*N-tert*-Butyldecahydro-2-[(2*R*,3*R*)-3-(3-hydroxy-
o-toluamido)-2-hydroxy-4-(phenylthio)butyl]isoquinoline-3-
carboxamide; $C_{32}H_{45}N_3O_4S$; *159989-64-7*
Protease inhibitor; antiviral (HIV)

Neocinchophen (rINN) see Appendix C

Neomycin (rINN) në·ö·*mï*·sin
Antimicrobial aminoglycosides produced by selected strains of
Streptomyces fradiae; neomycin B is framycetin; *1404-04-2*
● **Neomycin Sulfate** *1405-10-3*
Aminoglycoside antibacterial

Neostigmine (BAN) në·ö·*stig*·mën
3-(Dimethylcarbamoyloxy)trimethylanilinium ion; $C_{12}H_{19}N_2O_2$
● **Neostigmine Bromide** *114-80-7*
● **Neostigmine Metilsulfate** *51-60-5*
Cholinesterase inhibitor

Nepafenac (rINN) ne·pá·*fen*·ac
2-(2-Amino-3-benzoylphenyl)acetamide;
$C_{15}H_{14}N_2O_2$; *78281-72-8*;
Cyclo-oxygenase inhibitor; analgesic; anti-inflammatory

Netilmicin (rINN) ne·til·*mï*·sin
(1) 4-*O*-[(2*R*,3*R*)-*cis*-3-Amino-6-aminomethyl-3,4-dihydro-2*H*-pyran-2-yl]-2-deoxy-6-*O*-(3-deoxy-4-*C*-methyl-3-methyl¬amino-β-L-arabinopyranosyl)-1-*N*-ethylstreptamine;
(2) 2-Deoxy-6-*O*-(3-deoxy-4-*C*-methyl-3-methylamino-β-L-arabinopyranosyl)-4-*O*-(2,6-diamino-2,3,4,6-tetradeoxy-D-*glycero*-hex-4-enopyranosyl)-1-*N*-ethyl streptamine; (3) *N*[1]-ethylsissomicin; $C_{21}H_{41}N_5O_7$; *56391-56-1*
● **Netilmicin Sulfate** (2:5) *56391-57-2*

Aminoglycoside antibacterial

Netivudine (rINN) see Appendix C

Netobimin (rINN) ne·*tö*·bi·min
2-{3-Methoxycarbonyl-2-[2-nitro-5-(propylthio) phenyl]¬guanidino}ethanesulfonic acid; $C_{14}H_{20}N_4O_7S_2$; *88255-01-0*
Antihelminthic (veterinary)

Neutral Insulin Injection *see Insulin Injection*

● **Nevirapine** (rINN) ne·*vîr*·ra·pën
11-Cyclopropyl-5,11-dihydro-4-methyl-6*H*-dipyrido¬[3,2-*b*:2′,3′-*e*][1,4]diazepin-6-one; $C_{15}H_{14}N_4O$; *129618-40-2*
Non-nucleoside reverse transcriptase inhibitor; antiviral (HIV)

Nialamide (rINN) nï·*al*·a·mïd
N′-(2-Benzylcarbamoylethyl)isonicotinohydrazide; $C_{16}H_{18}N_4O_2$; *51-12-7*
Monoamine oxidase inhibitor; antidepressant

Nicametate (rINN) see Appendix C

Nicarbazin (BAN) nï·*kar*·ba·zin
1,3-Bis(4-nitrophenyl)urea-4,6-dimethylpyrimidin-2-ol; $C_{19}H_{18}N_6O_6$; *330-95-0*
Antiprotozoal

Nicardipine (rINN) nï·*kar*·di·pën
(*RS*)-2-[Benzyl(methyl)amino]ethyl methyl 1,4-dihydro-2,6-dimethyl-4-(3-nitrophenyl)pyridine-3,5-dicarboxylate; $C_{26}H_{29}N_3O_6$; *55985-32-5*
Nicardipine Hydrochloride *54527-84-3*
Calcium channel blocker

and enantiomer

● **Nicergoline** (rINN) nï·*ser*·go·lën
(8*R*)-10-Methoxy-1,6-dimethylergolin-8-ylmethyl 5-bromo¬nicotinate; $C_{24}H_{26}BrN_3O_3$; *27848-84-6*
Ergot derivative

Niceritrol (rINN) nï·*se*·ri·trol
Pentaerythritol tetranicotinate; $C_{29}H_{24}N_4O_8$; *5868-05-3*
Nicotinic acid derivative; lipid-regulating drug

Niclofolan (rINN) see Appendix C

● **Niclosamide** (rINN) ni·*klö*·sa·mïd
2′,5-Dichloro-4′-nitrosalicylanilide; $C_{13}H_{18}Cl_2N_2O_4$; *50-65-7*
  ● **Niclosamide Monohydrate**
Antihelminthic

Nicocodine (rINN) ni·kö·*kö*·dën
(1) (−)-(5*R*,6*S*)-4,5-Epoxy-3-methoxy-17-methylmorphin-7-
en-6-yl nicotinate; (2) 3-*O*-Methyl-6-*O*-nicotinoylmorphine;
$C_{24}H_{24}N_2O_4$; *3688-66-2*
Opioid receptor agonist

Nicodicodine (rINN) ni·kö·dï·*kö*·dën
(1) (−)-(5*R*,6*S*)-4,5-Epoxy-3-methoxy-17-methylmorphinan-
6-yl nicotinate; (2) 7,8-Dihydro-3-*O*-methyl-6-*O*-
nicotinoylmorphine; $C_{24}H_{26}N_2O_4$; *808-24-2*
Cough suppressant

Nicofuranose (rINN) see Appendix C

Nicomorphine (rINN) ni·kö·*mor*·fën
(1) (−)-(5*R*,6*S*)-4,5-Epoxy-17-methylmorphin-7-en-3,6-diyl
dinicotinate; (2) 3,6-Di-*O*-nicotinoylmorphine; $C_{29}H_{25}N_3O_5$;
639-48-5
Opioid receptor agonist

Nicorandil (rINN) ni·kö·*ran*·dil
N-[2-(Nitro-oxy)ethyl]nicotinamide; $C_8H_9N_3O_4$; *65141-46-0*
Potassium channel opener

● **Nicotinamide** (rINN) ni·kö·*ti*·na·mïd
Pyridine-3-carboxamide; $C_6H_6N_2O$; *98-92-0*
Vitamin B component

● **Nicotine** (BAN) ni·*kö*·tën
(*S*)-3-(1-Methylpyrrolidin-2-yl)pyridine; $C_{10}H_{14}N_2$; *54-11-5*;
Nicotine Ditartrate *65-31-6*
● **Nicotine Resinate**
Aid to smoking cessation

● **Nicotinic Acid** (rINN) ni·kö·*ti*·nik
Pyridine-3-carboxylic acid; $C_6H_5NO_2$; *59-67-6*
Vitamin B component

Nicotinyl Alcohol (BAN) ni·kö·*ti*·nïl
3-Pyridylmethanol; C_6H_7NO; *100-55-0*
Nicotinyl Alcohol Tartrate *6164-87-0*
Vasodilator

Nicoumalone *see Acenocoumarol*

● **Nifedipine** (rINN) nï·*fe*·di·pën
Dimethyl 1,4-dihydro-2,6-dimethyl-4-(2-nitrophenyl)pyridine-
3,5-dicarboxylate; $C_{17}H_{18}N_2O_6$; *21829-25-4*
Calcium channel blocker

Nifenazone (rINN) nï·*fe*·na·zön
N-(2,3-Dimethyl-5-oxo-1-phenyl-3-pyrazolin-4-yl)nicotinamide;
$C_{17}H_{16}N_4O_2$; *2139-47-1*
Cyclo-oxygenase inhibitor

The symbol '¬' in systematic chemical names signifies line continuation

● **Niflumic Acid** (rINN) nï·*floo*·mik
2-[[3-(Trifluoromethyl)phenyl]amino]pyridine-3-carboxylic acid;
$C_{13}H_9F_3N_2O_2$; *4394-00-7*
Cyclo-oxygenase inhibitor; analgesic; anti-inflammatory

Nifuratel (rINN) nï·*fûr*·ra·tel
5-Methylthiomethyl-3-(5-nitrofurfurylideneamino)-2-oxazolidone; $C_{10}H_{11}N_3O_5S$; *4936-47-4*
Antiprotozoal

Nifuroquine (rINN) nï·*fûr*·rö·kwën
4-(5-Nitro-2-furyl)quinoline-2-carboxylic acid 1-oxide;
$C_{14}H_8N_2O_6$; *57474-29-0*
Antibacterial

● **Nifuroxazide** (rINN) nï·*fûr*·*oks*·a·zïd
(*E*)-4-Hydroxy-*N'*-[(5-nitrofuran-2-yl)methylidene]-benzohydrazide; $C_{12}H_9N_3O_5$; *965-52-6*
Antibacterial

Nifursol (rINN) nï·*fûr*·sol
3,5-Dinitro-2′-(5-nitrofurfurylidene)salicylohydrazide;
$C_{12}H_7N_5O_9$; *16915-70-1*
Antifungal

Nifurtimox (rINN) nï·*fûr*·ti·moks
(*RS*)-Tetrahydro-3-methyl-4-(5-nitrofurfurylideneamino)-1,4-thiazine 1,1-dioxide; $C_{10}H_{13}N_3O_5S$; *23256-30-6*
Antiprotozoal

and enantiomer

● **Nikethamide** (rINN) ni·*ke*·tha·mïd
N,N-Diethylpyridine-3-carboxamide; $C_{10}H_{14}N_2O$; *59-26-7*
Central nervous system stimulant

Nilestriol (rINN) nï·*lës*·trë·ol
3-Cyclopentyloxy-19-nor-17α-pregna-1,3,5(10)-trien-20-yne-16α,17β-diol; $C_{25}H_{32}O_3$;
39791-20-3
Oestrogen

Nilotinib (rINN) nï·*lö*·tin·ib
4-Methyl-*N*-[3-(4-methyl-1*H*-imidazol-1-yl)-5-(trifluoromethyl)phenyl]-3-{[4-(pyridin-3-yl)pyrimidin-2-yl]amino}benzamide; $C_{28}H_{22}F_3N_7O$; *641571-10-0*;
Tyrosine kinase inhibitor; chronic myeloid leukaemia

Nilprazole (rINN) see Appendix C

Niludipine (rINN) nï·*lü*·di·pën
Bis(2-propoxyethyl) 1,4-dihydro-2,6-dimethyl-4-(3-nitrophenyl)pyridine-3,5-dicarboxylate; $C_{25}H_{34}N_2O_8$;
22609-73-0
Calcium channel blocker

● **Nilutamide** (rINN) nï·*loo*·ta·mïd
5,5-Dimethyl-3-(α,α,α-trifluoro-4-nitro-*m*-tolyl)-imidazolidine-2,4-dione; $C_{12}H_{10}F_3N_3O_4$; *63612-50-0*
Cytotoxic

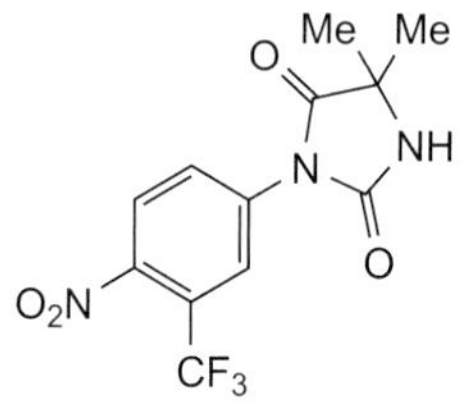

● **Nimesulide** (rINN) nï·*me*·sü·lïd
4′-Nitro-2′-phenoxymethanesulfonanilide; $C_{13}H_{12}N_2O_5S$; *51803-78-2*
Cyclo-oxygenase inhibitor; analgesic; anti-inflammatory

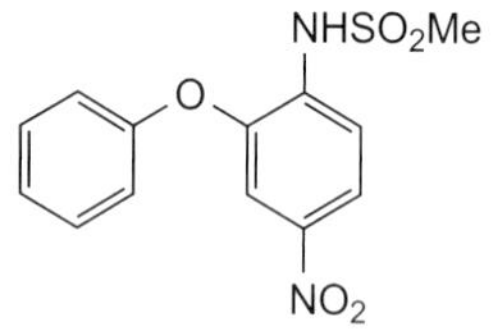

Nimodipine (rINN) ni·*mö*·di·pën
(*RS*)-Isopropyl 2-methoxyethyl 1,4-dihydro-2,6-dimethyl-4-(3-nitrophenyl)pyridine-3,5-dicarboxylate; $C_{21}H_{26}N_2O_7$; *66085-59-4*
Calcium channel blocker

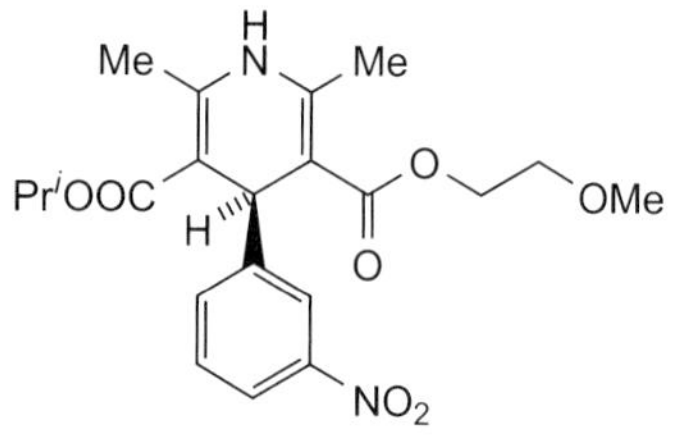

and enantiomer

Nimorazole (rINN) see Appendix C

Niridazole (rINN) nï·*ri*·da·zôl
1-(5-Nitro-1,3-thiazol-2-yl)imidazolidin-2-one; $C_6H_6N_4O_3S$; *61-57-4*
Antihelminthic

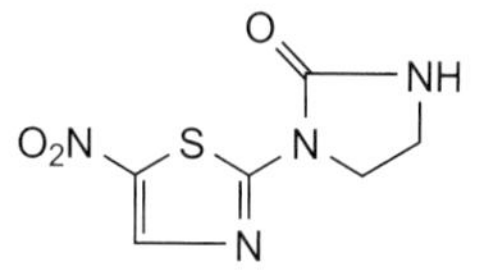

Nisoldipine (rINN) nï·*sol*·di·pën
(*RS*)-Isobutyl methyl 1,4-dihydro-2,6-dimethyl-4-(2-nitrophenyl)pyridine-3,5-dicarboxylate; $C_{20}H_{24}N_2O_6$; *63675-72-9*
Calcium channel blocker

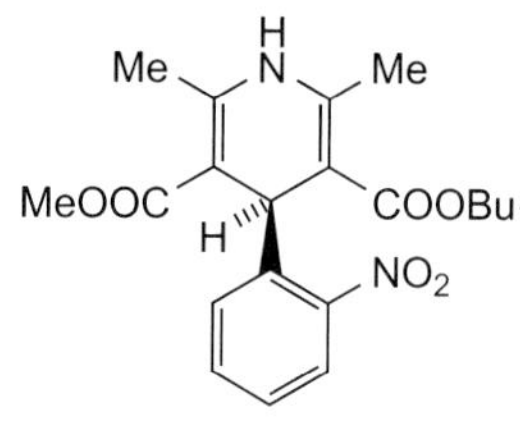

and enantiomer

● **Nitazoxanide** (rINN) nï·ta·*zoks*·a·nïd
2-(5-Nitro-1,3-thiazol-2-ylcarbamoyl)phenyl acetate; $C_{12}H_9N_3O_5S$; *55981-09-4*
Antiprotozoal

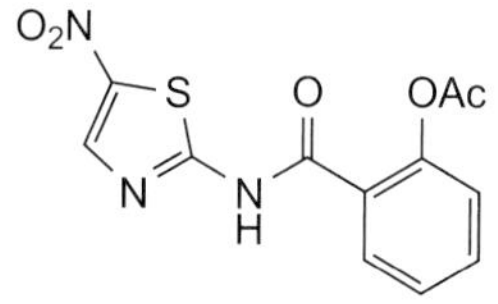

● **Nitrazepam** (rINN) nï·*trä*·ze·pam
1,3-Dihydro-7-nitro-5-phenyl-1,4-benzodiazepin-2-one; $C_{15}H_{11}N_3O_3$; *146-22-5*
Benzodiazepine

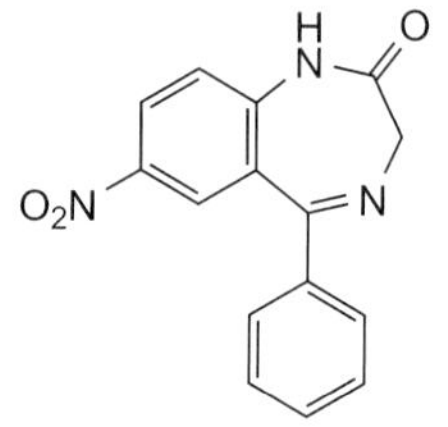

Nitrefazole (rINN) nï·*tref*·a·zôl
2-Methyl-4-nitro-1-(4-nitrophenyl)imidazole; $C_{10}H_8N_4O_4$; *21721-92-6*
Aldehyde dehydrogenase inhibitor; treatment of alcoholism

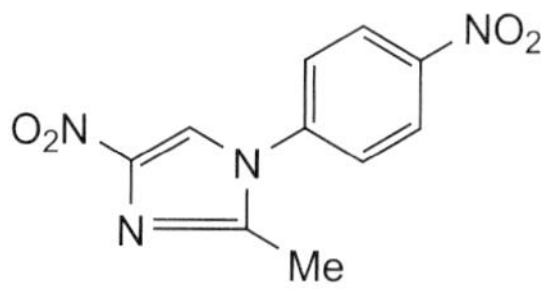

● **Nitrendipine** (rINN) nï·*tren*·di·pën
(*RS*)-Ethyl methyl 1,4-dihydro-2,6-dimethyl-4-(3-nitrophenyl)pyridine-3,5-dicarboxylate; $C_{18}H_{20}N_2O_6$; *39562-70-4*
Calcium channel blocker

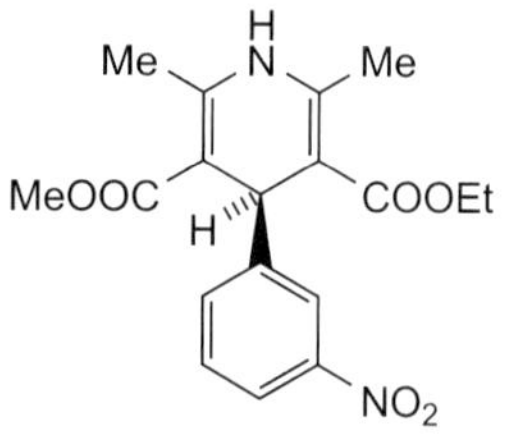

and enantiomer

The symbol '¬' in systematic chemical names signifies line continuation

Nitrocefin (BAN) nï·trö·*së*·fin
(7*R*)-3-[(*E*)-2,4-Dinitrostyryl]-7-(2-thienylacetamido)-3-cephem-4-carboxylic acid; $C_{21}H_{16}N_4O_8S_2$; *41906-86-9*
Nitrocefin Sodium
Detection of beta-lactamase activity in bacteria

● **Nitrofurantoin** (rINN) nï·trö·fûr·*ran*·tö·in
1-(5-Nitrofurfurylideneamino)hydantoin; $C_8H_6N_4O_5$; *67-20-9*
Antibacterial

● **Nitrofurazone** (rINN) nï·trö·*fûr*·ra·zön
5-Nitro-2-furaldehyde semicarbazone; nitrofural (pINN); $C_6H_6N_4O_4$; *59-87-0*
Antibacterial; topical antiprotozoal

Nitroscanate (rINN) nï·*tros*·ka·nät
4-(4-Nitrophenoxy)phenyl isothiocyanate; $C_{13}H_8N_2O_3S$; *19881-18-6*
Antihelminthic

Nitrovin (BAN) *nï*·trö·vin
(1) Bis[2-(5-nitro-2-furyl)vinyl]methylene¬hydrazinoformamidine; (2) 1,5-Bis(5-nitro-2-furyl)penta-1,4-dien-3-one amidinohydrazone; $C_{14}H_{12}N_6O_6$; *804-36-4*
Nitrovin Hydrochloride *2315-20-0*
Antibacterial

Nitroxinil (rINN) nï·*troks*·ë·nil
4-Hydroxy-3-iodo-5-nitrobenzonitrile; $C_7H_3IN_2O_3$; *1689-89-0*
Nitroxinil Eglumine *27917-82-4*
Antihelminthic

Nitroxoline (rINN) nï·*troks*·ö·lën
5-Nitroquinolin-8-ol; $C_9H_6N_2O_3$; *4008-48-4*
Antibacterial

Nitroxynil *see Nitroxinil*

Nivimedone (rINN) nï·*vi*·me·dön
5,6-Dimethyl-2-nitroindan-1,3-dione; $C_{11}H_9NO_4$; *49561-92-4*
Nivimedone Sodium
Antiallergic

● **Nizatidine** (rINN) nï·*za*·ti·dën
(1) *N*-[2-(2-Dimethylaminomethyl-1,3-thiazol-4-ylmethylthio]ethyl-*N'*-methyl-2-nitrovinylidenediamine;
(2) 4-[2-(1-Methylamino-2-nitrovinylamino)ethylthiomethyl]-1,3-thiazol-2-ylmethyl(dimethyl)amine;
$C_{12}H_{21}N_5O_2S_2$; *76963-41-2*
Histamine H_2 receptor antagonist; treatment of peptic ulcer

Noberastine (rINN) no·be·*ras*·tën
3-(5-Methylfurfuryl)-3*H*-imidazo[4,5-*b*]pyridin-2-yl(4-piperidyl)amine; $C_{17}H_{21}N_5O$; *110588-56-2*
Noberastine Maleate (1:2)
Histamine H_1 receptor antagonist; antihistamine

Nomegestrol (rINN) nö·me·*jes*·trol
6-Methyl-17α-hydroxy-19-norpregna-4,6-dien-3,20-dione; $C_{21}H_{28}O_3$; *58691-88-6*

● **Nomegestrol Acetate** *58652-20-3*
Progestogen

Nomifensine (rINN) no·mi·*fen*·sën

(*RS*)-1,2,3,4-Tetrahydro-2-methyl-4-phenylisoquinolin-8-ylamine; $C_{16}H_{18}N_2$; 24526-64-5

Nomifensine Maleate 32795-47-4

Monoamine reuptake inhibitor; antidepressant

and enantiomer

Nonabine (rINN) *non*·a·bën

7-(1,2-Dimethylheptyl)-2,2-dimethyl-4-(4-pyridyl)-2*H*-chromen-5-ol; $C_{25}H_{33}NO_2$; 16985-03-8

Cannabinoid

mixture of stereoisomers

Nonacog Alfa (rINN) *non*·a·kog al·fa

Blood coagulation factor IX (human), glycoform α; 113478-33-4

Recombinant factor IX

● **Nonoxinol** (rINN) no·*noks*·i·nol

α-(4-Nonylphenyl)-ω-hydroxypoly(oxyethylene)

Each nonoxinol name is followed by a number indicating the approximate number of oxyethylene groups present, *eg* nonoxinol 4, nonoxinol 9, and the individual chemical names may contain a specific numerical syllable for the same purpose

Spermatocide

Noracymethadol (rINN) see Appendix C

Noradrenaline /Norepinephrine (rINN)

nor·a·*dre*·na·lën/nor·e·pi·*ne*·frën

(*R*)-2-Amino-1-(3,4-dihydroxyphenyl)ethanol; $C_8H_{11}NO_3$; 51-41-2

● **Noradrenaline Acid Tartrate / Norepinephrine Acid Tartrate** Norepinephrine Bitartrate (USAN); 51-40-1 (anhydrous); 69815-49-2 (monohydrate)

● **Noradrenaline Hydrochloride / Norepinephrine Hydrochloride** 329-56-6

Alpha-adrenoceptor agonist

Norbudrine (rINN) *nor*·bü·drën

2-Cyclobutylamino-1-(3,4-dihydroxyphenyl)ethanol; $C_{12}H_{17}NO_3$; 15686-81-4

Bronchodilator

and enantiomer

Norcodeine (rINN) nor·*kö*·dën

(1) (−)-(5*R*,6*S*)-4,5-Epoxy-3-methoxymorphin-7-en-6-ol;
(2) 3-*O*-Methyl-17-normorphine; $C_{17}H_{19}NO_3$; 467-15-2

Opioid receptor agonist

Norelgestromin (rINN) nor·el·*jes*·trö·min

17-Hydroxy-18-homo-19-nor-17α-pregn-4-en-20-yn-3-one oxime; $C_{21}H_{29}NO_2$; 53016-31-2

Progestogen

Norethandrolone (rINN) see Appendix C

● **Norethisterone** (rINN) nor·e·*thi*·ste·rön

17β-Hydroxy-19-nor-17α-pregn-4-en-20-yn-3-one; norethindrone (USAN); $C_{20}H_{26}O_2$; 68-22-4

● **Norethisterone Acetate** Norethandrone Acetate (USAN) 51-98-9

Norethisterone Enantate

Progestogen

Noretynodrel (rINN) see Appendix C

● **Norfloxacin** (rINN) nor·*floks*·a·sin

1-Ethyl-6-fluoro-1,4-dihydro-4-oxo-7-piperazin-1-ylquinoline-3-carboxylic acid; $C_{16}H_{18}FN_3O_3$; 70458-96-7

Fluoroquinolone antibacterial

The symbol '¬' in systematic chemical names signifies line continuation

Norflurane (rINN) nor·*flûr*·rän
1,1,1,2-Tetrafluoroethane; $C_2H_2F_4$; *811-97-2*
General anaesthetic

● **Norgestimate** (rINN) nor·*jes*·ti·mät
13β-Ethyl-3-hydroxyimino-18,19-dinor-17α-pregn-4-en-20-yn-17β-yl acetate; $C_{23}H_{31}NO_3$; *35189-28-7*
Progestogen

Norgestomet (rINN) see Appendix C

● **Norgestrel** (rINN) nor·*jes*·trel
rac-13β-Ethyl-17β-hydroxy-18,19-dinor-17α-pregn-4-en-20-yn-3-one; DL-norgestrel; dl-norgestrel; $C_{21}H_{28}O_2$; *6533-00-2*
Progestogen

and enantiomer

Norletimol (rINN) see Appendix C

Norlevorphanol (rINN) nor·le·*vor*·fa·nol
(-)-Morphinan-3-ol; $C_{16}H_{21}NO$; *1531-12-0*
Opioid receptor agonist

Normethadone (rINN) nor·*me*·tha·dön
6-Dimethylamino-4,4-diphenylhexan-3-one; $C_{20}H_{25}NO$;
467-85-6
Opioid receptor agonist

Normorphine (rINN) nor·*mor*·fën
(−)-(5*R*,6*S*)-4,5-Epoxymorphin-7-en-3,6-diol; $C_{16}H_{17}NO_3$;
466-97-7
Opioid receptor agonist

Norpipanone (rINN) nor·*pi*·pa·nön
4,4-Diphenyl-6-piperidinohexan-3-one; $C_{23}H_{29}NO$; *561-48-8*
Opioid receptor agonist

Nortopixantrone (rINN) nor·to·piks·*an*·trön
2-{2-[(2-Hydroxyethyl)amino]ethyl}-5-{[2-(methylamino)¬ethyl]amino}indazolo[4,3-*gh*]isoquinolin-6(2*H*)-one;
$C_{20}H_{24}N_6O_2$
Nortopixantrone Hydrochloride
Cytotoxic

Nortriptyline (rINN) nor·*trip*·ti·lën
3-(10,11-Dihydro-5*H*-dibenzo[*a,d*]cyclohepten-5-ylidene)¬propyl(methyl)amine; $C_{19}H_{21}N$;
72-69-5
● **Nortriptyline Hydrochloride** *894-71-3*
Monoamine reuptake inhibitor; tricyclic antidepressant

Nosantine (rINN) *nö*·san·tën
9-{(1*R**)-1-[(*S**)-1-Hydroxyethyl]heptyl}hypoxanthine;
$C_{14}H_{22}N_4O_2$; *76600-30-1*
Immunomodulator

and enantiomer

● **Noscapine** (rINN) *nos·*ka·pën
(3S)-6,7-Dimethoxy-3-[(5R)-5,6,7,8-tetrahydro-4-methoxy-6-methyl-1,3-dioxolo[4,5-g]isoquinolin-5-yl]phthalide; *l*-α-narcotine; $C_{22}H_{23}NO_7$; *128-62-1*
  ● **Noscapine Hydrochloride** *912-60-7*
Opioid receptor agonist; cough suppressant

Nosiheptide (rINN) nö·si·*hep·*tïd
A peptide antibiotic obtained from cultures of *Streptomyces actuosus* 40037 or the same substance obtained by any other means; $C_{51}H_{43}N_{13}O_{12}S_6$; *56377-79-8*
Antibacterial

Novobiocin (rINN) nö·vö·*bï·*ö·sin
An antimicrobial substance produced by *Streptomyces niveus* and *S. spheroides* or related organisms; 4-hydroxy-3-[4-hydroxy-3-(3-methylbut-2-enyl)benzamido]-8-methylcoumarin-7-yl 3-*O*-carbamoyl-5,5-di-*C*-methyl-α-L-lyxopyranoside; $C_{31}H_{36}N_2O_{11}$; *303-81-1*
Novobiocin Sodium *1476-53-5*
Antibacterial

Noxiptiline (rINN) noks·*ip·*ti·lën
2-(10,11-Dihydro-5*H*-dibenzo[*a,d*]cyclohepten-5-ylidene¬amino-oxy)ethyldimethylamine; $C_{19}H_{22}N_2O$; *3362-45-6*
Noxiptiline Hydrochloride
Monoamine reuptake inhibitor; tricyclic antidepressant

Noxytiolin (rINN) noks·ë·*tï·*ö·lin
1-Hydroxymethyl-3-methyl-2-thiourea; $C_3H_8N_2OS$; *15599-39-0*
Monoamine reuptake inhibitor; tricyclic antidepressant

Nufenoxole (rINN) nü·fe·*noks·*ôl
2-[3-(2-Azabicyclo[2.2.2]octan-2-yl)-1,1-diphenylpropyl]-5-methyl-1,3,4-oxadiazole; $C_{25}H_{29}N_3O$; *57726-65-5*
Inhibitor of fluid secretion

Nupafant (rINN) *nü·*pa·fant
(S)-N-(1-Ethoxymethyl-3-methylbutyl)-N-methyl-α-(2-methyl-1*H*-imidazolo[4,5-*c*]pyridin-1-yl)-*p*-toluenesulfonamide; $C_{23}H_{32}N_4O_3S$; *139133-27-0*
Nupafant Hydrochloride *144736-31-2*
Platelet antagonist

Nylestriol *see Nilestriol*

● **Nystatin** (rINN) nï·*stat·*in
A mixture of polyenes produced by *Streptomyces noursei*; Nystatin A_1 is 19-(3-amino-3,6-dideoxy-β-D-mannopyranosyl¬oxy)-16-carboxy-3,5,7,10,11,15,17,35-octahydroxy-34,36-dimethyl-13-oxo-octatriaconta-20,22,24,26,30,32-hexaen-37-olide; *1400-61-9*
Antifungal

The symbol '¬' in systematic chemical names signifies line continuation

Ocaperidone (rINN) o·ka·pe·ri·dön
3-(2-[4-(6-Fluoro-1,2-benzoxazol-3-yl)piperidino]ethyl)-2,9-dimethylpyrido[1,2-*a*]pyrimidin-4-one; $C_{24}H_{25}FN_4O_2$; *129029-23-8*
Dopamine receptor antagonist; neuroleptic

Octacosactrin *see Tosactide*

Octafonium Chloride (rINN) ok·ta·*fö*·në·um
Benzyldiethyl-2-[4-(1,1,3,3-tetramethylbutyl)phenoxy]¬ethylammonium chloride; phenoctide; $C_{27}H_{42}ClNO$; *15687-40-8*
Antiseptic

Octatropine Methylbromide (rINN) ok·ta·*trö*·pën
(1*R*,3*r*,5*S*)-8-Methyl-3-(2-propylvaleryloxy)tropanium bromide; anistropine methylbromide (USAN); $C_{17}H_{32}BrNO_2$; *80-50-2*
Anticholinergic

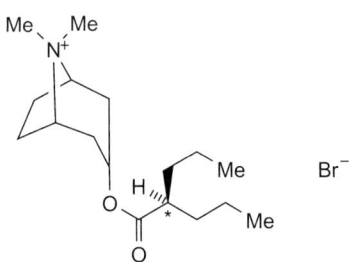

and enantiomer at C*

Octaverine (rINN) *see Appendix C*

Octenidine (rINN) ok·*te*·ni·dën
1,1′,4,4′-Tetrahydro-*N*,*N*′-dioctyl-1,1′-decamethylenedi-(4-pyridylideneamine); $C_{36}H_{62}N_4$; *71251-02-0*
Octenidine Hydrochloride *70775-75-6*
Octenidine Saccharin *86767-75-1*
Antiseptic

Octocog Alfa (rINN)
Recombinant human antihaemophilic factor VIII (without von Willebrand factor) derived from a cloned human factor VIII gene; factor VIII (rDNA)
Recombinant factor VIII

For labelling purposes the following three-letter code, to indicate the method of production, is approved:

(**bhk**) produced from genetically engineered baby hamster kidney cells

● **Octoxinol** (rINN) *see Appendix C*

Octreotide (rINN) ok·*trë*·ö·tïd
2-(D-Phenylalanyl-L-cystyl-L-phenylalanyl-D-tryptophyl-L-lysyl-L-threonyl-*N*-(2*R*,3*R*)-1,3-dihydroxybutyl]-L-cystinamide; $C_{49}H_{66}N_{10}O_{10}S_2$; *83150-76-9*
Octreotide Acetate
Somatostatin analogue; treatment of neuroendocrine tumours and acromegaly

D-Phe-Cys-Phe-D-Trp-Lys-Thr-Cys—NH

Oestradiol *see Estradiol*

Oestriol *see Estriol*

Oestrone *see Estrone*

Ofatumumab (rINN) off·á·*tü*·mü·mab
Immunoglobulin G1, anti-(human CD20 (antigen))(human monoclonal HuMax-CD20 heavy chain), disulfide with human monoclonal HuMax-CD20 κ-chain, dimer; *67981-59-8*
Monoclonal antibody (lymphocyte CD20); treatment of lymphoproliferative disorders

● **Ofloxacin** (rINN) ö·*floks*·a·sin
(±)-9-Fluoro-2,3-dihydro-3-methyl-10-(4-methylpiperazin-1-yl)-7-oxo-7*H*-pyrido[1,2,3-*de*][1,4]benzoxazine-6-carboxylic acid; $C_{18}H_{20}FN_3O_4$; *82419-36-1*
Fluoroquinolone antibacterial

and enantiomer

Olaflur (rINN) *o*·la·flûr
2,2′-{3-[*N*-(2-Hydroxyethyl)octadecylamino]propylimino}¬diethanol dihydrofluoride; $C_{27}H_{58}N_2O_3$,2HF; *6818-37-7*; *17671-49-1 (base)*
Fluoride analogue

Me [CH₂]₁₇ ... , 2HF

Olanzapine (rINN) ö·*lan*·za·pën

2-Methyl-4-(4-methylpiperazin-1-yl)-10*H*-thieno[2,3-*b*][1,5]¬
benzodiazepine; $C_{17}H_{20}N_4S$; *132539-06-1*
Dopamine D₂ receptor antagonist; serotonin 5HT₂ receptor
antagonist; neuroleptic

Olaquindox (rINN) o·la·*kwin*·doks

2-(2-Hydroxyethylcarbamoyl)-3-methylquinoxaline 1,4-dioxide;
$C_{12}H_{13}N_3O_4$; *23696-28-8*
Antibacterial

Oleandomycin (rINN) ö·lë·an·dö·*mï*·sin

An antibiotic produced by certain strains of *Streptomyces*
antibioticus; (2*R*,3*S*,4*R*,5*S*,6*S*,8*R*,10*R*,11*S*,12*R*,13*R*)-3-(2,6-
Dideoxy-3-*O*-methyl-α-L-*arabino*-hexopyranosyloxy)-8,8-
epoxymethano-11-hydroxy-2,4,6,10,12,13-hexamethyl-9-oxo-
5-(3,4,6-trideoxy-3-dimethylamino-β-D-*xylo*-hexopyranosyl¬
oxy)tridecan-13-olide; $C_{35}H_{61}NO_{12}$; *3922-90-5*
Macrolide antibacterial

Oletimol (rINN) see Appendix C

Olmesartan (rINN) ol·me·*sar*·tan

4-(2-Hydroxypropan-2-yl)-2-propyl-1-{[2'-(1*H*-tetrazol-5-
yl)biphenyl-4-yl]methyl}-1*H*-imidazole-5-carboxylic acid;
$C_{24}H_{26}N_6O_3$

Olmesartan medoxomil (rINN) *144689-63-4*

2,3-dihydroxy-2-butenyl 4-(1-hydroxy-1-methylethyl)-2-propyl-
1-[*p*-(*o*-1*H*-tetrazol-5-ylphenyl)benzyl]imidazole-5-carboxylate,
cayncglicio 2te,3n-scina rIbI orneaceteAngiotensin II (AT₁)
receptor antagonist

Olopatadine (rINN) o·lö·*pat*·a·dën

(*Z*)-11-[3-(Dimethylamino)propylidene]-6,11-
dihydrodibenz[*b,e*]oxepin-2-ylacetic acid; $C_{21}H_{23}NO_3$;
113806-05-6
Olopatadine Hydrochloride *140462-76-6*
Histamine H₁ receptor antagonist; treatment of allergic
conjuctivitis

Olsalazine (rINN) ol·*sa*·la·zën

5,5'-Azodisalicylic acid; $C_{14}H_{10}N_2O_6$; *15722-48-2*
● **Olsalazine Sodium** *6054-98-4*
Aminosalicylate; treatment of ulcerative colitis

Omalizumab (rINN) ö·ma·*liz*·ü·mab

Immunoglobulin G, anti-(human immunoglobulin E Fc region)
(human-mouse monoclonal E25 clone pSVIE26 γ1-chain)
disulfide, with human-mouse monoclonal E25 clone pSVIE26
κ-chain, dimer; *242138-07-4*
Monoclonal antibody (immunoglobulin E)

Omapatrilat (rINN) ö·ma·*pa*·tri·lat

(4*S*,7*S*,10a*S*)-Octahydro-4-[(*S*)-3-phenyl-2-sulfanylpropan¬
amido]-5-oxo-7*H*-pyrido[2,1-*b*][1,3]thiazepine-7-carboxylic
acid; $C_{19}H_{24}N_2O_4S_2$; *167305-00-2*
Endopeptidase inhibitor; treatment of hypertension

The symbol '¬' in systematic chemical names signifies line continuation

Omega-3 Marine Triglycerides (BAN)
A mixture of the triglycerides of the fatty acids from marine fish containing the equivalent of about 18% of eicosapenta-5,8,11,14,17-enoic acid and 12% of docosahexa-4,7,10,13,16,19-enoic acid
Lipid-regulating drug

● **Omeprazole** (rINN) ö·*me*·pra·zôl
5-Methoxy-2-(4-methoxy-3,5-dimethyl-2-pyridylmethylsulfinyl)benzimidazole; $C_{17}H_{19}N_3O_3S$; *73590-58-6*
  ● **Omeprazole Sodium** *95510-70-6*
  ● **Omeprazole Magnesium** *95382-33-5*
Proton pump inhibitor; treatment of peptic ulcer disease

Ondansetron (rINN) on·*dan*·se·tron
(*RS*)-1,2,3,9-Tetrahydro-9-methyl-3-(2-methylimidazol-1-ylmethyl)carbazol-4-one; $C_{18}H_{19}N_3O$; *99614-02-5*
  ● **Ondansetron Hydrochloride** *103639-04-9*
Serotonin 5HT$_3$ antagonist; treatment of nausea and vomiting

and enantiomer

Opebacan (rINN) ö·*peb*·a·kan
132-L-Alanine-1–193-bactericidal/permeability-increasing protein (human); *206254-79-7*
Bactericidal; permeability increasing protein

opebacan has the following amino acid sequence:

```
VNPGVVVRIS    QKGLDYASQQ    GTAALQKELK

RIKIPDYSDS    FKIKHLGKGH    YSFYSMDIRE

GQLPSSQISM    VPNVGLKFSI    SNANIKISGK

WKAQKRFLKM    SGNFDLSIEG    MSISADLKLG

SNPTSGKPTI    TASSCHSSIN    SVHVHISKSK

VGWLIQLFHK    KIESALRNKM    NSQVCEKVTN

SVSSELQPYF    QTL
```

Opipramol (rINN) ö·*pi*·pra·mol
2-[4-(3-5*H*-Dibenz[*b,f*]azepin-5-ylpropyl)piperazin-1-yl]¬ethanol; $C_{23}H_{29}N_3O$; *315-72-0*
Opipramol Hydrochloride *909-39-7*
Monoamine reuptake inhibitor; tricyclic antidepressant

♣ **Orbifloxacin** (rINN) or·bi·*floks*·a·sin
1-Cyclopropyl-7-(*cis*-3,5-dimethylpiperazin-1-yl)-5,6,8-trifluoro-4-oxo-1,4-dihydroquinoline-3-carboxylic acid; $C_{19}H_{20}F_3N_3O_3$; *113617-63-3*;
Antibacterial

Orciprenaline (rINN) or·si·*pren*·a·lën
1-(3,5-Dihydroxyphenyl)-2-isopropylaminoethanol; $C_{11}H_{17}NO_3$; *586-06-1*
  ● **Orciprenaline Sulfate** metaproterenol sulfate (USAN); *5874-97-5*
Beta$_2$-adrenoceptor agonist; bronchodilator

and enantiomer

Orgotein (rINN) or·gö·tën
A group of water-soluble metalloprotein congeners isolated from liver, red blood cells and other mammalian tissues; *9016-01-7*
Superoxide dismutase

Orlistat (rINN) or·li·stat
(*S*)-1-[(2*S*,3*S*)-3-Hexyl-4-oxo-oxetan-2-ylmethyl]dodecyl *N*-formyl-L-leucinate; $C_{29}H_{53}NO_5$; *96829-58-2*
Lipase inhibitor; treatment of obesity

Orotic Acid (rINN) o·*ro*·tik
1,2,3,6-Tetrahydro-2,6-dioxopyrimidine-4-carboxylic acid;
$C_5H_4N_2O_4$; *65-86-1*
Naturally occurring intermediate in the synthesis of pyrimidine
nucleotides

Orphenadrine (rINN) or·*fe*·na·drën
Dimethyl-2-(2-methylbenzhydryloxy)ethylamine; $C_{18}H_{23}NO$;
83-98-7

● **Orphenadrine Citrate** *4682-36-4*

● **Orphenadrine Hydrochloride** *341-69-5*
Anticholinergic

and enantiomer

● **Oseltamivir** (rINN) ö·sel·*ta*·mi·veer
Ethyl (3*R*,4*R*,5*S*)-4-acetamido-5-amino-3-(1-
ethylpropoxy)cyclohex-1-ene-1-carboxylate; $C_{16}H_{28}N_2O$;
RO 640796; *196618-13-0*
Treatment of influenza

Ospemifene (rINN) os·*pem*·if·ën
2-{-4-[(*Z*)-4-Chloro-1,2-diphenylbut-1-enyl]phenoxy}ethanol;
$C_{24}H_{23}ClO_2$; *128607-22-7*
Selective oestrogen receptor modulator

Ostreogrycin (rINN) see Appendix C

Otilonium Bromide (rINN) o·ti·*lö*·në·um brö·mïd
Diethyl(methyl){2-[4-(2-octyloxybenzamido)¬
benzoyloxy]ethyl}ammonium bromide; $C_{29}H_{43}BrN_2O_4$;
26095-59-0
Smooth muscle relaxant

Ovandrotone Albumin (rINN) ö·*van*·drö·tön *al*·bü·min
Pentadecakis- to pentatriacontakis[3-(3,17-dioxoandrost-4-en-
7α-ylthio)propionyl]albumin, [human serum]
To increase fecundity in ewes

HSA = Human Albmin

Ox Bile (BAN)
An alcoholic extract of ox bile reduced by evaporation and
containing bile salts
Pancreatic insufficiency

Oxacillin (rINN) oks·a·*si*·lin
6-(5-Methyl-3-phenyl-1,2-oxazole-4-carboxamido)penicillanic
acid; $C_{19}H_{19}N_3O_5S$; *66-79-5*

● **Oxacillin Sodium** *1173-88-2 (anhydrous)*;
7240-38-2 (monohydrate)
Penicillin antibacterial

● **Oxaliplatin** (rINN) oks·a·li·*pla*·tin
[(1*R*,2*R*)-1,2-Cyclohexanediamine-*N*,*N'*][oxalato(2−)]¬
platinum; $C_8H_{14}N_2O_4Pt$; *61825-94-3*
Platinum-containing cytotoxic

Oxamniquine (rINN) see Appendix C

Oxandrolone (rINN) oks·*an*·dro·lön
17β-Hydroxy-17α-methyl-2-oxa-5α-androstan-3-one;
$C_{19}H_{30}O_3$; *53-39-4*
Anabolic steroid; androgen

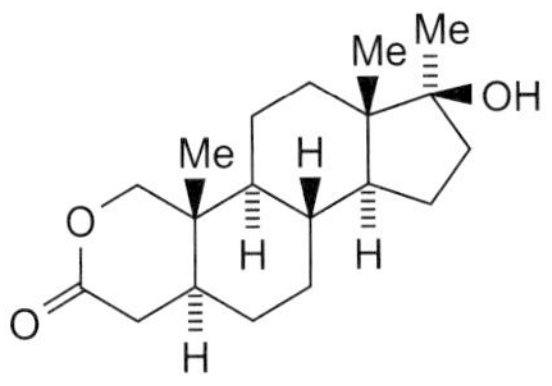

Oxantel (rINN) *oks·an·tel*

(*E*)-β-(1,4,5,6-Tetrahydro-1-methylpyrimidin-2-yl)styren-3-ol; $C_{13}H_{16}N_2O$; *36531-26-7*
Oxantel Embonate *42408-84-4*
Antihelminthic

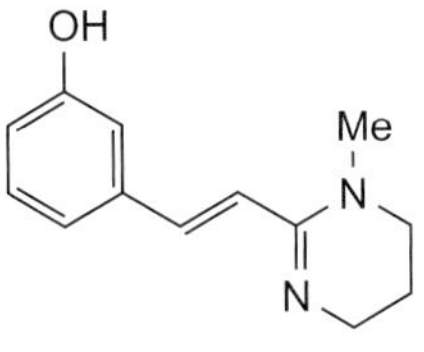

Oxaprozin (rINN) oks·a·*prö·*zin

3-(4,5-Diphenyl-1,3-oxazol-2-yl)propionic acid; $C_{18}H_{15}NO_3$; *21256-18-8*
Cyclo-oxygenase inhibitor; analgesic; anti-inflammatory

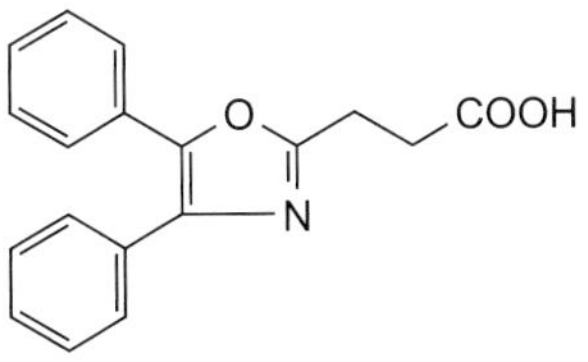

Oxatomide (rINN) see Appendix C

● **Oxazepam** (rINN) oks·*ä·*ze·pam

(*RS*)-7-Chloro-1,3-dihydro-3-hydroxy-5-phenyl-1,4-benzo¬
diaz epin-2-one; $C_{15}H_{11}ClN_2O_2$; *604-75-1*
Benzodiazepine

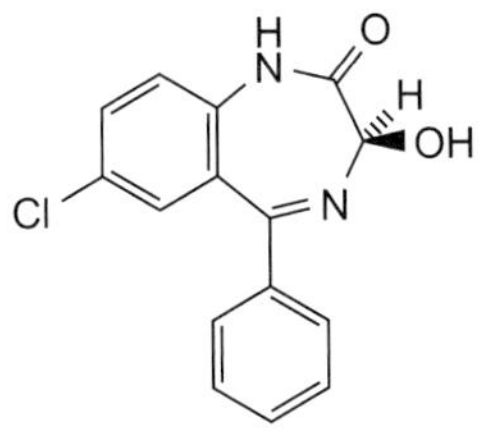

and enantiomer

Oxcarbazepine (rINN) oks·kar·*bä·*ze·pën

10,11-Dihydro-10-oxo-5*H*-dibenz[*b,f*]azepine-5-carboxamide; $C_{15}H_{12}N_2O_2$; *28721-07-5*
Antiepileptic

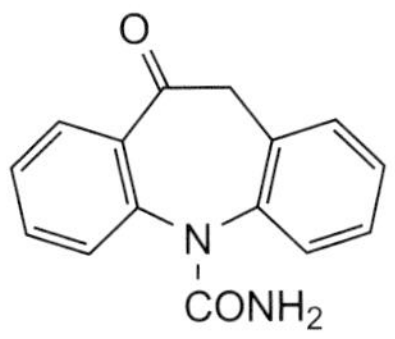

Oxedrine (rINN) *oks·*e·drën

(*RS*)-1-(4-Hydroxyphenyl)-2-(methylamino)ethanol; $C_9H_{13}NO_2$; *94-07-5*
Oxedrine Tartrate *16589-24-5*
Adrenoceptor agonist

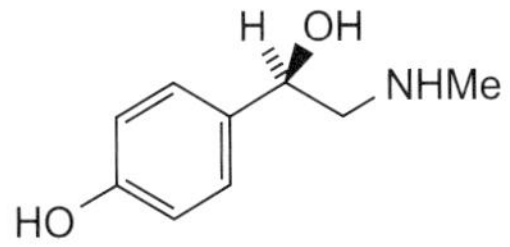

and enantiomer

● **Oxeladin** (rINN) oks·*e·*la·din

2-(2-Diethylaminoethoxy)ethyl 2-ethyl-2-phenylbutyrate; $C_{20}H_{33}NO_3$; *468-61-1*
● **Oxeladin Hydrogen Citrate** *52432-72-1*
Cough suppressant

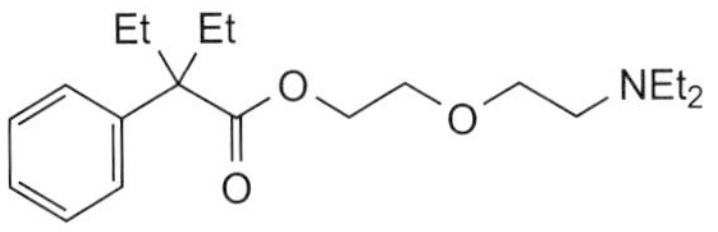

Oxerutins (BAN) oks·ë·*roo·*tins

A mixture of 5 different *O*-(β-hydroxyethyl) rutosides, not less than 45% of which is troxerutin
Treatment of venous disorders

● **Oxetacaine** (rINN) oks·*e·*ta·kän

2,2′-(2-Hydroxyethylimino)bis[*N*-(α,α-dimethylphenethyl)-*N*-methylacetamide]; $C_{28}H_{41}N_3O_3$; *126-27-6*
Local anaesthetic

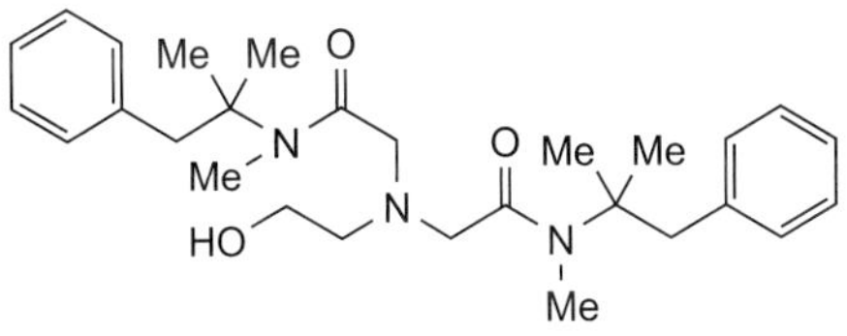

♣ **Oxfendazole** (rINN) oks·*fen·*da·zôl

Methyl 5-(phenylsulfinyl)-1*H*-benzimidazol-2-ylcarbamate; $C_{15}H_{13}N_3O_3S$; *53716-50-0*
Antihelminthic

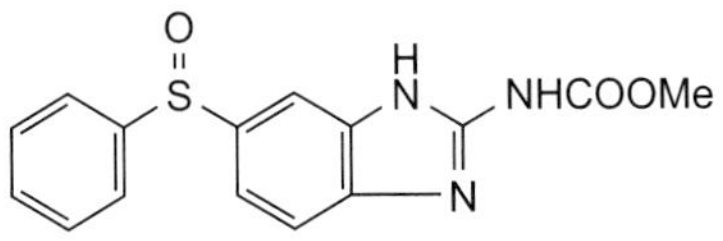

Oxfenicine (rINN) oks·*fe·*ni·sën

(*S*)-2-(4-Hydroxyphenyl)glycine; $C_8H_9NO_3$; *32462-30-9*
Carnitine-acyl transferase I inhibitor

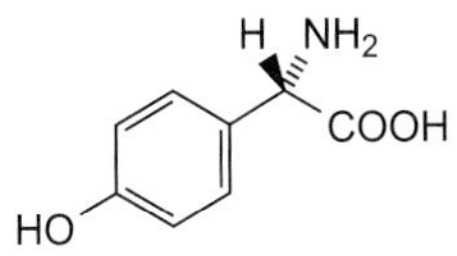

210

Oxibendazole (rINN) oks·ë·*ben*·da·zôl
  Methyl 5-propoxy-1*H*-benzimidazol-2-ylcarbamate;
  $C_{12}H_{15}N_3O_3$; *20559-55-1*
  Antihelminthic

Oxiconazole (rINN) oks·ë·*ko*·na·zôl
  2′,4′-Dichloro-2-(imidazol-1-yl)acetophenone (*Z*)-*O*-
  (2,4-dichlorobenzyl)oxime; $C_{18}H_{13}Cl_4N_3O$; *64211-45-6*
  Oxiconazole Nitrate *64211-46-7*
  Antifungal

Oxidronic Acid (rINN) oksë·*dro*·nik
  (Hydroxymethylene)diphosphonic acid; $CH_6O_7P_2$; *15468-10-7*
  Sodium Oxidronate *14255-61-9 (2Na)*
  Bisphosphonate; labelled with ^{99m}Tc for bone scanning

Oxipurinol (rINN) oks·ë·*pûr*·ri·nol
  1*H*-Pyrazolo[3,4-*d*]pyrimidine-4,6-diol; $C_5H_4N_4O_2$
  Xanthine oxidase inhibitor; treatment of gout

Oxiracetam (rINN) oks·ë·*ra*·se·tam
  (1) (*RS*)-2-(4-Hydroxy-2-oxopyrrolidin-1-yl)acetamide;
  (2) (*RS*)-*N*-Carbamoylmethyl-3-hydroxybutane-4-lactam;
  $C_6H_{10}N_2O_3$; *62613-82-5*
  Nootropic

and enantiomer

●**Oxitropium Bromide** (rINN) oks·ë·*trö*·pë·um
  (1*R*,3*s*,5*S*,6*R*,7*S*,8*r*)-8-Ethyl-3-[(*S*)-tropoyloxy]-6,7-
  epoxytropanium bromide; $C_{19}H_{26}BrNO_4$; *30286-75-0*
  Anticholinergic; reversible airways obstruction

Oxmetidine (rINN) oks·*me*·ti·dën
  2-[2-(5-Methylimidazol-4-ylmethylthio)ethylamino]-5-
  piperonylpyrimidin-4-(1*H*)-one; $C_{19}H_{21}N_5O_3S$; *72830-39-8*
  Histamine H_2 receptor antagonist

●**Oxolinic Acid** (rINN) oks·ö·*lin*·ik
  5-Ethyl-5,8-dihydro-8-oxo-1,3-dioxolo[4,5-*g*]quinoline-7-
  carboxylic acid; $C_{13}H_{11}NO_5$; *14698-29-4*
  Antibacterial

Oxoprostol (rINN) oks·ö·*prost*·ol
  (1) *trans*-2-(7-Hydroxyheptyl)-3-(3-oxo-4-phenoxybutyl)
  cyclopentanone; (2) *trans*-1-Hydroxy-16-phenoxy-ω-tetranor-
  prostane-9,15-dione; $C_{22}H_{32}O_4$; *69648-40-4*
  Prostaglandin

and enantiomer

Oxpentifylline *see Pentoxifylline*

Oxprenolol (rINN) oks·*pren*·o·lol
  1-*o*-Allyloxyphenoxy-3-isopropylaminopropan-2-ol;
  $C_{15}H_{23}NO_3$; *6452-71-7*
  ●**Oxprenolol Hydrochloride** *6452-73-9*
  Beta-adrenoceptor antagonist

and enantiomer

Oxybuprocaine (rINN) oks·ë·*bü*·prö·kän
2-Diethylaminoethyl 4-amino-3-butoxybenzoate; $C_{17}H_{28}N_2O_3$;
99-43-4
● **Oxybuprocaine Hydrochloride** *5987-82-6*
Local anaesthetic

Oxybutynin (rINN) oks·ë·*bü*·ti·nin
4-Diethylaminobut-2-ynyl 2-cyclohexyl-2-phenylglycolate;
$C_{22}H_{31}NO_3$; *5633-20-5*
● **Oxybutynin Hydrochloride** Oxybutynin chloride (USAN);
1508-65-2
Anticholinergic

Oxycinchophen (rINN) see Appendix C

♣ **Oxyclozanide** (rINN) oks·ö·*klö*·za·nïd
3,3′,5,5′,6-Pentachloro-2′-hydroxysalicylanilide; $C_{13}H_{16}Cl_5NO_3$;
2277-92-1
Antihelminthic

Oxycodone (rINN) oks·ë·*kö*·dön
(1) (−)-(5*R*,14*S*)-4,5-Epoxy-14-hydroxy-3-methoxy-17-
methylmorphinan-6-one; (2) 6-Deoxy-7,8-dihydro-14-
hydroxy-3-*O*-methyl-6-oxomorphine; $C_{18}H_{21}NO_4$; *76-42-6*
● **Oxycodone Hydrochloride** *124-90-3*
Opioid receptor agonist; analgesic

Oxyfedrine (rINN) oks·ë·*fe*·drën
3-(β-Hydroxy-α-methylphenethylamino)-3′-methoxy¬
propiophenone; $C_{19}H_{23}NO_3$; *15687-41-9*
Vasodilator

Oxymesterone (rINN) oks·ë·*mes*·te·rön
4,17β-Dihydroxy-17α-methylandrost-4-en-3-one; $C_{20}H_{30}O_3$;
145-12-0
Anabolic steroid; androgen

Oxymetazoline (rINN) oks·ë·me·*tä*·zö·lën
6-*tert*-Butyl-3-(2-imidazolin-2-ylmethyl)-2,4-xylenol;
$C_{16}H_{24}N_2O$; *1491-59-4*
● **Oxymetazoline Hydrochloride** *2315-02-8*
Alpha-adrenoceptor agonist; decongestant

● **Oxymetholone** (rINN) oks·ë·*me*·tho·lön
17β-Hydroxy-2-hydroxymethylene-17α-methyl-5α-androstan-
3-one; $C_{21}H_{32}O_3$; *434-07-1*
Anabolic steroid; androgen

Oxymorphone (rINN) oks·ë·*mor*·fön
(1) (−)-(5*R*,14*S*)-4,5-Epoxy-3,14-dihydroxy-17-methyl¬
morphinan-6-one; (2) 6-Deoxy-7,8-dihydro-14-hydroxy-6-
oxomorphine; $C_{17}H_{19}NO_4$; *76-41-5*
Opioid receptor agonist

Oxypertine (rINN) oks·ë·*per*·tën
5,6-Dimethoxy-2-methyl-3-[2-(4-phenylpiperazin-1-yl)¬
ethyl] indole; $C_{23}H_{29}N_3O_2$; *153-87-7*
Oxypertine Hydrochloride *40523-01-1*
Dopamine receptor antagonist; neuroleptic

Oxyphenbutazone (rINN) see Appendix C

Oxyphencyclimine (rINN) oks·ë·fen·*si*̈·kli·mën
1,4,5,6-Tetrahydro-1-methylpyrimidin-2-ylmethyl
α-cyclo hexylmandelate; $C_{20}H_{28}N_2O_3$; *125-53-1*
Anticholinergic

and enantiomer

Oxyphenisatine (rINN) oks·ë·fe·*ni*̈·sa·tën
3,3-Bis(4-hydroxyphenyl)indolin-2-one; $C_{20}H_{15}NO_3$; *125-13-3*
Oxyphenisatine Diacetate *115-33-3*
Stimulant laxative

Oxyphenonium Bromide (rINN) oks·ë·fe·*nö*·në·um
2-(α-Cyclohexylmandeloyloxy)ethyldiethylmethylammonium
bromide; $C_{21}H_{34}BrNO_3$; *50-10-2*
Anticholinergic

and enantiomer

Oxypurinol *see Oxipurinol*

● **Oxytetracycline** (rINN) oks·ë·te·tra·*si*̈·klën
(*1*) (4S,4aR,5S,5aR,6S,12aS)-4-Dimethylamino-1,4,4a,5,5a¬
,6,11,12a-octahydro-3,5,6,10,12,12a-hexahydroxy-6-methyl-
1,11-dioxonaphthacene-2-carboxamide; *(2)* 5β-
Hydroxytetracycline; $C_{22}H_{24}N_2O_9$; *79-57-2*
● **Oxytetracycline Calcium** *15251-48-6*
● **Oxytetracycline Dihydrate** *6153-64-6*
● **Oxytetracycline Hydrochloride** *2058-46-0*
Tetracycline antibacterial

● **Oxytocin** (rINN) oks·ë·*tö*·sin
$C_{43}H_{66}N_{12}O_{12}S_2$; *50-56-6*
Oxytocic

oxytocin has the following amino acid sequence:

```
Cys-Tyr-Ile-Gln-Asn-Cys-Pro-Leu-Gly-NH₂
```

● **Paclitaxel** (rINN) pa·kli·*taks*·el
(2S,5R,7S,10R,13S)-10,20-Bis(acetoxy)-2-benzoyloxy-1,7-
dihydroxy-9-oxo-5,20-epoxytax-11-en-13-yl (3S)-3-
benzoylamino-3-phenyl-D-lactate; $C_{47}H_{51}NO_{14}$; *33069-62-4*
Taxane cytotoxic

Pactimibe (rINN) p*ak*·ti·mïb
[7-(2,2-Dimethylpropanamido)-4,6-dimethyl-1-octylindol-5-
yl]acetic acid; $C_{25}H_{40}N_2O_3$; *189198-30-9*
Inhibitor of acyl-CoA cholesterol acyltransferase;
lipid-regulating drug

Padimate (rINN) *pa*·di·mät
A mixture of pentyl, isopentyl and 2-methylbutyl 4-dimethyl-
laminobenzoates; *14779-78-3*
Padimate O
2-ethylhexyl 4-dimethylaminobenzoate; $C_{17}H_{27}NO_2$; *21245-02-3*
Sunscreen

padimate O

The symbol '¬' in systematic chemical names signifies line continuation

Palatrigine (rINN) pa·*la*·tri·jën
6-(2,3-Dichlorophenyl)-2,3-dihydro-3-imino-2-isopropyl-1,2,4-triazin-5-ylamine; $C_{12}H_{13}Cl_2N_5$; *98410-36-7*
Class I antiarrhythmic

Palifermin (rINN) pa·li·*fer*·min
Human fibroblast growth factor-(24-163)-peptide;
$C_{724}H_{1147}N_{203}O_{206}S_9$; *162394-19-6*
Keratinocyte growth factor; treatment of mucositis

palifermin has the following amino acid sequence:

```
                      SYDYMEG    GDIRVRRLFC

RTQWYLRIDK  RGKVKGTQEM  KNNYNIMEIR  TVAVGIVAIK

GVESEFYLAM  NKEGKLYAKK  ECNEDCNFKE  LILENHYNTY

ASAKWTHNGG  EMFVALNQKG  IPVRGKKTKK  EQKTAHFLPM

AIT
```

Paliperidone (rINN) pa·li·*per*·ri·dön
rac-3-{2-[4-(6-Fluoro-1,2-benzoxazol-3-yl)piperidin-1-yl]ethyl}-9-hydroxy-2-methyl-6,7,8,9-tetrahydro-4*H*-pyrido[1,2-*a*]pyrimidin-4-one; $C_{23}H_{27}FN_4O_3$; *144598-75-4*
Dopamine D_2 receptor antagonist; serotonin $5HT_2$ receptor antagonist; neuroleptic

and enantiomer

Palivizumab (rINN) pa·li·*viz*·ü·mab
Immunoglobulin G 1 (human-mouse monoclonal MEDI-493γ1-chain antirespiratory syncytial virus protein F), disulfide with human-mouse monoclonal MEDI-493κ1-chain, dimer
Monoclonal antibody (respiratory syncytial virus)

Pamidronic Acid (rINN) pa·mi·*dro*·nik
3-Amino-1-hydroxypropylidenebis(phosphonic acid);
$C_3H_{11}NO_7P_2$; *40391-99-9*
● **Pamidronate Disodium** *57248-88-1*
Bisphosphonate; treatment of osteolytic lesions; Paget's disease; hypercalcaemia of malignancy

● **Pancreatin** (BAN) *pan*·krë·a·tin
A preparation of mammalian pancreas containing enzymes having protease, lipase and amylase activity; *8049-47-6*
Enzyme; treatment of pancreatic exocrine deficiency

Pancreozymin (BAN) see Appendix C

● **Pancuronium Bromide** (rINN) pan·kûr·*rö*·në·um
1,1′-(3α,17β-Diacetoxy-5α-androstan-2β,16β-ylene)bis(1-methylpiperidinium) dibromide; $C_{35}H_{60}Br_2N_2O_4$; *15500-66-0*
Non-depolarizing neuromuscular blocker

Panidazole (rINN) see Appendix C

Panitumumab (rINN) pa·ni·*tü*·mü·mab
Immunoglobulin, anti-(human epidermal growth factor receptor) (human monoclonal ABX-EGF heavy chain), disulfide with human monoclonal ABX-EGF light chain, dimer; *339177-26-3*;
Monoclonal antibody (human epidermal growth receptor); metastatic colorectal cancer

panitumumab has the following amino acid sequence:

Heavy Chain (Gamma)

```
QVQLQESGPG  LVKPSETLSL  TCTVSGGSVS  SGDYYWTWIR

QSPGKGLEWI  GHIYYSGNTN  YNPSLKSRLT  ISIDTSKTQF

SLKLSSVTAA  DTAIYYCVRD  RVTGAFDIWG  QGTMVTVSSA

STKGPSVFPL  APCSRSTSES  TAALGCLVKD  YFPEPVTVSW

NSGALTSGVH  TFPAVLQSSG  LYSLSSVVTV  PSSNFGTQTY

TCNVDHKPSN  TKVDKTVERK  CCVECPPCPA  PPVAGPSVFL

FPPKPKDTLM  ISRTPEVTCV  VVDVSHEDPE  VQFNWYVDGV

EVHNAKTKPR  EEQFNSTFRV  VSVLTVVHQD  WLNGKEYKCK

VSNKGLPAPI  EKTISKTKGQ  PREPQVYTLP  PSREEMTKNQ

VSLTCLVKGF  YPSDIAVEWE  SNGQPENNYK  TTPPMLDSDG

SFFLYSKLTV  DKSRWQQGNV  FSCSVMHEAL  HNHYTQKSLS

LSPGK
```

Light chain (Kappa)

```
DIQMTQSPSS  LSASVGDRVT  ITCQASQDIS  NYLNWYQQKP

GKAPKLLIYD  ASNLETGVPS  RFSGSGSGTD  FTFTISSLQP

EDIATYFCQH  FDHLPLAFGG  GTKVEIKRTV  AAPSVFIFPP

SDEQLKSGTA  SVVCLLNNFY  PREAKVQWKV  DNALQSGNSQ

ESVTEQDSKD  STYSLSSTLT  LSKADYEKHK  VYACEVTHQG

LSSPVTKSFN  RGEC
```

₂

Panthenol (rINN) *pan·*the·nol
(±)-2,4-Dihydroxy-*N*-(3-hydroxypropyl)-3,3-dimethyl¬
butyramide; pantothenyl alcohol; C₉H₁₉NO₄; *17307-32-3*
Pantothenic acid analogue

and enantiomer

Pantoprazole (rINN) pan·*to·*pra·zôl
5-Difluoromethoxybenzimidazol-2-yl 3,4-dimethoxy-2-
pyridylmethyl sulfoxide; C₁₆H₁₅F₂N₃O₄S; *102625-70-7*
● **Pantoprazole Sodium** *164579-32-2*
Proton pump inhibitor; treatment of peptic ulcer disease

Pantothenic Acid (BAN) pan·tö·*thë·*nik
(*R*)-*N*-(2,4-Dihydroxy-3,3-dimethylbutyryl)-β-alanine;
C₉H₁₈NO₅; *79-83-4*
● **Calcium Pantothenate** *137-08-6*
Vitamin B component

Panuramine (rINN) pan·*ûr·*ra·mën
(1) 1-Benzoyl-3-[1-(2-naphthylmethyl)4-piperidyl]urea; (2) *N*-
[1-(2-Naphthylmethyl)piperidin-4-ylaminocarbonyl]benzamide;
C₂₄H₂₅N₃O₂; *80349-58-2*
Panuramine Hydrochloride *80349-03-7*
Monoamine reuptake inhibitor; antidepressant

Papaveretum (BAN) pa·pa·ve·*rë·*tum
A mixture of 253 parts of morphine hydrochloride, 23 parts
of papaverine hydrochloride and 20 parts of codeine
hydrochloride; *8002-76-4*
Opioid receptor agonist; analgesic

Papaverine (BAN) pa·*pa·*ve·rën
1-(3,4-Dimethoxybenzyl)-6,7-dimethoxyisoquinoline;
C₂₀H₂₁NO₄; *58-74-2*
● **Papaverine Hydrochloride** *61-25-6*
Phosphodiesterase inhibitor; smooth muscle relaxant

Papaveroline (rINN) see Appendix C

● **Paracetamol** (rINN) pa·ra·*set·*a·mol
4′-Hydroxyacetanilide; acetaminophen (USAN); C₈H₉NO₂;
103-90-2
Analgesic; antipyretic

Parecoxib (rINN) pa·re·*koks·*ib
N-[4-(5-Methyl-3-phenyl-1,2-oxazol-4-
yl)phenylsulfonyl]propanamide; C₁₉H₁₈N₂O₄S; *198470-84-7*
Parecoxib Sodium
*Cyclo-oxygenase (COX-2) inhibitor; analgesic;
anti-inflammatory*

Paramethadione (rINN) see Appendix C

Paramethasone (rINN) pa·ra·*me·*tha·sön
6α-Fluoro-11β,17α,21-trihydroxy-16α-methylpregna-1,4-diene-
3,20-dione; C₂₂H₂₉FO₅; *53-33-8*
Paramethasone Acetate *1597-82-6*
Glucocorticoid

Parathyroid Hormone (rINN) pa·ra·*thï*·roid
Nonglycosylated human parathyroid hormone, the origin should be indicated between brackets after the INN, for example (*r. E.coli*) for the recombinant produced *Escherichia coli*; *345663-45-8*
Hormone

parathyroid hormone has the following amino acid sequence:

```
H-Ser-Val-Ser-Glu-Ile-Gln-Leu-Met-
   His-Asn-Leu-Gly-Lys-His-Leu-Asn-
   Ser-Met-Glu-Arg-Val-Gly-Trp-Leu-
   Arg-Lys-Lys-Leu-Gln-Asp-Val-His-
   Asn-Phe-Val-Ala-Leu-Gly-Ala-Pro-
   Leu-Ala-Pro-Arg-Asp-Ala-Gly-Ser-
   Gln-Arg-Pro-Arg-Lys-Lys-Glu-Asp-
   Asn-Val-Leu-Val-Glu-Ser-His-Glu-
   Lys-Ser-Leu-Gly-Glu-Ala-Asp-Lys-
   Ala-Asp-Val-Asn-Val-Leu-Thr-Lys-
   Ala-Lys-Ser-Gln-OH
```

Parbendazole (rINN) par·*ben*·da·zôl
Methyl 5-butylbenzimidazol-2-ylcarbamate; $C_{13}H_{17}N_3O_2$; *14255-87-9*
Antihelminthic

Pargyline (rINN) *par*·ji·lën
Benzyl(methylprop-2-ynyl)amine; $C_{11}H_{13}N$; *555-57-7*
Pargyline Hydrochloride *306-07-0*
Monoamine oxidase inhibitor; antidepressant

● **Parnaparin Sodium** (rINN) par·*na*·pa·rin
Sodium salt of depolymerised heparin obtained by hydrogen peroxide and copper(II) acetate degradation of heparin from pork intestinal mucosa; the majority of the components have a 2-*N*,6-*O*-disulfo-D-glucosamine structure at the reducing end of their chain; the molecular weight of these components lies between 4000 and 5000 (±20%); the degree of sulfation is 2.15 (±10%) per disaccharide unit
Low molecular weight heparin

Paromomycin (rINN) pa·rö·mö·*mï*·sin
Antimicrobial aminoglycosides produced by *Streptomyces rimosus* var. *paromomycinus*; *7542-37-2*
Aminoglycoside antibacterial

Paroxetine (rINN) pa·*roks*·e·tën
5-[(3*S*,4*R*)-4-*p*-Fluorophenyl-3-piperidylmethoxy]-1,3-benzodioxole; $C_{19}H_{20}FNO_3$; *61869-08-7*
● **Paroxetine Hydrochloride** *78246-49-8 (anhydrous); 110429-35-1 (hemihydrate)*
Selective serotonin reuptake inhibitor; antidepressant

Parvaquone (rINN) see Appendix C

Pazopanib (rINN) pa·*zop*·á·nib
5-({4-[(2,3-Dimethyl-2*H*-indazol-6-yl)methylamino]¬pyrimidin-2-yl}amino)-2-methylbenzenesulfonamide; $C_{21}H_{23}N_7O_2S$; *444731-52-6*;
Pazopanib Hydrochloride *635702-64-6*
Tyrosine kinase inhibitor; treatment of renal cell carcinoma

Pecazine (rINN) see Appendix C

Pecilocin (rINN) see Appendix C

Pefloxacin (rINN) pe·*floks*·a·sin
1-Ethyl-6-fluoro-1,4-dihydro-7-(4-methylpiperazin-1-yl)-4-oxo-quinoline-3-carboxylic acid; $C_{17}H_{20}FN_3O_3$; *70458-92-3*
● **Pefloxacin Mesilate** *70458-95-6*
Antibacterial

Pegaptanib (rINN) pe·*gap*·ta·nib
5'-Ester of (2'-deoxy-2'-fluoro)C-Gm-Gm-A-A-(2'-deoxy-2'-flouro)U-(2'-deoxy-2'-flouro)C-Am-Gm-(2'-deoxy-2'-flouro)U-Gm-Am-Am-(2'-deoxy-2'-fluoro)U-Gm-(2'-deoxy-2'-flouro)C-(2'-deoxy-2'-fluoro)U-(2'-deoxy-2'-fluoro)U-Am(2'-deoxy-2'-fluoro)U-Am-(2'-deoxy-2'-fluoro)C-Am-(2'-deoxy-2'-fluoro)U-(2'-deoxy-2'-flouro)C-(2'-deoxy-2'-fluoro)C-Gm-(3'→3')-dT with α,α'-[[(1*S*)-1-[[5 phosphonooxy)pentyl carbamoyl] pentane-1,5-diyl]bis(iminocarbonyl)]bis[ωmethoxypoly(oxyethane-1,2-diyl)]; $C_{294}H_{370}F_{13}N_{107}O_{188}P_{28}[C_2H_4O]_n$
Vascular endothelial growth factor; inhibitor of angiogenesis

Pegfilgrastim (rINN) peg·fil·*gras*·tim

N-(3-Hydroxypropyl)methionylcolony-stimulating factor
(human), 1-ether with a-methyl-w-hydroxypoly(oxyethylene);
208265-92-3
Recombinant methionyl human granulocyte colony-stimulating
factor

pegfilgrastim has the following amino acid sequence:

TPLGPASSLP	QSFLIKCLEQ	VRKIQGDGAA
LQEKLCATYK	LCHPEELVLL	GHSLGIPWAP
LSSCPSQALQ	LAGCLSQLHS	GLFLYQGLLQ
ALEGISPELG	PTLDTLQLDV	ADFATTIWQQ
MEELGMAPAL	QPTQGAMPAF	ASAFQRRAGG
VLVASHLQSF	LEVSYRVLRH	LAQP

Peginterferon Alfa-2a (rINN) peg·in·ter·*feer*·ron

Mono(*N²,N⁶*-dicarboxy-L-lysyl)interferon alfa-2a, diesters with
polyethylene glycol monomethyl ether.
The molecular weight of the pegylated part may be indicated in
the name by adding a number, *eg* peginterferon alfa-2a (40kD);
198153-51-4
Cytokine

peginterferon alfa-2a has the following amino acid sequence:

(M)CDLPQTHSLG	SRRTLMLLAQ	MRRISLFSCL
K̇DRHDFGFPQ	EEFGNQFQKA	ETIPVLHEMI
QQIFNLFSTK	DSSAAWDETL	LDKFYTELYQ
QLNDLEACVI	QGVGVTETPL	MKEDSILAVR
K̇YFQRITLYL	KEK̇KYSPCAW	EVVRAEIMRS
FSLSTNLQES	LRSKE	

* pegylation site

Peginterferon Alfa-2b (rINN)
Pegylated, recombinant interferon alfa-2b
Cytokine

peginterferon alfa-2b has the following amino acid sequence:

(M)ĊDLPQTHSLG	SRRTLMLLAQ	MRRISLFSCL
K̇DRHDFGFPQ	EEFGNQFQKA	ETIPVLHEMI
QQIFNLFSTK	DSSAAWDETL	LDKFYTELYQ
QLNDLEACVI	QGVGVTETPL	MKEDSILAVR
K̇YFQRITLYL	KEKKYSPĊAW	EVVRAEIMRS
FSLSTNLQES	LRSKE	

* potential pegylation site

Pegvisomant (rINN) peg·*vï*·zö·mant

18-L-Aspartic acid-21-L-asparagine-120-L-lysine-167-
L-asparagine-168-L-alanine-171-L-serine-172-L-arginine-174-
L-serine-179-L-threonine growth hormone (human), reaction
product with polyethylene glycol; *218620-50-9*;
Growth hormone analogue

pegvisomant has the following amino acid sequence:

ĊDLPQTHSLG	SRRTLMLLAQ	MRRISLFSCL	K̇DRHDFGFPQ
EEFGNQFQKA	ETIPVLHEMI	QQIFNLFSTK	DSSAAWDETL
LDKFYTELYQ	QLNDLEACVI	QGVGVTETPL	MKEDSILAVR
K̇YFQRITLYL	KEK̇KYSPCAW	EVVRAEIMRS	FSLSTNLQES
LRSKE			

* pegylation sites

Pemetrexed (rINN) pe·me·*treks*·ed

N-{4-[2-(2-Amino-4,7-dihydro-4-oxo-1*H*-pyrrolo[2,3-*d*]pyrim-
idin-5-yl)ethyl]benzoyl}-L-glutamic acid; $C_{20}H_{21}N_5O_6$;
137281-23-3
Thymidylate synthetase inhibitor; cytostatic

Pemoline (rINN) see Appendix C

Pempidine (rINN) *pem·pi·dën*
1,2,2,6,6-Pentamethylpiperidine; $C_{10}H_{21}N$; *79-55-0*
Ganglion blocker

Penamecillin (rINN) see Appendix C

Penbutolol (rINN) *pen·bü·to·lol*
(S)-1-*tert*-Butylamino-3-(2-cyclopentylphenoxy)propan-2-ol;
$C_{18}H_{29}NO_2$; *38363-40-5*
● **Penbutolol Sulfate** *38363-32-5*
Beta-adrenoceptor antagonist

Penciclovir (rINN) *pen·si·klö·veer*
9-[4-Hydroxy-3-(hydroxymethyl)butyl]guanine; $C_{10}H_{15}N_5O_3$;
39809-25-1
Purine nucleoside analogue; antiviral (herpesviruses)

Pendecamaine (rINN) see Appendix C

Pendetide *pen·de·tïd*
Glycyl-L-tyrosyl-N^6-[N-(2-{2-[bis(carboxymethyl)amino]¬
ethyl(carboxymethyl)amino}ethyl)-N-(carboxymethyl)glycyl]-
L-lysine; $C_{31}H_{47}N_7O_{14}$
*Molecule for linking radio-labels to monoclonal antibodies for
diagnostic purposes*

Penethamate (BAN) *pen·e·tha·mät*
2-Diethylaminoethyl 6-(2-phenylacetamido)penicillanate;
$C_{22}H_{31}N_3O_4S$
Penethamate Hydriodide *808-71-9*
Penicillin antibacterial (veterinary)

Penfluridol (rINN) *pen·flûr·ri·dol*
4-(4-Chloro-3-trifluoromethylphenyl)-1-[4,4-bis(4-fluo-
rophenyl)butyl]piperidin-4-ol; $C_{28}H_{27}ClF_5NO$; *26864-56-2*
Dopamine receptor antagonist; neuroleptic

● **Penicillamine** (rINN) *pe·ni·si·la·mën*
3,3-Dimethyl-D-cysteine; D-penicillamine; $C_5H_{11}NO_2S$; *52-67-5*
*Disease-modifying antirheumatic drug; chelating agent;
treatment of Wilson's disease; heavy metal poisoning; cystinuria*

Penicillinase (rINN) see Appendix C

Pentacosactride (BAN) see Appendix C

Pentacynium Metilsulfate (BAN) See Appendix C

● **Pentaerithrityl Tetranitrate** (rINN) *pen·ta·e·ri·thri·tïl*
2,2-Bis(hydroxymethyl)propane-1,3-diol tetranitrate;
$C_5H_8N_4O_{12}$; *78-11-5*
Vasodilator

Pentafluranol (rINN) see Appendix C

● **Pentagastrin** (rINN)

tert-Butyloxycarbonyl-[β-Ala^{13}]gastrin-(13-17)-pentapeptide
amide; $C_{37}H_{49}N_7O_9S$; *5534-95-2*
Gastrin analogue

```
Boc-β-Ala-Trp-Met-Asp-Phe-NH₂
```

Pentalamide (rINN) see Appendix C

Pentamethonium Bromide (rINN) pen·ta·me·*thö*·në·um
N,N′-Pentamethylenebis (trimethylammonium) dibromide;
$C_{11}H_{28}Br_2N_2$; *541-20-8*
Ganglion blocker

$Me_3\overset{+}{N}$———————$\overset{+}{N}Me_3$ $2Br^-$

Pentamethonium Iodide (rINN) see Appendix C

Pentamidine (rINN) pen·*ta*·mi·dën
4,4′-(Pentamethylenedioxy)dibenzamidine; $C_{19}H_{24}N_4O_2$;
100-33-4
● **Pentamidine Isetionate** *140-64-7*
Antiprotozoal

Pentapiperide (rINN) pen·ta·*pi*·per·rïd
1-Methylpiperidin-4-yl 3-methyl-2-phenylvalerate; $C_{18}H_{27}NO_2$;
7009-54-3
Anticholinergic

mixture of stereoisomers

Pentaquine (rINN) *pen*·ta·kwën
5-Isopropylaminopentyl(6-methoxy-8-quinolyl)amine;
$C_{18}H_{27}N_3O$; *86-78-2*
Antiprotozoal; treatment of malaria

Pentastarch (rINN) *pen*·ta·starch
A starch in which more than 90% of the amylopectin has been
etherified to the extent that on average 4 or 5 of the-OH groups
present in every 10 D-glucopyranose units of the starch polymer
have been converted to -OCH_2CH_2OH groups; *9005-27-0*
Plasma volume expander

● **Pentazocine** (rINN) pen·*tä*·zö·sën
(1) (2*R**,6*R**,11*R**)-1,2,3,4,5,6-Hexahydro-6,11-dimethyl-3-(3-
methylbut-2-enyl)-2,6-methano-3-benzazocin-8-ol;
(2) 17-(3-Methylbut-2-enyl)-6,7-dinormorphinan-3-ol;
$C_{19}H_{27}NO$; *359-83-1*
● **Pentazocine Hydrochloride** *64024-15-3*
● **Pentazocine Lactate** *17146-95-1*
Opioid receptor agonist; analgesic

and enantiomer

Pentetic Acid (rINN) pen·*te*·tik
[Carboxymethyliminobis(ethylenenitrilo)]tetra-acetic acid;
$C_{14}H_{23}N_3O_{10}$; *67-43-6*
Molecule used in radio-labelled form in diagnostic studies

Pentetrazol (rINN) pen·*te*·tra·zol
6,7,8,9-Tetrahydro-5*H*-tetrazolo[4,5-*a*]azepine; leptazol;
$C_6H_{10}N_4$; *54-95-5*
Respiratory stimulant

Pentetreotide (rINN) pen·*te*·trë·ö·tïd
N-{2-[{2-[Bis(carboxymethyl)amino]ethyl}(carboxymethyl)¬
amino]ethyl}-*N*-(carboxymethyl)glycyl-D-phenylalanyl-L-
cysteinyl-L-phenylalanyl-D-tryptophyl-L-lysyl-L-threonyl-L-
cysteinyl-(2*R*,3*R*)-threoninol cyclic disulfide (S³—S⁸);
$C_{63}H_{87}N_{13}O_{19}S_2$; *138661-02-6*
*Somatostatin analogue; diagnostic aid for neuroendocrine
tumours*

D-Phe-Cys-Phe-D-Trp-Lys-Thr-Cys

Penthienate (BAN) pen·*thï*·e·nät
2-Diethylaminoethyl 2-cyclopentyl-2-(2-thienyl)glycolate;
$C_{17}H_{27}NO_3S$; *22064-27-3*
Penthienate Bromide penthienate methobromide; *60-44-6*
Anticholinergic

Penthrichloral (rINN) pen·thri·*klor*·ral
5,5-Bis(hydroxymethyl)-2-trichloromethyl-1,3-dioxane;
$C_7H_{11}N_3O_4$; *5684-90-2*
Hypnotic

Pentifylline (rINN) pen·*ti*·fi·lën
1-Hexyl-3,7-dimethylxanthine; $C_{13}H_{20}N_4O_2$; *1028-33-7*
Vasodilator

● **Pentobarbital** (rINN) pen·tö·*bar*·bi·tal
5-Ethyl-5-(1-methylbutyl)barbituric acid; $C_{11}H_{18}N_2O_3$; *76-74-4*
● **Pentobarbital Sodium** *57-33-0*
Barbiturate

and enantiomer

Pentolonium Tartrate (rINN) pen·to·*lö*·në·um
N,N′-Pentamethylenebis(1-methylpyrrolidinium) di(hydrogen tartrate); $C_{23}H_{42}N_2O_{12}$; *52-62-0*
Ganglion blocker

Pentosalen (BAN) pen·*tö*·sa·len
9-(3-Methylbut-2-enyloxy)furo[3,2-g]chromen-7-one; ammidin; $C_{16}H_{14}O_4$; *482-44-0*
Aid to dermal pigmentation

Pentosan Polysulfate Sodium (rINN) *pen*·tö·san po·lë·*sul*·fät
A mixture of linear polymers of β-1→4-linked xylose, usually sulfated at the 2-and 3-positions and occasionally (approximately 1 in every 4 residues) substituted at the 2-position with 4-*O*-methyl-α-D-glucuronic acid 2,3-*O*-sulfate; the average molecular weight lies between 4000 and 6000 with a total molecular weight range of 1000 to 40000; *140207-93-8*
Heparinoid fibrinolytic

Pentostatin (rINN) pen·tö·*sta*·tin
1,2-Dideoxy-1-[*(R)*-3,6,7,8-tetrahydro-8-hydroxyimidazo[4,5-*d*][1,3]diazepin-3-yl]-D-*erythro*-pentofuranose; covidarabine; 2′-deoxycoformycin; deoxycoformycin; $C_{11}H_{16}N_4O_4$; *53910-25-1*
Purine analogue; cytostatic

● **Pentoxifylline** (rINN) pen·toks·*i*·fi·lën
3,7-Dimethyl-1-(5-oxohexyl)xanthine; $C_{13}H_{18}N_4O_3$; *6493-05-6*
Vasodilator

Pentoxyverine (rINN) pen·toks·*i*·ver·rën
2-[2-(Diethylamino)ethoxy]ethyl 1-phenylcyclopentane‐carboxylate; $C_{20}H_{31}NO_3$; *77-23-6*
● **Pentoxyverine Citrate** (1:1) *23142-01-1*
Cough suppressant

Peratizole (rINN) see Appendix C

Perfluamine (rINN) per·*floo*·a·mën
Tris(heptafluoropropyl)amine; $C_9F_{21}N$; *338-83-0*
Perfluorocarbon artificial oxygen carrier

Perflunafene (rINN) per·*floo*·na·fën
Perfluorodecahydronaphthalene; $C_{10}F_{18}$; *306-94-5*
Perfluorocarbon artificial oxygen carrier

Perflutren (rINN) pef·*floo*·tren

Octafluoropropane;

C_3F_8; *76-19-7*;

Imaging agent

Pergolide (rINN) *per*·gö·lïd

Methyl (8*R*,10*R*)-6-propylergolin-8-ylmethyl sulfide;

$C_{19}H_{26}N_2S$; *66104-22-1*

● **Pergolide Mesilate** *66104-23-2*

Dopamine receptor agonist; treatment of Parkinson's disease

Perhexiline (rINN) see Appendix C

Pericyazine (rINN) pe·ri·*sï*·a·zën

10-[3-(4-Hydroxypiperidino)propyl]phenothiazine-2-carbo¬
nitrile; periciazine (pINN); $C_{21}H_{23}N_3OS$; *2622-26-6*

Dopamine receptor antagonist; neuroleptic

Perindopril (rINN) per·*rin*·dö·pril

(2*S*,3a*S*,7a*S*)-1-{*N*-[(*S*)-1-(Ethoxycarbonyl)butyl]-L-alanyl}
perhydroindole-2-carboxylic acid; $C_{19}H_{32}N_2O_5$; *82834-16-0*

● **Perindopril Erbumine** *107133-36-8*

● **Perindopril Arginine**

Angiotensin converting enzyme inhibitor

Perindoprilat (rINN) per·rin·dö·*pri*·lat

(2*S*,3a*S*,7a*S*)-1-{*N*-[(*S*)-1-Carboxybutyl]-L-alanyl}¬
perhydroindole-2-carboxylic acid; $C_{17}H_{28}N_2O_5$;
95153-31-4; S-9780

Angiotensin converting enzyme inhibitor

Perlapine (rINN) see Appendix C

Permethrin (rINN) per·*mëth*·rin

3-Phenoxybenzyl *(1*RS*,3*RS*)-(1*RS*,3*SR*)-3-(2,2-dichlorovinyl)-
2,2-dimethylcyclopropanecarboxylate; $C_{21}H_{20}Cl_2O_3$;
52645-53-1

Insecticide

1R, 3S-isomer

● **Perphenazine** (rINN) per·*fen*·a·zën

2-{4-[3-(2-Chlorophenothiazin-10-yl)propyl]piperazin-1-yl}¬
ethanol; $C_{21}H_{26}ClN_3OS$; *58-39-9*

Dopamine receptor antagonist; neuroleptic

Pertuzumab (rINN) per·*too*·zü·mab

Immunoglobulin G1, anti-(human neu (receptor))
(human-mouse monoclonal 2C4 heavy chain), disulfide with
human-mouse monoclonal 2C4 k-chain, dimer; *380610-27-5*

Monoclonal antibody (HER-2)

pertuzumab has the following amino acid sequence:

The symbol '¬' in systematic chemical names signifies line continuation

```
DIQMTQSPSS    LSASVGDRVT    ITCKASQDVS
IGVAWYQQKP    GKAPKLLIYS    ASYRYTGVPS
RFSGSGSGTD    FTLTISSLQP    EDFATYYCQQ
YYIYPYTFGQ    GTKVEIKRTV    AAPSVFIFPP
SDEQLKSGTA    SVVCLLNNFY    PREAKVQWKV
DNALQSGNSQ    ESVTEQDSKD    STYSLSSTLT
LSKADYEKHK    VYACEVTHQG    LSSPVTKSFN
RGEC

EVQLVESGGG    LVQPGGSLRL    SCAASGFTFT
DYTMDWVRQA    PGKGLEWVAD    VNPNSGGSIY
NQRFKGRFTL    SVDRSKNTLY    LQMNSLRAED
TAVYYCARNL    GPSFYFDYWG    QGTLVTVSSA
STKGPSVFPL    APSSKSTSGG    TAALGCLVKD
YFPEPVTVSW    NSGALTSGVH    TFPAVLQSSG
LYSLSSVVTV    PSSSLGTQTY    ICNVNHKPSN
TKVDKKVEPK    SCDKTHTCPP    CPAPELLGGP
SVFLFPPKPK    DTLMISRTPE    VTCVVVDVSH
EDPEVKFNWY    VDGVEVHNAK    TKPREEQYNS
TYRVVSVLTV    LHQDWLNGKE    YKCKVSNKAL
PAPIEKTISK    AKGQPREPQV    YTLPPSREEM
TKNQVSLTCL    VKGFYPSDIA    VEWESNGQPE
NNYKTTPPVL    DSDGSFFLYS    KLTVDKSRWQ
QGNVFSCSVM    HEALHNHYTQ    KSLSLSPGK
```
2

Pethidine (rINN) *pe*·thi·dën
Ethyl 1-methyl-4-phenylpiperidine-4-carboxylate; $C_{15}H_{21}NO_2$; *57-42-1*
● **Pethidine Hydrochloride** meperidine hydrochloride (USAN); *50-13-5*
Opioid receptor agonist; analgesic

Pexelizumab (rINN) peks·e·*liz*·ü·mab
Immunoglobulin, anti-(human complement C5 α-chain) (human-mouse monoclonal 5G1.1-SC single chain); *219685-93-5*
Monoclonal antibody (CD-5 complement)

Plerixafor (rINN) ple·*riks*·á·for
1,1'-(1,4-phenylenebismethylene)bis(1,4,8,11-tetraazacyclotetradecane);$C_{28}H_{54}N_8$; *110078-46-1*;
CXCR4 chemokine receptor antagonist; immunostimulant

Phanquinone (rINN) *fan*·kwi·nön
4,7-Phenanthroline-5,6-dione; $C_{12}H_6N_2O_2$; *84-12-8*
Antiprotozoal

Phenacemide (rINN) see Appendix C

Phenactropinium Chloride (rINN) see Appendix C

Phenadoxone (rINN) see Appendix C

Phenaglycodol (rINN) fen·a·*gli*·kö·dol
2-(4-Chlorophenyl)-3-methylbutane-2,3-diol; $C_{11}H_{15}ClO_2$; *79-93-6*
Anxiolytic; sedative

mixture of stereoisomers

Phenampromide (rINN) fen·*am*·prö·mïd
N-(1-Methyl-2-piperidinoethyl)propionanilide; $C_{17}H_{26}N_2O$; *129-83-9*
Opioid receptor agonist

and enantiomer

Phenazocine (rINN) see Appendix C

and enantiomer

Phentermine (rINN) *fen·ter·mën*
  α,α-Dimethylphenethylamine; $C_{10}H_{15}N$; *122-09-8*
  Amfetamine analogue; appetite suppressant

Phentolamine (rINN) *fen·to·la·mën*
  3-[*N*-(2-Imidazolin-2-ylmethyl)-*p*-toluidino]phenol; $C_{17}H_{19}N_3O$;
  50-60-2
  ● **Phentolamine Mesilate** *65-28-1*
  Alpha-adrenoceptor antagonist

Phenyl Aminosalicylate *see Fenamisal*

● **Phenylbutazone** (rINN) *fë·nïl·bü·ta·zön*
  4-Butyl-1,2-diphenylpyrazolidine-3,5-dione; $C_{19}H_{20}N_2O_2$;
  50-33-9
  Cyclo-oxygenase inhibitor; pyrazolone analgesic

● **Phenylephrine** (rINN) *fë·nïl·e·frën*
  (*S*)-1-(3-Hydroxyphenyl)-2-methylaminoethanol; $C_9H_{13}NO_2$;
  59-42-7
  ● **Phenylephrine Hydrochloride** *61-76-7*
  Phenylephrine Tartrate
  Alpha-adrenoceptor agonist

Phenylpropanolamine (rINN) *fë·nïl·prö·pa·no·la·mën*
  (1*RS*,2*SR*)-2-Amino-1-phenylpropan-1-ol; $C_9H_{13}NO$;
  14838-15-4
  ● **Phenylpropanolamine Hydrochloride** *154-41-6*
  Adrenoceptor agonist

and enantiomer

Phenyltoloxamine (rINN) *fë·nïl·tol·oks·a·mën*
  2-(2-Benzylphenoxy)ethyldimethylamine; $C_{17}H_{21}NO$; *92-12-6*
  Phenyltoloxamine Citrate *1176-08-5*
  Histamine H_1 receptor antagonist; antihistamine

Phenyramidol *see Fenyramidol*

● **Phenytoin** (rINN) *fen·ë·tö·in*
  5,5-Diphenylimidazolidine-2,4-dione; $C_{15}H_{12}N_2O_2$; *57-41-0*
  ● **Phenytoin Sodium** *630-93-3*
  Antiepileptic

● **Phloroglucinol** (BAN) *flor·ö·gloo·sin·ol*
  Benzene-1,3,5-triol; $C_6H_6O_3$; *108-73-6*
  Antispasmodic

● **Pholcodine** (rINN) *fol·kö·dën*
  (1) (−)-(5*R*,6*S*)-4,5-Epoxy-17-methyl-3-(2-morpholino¬
  ethoxy) morphin-7-en-6-ol; (2) 3-*O*-(2-Morpholinoethyl)¬
  morphine; $C_{23}H_{30}N_2O_4$; *509-67-1*
  Opioid receptor agonist; cough suppressant

Pholedrine (rINN) *fol·e·drën*
  4-(2-Methylaminopropyl)phenol; $C_{10}H_{15}NO$; *370-14-9*
  Adrenoceptor agonist

Phosmet (BAN) *fos*·met
O,O-Dimethyl S-phthalimidomethyl phosphorodithioate;
$C_{11}H_{12}NO_4PS_2$; *732-11-6*
Organophosphorus insecticide

Phoxim (rINN) *foks*·im
O,O-Diethyl (a-cyanobenzylideneamino-oxy)¬
phosphorothionate; $C_{12}H_{15}N_2O_3PS$; *14816-18-3*
Ectoparasiticide; insecticide

Phthalylsulfacetamide (BAN) see Appendix C

● **Phthalylsulfathiazole** (rINN) ftha·lïl·sul·fa·*thï*·a·zôl
4′-(1,3-Thiazol-2-ylsulfamoyl)phthalanilic acid; $C_{17}H_{13}N_3O_5S_2$;
85-73-4
Antibacterial

Physostigmine (BAN) fï·sö·*stig*·mën
(3aS,8aR)-1,2,3,3a,8,8a-Hexahydro-1,3a,8-trimethylpyrrolo¬
[2,3,*b*]indol-5-yl methylcarbamate; eserine; $C_{15}H_{21}N_3O_2$;
57-47-6
● **Physostigmine Salicylate** *57-64-7*
● **Physostigmine Sulfate** *64-47-1*
Cholinesterase inhibitor

● **Phytomenadione** (rINN) fï·tö·men·a·*dï*·ön
A mixture of 2-methyl-3-[(2E,7R,11R)-3,7,11,15-
tetramethylhexadeca-2-enyl]naphthalene-1,4-dione and
'2Z'-isomer; vitamin K_1; phytonadione (USAN);
$C_{31}H_{46}O_2$; *84-80-0*
Vitamin K analogue

E-component

Piboserod (rINN) pï·*bö*·se·rod
N-[(1-Butyl-4-piperidyl)methyl]-3,4-dihydro-2H-[1,3]¬
oxazino[3,2-*a*]indole-10-carboxamide; $C_{22}H_{31}N_3O_2$;
152811-62-6
Piboserod Hydrochloride *178273-87-5*
Serotonin $5HT_4$ receptor antagonist; irritable bowel syndrome

Picloxydine (rINN) pi·*kloks*·ë·dën
1,1′-[Piperazine-1,4-diylbis(carbonimidoyl)]bis(3-*p*-chloro¬
phenylguanidine); $C_{20}H_{24}Cl_2N_{10}$; *5636-92-0*
Disinfectant

Picoplatin (rINN) pi·kö·*pla*·tin
cis-Amminedichloro(2-methylpyridine)platinum(II);
$C_6H_{10}Cl_2N_2Pt$; *181630-15-9*
Cytotoxic

● **Picotamide** (rINN) pi·*kot*·a·mïd
N,N′-Bis(3-pyridylmethyl)-4-methoxyisophthalamide;
$C_{21}H_{20}N_4O_3$; *32828-81-2*
Thromboxane synthetase inhibitor; thromboxane receptor antagonist; antiplatelet agent

Picumast (rINN) see Appendix C

226

Picumeterol (rINN) pi·kü·*me*·te·rol
(*R*)-1-(4-Amino-3,5-dichlorophenyl)-2-{6-[2-(2-pyridyl)¬
ethoxy]hexylamino}ethanol; C₂₁H₂₉Cl₂N₃O₂
Beta₂-adrenoceptor agonist; bronchodilator

Pidolic Acid (rINN) pi·*dol*·ik
(1) (*S*)-5-Oxopyrrolidine-2-carboxylic acid;
(2) 5-Oxo-ʟ-proline; C₅H₇NO₃; *98-79-3*
● **Magnesium Pidolate** *62003-27-4*
Source of magnesium

Pifenate (rINN) see Appendix C

Pilocarpine (BAN) pï·lö·*kar*·pën
(1) (2*S*,3*R*)-α-Ethyl-β-(1-methyl-1*H*-imidazol-5-ylmethyl)-γ-
butyrolactone; (2) (3*S*,4*R*)-3-Ethyl-4,5-dihydro-4-[(1-methyl-
1*H*-imidazol-5-yl)methyl]furan-2(3*H*)-one; C₁₁H₁₆N₂O₂;
92-13-7
● **Pilocarpine Hydrochloride** *54-71-7*
● **Pilocarpine Nitrate** *148-72-1*
Cholinoceptor agonist; treatment of glaucoma

Pimecrolimus (rINN) pi·me·krö·*lë*·mus
(3*S*,4*R*,5*S*,8*R*,9*E*,12*S*,14*S*,15*R*,16*S*,18*R*,19*R*,26a*S*,)-3-{[(*E*)-
2-[(1*R*,3*R*,4*S*)-4-Chloro-3-methoxycyclohexyl]-1-methylvinyl}-
8-ethyl-5,6,8,11,12,13,14,15,16,17,18,19,24,25,26,26a-
hexadecahydro-5,19-dihydroxy-14,16-dimethoxy-4,10,12,18-
tetramethyl-15,19-epoxy-3*H*-pyrido[2,1-*c*][1,4]oxa-
azacyclotricosine-1,7,20,21(4H,21H)-tetrone; C₄₃H₆₈ClNO₁₁;
137071-32-0
Calcineurin inhibitor; immunosuppressant

Piminodine (rINN) see Appendix C

● **Pimobendan** (rINN) pi·mo·*ben*·dan
6-[2-(4-Methoxyphenyl)-4,5-dihyrobenzimidazol-5-yl]-5-
methylpyridazin-3(2*H*)-one; C₁₉H₁₈N₄O₂; *118428-36-7*
Inhibitor of phosphodiesterase type III; calcium sensitizer

and enantiomer

Pimonidazole (rINN) see Appendix C

● **Pimozide** (rINN) *pi*·mö·zïd
1-{1-[4,4′-bis(fluorophenyl)butyl]-4-piperidyl}-1,3-
dihydrobenzimidazol-2-one; C₂₈H₂₉F₂N₃O; *2062-78-4*
Dopamine receptor antagonist; neuroleptic

● **Pindolol** (rINN) *pin*·do·lol
1-(Indol-4-yloxy)-3-isopropylaminopropan-2-ol; C₁₄H₂₀N₂O₂;
13523-86-9
Beta-adrenoceptor antagonist

and enantiomer

Pioglitazone (rINN) pï·ö·*gli*·ta·zön
(*RS*)-5-{4-[2-(5-Ethyl-2-pyridyl)ethoxy]benzyl}-1,3-thiazo¬
lidin-2,4-dione; C₁₉H₂₀N₂O₃S; *111025-46-8*
*Peroxisome proliferator-activated receptor (PPAR)-gamma
agonist; treatment of diabetes mellitus*

and enantiomer

Pipamazine (rINN) see Appendix C

Pipamperone (rINN) pi·*pam*·pe·rön
1-[3-(4-Fluorobenzoyl)propyl]-4-piperidinopiperidine-4-
carboxamide; $C_{21}H_{30}FN_3O_2$; *1893-33-0*
Dopamine receptor antagonist

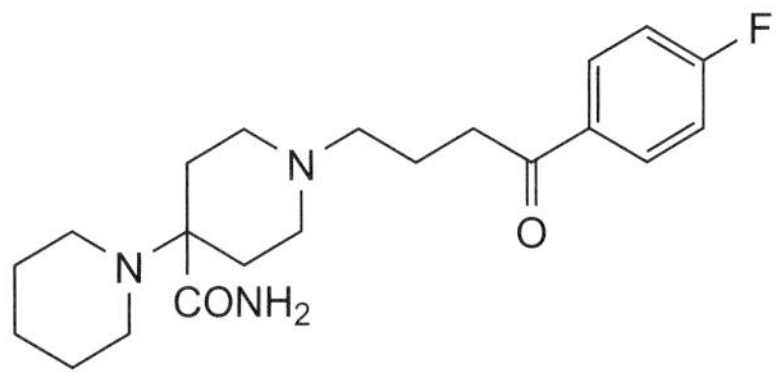

Pipazetate (rINN) pi·*pa*·ze·tät
2-(2-Piperidinoethoxy)ethyl pyrido[3,2-*b*][1,4]benzothiazine-
10-carboxylate; $C_{21}H_{25}N_3O_3S$; *2167-85-3*
Cough suppressant

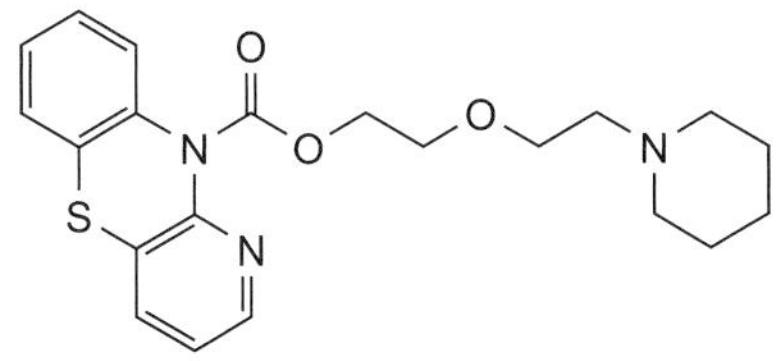

Pipecuronium Bromide (rINN) pi·pe·kûr·*rö*·në·um
1,1,1′,1′-Tetramethyl-4,4′-(3α,17β-diacetoxy-5α-
androstan-2β,16β-diyl)dipiperazinium dibromide;
$C_{35}H_{62}Br_2N_4O_4$; *68399-57-5 (dihydrate)*
Non-depolarizing neuromuscular blocker

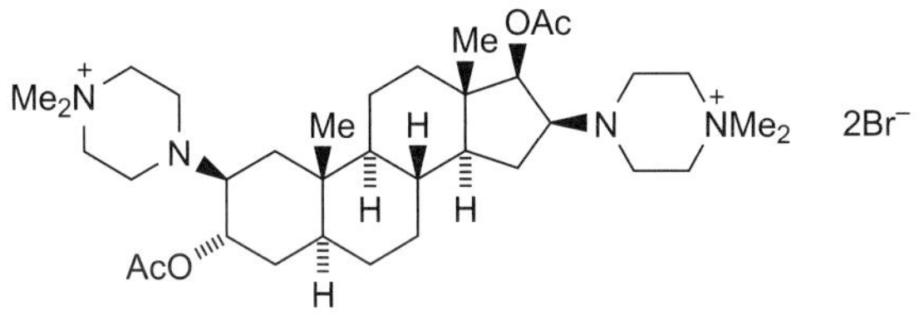

● **Pipemidic Acid** (rINN) pi·pe·*mi*·dik
8-Ethyl-5,8-dihydro-5-oxo-2-(piperazin-1-yl)pyrido[2,3-*d*]¬
pyrimidine-6-carboxylic acid; $C_{14}H_{17}N_5O_3$; *51940-44-4;*
72571-82-5 (trihydrate)
Antibacterial

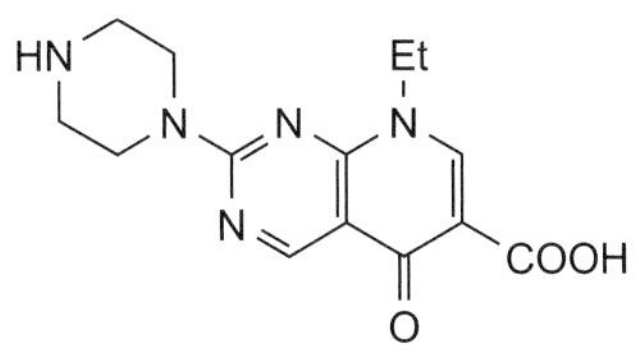

Pipenzolate Bromide (rINN) see Appendix C

● **Piperacillin** (rINN) pi·pe·ra·*si*·lin
6-[(*R*)-2-(4-Ethyl-2,3-dioxopiperazine-1-carboxamido)-2-
phenylacetamido]penicillanic acid; $C_{23}H_{27}N_5O_7S$; *59703-84-3*
● **Piperacillin Sodium**
Penicillin antibacterial

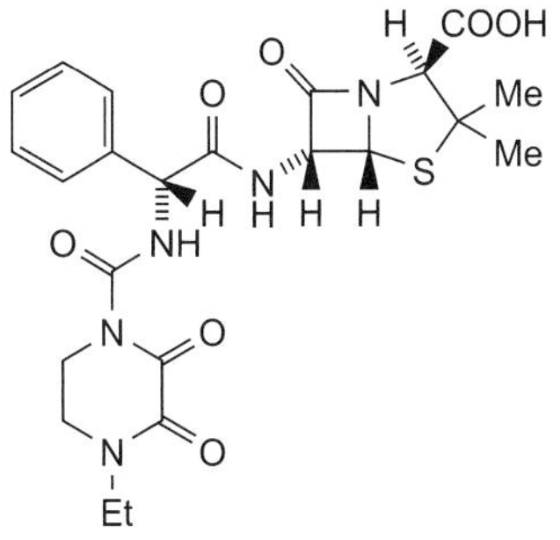

Piperazine Calcium Edetate (rINN)
Calcium piperazine-1,4-diylium ethylenediaminetetra-acetate;
$C_{14}H_{24}CaN_4O_8$; *12002-30-1*
Antihelminthic

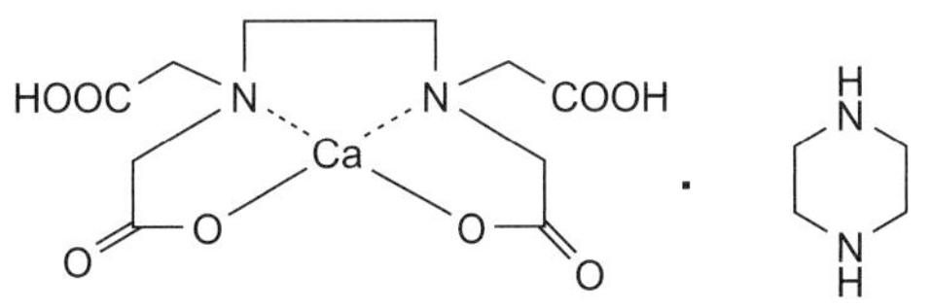

Piperidolate (rINN) pi·pe·*ri*·dö·lät
(*RS*)-1-Ethyl-3-piperidyl diphenylacetate; $C_{21}H_{25}NO_2$; *82-98-4*
Piperidolate Hydrochloride *129-77-1*
Anticholinergic

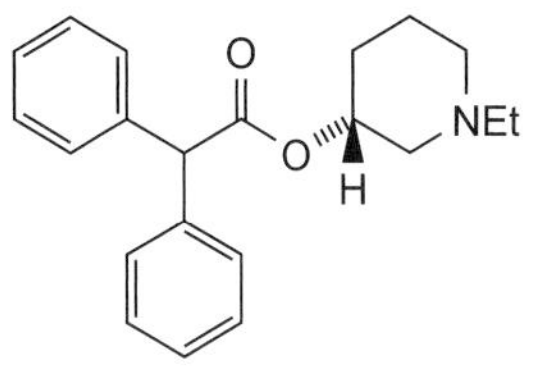

and enantiomer

Piperocaine (rINN) pi·*pe*·rö·kän
(*RS*)-3-(2-Methylpiperidino)propyl benzoate; $C_{16}H_{23}NO_2$;
136-82-3
Local anaesthetic

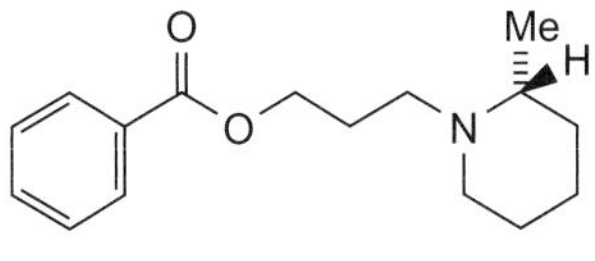

and enantiomer

♣ **Piperonyl Butoxide** (BAN) pi·*pe*·ro·nïl bü·*toks*·ïd
5-[2-(2-*tert*-Butoxyethoxy)ethoxymethyl]-6-propyl-1,3-
benzodioxole; $C_{19}H_{30}O_5$; *51-03-6*
Insecticide

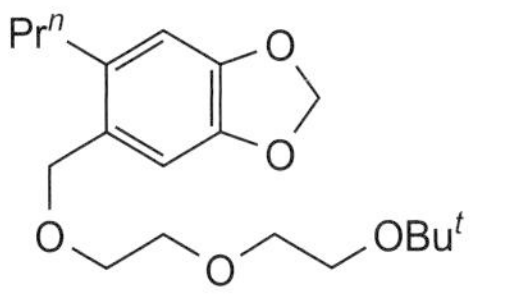

Piperoxan (rINN) see Appendix C

Pipotiazine (rINN) pi·pö·*ti*·a·zën
  10-{3-[4-(2-Hydroxyethyl)piperidino]propyl}-*N,N*-dimethyl¬
  phenothiazine-2-sulfonamide; $C_{24}H_{33}N_3O_3S_2$; *39860-99-6*
  Pipotiazine Palmitate (ester); *37517-26-3*
  Dopamine receptor antagonist; neuroleptic

Pipoxolan (rINN) see Appendix C

Pipradrol (rINN) see Appendix C

Piprinhydrinate (rINN) see Appendix C

●**Piracetam** (rINN) pi·*ra*·së·tam
  2-(2-Oxopyrrolidin-1-yl)acetamide; $C_6H_{10}N_2O_2$; *7491-74-9*
  Nootropic; cortical myoclonus

Pirazolac (rINN) pi·*ra*·zö·lak
  4-(4-Chlorophenyl)-1-(4-fluorophenyl)pyrazol-3-ylacetic acid;
  $C_{17}H_{12}ClFN_2O_2$; *71002-09-0*
  Cyclo-oxygenase inhibitor; analgesic; anti-inflammatory

Pirbuterol (rINN) see Appendix C

Pirenperone (rINN) see Appendix C

Pirenzepine (rINN) pi·*ren*·ze·pën
  5,11-Dihydro-11-(4-methylpiperazin-1-ylacetyl)pyrido¬
  [2,3-*b*][1,4]benzodiazepin-6-one; $C_{19}H_{21}N_5O_2$; *28797-61-7*
  ●**Pirenzepine Hydrochloride** *29868-61-7*
  Muscarinic M_3 receptor antagonist

●**Piretanide** (rINN) pi·*re*·ta·nïd
  4-Phenoxy-3-pyrrolidin-1-yl-5-sulfamoylbenzoic acid;
  $C_{17}H_{18}N_2O_5S$; *55837-27-9*; Hoe 118
  Thiazide diuretic

Piridoxilate (rINN) pi·ri·*doks*·i·lät
  2-(5-Hydroxy-4-hydroxymethyl-6-methyl-3-
  pyridylmethoxy)glycolic acid—2-[4,5-bis(hydroxymethyl)-2-
  methyl-3-pyridyloxy]glycolic acid (1:1); $C_{20}H_{26}N_2O_{12}$;
  24340-35-0
  Vasodilator

Pirimiphos-ethyl (BAN) pi·*rim*·i·fos-ë·thïl
  O-(2-Diethylamino-6-methylpyrimidin-4-yl) *O,O*-diethyl
  phosphorothioate; $C_{13}H_{24}N_3O_3PS$; *23505-41-1*
  Organophosphorus insecticide

Piritramide (rINN) pi·*ri*·tra·mïd
  1-(3-Cyano-3,3-diphenylpropyl)-4,4′-bipiperidine-4-
  carboxamide; $C_{27}H_{34}N_4O$; *302-41-0*
  Opioid receptor agonist

Pirodavir (rINN) pi·*ro*·da·veer
  Ethyl 4-{2-[1-(6-methylpyridazin-3-yl)-4-piperidyl]¬
  ethoxy}benzoate; $C_{21}H_{27}N_3O_3$; *124436-59-5*
  Antiviral (rhinoviruses)

The symbol '¬' in systematic chemical names signifies line continuation

● **Piroxicam** (rINN) pi·*roks*·i·kam
4-Hydroxy-2-methyl-*N*-2-pyridyl-2*H*-1,2-benzothiazine-3-carboxamide 1,1-dioxide; $C_{15}H_{13}N_3O_4S$; *36322-90-4*
Piroxicam Betadex
Cyclo-oxygenase inhibitor; analgesic; anti-inflammatory

Piroximone (rINN) pi·*roks*·i·mön
4-Ethyl-5-isonicotinoyl-4-imidazolin-2-one; $C_{11}H_{11}N_3O_2$; *84490-12-0*
Inhibitor of phosphodiesterase type III; positive inotrope

Pirprofen (rINN) *per*·prö·fen
2-[3-Chloro-4-(3-pyrrolin-1-yl)phenyl]propionic acid; $C_{13}H_{14}ClNO_2$; *31793-07-4*
Cyclo-oxygenase inhibitor; analgesic; anti-inflammatory

and enantiomer

Pirquinozol (rINN) see Appendix C

Pituitary Extract (Posterior) (BAN) see Appendix C

● **Pivampicillin** (rINN) pi·*vam*·pi·si·lin
Pivaloyloxymethyl 6-(D-phenylglycylamino)penicillanate; $C_{22}H_{29}N_3O_6S$; *33817-20-8*

● **Pivampicillin Hydrochloride** *26309-95-5*
Antibacterial

Pivhydrazine (BAN) see Appendix C

Pivmecillinam (rINN) piv·me·*si*·li·nam
Pivaloyloxymethyl 6-(azepan-1-ylmethyleneamino)¬penicillanate; amdinocillin pivoxil (USAN); $C_{21}H_{33}N_3O_5S$; *32886-97-8*
● **Pivmecillinam Hydrochloride**
Penicillin antibacterial

Pivsulbactam (BAN) piv·sul·*bak*·tam
(1) Pivaloyloxymethyl penicillanate 1,1-dioxide; (2) Pivaloyloxymethyl (2*S*,5*R*)-3,3-dimethyl-7-oxo-4-thia-1-azabicyclo[3.2.0]heptane-2-carboxylate 1,1-dioxide; sulbactam pivoxil (USAN); $C_{14}H_{21}NO_7S$; *69388-79-0*
Beta-lactamase inhibitor

Pixantrone (rINN) piks·*an*·trön
6,9-Bis[(2-aminoethyl)amino]benzo[*g*]isoquinoline-5,10-dione; $C_{17}H_{19}N_5O_2$; *144510-96-3*
Pixantrone Maleate (1:2) *144675-97-8*
Cytotoxic

Pizotifen (rINN) pi·*zo*·ti·fen
9,10-Dihydro-4-(1-methylpiperidin-4-ylidene)-4*H*-benzo¬[4,5]cyclohepta[1,2-*b*]thiophene; pizotyline (USAN); $C_{19}H_{21}NS$; *15574-96-6*
● **Pizotifen Malate** *5189-11-7*
Serotonin (5HT) receptor partial agonist; prophylaxis of migraine

Plasmin *see Fibrinolysin (human)*

Plasminogen (BAN) plaz·*mi*·nö·jen
The specific substance derived from plasma which, when activated, has the property of lysing fibrinogen, fibrin and some other proteins.
Fibrinolytic

Plevitrexed (rINN) ple·vi·*treks*·ed
(*S*)-2-[(4-{[(3,4-Dihydro-2,7-dimethyl-4-oxoquinazolin-6-
yl)methyl](prop-2-ynyl)amino}-2-fluorobenzamido-4-
(1*H*-1,2,3,4-tetrazol-5-yl)butanoic acid;
$C_{26}H_{25}FN_8O_4$; *153537-73-6*
Thymidylate synthase inhibitor; treatment of solid tumours

Plicamycin (rINN) see Appendix C

Plitidepsin (rINN) pli·tï·*dep*·sin
3,6-Anhydro(*N*-{(2*S*,4*S*)-4-[(3*S*,4*R*,5*S*)-3-hydroxy-4-{[*N*-(2-
oxopropanoyl)-L-prolyl-*N*-methyl-D-leucyl-L-threonyl]amino}-
5-methylheptanoyloxy]-2,5-dimethyl-3-oxohexanoyl}-
L-leucyl-L-propyl-*N*,*O*-dimethyl-L-tyrosine); $C_{57}H_{87}N_7O_{15}$;
137219-37-5
Cytotoxic

Podophyllotoxin (BAN) pö·dö·fï·lö·*toks*·in
(5*R*,5a*R*,8a*R*,9*R*)-5,5a,6,8,8a,9-Hexahydro-9-hydroxy-5-
(3,4,5-trimethoxyphenyl)furo[3′4′:6,7]naphtho[2,3-*d*]-
1,3-dioxol-6-one; $C_{22}H_{22}O_8$; *518-28-5*
Inhibitor of DNA topoisomerase type II

● **Poldine Metilsulfate** (BAN) *pol*·dën
(*RS*)-2-Benziloyloxymethyl-1,1-dimethylpyrrolidinium
methylsulfate; $C_{22}H_{29}NO_7S$; *545-80-2*
Anticholinergic

and enantiomer

Polidexide (BAN) see Appendix C

Polidronium Chloride (rINN) po·lë-*drö*·në·um
α-{ (*E*)–4–[Tris(2-hydroxyethyl)ammonio]but-2-enyl}-ω-[tris(2-
hydroxyethyl)ammonio]poly[(dimethyliminio)(*E*)-but-2-enylene
chloride] dichloride; $C_{16}H_{36}Cl_2N_2O_6$ $(C_6H_{12}ClN)_n$; *75345-27-6*
Antibacterial

Poliglecaprone (rINN) po·lë·*gle*·ka·prön
Poly[oxy(1-oxoethylene)]-*block*-poly[oxy(1-oxohexa¬
methylene)]; $[C_2H_2O_2]_m[C_6H_{10}O_2]_n$; *41706-81-4*
Synthetic absorbable suture

Polihexanide (rINN) po·lë-*heks*·a·nïd
Poly(biguanide-1,5-diylhexamethylene) hydrochloride;
32289-58-0
Disinfectant

Poloxalene (rINN) pol·*oks*·a·lën
A block co-polymer of oxyethylene and oxypropylene having a
molecular weight of approximately 3000; *9003-11-6*
Non-ionic surfactant

● **Poloxamer** (rINN) pol·*oks*·a·mer
a-Hydro-ω-hydroxypoly[oxyethyleneoxy(1-methylethylene)¬
oxyethylene] block copolymer.
Each poloxamer name is followed by a number, *eg*, poloxamer
188, 331, 407 etc. The first two digits multiplied by 100
correspond to the approximate average molecular weight of the
poly(oxypropylene) portion; the third digit multiplied by 10
corresponds to the percentage by weight of the
poly(oxyethylene) portion; *9003-11-6*
Non-ionic surfactant

The symbol '¬' in systematic chemical names signifies line continuation

Poloxyl Lanolin (BAN) po·*loks*·ïl
A polyoxyethylene condensation product of anhydrous lanolin.
Ethoxylated lanolin; emollient

Polycarbophil (rINN) po·lë·*kar*·bö·fil
Polyacrylic acid cross-linked with divinyl glycol; *9003-97-8*
Polycarbophil Calcium
Bulk laxative

Polydioxanone (BAN) po·lë·dï·*oks*·a·nön
Poly[oxy(1-oxoethylene)oxyethylene]; $(C_4H_6O_3)_n$; *31621-87-1*;
PDS
Synthetic absorbable suture

Polyestradiol Phosphate (rINN) see Appendix C

Polygeline (rINN) po·*li*·je·lën
A polymer prepared by cross-linking polypeptides derived from
denatured gelatin with a di-isocyanate to form urea bridges;
9015-56-9
Plasma volume expander

Polyglactin (BAN) pol·ë·*glak*·tin
Lactic acid polyester with glycollic acid; *26780-50-7*
Synthetic absorbable suture

Polyglycolic Acid (rINN) pol·ë·glï·*ko*·lik
Poly(glycollic acid); *26009-03-0*
Synthetic absorbable suture

Polyglyconate (BAN) pol·ë·*glï*·kö·nät
A co-polymer of 1,4-dioxane-2,5-dione and trimethylene
carbonate; *75734-93-9*
Synthetic absorbable suture

Polyhexanide *see Polihexanide*

Polymyxin B (rINN) po·lë·*miks*·in
Antimicrobial polypeptides produced by strains of *Bacillus
polymyxa*; polymyxin E is Colistin; *1404-26-8*

● **Polymyxin B Sulfate** *1405-20-5*
Antibacterial

Polynoxylin (rINN) po·lë·*noks*·i·lin
Poly{[bis(hydroxymethyl)ureylene]methylene}; *9011-05-6*
Antiseptic

Polyoxyl 8 Stearate *see Macrogol 8 Stearate*

Polyoxyl 40 Stearate *see Macrogol 40 Stearate*

Polysorbate (rINN) po·lë·*sor*·bät
Polyoxyethylene derivatives of cyclic sorbitol anhydrides
partially esterified with a fatty acid
The numbered polysorbates indicated below refer to the
following compounds: *eg*

● *polysorbate 20:* polyoxyethylene 20 sorbitan monolaurate;
9005-64-5
polysorbate 40: polyoxyethylene 20 sorbitan monopalmitate;
9005-66-7

● *polysorbate 60:* polyoxyethylene 20 sorbitan monostearate;
9005-67-8
polysorbate 65: polyoxyethylene 20 sorbitan tristearate;
9005-71-4

● *polysorbate 80*: polyoxyethylene 20 sorbitan mono-oleate;
9005-65-6
polysorbate 85: polyoxyethylene 20 sorbitan trioleate;
9005-70-3
polyoxyethylene 20 sorbitan corresponds to tris(polyethylene
glycol 300) sorbitan ethers.
Non-ionic surfactants

● **Polythiazide** (rINN) po·lë·*thï*·a·zïd
(*RS*)-6-Chloro-3,4-dihydro-2-methyl-3-(2,2,2-trifluoro‐
ethylthiomethyl)-2*H*-1,2,4-benzothiadiazine-7-sulfonamide 1,1-
dioxide; $C_{11}H_{13}ClF_3N_3O_4S_3$; *346-18-9*
Thiazide diuretic

and enantiomer

Polyvinox (BAN) see Appendix C

Ponalrestat (rINN) po·*nal*·re·stat
3-(4-Bromo-2-fluorobenzyl)-3,4-dihydro-4-oxophthalazin-1-
ylacetic acid; $C_{17}H_{12}BrFN_2O_3$; *72702-95-5*
Aldose reductase inhibitor; treatment of diabetes mellitus

Poractant Alfa (BAN) por·*rak*·tant
An extract of porcine lung containing not less than 90% of phospholipids, about 1% of hydrophobic proteins (SP-B and SP-C) and about 9% of other lipids; *129069-19-8*
Lung surfactant

Porfimer Sodium (rINN) see Appendix C

Porfiromycin (rINN) see Appendix C

Posaconazole (rINN) po·sa·*kon*·a·zôl
4-[4-(4-{4-[(3R,5R)-5-(2,4-Difluorophenyl)tetrahydro-5-(1H-1,2,4-triazol-1-ylmethyl)-3-furylmethoxy]phenyl}piperazin-1-yl)phenyl]-2-[(1S,2S)-1-ethyl-2-hydroxypropyl]-2,4-dihydro-3H-1,2,4-triazol-3-one; $C_{37}H_{42}F_2N_8O_4$; *171228-49-2*
Azole antifungal

Posizolid (rINN) po·*si*·zö·lid
(5R)-3-(4-{1-[(2S)-2,3-Dihydroxypropanoyl]-1,2,3,6-tetrahydro-4-pyridyl}-3,5-difluorophenyl)-5-(1,2-oxazol-3-yloxymethyl)-1,3-oxazolan-2-one; $C_{21}H_{21}F_2N_3O_7$; *252260-06-3*
Posizolid Disodium Phosphate
Antibacterial

Poskine (rINN) see Appendix C

Potassium Menaphthosulphate *see Menadiol Potassium Sulfate*

● **Povidone** (rINN) *po*·vi·dön
Poly[1-(2-oxopyrrolidin-1-yl)ethylene]; polyvidone (pINN); *9003-39-8*
Disinfectant; excipient

● **Povidone–Iodine** (BAN)
Poly[1-(2-oxopyrrolidin-1-yl)ethylene]–iodine complex; iodinated povidone; *25655-41-8*
Disinfectant

Practolol (rINN) *prak*·to·lol
4′-(2-Hydroxy-3-isopropylaminopropoxy)acetanilide; $C_{14}H_{22}N_2O_3$; *6673-35-4*
Beta-adrenoceptor antagonist

and enantiomer

Prajmalium Bitartrate (rINN) praj·*mal*·ë·um
N-Propylajmalinium hydrogen tartrate; $C_{27}H_{38}N_2O_8$; *2589-47-1*
Class I antiarrhythmic

Pralidoxime (rINN) pra·li·*doks*·ëm
2-Hydroxyiminomethyl-1-methylpyridinium (cation); $C_7H_9N_2O$; *495-94-3*
Pralidoxime Iodide *94-63-3*
Cholinesterase reactivator; treatment of organophosphorus poisoning

Pramipexole (rINN) pra·mi·*peks*·ôl
(S)-2-Amino-4,5,6,7-tetrahydro-1,3-benzothiazole-6-yl(propyl) amine; $C_{10}H_{17}N_3S$; *104632-26-0*

● **Pramipexole Hydrochloride** (2HCl) *104632-25-9*
Dopamine receptor agonist; treatment of Parkinson's disease

Pramiverine (rINN) pra·*mi*·ver·rën
(4,4-Diphenylcyclohexyl)isopropylamine; $C_{21}H_{27}N$; *14334-40-8*
Antispasmodic

The symbol '¬' in systematic chemical names signifies line continuation

Pramlintide (rINN) *pram·lin·tïd*
151126-32-8
Pramlintide Acetate
Amylin analogue

Pramlintide has the amino acid sequence shown below

```
Lys-Cys-Asn-Thr-Ala-Thr-Cys-Ala-Thr-
Gln-Arg-Leu-Ala-Asn-Phe-Leu-Val-His-
Ser-Ser-Asn-Asn-Phe-Gly-Pro-Ile-Leu-
Pro-Pro-Thr-Asn-Val-Gly-Ser-Asn-Thr-
Tyr-NH₂
```

Pramocaine (rINN) *pra·mö·kän*
4-[3-(4-Butoxyphenoxy)propyl]morpholine; pramocaine (rINN);
$C_{17}H_{27}NO_3$; *140-65-8*
Pramocaine Hydrochloride *637-58-1*
Local anaesthetic

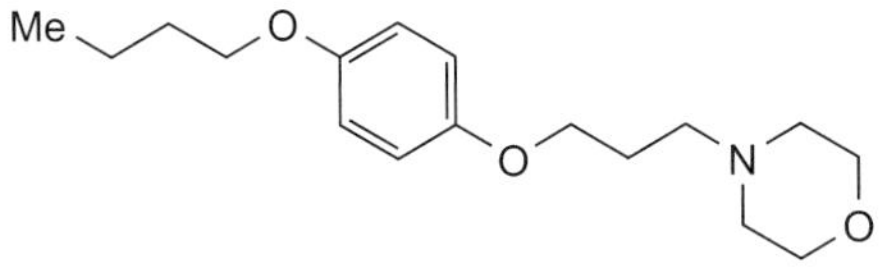

Prampine see Appendix C

Pranlukast (rINN) *pran·loo·kast*
N-[4-Oxo-2-(1H-tetrazol-5-yl)-4H-chromen-8-yl]-4-(4-phenyl-butoxy)benzamide; $C_{27}H_{23}N_5O_4$; *103177-37-3*
Leukotriene CysLT₁ receptor antagonist; treatment of asthma

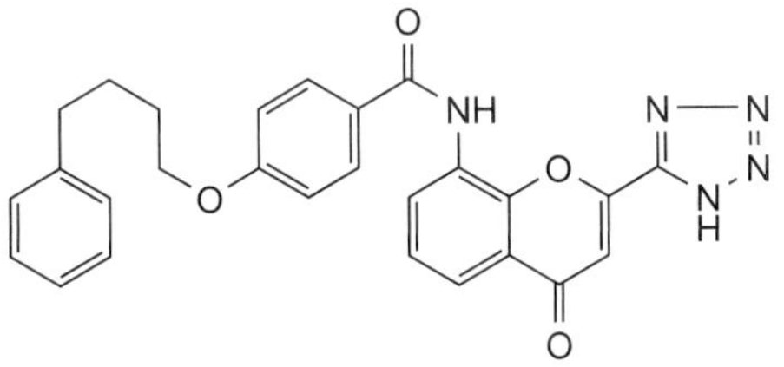

Prasugrel (rINN) *praz·ü·grel*
5-[(1RS)-2-cyclopropyl-1-(2-fluorophenyl)-2-oxoethyl]-4,5,6,7-tetrahydrothieno[3,2-c]pyridin-2-yl acetate;
$C_{20}H_{20}FNO_3S$; *150322-43-3*
Prasugrel Hydrochloride *389574-19-0*
Inhibitor of ADP-mediated platelet aggregation

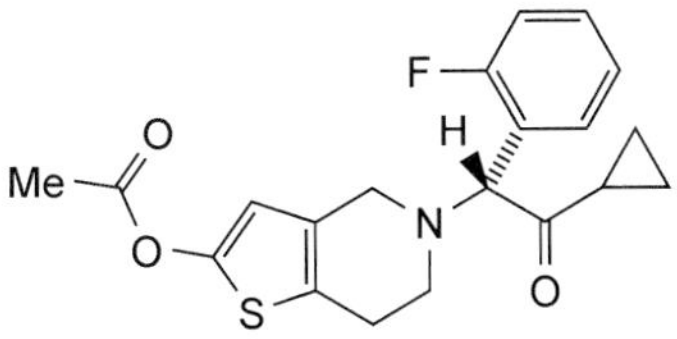

and enantiomer

Pravastatin (rINN) *pra·va·sta·tin*
(3R,5R)-7-{(1S,2S,6S,8S,8aR)-1,2,6,7,8,8a-Hexahydro-6-hydroxy-2-methyl-8-[(S)-2-methylbutyryloxy]-1-naphthyl}3,5-dihydroxyheptanoic acid; $C_{23}H_{36}O_7$; *81093-37-0*
Pravastatin Sodium *81131-70-6*
HMG Co-A reductase inhibitor; lipid-regulating drug

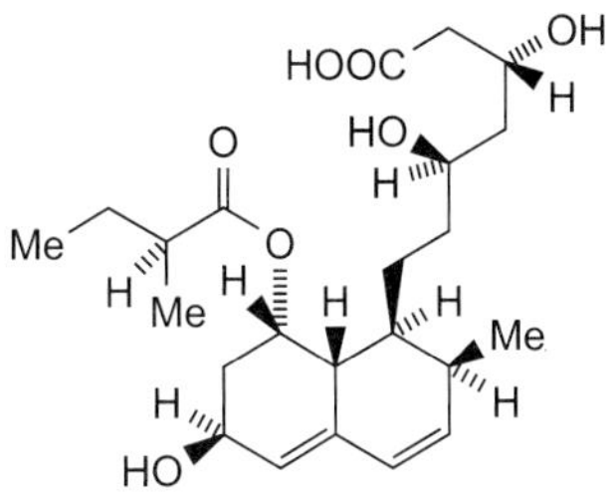

Prazepam (rINN) *prä·ze·pam*
7-Chloro-1-(cyclopropylmethyl)-1,3-dihydro-5-phenyl-1,4-benzodiazepin-2-one; $C_{19}H_{17}ClN_2O$; *2955-38-6*
Anxiolytic

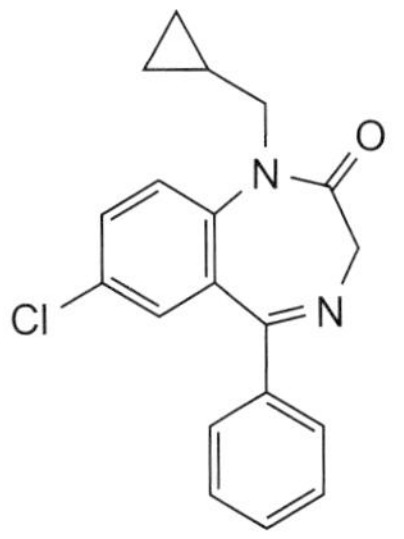

Praziquantel (rINN) *prä·zi·kwan·tel*
2-Cyclohexylcarbonyl-1,2,3,6,7,11b-hexahydropyrazino[2,1-a]isoquinolin-4-one; $C_{19}H_{24}N_2O_2$; *55268-74-1*
Antihelminthic

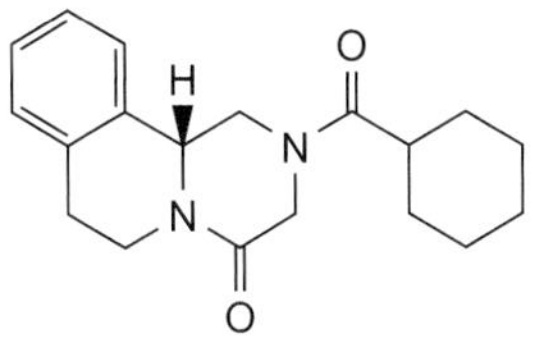

and enantiomer

Prazitone (rINN) see Appendix C

Prazosin (rINN) *prä·zö·sin*
2-[4-(2-Furoyl)piperazin-1-yl]-6,7-dimethoxyquinazolin-4-ylamine; $C_{19}H_{21}N_5O_4$; *19216-56-9*
Prazosin Hydrochloride *19237-84-4*
Alpha₁-adrenoceptor antagonist

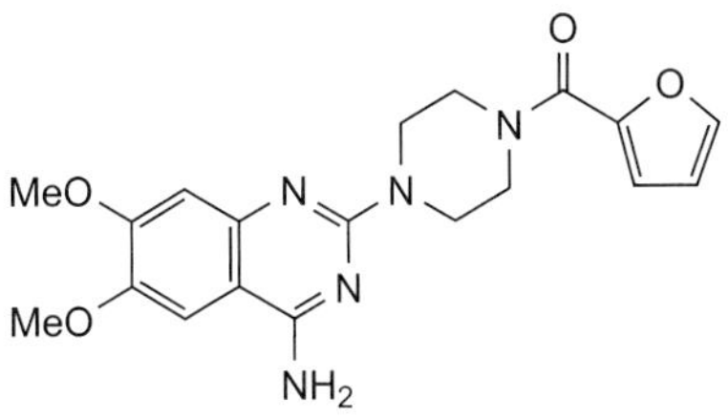

Prednicarbate (rINN) *pred·ni·kar·bät*
Ethyl 11β-hydroxy-3,20-dioxopregna-1,4-diene-17,21-diyl 17-carbonate 21-propanoate; $C_{27}H_{36}O_8$; *73771-04-7*
Glucocorticoid

234

Prednisolamate (rINN) pred·ni·*so*·la·mät
11β,17α-Dihydroxy-3,20-dioxopregna-1,4-dien-21-yl
diethylaminoacetate; prednisolone 21-diethylaminoacetate;
$C_{27}H_{39}NO_6$; *5626-34-6*
Glucocorticoid

● **Prednisolone** (rINN) pred·*nis*·o·lön

11β,17α,21-Trihydroxypregna-1,4-diene-3,20-dione; $C_{21}H_{28}O_5$;
50-24-8
 ● **Prednisolone Acetate** *52-21-1*
 Prednisolone Hexanoate
 Prednisolone Metasulfobenzoate Sodium *630-67-1*
 ● **Prednisolone Pivalate** *1107-99-9*
 ● **Prednisolone Sodium Phosphate** *125-02-0*

Glucocorticoid

Prednisolone Steaglate (rINN) pred·*ni*·so·lön *stë*·a·glät
11β,17α-Dihydroxy-3,20-dioxopregna-1,4-dien-21-yl
stearoylglycollate; $C_{41}H_{64}O_8$; *5060-55-9*
Glucocorticoid

● **Prednisone** (rINN) *pred*·nis·ön
17α,21-Dihydroxypregna-1,4-diene-3,11,20-trione; $C_{21}H_{26}O_5$;
53-03-2
 Prednisone Acetate *125-10-0*
Glucocorticoid

Prednylidene (rINN) pred·*ni*·li·dën
11β,17α,21-Trihydroxy-16-methylenepregna-1,4-diene-3,20-
dione; $C_{22}H_{28}O_5$; *599-33-7*
Glucocorticoid

Pregabalin (rINN) prë·*gá*·ba·lin
(*S*)-3-(Aminomethyl)-5-methylhexanoic acid; $C_8H_{17}NO_2$;
148553-50-9
Antiepileptic

Pregnenolone (rINN) see Appendix C

Premazepam (rINN) prë·*mä*·ze·pam
1,2,3,7-Tetrahydro-6,7-dimethyl-5-phenylpyrrolo[3,4-*e*][1,4]¬
diazepin-2-one; $C_{15}H_{15}N_3O$; *57435-86-6*
Benzodiazepine

Prenalterol (rINN) pre·*nal*·te·rol
(*S*)-1-(4-Hydroxyphenoxy)-3-isopropylaminopropan-2-ol;
$C_{12}H_{19}NO_3$; *57526-81-5*
 Prenalterol Hydrochloride *61260-05-7*
Beta₁-adrenoceptor agonist

Prenylamine (rINN) pre·*ni*·la·mën
(*RS*)-2-Benzhydrylethyl(α-methylphenethyl)amine; $C_{24}H_{27}N$;
390-64-7
 Prenylamine Lactate *69-43-2*
Calcium channel blocker

The symbol '¬' in systematic chemical names signifies line continuation

and enantiomer

Pretamazium Iodide (rINN) see Appendix C

● **Prilocaine** (rINN) *prï·lö·kän*
2-Propylaminopropiono-*o*-toluidide; $C_{13}H_{20}N_2O$; *721-50-6*
● **Prilocaine Hydrochloride** *1786-81-8*
Local anaesthetic

and enantiomer

Primaquine (rINN) *prim·a·kwën*
4-Amino-1-methylbutyl(6-methoxy-8-quinolyl)amine;
$C_{15}H_{21}N_3O$; *90-34-6*
● **Primaquine Phosphate** *63-45-6*
Antiprotozoal (malaria)

and enantiomer

Primidolol (rINN) *pri·mï·do·lol*
1-[2-(2-Hydroxy-3-*o*-tolyloxypropylamino)ethyl]-5-methyl
uracil; $C_{17}H_{23}N_3O_4$; *67227-55-8*
Beta-adrenoceptor antagonist

and enantiomer

● **Primidone** (rINN) *pri·mi·dön*
5-Ethyl-5-phenylperhydropyrimidine-4,6-dione; $C_{12}H_{14}N_2O_2$;
125-33-7
Antiepileptic

Pristinamycin (rINN) *pris·ti·na·mï·sin*
Antimicrobial substances produced by *Streptomyces pristina
spiralis*; *11006-76-1*; certain components are identical with
some constituents of mikamycin, ostreogrycin and
virginiamycin
Streptogramin antibacterial

Prizidilol (rINN) *pri·zi·di·lol*
1-*tert*-Butylamino-3-[2-(6-hydrazinopyridazin-3-yl)phenoxy]⌐
propan-2-ol; $C_{17}H_{25}N_5O_2$; *59010-44-5*
Beta-adrenoceptor antagonist

and enantiomer

● **Probenecid** (rINN) *prö·be·ne·sid*
4-(Dipropylsulfamoyl)benzoic acid; $C_{13}H_{19}NO_4S$; *57-66-9*;
Uricosuric drug

Probucol (rINN) *prö·bü·kol*
4,4′-Isopropylidenedithiobis(2,6-di-*tert*-butylphenol);
$C_{31}H_{48}O_2S_2$; *23288-49-5*
Lipid-regulating drug

Procainamide (rINN) *prö·kä·na·mïd*
4-Amino-*N*-(2-diethylaminoethyl)benzamide; $C_{13}H_{21}N_3O$;
51-06-9;
● **Procainamide Hydrochloride** *614-39-1*
Class I antiarrhythmic

Procaine (rINN) *prö·kän*
2-Diethylaminoethyl 4-aminobenzoate; $C_{13}H_{20}N_2O_2$; *59-46-1*
● **Procaine Hydrochloride** *51-05-8*
Local anaesthetic

● **Procaine Benzylpenicillin** (rINN) prö·kän
2-(4-Aminobenzoyloxy)ethyldiethylammonium 6-(2-phenyl-acetamido)penicillanate; procaine penicillin G;
$C_{29}H_{38}N_4O_6S$; *54-35-3*
Penicillin antibacterial

Procaine Penicillin *see Procaine Benzylpenicillin*

Procarbazine (rINN) see Appendix C

Procaterol (rINN) prö·*ka*·te·rol
8-Hydroxy-5-[(1*R**,2*S**)-1-hydroxy-2-isopropylaminobutyl]-2-quinolone; $C_{16}H_{22}N_2O_3$; *60443-17-6*; *72332-33-3*
Procaterol Hydrochloride *59828-07-8*; OPC-2009
Beta$_2$-adrenoceptor agonist; bronchodilator

and enantiomer

Prochlorperazine (rINN) prö·klor·*pe*·ra·zën
2-Chloro-10-[3-(4-methylpiperazin-1-yl)propyl]phenothiazine;
$C_{20}H_{24}ClN_3S$; *58-38-8*
● **Prochlorperazine Maleate** *84-02-6*
● **Prochlorperazine Mesilate** *5132-55-8*
Dopamine receptor antagonist; neuroleptic

Proclonol (rINN) see Appendix C

Procromil (BAN) prö·kro·mil
6,7,8,9-Tetrahydro-4-oxo-10-propyl-4*H*-benzo[*g*]chromene-2-carboxylic acid; $C_{17}H_{18}O_4$; *60400-86-4*
Cromone; treatment of asthma; food allergy;
allergic conjunctivitis; rhinitis

Procyclidine (rINN) prö·*si*·kli·dën
(*RS*)-1-Cyclohexyl-1-phenyl-3-(pyrrolidin-1-yl)propan-1-ol;
$C_{19}H_{29}NO$; *77-37-2*
● **Procyclidine Hydrochloride** *1508-76-5*
Anticholinergic

and enantiomer

Profadol (rINN) see Appendix C

Profenamine (rINN) prö·*fen*·a·mën
(*RS*)-[1-Methyl-2-(phenothiazin-10-yl)ethyl]diethylamine;
$C_{19}H_{24}N_2S$; *522-00-9*
Anticholinergic

and enantiomer

Progabide (rINN) *prö*·ga·bïd
4-(4′-Chloro-5-fluoro-2-hydroxybenzhydrylideneamino)¬
butyramide; $C_{17}H_{16}ClFN_2O_2$; *62666-20-0*
Antiepileptic

● **Progesterone** (rINN) prö·*je*·ster·rön
Pregn-4-ene-3,20-dione; $C_{21}H_{30}O_2$; *57-83-0*
Progestogen

Proglumetacin (rINN) prö·gloo·*me*·ta·sin
3-{4-[2-(1-*p*-Chlorobenzoyl-5-methoxy-2-methylindol-3-
ylacetoxy)ethyl]piperazin-1-yl}propyl 4-benzamido-*N,N*-
dipropylglutaramate; $C_{46}H_{58}ClN_5O_8$; *57132-53-3*
Cyclo-oxygenase inhibitor; analgesic; anti-inflammatory

and enantiomer

Proglumide (rINN) *prö*·gloo·mïd
4-Benzamido-*N,N*-dipropylglutaramic acid; $C_{18}H_{26}N_2O_4$;
6620-60-6
Cholecystokynin antagonist

and enantiomer

Proguanil (rINN) *prö*·gwa·nil
1-(4-Chlorophenyl)-5-isopropylbiguanide; $C_{11}H_{16}ClN_5$;
500-92-5
● **Proguanil Hydrochloride** *637-32-1*
Antiprotozoal (malaria)

Proheptazine (rINN) *prö*·hep·ta·zën
(*RS*)-1,3-Dimethyl-4-phenylazepan-4-yl propionate; $C_{17}H_{25}NO_2$;
77-14-5
Opioid receptor agonist

and enantiomer

Proligestone (rINN) prö·li·*jes*·tön
14α,17α-Propylidenedioxypregn-4-ene-3,20-dione; $C_{24}H_{34}O_4$;
23873-85-0
Progestogen

● **Proline** (rINN) *Prö*·lën
L-Proline; (*S*)-Pyrrolidine-2-carboxylic acid; $C_5H_9NO_2$;
147-85-3;
Amino acid

Prolintane (rINN) see Appendix C

Promazine (rINN) *prö*·ma·zën
Dimethyl(3-phenothiazin-10-ylpropyl)amine; $C_{17}H_{20}N_2S$;
58-40-2
● **Promazine Hydrochloride** *53-60-1*
Dopamine receptor antagonist; neuroleptic

Promethazine (rINN) prö·*me*·tha·zën
Dimethyl(1-methyl-2-phenothiazin-10-ylethyl)amine;
$C_{17}H_{20}N_2S$; *60-87-7*
● **Promethazine Hydrochloride** *58-33-3*
Histamine H_1 receptor antagonist; antihistamine

and enantiomer

● **Promethazine Teoclate** (rINN)
Promethazine salt of 8-chlorotheophylline; $C_{24}H_{27}ClN_6O_2S$;
17693-51-5
Histamine H_1 receptor antagonist; antihistamine

Promethoestrol *see Methestrol*

Promoxolane (rINN) see Appendix C

Pronetalol (rINN) see Appendix C

Propacetamol (rINN) prö·pa·*set*·a·mol
4-Acetamidophenyl diethylaminoacetate; $C_{14}H_{20}N_2O_3$; *66532-85-2*
● **Propacetamol Hydrochloride** *66532-86-3*
Analgesic; antipyretic

Propafenone (rINN) prö·*pa*·fe·nön
2′-(2-Hydroxy-3-propylaminopropoxy)-3-phenylpropio¬
phenone; $C_{21}H_{27}NO_3$; *54063-53-5*
● **Propafenone Hydrochloride** *34183-22-7*
Class I antiarrhythmic

and enantiomer

Propamidine (rINN) prö·*pa*·mi·dën
4,4′-(Trimethylenedioxy)dibenzamidine; $C_{17}H_{20}N_4O_2$; *104-32-5*
Propamidine Isetionate *140-63-6*
Antiseptic

Propanidid (rINN) see Appendix C

● **Propantheline Bromide** (rINN) prö·*pan*·the·lën
Di-isopropylmethyl-2-(xanthen-9-ylcarbonyloxy)¬
ethylammonium bromide; $C_{23}H_{30}BrNO_3$;*50-34-0*
Anticholinergic

Propatylnitrate (rINN) prö·pa·til·*ni*·trät
1,1,1-Tris(nitratomethyl)propane; $C_6H_{11}N_3O_9$; *2921-92-8*
Nitric oxide analogue

Propentofylline (rINN) prö·pen·*to*·fi·lën
3-Methyl-1-(5-oxohexyl)-7-propyl-7*H*-purine-2,6(1*H*,3*H*)-
dione; $C_{15}H_{22}N_4O_3$; *55242-55-2*
Non-selective phosphodiesterase inhibitor; treatment of reversible airways obstruction

Properidine (rINN) see Appendix C

Propetamphos (BAN) prö·pe·*tam*·fos
Isopropyl (*E*)-3-[(ethylamino)(methoxy) phosphino¬
thioyloxy]but-2-enoate; $C_{10}H_{20}NO_4PS$; *31218-83-4*
Organophosphorus insecticide; ectoparasiticide

Propicillin (rINN) prö·pi·*si*·lin
6-(2-Phenoxybutyramido)penicillanic acid; $C_{18}H_{22}N_2O_5S$; *551-27-9*
Propicillin Potassium *1245-44-9*
Penicillin antibacterial

and enantiomer at C*

Propiolactone (rINN) prö·pë·ö·*lak*·tön
Propan-3-olide; $C_3H_4O_2$; *57-57-8*
Disinfectant

Propiomazine (rINN) prö·pë·*ö*·ma·zën
1-{10-[2-(Dimethylamino)propyl]phenothiazin-2-yl}propan-
1-one; $C_{20}H_{24}N_2OS$; *362-29-8*
Histamine H_1 receptor antagonist; antihistamine

and enantiomer

Propiram (rINN) *prö*·pi·ram
N-(1-Methyl-2-piperidinoethyl)-*N*-(2-pyridyl)propionamide;
$C_{16}H_{25}N_3O$; *15686-91-6*
Propiram Fumarate *13717-04-9*
Opioid receptor partial agonist; analgesic

and enantiomer

and enantiomer

Propiverine (rINN) prö·*pi*·ve·rën
1-Methyl-4-piperidyl diphenyl(propoxy)acetate; $C_{23}H_{29}NO_3$; *60569-19-9*

Propiverine Hydrochloride *54556-98-8*
Anticholinergic

● **Propofol** (rINN) *prö*·po·fol
2,6-Di-isopropylphenol; $C_{12}H_{18}O$; *2078-54-8*
Intravenous general anaesthetic

Propoxur (rINN) prö·poks·ûr
2-Isopropoxyphenyl methylcarbamate; $C_{11}H_{15}NO_3$; *114-26-1*
Carbamate insecticide; ectoparasiticide

Propranolol (rINN) prö·*pran*·o·lol
1-Isopropylamino-3-(1-naphthyloxy)propan-2-ol; $C_{16}H_{21}NO_2$; *525-66-6*
● **Propranolol Hydrochloride** *318-98-9*
Beta-adrenoceptor antagonist

and enantiomer

Propyl Docetrizoate (rINN) see Appendix C

Propylhexedrine (rINN) prö·pïl·*heks*·e·drën
2-Cyclohexyl-1-methylethyl(methyl)amine; $C_{10}H_{21}N$; *3595-11-7*
Appetite suppressant

Propyliodone (rINN) prö·pïl·*ï*·ö·dön
Propyl 1,4-dihydro-3,5-di-iodo-4-oxo-1-pyridylacetate; $C_{10}H_{11}I_2NO_3$; *587-61-1*
Iodinated contrast medium

● **Propylthiouracil** (rINN) prö·pïl·thï·ö·*ûr*·ra·sil
2,3-Dihydro-6-propyl-2-thioxopyrimidin-4(1*H*)-one; $C_7H_{10}N_2OS$; *51-52-5*
Thiourea antithyroid drug

● **Propyphenazone** (rINN) prö·pë·*fe*·na·zön
4-Isopropyl-2,3-dimethyl-1-phenyl-3-pyrazolin-5-one; $C_{14}H_{18}N_2O$; *479-92-5*
Pyrazolone analgesic

Proquamezine *see Aminopromazine*

Proquazone (rINN) *pro*·kwa·zön
1-Isopropyl-7-methyl-4-phenylquinazolin-2(1*H*)-one; $C_{18}H_{18}N_2O$; *22760-18-5*
Cyclo-oxygenase inhibitor; analgesic; anti-inflammatory

Prorenoate Potassium (rINN) prö·*ren*·ö·ät
Potassium 6α,7α-dihydro-17β-hydroxy-3-oxo-3'*H*-cyclopropa[6,7]-21,24-dinor-17α-chol-4-en-23-oate; $C_{23}H_{31}KO_4$; *49847-97-4*
Aldosterone receptor antagonist; potassium-sparing diuretic

Proscillaridin (rINN) prö·si·*la*·ri·din
14-Hydroxy-3β-(α-L-rhamnopyranosyloxy)-14β-bufa-4,20,22-trienolide; $C_{30}H_{42}O_8$; *466-06-8*
Na/K-ATPase inhibitor; cardiac glycoside

Prostalene (rINN) *pros*·ta·lën
(1) (±)-Methyl 7-{(1R,2R,3R,5S)-3,5-dihydroxy-2-[(E)-3-hydroxy-3-methyloct-1-enyl]cyclopentyl}hepta-4,5-dienoate;
(2) (±)-Methyl (13E)-(9S,11R,15R)-9,11,15-trihydroxy-15-methylprosta-4,5,13-trienoate; $C_{22}H_{36}O_5$; *54120-61-5*
Prostaglandin (PGF₁) analogue

and epimer at C*

● **Protamine Hydrochloride**
Antidote to heparin

● **Protamine Sulfate** (BAN) *prö*·ta·mën sul·fät
A purified mixture of the sulfates of basic peptides prepared from the sperm or mature testes of fish, usually species of Cluperidae or Salmonidae; *9009-65-8*
Antidote to heparin

Prothionamide *see Protionamide*

Prothipendyl (rINN) see Appendix C

Protionamide (rINN) prö·ti·*on*·a·mïd
2-Propylpyridine-4-carbothioamide; $C_9H_{12}N_2S$; *14222-60-7*
Treatment of tuberculosis

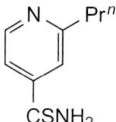

● **Protirelin** (rINN) prö·*ti*·re·lin
1-[*N*-(5-Oxo-L-prolyl)-L-histidyl]-L-prolinamide; TRH; $C_{16}H_{22}N_6O_4$; *24305-27-9*
Thyrotrophin-releasing hormone

oxoPro-His-Pro-NH₂

Protokylol (rINN) prö·tö·*ki̇*·lol
2-[2-(1,3-Benzodioxol-5-yl)-1-methylethyl]amino-1-(3,4-dihydroxyphenyl)ethanol; $C_{18}H_{21}NO_5$; *136-70-9*
Beta₂-adrenoceptor agonist

mixture of stereoisomers

Protriptyline (rINN) prö·*trip*·ti·lën
3-(5*H*-Dibenzo[*a*,*d*]cyclohepten-5-yl)propyl(methyl)amine; $C_{19}H_{21}N$; *438-60-8*
● **Protriptyline Hydrochloride** *1225-55-4*;
Monoamine reuptake inhibitor; tricyclic antidepressant

Proxicromil (rINN) see Appendix C

Proxymetacaine (rINN) proks·ë·*me*·ta·kän
2-Diethylaminoethyl 3-amino-4-propoxybenzoate; $C_{16}H_{26}N_2O_3$; *499-67-2*
● **Proxymetacaine Hydrochloride** proparacaine hydrochloride (USAN); *5875-06-9*
Local anaesthetic

● **Proxyphylline** (rINN)
7-(2-Hydroxypropyl)theophylline; $C_{10}H_{14}N_4O_3$; *603-00-9*
Non-selective phosphodiesterase inhibitor; treatment of reversible airways obstruction

The symbol '¬' in systematic chemical names signifies line continuation

and enantiomer

Prucalopride (rINN) proo·*kal*·ö·prïd
4-Amino-5-chloro-2,3-dihydro-*N*-[1-(3-methoxypropyl)-4-piperidyl][1]benzofuran-7-carboxamide; $C_{18}H_{26}ClN_3O_3$; *179474-81-8*
Serotonin 5HT$_4$ receptor agonist; enterokinetic agent

Pseudoephedrine (rINN) sü·dö·*e*·fe·drën
(+)-(1*S*,2*S*)-2-Methylamino-1-phenylpropan-1-ol; $C_{10}H_{15}NO$; *90-82-4*
● **Pseudoephedrine Hydrochloride** *345-78-8*; present in many proprietary preparations
Adrenoceptor agonist

Psilocybine (rINN) sï·lö·*sï*·bën
3-(2-Dimethylaminoethyl)indol-4-yl dihydrogen phosphate; $C_{12}H_{17}N_2O_4P$; *520-52-5*
Psychotomimetic

Pumactant (BAN) pü·*mak*·tant
A mixture of 7 parts by weight of 1,2-dipalmitoyl-*sn*-glycero(3)phosphocholine (DPPC) and 3 parts by weight of 2-oleoyl-1-palmitoyl-*sn*-glycero(3)phospho(1)-*sn*-glycerol (PG); artificial lung surfactant
Pulmonary surfactant

Puromycin (rINN) pûr·rö·*mï*·sin
(*S*)-3′-[2-Amino-3-(4-methoxyphenyl)propionamido]-3′-deoxy-*N*,*N*-dimethyladenosine; $C_{22}H_{29}N_7O_5$; *53-79-2*
Antibacterial

Pyrantel (rINN) *pi*·ran·tel
1,4,5,6-Tetrahydro-1-methyl-2-[(*E*)-2-(2-thienyl)vinyl]pyrimidine; $C_{11}H_{14}N_2S$; *15686-83-6*
● **Pyrantel Embonate** *22204-24-5*
Anthelminthic

● **Pyrazinamide** (rINN) pi·ra·*zi*·na·mïd
Pyrazine-2-carboxamide; $C_5H_5N_3O$; *98-96-4*
Antituberculosis drug

● **Pyridostigmine Bromide** (rINN) pi·ri·dö·*stig*·mën
3-Dimethylcarbamoyloxy-1-methylpyridinium bromide; $C_9H_{13}BrN_2O_2$; *101-26-8*
Cholinesterase inhibitor

Pyridoxine (rINN) pi·ri·*doks*·ën
5-Hydroxy-6-methylpyridine-3,4-diyldimethanol; $C_8H_{11}NO_3$; *65-23-6*
● **Pyridoxine Hydrochloride** Vitamin B$_6$; *58-56-0*
Vitamin B$_6$

● **Pyrimethamine** (rINN) pi·ri·*me*·tha·mën
5-(4-Chlorophenyl)-6-ethylpyrimidine-2,4-diyldiamine; $C_{12}H_{13}ClN_4$; *58-14-0*
Dihydrofolate reductase inhibitor; antiprotozoal (malaria)

Pyrimitate (rINN) pi·*ri*·mi·tät
O-2-Dimethylamino-6-methylpyrimidin-4-yl O,O-diethyl
phosphorothioate; $C_{11}H_{20}N_3O_3PS$; *5221-49-8*
Organophosphorus insecticide

Pyritinol (rINN) pi·*ri*·ti·nol
[Dithiodimethylenebis(5-hydroxy-6-methylpyridine-3,4-diyl)]¬
dimethanol; $C_{16}H_{20}N_2O_4S_2$; *1098-97-1*
Nootropic

Pyrrobutamine (BAN) pi·rö·*bü*·ta·mën
1-[4-(4-Chlorophenyl)-3-phenylbut-2-enyl]pyrrolidine;
$C_{20}H_{22}ClN$; *91-87-7*
Histamine H₁ receptor antagonist; antihistamine

Pyrrocaine (rINN) see Appendix C

Pyrvinium Pamoate (rINN) see Appendix C

Quadazocine (rINN) kwo·*dä*·zö·sën
1-Cyclopentyl-5-(2R,6S,11S)-(1,2,3,4,5,6-hexahydro-8-hydroxy-
3,6,11-trimethyl-2,6-methano-3-benzazocin-11-yl)pentan-3-one;
$C_{25}H_{37}NO_2$; *71276-43-2*
Quadazocine Mesilate *71276-44-3*
Opioid receptor antagonist

Quadrosilan (rINN) see Appendix C

Quazepam (rINN) *kwä*·ze·pam
7-Chloro-5-(2-fluorophenyl)-1,3-dihydro-1-(2,2,2-trifluoro¬
ethyl)-1,4-benzodiazepine-2-thione; $C_{17}H_{11}ClF_4N_2S$; *36735-22-5*
Benzodiazepine

Quetiapine (rINN) kwe·*ti*·a·pën
2-{2-[4-(Dibenzo[b,f][1,4]thiazepin-11-yl)piperazin-1-
yl]ethoxy}ethanol; $C_{21}H_{25}O_2N_3S$
Quetiapine Fumarate *111974-72-2*
Dopamine receptor antagonist; neuroleptic

Quinacillin (rINN) kwi·na·*si*·lin
6-(3-Carboxyquinoxalin-2-ylcarboxamido)penicillanic acid;
$C_{18}H_{16}N_4O_6S$; *1596-63-0*
Penicillin antibacterial

Quinagolide (rINN) kwi·*na*·gö·lïd
(3S,4aS,10aR)-3-Diethylaminosulfonylamino-1,2,3,4,4a,¬
5,10,10a-octahydro-1-propylbenzo[g]quinolin-6-ol;
$C_{20}H_{33}N_3O_3S$
Quinagolide Hydrochloride *94424-50-7*
Dopamine receptor agonist; treatment of Parkinson's disease

Quinalbarbitone Sodium *see Secobarbital Sodium*

Quinapril (rINN) *kwi*·na·pril
(3S)-2-{N-[(S)-1-Ethoxycarbonyl-3-phenylpropyl]-ʟ-alanyl}-
1,2,3,4-tetrahydroisoquinoline-3-carboxylic acid; $C_{25}H_{30}N_2O_5$;
85441-61-8
Quinapril Hydrochloride
Angiotensin converting enzyme inhibitor

The symbol '¬' in systematic chemical names signifies line continuation

and enantiomer

Quindoxin (rINN) kwin·*doks*·in
Quinoxaline 1,4-dioxide; $C_8H_6N_2O_2$; *2423-66-7*
Antibacterial

Quingestanol (rINN) kwin·*jes*·ta·nol
3-Cyclopentyloxy-19-nor-17α-pregna-3,5-dien-20-yn-17α-ol;
$C_{25}H_{32}O_2$; *10592-65-1*
Oestrogen

Quinelorane (rINN) kwi·*ne*·lor·rän
(5aR,9aR)-5,5a,6,7,8,9,9a,10-Octahydro-6-propylpyrido[2,3-g]quinazolin-2-ylamine; $C_{14}H_{22}N_4$; *97466-90-5*
Quinelorane Hydrochloride *97548-97-5* (2HCl)
Dopamine D_2 receptor agonist

Quinidine (BAN) *kwi*·ni·dën
(8R,9S)-6′-Methoxycinchonan-9-ol; $C_{20}H_{24}N_2O_2$; *56-54-2*
● **Quinidine Bisulfate** *50-54-4*
● **Quinidine Sulfate** *6591-63-5*
Class I antiarrhythmic

Quinestradol (rINN) kwi·*nës*·tra·dol
3-Cyclopentyloxyestra-1,3,5(10)-triene-16α,17β-diol; $C_{23}H_{32}O_3$; *1169-79-5*
Oestrogen

Quinine (BAN) kwi·nën
(8S,9R)-6′-Methoxycinchonan-9-ol; $C_{20}H_{24}N_2O_2$; *130-95-0*
● **Quinine Bisulfate** *549-56-4*
● **Quinine Dihydrochloride** *60-93-5*
● **Quinine Hydrochloride** *130-89-2*
● **Quinine Sulfate** *6119-70-6*
Antiprotozoal (malaria)

Quinestrol (rINN) kwi·*nës*·trol
3-Cyclopentyloxy-19-nor-17α-pregna-1,3,5(10)-trien-20-yn-17β-ol; $C_{25}H_{32}O_2$; *152-43-2*
Oestrogen

Quinisocaine (rINN) kwin·*i*·sö·kän
2-(3-Butyl-1-isoquinolyloxy)ethyldimethylamine; $C_{17}H_{24}N_2O$; *86-80-6*
Local anaesthetic

Quinethazone (rINN) kwi·*ne*·tha·zön
(RS)-7-Chloro-2-ethyl-1,2,3,4-tetrahydro-4-oxoquinazoline-6-sulfonamide; $C_{10}H_{12}ClN_3O_3S$; *73-49-4*
Thiazide-like diuretic

Quintiofos (rINN) kwin·tï·ö·fos

O-Ethyl *O*-8-quinolyl phenylphosphonothioate; $C_{17}H_{16}NO_2PS$; *1776-83-6*

Insecticide

Quinupristin (rINN) kwin·ü·*pris*·tin

N-[(3*R*,6*S*,7*R*,10*S*,13*S*,16*R*,20*S*,23*S*)-20-[(4-(Dimethylamino)¬benzyl]-3-ethyl-7,21-dimethyl-2,5,9,15,19,22-hexaoxo-10-phenyl-16-{[(3*S*)-quinuclidin-3-ylthio]methyl}-8-oxa-1,4,11,18,21-penta-azatricyclo[21.3.0.0^{13,18}]hexacosan-6-yl]-3-hydroxypyridine-2-carboxamide; $C_{53}H_{67}N_9O_{10}S$; *120138-50-3*

Quinupristin Mesilate

Streptogramin antibacterial

Rabeprazole (rINN) ra·*be*·pra·zôl

2-{[4-(3-Methoxypropoxy)-3-methyl-2-pyridyl] methyl¬sulfinyl}-1*H*-benzimidazole; $C_{18}H_{21}N_3O_3S$; *117976-89-3*

Rabeprazole Sodium *117976-90-6*

Proton pump inhibitor; treatment of peptic ulcer disease

● **Racecadotril** (rINN) ra·së·*ka*·dö·tril

Benzyl *rac*-{2-[(acetylsulfanyl)methyl]-3-phenyl¬propanamido}acetate; $C_{21}H_{23}NO_4S$; *81110-73-8*;

Enkephalinase inhibitor: treatment of diarrhoea

● **Racementhol** (rINN) ra·së·*men*·thol

(1*RS*,2*SR*,5*RS*)-2-Isopropyl-5-methylcyclohexanol; $C_{10}H_{20}O$; *15356-70-4*

Racemic menthol; relief of the symptoms of upper respiratory tract diseases; relief of itching

Racemethorphan (rINN) see Appendix C

Racemoramide (rINN) ra·së·*mo*·ra·mïd

(*RS*)-1-(3-Methyl-4-morpholino-2,2-diphenylbutyryl)¬pyrrolidine; $C_{25}H_{32}N_2O_2$; *545-59-5*

Opioid receptor agonist

Racemorphan (rINN) ra·së·*mor*·fan

(±)-17-Methylmorphinan-3-ol; $C_{17}H_{23}NO$; *297-90-5*

Opioid receptor agonist

Racephedrine (rINN) ra·*se*·fe·drën

(1*RS*,2*SR*)-2-Methylamino-1-phenylpropan-1-ol; $C_{10}H_{15}NO$; *90-81-3*

● **Racephedrine Hydrochloride** *134-71-4*

Adrenoceptor agonist

The symbol '¬' in systematic chemical names signifies line continuation

Raclopride (rINN) *ra*·klö·prïd
(*S*)-3,5-Dichloro-*N*-(1-ethylpyrrolidin-2-ylmethyl)-6-
methoxysalicylamide; $C_{15}H_{20}Cl_2N_2O_3$; *84225-95-6*
Raclopride Tartrate *98185-20-7*
Dopamine D_2 receptor antagonist; neuroleptic

♣ **Rafoxanide** (rINN) ra·*foks*·a·nïd
3′-Chloro-4′-(4-chlorophenoxy)-3,5-di-iodosalicylanilide;
$C_{19}H_{11}Cl_2I_2NO_3$; *22662-39-1*
Antihelminthic (veterinary)

Raloxifene (rINN) ra·*loks*·i·fën
[6-Hydroxy-2-(4-hydroxyphenyl)benzo[*b*]thien-3-yl][4-(2-
piperidinoethoxy)phenyl]methanone; $C_{28}H_{27}NO_4S$; *84449-90-1*
● **Raloxifene Hydrochloride** *82640-04-8*
Selective oestrogen receptor modulator

Raltegravir (rINN) rál·të·*gra*·vïr
N-[(4-Fluorophenyl)methyl]-5-hydroxy-1-methyl-2-[2-(5-
methyl-1,3,4-oxadiazole-2-carboxamido)propan-2-yl]-6-oxo-
1,6-dihydropyrimidine-4-carboxamide; $C_{20}H_{21}FN_6O_5$;
518048-05-0
Raltegravir Potassium *871038-72-1*
Antiviral (HIV)

Raltitrexed (rINN) ral·ti·*treks*·ed
N-{5-[3,4-Dihydro-2-methyl-4-oxoquinazolin-6-ylmethyl¬
(methyl)amino]-2-thenoyl}-L-glutamic acid; $C_{21}H_{22}N_4O_6S$;
112887-68-0
Thymidylate synthetase inhibitor; cytostatic

Ramatroban (rINN) ra·*ma*·trö·ban
(*R*)-3-[3-(4-Fluorophenylsulfonylamino)-1,2,3,4-tetra¬
hydrocarbazol-9-yl]propionic acid; $C_{21}H_{21}FN_2O_4S$;
116649-85-5
*Thromboxane (A_2) receptor antagonist; antagonist at
chemoattractant receptor - homologous molecule expressed
at TH_2 cells ($CRTH_2$); anticoagulant*

Ramelteon (rINN) ram·*el*·të·on
N-{2-[(8*S*)-1,6,7,8-Tetrahydro-2*H*-indeno[5,4-*b*]furan-8-
yl]ethyl}propanamide; $C_{16}H_{21}NO_2$; *196597-26-9*
Melatonin receptor agonist; hypnotic

● **Ramipril** (rINN) *ra*·mi·pril
(1) (2*S*,3a*S*,6a*S*)-1-{*N*-[(*S*)-1-ethoxycarbonyl-3-phenylpropyl]-L-
alanyl}perhydrocyclopenta[*b*]pyrrole-2-carboxylic acid;
(2) (1*S*,3*S*,5*S*)-2-{*N*-[(*S*)-1-ethoxycarbonyl-3-phenylpropyl]-
L-alanyl}-2-azabicyclo[3.3.0]octane-3-carboxylic acid;
$C_{23}H_{32}N_2O_5$; *87333-19-5*
Angiotensin converting enzyme inhibitor

Ranibizumab (rINN) ra·ni·*bi*·zü·mab
Immunoglobulin g1, anti-(human vascular endothelial growth
factor) Fab fragment (human-mouse monoclonal rhuFAB V2
g1 chain), disulfide with human-mouse monoclonal rhuFAB V2
k-chain; *347396-82-1*
Monoclonal antibody (VEGF)

ranibizumab has the following amino acid sequence:

```
DIQLTQSPSS    LSASVGDRVT    ITCSASQDIS
NYLNWYQQKP    GKAPKVLIYF    TSSLHSGVPS
RFSGSGSGTD    FTLTISSLQP    EDFATYYCQQ
YSTVPWTFGQ    GTKVEIKRTV    AAPSVFIFPP
SDEQLKSGTA    SVVCLLNNFY    PREAKVQWKV
DNALQSGNSQ    ESVTEQDSKD    STYSLSSTLT
LSKADYEKHK    VYACEVTHQG    LSSPVTKSFN
RGEC

EVQLVESGGG    LVQPGGSLRL    SCAASGYDFT
HYGMNWVRQA    PGKGLEWVGW    INTYTGEPTY
AADFKRRFTF    SLDTSKSTAY    LQMNSLRAED
TAVYYCAKYP    YYYGTSHWYF    DVWGQDTLVT
VSSASTKGPS    VFPLAPSSKS    TSGGTAALGC
LVKDYFPEPV    TVSWNSGALT    SGVHTFPAVL
QSSGLYSLSS    VVTVPSSSLG    TQTYICNVNH
KPSNTKVDKK    VEPKSCDKTH    L
```

Ranitidine (rINN) ra·*ni*·ti·dën

Dimethyl{5-[2-(1-methylamino-2-nitrovinylamino)¬
ethylthiomethyl]-furfuryl}amine; $C_{13}H_{22}N_4O_3S$; *66357-35-5*

● Ranitidine Hydrochloride

Histamine H_2 receptor antagonist; treatment of peptic ulcer disease

Ranitidine Bismuth Citrate (BAN)

Bismuth(III) citrate—(*E*)-*N*-{2-[5-(dimethylaminomethyl)¬
furfurylthio]ethyl}-*N*′-methyl-2-nitrovinylidenediamine
(ranitidine); ranitidine bismutrex; $C_{13}H_{22}N_4O_3S \cdot Bi \cdot C_6H_5O_7$;
128345-62-0

Histamine H_2 receptor antagonist; treatment of peptic ulcer disease

Ranolazine (rINN) ran·*öl*·á·zën

N-(2,6-Dimethylphenyl)2-{4-[(2*RS*)-2-hydroxy-3-
(2-methoxyphenoxy)propyl]piperazin-1-yl}acetamide;
$C_{24}H_{33}N_3O_4$; *95635-55-5*;
Inhibitor of late sodium currents; treatment of angina pectoris

and enantiomer

Rapacuronium Bromide (rINN) ra·pa·kûr·*rö*·në·um

1-(3α-Acetoxy-2β-piperidino-17β-propionyloxy-5α-
androstan-16β-yl)-1-allylpiperidinium bromide; $C_{37}H_{61}BrN_2O_4$;
156137-99-4
Non-depolarizing neuromuscular blocker

Rasburicase (rINN) ras·*bûr*·ri·käs

A recombinant urate oxidase obtained from *Aspergillus flavus*,
expressed in yeast strain *Saccharomyces cerevisiae*;
139774-45-1
*Enzyme (recombinant urate oxidase); treatment and prophylaxis
of hyperuricaemia*

rasburicase has the following amino acid sequence:

```
Ac
|
SAVKAARYGK    DNVRVYKVHK    DEKTGVQTVY
EMTVCVLLEG    EIETSYTKAD    NSVIVATDSI
KNTIYITAKQ    NPVTPPELFG    SILGTHFIEK
YNHIHAAHVN    IVCHRWTRMD    IDGKPHPHSF
IRDSEEKRNV    QVDVVEGKGI    DIKSSLSGLT
VLKSTNSQFW    GFLRDEYTTL    KETWDRILST
DVDATWQWKN    FSGLQEVRSH    VPKFDATWAT
AREVTLKTFA    EDNSASCQAT    MYKMAEQILA
RQQLIETVEY    SLPNKHYFEI    DLSWHKGLQN
TGKNAEVFAP    QSDPNGLIKC    TVGRSSLKSK
L
```

Razoxane (rINN) see Appendix C

Reboxetine (rINN) re·*boks*·e·tën

(±)-(2*RS*)-2-[(α*RS*)-α-(2-Ethoxyphenoxy)benzyl]morpholine;
$C_{19}H_{23}NO_3$; *71620-89-8*

Reboxetine Mesilate *98769-84-7*

Noradrenaline reuptake inhibitor; antidepressant

and enantiomer

The symbol '¬' in systematic chemical names signifies line continuation

Recainam (rINN) *re·kä·nam*

1-[3-(Isopropylamino)propyl]-3-(2,6-xylyl)urea; $C_{15}H_{25}N_3O$; *74738-24-2*

Recainam Hydrochloride *74752-07-1*

Recainam Tosilate *74752-08-2*

Class I antiarrhythmic

Regadenoson (rINN) *re·gá·de·nö·son*

1-[6-Amino-9-(b-D-ribofuranosyl)-9*H*-purin-2-yl]-*N*-methyl-1*H*-pyrazole-4-carboxamide; $C_{15}H_{18}N_8O_5$; *313348-27-5*

Adenosine A_{2A} receptor agonist

Remifentanil (rINN) *re·mi·fen·ta·nil*

Methyl 1-(2-methoxycarbonylethyl)-4-(*N*-phenylpropion¬amido)piperidine-4-carboxylate; $C_{20}H_{28}N_2O_5$; *132875-61-7*

Remifentanil Hydrochloride *132539-07-2*

Opioid receptor agonist; analgesic

Remoxipride (rINN) see Appendix C

Renzapride (rINN) *ren·za·prïd*

(±)-*endo*-4-Amino-*N*-(1-azabicyclo[3.3.1]non-4-yl)-5-chloro-*o*-anisamide; $C_{16}H_{22}ClN_3O_2$; *11727-80-7*;

Renzapride Hydrochloride *88721-77-1*

Enterokinetic

and enantiomer

• **Repaglinide** (rINN) *re·pa·gli·nïde*

(*S*)-2-Ethoxy-4-{[1-(*o*-piperidinophenyl)-3-methylbutyl]¬carbamoylmethyl}benzoic acid; $C_{27}H_{36}N_2O_4$; *135062-92-1*

Stimulates insulin release; treatment of diabetes mellitus

Reproterol (rINN) *re·prö·te·rol*

7-[3-(β,3,5-Trihydroxyphenethylamino)propyl]theophylline; $C_{18}H_{23}N_5O_5$; *54063-54-6*

Reproterol Hydrochloride *13055-82-8*

Beta$_2$-adrenoceptor agonist; bronchodilator

and enantiomer

Rescinnamine (rINN) *re·si·na·mën*

Methyl-*O*-(3,4,5-trimethoxycinnamoyl)reserpate; $C_{35}H_{42}N_2O_9$; *24815-24-5*

Rauwolfia alkaloid; treatment of hypertension

• **Reserpine** (rINN) *re·ser·pën*

An alkaloid obtained from *Rauwolfia serpentina* Benth; (1) methyl 11,17α-dimethoxy-18β-(3,4,5-trimethoxybenzoyloxy)-3β,20α-yohimbane-16β-carboxylate; (2) Methyl *O*-(3,4,5-trimethoxybenzoyl)reserpate; $C_{33}H_{40}N_2O_9$; *50-55-5*

Rauwolfia alkaloid; treatment of hypertension

Retapamulin (rINN) *re·ta·pa·mü·lin*

(3a*S*,4*R*,5*S*,6*S*,8*R*,9*R*,9a*R*,10*R*)-6-Ethenyl-5-hydroxy-4,6,9,10-tetramethyl-1-oxodecahydro-3a,9-propanocyclopenta[8]annulen-8-yl{[(1*R*,3*s*,5*S*)-8-methyl-8-azabicyclo[3.2.1]octan-3-yl]sulfanyl}acetate; $C_{30}H_{47}NO_4S$; *224452-66-8*;

Antibacterials

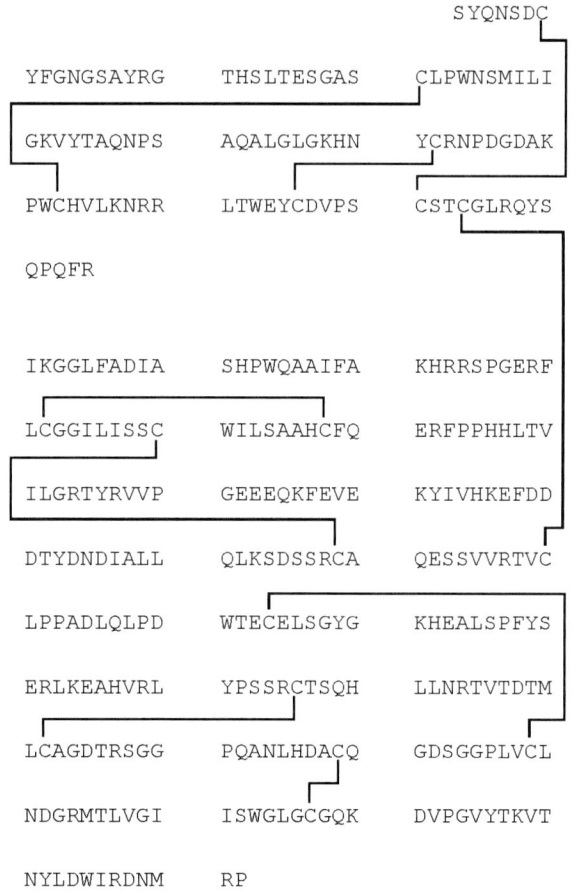

Reteplase (rINN) *re·te·pläz*
173-L-Serine-174-L-tyrosine-175-L-glutamine-173-
527-plasminogen activator (human tissue-type);
133652-38-7
Tissue-type plasminogen activator; fibrinolytic

reteplase has the following amino acid sequence (cf alteplase):

```
                              SYQNSDC

YFGNGSAYRG    THSLTESGAS    CLPWNSMILI

GKVYTAQNPS    AQALGLGKHN    YCRNPDGDAK

PWCHVLKNRR    LTWEYCDVPS    CSTCGLRQYS

QPQFR


IKGGLFADIA    SHPWQAAIFA    KHRRSPGERF

LCGGILISSC    WILSAAHCFQ    ERFPPHHLTV

ILGRTYRVVP    GEEEQKFEVE    KYIVHKEFDD

DTYDNDIALL    QLKSDSSRCA    QESSVVRTVC

LPPADLQLPD    WTECELSGYG    KHEALSPFYS

ERLKEAHVRL    YPSSRCTSQH    LLNRTVTDTM

LCAGDTRSGG    PQANLHDACQ    GDSGGPLVCL

NDGRMTLVGI    ISWGLGCGQK    DVPGVYTKVT

NYLDWIRDNM    RP
```

●**Retinol** (rINN) *re·ti·nol*
(1) 15-Apo-β-caroten-15-ol; (2) *all-trans*-3,7-dimethyl-9-
(2,6,6-trimethylcyclohex-1-enyl)nona-2,4,6,8-tetraen-1-ol;
vitamin A alcohol; $C_{20}H_{30}O$; *68-26-8*
Vitamin A

Revatropate (rINN) *re·va·trö·pät*
(*R*)-3-Quinuclidinyl (2*S*)-2-hydroxymethyl-4-(*R*)-methyl¬
sulfinyl-2-phenylbutyrate; $C_{19}H_{27}NO_4S$; *149926-91-0*
Revatropate Hydrobromide
Anticholinergic

Reviparin Sodium (rINN) *re·vi·pa·rin sö·dë·um*
Sodium salt of a low molecular weight heparin that is obtained
by nitrous acid depolymerisation of heparin from porcine
intestinal mucosa; the majority of the components have a
2-*O*-sulfo-α-L-idopyranosuronic acid structure at the
non-reducingend and a 6-*O*-sulfo-2,5-anhydro-D-mannitol
structure at the reducing end of their chain; the weight-average
molecular weight ranges between 3150 and 5150, with a
characteristic value of about 4250; the degree of sulfation is
about 2.1 per disaccharide unit
Low molecular weight heparin

Revospirone (rINN) *re·vö·spï·rön*
2-{3-[4-(Pyrimidin-2-yl)piperazin-1-yl]propyl}-1,2-
benzothiazol-3(2*H*)-one 1,1-dioxide; $C_{18}H_{21}N_5O_3S$; *95847-87-3*
Hypnotic (veterinary)

●**Ribavirin** (rINN) *rï·ba·vîr·rin*
1-β-D-Ribofuranosyl-1*H*-1,2,4-triazole-3-carboxamide;
$C_8H_{12}N_4O_5$; *36791-04-5*
Antiviral (hepatitis C, respiratory syncytial virus)

●**Riboflavin** (rINN) *rï·bö·flä·vin*
7,8-Dimethyl-10-(1'-D-ribityl)isoalloxazine; $C_{17}H_{20}N_4O_6$;
83-88-5; component in many proprietary preparations
●**Riboflavin Sodium Phosphate** *130-40-5*
Vitamin B₂

The symbol '¬' in systematic chemical names signifies line continuation

Ribostamycin (rINN) see Appendix C

Ricasetron (rINN) ri·*ka*·se·tron
2,3-Dihydro-3,3-dimethyl-*N*-[(3*r*)-8-methyl-8-azabicyclo¬
[3.2.1]octan-3-yl]indole-1-carboxamide; C$_{19}$H$_{27}$N$_3$O;
117086-68-7
Ricasetron Hydrochloride *140865-88-9*
Serotonin 5HT$_3$ receptor antagonist

Ridogrel (rINN) *ri*·dö·grel
(*E*)-5-[α-(3-Pyridyl)-3-trifluoromethylbenzylideneamino¬
oxy]pentanoic acid; C$_{18}$H$_{17}$F$_3$N$_2$O$_3$; *110140-89-1*
Thromboxane synthetase inhibitor

● **Rifabutin** (rINN) ri·fa·*bü*·tin
(12*E*,22*E*,24*Z*)(9*S*,14*S*,15*R*,16*S*,17*R*,18*R*,19*R*,20*S*,21*S*)-3,5,9,10-
Tetrahydro-6,18,20-trihydroxy-1′-isobutyl-14-methoxy-
7,9,15,17,19,21,25-heptamethyl-5,10,26-trioxospiro[9,4-
(epoxypentadeca[1,11,13]trienimino)-2*H*-furo[2′,3′:7,8]-
naphtho[1,2-*d*]imidazole-2,4′-piperidin]-16-yl acetate;
C$_{46}$H$_{62}$N$_4$O$_{11}$; *72559-06-9*
Rifamycin antituberculosis drug

Rifamide (rINN) *ri*·fa·mïd
Rifamycin B *N,N*-diethylamide; C$_{43}$H$_{58}$N$_2$O$_{13}$; *2750-76-7*
Rifamycin antituberculosis drug

● **Rifampicin** (rINN) ri·*fam*·pi·sin
(1) (12*Z*,14*E*,24*E*)-(2*S*,16*S*,17*S*,18*R*,19*R*,20*R*,21*S*,22*R*,23*S*)-1,2-
Dihydro-5,6,9,17,19-pentahydroxy-23-methoxy-2,4,12,16,¬
18,20,22-heptamethyl-8-(4-methylpiperazin-1-yliminomethyl)-
1,11-dioxo-2,7-(epoxypentadeca-1,11,13-trienoimino)naphtho¬
[2,1-*b*]furan-21-yl acetate; (2) 3-(4-methylpiperazin-1-
yliminomethyl)rifamycin SV; rifampin (USAN); C$_{43}$H$_{58}$N$_4$O$_{12}$;
13292-46-1
Rifamycin antituberculosis drug

Rifamycin (rINN) ri·fa·*mï*·sin
An ansamycin antibiotic produced by certain strains of
Streptomyces mediterranei; (12*Z*,14*E*,24*E*)-(2*S*,16*S*,17*S*,¬
18*R*,19*R*,20*R*,21*S*,22*R*,23*S*)-1,2-Dihydro-5,6,9,17,19-
pentahydroxy-23-methoxy-2,4,12,16,18,20,22-heptamethyl-
1,11-dioxo-2,7-(epoxypentadeca-1,11,13-trienoimino)-
naphtho[2,1-*b*]furan-21-yl acetate; rifamycin SV; C$_{37}$H$_{47}$NO$_{12}$;
6998-60-3
● **Rifamycin Sodium** *14897-39-3*
Rifamycin antituberculosis drug

Rifapentine (rINN) ri·fa·*pen*·tën

(4Z,6E,16E)-(8S,9S,10R,11R,12R,13S,14R,15S,19S)-26-[N-(4-Cyclopentylpiperazin-1-yl)formimidoyl]-9,11,23,25,27-pentahydroxy-15-methoxy-4,8,10,12,14,19,22-heptamethyl-3,30-dioxo-18,20-dioxa-2 azatetracyclo [17.6.5.0²¹,²⁹·0²⁴,²⁸]¬ triaconta-1(25),4,6,16,21(29),22, 24(28),26-octaen-13-yl acetate; $C_{47}H_{64}N_4O_{12}$; *61379-65-5*
Rifamycin antituberculosis drug

● **Rifaximin** (rINN) ri·*fak*·sim·min

(2S,16Z,18E,20S,21S,22R,23R,24R,25S,26R,27S,28E)-25-Acetyloxy-5,6,21,23-tetrahydroxy-27-methoxy-2,4,11,16,20,22,24,26-octamethyl-2,7-(epoxypentadeca[1,11,13]trienimino)furo[2″,3″:7′,8′]¬ naptho[1′,2′:4,5]imidazo[1,2-a]pyridine-1,15(2H)-dione; $C_{43}H_{51}N_3O_{11}$; *80621-81-4*;
Antibacterial; treatment of infective diarrhoea

Riluzole (rINN) ri·lü·zôl

6-Trifluoromethoxy-1,3-benzothiazol-2-ylamine; $C_8H_5F_3N_2OS$; *1744-22-5*
Glutamate receptor antagonist; treatment of amyotrophic lateral sclerosis

Rimantadine (rINN) ri·*man*·ta·dën

(RS)-1-(Adamantan-1-yl)ethylamine; $C_{12}H_{21}N$; *13392-28-4*
Rimantadine Hydrochloride *1501-84-4*
Viral replication inhibitor (influenza A)

and enantiomer

Rimexolone (rINN) ri·*meks*·o·lön

11β-Hydroxy-16α,17α-dimethyl-17β-propionylandrosta-1,4-dien-3-one; $C_{24}H_{34}O_3$; *49697-38-3*
Glucocorticoid

Rimiterol (rINN) see Appendix C

Rioprostil (rINN) rï·ö·*pros*·til

(E)-(2R,3R,4R)-4-Hydroxy-2-(7-hydroxyheptyl)-3-(4-hydroxy-4-methyloct-1-enyl)cyclopentanone; $C_{21}H_{38}O_4$; *77287-05-9*
Prostaglandin (PGE₁) analogue

Risedronic Acid (rINN) rï·se·*dro*·nik

1-Hydroxy-2-(3-pyridyl)ethane-1,1-diylbis(phosphonic acid); $C_7H_{11}NO_7P_2$; *105462-24-6*
Risedronate Sodium (monosodium) *115436-72-1*
Bisphosphonate; treatment of osteoporosis, Paget's disease

● **Risperidone** (rINN) ris·*per*·ri·dön

3-{2-[4-(6-Fluoro-1,2-benzoxazol-3-yl)piperidino]ethyl}-6,7,8,9-tetrahydro-2-methylpyrido[1,2-a]pyrimidin-4-one; $C_{23}H_{27}FN_4O_2$; *106266-06-2*
Dopamine D₂ receptor antagonist; serotonin 5HT₂ receptor antagonist; neuroleptic

Ristianol (rINN) ris·*tï*·a·nol

2-(4-Pyridylmethylthio)ethanol; $C_8H_{11}NOS$; *78092-65-6*
Ristianol Phosphate *78092-66-7*
Immunomodulator

The symbol '¬' in systematic chemical names signifies line continuation

Ristocetin (rINN) ris·tö·*së*·tin
　Antimicrobial glycopeptides produced by *Nocardia lurida*;
　1404-55-3
　Antibacterial

Ritanserin (rINN) ri·*tan*·ser·rin
　6-{2-[4-(4,4′-Difluorobenzhydrylidene)piperidino]ethyl}-7-
　methyl-[1,3]thiazolo[3,2-*a*]pyrimidin-5-one; $C_{27}H_{25}F_2N_3OS$;
　87051-43-2
　Serotonin 5HT$_2$ receptor antagonist

Ritodrine (rINN) *ri*·tö·drën
　(±)-*erythro*-1-(4-Hydroxyphenyl)-2-(4-hydroxyphenethyl¬
　amino)propan-1-ol; $C_{17}H_{21}NO_3$; *26652-09-5*
　● **Ritodrine Hydrochloride** *23239-51-2*
　Beta$_2$-adrenoceptor agonist; bronchodilator

and enantiomer

● **Ritonavir** (rINN) ri·*to*·na·veer
　N^1-[(1*S*,3*S*,4*S*)-1-Benzyl-3-hydroxy-5-phenyl-4-(1,3-thiazol-5-
　ylmethoxycarbonylamino)pentyl]-N^2-{[(2-isopropyl-1,3-thiazol-
　4-yl)methyl](methyl)carbamoyl}-L-valinamide; $C_{37}H_{48}N_6O_5S_2$;
　155213-67-5
　Protease inhibitor; antiviral (HIV)

Rituximab (rINN) ri·*tuks*·i·mab
　Immunoglobulin G1, human/mouse monoclonal antibody
　IDEC-C2B8 directed against the human antigen CD20
　consisting of murine variable domains with human κ light
　chains and γ1 heavy chains; anti-CD20 mab
　Monoclonal antibody (CD20 receptors on tumour cells)

Rivaroxaban (rINN) ri·*va*·roks·á·ban
　5-Chloro-*N*-({(5*S*)-2-oxo-3-[4-(3-oxomorpholin-4-yl)phenyl]-
　1,3-oxazolidin-5-yl}methyl)thiophene-2-carboxamide;
　$C_{19}H_{18}ClN_3O_5S$; *366789-02-8*
　Factor Xa inhibitor; anticoagulant

Rivastigmine (rINN) ri·va·*stig*·mën
　3-[(*S*)-1-(Dimethylamino)ethyl]phenyl ethyl(methyl)carbamate;
　$C_{14}H_{22}N_2O_2$; *123441-03-2*
　Cholinesterase inhibitor; treatment of Alzheimer's disease

Rizatriptan (rINN) ri·za·*trip*·tan
　Dimethyl{2-[5-(1*H*-1,2,4-triazol-1-ylmethyl)indol-3-yl]¬
　ethyl}amine; $C_{15}H_{19}N_5$; *144034-80-0*
　Rizatriptan Benzoate *145202-66-0*
　Serotonin 5HT$_1$ receptor agonist; treatment of migraine

Robalzotan (rINN) rö·*bal*·zö·tan
　(*R*)-3-(Dicyclobutylamino)-8-fluoro-5-chromancarboxamide;
　$C_{18}H_{23}FN_2O_2$; *169758-66-1*
　Serotonin 5HT$_{1A}$ receptor antagonist

Robenidine (rINN) rö·*be*·ni·dën
　1,3-Bis(4-chlorobenzylideneamino)guanidine; $C_{15}H_{13}Cl_2N_5$;
　25875-51-8
　Antiprotozoal (veterinary)

● **Rocuronium Bromide** (rINN) ro·k ûr·*rö*·në·um
　1-(17β-Acetoxy-3α-hydroxy-2β-morpholino-5α-androstan-
　16β-yl)-1-allylpyrrolidinium bromide; $C_{32}H_{53}BrN_2O_4$;
　119302-91-9
　Non-depolarizing neuromuscular blocker

Rofecoxib (rINN) rö·fë·*koks*·ib
4-(4-Mesylphenyl)-3-phenylfuran-2(5*H*)-one; $C_{17}H_{14}O_4S$; *162011-90-7*
Cyclo-oxygenase (COX-2) inhibitor; analgesic; anti-inflammatory

Rogletimide (rINN) rö·*gle*·ti·mïd
(*RS*)-2-Ethyl-2-(4-pyridyl)glutarimide; $C_{12}H_{14}N_2O_2$; *121840-95-7*
Aromatase inhibitor; treatment of breast cancer

and enantiomer

Rolgamidine (rINN) see Appendix C

Rolicyprine (rINN) see Appendix C

Rolitetracycline (rINN) rö·li·te·tra·*si*·klën
N^2-(Pyrrolidin-1-ylmethyl)tetracycline; $C_{27}H_{33}N_3O_8$; *751-97-3*
Rolitetracycline Nitrate *7681-32-5*
Tetracycline antibacterial

Rolziracetam (rINN) rol·zi·*ra*·se·tam
Perhydropyrrolizine-3,5-dione; $C_7H_9NO_2$; *18356-28-0*
Nootropic

Romazarit (rINN) ro·*ma*·za·rit
2-(2-*p*-Chlorophenyl-4-methyl-1,3-oxazol-5-ylmethoxy)-2-methylpropionic acid; $C_{15}H_{16}ClNO_4$; *109543-76-2*
Romazarit Sodium *109544-09-4*
Anti-inflammatory

Romifidine (rINN) ro·*mi*·fi·dën
2-Bromo-6-fluoro-*N*-(1-imidazolin-2-yl)aniline; $C_9H_9BrFN_3$; *65896-16-4*
Romifidine Hydrochloride *65896-14-2*
Alpha₂-adrenoceptor agonist

Romiplostim (rINN) *rom*·ë·*plos*·tim
L-Methionyl[human immunogloblin heavy constant gamma 1-(227 *C*-terminal residues)-peptide (Fc fragment)] fusion protein with 41 amino acids peptide, (7-7′:10,10′)-bisdisulfide dimer;
267639-76-9;
Fusion protein analogue of thrombopoietin; treatment of idiopathic thrombocytopenic purpura

romiplostim has the following amino acid sequence:

```
MDKTHTCPPC   PAPELLGGPS   VFLFPPKPKD
TLMISRTPEV   TCVVVDVSHE   DPEVKFNWYV
DGVEVHNAKT   KPREEQYNST   YRVVSVLTVL
HQDWLNGKEY   KCKVSNKALP   APIEKTISKA
KGQPREPQVY   TLPPSRDELT   KNQVSLTCLV
KGFYPSDIAV   EWESNGQPEN   NYKTTPPVLD
SDGSFFLYSK   LTVDKSRWQQ   GNVFSCSVMH
EALHNHYTQK   SLSLSPGKGG   GGGIEGPTLR
QWLAARAGGG   GGGGGIEGPT   LRQWLAARA
```

disulfide bridges at locations 7-7′, 10-10′, 42-102, 42′-102′, 148-206, 148′-206′

♣ **Ronidazole** (rINN) ro·*nïd*·a·zôl
(1-Methyl-5-nitroimidazol-2-yl)methyl carbamate;
$C_6H_8N_4O_4$; *7681-76-7*
Antiprotozoal

The symbol '¬' in systematic chemical names signifies line continuation

Ropinirole (rINN) rö·*pi*·ni·rôl
4-[2-(Dipropylamino)ethyl]indolin-2-one; $C_{16}H_{24}N_2O$;
91374-21-9
Ropinirole Hydrochloride *91374-20-8*
Dopamine receptor agonist

Ropivacaine (rINN) rö·*pi*·va·kän
(*S*)-2′,6′-Dimethyl-1-propylpiperidine-2-carboxanilide;
$C_{17}H_{26}N_2O$; *84057-95-4*
● **Ropivacaine Hydrochloride** *98717-15-8 (anhydrous)*,
132112-35-7 (monohydrate)
Local anaesthetic

Rosaramicin (rINN) rös·a·ra·*mï*·sin
(*E*)-3-Ethyl-10-(formylmethyl)-7-hydroxy-2,8,12,16-
tetramethyl-9-(3,4,6-trideoxy-3-dimethylamino-β-D-*xylo*-
hexopyranosyloxy)-4,17-dioxabicyclo[14.1.0]heptadec-14-
ene-5,13-dione; $C_{31}H_{51}NO_9$; *35834-26-5*
Macrolide antibacterial

Rosiglitazone (rINN) rö·si·*gli*·ta·zön
(*RS*)-5-(4-{2-[Methyl(2-pyridyl)amino]ethoxy}benzyl)-1,3-
thiazolidine-2,4-dione; $C_{18}H_{19}N_3O_3S$; *122320-73-4*
*Peroxisome proliferator-activated receptor (PPAR)-gamma
agonist; treatment of diabetes mellitus*

and enantiomer

Rosoxacin (rINN) see Appendix C

Rosuvastatin (rINN) ro·sü·va·*sta*·tin
(*E*)-(3*R*,5*S*)-7-{4-(4-Fluorophenyl)-6-isopropyl-2-[methyl¬
(methylsulfonyl)amino]pyrimidin-5-yl}-3,5-dihydroxyhept-6-
enoic acid; $C_{22}H_{28}FN_3O_6S$
Rosuvastatin Calcium *147098-20-2*
HMG Co-A reductase inhibitor; lipid-regulating drug

Rotigotine (rINN) rö·*ti*·gö·tën
(6*S*)-6-[Propyl[2-(thiophen-2-yl)ethyl]amino]-5,6,7,8-
tetrahydronaphthalen-1-ol; $C_{19}H_{25}NOS$; *99755-59-6*
*Dopamine D_2 receptor agonist; treatment of Parkinson's
disease and restless legs syndrome*

Roxarsone (rINN) roks·*ar*·sön
4-Hydroxy-3-nitrophenylarsonic acid; $C_6H_6AsNO_6$; *121-19-7*
Antiprotozoal

Roxatidine (rINN) roks·*a*·ti·dën
N-[3-(α-Piperidino-*m*-tolyloxy)propyl]glycolamide;
$C_{17}H_{26}N_2O_3$; *97900-88-4*
*Histamine H_2 receptor antagonist; treatment of peptic ulcer
disease*

Roxatidine Acetate (rINN) roks·*a*·ti·dën *a*·së·tät
3-(a-Piperidino-*m*-tolyloxy)propylcarbamoylmethyl acetate;
$C_{19}H_{28}N_2O_4$; *78628-28-1*
Roxatidine Acetate Hydrochloride *93793-83-0*
*Histamine H_2 receptor antagonist; treatment of peptic ulcer
disease*

Roxithromycin (rINN) roks·i·thrö·mï·sint
(3*R*,4*S*,5*S*,6*R*,7*R*,9*R*,11*S*,12*R*,13*S*,14*R*)-4-[(2,6-Dideoxy-3-*C*-methyl-3-*O*-methyl-α-L-ribo-hexopyranosyl)oxy]-14-ethyl-7,12,13-trihydroxy-10-[(*E*)-[(2-methoxyethoxy)methoxy]¬imino]-3,5,7,9,11,13-hexamethyl-6-[[3,4,6-trideoxy-3-(dimethylamino)-β-D-xylo-hexopyranosyl]oxy]¬oxacyclotetradecan-2-one (erythromycin 9-(*E*)-[*O*-[(2-methoxyethoxy)methyl]oxime]); C₄₁H₇₆N₂O₁₅; *80214-83-1*
Macrolide antibacterial

Rufinamide (rINN) rü·*fin*·a·mïd
1-(2,6-Difluorobenzyl)-1*H*-1,2,3-triazole-4-carboxamide; C₁₀H₈F₂N₄O; *106308-44-5*
Antiepileptic

Rufloxacin (rINN) roo·*floks*·a·sin
9-Fluoro-2,3-dihydro-10-(4-methylpiperazin-1-yl)-7-oxo-7*H*-pyrido[1,2,3-*de*]-1,4-benzothiazine-6-carboxylic acid; C₁₇H₁₈FN₃O₃S; *101363-10-4*
Fluoroquinolone antibacterial

Rufocromomycin (rINN) see Appendix C

Rutoside (rINN) *roo*·tö·sïd

2-(3,4-Dihydroxyphenyl)-5,7-dihydroxy-4-oxo-4*H*-chromen-3-yl 6-*O*-(α-L-rhamnosyl)-β-D-glucoside; rutin; C₂₇H₃₀O₁₆; *153-18-2-4*
Bioflavinoid

Sabcomeline (rINN) sab·*kö*·me·lën
(*Z*)-[(*R*)-Quinuclidin-3-yl](methoxyimino)acetonitrile; C₁₀H₁₅N₃O; *159912-53-5*
Sabcomeline Hydrochloride
Muscarinic M₁ receptor partial agonist; treatment of Alzheimer's disease

Sabeluzole (rINN) see Appendix C

Salazosulfadimidine (rINN) sa·lä·zö·sul·fa·*dï*·mi·dën
4′-(4,6-Dimethylpyrimidin-2-ylsulfamoyl)-4-hydroxyazo¬benzene-3-carboxylic acid; C₁₉H₁₇N₅O₅S; *2315-08-4*
Aminosalicylate

Salbutamol (rINN) sal·*bü*·ta·mol
1-(4-Hydroxy-3-hydroxymethylphenyl)-2-(*tert*-butylamino)¬ethanol; albuterol (USAN); C₁₃H₂₁NO₃; *18559-94-9*
Salbutamol Sulfate *51022-70-9*
Beta₂-adrenoceptor agonist; bronchodilator

and enantiomer

Salcatonin *see Calcitonin (Salmon)*

Salicylamide (rINN) sa·li·*sï*·la·mïd
2-Hydroxybenzamide; C₇H₇NO₂; *65-45-2*
Salicylate; non-selective cyclo-oxygenase inhibitor; antipyretic; analgesic; anti-inflammatory

---

The symbol '¬' in systematic chemical names signifies line continuation

Salinazid (rINN) see Appendix C

Salinomycin (rINN) sa·li·nö·*mi*·sin
(2*R*)-2-{(2*R*,5*S*,6*R*)-6-[(1*S*,2*S*,3*S*,5*R*)-5-{2*S*,5*S*,7*R*,¬
9*S*,10*S*,12*R*,15*R*)-2-[(2*R*,5*R*,6*S*)-5-Ethyltetrahydro-5-hydroxy-
6-methylpyran-2-yl]-15-hydroxy-2,10,12-trimethyl-1,6,8-
trioxadispiro[4.1.5.3]pentadec-13-en-9-yl}-2-hydroxy-1,3-
dimethyl-4-oxoheptyl]tetrahydro-5-methylpyran-2-yl}butyric
acid; C₄₂H₇₀O₁₁; *53003-10-4*
Antiprotozoal (veterinary)

Salmefamol (rINN) sal·*me*·fa·mol
1-(4-Hydroxy-3-hydroxymethylphenyl)-2-(4-methoxy-α-
methylphenethylamino)ethanol; C₁₉H₂₅NO₄; *18910-65-1*
Beta₂-adrenoceptor agonist; bronchodilator

mixture of stereoisomers

Salmeterol (rINN) sal·*me*·te·rol
(*RS*)-5-{1-Hydroxy-2-[6-(4-phenylbutoxy)hexylamino]¬
ethyl}salicyl alcohol; C₂₅H₃₇NO₄; *89365-50-4*
● **Salmeterol Xinafoate** *94749-08-3*
Beta₂-adrenoceptor agonist; bronchodilator

and enantiomer

Salsalate (rINN) see Appendix C

Sampatrilat (rINN) sam·*pa*·tri·lat
N-{1-[(*S*)-2-Carboxy-3-(*N²*-mesyl-L-lysylamino)propyl]¬
cyclopentylcarbonyl}-L-tyrosine; C₂₆H₄₀N₄O₉S;
129981-36-8
Vasopeptidase inhibitor; treatment of hypertension

Sanfetrinem (rINN) san·*fe*·tri·nem
(1*S*,5*S*,8a*S*,8b*R*)-1,2,5,6,7,8,8a,8b-Octahydro-1-[(*R*)-1-hydroxy¬
ethyl]-5-methoxy-2-oxoazeto[2,1-*a*]isoindole-4-carboxylate;
C₁₄H₁₉NO₅; *141611-76-9*
Sanfetrinem Cilexetil; *141646-08-4*
Sanfetrinem Sodium *141611-76-9*
Trinem antibacterial

Saperconazole (rINN) sa·per·*ko*·na·zôl
(±)-2-*sec*-Butyl-4-[4-(4-{4-[(2*RS*,4*SR*)-2-(2,4-difluorophenyl)-2-
(1*H*-1,2,4-triazol-1-ylmethyl)-1,3-dioxolan-4-ylmethoxy]¬
phenyl}piperazin-1-yl)-phenyl]-2,4-dihydro-1,2,4-triazol-3-one;
C₃₅H₃₈F₂N₈O₄; *110588-57-3*
Antifungal

mixture of 4 isomers

Saprisartan (rINN) sa·pri·*sar*·tan
1-{3-Bromo-2-[2-trifluoromethylsulfonylamino)phenyl]¬
benzo[*b*]furan-5-ylmethyl}-4-cyclopropyl-2-ethyl-1*H*-
imidazole-5-carboxamide; C₂₅H₂₁BrF₃N₄O₄S
Saprisartan Potassium *146623-69-0*
Angiotensin II (AT₁) receptor antagonist

Sapropterin (rINN) sa·*prop*·ter·in
(6*R*)-2-Amino-6-[(1*R*,2*S*)-1,2-dihydroxypropyl]-5,6,7,8-
tetrahydropteridin-4(3*H*)-one; C₉H₁₅N₅O₃; *62989-33-7*;
Sapropterin Dihydrochloride *69056-38-8*
Tetrahydrobiopterin analogue; treatment of phenylketonuria

Saquinavir (rINN) sa·*kwi*·na·veer

N^1-{(1S,2R)-1-Benzyl-3-[(3S,4aS,8aS)-3-(*tert*-butyl¬ carbamoyl)perhydroisoquinolin-2-yl]-2-hydroxypropyl}-N^2-(2-quinolylcarbonyl)-L-aspartamide; $C_{38}H_{50}N_6O_5$; *127779-20-8*

●**Saquinavir Mesilate** *149845-06-7*
Protease inhibitor; antiviral (HIV)

Sarafloxacin (rINN) sa·ra·*floks*·a·sin

6-Fluoro-1-(4-fluorophenyl)-1,4-dihydro-4-oxo-7-piperazin-1-ylquinoline-3-carboxylic acid; $C_{20}H_{17}F_2N_3O_3$; *98105-99-8*
Sarafloxacin Hydrochloride *91296-87-6*
Fluoroquinolone antibacterial

Saralasin (rINN) sa·ra·*lä*·sin

[1-(N-Methylglycine),5-valine,8-alanine]angiotensin; $C_{42}H_{65}N_{13}O_{10}$; *34273-10-4*
Saralasin Acetate *39698-78-7*
Angiotensin converting enzyme inhibitor

```
Sar-Arg-Val-Tyr-Val-His-Pro-Ala
```

Sargramostim (rINN) sar·gra·*mos*·tim

Recombinant granulocyte macrophage colony stimulating factor; a glycosylated recombinant analogue expressed by *Saccharomyces cerevisiae*; GM-CSF; *83869-56-1*
Recombinant human granulocyte macrophage colony-stimulating factor

For labelling purposes the following three-letter code, to indicate the method of production, is approved:
(rys) produced by fermentation using *Saccharomyces cerevisiae* containing a recombinant plasmid

sargramostim has the following amino acid sequence:

```
APARSPSPST   QPWEHVNAIQ   EALRLLNLSR
DTAAEMNETV   EVISEMFDLQ   EPTCLQTRLE
LYKQGLRGSL   TKLKGPLTMM   ASHYKQHCPP
TPETSCATQI   ITFESFKENL   KDFLLVIPFD
CWEPVQE
```

Saruplase (rINN) *sa*·roo·pläs

Prourokinase (enzyme-activating) (human clone pA3/pD2/pF1 protein moiety), non-glycosylated; *99149-95-8*
Urokinase-type plasminogen activator; thrombolytic

saruplase has the following amino acid sequence (Cys—Cys bridging not shown):

```
SNELHQVPSN   CDCLNGGTCV   SNKYFSNIHW
CNCPKKFGGQ   HCEIDKSKTC   YEGNGHFYRG
KASTDTMGRP   CLPWNSATVL   QQTYHAHRSD
ALQLGLGKHN   YCRNPDNRRR   PWCYVQVGLK
PLVQECMVHD   CADGKKPSSP   PEELKFQCGQ
KTLRPRFKII   GGEFTTIENQ   PWFAAIYRRH
RGGSVTYVCG   GSLISPCWVI   SATHCFIDYP
KKEDYIVYLG   RSRLNSNTQG   EMKFEVENLI
LHKDYSADTL   AHHNDIALLK   IRSKEGRCAQ
PSRTIQTICL   PSMYNDPQFG   TSCEITGFGK
ENSTDYLYPE   QLKMTVVKLI   SHRECQQPHY
YGSEVTTKML   CAADPQWKTD   SCQGDSGGPL
VCSLQGRMTL   TGIVSWGRGC   ALKDKPGVYT
RVSHFLPWIR   SHTKEENGLA   L
```

Satumomab (rINN) sa·*tü*·mö·mab

Mouse IgG 1 cell monoclonal immunoglobulin
Indium[¹¹¹In] Satumomab Pendetide
Monoclonal antibody (colorectal and ovarian tumour-associated antigens)

Saxagliptin (rINN) saks·á·glip·tin

(1S,3S,5S)-2-{(2S)-2-Amino-2-(3-hydroxyadamantan-1-yl)acetyl}-2-azabicyclo[3.1.0]hexane-3-carbonitrile; $C_{18}H_{25}N_3O_2$; *361442-04-8*;
Saxagliptin Hydrochloride *709031-78-7*
Dipeptidylpeptidase-4 inhibitor; treatment of type 2 diabetes mellitus

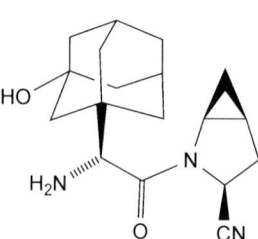

Secalciferol (rINN) se·kal·*si*·fe·rol

(1) (5Z,7E)-(3S,24R)-9,10-Secocholesta-5,7,10(19)-triene-3,24,25-triol; (2) (24R)-24,25-dihydroxycholecalciferol;
$C_{27}H_{44}O_3$; *55721-11-4*
Vitamin D analogue

The symbol '¬' in systematic chemical names signifies line continuation

Secbutabarbital (rINN) see Appendix C

Secnidazole (rINN) sek·*nï*·da·zôl
1-(2-Methyl-5-nitroimidazol-1-yl)propan-2-ol; $C_7H_{11}N_3O_3$;
3366-95-8
Antiprotozoal

and enantiomer

● **Secobarbital Sodium** (rINN) se·kö·*bar*·bi·tal
Sodium 5-allyl-5-(1-methylbutyl)barbiturate; $C_{12}H_{17}N_2NaO_3$;
309-43-3
Barbiturate

and enantiomer

Secretin (rINN) se·*krë*·tin
A polypeptide hormone, obtained from duodenal mucosa, that
activates pancreatic secretion and lowers the blood sugar level;
1393-25-5
Polypeptide hormone

Seganserin (rINN) se·*gan*·ser·rin
3-{2-[4-(4,4′-Difluorobenzhydrylidene)piperidino]ethyl}-2-
methylpyrido[1,2-*a*]pyrimidin-4-one; $C_{29}H_{27}F_2N_3O$;
87729-89-3
Seganserin Hydrochloride *97939-66-1*
Serotonin 5HT$_2$ receptor antagonist

♣ **Selamectin** (rINN) se·lá·*mek*·tin
(2a*E*,2′*R*,4*E*,5′*S*,6*S*,6′*S*,7*S*,8*E*,11*R*,15*S*,17a*R*,20*Z*,20a*R*,20b*S*)-
6′-Cyclohexyl-7-[(2,6-dideoxy-3-*O*-methyl-α-L-
arabinohexopyranosyl)oxy]-20b-hydroxy-20-(hydroxyimino)-
5′,6,8,19-tetramethyl-3′,4′,5′,6,6′,7,10,11,14,15,17a,20,¬
20a,20b-tetradecahydro-2*H*,17*H*-spiro[11,15-methanofuro[4,3,2-
pq][2,6]benzodioxacyclooctadecine-13,2′-pyran]-17-one;
((5*Z*,25*S*)-25-cyclohexyl-4′-*O*-de(2,6-dideoxy-3-*O*-methyl-α-L-
arabino-hexopyranosyl)-5-demethoxy-25-de(1-methylpropyl)-
22,23-dihydro-5-(hydroxyimino)avermectin A1a); $C_{43}H_{63}NO_{11}$;
165108-07-6
Antihelminthic (veterinary)

Selegiline (rINN) se·*lej*·i·lën
(*R*)-Methyl(α-methylphenethyl)prop-2-ynylamine; $C_{13}H_{17}N$;
14611-51-9
● **Selegiline Hydrochloride** *14611-52-0*
*Monoamine oxidase type B inhibitor; treatment of Parkinson's
disease*

Semduramicin (rINN) sem·*dûr*·ra·*mï*·sin
(2*R*,3*S*,4*S*,5*R*,6*S*)-Tetrahydro-2,4-dihydroxy-6-{(*R*)-1-
[(2*S*,5*R*,7*S*,8*R*,9*S*)-9-hydroxy-2,8-dimethyl-2-{(2*S*,2′*R*,3′¬
S,5*R*,5′*R*)-octahydro-2-methyl-5′-[(2*S*,3*S*,5*R*,6*S*)-tetrahydro-6-
hydroxy-3,5,6-trimethyl-2*H*-pyran-2-yl]-3′-[(2*S*,5*S*,6*R*)-tetrahy-
dro-5-methoxy-6-methyl-2*H*-pyran-2-yloxy]-2,2′-bifuran-5-yl}-
1,6-dioxaspiro[4.5]dec-7-yl]ethyl}-5-methoxy-3-methyl-2*H*-
pyran-2-ylacetic acid; $C_{45}H_{76}O_{16}$; *113378-31-7*
Antiprotozoal (veterinary)

Semisodium Valproate (BAN) se·mi·sö·dë·um *val*·prö·ät
2-Propylvaleric acid—sodium 2-propylvalerate (1:1);
divalproex sodium (USAN); $C_{16}H_{31}NaO_4$; *76584-70-8*
Antiepileptic

Me $\diagdown$ Me

COOH

COONa

Me $\diagdown$ Me

Senlizumab (rINN) sen·*li*·zü·mab

Humanised monoclonal anti-TNF alpha antibody; a glycoprotein consisting of 2 identical light chains and 2 identical heavy chains; the heavy chain is normally glycosylated; *336128-48-4*

Monoclonal antibody (TNF alfa); treatment of Crohn's disease and rheumatoid arthritis

senlizumab has the following amino acid sequence:

Heavy chain sequence:

QVQLVQSGAE	VVKPGSSVKV	SCKASGYTFT
DYNVDWVKQA	PGQGLQWIGN	INPNNGGTIY
NQKFKGKGTL	TVDKSTSTAY	MELSSLTSED
TAVYYCARSA	FYNNYEYFDV	WGQGTTVTVS
SASTKGPSVF	PLAPCSRSTS	ESTAALGCLV
KDYFPEPVTV	SWNSGALTSG	VHTFPAVLQS
SGLYSLSSVV	TVPSSSLGTK	TYTCNVDHKP
SNTKVDKRVE	SKYGPPCPSC	PAPEFLGGPS
VFLFPPKPKD	TLMISRTPEV	TCVVVDVSQE
DPEVQFNWYV	DGVEVHNAKT	KPREEQFNST
YRVVSVLTVL	HQDWLNGKEY	KCKVSNKGLP
SSIEKTISKA	KGQPREPQVY	TLPPSQEEMT
KNQVSLTCLV	KGFYPSDIAV	EWESNGQPEN
NYKTTPPVLD	SDGSFFLYSR	LTVDKSRWQE
GNVFSCSVMH	EALHNHYTQK	SLSLSLGK

Light chain sequence:

DIMMTQSPST	LSASVGDRVT	ITCKSSQSLL
YSNNQKNYLA	WYQQKPGQAP	KLLISWASTR
ESGVPSRFIG	SGSGTEFTLT	ISSLQPDDVA
TYYCQQYYDY	PWTFGQGTKV	EIKRTVAAPS
VFIFPPSDEQ	LKSGTASVVC	LLNNFYPREA
KVQWKVDNAL	QSGNSQESVT	EQDSKDSTYS
LSSTLTLSKA	DYEKHKVYAC	EVTHQGLSSP
VTKSFNRGEC		

Seocalcitol (rINN) së·ö·*kal*·si·tol

(5Z,7E,22E,24E)-(1S,3R)-24a,26a,27a-Trihomo-9,10-secocholesta-5,7,10(19),22,24-pentaene-1,3,25-triol; $C_{30}H_{46}O_3$; *134404-52-7*

Vitamin D analogue

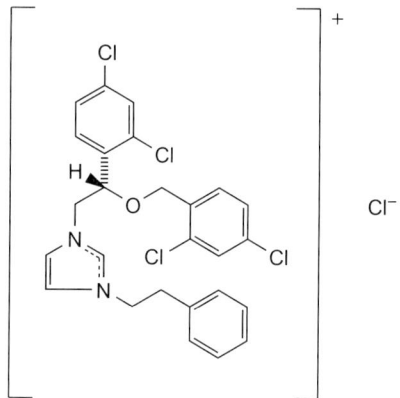

Sepazonium Chloride (rINN) se·pa·zö·*në*·um

(RS)-1-[2,4-Dichloro-β-(2,4-dichlorobenzyloxy)phenethyl]-3-phenethylimidazolium chloride; $C_{26}H_{23}Cl_5N_2O$; *54143-54-3*

Antiseptic

and enantiomer

Seractide (rINN) se·*rak*·tïd

[31-Serine]corticotrophin; *12279-41-3*

Corticotrophic peptide

seractide has the following amino acid sequence:

Ser-Tyr-Ser-Met-Glu-His-Phe-Arg-
Trp-Gly-Lys-Pro-Val-Gly-Lys-Lys-
Arg-Arg-Pro-Val-Lys-Val-Tyr-Pro-
Asp-Ala-Gly-Glu-Asp-Gln-Ser-Ala-
Glu-Ala-Phe-Pro-Leu-Glu-Phe

● **Serine** (rINN) *Se*·rën

L-Serine; (S)-2-Amino-3-hydroxypropanoic acid; $C_3H_7NO_3$; *56-45-1*;

Amino acid

The symbol '¬' in systematic chemical names signifies line continuation

Sermorelin (rINN) ser·mo·*rë*·lin
86168-78-7
Somatorelin (growth hormone releasing hormone) analogue sermorelin has the following amino acid sequence:

```
Tyr-Ala-Asp-Ala-Ile-Phe-Thr-Asn-

Ser-Tyr-Arg-Lys-Val-Leu-Gly-Gln-

Leu-Ser-Ala-Arg-Lys-Leu-Leu-Gln-

Asp-Ile-Met-Ser-Arg-NH₂
```

Sertaconazole (rINN) ser·ta·*kon*·a·zôl
(*RS*)-1-{2-[(7-Chloro-1-benzothien-3-yl)methoxy]-2-(2,4-dichlorophenyl)ethyl}imidazole; $C_{20}H_{15}Cl_3N_2OS$; *99592-32-2*
● **Sertaconazole Nitrate** *99592-39-9*
Antifungal

and enantiomer

Sertindole (rINN) *ser*·tin·dôl
1-(2-{4-[5-Chloro-1-(4-fluorophenyl)indol-3-yl]piperidino}ethyl)imidazolidin-2-one; $C_{24}H_{26}ClFN_4O$; *106516-24-9*
Dopamine D_2 receptor antagonist; serotonin $5HT_2$ receptor antagonist; neuroleptic

Sertraline (rINN) *ser*·tra·lën
(1*S*,4*S*)-4-(3,4-Dichlorophenyl)-1,2,3,4-tetrahydro-1-naphthyl(methyl)amine; $C_{17}H_{17}Cl_2N$; *79617-96-2*
● **Sertraline Hydrochloride** *79559-97-0*
Selective serotonin reuptake inhibitor; antidepressant

♣ **Serum Gonadotrophin** (rINN)
A preparation of a glycoprotein fraction obtained from the serum or plasma of the pregnant mare capable of stimulating the follicles in the mammalian ovary
Equine serum gonadotrophin (veterinary)

Setazindol (rINN) se·*ta*·zin·dol
4′-Chloro-2-[(methylamino)methyl]benzhydryl alcohol; $C_{15}H_{16}ClNO$; *56481-43-7*
Appetite suppressant

Sevelamer (rINN) se·*ve*·la·mer
Allylamine polymer with 2-chloroethyloxirane; $(C_3H_7N)_m·(C_3H_5ClO)_n$; *52757-95-6*
Sevelamer Hydrochloride *182683-00-7*
Phosphate binder; treatment of hyperphosphataemia

● **Sevoflurane** (rINN) se·vö·*flûr*·rän
1,1,1,3,3,3-Hexafluoro-2-fluoromethoxypropane; $C_4H_3F_7O$; *28523-86-6*
General anaesthetic

Sibenadet (rINN) sï·*ben*·a·det
4-Hydroxy-7-(2-{2-[3-(2-phenylethoxy)propylsulfonyl]¬ethyl}amino)ethyl-1,3-benzothiazol-2(3*H*)-one; $C_{22}H_{28}N_2O_5S_2$
Sibenadet Hydrochloride *154189-24-9*
Dopamine D_2 receptor agonist; beta₂-adrenoceptor agonist; treatment of chronic obstructive pulmonary disease

Sibrafiban (rINN) sï·*bra*·fi·ban
Ethyl (*Z*)-({*N*-[1-(*N*-hydroxycarbamimidoyl)benzoyl]-L-alanyl}-4-piperidyloxy)acetate; $C_{20}H_{28}N_4O_6$; *172927-65-0*
Glycoprotein IIb/IIIa receptor inhibitor; antiplatelet drug

Sibutramine (rINN) sï·*bü*·tra·mën

1-(1-*p*-Chlorophenylcyclobutyl)-3-methylbutyldimethylamine;
$C_{17}H_{26}ClN$; *106650-56-0*
Sibutramine Hydrochloride *84485-00-7*
*Inhibition of 5HT and noradrenaline reuptake;
appetite suppressant*

and enantiomer

Siguazodan (rINN) sï·*gwa*·zö·dan

(*RS*)-2-Cyano-1-methyl-3-[4-(4-methyl-6-oxo-1,4,5,6-tetra-
hydropyridazin-3-yl)phenyl]guanidine; $C_{14}H_{16}N_6O$;
115344-47-3; *99591-83-0*
Inhibitor of phosphodiesterase IV; positive inotrope

and enantiomer

Sildenafil (rINN) sil·*de*·na·fil

5-[2-Ethoxy-5-(4-methylpiperazin-1-ylsulfonyl)phenyl]-1,6-
dihydro-1-methyl-3-propylpyrazolo[4,3-*d*]pyrimidin-7-one;
$C_{22}H_{30}N_6O_4S$; *139755-83-2*
Sildenafil Citrate
*Selective inhibitor of cyclic GMP specific phosphodiesterase
(Type V) with vasodilator action; treatment of male erectile
dysfunction*

Silodosin (rINN) sï·*lö*·dö·sin

1-(3-Hydroxypropyl)-5-[(2*R*)-2-[[2-[2-(2,2,2-
trifluoroethoxy)phenoxy]ethyl]amino]propyl]-2,3-
dihydro-1*H*-indole-7-carboxamide; $C_{25}H_{32}F_3N_3O_4$;
361442-04-8;
*Alpha$_1$-adrenoceptor antagonist; treatment of benign prostatic
hyperplasia*

Simeticone (rINN) sï·*me*·ti·kön

α-(Trimethylsilyl)-ω-methylpoly[oxy(dimethylsilylene)],
mixture with silicon dioxide; *8050-81-5*
Silicon dioxide analogue; defoaming agent

Simvastatin (rINN) sim·va·*sta*·tin

(1*S*,3*R*,7*S*,8*S*,8a*R*)-1,2,3,7,8,8a-Hexahydro-3,7-dimethyl-8-{2-
[(2*R*,4*R*)-tetrahydro-4-hydroxy-6-oxo-2*H*-pyran-2-yl]ethyl}-1-
naphthyl 2,2-dimethylbutyrate; $C_{25}H_{38}O_5$; *79902-63-9*
HMG Co-A reductase inhibitor; lipid-regulating drug

Sincalide (rINN) *sin*·ka·lïd

De-1-(5-oxo-L-proline)-de-2-L-glutamine-5-
methionine-caerulein; $C_{49}H_{62}N_{10}O_{16}S_3$; *25126-32-3*
Cholecystokinin analogue

```
Asp-Tyr(SO3H)-Met-Gly-Trp-Met-Asp-Phe-NH2
```

Sipatrigine (rINN) si·*pa*·tri·jën

2-(4-methylpiperazin-1-yl)-5-(2,3,5-trichlorophenyl)-
pyrimidin-4-amine; $C_{15}H_{16}Cl_3N_5$;
130800-90-7
Neuroprotective agent

Sirolimus (rINN) si·*ro*·li·mus

(14*E*,16*E*,18*E*,26*E*)-(7*R*,8*R*,11*S*,13*S*,20*S*,22*R*,24*R*,25-
R,28*R*,31*S*,33a*S*)-1,2,3,4,6,7,8,9,10,11,12,13,20,21,-
22,23,24,25,28,29,30,31,33,33a-tetracosahydro-7,25-dihydroxy-
31-{(*R*)-2-[(1*S*,3*R*,4*R*)-4-hydroxy-3-methoxycyclohexyl]-1-
methylethyl}-13,24-dimethoxy-8,14,20,22,26,28-hexamethyl-
7,11-epoxy-5*H*-32-oxa-4a-aza-benzocyclohentriacontene-
5,6,23,29,33-pentone;
$C_{51}H_{79}NO_{13}$; *53123-88-9*
Calcineurin inhibitor; immunosuppressant

The symbol '¬' in systematic chemical names signifies line continuation

Sisomicin (rINN) sis·ö·*mi*·sin

An antimicrobial base produced by *Micromonospora inyoensis*
(1) 4-*O*-[(2*R*,3*R*)-*cis*-3-amino-6-aminomethyl-3,4-dihydro-2*H*-
pyran-2-yl]-2-deoxy-6-*O*-(3-deoxy-4-*C*-methyl-3-methyl¬
amino-β-L-arabinopyranosyl)streptamine; (2) 2-deoxy-6-*O*-(3-
deoxy-4-*C*-methyl-3-methylamino-β-L-arabinopyranosyl)-4-*O*-
(2,6-diamino-2,3,4,6-tetradeoxy-D-*glycero*-hex-4-enopyranosyl)-
D-streptamine; C₁₉H₃₇N₅O₇; 32385-11-8
Aminoglycoside antibacterial

Sitagliptin (rINN) *si*·ta·glip·tin
(3*R*)-3-Amino-1-[3-(trifluoromethyl)-5,6,7,8-tetrahydro¬
[1,2,4]triazolo[4,3-*a*]pyrazin-7-yl]-4-(2,4,5-trifluorophenyl)¬
butan-1-one; C₁₆H₁₅F₆N₅O; 486460-32-6
Sitagliptin phosphate 654671-78-0
Dipeptidylpeptidase-4 inhibitor; treatment of diabetes mellitus

Sitamaquine (rINN) sï·*tam*·a·quën
N,*N*-Diethyl-*N*′-(6-methoxy-4-methyl-8-quinolyl)hexane-1,6-
diamine; C₂₁H₃₃N₃O; 57695-04-2
Sitamaquine Hydrochloride (2HCl) 5330-29-0
Antiprotozoal; treatment of leishmaniasis

Sodium Acetrizoate (rINN) sö·dë·um a·së·*trï*·zö·ät
Sodium 3-acetamido-2,4,6-tri-iodobenzoate; C₉H₅I₃NNaO₃;
129-63-5
Iodinated contrast medium

Sodium Anoxynaphthonate (rINN) sö·dë·um a·noks·ë·*naf*·thö·nät
Trisodium 4′-anilino-8-hydroxy-1,1′-azonaphthalene-3,5′,6-
trisulfonate; anazolene sodium (pINN; USAN);
Coomassie Blue; C₂₆H₁₆N₆Na₃O₁₀S₃; 3861-73-2
Investigation of cardiac disease

Sodium Antimonylgluconate (rINN)
sö·dë·um an·ti·mo·nïl·*gloo*·ko·nät
Sodium salt of an antimony(III) derivative of gluconic acid;
C₆H₈NaO₇Sb; 16307-91-5
Antihelminthic

Sodium Apolate (rINN) sö·dë·um *a*·po·lät
Poly(sodium ethylenesulfonate); sodium lyapolate; 25053-27-4
Heparinoid; anticoagulant

●**Sodium Calcium Edetate** (rINN) sö·dë·um kal·së·um *e*·de·tät
Calcium disodium ethylenediaminetetra-acetate; calcium
disodium versenate; C₁₀H₁₂CaN₂Na₂O₈; 62-33-9
Chelating agent

262

● **Sodium Cyclamate** (rINN) sö·dë·um *si̇̈*·kla·mät
  Sodium *N*-cyclohexylsulfamate; $C_6H_{12}NNaO_3S$; *139-05-9*
  Sweetening agent

Sodium Dibunate (rINN) sö·dë·um *di̇̈*·bü·nät
  Sodium 2,6-di-*tert*-butylnaphthalene-1-sulfonate; $C_{18}H_{23}NaO_3S$;
  14992-59-7
  Cough suppressant

Sodium Diprotrizoate (rINN) sö·dë·um di̇̈·prö·*tri̇̈*·zö·ät
  Sodium 3,5-dipropionamido-2,4,6-tri-iodobenzoate;
  $C_{13}H_{12}I_3N_2NaO_4$; *129-57-7*
  Iodinated contrast medium

● **Sodium Feredetate** (rINN) sö·dë·um fer·*e*·de·tät
  Iron(III) sodium ethylenediaminetetra-acetate; $C_{10}H_{21}FeN_2NaO_8$;
  15708-41-5
  Source of iron

Sodium Glucaldrate (BAN)
  Sodium diaquagluconato(2−)-O^1,O^2-dihydroxoaluminate
  Antacid chelate

Sodium Glucaspaldrate (rINN) see Appendix C

Sodium Iopodate (rINN) sö·dë·um *i̇̈*·ö·pö·dät
  Sodium 3-(3-dimethylaminomethyleneamino-2,4,6-
  tri-iodophenyl)propionate; $C_{12}H_{12}I_3N_2NaO_2$; *1221-56-3*
  Iodinated contrast medium

Sodium Ironedetate *see Sodium Feredetate*

Sodium Metrizoate (rINN) sö·dë·um me·*tri̇̈*·zö·ät
  Sodium 3-acetamido-2,4,6-tri-iodo-5-*N*-
  methylacetamidobenzoate; $C_{12}H_{10}I_3N_2NaO_4$; *7225-61-8*
  Iodinated contrast medium

● **Sodium Phenylbutyrate** (BAN)
  Sodium 4-phenylbutyrate; $C_{10}H_{11}NaO_2$; *1716-12-7*
  Glutamine conjugate; treatment of hyperammonaemia

● **Sodium Picosulfate** (rINN) sö·dë·um·pi·kö·*sul*·fät
  Disodium 4,4′-(2-pyridyl)methylenedi(phenyl sulfate);
  $C_{18}H_{13}NNa_2O_8S_2$; *10040-45-6*
  Stimulant laxative

Sodium Stibocaptate (rINN) sö·dë·um sti·bö·*kap*·tät
  Hexasodium salt of 2,2′-(*meso*-1,2-dicarboxy ethyl¬
  enedithio)bis(1,3,2-dithiastibolane-4,5-dicarboxylic acid);
  $C_{12}H_6Na_6O_{12}S_6Sb_2$; *3064-61-7*
  Trivalent ammonium compound; anthelminthic

● **Sodium Stibogluconate** (rINN) sö·dë·um sti·bö·*gloo*·ko·nät
  Disodium salt of μ-oxy-bis[gluconato(3−)-O^2,O^3,O^4-
  hydroxoantimony]; $C_{12}H_{18}Na_2O_{17}Sb_2$ (approximate);
  16037-91-5
  Trivalent ammonium compound; antihelminthic

The symbol '¬' in systematic chemical names signifies line continuation

Sodium Timerfonate (rINN) *sö·dë·um ti·mer·fo·nät*
Sodium 4-(ethylmercurithio)benzenesulfonate; $C_8H_9HgNaO_3S_2$;
5964-24-9
Preservative

Sodium Tyropanoate (rINN) *sö·dë·um tîr·rö·pan·ö·ät*
Sodium 2-(3-butyramido-2,4,6-tri-iodobenzyl)butyrate;
$C_{15}H_{17}I_3NNaO_3$; *7246-21-1*
Iodinated contrast medium

and enantiomer

Solapsone (BAN) *so·lap·sön*
Tetrasodium 3,3′-diphenyl-4,4′-sulfonylbis(1-anilinopropane-
1,3-disulfonate); solasulfone (pINN); $C_{30}H_{28}N_2Na_4O_{14}S_5$;
133-65-3
Sulfone antibacterial; antileprosy drug

mixture of isomers

Solifenacin (rINN) *so·li·fen·á·sin*
(3*R*)-1-Azabicyclo[2.2.2]oct-3-yl(1*S*)-1-phenyl-3,4-dihydro-
isoquinoline-2(1*H*)-carboxylate; $C_{23}H_{26}N_2O_2$; *242478-37-1*
Muscarinic M_3 receptor antagonist; anticholinergic

Solimastat (rINN) *so·lim·a·stat*
(2*S*,3*R*)-3-[(1*S*)-(2,2-Dimethyl-1-(2-pyridylcarbamoyl)-
propylcarbamoyl]-2-methoxy-5-methylhexanohydroxamic acid;
$C_{20}H_{32}N_4O_5$
Matrix metalloproteinase inhibitor

Somalapor (rINN) *sö·ma·la·por*
L-Alanyl-somatotropin (porcine);
106282-98-8
Porcine somatotropin derivative (veterinary)

somalapor has the following amino acid sequence:

```
AFPAMPLSSL   FANAVLRAQH   LHQLAADTYK

EFERAYIPEG   QRYSIQNAQA   AFCFSETIPA

PTGKDEAQQR   SDVELLRFSL   LLIQSWLGPV

QFLSRVFTNS   LVFGTSDRVY   EKLKDLEEGI

QALMRELEDG   SPRAGQILKQ   TYDKFDTNLR

SDDALLKNYG   LLSCFKKDLH   KAETYLRVMK

CRRFVESSCA   F
```

Somatostatin (rINN) *sö·ma·tö·sta·tin*
$C_{76}H_{104}N_{18}O_{19}S_2$; *38916-34-6*
Growth hormone release inhibiting hormone

somatostatin has the following amino acid sequence:

```
Ala-Gly-Cys-Lys-Asn-Phe-Phe-Trp-

Lys-Thr-Phe-Thr-Ser-Cys
```

Somatrem (rINN) *sö·ma·trem*
Methionyl human growth hormone; *82030-87-3*
Growth hormone analogue

somatrem has the following amino acid sequence:

```
MFPTIPSRLF   DNAMLRLAHR   LHQLAFDTYQ

EFEEAYIPKE   QKYSFLQNPQ   TSLCFSESIP

TPSNREETQQ   KSNLELLRIS   LLLIQSWLEP

VQFLRSVFAN   SLVYGASDSN   VYDLLKDLEE

GIQTLMGRLE   DGSPRTGQIF   KQTYSKFDTN

SHNDDALLKN   YGLLYCFRKD   MDKVETFLRI

VQCRSVEGSC   GF
```

- **Somatropin** (rINN) sö·*ma*·trö·pin
Synthetic human growth hormone; a protein having the normal structure of the major (22K) component of natural human growth hormone produced by the pituitary. When produced by synthesis or other artificial means the name, for labelling purposes, carries in parentheses an approved code in lower case letters indicative of the method of production;
12629-01-5
Growth hormone

The following codes are approved and others will be made available as the need arises:
(**epr**) produced by enzymatic conversion of a precursor produced by a bacterium genetically modified by recombinant DNA technology
(**rbe**) produced from bacteria genetically modified by recombinant DNA technology
(**rmc**) produced from genetically engineered and transformed mammalian (mouse) cells;

somatropin has the following amino acid sequence:

```
FPTIPLSRLF   DNAMLRAHRL   HQLAFDTYQE
FEEAYIPKEQ   KYSFLQNPQT   SLCFSESIPT
PSNREETQQK   SNLELLRISL   LLIQSWLEPV
QFLRSVFANS   LVYGASDSNV   YDLLKDLEEG
IQTLMGRLED   GSPRTGQIFK   QTYSKFDTNS
HNDDALLKNY   GLLYCFRKDM   DKVETFLRIV
QCRSVEGSCG   F
```

Somenopor (rINN) sö·*me*·nö·por
L-Alanyl-des-(32-38)-somatotropin (porcine);
119693-74-2
Porcine somatotropin derivative (veterinary)

somenopor has the following amino acid sequence:

```
AFPAMPLSSL   FANAVLRAQH   LHQLAADTYK
EFGQRYSIQN   AQAAFCFSET   IPAPTGKDEA
QQRSDVELLR   FSLLLIQSWL   GPVQFLSRVF
TNSLVFGTSD   RVYEKLKDLE   EGIQALMREL
EDGSPRAGQI   LKQTYDKFDT   NLRSDDALLK
NYGLLSCFKK   DLHKAETYLR   VMKCRRFVES
SCAF
```

Sometribove (rINN) sö·*me*·tri·böv
Methionyl bovine growth hormone; *102744-97-8*
Bovine somatotropin derivative (veterinary)

sometribove has the following amino acid sequence:

```
MFPAMSLSGL   FANAVLRAQH   LHQLAADTFK
EFERTYIPEG   QRYSIQNTQV   AFCFSETIPA
PTGKNEAQQK   SDLELLRISL   LLIQSWLGPL
QFLSRVFTNS   LVFGTSDRVY   EKLKDLEEGI
LALMRELEDG   TPRAGQILKQ   TYDKFDTNMR
SDDALLKNYG   LLSCFRKDLH   KTETYLRVMK
CRRFGEASCA   F
```

Sometripor (rINN) sö·*me*·tri·por
Methionyl porcine growth hormone; *102733-72-2*
Porcine somatotropin derivative (veterinary)

sometripor has the following amino acid sequence:

```
MFPAMSLSGL   FANAVLRAQH   LHQLAADTFK
EFERTYIPEG   QRYSIQNTAV   AFCFSETIPA
PTGKNEAQQK   SDLELLRISL   LLIQSWLGPL
QFLSRVFTNS   LVFGTSDRVY   EKLKDLEEGI
LALMRELEDG   TPRAGQILKQ   TYDKFDTNMR
SDDALLKNYG   LLSCFRKDLH   KTETYLRVMK
CRRFGEASCA   F
```

Somidobove (rINN) sö·*mï*·dö·böv
Synthetic bovine growth hormone; *89383-13-1*
Bovine somatotropin derivative (veterinary)

somidobove has the following amino acid sequence:

```
MFPLDDDDKF   PAMSLSGLFA   NAVLRAQHLH
QLAADTFKEF   ERTYIPEGQR   YSIQNTQVAF
CFSETIPAPT   GKNEAQQKSD   LELLRISLLL
IQSWLGPLQF   LSRVFTNSLV   FGTSDRVYEK
LKDLELGILA   LMRELEDGTP   RAGQILKQTY
DKFDTNMRSD   DALLKNYGLL   SCFRKDLHKT
ETYLRVMKCR   RFGEASCAF
```

Sorafenib (rINN) so·rá·*fe*·nib
4-(4-{3-[4-Chloro-3-(trifluoromethyl)phenyl]carbamoyl amino}phenoxy)-*N*-methylpyridine-2-carboxamide;
$C_{21}H_{16}ClF_3N_4O_3$; *284461-73-0*;
Sorafenib Tosilate *475207-59-1*
Tyrosine kinase inhibitor; treatment of renal cell carcinoma

Sorbinil (rINN) *sor·bi·nil*
(S)-6-Fluorospiro[chroman-4,4′-imidazolidine]-2′,5′-dione;
$C_{11}H_9FN_2O_3$; *68367-52-2*
Aldose reductase inhibitor

● **Sorbitan Laurate** (rINN) *sor·bi·tan lor·rät*
Sorbitan monolaurate; $C_{18}H_{34}O_6$; *1338-39-2*
Non-ionic surfactant

● **Sorbitan Oleate** (rINN) *sor·bi·tan ö·lë·ät*
Sorbitan mono-oleate; $C_{24}H_{44}O_6$ (approximate); *1338-43-8*
Non-ionic surfactant

● **Sorbitan Palmitate** (rINN) *sor·bi·tan parl·mi·tät*
Sorbitan monopalmitate; $C_{22}H_{42}O_6$ (approximate); *26266-57-9*
Non-ionic surfactant

● **Sorbitan Sesquioleate** (rINN) *sor·bi·tan ses·kwë·ö·lë·ät*
Sorbitan sesquioleate; $C_{33}H_{60}O_{6·5}$ (approximate); *8007-43-0*
Non-ionic surfactant

● **Sorbitan Stearate** (rINN) *sor·bi·tan steer·rät*
Sorbitan monostearate; $C_{24}H_{46}O_6$ (approximate); *1338-41-6*
Non-ionic surfactant

● **Sorbitan Trioleate** (rINN) *sor·bi·tan trï·ö·lë·ät*
Sorbitan trioleate; $C_{60}H_{108}O_8$; *5960-06-5*
Non-ionic surfactant

Sorbitan Tristearate (rINN) *sor·bi·tan trï·steer·rät*
Sorbitan tristearate; $C_{60}H_{114}O_8$; *26658-19-5*
Non-ionic surfactant

Sorivudine (rINN) *sor·ri·vü·dën*
(E)-1-β-D-Arabinofuranosyl-5-(2-bromovinyl)uracil;
$C_{11}H_{13}BrN_2O_6$; *77181-69-2*
Antiviral (varicella zoster)

Sotalol (rINN) *sö·ta·lol*
4′-(1-Hydroxy-2-isopropylaminoethyl)methanesulfonanilide;
$C_{12}H_{20}N_2O_3S$; *3930-20-9*
● **Sotalol Hydrochloride** *959-24-0*
Beta-adrenoceptor antagonist; class II and class III antiarrhythmic

and enantiomer

Sparfloxacin (rINN) *spar·floks·a·sin*
5-Amino-l-cyclopropyl-7-(cis-3,5-dimethylpiperazin-l-yl)-6,8-difluoro-l,4-dihydro-4-oxoquinoline-3-carboxylic acid;
$C_{19}H_{22}F_2N_4O_3$; *110871-86-8*
Fluoroquinolone antibacterial

Spectinomycin (rINN) *spek·tin·ö·mï·sin*
An antimicrobial substance produced by *Streptomyces spectabillis*; [(2R)-(2a,4ab,5b,6b,7b,8b,9a,9aa,10ab)]-perhydro-4a,7,9-trihydroxy-2-methyl-6,8-bis(methylamino)pyrano[2,3-b][1,4]benzodioxin-4-one; $C_{14}H_{24}N_2O_7$; *1695-77-8*
● **Spectinomycin Hydrochloride** *22189-32-8 (pentahydrate)*; *21736-83-4 (anhydrous)*
♣ **Spectinomycin Sulfate**
Aminocyclotol antibacterial

Spiperone (rINN) *spï*·pe·rön
8-[3-(4-Fluorobenzoyl)propyl]-1-phenyl-1,3,8-triazaspiro¬
[4.5]decan-4-one; $C_{23}H_{26}FN_3O_2$; *749-02-0*
Dopamine receptor antagonist; neuroprotective agent

● **Spiramycin** (rINN) spïr·ra·*mï*·sin
An antimicrobial macrolide antibiotic produced by *Streptomyces ambofaciens*; *8025-81-8*
Antibacterial

Spirapril (rINN) *spir*·ra·pril
(*S*)-7-{*N*-(*S*)-1-Ethoxycarbonyl-3-phenylpropyl-L-alanyl}-1,4-
dithia-7-azaspiro[4.4]nonane-8-carboxylic acid; $C_{22}H_{30}N_2O_5S_2$;
83647-97-6
  ● **Spirapril Hydrochloride** *94841-17-5*
  Angiotensin converting enzyme inhibitor

Spirilene (rINN) see Appendix C

Spirogermanium (rINN) spïr·rö·jer·*mä*·në·um
3-(8,8-Diethyl-2-aza-8-germaspiro[4.5]dec-2-yl)propyl¬
dimethylamine; $C_{17}H_{36}GeN_2$; *41992-23-8*
  Spirogermanium Hydrochloride *41992-22-7*
  Cytotoxic

● **Spironolactone** (rINN) spïr·rö·nö·*lak*·tön
7α-Acetylthio-3-oxo-17α-pregn-4-ene-21,17β-carbolactone;
$C_{24}H_{32}O_4S$; *52-01-7*
Aldosterone receptor antagonist; potassium-sparing diuretic

Spiroplatin (rINN) spïr·rö·*pla*·tin
cis-(Cyclohexylidenedimethylenediamine-*N*,*N'*)(sulfato)¬
platinum; $C_8H_{18}N_2O_4PtS$; *74790-08-2*
Platinum-containing cytotoxic

Stanolone *see Androstanolone*

● **Stanozolol** (rINN) sta·*nö*·zö·lol
17α-Methyl-2'*H*-5α-androst-2-eno[3,2-*c*]pyrazol-17β-ol;
$C_{21}H_{32}N_2O$; *10418-03-8*
Anabolic steroid; androgen

● **Stavudine** (rINN) sta·vü·dën
1-(2,3-Dideoxy-β-D-*glycero*-pent-2-enofuranosyl)-5-methyl¬
uracil; $C_{10}H_{12}N_2O_4$; *3056-17-5*
*Nucleoside analogue reverse transcriptase inhibitor;
antiviral (HIV)*

Stibamine Glucoside (rINN) *sti*·ba·mën *gloo*·kö·sïd
Sodium [4-(glucopyranosylamino)phenyl]trioxoantimonate;
$C_{36}H_{49}N_3NaO_{22}Sb_3$; *1344-34-9*
Antiprotozoal

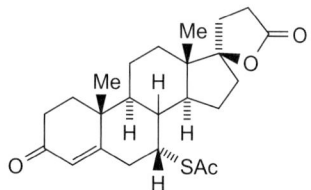

R = $C_6H_{11}O_5$

Stibocaptate *see Sodium Stibocaptate*

Stilbamidine Isetionate (rINN) stil·*ba*·mi·dën
Stilbene-4,4'-dicarboxamidine di-(2-hydroxyethane)-sulfonate;
$C_{20}H_{28}N_4O_8S_2$; *140-59-0*
Antiprotozoal; treatment of leishmaniasis

The symbol '¬' in systematic chemical names signifies line continuation

Stilbazium Iodide (rINN) stil·*bä*·zë·um
β,β′-(1-Ethylpyridinium-2,6-diyl)bis(4-pyrrolidin-1-ylstyrene) iodide; C₃₁H₃₆IN₃; *3784-99-4*
Antihelminthic

Stilboestrol *see Diethylstilbestrol*

Stirimazole (rINN) see Appendix C

Streptodornase (rINN) strep·tö·*dor*·näz
An enzyme obtained from cultures of various strains of *Streptococcus haemolyticus* and capable of catalysing the depolymerisation of polymerised deoxyribonucleoproteins; *37340-82-2*
Fibrinolytic enzyme

Streptoduocin (BAN) strep·tö·*duo*·sin
A mixture of equal parts of dihydrostreptomycin sulfate and streptomycin sulfate
Antibacterial; antituberculosis drug

●**Streptokinase** (rINN) strep·tö·*ki*·näz
An enzyme obtained from cultures of various strains of *Streptococcus haemolyticus* and capable of changing plasminogen into plasmin; *9002-02-1*
Plasminogen activator; fibrinolytic

Streptomycin (rINN) strep·tö·*mi*·sin
O-2-Deoxy-2-methylamino-α-L-glucopyranosyl-(1→2)-*O*-5-deoxy-3-*C*-formyl-α-L-lyxofuranosyl-(1→4)-*N*³,*N*³-diamidino-D-streptamine; C₂₁H₃₉N₇O₁₂; *57-92-1*
●**Streptomycin Sulfate** *3810-74-0*
Aminoglycoside antibacterial; antituberculosis drug

Streptoniazid (rINN) see Appendix C

Styramate (rINN) see Appendix C

Succimer (rINN) *suks*·i·mer
meso-2,3-Dimercaptosuccinic acid; C₄H₆O₄S₂; *304-55-2*
Lead chelator

●**Succinylsulfathiazole** (rINN) suks·i·nïl·sul·fa·*thï*·a·zôl
4′-(1,3-Thiazol-2-ylsulfamoyl)succinanilic acid; C₁₃H₁₃N₃O₅S₂; *166-43-8*
Sulfonamide antibacterial

Suclofenide (rINN) sü·*klö*·fe·nid
(*RS*)-3-Chloro-4-(2-phenylsuccinimido)benzenesulfonamide; C₁₆H₁₃ClN₂O₄S; *30279-49-3*
Antiepileptic

and enantiomer

●**Sucralfate** (rINN) *sü*·kral·fät
β-D-Fructofuranosyl-α-D-glucopyranoside octakis(hydrogen sulfate), aluminium complex; *54182-58-0*
Treatment of gastric and duodenal ulcers

R = SO₃Al(OH)₂

[Al(OH)₃]ₓ [H₂O]ᵧ

• **Sucralose** (BAN) *sü·*kra·lös
1,6-Dichloro-1,6-dideoxy-β-D-fructofuranosyl 4-chloro-4-deoxy-α-D-galactopyranoside; *56038-13-2*; $C_{12}H_{19}Cl_3O_8$
Sweetening agent

Sucralox (rINN) see Appendix C

Sudoxicam (rINN) sü·*doks·*i·kam
4-Hydroxy-2-methyl-*N*-(1,3-thiazol-2-yl)-1,2-benzothiazine-3-carboxamide 1,1-dioxide; $C_{13}H_{11}N_3O_4S_2$; *34042-85-8*
Cyclo-oxygenase inhibitor; analgesic; anti-inflammatory

• **Sufentanil** (rINN) sü·*fen·*ta·nil
N-{4-(Methoxymethyl)-1-[2-(2-thienyl)ethyl]-4-piperidyl}¬propionanilide; $C_{22}H_{30}N_2O_2S$; *56030-54-7*
• **Sufentanil Citrate** *60561-17-3*
Opioid receptor agonist; analgesic

Sufugolix (rINN) su·*fü·*gö·liks
5-{[Benzyl(methyl)amino]methyl}-1-(2,6-difluorobenzyl)-6-[4-(3-methoxyureido)phenyl]-3-phenylthieno[2,3-*d*]pyrimidine-2,4(1*H*,3*H*)-dione; $C_{36}H_{31}F_2N_5O_4S$; *308831-61-0*
Luteinizing hormone-releasing hormone (LHRH) antagonist

Sufotidine (rINN) su·*fo·*ti·dën
1-Methyl-3-(mesylmethyl)-1*H*-1,2,4-triazol-5-yl[3-(α-piperidino-*m*-tolyloxy)propyl]amine; $C_{20}H_{31}N_5O_3S$; *80343-63-1*
Histamine H_2 receptor antagonist

Sugammadex (rINN) sü·*gam·*má·deks
Cyclooctakis-(1→4)-[6-*S*-(2-carboxyethyl)-6-thio-α-D-glucopyranosyl]; $C_{72}H_{112}O_{48}S_8$; *343306-71-8*;
Sugammadex Sodium *343306-79-6*
Modified gamma cyclodextrin; reversal of neuromuscular blockade in general anaesthesia

Sulbactam (rINN) sul·*bak·*tam
(1) (2*S*,5*R*)-3,3-Dimethyl-7-oxo-4-thia-1-azabicyclo [3.2.0]¬heptane-2-carboxylic acid 4,4-dioxide; (2) Penicillanic acid 1,1-dioxide; $C_8H_{11}NO_5S$; *68373-14-8*
• **Sulbactam Sodium** *69388-84-7*
Beta-lactam antibacterial

The symbol '¬' in systematic chemical names signifies line continuation

Sulconazole (rINN) sul·*kon*·a·zôl
1-[2,4-Dichloro-β-(4-chlorobenzylthio)phenethyl]imidazole;
$C_{18}H_{15}Cl_3N_2S$; *61318-90-9*
Sulconazole Nitrate *61318-91-0*
Azole antifungal

and enantiomer

Sulesomab (rINN) soo·*le·zö*·mab
Immunoglobulin G1, anti-(human NCA-90 granulocyte cell
antigen) Fab' fragment (mouse monoclaonal IMMU-MN3
γ-chain), disulfide with mouse monoclonal IMMU-MN3 light
chain; *167747-19-5*;
Monoclonal antibody (technetium-99m); imaging osteomyelitis

Sulfabenzamide (rINN) sul·fa·*ben*·za·mïd
N-Sulfanilylbenzamide; $C_{13}H_{12}N_2O_3S$; *127-71-9*
Sulfonamide antibacterial

Sulfacarbamide (rINN) sul·fa·*kar*·ba·mïd
Sulfanilylurea; $C_7H_9N_3O_3S$; *547-44-4*
Sulfonamide antibacterial

Sulfacetamide (rINN) sul·fa·*set*·a·mïd
N-Sulfaniloylacetamide; $C_8H_{10}N_2O_3S$; *144-80-9*
●**Sulfacetamide Sodium** *6209-17-2*
Sulfonamide antibacterial

Sulfachlorpyridazine (rINN) sul·fa·klor·pi·*ri*·da·zën
N-(6-Chloropyridazin-3-yl)sulfanilamide; $C_{10}H_9ClN_4O_2S$;
80-32-0
Sulfachlorpyridazine Sodium
Sulfonamide antibacterial

Sulfacytine (rINN) sul·fa·*si*·tën
(1) *N*[1]-(1-Ethyl-1,2-dihydro-2-oxopyrimidin-4-yl)sulfanilamide;
(2) 1-ethyl-*N*-sulfanilylcytosine; sulfacitine (pINN);
$C_{12}H_{14}N_4O_3S$; *17784-12-2*
Sulfonamide antibacterial

●**Sulfadiazine** (rINN) sul·fa·*di*·a·zën
N[1]-(Pyrimidin-2-yl)sulfanilamide; $C_{10}H_{10}N_4O_2S$; *68-35-9*
Sulfadiazine Silver *22119-08-2*
Sulfonamide antibacterial

Sulfadimethoxine (rINN) sul·fa·di·me·*thoks*·ën
N[1]-(2,6-Dimethoxypyrimidin-4-yl)sulfanilamide; $C_{12}H_{14}N_4O_4S$;
122-11-2
Sulfonamide antibacterial

●**Sulfadimidine** (rINN) sul·fa·*di*·mi·dën
N[1]-(4,6-Dimethylpyrimidin-2-yl)sulfanilamide; sulfamethazine
(USAN); $C_{12}H_{14}N_4O_2S$; *57-68-1*
●**Sulfadimidine Sodium**
Sulfonamide antibacterial

●**Sulfadoxine** (rINN) sul·fa·*doks*·ën
N[1]-(5,6-Dimethoxypyrimidin-4-yl)sulfanilamide; $C_{12}H_{14}N_4O_4S$;
2447-57-6
Sulfonamide antibacterial

Sulfaethidole (rINN) sul·fa·*e*·thi·dôl
N[1]-(5-Ethyl-1,3,4-thiadiazol-2-yl)sulfanilamide; $C_{10}H_{12}N_4O_2S_2$;
94-19-9
Sulfonamide antibacterial

Sulfafurazole (rINN) sul·fa·*fûr*·ra·zôl
N^1-(3,4-Dimethyl-1,2-oxazol-5-yl)sulfanilamide; sulfisoxazole (USAN); $C_{11}H_{13}N_3O_3S$; *127-69-5*
Sulfonamide antibacterial

Sulfaguanidine (rINN) sul·fa·*gwan*·i·dën
1-Sulfanilylguanidine; $C_7H_{10}N_4O_2S$; *56-67-0*
Sulfonamide antibacterial

Sulfaloxic Acid (rINN) sul·fa·*loks*·ik
4′-[(Hydroxymethylcarbamoyl)sulfamoyl]phthalanilic acid; $C_{16}H_{15}N_3O_7S$; *14376-16-0*
Calcium Sulfaloxate
Sulfonamide antibacterial

Sulfamerazine (rINN) see Appendix C

Sulfamethizole (rINN) sul·fa·*me*·thi·zôl
N^1-(5-Methyl-1,3,4-thiadiazol-2-yl)sulfanilamide; $C_9H_{10}N_4O_2S_2$; *144-82-1*
Sulfonamide antibacterial

Sulfamethoxazole (rINN) sul·fa·me·*thoks*·a·zôl
N^1-(5-Methyl-1,2-oxazol-3-yl)sulfanilamide; $C_{10}H_{11}N_3O_3S$; *723-46-6*
Sulfonamide antibacterial

♣ **Sulfamethoxypyridazine** (rINN) sul·fa·me·thoks·ë·pi·*ri*·da·zën
N^1-(6-Methoxypyridazin-3-yl)sulfanilamide; $C_{11}H_{12}N_4O_3S$; *80-35-3*
Sulfonamide antibacterial

Sulfametopyrazine (rINN) sul·fa·me·tö·*pï*·ra·zën
N^1-(3-Methoxypyrazin-2-yl)sulfanilamide; sulfalene (pINN; USAN); $C_{11}H_{12}N_4O_3S$; *152-47-6*
Sulfonamide antibacterial

Sulfametoxydiazine (rINN) sul·fa·me·toks·ë·*dï*·a·zën
N^1-(5-Methoxypyrimidin-2-yl)sulfanilamide; sulfameter (USAN); $C_{11}H_{12}N_4O_3S$; *651-06-9*
Sulfonamide antibacterial

Sulfametrole (rINN) sul·*fa*·me·trôl
N^1-(4-Methoxy-1,2,5-thiadiazol-3-yl)sulfanilamide; $C_9H_{10}N_4O_3S_2$; *32909-92-5*
Sulfonamide antibacterial

Sulfamonomethoxine (rINN) sul·fa·mo·nö·me·*thoks*·ën
N^1-(6-Methoxypyrimidin-4-yl)sulfanilamide; $C_{11}H_{12}N_4O_3S$; *1220-83-3*
Sulfamonomethoxine Sodium *38006-08-5*
Sulfonamide antibacterial

Sulfamoprine (BAN) see Appendix C

Sulfamoxole (rINN) sul·fa·*moks*·ôl
N^1-(4,5-Dimethyl-1,3-oxazol-2-yl)sulfanilamide; $C_{11}H_{13}N_3O_3S$; *729-99-7*
Sulfonamide antibacterial

Sulfan Blue (BAN)

Sodium α-(4-Diethylaminophenyl)-α-(4-diethyliminiocyclo¬
hexa-2,5-dienylidene)toluene-2,5-disulfonate; isosulfan blue
(USAN); Blue VRS; $C_{27}H_{31}N_2NaO_6S_2$; *68238-36-8*
Dyestuff used in lymphangiography

Sulfanitran (rINN) sul·fa·*nï*·tran

4′-(4-Nitrophenylsulfamoyl)acetanilide; $C_{14}H_{13}N_3O_5S$;
122-16-7
Antiprotozoal

Sulfaphenazole (rINN) sul·fa·*fe*·na·zôl

N^1-(1-Phenylpyrazol-5-yl)sulfanilamide; $C_{15}H_{14}N_4O_2S$;
526-08-9
Sulfonamide antibacterial

Sulfaproxyline (rINN) sul·fa·*proks*·ë·lën

N^1-(4-Isopropoxybenzoyl)sulfanilamide; $C_{16}H_{18}N_2O_4S$;
116-42-7
Sulfonamide antibacterial

Sulfapyrazole (rINN) see Appendix C

Sulfapyridine (rINN) see Appendix C

♣ **Sulfaquinoxaline** sul·fa·kwi·*noks*·a·lën

N^1-Quinoxalin-2-ylsulfanilamide; $C_{14}H_{12}N_4O_2S$; *59-40-5*
Sulfaquinoxaline Sodium *967-80-6*
Sulfonamide antibacterial (veterinary)

● **Sulfasalazine** (rINN) sul·fa·*sal*·a·zën

4-Hydroxy-4′-(2-pyridylsulfamoyl)azobenzene-3-carboxylic
acid; salazosulfapyridine (pINN); salicylazosulfapyridine;
$C_{18}H_{14}N_4O_5S$; *599-79-1*
Sulfonamide aminosalicylate; treatment of ulcerative colitis

Sulfasomizole (rINN) see Appendix C

● **Sulfathiazole** (rINN) sul·fa·*thï*·a·zôl

N^1-(1,3-Thiazol-2-yl)sulfanilamide; $C_9H_9N_3O_2S_2$; *72-14-0*
♣ **Sulfathiazole Sodium** *144-747-1*;
6791-71-5 (pentahydrate)
Sulfonamide antibacterial (veterinary)

Sulfathiourea (rINN) sul·fa·thï·ö·ûr·*rë*·a

Sulfanilylthiourea; $C_7H_9N_3O_2S_2$; *515-49-1*
Sulfonamide antibacterial

Sulfatolamide (rINN) sul·fa·*tol*·a·mïd

Sulfanilylthiourea salt of α-amino-*p*-toluenesulfonamide;
$C_7H_9N_3O_2S_2.C_7H_{10}N_2O_2S$; *1161-88-2*
Sulfonamide antibacterial

Sulfatroxazole (rINN) sul·fa·*troks*·a·zôl

N^1-(4,5-Dimethy-1,2-oxazol-3-yl)sulfanilamide; $C_{11}H_{13}N_3O_3S$;
23256-23-7
Sulfonamide antibacterial

Sulfaurea *see Sulfacarbamide*

● **Sulfinpyrazone** (rINN) sul·fin·*pi*·ra·zön
1,2-Diphenyl-4-(2-phenylsulfinylethyl)pyrazolidine-3,5-dione;
$C_{23}H_{20}N_2O_3S$; *57-96-5*
Uricosuric

● **Sulfiram** (rINN) *sul*·fi·ram
Tetraethylthiuram monosulfide; $C_{10}H_{20}N_2S_3$; *95-05-6*
Aldehyde reductase inhibitor; acaricide

♣ **Sulfisomidine** (rINN) sul·fi·*so*·mi·dën
N^1-(2,6-Dimethylpyrimidin-4-yl)sulfanilamide; $C_{12}H_{14}N_4O_2S$;
515-64-0
Sulfonamide antibacterial

Sulfobromophthalein (BAN) sul·fö·brö·mö·*fthä*·lën
5,5′-(4,5,6,7-Tetrabromo-3-oxo-(3*H*)-isobenzofuran-1-ylidene)-
bis-(2-hydroxybenzenesulfonic acid); $C_{20}H_{10}Br_4O_{10}S_2$; *297-83-6*
Sulfobromophthalein Sodium *71-67-0*
Measurement of liver function

Sulfomyxin Sodium (rINN) sul·fö·*miks*·in
A mixture of sulfomethylated polymyxin B and sodium
bisulfite; $C_{61}H_{103}N_{16}Na_5O_{28}S$; *1405-52-3*
Sulfonamide antibacterial

Sulglicotide (rINN) sul·*gli*·kö·tïd
The sulfuric polyester of a glycopeptide isolated from pig
duodenum; *54182-59-1*
Sulglicotide Sodium
Treatment of peptic ulcer disease

● **Sulindac** (rINN) *sul*·in·dak
(*Z*)-5-Fluoro-2-methyl-1-(4-methylsulfinylbenzylidene)indene-
3-acetic acid; $C_{20}H_{17}FO_3S$; *38194-50-2*
Cyclo-oxygenase inhibitor; analgesic; anti-inflammatory

● **Suloctidil** (rINN) su·*lok*·ti·dil
Erythro-1-[4-(Isopropylthio)phenyl]-2-octylaminopropan-1-ol;
$C_{20}H_{35}NOS$; *54063-56-8*
Vasodilator

and enantiomer

● **Sulofenur** (rINN) sü·*lö*·fe·nûr
1-(4-Chlorophenyl)-3-(indan-5-ylsulfonyl)urea; $C_{16}H_{15}ClN_2O_3S$;
110311-27-8
Sulfonylurea cytotoxic

● **Sulotroban** (rINN) sü·*lö*·trö·ban
4-(2-Phenylsulfonylaminoethyl)phenoxyacetic acid;
$C_{16}H_{17}NO_5S$; *72131-33-0*
Thromboxane A_2 antagonist

Sulpha drugs *see corresponding name beginning 'Sulfa-'*

Sulphan Blue *see Sulfan Blue*

Sulphobromophthalein *see Sulfobromophthalein*

● **Sulpiride** (rINN) *sul*·pi·rïd
(*RS*)-*N*-(1-Ethylpyrrolidin-2-ylmethyl)-2-methoxy-5-
sulfamoylbenzamide; $C_{15}H_{23}N_3O_4S$; *15676-16-1*
Dopamine receptor antagonist; neuroleptic

and enantiomer

● **Sultamicillin** (rINN) see Appendix C

The symbol '¬' in systematic chemical names signifies line continuation

Sultiame (rINN) sul·*ti*·äm
4-(Tetrahydro-2*H*-1,2-thiazin-2-yl)benzenesulfonamide *S,S*-dioxide; $C_{10}H_{14}N_2O_4S_2$; *61-56-3*
Antiepileptic

Sumacetamol (rINN) sü·ma·*se*·ta·mol
4-Acetamidophenyl *N*-acetyl-DL-methioninate; $C_{15}H_{20}N_2O_4S$; *69217-67-0*
Analgesic; antipyretic

and enantiomer

Sumatriptan (rINN) sü·ma·*trip*·tan
3-(2-Dimethylaminoethyl)indol-5-yl-*N*-methylmethane¬sulfonamide; $C_{14}H_{21}N_3O_2S$; *103628-46-2*
● **Sumatriptan Succinate** *103628-48-4*
Serotonin 5HT$_1$ receptor agonist; treatment of migraine

Sunitinib (rINN) sun·i·*tin*·nib
N-[2-(Diethylamino)ethyl]-5-[(*Z*)-(5-fluoro-2-oxo-1,2-dihydro-3*H*-indol-3-ylidene)methyl]-2,4-dimethyl-1*H*-pyrrole-3-carboxamide; $C_{22}H_{27}FN_4O_2$; *557795-19-4*;
Sunitinib Malate *341031-54-7*
Tyrosine kinase inhibitor; antineoplastic

Suprofen (rINN) sü·prö·fen
2-[4-(2-Thenoyl)phenyl]propionic acid; $C_{14}H_{12}O_3S$; *40828-46-4*
Cyclo-oxygenase inhibitor; analgesic; anti-inflammatory

and enantiomer

Suriclone (rINN) *sûr*·ri·klön
(*RS*)-6-(7-Chloro-1,8-naphthyridin-2-yl)-2,3,6,7-tetrahydro-7-oxo-5*H*-[1,4]dithi-ino[2,3-*c*]pyrrol-5-yl 4-methylpiperazine-1-carboxylate; $C_{20}H_{20}ClN_5O_3S_2$; *53813-83-5*
Non-benzodiazepine hypnotic

and enantiomer

Sutilains (rINN) see Appendix C

Suxamethonium Bromide (rINN) suks·a·me·*thö*·në·um
2,2′-Succinyldioxybis(ethyltrimethylammonium) dibromide; $C_{14}H_{30}Br_2N_2O_4$; *55-94-7*
Depolarizing neuromuscular blocker

● **Suxamethonium Chloride** (rINN) suks·a·me·*thö*·në·um
2,2′-Succinyldioxybis(ethyltrimethylammonium) dichloride; succinylcholine chloride (USAN); $C_{14}H_{30}Cl_2N_2O_4$; *71-27-2; (anhydrous); 6101-15-1 (dihydrate)*
Depolarizing neuromuscular blocker

Suxethonium Bromide (rINN) suks·e·*thö*·në·um
2,2′-Succinyldioxybis(diethyldimethylammonium) dibromide; $C_{16}H_{34}Br_2N_2O_4$; *54063-57-9*
Depolarizing neuromuscular blocker

● **Suxibuzone** (rINN) suks·i·*bü*·zön
4-[(4-Butyl-3,5-dioxo-1,2-diphenylpyrazolidin-4-yl)methyl hydrogen succinate; $C_{24}H_{26}N_2O_6$; *27470-51-5*
Cyclo-oxygenase inhibitor; analgesic; anti-inflammatory

Syrosingopine (rINN) see Appendix C

Tacalcitol (rINN) ta·*kal*·si·tol
(5Z,7E)-(1S,3R,24R)-9,10-Secocholesta-5,7,10(19)-triene-
1,3,24-triol; $C_{27}H_{44}O_3$; *57333-96-7*
Vitamin D_3 analogue

Tacrine (rINN) *ta*·krën
1,2,3,4-Tetrahydroacridin-9-ylamine; $C_{13}H_{14}N_2$; *321-64-2*
Tacrine Hydrochloride *1684-40-8*
Cholinesterase inhibitor

Tacrolimus (rINN) ta·*kro*·li·mus
(E)-(7R,8R,10S,11R,12S,14S,18R,21S,22R,23S)-18-allyl-
1,2,3,4,6,7,8,9,10,11,12,13,14,15,18,19,20,21,22,23,25,25a-
Docosahydro-7,21-dihydroxy-23-{(E)-2-[(1R,3R,4R)-4-hydroxy-
3-methoxycyclohexyl]-1-methylvinyl}-10,12-dimethoxy-
8,14,16,22-tetramethyl-7,11-epoxy-5H-24-oxa-4a-azabenzo¬
cyclotricosene-5,6,19,25-tetrone; $C_{44}H_{69}NO_{12}$; *104987-11-3*
Calcineurin inhibitor; immunosuppressant

Tadalafil (rINN) tá·*da*·la·fil
(6R,12aR)-6-(1,3-Benzodioxol-5-yl)-2-methyl-2,3,6,7,12,12a-
hexahydropyrazino[1',2':1,6]pyrido[3,4-*b*]indole-1,4-dione;
$C_{22}H_{19}N_3O_4$; *171596-29-5*
*Selective inhibitor of cyclic GMP-specific phosphodiesterase type
V with vasodilator action; treatment of male erectile dysfunction*

Tafenoquine (rINN) ta·*fen*·ö·kwën
(RS)-N^4-[2,6-Dimethoxy-4-methyl-5-(3-trifluoromethyl¬
phenoxy)quinolin-8-yl]pentane-1,4-diamine; $C_{24}H_{28}F_3N_3O_3$;
106635-80-7
Tafenoquine Succinate *106635-81-8*
Antibacterial

and enantiomer

Tafluprost (rINN) ta·flu·*prost*
Isopropyl (5Z)-7-{(1R,2R,3R,5S)-2-[(1E)-3,3-difluoro-4-
phenoxybut-1-enyl]-3,5-dihydroxycyclopentyl}hept-5-enoate;
$C_{25}H_{34}F_2O_5$; *209860-87-7*
Prostaglandin analogue; treatment of glaucoma

Talampicillin (rINN) see Appendix C

Talizumab (rINN) ta·*li*·zü·mab
Immunoglobulin G, anti-(human immunoglobulin E Fc region)
(human-mouse monoclonal Hu901 a-chain), disulfide with
human-mouse monoclonal Hu901 k-chain, dimer; *380610-22-0*
Monoclonal antibody (human immunoglobulin E Fc region)

Taloximine (rINN) see Appendix C

Tameridone (rINN) see Appendix C

Tamitinol (rINN) ta·*mi*·ti·nol
4-(Ethylaminomethyl)-2-methyl-5-(methylthiomethyl)pyridin-3-
ol; $C_{11}H_{18}N_2OS$; *59429-50-4*
Nootropic

Tamoxifen (rINN) ta·*moks*·i·fen
(Z)-2-[p-(1,2-Diphenylbut-1-enyl)phenoxy]ethyldimethylamine;
C₂₆H₂₉NO; *10540-29-1*
● **Tamoxifen Citrate** *54965-24-1*
Selective oestrogen receptor modulator

Tamsulosin (rINN) tam·sü·*lö*·sin
(R)-5-{2-[2-(2-Ethoxyphenoxy)ethylamino]propyl}-2-methoxybenzenesulfonamide; C₂₀H₂₈N₂O₅S; *106133-20-4*
● **Tamsulosin Hydrochloride** *106463-17-6*
Alpha₁-adrenoceptor antagonist

Tandospirone (rINN) tan·*do*·spi·rön
(1R′,2S′,3R′,4S′)-N-{4-[4-(Pyrimidin-2-yl)piperazin-1-yl]butyl}-8,9,10-trinorbornane-2,3-dicarboximide (1:1);
C₂₁H₂₉N₅O₂; *87760-53-0*
Tandospirone Citrate *112457-95-1*
Serotonin 5HT₁A receptor partial agonist; anxiolytic

Taprizosin (rINN) ta·*prï*·zö·sin
N-{2-[4-Amino-6,7-dimethoxy-5-(2-pyridyl)quinazolin-2-yl]-1,2,3,4-tetrahydro-5-isoquinolyl}methanesulfonamide;
C₂₅H₂₆N₆O₄S; *210538-44-6*
Alpha₁-adrenoceptor antagonist

Targinine (rINN) tar·ji·nën
Nω-Methyl-L-arginine; C₇H₁₆N₄O₂; *17035-90-4*
Nitric oxide synthase inhibitor

Tariquidar (rINN) ta·*ri*·kwid·ar
N-[-({4-[2-(6,7-Dimethoxy-1,2,3,4-tetrahydroisoquinolin-2-yl)ethyl]phenyl}carbamoyl)-4,5-dimethoxyphenyl]quinoline-3-carboxamide; C₃₈H₃₈N₄O₆; *206873-63-4*
Inhibitor of multidrug resistance (P glycoprotein)

Tasonermin (rINN) ta·*son*·er·min
Tumour necrosis factor (TNF) alfa-1a (human); *94948-59-1*
Recombinant tumour necrosis factor

tasonermin has the following amino acid sequence:

```
VRSSSRTPSD   KPVAHVVANP   QAEGQLQWLN
RRANALLANG   VELRDNQLVV   PSEGLYLIYS
QVLFKGQGCP   STHVLLTHTI   SRIAVSYQTK
NVLLSAIKSP   CQRETPEGAE   AKPWYEPIYL
GGVFQLEKGD   RLSAEINRPD   YLDFAESGQV
YFGIIAL
```

Tasosartan (rINN) ta·sö·*sar*·tan
5,8-Dihydro-2,4-dimethyl-8-[4-(o-1H-tetrazol-5-ylphenyl)benzyl]pyrido-[2,3-d]pyrimidin-7(6H)-one; C₂₃H₂₁N₇O;
145733-36-4
Recombinant tumour necrosis factor

Taurine (rINN) *tor*·rën
2-Aminoethanesulfonic acid; C₂H₇NO₃S; *107-35-7;*
Amino acid

Taurolidine (rINN) see Appendix C

Tauroselcholic Acid (rINN) tor·rö·sel·*kö*·lik
N-[3α,7α,12α-Trihydroxy-23,24-dinor-5β-cholan-22-ylselenoacetyl]taurine; C$_{26}$H$_{45}$NO$_7$SSe; *75018-71-2*
Measurement of bile acid absorption

Taurultam (rINN) *tor*·rul·tam
Perhydro-1,2,4-thiadiazine 1,1-dioxide; C$_3$H$_8$N$_2$O$_2$S;
38668-01-8
Antibacterial

Tazarotene (rINN) ta·*za*·rö·tën
Ethyl 6-[(4,4-dimethylthiochroman-6-yl)ethynyl]nicotinate;
C$_{21}$H$_{21}$NO$_2$S; *118292-40-3*
Vitamin A analogue (retinoid); treatment of psoriasis

Tazasubrate (rINN) tä·za·*sü*·brät
2-[(6-Ethoxy-1,3-benzothiazol-2-yl)thio]-2-phenylpropionic
acid; C$_{18}$H$_{13}$NO$_3$S$_2$; *79071-15-1*
Lipid-regulating agent

and enantiomer

Tazobactam (rINN) ta·zö·*bak*·tam
(1) (2*S*,3*S*,5*R*)-3-Methyl-7-oxo-3-(1*H*-1,2,3-triazol-1-ylmethyl)-4-thia-1-azabicyclo[3.2.0]heptane-2-carboxylic acid 4,4-dioxide;
(2) (2*S*)-C^2-(1*H*-1,2,3-triazol-1-yl)penicillinic acid *S*,*S*-dioxide;
C$_{10}$H$_{12}$N$_4$O$_5$S; *89786-04-9*
Beta-lactam antibacterial

Teceleukin (rINN) te·se·*loo*·kin
Methionyl interleukin-2; *94218-75-4*
Recombinant interleukin II

teceleukin has the following amino acid sequence:

```
MAPTSSSTKK   TQLQLEHLLL   DLQMILNGIN

NYKNPKLTRM   LTFKFYMPKK   ATELKHLQCL

EEELKPLEEV   LNLAQSKNFH   LRPRDLISNI

NVIVLELKGS   ETTFMCEYAD   ETATIVEFLN

RWITFCQSII   STLT
```

Technetium[^{99m}Tc] Bicisate (rINN) tek·*në*·së·um *bi*·si·sät
(SPY-5-23)-[*N*,*N*′-Ethylenebis(ethyl L-cysteinato)-*S*,*S*′,*N*,*N*′-(3)]oxo[^{99m}Tc]technetium(v); C$_{12}$H$_{21}$N$_2$O$_5$S$_2$Tc; *121281-41-2*
Imaging agent

Technetium[^{99m}Tc] Sestamibi (rINN) tek·*në*·së·um ses·*ta*·mi·bë
Hexakis(2-methoxy-2-methylpropylisocyanide)¬
technetium(I)[^{99m}Tc] cation; ^{99m}Tc[C$_6$H$_{11}$NO]$_6$$^+$; *109581-73-9*
Imaging agent

Technetium[^{99m}Tc] Teboroxime (rINN)
tek·*në*·së·um te·bor·*roks*·ëm
(TPRS-7-1-232′4′54)-Bis[(1,2-cyclohexanedione dioximato)¬
(1−)-*O*][(1,2-cyclohexanedione dioximato)(2−)-*O*]¬
methylborato(2−)-*N*,*N*′,*N*′′,*N*′′′,*N*′′′′,*N*′′′′′]-chloro[^{99m}Tc]¬
technetium(III); C$_{19}$H$_{29}$BClN$_6$O$_6$Tc; *104716-22-5*
Imaging agent

The symbol '¬' in systematic chemical names signifies line continuation

Technetium[⁹⁹ᵐTc] Tiatide (rINN) tek·*në*·së·um *tï*·a·tïd
Sodium [*N*-(mercaptoacetyl)glycylglycylglycinato(1−)-
N,N′,N′′,S]oxotechnetate(2−); $C_8H_8N_3NaO_6STc$; *104348-91-6*
(anion)
Imaging agent

Teclothiazide (rINN) te·klö·*thï*·a·zïd
(*RS*)-6-Chloro-3,4-dihydro-3-trichloromethyl-2*H*-1,2,4-
benzothiadiazine-7-sulfonamide 1,1-dioxide; $C_8H_7Cl_4N_3O_4S_2$;
4267-05-4
Thiazide diuretic

and enantiomer

Tedisamil (rINN) te·*di*·sa·mil
3′,7′-Bis(cyclopropylmethyl)spiro[cyclopentane-1,9′-[3,7]¬
diazabicyclo[3.3.1]nonane]; $C_{19}H_{32}N_2$; *90961-53-8*;
Antiarrhythmic; anti-ischaemic

Teduglutide (rINN) te·*du*·gloo·tïd
[2-Glycine] (1-33)-peptide 2 analogue of human glucagon
(GLP-2); *287714-30-1*

teduglutide has the following amino acid sequence:

```
H-His-Gly-Asp-Gly-Ser-Phe-Ser-Asp-Glu-Met-
                                            10
   Asn-Thr-Ile-Leu-Asp-Asn-Leu-Ala-Ala-Arg-
                                            20
   Asp-Phe-Ile-Asn-Trp-Leu-Ile-Gln-Thr-Lys-
                                            30
   Ile-Thr-Asp-OH
```

Tegafur (rINN) *teg*·a·fûr
5-Fluoro-1-(tetrahydro-2-furyl)uracil; $C_8H_9FN_2O_3$; *17902-23-7*
Pyrimidine analogue; cytotoxic

Tegaserod (rINN) te·*ga*·ser·rod
1-[(5-Methoxyindol-3-yl)methyleneamino]-3-pentylguanidine;
$C_{16}H_{23}N_5O$; *145158-71-0*
Serotonin 5HT₄ receptor partial agonist

●**Teicoplanin** (rINN) tï·kö·*plä*·nin
An antibiotic obtained from cultures of *Actinoplanes
teichomyceticus*, or the same substance obtained by any other
means; *61036-64-4*; Teichomycin A2
Glycopeptide antibacterial

Telbivudine (rINN) tel·*bi*·vü·dën
1-(2-Deoxy-ʙ-ʟ-*erythro*-pentofuranosyl)-5-methylpyrimidine-
2,4(1*H*,3*H*)-dione; $C_{10}H_{14}N_2O_5$; *3424-98-4*
Antiviral (hepatitis B)

Telithromycin (rINN) te·li·thrö·*mï*·sin
(3a*S*,4*R*,7*R*,9*R*,10*R*,11*R*,13*R*,15*R*,15a*R*)-4-Ethyloctahydro-11-
methoxy-3a,7,9,11,13,15-hexamethyl-1-{4-[4-(3-pyridyl)¬
imidazol-1-yl]butyl}-10-[(3,4,6-trideoxy-3-dimethylamino-
β-ᴅ-*xylo*-hexopyranosyl)oxy]-2*H*-oxacyclotetradecino¬
[4,3-*d*][1,3]oxazole-2,6,8,14(1*H*,7*H*,9*H*)-tetrone;
$C_{43}H_{65}N_5O_{10}$; *173838-31-8*
Macrolide antibacterial

● **Telmisartan** (rINN) tel·mi·*sar*·tan
4′-{[4-Methyl-6-(1-methylbenzimidazol-2-yl)-2-propyl¬
benzimidazol-1-yl]methyl}biphenyl-2-carboxylic acid;
$C_{33}H_{30}N_4O_2$; *144701-48-4*
Angiotensin II (AT$_1$) receptor antagonist

Teludipine (rINN) ta·*lü*·di·pën
Diethyl (4*RS*)-(*E*)-4-[2-(2-*tert*-butoxycarbonylvinyl)phenyl]-2-
dimethylaminomethyl-1,4-dihydro-6-methylpyridine-3,5-
dicarboxylate; $C_{28}H_{38}N_2O_6$; *108687-08-7*
Teludipine Hydrochloride *108700-03-4*
Calcium channel blocker

and enantiomer

Temafloxacin (rINN) te·ma·*floks*·a·sin
(*RS*)-1-(2,4-Difluorophenyl)-6-fluoro-1,4-dihydro-7-(3-
methylpiperazin-1-yl)-4-oxoquinoline-3-carboxylic acid;
$C_{21}H_{18}F_3N_3O_3$; *108319-06-8*
Temafloxacin Hydrochloride *105784-61-0*
Fluoroquinolone antibacterial

and enantiomer

● **Temazepam** (rINN) te·*mä*·ze·pam
7-Chloro-1,3-dihydro-3-hydroxy-1-methyl-5-phenyl-1,4-
benzodiazepin-2-one; $C_{16}H_{13}ClN_2O_2$; *846-50-4*
Benzodiazepine

Temelastine (rINN) te·me·*las*·tën
2-[4-(5-Bromo-3-methyl-2-pyridyl)butylamino]-5-(6-methyl-3-
pyridylmethyl)pyrimidin-4(1*H*)-one; $C_{21}H_{24}BrN_5O$;
86181-42-2
Histamine H$_1$ receptor antagonist; antihistamine

Temocapril (rINN) te·mö·*ka*·pril
(+)-[(2*S*,6*R*)-6-{[(*S*)-1-(Ethoxycarbonyl)-3-phenylpropyl]¬
amino}-5-oxo-2-(2-thienyl)-1,4-thiazepan-4-yl]acetic acid;
$C_{23}H_{28}N_2O_5S_2$; *111902-57-9*
Temocapril Hydrochloride *110221-44-8*
Angiotensin converting enzyme inhibitor

Temocaprilat (rINN) te·mö·*ka*·pri·lat
(+)-[(2*S*,6*R*)-6-{[(*S*)-1-Carboxy-3-phenylpropyl]amino}-5-oxo-2-(2-
thienyl)-1,4-thiazepan-4-yl]acetic acid; *118292-40-3*; $C_{21}H_{24}N_2O_5S_2$
Angiotensin converting enzyme inhibitor

Temocillin (rINN) te·mö·*si*·lin
(6*S*)-6-[2-Carboxy-2-(3-thienyl)acetamido]-6-methoxy¬
penicillanic acid; $C_{16}H_{18}N_2O_7S_2$; *66148-78-5*
Temocillin Sodium *61545-06-0*
Penicillin antibacterial

and epimer at C*

Temoporfin (rINN) te·mö·*por*·fin
7,8-Dihydro-5,10,15,20-tetrakis(3-hydroxyphenyl)porphyrin;
$C_{44}H_{32}N_4O_4$; *122341-38-2*
Porphyrin derivative; photosensitiser

The symbol '¬' in systematic chemical names signifies line continuation

Temozolomide (rINN) te·mö·*zo*·lö·mïd

3,4-Dihydro-3-methyl-4-oxoimidazo[5,1-*d*][1,2,3,5]tetrazine-8-carboxamide; $C_6H_6N_6O_2$; *85622-93-1*
Cytotoxic alkylating agent

Temsirolimus (rINN) *tem*·sir·ö·*lim*·us

(1*R*,2*R*,4*S*)-4-{(2*R*)-2-[(3*S*,6*R*,7*E*, 9*R*,10*R*,12*R*,14*S*,15*E*,¬17*E*,19*E*,21*S*,23*S*,26*R*,27*R*,34a*S*)-9,27-Dihydroxy-10,21-dimethoxy-6,8,12,14,20,26-hexamethyl-1,5,11,28,29-pentaoxo-1,4,5,6,9,10,11,12,13, 14,21,¬22,23,24,25,26,27,28,29,31,32,33,34,34a-tetracosahydro-3*H*-23,27-epoxypyrido[2,1-*c*][1,4]-oxazacyclohentriacontin-3-yl]propyl}-2-ethoxycyclohexyl 3-hydroxy-2-(hydroxymethyl)-2-methylpropanoate; $C_{56}H_{87}NO_{16}$;
162635-04-3

Calcineurin inhibitor; immunosuppressant

Temurtide (rINN) *te*·mûr·tïd

N-{(*R*)-2-[(3*R*,4*R*,5*S*,6*R*)-3-Acetamidotetrahydro-2,5-dihydroxy-6-hydroxymethylpyran-4-yloxy]propionyl}-L-threonyl-D-isoglutamine; $C_{20}H_{34}N_4O_{12}$; *66112-59-2*
Vaccine adjuvant

Tenecteplase (rINN) te·*nek*·te·pläs

[103-L-asparagine,117-L-glutamine,296-L-alanine,297-L-alanine,298-L-alanine,299-L-alanine]plasminogen activator (human tissue-type); *191588-94-0*
Tissue-type plasminogen activator; fibrinolytic

tenecteplase has the following glycosylated amino acid sequence:

SYQVICRDEK	TQMIYQQHQS	WLRPVLRSNR
VEYCWCNSGR	AQCHSVPVKS	CSEPRCFNGG
TCQQALYFSD	FVCQCPEGFA	GKCCEIDTRA
TCYEDQGISY	RGTWSTAESG	AECTNWNQSA
LAQKPYSGRR	PDAIRLGLGN	HNYCRNPDRD
SKPWCYVFKA	GKYSSEFCSY	PACSEGNSDC
YFGNGSAYRG	THSLTESGAS	CLPWNSMILI
GKVYTAQNPS	AQALGLGKHN	YCRNPDGDAK
PWCHVLKNRR	LTWEYCDVPS	CSTCGLRQYS
QPQFR		
IKGGLFADIA	SHPWQAAIFA	KHRRSPGERF
LCGGILISSC	WILSAAHCFQ	ERFPPHHLTV
ILGRTYRVVP	GEEEQKFEVE	KYIVHKEFDD
DTYDNDIALL	QLKSDSSRCA	QESSVVRTVC
LPPADLQLPD	WTECELSGYG	KHEALSPFYS
ERLKEAHVRL	YPSSRCTSQH	LLNRTVTDNM
LCAGDTRSGG	PQANLHDACQ	GDSGGPLVCL
NDGRMTLVGI	ISWGLGCGQK	DVPGVYTKVT
NYLDWIRDNM	RP	

Tenidap (rINN) *te*·ni·dap

(*Z*)-5-Chloro-3-(α-hydroxy-2-thenylidene)-2-oxoindoline-1-carboxamide; $C_{14}H_9ClN_2O_3S$; *120210-48-2*
Tenidap Sodium *119784-94-0*
Cyclo-oxygenase inhibitor; analgesic; anti-inflammatory

Teniposide (rINN) te·*ni*·pö·sïd
(5*S*,5a*R*,8a*R*,9*S*)-5,8,8a,9-Tetrahydro-5-(4-hydroxy-3,5-
dimethoxyphenyl)-9-[(*R*)-4,6-*O*-thenylidene-β-D-gluco¬
pyranosyloxy]isobenzofuro[5,6-*f*][1,3]benzodioxol-6(5a*H*)-
one; $C_{32}H_{32}N_{13}S$; *29767-20-2*
Inhibitor of DNA topoisomerase type II; cytotoxic

Tenofovir (rINN) te·*nö*·fö·veer
{[(*R*)-2-(6-Amino-9*H*-purin-9-yl)-1-methylethoxy]methyl}¬
phosphonic acid; $C_9H_{14}N_5O_4P$; *147137-20-6*
Tenofovir Disoproxil
Nucleoside reverse transcriptase inhibitor; antiviral (HIV)

● **Tenoxicam** (rINN) te·*noks*·i·kam
4-Hydroxy-2-methyl-*N*-(2-pyridyl)-2*H*-thieno[2,3-*e*][1,2]¬
thiazine-3-carboxamide 1,1-dioxide; $C_{13}H_{11}N_3O_4S_2$; *59804-37-4*
Cyclo-oxygenase inhibitor; analgesic; anti-inflammatory

Teprotide (rINN) *te*·prö·tïd
$C_{53}H_{76}N_{14}O_{12}$; *35115-60-7*
Angiotensin converting enzyme inhibitor

<Glu-Trp-Pro-Arg-Pro-Gln-Ile-Pro-Pro

Terazosin (rINN) te·*rä*·zö·sin
(±)-6,7-Dimethoxy-2-[4-(tetrahydrofuran-2-carbonyl)¬
piperazin-1-yl]quinazolin-4-ylamine; $C_{19}H_{25}N_5O_4$; *63590-64-7*
● **Terazosin Hydrochloride** *70024-40-7 (hydrate)*;
63074-08-8 (anhydrous)
Alpha$_1$-adrenoceptor antagonist

mixture of 4 stereoisomers

Terbinafine (rINN) ter·*bi*·na·fën
(*E*)-6,6-Dimethylhept-2-en-4-ynyl(methyl)(1-naphthyl¬
methyl)amine; $C_{21}H_{25}N$; *91161-71-6*
● **Terbinafine Hydrochloride** *78628-80-5*
Antifungal

Terbucromil (rINN) ter·*bü*·krö·mil
6,8-Di-*tert*-butyl-4-oxochromene-2-carboxylic acid; $C_{18}H_{22}O_4$;
37456-21-6
*Cromone; treatment of asthma, food allergy,
allergic conjunctivitis, rhinitis*

Terbutaline (rINN) ter·*bü*·ta·lën
2-(*tert*-Butylamino)-1-(3,5-dihydroxyphenyl)ethanol;
$C_{12}H_{19}NO_3$; *23031-25-6*
● **Terbutaline Sulfate** *23031-32-5*
Beta$_2$-adrenoceptor agonist; bronchodilator

and enantiomer

● **Terconazole** (rINN) ter·*ko*·na·zôl
1-{4-[2-(2,4-Dichlorophenyl)-*r*-2-(1*H*-1,2,4-triazol-1-ylmethyl)-
1,3-dioxolan-*c*-4-ylmethoxy]phenyl}-4-isopropylpiperazine;
$C_{26}H_{31}Cl_2N_5O_3$; *67915-31-5*
Antifungal

The symbol '¬' in systematic chemical names signifies line continuation

and enantiomer

● **Terfenadine** (rINN) ter·*fe*·na·dën
1-(4-*tert*-Butylphenyl)-4-[4-(α-hydroxybenzhydryl)¬
piperidino]butan-1-ol; $C_{32}H_{41}NO_2$; *50679-08-8*
Histamine H_1 receptor antagonist; antihistamine

and enantiomer

Terfluranol (rINN) ter·*flûr*·ra·nol
4,4′-[(1*R*,2*S*)-1-Methyl-2-(2,2,2-trifluoroethyl)ethylene]¬
diphenol; $C_{17}H_{17}F_3O_2$; *64396-09-4*
Treatment of breast cancer

Teriparatide (rINN) te·ri·*pa*·rá·tïd
L-Seryl-L-valyl-L-seryl-L-glutamyl-L-isoleucyl-L-glutaminyl-
L-leucyl-L-methionyl-L-glutamyl-L-arginyl-L-valyl-L-glutamyl-
L-arginyl-L-valyl-L-glutamyl-L-tryptophyl-L-leucyl-L-arginyl-
L-lysyl-L-lysyl-L-leucyl-L-glutaminyl-L-aspartyl-L-valyl-
L-histidyl-L-asparginyl-L-phenylalanine; *52232-67-4*;
Teriparatide Acetate *99294-94-7*
Parathyroid hormone analogue; treatment of osteoporosis

teriparatide has the following amino acid sequence:

```
Ser-Val-Ser-Glu-Ile-Gln-Leu-Met-His-Asn-

Leu-Gly-Lys-His-Leu-Asn-Ser-Met-Glu-Arg-

Val-Glu-Trp-Leu-Arg-Lys-Lys-Leu-Gln-Asp-

Val-His-Asn-Phe
```

Terlipressin (rINN) ter·li·*pres*·sin
N-[*N*-(*N*-Glycylglycyl)glycyl]-8-L-lysine vasopressin;
14636-12-5
*Vasopressin analogue; treatment of diabetes insipidus, bleeding
from varices, dialysis*
Terlipressin Acetate

```
Gly-Gly-Gly-Cys-Tyr-Phe-Gln-Asn-
      └─────────────────────────
Cys-Pro-Lys-Gly-NH₂
```

Terodiline (rINN) see Appendix C

Terpin (rINN) *ter*·pin (BAN)
cis-p-Menthane-1,8-diol; $C_{10}H_{20}O_2$; *80-53-5*
Terpin Hydrate *2451-01-6*; component in many proprietary
preparations
Expectorant

Tertatolol (rINN) ter·*ta*·to·lol
1-*tert*-Butylamino-3-(3,4-dihydro-2*H*-1-benzothiin-8-yloxy)¬
propan-2-ol; $C_{16}H_{25}NO_2S$; *34784-64-0*
Beta-adrenoceptor antagonist

and enantiomer

● **Testosterone** (rINN) tes·*to*·ste·rön
17β-Hydroxyandrost-4-en-3-one; $C_{19}H_{28}O_2$; *58-22-0*

● **Testosterone Decanoate** *5721-91-5*

● **Testosterone Enanthate** *315-37-7*

● **Testosterone Isocaproate** *15262-86-9*

♣ **Testosterone Phenylpropionate** *1255-49-8*

● **Testosterone Propionate** *57-85-2*

Testosterone Undecanoate
Androgen

Tetrabenazine (rINN) te·tra·*ben*·á·zën
9,10-Dimethoxy-3-(2-methylpropyl)-1,3,4,6,7,11b-hexahydro-
2*H*-benzo[*a*]quinolizin-2-one; $C_{19}H_{27}NO_3$; *58-46-8*;
Movement disorder control

mixture of 4 stereoisomers

Tetracaine (rINN) te·tra·kän
2-Dimethylaminoethyl 4-butylaminobenzoate;
$C_{15}H_{24}N_2O_2$; *94-24-6*
● **Tetracaine Hydrochloride** *136-47-0*
Local anaesthetic

Tetracosactide (rINN) te·tra·kos·*ak*·tïd
Corticotrophin-(1-24)-tetracosapeptide; cosyntropin (USAN);
16960-16-0
Tetracosactide Acetate
Corticotropic peptide

```
Ser-Tyr-Ser-Met-Glu-His-Phe-Arg-Trp-Gly-

Lys-Pro-Val-Gly-Lys-Lys-Arg-Arg-Pro-Val-

Lys-Val-Tyr-Pro
```

● **Tetracycline** (rINN) te·tra·*sï*·klën
(4*S*,4a*S*,5a*S*,6*S*,12a*S*)-4-Dimethylamino-1,4,4a,5,5a,6,11,12a-
octahydro-3,6,10,12,12a-pentahydroxy-6-methyl-1,11-
dioxonaphthacene-2-carboxamide; $C_{22}H_{24}N_2O_8$; *60-54-8*
● **Tetracycline Hydrochloride** *64-75-5*
Tetracycline antibacterial

Tetracycline Phosphate Complex (BAN)
A sparingly soluble complex of sodium metaphosphate and
tetracyline; *1336-20-5*
Antihelminthic

Tetrahydrozoline *see Tetryzoline*

Tetramisole (rINN) te·*tra*·mi·sôl
2,3,5,6-Tetrahydro-6-phenylimadazo[2,1-*b*][1,3]thiazole;
$C_{11}H_{12}N_2S$; *5036-02-2*
Tetramisole Hydrochloride *5386-74-8*
Antihelmintic

and enantiomer

● **Tetrazepam** (rINN) te·*trä*·zë·pam
7-Chloro-5-(cyclohexen-1-yl)-1-methyl-1,3-dihydro-2*H*-1,4-
benzodiazepin-2-one; $C_{16}H_{17}ClN_2O$; *10379-14-3*
Benzodiazepine; hypnotic

Tetrofosmin (rINN) te·trö·*fos*·min
(1) *P,P,P´,P´*-Tetrakis(2-ethoxyethyl)ethylenebisphosphane;
(2) 6,9-bis(2-ethoxyethyl)-3,12-dioxa-6,9-diphosphatetradecane;
$C_{18}H_{40}O_4P_2$; *127502-06-1*
Imaging agent for radiography

Tetronasin (rINN) te·*tro*·na·sin
Tetrahydro-3-[(*S*)-1-hydroxy-2-{(1*S*,2*S*,6*R*)-2-[(*E*)-3-hydroxy-2-
{(2*R*, 3*R*,6*S*)-tetrahydro-3-methyl-6-[(*E*)-(*S*)-3-{(2*R*,3*S*,5*R*)-
tetrahydro-5-[(*R*)-1-methoxyethyl]-2-furyl}but-1-enyl]-3-
methyl-2*H*-pyran-2-yl}prop-1-enyl]-6-methylcyclohexyl}¬
propylidene]furan-2,4-dione; $C_{35}H_{54}O_8$; *75139-06-9*;
ICI 139603
Tetronasin Sodium *75139-05-8*
Ionophore antimicrobial

Tetroxoprim (rINN) te·*troks*·ö·prim
5-[3,5-Dimethyloxy-4-(2-methoxyethoxy)benzyl]pyrimidine-
2,4-diyldiamine; $C_{16}H_{22}N_4O_4$; *53808-87-0*
Dihydrofolate reductase inhibitor

Tetryzoline (rINN) te·*trï*·zö·lën
(*RS*)-2-(1,2,3,4-Tetrahydro-1-naphthyl)-2-imidazoline;
$C_{13}H_{16}N_2$; *84-22-0*
● **Tetryzoline Hydrochloride** *552-48-5*
Adrenoceptor agonist; decongestant

and enantiomer

The symbol '¬' in systematic chemical names signifies line continuation

Tezosentan (rINN) te·zö·*zen*·tan

N-{6-(2-Hydroxyethoxy)-5-(2-methoxyphenoxy)-2-[2-(1*H*-tetrazol-5-yl)pyridin-4-yl]pyrimidin-4-yl}-5- isopropyl¬pyridine-2-sulfonamide; $C_{27}H_{27}N_9O_6S$; *180384-57-0*
Endothelin A/B receptor antagonist

Thalidomide (rINN) tha·*li*·dö·mïd

(*RS*)-2-Phthalimidoglutarimide; $C_{13}H_{10}N_2O_4$; *50-35-1*
Immunomodulator

and enantiomer

Thaumatin (BAN) *thor*·ma·tin

A mixture in the ratio 2:1 of two polypeptides, thaumatin I and II, each consisting of 207 amino acid residues and having a molecular weight of about 22,000, extracted from the aril of the tropical fruit *Thaumatococcus daniellii* Benth; *53850-34-3*
Sweetening agent

Thebacon (rINN) *the*·ba·kon

(1) (−)-(5*R*,6*S*)-4,5-Epoxy-3-methoxy-17-methylmorphin-6-en-6-yl acetate; (2) 6-*O*-Acetyl-7,8-dihydro-3-*O*-methyl-6,7-didehydromorphine; $C_{20}H_{23}NO_4$; *466-90-0*
Opioid receptor agonist; cough suppressant

Thenalidine (rINN) the·*na*·li·dën

N-(1-Methyl-4-piperidyl)-*N*-(2-thenyl)aniline; $C_{17}H_{22}N_2S$; *86-12-4*
Histamine H_1 receptor antagonist; antihistamine

♣ **Thenium Closilate** (rINN) *thë*·në·um *klö*·si·lät

Dimethyl(2-phenoxyethyl)2-thenylammonium¬4-chlorobenzenesulfonate; $C_{21}H_{24}ClNO_4S_2$; *4304-40-9*
Antihelmintic (veterinary)

Thenyldiamine (rINN) the·nïl·*di*·a·mën

2-(*N*-2-Pyridyl-*N*-3-thenylamino)ethyldimethylamine; $C_{14}H_{19}N_3S$; *91-79-2*
Thenyldiamine Hydrochloride *958-93-0*
Histamine H_1 receptor antagonist; antihistamine

● **Theobromine** (rINN) thë·ö·*brö*·mën

3,7-Dihydro-3,7-dimethylpurine-2,6(1*H*)-dione; $C_7H_8N_4O_2$; *83-67-0*
Non-selective phosphodiesterase inhibitor (xanthine); treatment of reversible airways obstruction

Theodrenaline (rINN) thë·ö·*dren*·a·lën

7-[2-(3,4,β-Trihydroxyphenethylamino)ethyl]theophylline; $C_{17}H_{21}N_5O_5$; *13460-98-5*
Vasopressor

and enantiomer

● **Theophylline** (BAN) thë·*o*·fi·lën

3,7-Dihydro-1,3-dimethylpurine-2,6(1*H*)-dione; $C_7H_8N_4O_2$; *58-55-9*
● **Theophylline Hydrate** (monohydrate); *5967-84-0*
Non-selective phosphodiesterase inhibitor (xanthine); treatment of reversible airways obstruction

Thiabendazole *see Tiabendazole*

284

Thiacetazone *see Thioacetazone*

Thialbarbital (rINN) thï·al·*bar*·bi·tal
5-Allyl-5-(cyclohex-2-enyl)-2-thiobarbituric acid; $C_{13}H_{16}N_2O_2S$;
467-36-7
Barbiturate

● **Thiamazole** (rINN) thï·*am*·a·zôl
1-Methylimidazole-2-thiol;
$C_4H_6N_2S$; *60-56-0*
Thionamide antithyroid

Thiambutosine (rINN) thï·am·*bü*·tö·sën
1-(4-Butoxyphenyl)-3-(4-dimethylaminophenyl)thiourea;
$C_{19}H_{25}N_3OS$; *500-89-0*
Antileprosy drug

Thiamine (rINN) *thï*·a·mën
3-(4-Amino-2-methylpyrimidin-5-ylmethyl)-5-(2-hydroxy¬
ethyl)-4-methyl-1,3-thiazolium hydroxide; vitamin B1;
$C_{12}H_{18}N_4O_2S$; *59-43-8*
● **Thiamine Hydrochloride** *67-03-8*
● **Thiamine Nitrate** *532-43-4*
Vitamin B₁

● **Thiamphenicol** (rINN) thï·am·*fe*·ni·kol
($\alpha R,\beta R$)-2,2-Dichloro-*N*-(β-hydroxy-α-hydroxymethyl-4-
methylsulfonylphenethyl)acetamide; $C_{12}H_{15}Cl_2NO_5S$;
15318-45-3
Antibacterial

Thiazesim *see Tiazesim*

Thiethylperazine (rINN) see Appendix C

Thioacetazone (rINN) thï·ö·a·*set*·a·zön
4-Acetamidobenzaldehyde thiosemicarbazone; $C_{10}H_{12}N_4OS$;
104-06-3
Antituberculosis drug

Thiocarlide *see Tiocarlide*

● **Thioctic Acid** (rINN) thï·*ok*·tik
5-[(3*RS*)-1,2-Dithiolan-3-yl]pentanoic acid; $C_8H_{14}O_2S_2$;
62-46-4
Antioxidant

and enantiomer

Thioguanine *see Tioguanine*

● **Thiomersal** (rINN) thï·ö·*mer*·sal
Sodium salt of (2-carboxyphenylthio)ethylmercury; thimerosal;
thiomersalate; $C_9H_9HgNaO_2S$; *54-64-8*
Antiseptic; adjuvant in vaccine formulations

Thiomesterone *see Tiomesterone*

Thiopental (rINN) thï·ö·*pen*·tal
5-Ethyl-5-(1-methylbutyl)-2-thiobarbituric acid; $C_{11}H_{18}N_2O_2S$;
76-75-5
● **Thiopental Sodium** *71-73-8*
Intravenous barbiturate; general anaesthetic

Thiophanate (BAN) thï·*o*·fa·nät
(1) 4,4′-*o*-Phenylenebis(ethyl 3-thioallophanate);
(2) 4,4′-*o*-phenylenebis(3-ethoxycarbonyl-2-thiourea);
$C_{14}H_{18}N_4O_4S_2$; *23564-06-9*
Antihelmintic

Thiopropazate (rINN) see Appendix C

The symbol '¬' in systematic chemical names signifies line continuation

Thioproperazine (rINN) thï·ö·prö·*pe*·ra·zën
N,N-Dimethyl-10-[3-(4-methylpiperazin-1-yl)propyl]pheno‐
thiazine-2-sulfonamide; $C_{22}H_{30}N_4O_2S_2$; *316-81-4*
Thioproperazine Mesilate *2347-80-0*
Dopamine receptor antagonist; neuroleptic

● **Thioridazine** (rINN) thï·ö·*rid*·a·zën
(*RS*)-10-[2-(1-Methyl-2-piperidyl)ethyl]-2-methyl thio‐
phenothiazine; $C_{21}H_{26}N_2S_2$; *50-52-2*
● **Thioridazine Hydrochloride** *130-61-0*
Dopamine receptor antagonist; neuroleptic

and enantiomer

● **Thiotepa** (rINN) thï·ö·*të*·pa
Phosphorothioic tri(ethyleneamide); $C_6H_{12}N_3PS$; *52-24-4*
Cytotoxic alkylating agent

Thiothixene *see Tiotixene*

Thioxolone *see Tioxolone*

Thonzylamine (rINN)
2-[*p*-Anisyl(pyrimidin-2-yl)amino]ethyldimethylamine;
$C_{16}H_{22}N_4O$; *91-85-0*
Histamine H_1 receptor antagonist; antihistamine

● **Threonine** (rINN) *thrë*·ö·nïn
L-Threonine; (2S,3R)-2-Amino-3-hydroxybutanoic acid;
$C_4H_9NO_3$; *72-19-5;*
Amino acid

Thurfyl Nicotinate (BAN) *ther*·fïl
Tetrahydrofurfuryl nicotinate; $C_{11}H_{13}NO_3$; *70-19-9*
Vasodilator

Thymopentin (rINN) thï·mö·*pen*·tin
L-arginyl-L-lysyl-α-L-aspartyl-L-valyl-L-tyrosine; $C_{30}H_{49}N_9O_9$;
69558-55-0
Thymopoietin pentapeptide; immunomodulator

```
Arg-Lys-Asp-Val
```

Thymoxamine *see Moxisylyte*

Thyrotrophin (rINN) thï·rö·*trö*·fïn
Thyrotrophic hormone; *9002-71-5*
Thyroid stimulating hormone (TSH)

Thyrotropin Alfa (rINN) thî·rö·*trö*·pin al·fa
Thyrotropin (human β-subunit protein moiety), complex with
chorionic gonadotropin (human α-subunit protein moiety);
194100-83-9
Recombinant thyroid stimulating hormone

*thyrotropin alfa has the following amino acid sequence
(Cys—Cys bridging not shown):*

```
α-subunit:
  APDVQDCPEC    TLQENPFFSQ    PGAPILQCMG

  CCFSRAYPTP    LRSKKTMLVQ    KNVTSESTCC

  VAKSYNRVTV    MGGFKVENHT    ACHCSTCYYH

  KS


β-subunit:
  FCIPTEYTMH    IERRECAYCL    TINTTICAGY

  CMTRDINGKL    FLPKYALSQD    VCTYRDFIYR

  TVEIPGCPLH    VAPYFSYPVA    LSCKCGKCNT

  DYSDCIHEAI    KTNYCTKPQK    SYLVGFSV
```

Thyroxine *see Levothyroxine*

● **Tiabendazole** (rINN) tï·a·*ben*·da·zôl
2-(1,3-Thiazol-4-yl)benzimidazole; $C_{10}H_7N_3S$; *148-79-8*
Benzimidazole antihelminthic

Tiagabine (rINN) ti·*a*·ga·bën
(*R*)-1-[4,4-Bis(3-methyl-2-thienyl)but-3-enyl]piperidine-3-carboxylic acid; $C_{20}H_{25}NO_2S_2$; *115103-54-3*
Tiagabine Hydrochloride *145821-59-6*
Antiepileptic

Tiamenidine (rINN) ti·a·*me*·ni·dën
2-Chloro-4-methyl-3-thienyl(2-imidazolin-2-yl)amine; $C_8H_{10}ClN_3S$; *31428-61-2*
Tiamenidine Hydrochloride *31428-62-3*
Alpha₂-adrenoceptor agonist; treatment of hypertension

♣ **Tiamulin** (rINN) ti·*a*·mü·lin
11-Hydroxy-6,7,10,12-tetramethyl-1-oxo-10-vinylperhydro-3a,7-pentanoinden-8-yl (2-diethylaminoethylthio)acetate; $C_{28}H_{47}NO_4S$; *56142-71-3*
♣ **Tiamulin Hydrogen Fumarate** *55297-96-6*
Antibacterial

Tiapamil (rINN) ti·*a*·pa·mil
(*RS*)-3,4-Dimethoxyphenethyl{3-[2-(3,4-dimethoxyphenyl)-1,3-dithian-2-yl]propyl}methylamine *S,S,S′,S′*-tetraoxide; $C_{26}H_{37}NO_8S_2$; *57010-31-8*
Calcium channel blocker

and enantiomer

Tiapride (rINN) *ti*·a·prïd
N-(2-Diethylaminoethyl)-2-methoxy-5-methylsulfonyl¬benzamide; $C_{15}H_{24}N_2O_4S$; *51012-32-9*
● **Tiapride Hydrochloride** *51012-33-0*
Dopamine receptor antagonist; neuroleptic

● **Tiaprofenic Acid** (rINN) ti·a·*prö*·fë·nik
2-(5-Benzoyl-2-thienyl)propionic acid; $C_{14}H_{12}O_3S$; *33005-97-7*
Cyclo-oxygenase inhibitor; analgesic; anti-inflammatory

and enantiomer

Tiaprost (rINN) *ti*·a·prost
(1) (5*Z*,13*E*)-(9*S*,11*R*,15*RS*)-9,11,15-Trihydroxy-16-(3-thienyloxy)-17,18,19,20 tetranorprosta-5,13-dienoic acid;
(2) (*Z*)-7-{(1*R*,2*R*,3*R*,5*S*)-3,5-Dihydroxy-2-[(*E*)-(3*RS*)-3-hydroxy-4-(3-thienyloxy)buten-1-yl]cyclopentyl}hept-5-enoic acid; $C_{20}H_{28}O_6S$; *71116-82-0*
Prostaglandin (PGF₂ₐ) analogue

and epimer at C*

Tiaramide (rINN) ti·*a*·ra·mïd
5-Chloro-3-[4-(2-hydroxyethyl)piperazin-1-ylcarbonylmethyl]-1,3-benzothiazol-2(3*H*)-one; $C_{15}H_{18}ClN_3O_3S$; *32527-55-2*
Cyclo-oxygenase inhibitor; analgesic; anti-inflammatory

Tiazesim (rINN) ti·*a*·ze·sim
5-(2-Dimethylaminoethyl)-2,3-dihydro-2-phenyl-1,5-benzo¬thiazepin-4(5*H*)-one; $C_{19}H_{22}N_2OS$; *5845-26-1*
Antidepressant

● **Tibolone** (rINN) *ti*·bo·lön
17β-Hydroxy-7α-methyl-19-nor-17α-pregn-5(10)-en-20-yn-3-one; $C_{21}H_{28}O_2$; *5630-53-5*
Steroid with oestrogenic and progestogenic properties

The symbol '¬' in systematic chemical names signifies line continuation

Tibric Acid (rINN) *ti*·brik

2-Chloro-5-(*cis*-3,5-dimethylpiperidinosulfonyl)benzoic acid; $C_{14}H_{18}ClNO_4S$; *37087-94-8*
Fibrate; lipid-regulating drug

Ticagrelor (rINN) ti·*ká*·gre·lor

(1S,2S,3R,5S)-3-(7-{[(1S,2R)-2-(3,4-Difluorophenyl)¬
cyclopropyl]amino}-5-(propanesulfanyl)-3H-[1,2,3]¬
triazolo[4,5-d]pyrimidin-3-yl)-5-(2-hydroxethoxy)¬
cyclopentane-1,2-diol; $C_{23}H_{28}F_2N_6O_4S$; *274693-27-5*;
Platelet aggregation inhibitor

Ticarbodine (rINN) see Appendix C

Ticarcillin (rINN) tï·kar·*si*·lin

6-[2-Carboxy-2-(3-thienyl)acetamido]penicillanic acid;
$C_{15}H_{16}N_2O_6S_2$; *3973-04-4*

● **Ticarcillin Sodium** *4697-14-7*
Penicillin antibacterial

and enantiomer at C*

Ticlopidine (rINN) tï·*klö*·pi·dën

5-(2-Chlorobenzyl)-4,5,6,7-tetrahydrothieno[3,2-c]pyridine;
$C_{14}H_{14}ClNS$; *55142-85-3*

● **Ticlopidine Hydrochloride** *53885-35-1*

Inhibition of adenosine diphosphate (ADP)-mediated platelet aggregation; antiplatelet drug

Tiemonium Iodide (rINN) tï·e·*mö*·në·um

4-[3-Hydroxy-3-phenyl-3-(2-thienyl)propyl]-4-methyl¬
morpholinium iodide; $C_{18}H_{24}INO_2S$; *144-12-7*
Anticholinergic

and enantiomer

Tienilic Acid (rINN) tï·e·*ni*·lik

[2,3-Dichloro-4-(2-thenoyl)phenoxy]acetic acid; $C_{13}H_8Cl_2O_4S$;
40180-04-9
Thiazide-like diuretic

Tiformin (rINN) tï·*for*·min

4-Guanidinobutyramide; $C_5H_{12}N_4O$; *4210-97-3*
Biguanide; treatment of diabetes mellitus

Tigecycline (rINN) ti·ge·*sik*·lën

(4S,4aS,5aR,12aS)-4,7-Bis(dimethylamino)-9-[2-(*tert*-
butylamino)acetamido]-3,10,12,12a-tetrahydroxy-1,11-dioxo-
1,4,4a,5,5a,6,11,12a-octahydrotetracene-2-carboxamide;
$C_{29}H_{39}N_5O_8$; *220620-09-7*;
Antibacterial

Tigloidine (rINN) see Appendix C

Tiletamine (rINN) tï·*le*·ta·mën

(RS)-2-Ethylamino-2-(2-thienyl)cyclohexanone; $C_{12}H_{17}NOS$;
14176-49-9
Tiletamine Hydrochloride *14176-50-2*
General anaesthetic

and enantiomer

Tilidate (rINN) see Appendix C

Tilmicosin (rINN) til·*mï*·kö·sin
(10*E*,12*E*)-(3*R*,4*S*,5*S*,6*R*,8*R*,14*R*,15*R*)-14-(6-Deoxy-2,3-di-*O*-methyl-β-D-*allo*-hexopyranosyloxymethyl)-5-(3,6-dideoxy-3-dimethylamino-β-D-*gluco*hexopyranosyloxy)-6-[2-(*cis*-3,5-dimethylpiperidino)ethyl]-3-hydroxy-4,8,12-trimethyl-9-oxo-heptadeca-10,12-dien-15-olide; $C_{46}H_{80}N_2O_{13}$; *108050-54-0*
Macrolide antibacterial

Tiludronic Acid (rINN) tï·lü·*dro*·nik
(4-Chlorophenylthiomethylene)bisphosphonic acid; $C_7H_9ClO_6P_2S$; *89987-06-4*
Tiludronate Sodium (2Na) *149845-07-8*
Bisphosphonate; treatment of Paget's disease

Timolol (rINN) *tï*·mo·lol
(*S*)-1-*tert*-Butylamino-3-(4-morpholino-1,2,5-thiadiazol-3-yloxy)propan-2-ol; $C_{13}H_{24}N_4O_3S$; *26839-75-8*
Timolol Maleate *26921-17-5*
Beta-adrenoceptor antagonist

Tinidazole (rINN) ti·*nï*·da·zôl
1-[2-(Ethylsulfony)ethyl]-2-methyl-5-nitroimidazole; $C_8H_{13}N_3O_4S$; *19387-91-8*
Antiprotozoal; antibacterial

Tinzaparin Sodium (rINN) tin·*za*·pa·rin
Sodium salt of depolymerised heparin obtained by enzymatic degradation of heparin from pork intestinal mucosa; the majority of the components have a 2-*O*-sulfo-4-enopyr¬anosuronic acid structure at the non-reducing end of their chain and a 2-*N*,6-*O*-disulfo-D-glucosamine structure at the reducing end; the molecular weight of 70% of the components lies between 1,500 and 10,000 and the average molecular weight is about 4,500; the degree of sulfation is 2·0 to 2·5 per disaccharide unit
Low molecular weight heparin

Tiocarlide (rINN) see Appendix C

Tioconazole (rINN) tï·ö·*ko*·na·zôl
1-[2,4-Dichloro-β-(2-chloro-3-thenyloxy)phenethyl]imidazole; $C_{16}H_{13}Cl_3N_2OS$; *65899-73-2*
Antifungal

and enantiomer

Tioguanine (rINN) tï·o·*gwa*·nën
2-Aminopurine-6-thiol; $C_5H_5N_5S$; *154-42-7*
Purine analogue; cytostatic

Tiomesterone (rINN) tï·ö·*mes*·te·rön
1α,7α-Bis(acetylthio)-17β-hydroxy-17α-methylandrost-4-en-3-one; $C_{24}H_{34}O_4S_2$; *2205-73-4*
Anabolic steroid

Tiopinac (rINN) tï·ö·pi·nak
6,11-Dihydro-11-oxodibenzo[*b,e*]thiepin-3-acetic acid; $C_{16}H_{12}O_3S$; *61220-69-7*
Cyclo-oxygenase inhibitor; analgesic; anti-inflammatory

Tiotixene (rINN) tï·ö·*tiks*·ën
(*Z*)-*N*,*N*-Dimethyl-9-[3-(4-methylpiperazin-1-
yl)propylidene]thioxanthene-2-sulfonamide; $C_{23}H_{29}N_3O_2S_2$;
3313-26-6
Dopamine receptor antagonist; neuroleptic

● **Tiotropium Bromide** (rINN) tï·ö·*trö*·pë·um brö·mïd
(1*S*,3*s*,5*R*,6*R*,7*S*)-6,7-Epoxy-3-(2-hydroxy-2,2-di-2-thienyl¬
acetoxy)-8-methyltropanium bromide; $C_{19}H_{22}BrNO_4S_2$;
139404-48-1
Anticholinergic (antimuscarinic) bronchodilator

Tioxaprofen (rINN) tï·oks·a·*prö*·fen
2-[4,5-Bis(4-chlorophenyl)-1,3-oxazol-2-ylthio]propionic acid;
$C_{18}H_{13}Cl_2NO_3S$; *40198-53-6*
Cyclo-oxygenase inhibitor; analgesic; anti-inflammatory

and enantiomer

Tioxolone (rINN) tï·*oks*·o·lön
6-Hydroxy-1,3-benzoxathiol-2-one; $C_7H_4O_3S$; *4991-65-5*
Keratolytic

Tipentosin (rINN) see Appendix C

Tipranavir (rINN) tï·*pran*·a·veer
N-(3-{(*R*)-1-[(*R*)-5,6-Dihydro-4-hydroxy-2-oxo-6-phenethyl-6-
propyl-2*H*-pyran-3-yl]propyl}phenyl)-5-trifluoro¬
methyl pyridine-2-sulfonamide; $C_{31}H_{33}F_3N_2O_5S$; *164484-41-4*
Protease inhibitor; antiviral (HIV)

Tipredane (rINN) *ti*·pre·dän
17α-(Ethylthio)-9α-fluoro-11β-hydroxy-17β-(methylthio)¬
androsta-1,4-dien-3-one; $C_{22}H_{31}FO_2S_2$; *85197-77-9*
Glucocorticoid

Tiprenolol (rINN) tï·*pren*·o·lol
3-Isopropylamino-1-[2-(methylthio)phenoxy]propan-2-ol;
$C_{13}H_{21}NO_2S$; *26481-51-6*
Tiprenolol Hydrochloride *39832-43-4*
Beta-adrenoceptor antagonist

and enantiomer

Tiprostanide (rINN) see Appendix C

Tiquinamide (rINN) tï·*kwi*·na·mïd
5,6,7,8-Tetrahydro-3-methylquinoline-8-carbothioamide;
$C_{11}H_{14}N_2S$; *53400-67-2*
Tiquinamide Hydrochloride *53400-68-3*
Inhibitor of gastric acid secretion

Tirilazad (rINN) ti·*ri*·la·zad
21-{4-[2,6-(Dipyrrolidin-1-yl)pyrimidin-4-yl]piperazin-1-yl}-
16α-methylpregna-1,4,9(11)-triene-3,20-dione; $C_{38}H_{52}N_6O_2$;
110101-66-1
Tirilazad Mesilate *111793-42-1*
Inhibitor of lipid peroxidation

Tirofiban (rINN) tï·rö·*fi*·ban
N-(Butylsulfonyl)-*O*-[4-(piperidin-4-yl)butyl]-L-tyrosine;
$C_{22}H_{36}N_2O_5S$; *144494-65-5*
Tirofiban Hydrochloride *150915-40-5*
Glycoprotein IIb/IIIa receptor antagonist; antiplatelet drug

Tixocortol (rINN) tiks·ö·*kor*·tol
11β,17α-Dihydroxy-21-mercaptopregn-4-ene-3,20-dione;
$C_{21}H_{30}O_4S$; *61951-99-3*
Tixocortol Pivalate
Glucocorticoid

Tizanidine (rINN) tï·*za*·ni·dën
5-Chloro-2,1,3-benzothiadiazol-4-yl(2-imidazolin-2-yl)amine;
$C_9H_8ClN_5S$; *51322-75-9*
Tizanidine Hydrochloride
Alpha₂-adrenoceptor agonist; skeletal muscle relaxant

Tizolemide (rINN) tï·*zo*·le·mïd
(*RS*)-2-Chloro-5-[4-hydroxy-3-methyl-2-(methylimino)-1,3-
thiazolidin-4-yl]-benzenesulfonamide; $C_{11}H_{14}ClN_3O_3S_2$;
56488-58-5
Tizolemide Hydrochloride
Loop diuretic

and enantiomer

● **Tobramycin** (rINN) to·bra·*mï*·sin
An antimicrobial base produced by *Streptomyces tenebrarius*;
6-*O*-(3-amino-3-deoxy-α-D-glucopyranosyl)-2-deoxy-4-*O*-(2,6-
diamino-2,3,6-trideoxy-α-D-*ribo*-hexopyranosyl)-D-streptamine;
$C_{18}H_{37}N_5O_9$; *32986-56-4*
Tobramycin Sulfate *49842-07-1*
Aminoglycoside antibacterial

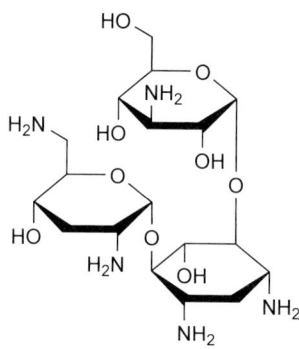

Tocainide (rINN) see Appendix C

Tocladesine (rINN) to·*kla*·de·sën
8-Chloroadenosine 3′,5′-(hydrogen phosphate);
$C_{10}H_{11}ClN_5O_6P$; *41941-56-4*
Immunomodulator

Tocofersolan (rINN) tok·ö·*fir*·sö·lan
α-Hydropoly(oxyethan-1,2-diyl) 2,5,7,8-tetramethyl-2-(4,8,12-
trimethyltridecyl)chroman-6-yl succinate;
$C_{33}H_{54}O_5(C_2H_4O)_n$; *52232-67-4*;
Vitamin E analogue

Todralazine (rINN) to·*dra*·la·zën
Ethyl 3-(phthalazin-1-yl)carbazate; $C_{11}H_{12}N_4O_2$; *14679-73-3*
Vasodilator; treatment of hypertension

Tofenacin (rINN) see Appendix C

Tolamolol (rINN) to·*lam*·o·lol
(*RS*)-4-[2-(2-Hydroxy-3-*o*-tolyloxypropylamino)ethoxy]¬
benzamide; $C_{19}H_{24}N_2O_4$; *38103-61-6*
Tolamolol Hydrochloride *51599-37-2*
Beta-adrenoceptor antagonist

The symbol '¬' in systematic chemical names signifies line continuation

and enantiomer

● **Tolazamide** (rINN) tol·*ä*·za·mïd
1-(Perhydroazepin-1-yl)-3-*p*-tolylsulfonylurea; $C_{14}H_{21}N_3O_3S$;
1156-19-0
*Inhibition of ATP-dependent potassium channels
(sulfonylurea); treatment of diabetes mellitus*

Tolazoline (rINN) tol·*ä*·zö·lën
2-Benzyl-2-imidazoline; $C_{10}H_{12}N_2$; *59-98-3*
Tolazoline Hydrochloride *59-97-2*
Alpha-adrenoceptor agonist

● **Tolbutamide** (rINN) tol·*bü*·ta·mïd
1-Butyl-3-tosylurea; $C_{12}H_{18}N_2O_3S$; *64-77-7*
*Inhibition of ATP-dependent potassium channels (sulfonylurea);
treatment of diabetes mellitus*

Tolcapone (rINN) see Appendix C

Toldimfos (rINN) tol·*dim*·fos
4-Dimethylamino-*o*-tolylphosphinic acid; $C_9H_{14}NO_2P$;
57808-64-7
Toldimfos Sodium *5787-63-3*
Source of phosphate

● **Tolfenamic Acid** (rINN) tol·fe·*nam*·ik
N-(3-Chloro-*o*-tolyl)anthranilic acid; $C_{14}H_{12}ClNO_2$; *13710-19-5*
Cyclo-oxygenase inhibitor; analgesic; anti-inflammatory

Tolgabide (rINN) *tol*·ga·bïd
(*E*)-4-(4′,5-Dichloro-2-hydroxy-3-methylbenzhydrylidene¬
amino)butyramide; $C_{18}H_{18}Cl_2N_2O_2$; *86914-11-6*
Antiepileptic

Tolmesoxide (rINN) tol·me·*soks*·ïd
4,5-Dimethyoxy-*o*-tolyl methyl sulfoxide; $C_{10}H_{14}O_3S$;
38452-29-8
Vasodilator

Tolmetin (rINN) see Appendix C

● **Tolnaftate** (rINN) *tol*·naf·tät
O-2-Naphthyl *N*-methyl-*m*-tolylthiocarbamate; $C_{19}H_{17}NOS$;
2398-96-1
Antifungal

Tolpentamide (rINN) tol·*pen*·ta·mïd
1-Cyclopentyl-3-tosylurea; $C_{13}H_{18}N_2O_3S$; *1027-87-8*
Treatment of diabetes mellitus

Tolperisone (rINN) tol·*pe*·ri·sön
(*RS*)-2,4′-Dimethyl-3-piperidinopropiophenone; $C_{16}H_{23}NO$;
728-88-1
Skeletal muscle relaxant

and enantiomer

Tolpiprazole (rINN) see Appendix C

Tolpronine (rINN) *tol*·prö·nën
(*RS*)-1-(1,2,3,6-Tetrahydro-1-pyridyl)-3-*o*-tolyloxypropan-2-ol;
$C_{15}H_{21}NO_2$; *97-57-4*
Analgesic

and enantiomer

Tolpropamine (rINN) see Appendix C

Tolrestat (rINN) *tol*·res·tat
N-[6-Methoxy-5-trifluoromethyl-1-naphthyl(thiocarbonyl)]-*N*-
methylglycine; $C_{16}H_{14}F_3NO_3S$; *82964-04-3*
Aldose reductase inhibitor; treatment of diabetes mellitus

Tolterodine (rINN) tol·*te*·rö·dën
(*R*)-2-[3-(Di-isopropylamino)-1-phenylpropyl]-*p*-cresol;
$C_{22}H_{31}O$; *124937-51-5*
Tolterodine Tartrate
Anticholinergic

Toltrazuril (rINN) tol·*tra*·zûr·ril
1-Methyl-3-{4-[4-(trifluoromethylthio)phenoxy]-*m*-tolyl}-1,3,5-
triazinane2,4,6-trione; $C_{18}H_{14}F_3N_3O_4S$; *69004-03-1*
Antiprotozoal

Tolvaptan (rINN) tol·*vap*·tan
N-{4-[(5*RS*)-7-Chloro-5-hydroxy-2,3,4,5-tetrahydro-1*H*-1-
benzazepin-1-yl]-3-methylphenyl}-2-methylbenzamide;
$C_{26}H_{25}ClN_2O_3$; *150683-30-0*;
*Vasopressin V₂ receptor antagonist; treatment of the syndrome
of inappropriate ADH secretion*

and enantiomer

Tolycaine (rINN) *tol*·ë·kän
Methyl 2-diethylaminoacetamido-*m*-toluate; $C_{15}H_{22}N_2O_3$;
3886-58-6
Tolycaine Hydrochloride *7210-92-6*
Local anaesthetic

Tonabersat (rINN) to·*nab*·er·sat
N-[(3*S*,4*S*)-6-Acetyl-3-hydroxy-2,2-dimethylchroman-4-yl]-3-
chloro-4-fluorobenzamide; $C_{20}H_{19}ClFNO_4$; *175013-84-0*
Treatment of migraine

Topiramate (rINN) to·*pï*·ra·mät
2,3:4,5-Di-*O*-(isopropylidene)-β-D-fructopyranose sulfamate;
$C_{12}H_{21}NO_8S$; *97240-79-4*
Antiepileptic

Topixantrone (rINN) to·piks·*an*·trön
5-{[2-(Dimethylamino)ethyl]amino}-2-{2-[(2-hydroxyethyl)¬
amino]ethyl}inazolo[4,3-*gh*]isoquinolin-6(2*H*)-one; $C_{21}H_{26}N_6O_2$
Topixantrone Hydrochloride (2:1)
Cytotoxic

The symbol '¬' in systematic chemical names signifies line continuation

Topotecan (rINN) to·*po*·te·kan
(*S*)-10-Dimethylaminomethyl-4-ethyl-4,9-dihydroxy-1*H*-pyrano[3′,4′:6,7]-indolizino[1,2-*b*]quinoline-3,14(4*H*,12*H*)-dione; $C_{23}H_{23}N_3O_5$; *123948-87-8*
Topotecan Hydrochloride *119413-54-6*
Inhibitor of DNA topoisomerase type I; cytotoxic

Torasemide (rINN) tor·*ra*·se·mïd
1-Isopropyl-3-(4-*m*-toluidinopyridine-3-sulfonyl)urea;
$C_{16}H_{20}N_4O_3S$; *56211-40-6*
Torasemide Sodium *72810-59-4*
Thiazide-like diuretic

Toremifene (rINN) tor·*re*·mi·fën
(*Z*)-2-[4-(4-Chloro-1,2-diphenylbut-1-enyl)phenoxy]ethyl⌐
dimethylamine; $C_{26}H_{28}ClNO$; *89778-26-7*
Selective oestrogen receptor modulator

Tosactide (rINN) to·*sak*·tïd
[25-Aspartic acid,26-alanine,27-glycine]corticotrophin-(1-28)-octacosapeptide; $C_{150}H_{230}N_{44}O_{38}S$; *47931-80-6*
Corticotropin analogue

```
Ser-Tyr-Ser-Met-Glu-His-Phe-Arg-Trp-Gly-
Lys-Pro-Val-Gly-Lys-Lys-Arg-Arg-Pro-Val-
Lys-Val-Tyr-Pro-Asp-Ala-Gly-Glu
```

Tosylchloramide Sodium (rINN) tö·sïl·*klor*·ra·mïd *sö*·dë·um
N-Chlorotoluene-*p*-sulfonamide trihydrate, sodium salt;
chloramine-T (USAN); $C_7H_7ClNNaO_2S,3H_2O$; *127-65-1*
Antiseptic

Trabectedin (rINN) tra·*bek*·ted·in
(1′*R*,6*R*,6a*R*,7*R*,13*S*,14*S*,16*R*)-6′,8,14-trihydroxy-7′,9-dimethoxy-4,10,23-trimethyl-19-oxo-3′,4′,6,7,12,13,14,16-octahydrospiro[6,16-(epithiopropanooxymethano)-7,13-imino-6a*H*-1,3-dioxolo[7,8]isoquinolino[3,2-*b*][3]benzazocine-20,1′(2′*H*)-isoquinolin]-5-yl acetate;
$C_{39}H_{43}N_3O_{11}S$; *114899-77-3*;
Treatment of soft-tissue sarcomas

Trabedersen (rINN) tra·be·*der*·sen
2′-Deoxy-*P*-thiocytidylyl-(3′→5′)-2′-deoxy-*P*-thioguanylyl-(3′→5′)-2′-deoxy-*P*-thioguanylyl-(3′→5′)-2′-deoxy-*P*-thiocytidylyl-(3′→5′)-2′-deoxy-*P*-thioadenylyl-(3′→5′)-*P*-thiothymidylyl-(3′→5′)-2′-deoxy-*P*-thioguanylyl-(3′→5′)-*P*-thiothymidylyl-(3′→5′)-2′-deoxy-*P*-thiocytidylyl-(3′→5′)-*P*-thiothymidylyl-(3′→5′)-2′-deoxy-*P*-thioadenylyl-(3′→5′)-*P*-thiothymidylyl-(3′→5′)-*P*-thiothymidylyl-(3′→5′)-*P*-thiothymidylyl-(3′→5′)-2′-deoxy-*P*-thioguanylyl-(3′→5′)-*P*-thiothymidylyl-(3′→5′)-2′-deoxyadenosine; $C_{177}H_{225}N_{60}O_{94}P_{17}S_{17}$; *5681-61-4*;
Antisense oligonucleotide (TGF beta-2); treatment of tumours

Tracazolate (rINN) tra·*kaz*·ö·lät
Ethyl 4-butylamino-1-ethyl-6-methyl-1*H*-pyrazolo[3,4-*b*]⌐
pyridine-5-carboxylate; $C_{16}H_{24}N_4O_2$; *41094-88-6*
*Gamma-aminobutyric acid (GABA$_A$) receptor modulator;
anxiolytic*

Tramadol (rINN) *tra*·ma·dol
(±)-*cis*-2-Dimethylaminomethyl-1-(3-methoxy phenyl)⌐
cyclohexanol; $C_{16}H_{25}NO_2$; *27203-92-5*
Tramadol Hydrochloride *36282-47-0*
*Opioid receptor agonist; noradrenaline reuptake inhibitor;
analgesic*

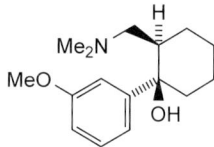

and enantiomer

Tramazoline (rINN) tra·mä·zö·lën
2-Imidazolin-2-yl(5,6,7,8-tetrahydro-1-naphthyl)amine;
$C_{13}H_{17}N_3$; *1082-57-1*
- **Tramazoline Hydrochloride** *3715-90-0*
Adrenoceptor agonist; decongestant

- **Trandolapril** (rINN) tran·do·la·pril
(2S,3aR,7aS)-1-{N-[(S)-1-Ethoxycarbonyl-3-phenylpropyl]-L-
alanyl}perhydroindole-2-carboxylic acid; $C_{24}H_{34}N_2O_5$;
87679-37-6
Angiotensin converting enzyme inhibitor

- **Tranexamic Acid** (rINN) tran·eks·a·mik
trans-4-Aminomethylcyclohexanecarboxylic acid; $C_8H_{15}NO_2$;
1197-18-8
Antifibrinolytic

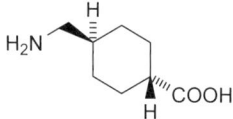

and enantiomer

Tranylcypromine (rINN) tra·nïl·sï·prö·mën
trans-2-Phenylcyclopropylamine; $(C_9H_{11}N)_2$; *155-09-9*
- **Tranylcypromine Sulfate** *13492-01-8*
Monoamine oxidase inhibitor; antidepressant

and enantiomer

- **Trapidil** (rINN) tra·pi·dil
N,N-Diethyl-5-methyl-[1,2,4]triazolo[1,5-*a*]pyrimidin-7-amine;
$C_{10}H_{15}N_5$; *15421-84-8*
Antiplatelet agent; vasodilator

Trastuzumab (rINN) tra·stü·zoo·mab
Immunoglobulin G 1 (human–mouse monoclonal rhuMab
HER2γ₁-chain antihuman p185ᶜ⁻ᵉʳᵇᴮ² receptor), disulfide with
human–mouse monoclonal rhuMab HER2-light chain, dimer;
180288-69-1
*Monoclonal antibody (Human Epidermal growth factor
Receptor II; HER2)*

Travoprost (rINN) tra·vö·prost
(1) Isopropyl (Z)-7-[(1R,2R,3R,5S)-3,5-dihydroxy-2-{(1E,3R)-
3-hydroxy-4-[3-(trifluoromethyl)phenyloxy]but-1-
enyl}cyclopentyl]hept-5-enoate;
(2) Isopropyl (5Z,13E)-(9S,11R,15R)-9,11,15-trihydroxy-16-[3-
(trifluoromethyl)phenyloxy]-17,18,19,20-tetranorprosta-5,13-
dienoate; $C_{26}H_{35}F_3O_6$; *157283-68-6*
Prostaglandin (PGF$_{2\alpha}$) analogue

Trazodone (rINN) tra·zö·dön
2-[3-(4-*m*-Chlorophenylpiperazin-1-yl)propyl]-1,2,4-triazolo¬
[4,3-*a*]pyridin-3(2*H*)-one; $C_{19}H_{22}ClN_5O$; *19794-93*
- **Trazodone Hydrochloride** *25332-39-2*
Monoamine reuptake inhibitor; antidepressant

- **Trehalose** (rINN) trë·ha·lös
α-D-Glucopyranosyl α-D-glucopyranoside;
$C_{12}H_{22}O_{11}$; *99-20-7*;
Excipient

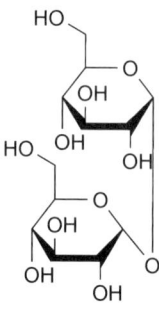

The symbol '¬' in systematic chemical names signifies line continuation

Trenbolone (rINN) *tren·bo·lön*
17β-Hydroxyestra-4,9,11-trien-3-one; $C_{18}H_{22}O_2$; *10161-33-8*
Trenbolone Acetate *10161-34-9*;
Anabolic steroid; androgen

Treosulfan (rINN) *trë·ö·sul·fan*
L-Threitol 1,4-dimethanesulfonate; $C_6H_{14}N_8S_2$; *299-75-2*
Cytotoxic alkylating agent

Tresperimus (rINN) *tre·spe·ri·mus*
[(6-Guanidinohexyl)carbamoyl]methyl *N*-{4-[(3-aminopropyl)amino]butyl}carbamate; $C_{17}H_{37}N_7O_3$;
160677-67-8
Immunosuppressant

Tretamine (rINN) see Appendix C

Trethinium Tosilate (rINN) see Appendix C

● **Tretinoin** (rINN) *tre·tin·ö·in*
(1) 15-Apo-β-caroten-15-oic acid; (2) 3,7-dimethyl-9-(2,6,6-trimethylcyclohex-1-enyl)nona-2,4,6,8-*all-trans*-tetraenoic acid;
(3) *all-trans*-retinoic acid; $C_{20}H_{28}O_2$; *302-79-4*
Vitamin A analogue (retinoid); treatment of acne

● **Triacetin** (rINN) *tri·a·së·tin*
Propane-1,2,3-triyl triacetate; $C_9H_{14}O_6$; *102-76-1*
Antifungal

Triacetyloleandomycin *see Troleandomycin*

● **Triamcinolone** (rINN) *tri·am·sin·o·lön*
9α-Fluoro-11β,16α,17α,21-tetrahydroxypregna-1,4-diene-3,20-dione; $C_{21}H_{27}FO_6$; *124-94-7*
Glucocorticoid

● **Triamcinolone Acetonide** (rINN) *tri·am·sin·o·lön*
9α-Fluoro-11β,21-dihydroxy-16α,17α-isopropylidenedioxy-pregna-1,4-diene-3,20-dione; $C_{24}H_{31}FO_6$; *76-25-5*
Glucocorticoid

Triamcinolone Hexacetonide (rINN) *tri·am·sin·o·lön*
9α-Fluoro-11β-hydroxy-16α,17α-isopropylidenedioxy-3,20-dioxopregna-1,4-diene-21-yl 3,3-dimethylbutyrate; $C_{30}H_{41}FO_7$;
5611-51-8
Glucocorticoid

● **Triamterene** (rINN) *tri·am·te·rën*
6-Phenylpteridine-2,4,7-triamine; $C_{12}H_{11}N_7$; *396-01-0*
Sodium channel blocker; potassium-sparing diuretic

Triaziquone (rINN) see Appendix C

Triazolam (rINN) see Appendix C

Tribavirin *see Ribavirin*

● **Tribenoside** (rINN) trï·*ben*·ö·sïd
Ethyl 3,5,6-tri-*O*-benzyl-D-glucofuranoside; $C_{29}H_{34}O_6$;
10310-32-4
Sclerosing agent

and anomer at C*

Tribromsalan (rINN) trï·*brom*·sa·lan
3,4′,5-Tribromosalicylanilide; $C_{13}H_8Br_3NO_2$; *87-10-5*
Antihelmintic

Trichlormethine (rINN) trï·klor·*me*·thën
Tris(2-chloroethyl)amine; $C_6H_{12}Cl_3N$; *555-77-1*
Cytotoxic alkylating agent

Triclabendazole (rINN) trï·kla·*ben*·da·zôl
5-Chloro-6-(2,3-dichlorophenoxy)-2-(methylthio)-1*H*-
benzimidazole; $C_{14}H_9Cl_3N_2OS$; *68786-66-3*
Benzimidazole antihelminthic

Triclofenol Piperazine (rINN) trï·klö·*fë*·nol pi·*pe*·ra·zën
Piperazine bis(2,4,5-trichlorophenoxide); $C_{16}H_{16}Cl_6N_2$;
5714-82-9
Antihelmintic

Triclofos (rINN) trï·klö·fos
2,2,2-Trichloroethyl dihydrogen phosphate; $C_2H_4Cl_3O_4P$;
306-52-5

● **Triclofos Sodium** *7246-20-0*
Hypnotic

Triclosan (rINN) trï·klö·san
5-Chloro-2-(2,4-dichlorophenoxy)phenol; $C_{12}H_7Cl_3O_2$;
3380-34-5
Antiseptic

Tricyclamol Chloride (rINN) see Appendix C

Tridihexethyl Chloride (rINN) trï·dï·heks·*ë*·thïl
(*RS*)-(3-Cyclohexyl-3-hydroxy-3-phenylpropyl)¬
triethylammonium chloride; $C_{21}H_{36}ClNO$; *125-99-5*
Anticholinergic

and enantiomer

Trientine Dihydrochloride (rINN) *trï*·en·tën
2,2-Ethylenedi-iminobis(ethylamine) dihydrochloride;
trientine hydrochloride; $C_6H_{18}N_4$,2HCl; *38260-01-4*
Copper chelating agent

Trifluomeprazine (rINN) tri·floo·o·*me*·pra·zën
(*RS*)-Dimethyl[2-methyl-3-(2-trifluoromethylphenothiazin-
10-yl)propyl]amine; $C_{19}H_{21}F_3N_2S$; *2622-37-9*

♣ **Trifluomeprazine Maleate**
Dopamine receptor antagonist; neuroleptic

and enantiomer

Trifluoperazine (rINN) trï·floo·ö·*pe*·ra·zën
10-[3-(4-Methylpiperazin-1-yl)propyl]-2-trifluoromethyl¬
phenothiazine; $C_{21}H_{24}F_3N_3S$; *117-89-5*

● **Trifluoperazine Hydrochloride** *440-17-5*
Dopamine receptor antagonist; neuroleptic

The symbol '¬' in systematic chemical names signifies line continuation

Trifluperidol (rINN) see Appendix C

Triflupromazine (rINN) trï·floo-*prö*·ma·zën
Dimethyl[3-(2-trifluoromethylphenothiazin-10-yl)propyl]¬
amine; $C_{18}H_{19}F_3N_2S$; *146-54-3*
Dopamine receptor antagonist; neuroleptic

● **Triflusal** (rINN) trï·floo·sal
O-Acetyl-4-(trifluoromethyl)salicylic acid; $C_{10}H_7F_3O_4$;
322-79-2
Thromboxane synthesis inhibitor; antiplatelet drug

Trifosmin (rINN) tri-*fos*·min
Tris(3-methoxypropyl)phosphine; $C_{12}H_{27}O_3P$; *83622-85-9*
Diagnostic agent

Trihexyphenidyl (rINN) trï·heks·ë·*fe*·ni·dïl
(*RS*)-1-Cyclohexyl-1-phenyl-3-piperidinopropan-1-ol;
$C_{20}H_{31}NO$; *144-11-6*
● **Trihexyphenidyl Hydrochloride** *52-49-3*
Anticholinergic

and enantiomer

Trilostane (rINN) *trï*·lö·stän
4α,5α-Epoxy-17β-hydroxy-3-oxoandrostane-2α-carbonitrile;
$C_{20}H_{27}NO_3$; *13647-35-3*
*Inhibitor of adrenal steroid synthesis by inhibition of
3-beta-hydroxysteroid dehydrogenase; enzyme inhibitor*

Trimazosin (rINN) trï·*mä*·zö·sin
2-Hydroxy-2-methylpropyl 4-(4-amino-6,7,8-trimethoxyquin¬
azolin-2-yl)piperazine-1-carboxylate; $C_{20}H_{29}N_5O_6$; *35795-16-5*
Trimazosin Hydrochloride *35795-17-6*;
53746-46-6 (monohydrate)
Alpha₁-adrenoceptor agonist

Trimebutine (rINN) trï·*me*·bü·tën
(*RS*)-2-Dimethylamino-2-phenylbutyl 3,4,5-trimethoxy¬
benzoate; $C_{22}H_{29}NO_5$; *39133-31-8*
Treatment of irritable bowel syndrome
● **Trimebutine Maleate** *34140-59-5*

and enantiomer

Trimegestone (rINN) tri·me·*jes*·tön
17β-[(*S*)-2-Hydroxypropionyl]-17α-methylestra-4,9-dien-3-one;
$C_{22}H_{30}O_3$; *74513-62-5*
Progestogen

Trimeperidine (rINN) trï·me·*pe*·ri·dën
1,2,5-Trimethyl-4-phenyl-4-piperidyl propionate; $C_{17}H_{25}NO_2$;
64-39-1
Opioid receptor agonist

mixture of 8 stereoisomers

Trimeprazine *see Alimemazine*

Trimetaphan Camsilate (rINN) see Appendix C

Trimetazidine (rINN) trï·me·*ta*·zi·dën
1-(2,3,4-Trimethoxybenzyl)piperazine; $C_{14}H_{22}N_2O_3$; *5011-34-7*
● **Trimetazidine Hydrochloride** *13171-25-0*
Vasodilator

●Trimethadione (rINN)
3,5,5-Trimethyl-1,3-oxazolidine-2,4-dione; $C_6H_9NO_3$; *127-48-0*
Antiepileptic

Trimethidinium Methosulfate (rINN) see Appendix C

●Trimethoprim (rINN) trï·*me*·thö·prim
5-(3,4,5-Trimethoxybenzyl)pyrimidine-2,4-diyldiamine;
$C_{14}H_{18}N_4O_3$; *738-70-5*
Dihydrofolate reductase inhibitor; antibacterial

Trimetrexate (rINN) trï·me·*treks*·ät
5-Methyl-6-(3,4,5-trimethoxyanilinomethyl)quinazoline-2,4-
diyldiamine; $C_{19}H_{23}N_5O_3$; *52128-35-5*
*Dihydrofolate reductase inhibitor; antifungal
(Pneumocystis jiroveci)*

Trimipramine (rINN) trï·*mi*·pra·mën
(*RS*)-Dimethyl[3-(10,11-dihydro-5*H*-dibenz[*b,f*]azepin-5-yl)-2-
methylpropyl]amine; $C_{20}H_{26}N_2$; *739-71-9*
● **Trimipramine Maleate** *521-78-8*
Monoamine reuptake inhibitor; tricyclic antidepressant

and enantiomer

Trimustine *see Trichlormethine*

Triparanol (rINN) see Appendix C

Tripelennamine (rINN) see Appendix C

Triplatin Tetranitrate (rINN) trï·*pla*·tin te·tra·*nï*·trät
(SP-4-1)-Diamminebis[*(SP-4-2)*-diamminechloroplatinum(II)
(μ-hexane-1,6-diamine)]platinum tetranitrate;
$C_{12}H_{50}Cl_2N_{14}O_{12}Pt_3$; *172903-00-3*
Platinum-containing cytotoxic

Triprolidine (rINN) trï·*pro*·li·dën
(*E*)-2-[3-(Pyrrolidin-1-yl)-1-*p*-tolylprop-1-enyl]pyridine;
$C_{19}H_{22}N_2$; *486-12-4*
● **Triprolidine Hydrochloride** *6138-79-0*
Histamine H_1 receptor antagonist; antihistamine

Triptorelin (rINN) trip·tö·*rë*·lin
[6-D-Tryptophan] luteinising hormone-releasing factor;
$C_{64}H_{82}N_{18}O_{13}$; *57773-63-4*
*Gonadotropin releasing hormone (gonadorelin) analogue;
treatment of prostate cancer*

```
<Glu-His-Trp-Ser-Tyr-D-Trp-Leu-Arg-Pro-Gly-NH₂
```

Troglitazone (rINN) see Appendix C

Troleandomycin (rINN) trö·lë·an·dö·*mï*·sin
(2*R*,3*S*,4*R*,5*S*,6*S*,8*R*,10*R*,11*S*,12*R*,13*R*)-11-Acetoxy-3-(4-*O*-
acetyl-2,6-dideoxy-3-*O*-methyl-α-L-*arabino*-hexopyranosyl¬
oxy)-5-(2-*O*-acetyl-3,4,6-trideoxy-3-dimethylamino-β-D-*xylo*-
hexopyranosyloxy)-8,8-epoxymethano-2,4,6,10,12,13-hexa¬
methyl-9-oxotetradecan-13-olide; $C_{41}H_{67}NO_{15}$; *2751-09-9*
Macrolide antibacterial

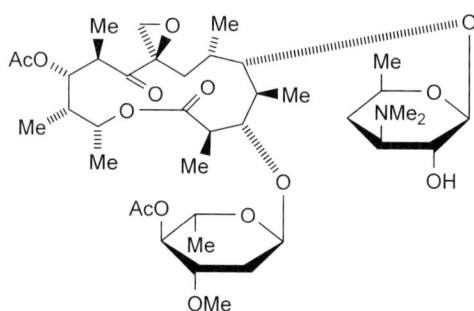

Trolnitrate Phosphate (rINN) see Appendix C

The symbol '¬' in systematic chemical names signifies line continuation

- **Trometamol** (rINN) trö·me·ta·mol
  2-Amino-2-hydroxymethylpropane-1,3-diol; tromethamine
  (USAN); $C_4H_{11}NO_3$; 77-86-1; component of several proprietary
  preparations
  Organic amine proton acceptor; alkalinizing agent

Tropanserin (rINN) trö·pan·ser·rin
  (8S)-Tropan-3-yl 3,5-dimethylbenzoate; $C_{17}H_{23}NO_2$;
  85181-40-4
  Tropanserin Hydrochloride 85181-38-0
  Serotonin $5HT_{2a}$ receptor antagonist

- **Tropicamide** (rINN) trö·pi·ka·mïd
  (RS)-N-Ethyl-N-(4-pyridylmethyl)tropamide; $C_{17}H_{20}N_2O_2$;
  1508-75-4
  Anticholinergic

and enantiomer

Tropigline (rINN) trö·pi·glën
  (E)-(1R,3r,5S)-3-(Methylmethacryloyloxy)tropane; $C_{13}H_{21}NO_2$;
  533-08-4
  Treatment of Parkinson's disease

Tropisetron (rINN) trö·pi·se·tron
  (3r)-Tropan-3-yl indole-3-carboxylate; $C_{17}H_{20}N_2O_2$;
  89565-68-4
  Tropisetron Hydrochloride 105826-92-4
  Serotonin $5HT_3$ receptor antagonist; antiemetic

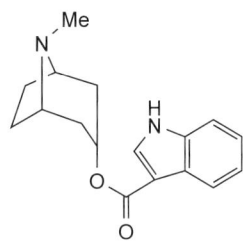

Trospectomycin (rINN) trö·spek·tö·mï·sin
  (2R,4aR,5aR,6S,7S,8R,9S,9aR,10aS)-2-Butyl-4a,7,9-trihydroxy-
  6,8-bis(methylamino)perhydropyrano[2,3-b][1,4]benzodioxin-4-
  one; $C_{17}H_{30}N_2O_7$; 88669-04-9
  Trospectomycin Sulfate 88851-61-0
  Aminocyclotol antibacterial

- **Trospium Chloride** (rINN) trö·spë·um klor·rïd
  (1) (3r)-3-(Hydroxydiphenylacetoxy)-8λ^5-spiro[8-azabicyclo⌐
  [3.2.1]octane-8,1′-pyrrolidin]-8-ylium chloride;
  (2) 3α-hydroxyspiro[1αH-nortropane-8,1′-pyrrolidinium]
  chloride benzilate; $C_{25}H_{30}ClNO_3$; 10405-02-4
  Anticholinergic

- **Troxerutin** (rINN) troks·ë·roo·tin
  (1) 5-Hydroxy-7-(2-hydroxyethoxy)-2-[3,4-bis(2-hydroxy⌐
  ethoxy)phenyl]-4-oxo-4H-chromen-3-yl rutinoside;
  (2) 3′,4′,7-tris[O-(2-hydroxyethyl)]rutin; $C_{33}H_{42}O_{19}$; 7085-55-4
  Bioflavonoid

Troxidone *see Trimethadione*

Troxonium Tosilate (BAN) see Appendix C

Troxypyrrolium Tosilate (BAN) troks·ë·pi·rö·lë·um
  N-Ethyl-N-2-(3,4,5-trimethoxybenzoyloxy)ethylpyrrolidinium
  p-toluenesulfonate; $C_{25}H_{35}NO_8S$; 3612-98-4
  Choline uptake inhibitor

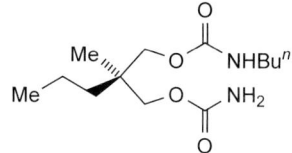

and enantiomer

● **Trypsin** (rINN) *trip*·sin

A protease obtained from the pancreas of mammals by the extraction and subsequent activation of trypsinogen; *9002-07-7*
Proteolytic enzyme

Tyformin *see Tiformin*

♣ **Tylosin** (rINN) *tï*·lö·sin

A macrolide antibiotic derived from an actinomycete resembling *Streptomyces fradiae*; *1401-69-0*
Tylosin Phosphate
♣ **Tylosin Tartrate**
Macrolide antibacterial (veterinary)

● **Tryptophan** (rINN) trip·*tö*·fan

L-Tryptophan; L-2-Amino-3-(indol-3-yl)propionic acid; $C_{11}H_{12}N_2O_2$; *61-90-5*;
Amino acid; treatment of depression

Tuaminoheptane (rINN) see Appendix C

● **Tubocurarine Chloride** (rINN) tü·bö·kûr·*rar*·rën

7′,12′-Dihydroxy-6,6′-dimethoxy-2,2′,2′-trimethyl¬
tubocuraranium chloride hydrochloride; $C_{37}H_{42}Cl_2N_2O_6$;
57-94-3
Non-depolarizing neuromuscular blocker

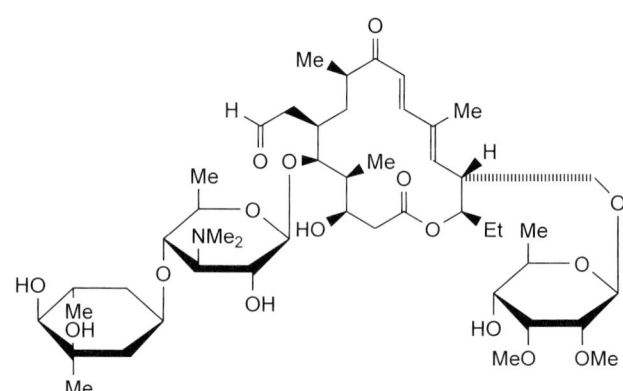

tylosin A

Tucaresol (rINN) tü·*ka*·re·sol

α-(2-Formyl-3-hydroxyphenoxy)-*p*-toluic acid; $C_{15}H_{12}O_5$
Treatment of sickle-cell anaemia

Tyloxapol (rINN) tï·*loks*·a·pol

4-(1,1,3,3-Tetramethylbutyl)phenol polymer with ethylene oxide and formaldehyde; *25301-02-4*
Non-ionic surfactant

R = CH₂CH₂O—[CH₂CH₂O]ₙ—OCH₂CH₂OH

$m < 6$ $n = 6\text{-}8$

Tulobuterol (rINN) see Appendix C

Tybamate (rINN) *tï*·ba·mät

(*RS*)-2-Methyl-2-propyltrimethylene butylcarbamate carbamate;
$C_{13}H_{26}N_2O_4$; *4268-36-4*
Anxiolytic

● **Tymazoline** (BAN) tï·*mä*·zö·lën

2-(2-Isopropyl-5-methylphenoxymethyl)-2-imidazoline;
$C_{14}H_{20}N_2O$; *24243-97-8*
Adrenoceptor agonist; decongestant

The symbol '¬' in systematic chemical names signifies line continuation

● **Tyrosine** (rINN) *tï·rö·sën*
L-Tyrosine; L-2-Amino-3-(4-hydroxyphenyl)propionic acid;
$C_9H_{11}NO_3$; *60-18-4*;
Amino acid

Tyrothricin (rINN) *tï·rö·thrï·sin*
A mixture of antimicrobial polypeptides, including gramicidin and tyrocidine, produced by *Bacillus brevis*; *1404-88-2*
Polypeptide antibacterial

● **Ubidecarenone** (rINN) *ü·bi·de·ka·re·nön*
2-[(*all-E*)-3,7,11,15,19,23,27,31,35,39-decamethyltetraconta-2,6,10,14,18,22,26,30,34,38-decaenyl]-5,6-dimethoxy-3-methyl-*p*-benzoquinone; $C_{59}H_{90}O_4$; *303-98-0*
Co-enzyme in mitochondrial electron transport

Ubisindine (rINN) *ü·bi·sin·dën*
(1) (*RS*)-2-(2-Diethylaminoethyl)-3-phenylisoindolin-1-one;
(2) (*RS*)-2-(2-diethylaminoethyl)-3-phenylphthalimidine;
$C_{20}H_{24}N_2O$; *26070-78-0*
Antiarrhythmic

and enantiomer

Ulipristal (rINN) *ü·li·priss·tal*
11β-[4-(Dimethylamino)phenyl]-17-hydroxy-19-norpregna-4,9-diene-3,20-dione; $C_{28}H_{35}NO_3$; *159811-51-5*;
Ulipristal Acetate *126784-99-4*
Progestogen; post-coital contraceptive

Upenazime (rINN) *ü·pen·a·zëm*
(*E,E*)-3,3′-Dimethyl-3,3′-(butane-1,4-diyldi-imino)bis(butan-2-one oxime); $C_{14}H_{30}N_4O_2$; *95268-62-5*
Diagnostic agent

Uramustine (rINN) *ûr·ra·mus·tën*
5-[Bis(2-chloroethyl)amino]uracil; uracil mustard (USAN);
$C_8H_{11}ClN_3O_2$; *66-75-1*
Cytotoxic alkylating agent

Urapidil (rINN) *ûr·rap·i·dil*
6-[3-(4-*o*-Methoxyphenylpiperazin-1-yl)propylamino]-1,3-dimethyluracil; $C_{20}H_{29}N_5O_3$; *34661-75-1*
Alpha_1-adrenoceptor antagonist

Uredofos (rINN) *ûr·rë·dö·fos*
Diethyl 3-[2-(3-tosylureido)phenyl]-2-thioureidophosphonate;
$C_{19}H_{25}N_4O_6PS_2$; *52406-01-6*
Antihelmintic

● **Urofollitropin** (rINN) *ûr·rö·fol·li·trö·pin*
A preparation of menopausal gonadotrophin extracted from human urine, but possessing negligible luteinising hormone (LH) activity
Follicle-stimulating hormone

● **Urokinase** (rINN) *ûr·rö·kï·näz*
An enzyme isolated from human urine that converts plasminogen to plasmin; EC 3.4.21.31;
9039-53-6
Plasminogen activator; fibrinolytic enzyme

Vapiprost (rINN) *va·pi·prost*
(1) (Z)-(1R,2R,3S,5S)-7-[5-(Biphenyl-4-ylmethoxy)-3-hydroxy-
2-piperidinocyclopentyl]hept-4-enoic acid;
(2) (Z)-(9S,11S,12R) -9-biphenyl-4-ylmethoxy-11-hydroxy-12-
piperidino-(13—20)octanorprost-4-enoic acid;
$C_{30}H_{39}NO_4$; 85505-64-2
Vapiprost Hydrochloride 87248-13-3
Thromboxane A_2 inhibitor

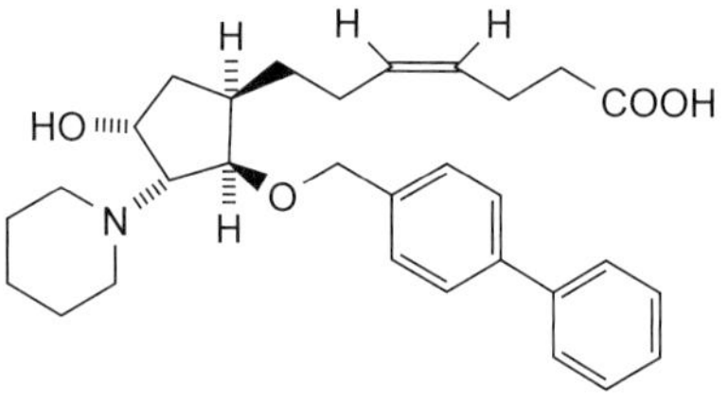

Vapreotide (rINN) *va·prë·ö·tïd*
$C_{57}H_{70}N_{12}O_9S_2$; 103222-11-3
Vapreotide Acetate
*Somatostatin analogue; treatment of neuroendocrine tumours,
acromegaly, bleeding varices*

Vapreotide has the amino acid sequence shown below:

```
D-Phe-Cys-Tyr-D-Trp-Lys-Val-Cys-Trp -NH2
```

Vardenafil (rINN) *var·den·a·fil*
2-[2-Ethoxy-5-(4-ethylpiperazine-1-ylsulfonyl)phenyl]-5-
methyl-7-propylimidazo[5,1-f][1,2,4]triazin-4(3H)-one;
$C_{23}H_{32}N_6O_4S$; 224785-90-4
*Selective inhibitor of cyclic GMP-specific phosphodiesterase
type V with vasodilator action; treatment of erectile dysfunction*

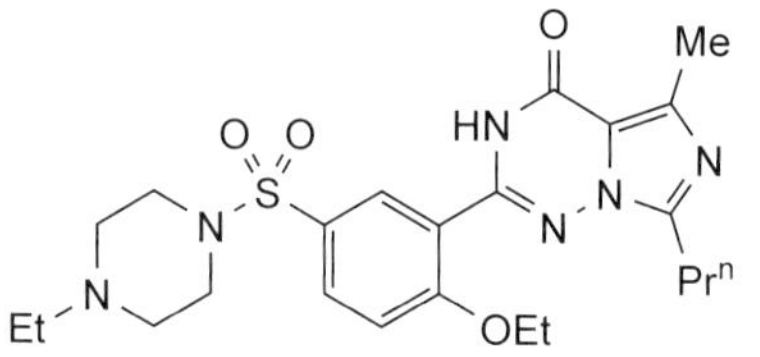

Varenicline (rINN) *va·re·nik·lën*
7,8,9,10-Tetrahydro-6H-6,10-methanoazepino[4,5g]¬
quinoxaline; $C_{13}H_{13}N_3$; 249296-44-4
Nicotinic receptor agonist

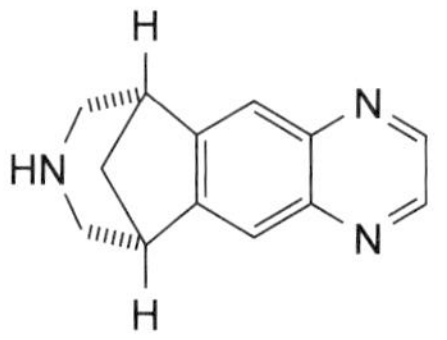

● **Vecuronium Bromide** (rINN) *ve·kûr·rö·në·um*
1-(3α,17β-Diacetoxy-2β-piperidino-5α-androstan-16β-yl)-1-
methylpiperidinium bromide; $C_{34}H_{57}BrN_2O_4$; 50700-72-6
Non-depolarizing neuromuscular blocker

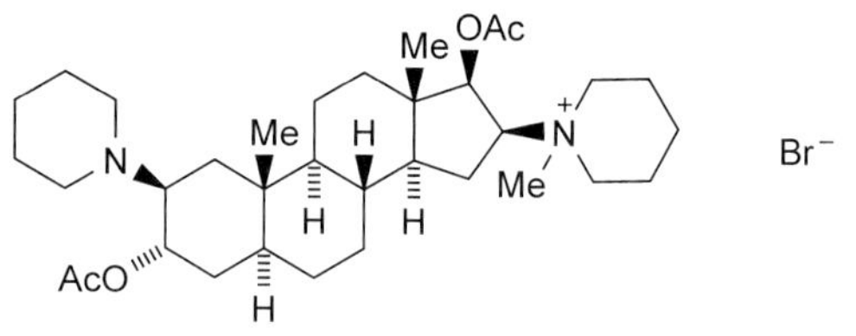

♣ **Vedaprofen** (rINN) *vë·da·prö·fen*
(RS)-2-(4-Cyclohexyl-1-naphthyl)propionic acid; $C_{19}H_{22}O_2$;
71109-09-6
*Cyclo-oxygenase inhibitor; analgesic; anti-inflammatory
(veterinary)*

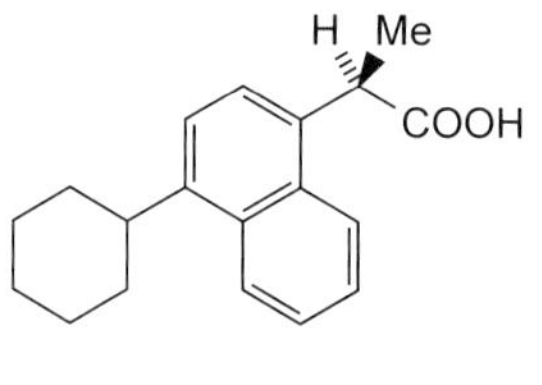

and enantiomer

Velaglucerase alfa (rINN) *ve·lá·gloo·ser·äs*
Human glucosylceramidase (EC 3.2.1.45 or
beta-glucocerebrosidase), glycoform α; 884604-91-5;
β-Glucocerebrosidase enzyme; treatment of Gaucher's disease

velaglucerase alfa has the following amino acid sequence:

ARPCIPKSFG	YSSVVCVCNA	TYCDSFDPPT	FPALGTFSRY
ESTRSGRRME	LSMGPIQANH	TGTGLLLTLQ	PEQKFQKVKG
FGGAMTDAAA	LNILALSPPA	QNLLLKSYFS	EEGIGYNIIR
VPMASCDFSI	RTYTYADTPD	DFQLHNFSLP	EEDTKLKIPL
IHRALQLAQR	PVSLLASPWT	SPTWLKTNGA	VNGKGSLKGQ
PGDIYHQTWA	RYFVKFLDAY	AEHKLQFWAV	TAENEPSAGL
LSGYPFQCLG	FTPEHQRDFI	ARDLGPTLAN	STHHNVRLLM
LDDQRLLLPH	WAKVVLTDPE	AAKYVHGIAV	HWYLDFLAPA
KATLGETHRL	FPNTMLFASE	ACVGSKFWEQ	SVRLGSWDRG
MQYSHSIITN	LLYHVVGWTD	WNLALNPEGG	PNWVRNFVDS
PIIVDITKDT	FYKQPMFYHL	GHFSKFIPEG	SQRVGLVASQ
KNDLDAVALM	HPDGSAVVVV	LNRSSKDVPL	TIKDPAVGFL
ETISPGYSIH	TYLWRRQ		

* glycosylation site

Velaresol (rINN) *ve·la·re·sol*
5-(2-Formyl-3-hydroxyphenoxy)valeric acid; $C_{12}H_{14}O_5$;
77858-21-0
Treatment of sickle cell disease

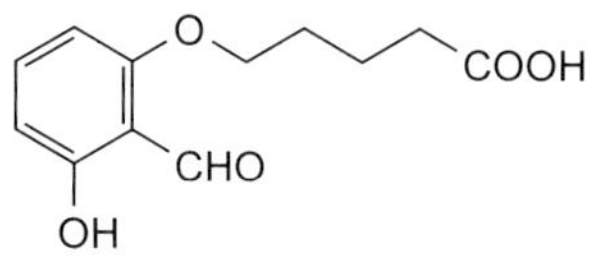

The symbol '¬' in systematic chemical names signifies line continuation

Velnacrine (rINN) see Appendix C

Venlafaxine (rINN) ven·la·*faks*·ën
(*RS*)-1-(2-Dimethylamino-1-*p*-methoxyphenyl ethyl)cyclo¬
hexanol; $C_{17}H_{27}NO_2$; *93413-69-5*
- **Venlafaxine Hydrochloride** *99300-78-4*
Inhibition of 5HT and noradrenaline reuptake; antidepressant

and enantiomer

Verapamil (rINN) ve·*ra*·pa·mil
(*RS*)-5-[*N*-(3,4-Dimethoxyphenethyl)methylamino]-2-(3,4-
dimethoxyphenyl)-2-isopropylvaleronitrile; $C_{27}H_{38}N_2O_4$;
52-53-9
- **Verapamil Hydrochloride** *152-11-4*
Calcium channel blocker

and enantiomer

Verazide (rINN) see Appendix C

Verteporfin (rINN) ver·te·*por*·fin
A 50:50 mixture of ($2^4RS,3RS$)-2^4,3-dihydro-2^3,2^4-
bis(methoxycarbonyl)-12-[2-(methoxycarbonyl)ethyl]-
3,7,13,18-tetramethyl-17-vinylbenzo[*b*]porphyrin-8-propionic
acid and ($2^4RS,3RS$)-2^4,3-dihydro-2^3,2^4-
bis(methoxycarbonyl)-8-[2-(methoxycarbonyl)ethyl]-
3,7,13,18-tetramethyl-17-vinylbenzo[*b*] porphyrin-12-
propionic acid; $C_{41}H_{42}N_4O_8$ *(both components)*; *129497-78-5*
Porphyrin analogue; photosensitizing agent

and enantiomer

+

and enantiomer

Vernakalant (rINN) ver·nak·á·lant
(3*R*)-1-{(1*R*,2*R*)-2-[2-(3,4-Dimethoxyphenyl)ethoxy]¬
cyclohexyl}pyrrolidin-3-ol; $C_{20}H_{31}NO_4$; *794466-70-9*;
Vernakalant Hydrochloride *748810-28-8*
Potassium channel blocker; antiarrhythmic

Vetrabutine (rINN) ve·tra·*bü*·tën
(*RS*)-Dimethyl-α-3-phenylpropylveratrylamine; $C_{20}H_{27}NO_2$;
3735-45-3
Vetrabutine Hydrochloride *5974-09-4*
Uterus relaxant

and enantiomer

Vidarabine (rINN) see Appendix C

Vigabatrin (rINN) vï·*ga*·ba·trin
4-Aminohex-5-enoic acid; $C_6H_{11}NO_2$; *60643-86-9*
Antiepileptic

and enantiomer

Vildagliptin (rINN) vil·*dá*·glip·tin
(2*S*)-1-{[(3-Hydroxyadamantan-1-yl)amino]acetyl}pyrrolidine-
2-carbonitrile; $C_{17}H_{25}N_3O_2$; *274901-16-5*;
*Dipeptidyl peptidase IV inhibitor; treatment of type 2 diabetes
mellitus*

Viloxazine (rINN) see Appendix C

Vinbarbital (rINN) vin·*bar*·bi·tal
5-Ethyl-5-(1-methylbut-1-enyl)barbituric acid; $C_{11}H_{16}N_2O_3$;
125-42-8
Barbiturate

Vinblastine (rINN) vin·*blas*·tën

An alkaloid extracted from *Vinca rosea*; methyl (3a*R*,4*R*,¬ 5*S*,5a*R*,10b*R*, 13a*R*)-4-acetoxy-3a-ethyl-9-[(5*S*,7*S*,9*S*)-5-ethyl-5-hydroxy-9-methoxycarbonyl-1,4,5,6,7,8,9,10-octahydro-2*H*-3,7-methanoazacycloundecino[5,4-*b*]indol-9-yl]-5-hydroxy-8-methoxy-6-methyl-3a,4,5,5a,6,11,12,13a-octahydro-1*H*-indolizino[8,1-*cd*]carbazole-5-carboxylate; vincaleukoblastine; $C_{46}H_{58}N_4O_9$; *865-21-4*

● **Vinblastine Sulfate** *143-67-9*
Vinca alkaloid cytotoxic

Vincamine (rINN) *vin*·ka·mën

An alkaloid obtained from *Vinca minor*; methyl (3α,14β,¬ 16α-)14,15-dihydro-14-hydroxyeburnamenine-14-carboxylate; $C_{21}H_{26}N_2O_3$; *1617-90-9*
Vasodilator

Vincristine (rINN) vin·*kris*·tën

An alkaloid extracted from *Vinca rosea*; methyl (3a*R*,4*R*,5*S*,5a*R*,10b*R*,13a*R*)-4-acetoxy-3a-ethyl-9-[(5*S*,7*S*,9*S*)-5-ethyl-5-hydroxy-9-methoxycarbonyl-1,4,5,6,7,8,9,10-octahydro-2*H*-3,7-methanoazacycloundecino[5,4-*b*]indol-9-yl]-6-formyl-5-hydroxy-8-methoxy-3a,4,5,5a, 6,11,12,13a-octahydro-1*H*-indolizino[8,1-*cd*]carbazole-5-carboxylate; 22-oxovincaleukoblastine; $C_{46}H_{56}N_4O_{10}$; *57-22-7*

● **Vincristine Sulfate** *2068-78-2*
Vinca alkaloid cytotoxic

Vindesine (rINN) *vin*·de·sën

3-Carbamoyl-4-*O*-deacetyl-3-de(methoxycarbonyl)¬ vincaleukoblastine; $C_{43}H_{55}N_5O_7$; *53643-48-4*

● **Vindesine Sulfate** *59917-39-4*
Vinca alkaloid cytotoxic

Vinflunine (rINN) vin·*floo*·nïn

4'-Deoxy-20',20'-difluoro-8'-norvincaleukoblastine; $C_{45}H_{54}F_2N_4O_8$; *162652-95-1*;

Vinflunine Ditartrate *194468-36-5*
Vinca alkaloid; cytotoxic

Vinorelbine (rINN) vin·*or*·rel·bën

3′,4′-Didehydro-4′-deoxy-8′-norvincaleukoblastine; $C_{45}H_{54}N_4O_8$; *71486-22-1*

● **Vinorelbine Tartrate** *125317-39-7*
Vinca alkaloid cytotoxic

● **Vinpocetine** (rINN) vin·pö·*set*·ën

Ethyl (13a*S*,13b*S*)-13a-ethyl-2,3,5,6,13a,13b-hexahydro-1*H*-indolo[3,2,1-*de*]pyrido[3,2,1-*ij*][1,5]naphthyridine-12-carboxylate; $C_{22}H_{26}N_2O_2$; *42971-09-5*
Vincamine derivative

Vinylbital (rINN) vï·*nil*·bi·tal
(*RS*)-5-(1-Methylbutyl)-5-vinylbarbituric acid; $C_{11}H_{16}N_2O_3$; 2430-49-1
Hypnotic

and enantiomer

Viomycin (rINN) see Appendix C

Viprostol (rINN) vï·*pros*·tol
(1) Methyl (5*Z*,13*E*)-(11*R*,16*RS*)-11,16-dihydroxy-9-oxo-16-vinylprosta-5,13-dienoate; (2) methyl (*Z*)-7-[(1*R*,2*R*,3*R*)-2-[(*E*)-(4*RS*)-butyl-4-hydroxyhexa-1,5-dienyl]-3-hydroxy-5-oxocyclopentyl]hept-5-enoate; $C_{23}H_{36}O_5$; 73621-92-8
Prostaglandin (PGE$_2$) analogue

and epimer at C*

Viprynium Embonate *see Pyrvinium Pamoate*

Virginiamycin (rINN) ver·jin·e·a·*mï*·sin
Antimicrobial substances produced by *Streptomyces virginiae*; certain components are identical with some constituents of mikamycin, ostreogrycin and pristinamycin; 11006-76-1
Streptogramin antibacterial (veterinary)

Visnadine (rINN) *vis*·na·dën
(9*R*,10*R*)-10-Acetoxy-9,10-dihydro-8,8-dimethyl-2-oxo-2*H*,8*H*-pyrano[2,3-*f*]chromen-9-yl (*R*)-2-methylbutyrate; $C_{21}H_{24}O_7$; 477-32-7
Vasodilator

Voriconazole (rINN) vo·ri·*kon*·a·zôl
(2*R*,3*S*)-2-(2,4-Difluorophenyl)-3-(5-fluoropyrimidin-4-yl)-1-(1,2,4-triazol-1-yl)butan-2-ol; $C_{16}H_{14}N_5F_3O$; 137234-62-9
Antifungal

Vorozole (rINN) *vo*·rö·zôl
(*S*)-6-[4-Chloro-α-(1,2,4-triazol-1-yl)benzyl]-1-methyl-1*H*-benzotriazole; $C_{16}H_{13}ClN_6$; 129731-10-8; R83842
Aromatase (testosterone) inhibitor

Votumumab (rINN) vo·*tü*·mü·mab
Gamma immunoglobulin chain (human monoclonal antibody 88BV59 anti-tumour antigen); 148189-70-2
Monoclonal antibody (colorectal tumour-associated antigens)

Warfarin (rINN) *wor*·fa·rin
(*RS*)-4-Hydroxy-3-(3-oxo-1-phenylbutyl)coumarin; $C_{19}H_{16}O_4$; 81-81-2
● **Warfarin Sodium** 129-06-6
● **Warfarin Sodium Clathrate**
Vitamin K epoxide reductase inhibitor; oral anticoagulant (coumarin)

and enantiomer

Xaliproden (rINN) za·*li*·prö·den
1,2,3,6-Tetrahydro-1-[2-(2-naphthyl)ethyl]-4-(3-trifluoro-methylphenyl)pyridine; $C_{24}H_{22}F_3N$; 134354-02-8
Nootropic agent; treatment of neurodegenerative diseases

Xamoterol (rINN) see Appendix C

Xantinol Nicotinate (rINN) *zan*·ti·nol ni·kö·*ti*·nät
(*RS*)-7-{2-Hydroxy-3-[2-hydroxyethyl(methyl)amino]¬
propyl}theophylline—nicotinic acid (1:1);
$C_{13}H_{21}N_5O_4,C_6H_5NO_2$; *437-74-1*
Nicotinic acid analogue; vasodilator

and enantiomer

Xantocillin (rINN) zan·tö·*si*·lin
Antibiotics obtained from the mycelium of *Penicillium notatum*
(xantocillin X is 2,3-di-isocyano-1,4-bis(4-hydroxyphenyl)buta-
1,3-diene); $C_{18}H_{12}N_2O_2$; *580-74-5*
Penicillin antibacterial

Xenysalate (rINN) ze·*ni*·sa·lät
2-Diethylaminoethyl 2-hydroxybiphenyl-3-carboxylate;
biphenamine (USAN); $C_{19}H_{23}NO_3$; *3572-52-9*
Seborrhoeic dermatitis

Xibornol (rINN) *zi*·bor·nol
6-[(1*R*,2*S*,4*S*)-Born-2-yl]-3,4-xylenol; $C_{18}H_{26}O$; *13741-18-9*
Antibacterial

Xipamide (rINN) *zip*·a·mïd
4-Chloro-5-sulfamoylsalicylo-2′,6′-xylidide; $C_{15}H_{15}ClN_2O_4S$;
14293-44-8
Thiazide-like diuretic

Xylamide Tosilate (rINN) see Appendix C

Xylazine (rINN) *zï*·la·zën
N-(5,6-Dihydro-4*H*-1,3-thiazin-2-yl)-2,6-xylidine; $C_{12}H_{16}N_2S$;
7361-61-7
♣ **Xylazine Hydrochloride** *23076-35-9*
Analgesic (veterinary)

⦿**Xylitol** (rINN) *zï*·li·tol
Xylitol; $C_5H_{12}O_5$; *87-99-0*
Sweetening agent

Xylometazoline (rINN) *zï*·lö·me·*täz*·ö·lën
2-(4-*tert*-Butyl-2,6-dimethylbenzyl)-2-imidazoline; $C_{16}H_{24}N_2$;
526-36-3
⦿**Xylometazoline Hydrochloride** *1218-35-5*
Alpha-adrenoceptor agonist

Yttrium (⁹⁰Y) Tacatuzumab Tetraxetan (rINN) *it*·trë·um
ta·ka·*too*·zü·mab te·traks·it·an
Immunoglobulin G1, anti-(human α-fetoprotein) (human-mouse
monoclonal hAFP-31 γ1-chain), disulfide with human-mouse
monoclonal hAFP-31 κ-chain, dimer, 1,4,7,10-
tetraazacyclododecane-1,4,7,10-tetraacetic acid conjugate,
yttrium-⁹⁰Y chelate;
$C_{6470}H_{9971}N_{1712}O_{2007}S_{42}{}^{90}Y$; *476413-07-7*
Monoclonal antibody (alfa fetoprotein)

The symbol '¬' in systematic chemical names signifies line continuation

Yohimbic Acid (rINN) yo·*him*·bik
17α-hydroxyyohimban-16α-carboxylic acid; $C_{20}H_{24}N_2O_3$
● **Yohimbine hydrochloride** *65-19-0*
Alpha$_2$-adrenoceptor antagonist

Zafirlukast (rINN) za·*feer*·loo·kast
Cyclopentyl {3-[2-methoxy-4-(*o*-tolylsulfonylamino¬
carbonyl)benzyl]-1-methylindol-5-yl}carbamate; $C_{31}H_{33}N_3O_6S$;
107753-78-6
Leukotriene CysLT$_1$ receptor antagonist; treatment of asthma

Zalcitabine (rINN) zal·*sï*·ta·bën
2′,3′-Dideoxycytidine; $C_9H_{13}N_3O_3$; *7481-89-2*
Nucleoside reverse transcriptase inhibitor; antiviral (HIV)

Zaleplon (rINN) *zal*·e·plon
3′-(3-Cyanopyrazolo[1,5-*a*]pyrimidin-7-yl)-*N*-ethylacetanilide;
$C_{17}H_{15}N_5O$; *151319-34-5*
Non-benzodiazepine hypnotic

Zaltidine (rINN) *zal*·ti·dën
2-{[4-(2-Methyl-1*H*-imidazol-4-yl)-1,3-thiazol-2-yl]}¬
guanidine; $C_8H_{10}N_6S$; *85604-00-8*
Zaltidine Hydrochloride *90274-23-0 (2HCl)*; CP-57361-01
Histamine H$_2$ receptor antagonist; treatment of peptic ulcer disease

Zanamivir (rINN) za·*na*·mi·veer
5-Acetamido-2,6-anhydro-3,4,5-trideoxy-4-guanidino-D-
glycero-D-*galacto*-non-2-enonic acid; $C_{12}H_{20}N_4O_7$; *139110-80-8*
Neuraminidase inhibitor; treatment of influenza

Zaprinast (rINN) see Appendix C

Zatosetron (rINN) za·*tö*·se·tron
(3*r*)-5-Chloro-2,3-dihydro-2,2-dimethyl-*N*-tropan-3-ylbenzo¬
[*b*]furan-7-carboxamide; $C_{19}H_{25}ClN_2O_2$; *123482-22-4*
Zatosetron Maleate *123482-23-5*
Serotonin 5HT$_3$ receptor antagonist; antiemetic

Zeranol (rINN) *ze*·ra·nol
(3*S*,7*R*)-3,4,5,6,7,8,9,10,11,12-Decahydro-7,14,16-trihydroxy-
3-methyl-1*H*-2-benzoxacyclotetradecin-1-one; $C_{18}H_{26}O_5$;
26538-44-3
Non-steroidal oestrogen

Zetidoline (rINN) ze·*tïd*·o·len
1-(3-Chlorophenyl)-3-[2-(3,3-dimethylazetidin-1-yl)ethyl]-2-
imidazolidone; $C_{16}H_{22}ClN_3O$; *51940-78-4*
Zetidoline Hydrochloride *74315-62-1*
Dopamine receptor antagonist; neuroleptic

● **Zidovudine** (rINN) zï·*do*·vü·dën
3′-Azido-3′-deoxythymidine; azidothymidine; AZT;
$C_{10}H_{13}N_5O_4$; *30516-87-1*
Nucleoside reverse transcriptase inhibitor; antiviral (HIV)

Zileuton (rINN) *zï·lü·*tron
(*RS*)-1-[1-(Benzo[*b*]thien-2-yl)ethyl]-1-hydroxyurea;
$C_{11}H_{12}N_2O_2S$; *111406-87-2*
5-lipoxygenase inhibitor; chronic asthma

and enantiomer

Zimeldine (rINN) see Appendix C

Ziprasidone (rINN) zï·*pra·*si·dön
5-{2-[4-(1,2-Benzothiazol-3-yl)piperazin-1-yl]ethyl}-6-chloro-
1,3-dihydroindol-2-one; $C_{21}H_{21}ClN_4OS$; *146939-27-7*
● **Ziprasidone Hydrochloride**
*Dopamine D_2 receptor antagonist; serotonin $5HT_2$ receptor
antagonist; neuroleptic*

Zofenopril (rINN) zo·*fe·*nö·pril
(4*S*)-1-[(2*S*)-3-(Benzoylthio)-2-methylpropionyl]-4-
phenylthio-L-proline; $C_{22}H_{23}NO_4S_2$; *81872-10-8*
Zofenopril Calcium *81938-43-4*
Angiotensin converting enzyme inhibitor

Zolasartan (rINN) zö·la·*sar·*tan
1-{3-Bromo-2-[2-(1*H*-tetrazol-5-yl)phenyl]benzo[*b*]furan-5-
ylmethyl}-2-butyl-4-chloro-1*H*-imidazole-5-carboxylic acid;
$C_{24}H_{20}BrClN_6O_3$; *145781-32-4*
Angiotensin II (AT₁) receptor antagonist

Zolazepam (rINN) zö·*läz·*e·pam
4-(2-Fluorophenyl)-1,6,7,8-tetrahydro-1,3,8-trimethyl¬
pyrazolo[3,4-*e*][1,4]diazepin-7-one; $C_{15}H_{15}FN_4O$; *31352-82-6*
Zolazepam Hydrochloride *33745-44-3*
Benzodiazepine

Zoledronic Acid (rINN) zö·le·*dro·*nik
1-Hydroxy-2-(imidazol-1-yl)ethane-1,1-diyldiphosphonic acid;
$C_5H_{10}N_2O_7P_2$; *118072-93-8*
Bisphosphonate; treatment of osteolytic lesions, hypercalcaemia

Zolmitriptan (rINN) zol·mi·*trip·*tan
(*S*)-4-{3-[2-(Dimethylamino)ethyl]indol-5-ylmethyl}-1,3-
oxazolidin-2-one; $C_{16}H_{21}N_3O_2$; *139264-17-8*
Serotonin $5HT_1$ receptor agonist; treatment of migraine

Zolpidem (rINN) zol·pi·dem
N, *N*-Dimethyl-2-(6-methyl-2-*p*-tolylimidazo[1,2-*a*]pyridin-3-
yl)acetamide; $C_{19}H_{21}N_3O$; *82626-48-0*
● **Zolpidem Tartrate**
Non-benzodiazepine hypnotic

Zomepirac (rINN) zö·*me·*pi·rak
5-(4-Chlorobenzoyl)-1,4-dimethylpyrrol-2-ylacetic acid;
$C_{15}H_{14}ClNO_3$; *33369-31-2*
Zomepirac Sodium *64092-48-4*
Cyclo-oxygenase inhibitor; analgesic; anti-inflammatory

The symbol '¬' in systematic chemical names signifies line continuation

Zoniporide (rINN) zö·ni·por·ïd
N-Carbamimidoyl-5-cyclopropyl-1-(quinolin-5-yl)-1H-pyrazole-4-carboxamide; $C_{17}H_{16}N_6O$; 241800-98-6
Na$^+$/H$^+$ antiport inhibitor

Zonisamide (rINN) zo·ni·sa·mïd
1-(1,2-Benzoxazol-3-yl)methanesulfonamide; $C_8H_8N_2O_3S$; 68291-97-4
Hypnotic

●**Zopiclone** (rINN) zo·pi·klön
(R,S)-6-(5-Chloro-2-pyridyl)-6,7-dihydro-7-oxo-5H-pyrrolo[3,4-b]pyrazin-5-yl 4-methylpiperazine-1-carboxylate; $C_{17}H_{17}ClN_6O_3$; 43200-80-2
Non-benzodiazepine hypnotic

and enantiomer

Zopolrestat (rINN) zö·pol·re·stat
3,4-Dihydro-4-oxo-3-(5-trifluoromethyl-1,3-benzothiazol-2-ylmethyl)phthalazin-1-ylacetic acid; $C_{19}H_{12}F_3N_3O_3S$; 110703-94-1
Aldose reductase inhibitor; treatment of diabetes

Zotepine (rINN) zö·te·pën
[2-(8-Chlorodibenzo[b,f]thiepin-10-yloxy)ethyl]dimethylamine; $C_{18}H_{18}ClNOS$; 26615-21-4
Dopamine D$_2$ receptor antagonist; Serotonin 5HT$_2$ receptor antagonist; neuroleptic

Zoticasone (rINN) zö·ti·ka·sön
S-[(R)-2-Oxotetrahydro-3-furyl] 6α,9α-difluoro-11β,17α-dihydroxy-16α-methyl-3-oxoandrosta-1,4-diene-17β-carbothioate; $C_{25}H_{30}F_2O_6S$
Zoticasone Propionate 192056-77-2
Glucocorticoid; treatment of allergic rhinitis

Zoxazolamine (rINN) see Appendix C

Zuclopenthixol (rINN) zoo·klö·pen·thiks·ol
(Z)-2-{4-[3-(2-Chloro-10H-dibenzo[b,e]thiin-10-ylidene)propyl]piperazin-1-yl}ethanol; Z-clopenthixol; $C_{22}H_{25}ClN_2OS$; 53772-83-1
●**Zuclopenthixol Acetate** 85721-05-7
●**Zuclopenthixol Decanoate** 64053-00-5
●**Zuclopenthixol Hydrochloride** 633-59-0
Dopamine receptor antagonist; neuroleptic

Names for Combinations of Substances

In the prescribing and dispensing of compounded preparations containing two active ingredients, and for which the following names are provided, the nominal amounts of the components per unit dose or per single-dose container are indicated, where necessary, in the form x/y where x and y are the respective amounts in milligrams of the components in the order implied in the name. For oral liquid preparations a unit dose is taken as 5 millilitres. For parenteral preparations x and y are the nominal amounts in milligrams of the components in the container.

Examples

Tablets containing 5 mg of amiloride hydrochloride and 50 mg of hydrochlorothiazide are described as *co-amilozide 5/50 tablets*.

An oral suspension containing 125 mg of amoxycillin trihydrate and 31 mg of clavulanic acid (as the potassium salt) in 5 ml is described as *co-amoxiclav 125/31 oral suspension*; an injection containing 500 mg and 100 mg respectively in 10 ml is described as *co-amoxiclav 500/100 injection*.

● **Co-amilofruse** kö-a·*mi*·lö·früs
Amiloride hydrochloride and furosemide in the proportions, by weight, 1 part to 8 parts respectively.
Potassium-sparing diuretic + loop diuretic

● **Co-amilozide** kö-a·*mi*·lö·zid
Amiloride hydrochloride and hydrochlorothiazide in the proportions, by weight, 1 part to 10 parts respectively.
Potassium-sparing diuretic + thiazide diuretic

● **Co-amoxiclav** kö-a·*moks*·i·klav
Amoxicillin (as the trihydrate or as the sodium salt) and clavulanic acid (as potassium clavulanate); the proportions are expressed in the form x/y where x and y are the strength in milligrams of amoxicillin and clavulanic acid respectively.
Penicillin antibacterial + beta-lactamase inhibitor

● **Co-beneldopa** kö-ben·el·*dö*·pa
Benserazide (as the hydrochloride) and levodopa in the proportions, by weight, 1 part to 4 parts respectively.
Dopa decarboxylase inhibitor + dopamine precursor; treatment of Parkinson's disease

● **Co-careldopa** kö-ka·rel·*dö*·pa
Carbidopa and levodopa; the proportions are expressed in the form x/y, where x and y are the strengths in milligrams of carbidopa and levodopa respectively.
Dopa decarboxylase inhibitor + dopamine precursor; treatment of Parkinson's disease

● **Co-codamol** kö-*kö*·da·mol
Codeine phosphate and paracetamol; the proportions are expressed in the form x/y where x and y are the strengths in milligrams of codeine phosphate and paracetamol respectively.
Opioid analgesic + analgesic; antipyretic

● **Co-codaprin** kö-*kö*·da·prin
Codeine phosphate and aspirin in the proportions, by weight, 1 part to 50 parts respectively.
Opioid analgesic + antipyretic; analgesic; anti-inflammatory

Co-cyprindiol kö-sï·prin·*di*·ol
Cyproterone acetate and ethinylestradiol in the proportions by weight, 2000 parts to 35 parts respectively.
Treatment of acne

● **Co-danthramer** kö-*dan*·thra·mer
Dantron and poloxamer 188; the proportions are expressed in the form x/y, where x and y are the strengths in milligrams of dantron and poloxamer respectively.
Stimulant laxative

● **Co-danthrusate** kö-dan·throo·sät
Dantron and docusate sodium in the proportions by weight, 5 parts to 6 parts respectively.
Stimulant laxative

● **Co-dydramol** kö-*dï*·dra·mol
Dihydrocodeine tartrate and paracetamol in the proportions, by weight, 1 part to 50 parts respectively.
Opioid analgesic + analgesic; antipyretic

Co-fluampicil kö-floo·*am*·pi·sil
Flucloxacillin and ampicillin in equal proportions by weight.
Penicillin antibacterial

Co-flumactone kö-floo·*mak*·tön
Hydroflumethiazide and spironolactone in equal proportions by weight.
Thiazide diuretic + potassium-sparing diuretic

Co-magaldrox kö-*ma*·gal·droks
Magnesium hydroxide and aluminium hydroxide; the proportions are expressed in the form *x/y* where *x* and *y* are the strengths in milligrams per unit dose of magnesium hydroxide and aluminium hydroxide respectively.
Antacid

Co-methiamol kö-me-*thï*·a·mol
DL-Methionine and paracetamol; the proportions are expressed in the form *x/y* where *x* and *y* are the strength in milligrams of DL-methionine and paracetamol respectively.
Antidote to paracetamol poisoning + analgesic; antipyretic

Co-phenotrope kö-*fe*·nö·tröp
Diphenoxylate hydrochloride and atropine sulphate in the proportions, by weight, 100 parts to 1 part respectively.
Treatment of diarrhoea

Co-prenozide kö-*pre*·nö·zïd
Oxprenolol hydrochloride and cyclopenthiazide in the proportions, by weight, 640 parts to 1 part respectively.
Beta-adrenoceptor antagonist + thiazide diuretic

● **Co-proxamol** kö-*proks*·a·mol
Dextropropoxyphene hydrochloride and paracetamol in the proportions, by weight, 1 part to 10 parts respectively.
Opioid analgesic + analgesic; antipyretic

Co-simalcite kö-*sï*·mal·sït
Activated dimeticone and hydrotalcite; the proportions are expressed in the form *x/y*, where *x* and *y* are the strengths in milligrams of activated dimeticone and hydrotalcite respectively.
Treatment of diarrhoea

● **Co-tenidone** kö-*te*·ni·dön
Atenolol and chlortalidone in the proportions, by weight, 4 parts to 1 part respectively.
Beta-adrenoreceptor antagonist + thiazide-like diuretic

Co-tetroxazine kö-te-*troks*·a·zën
Tetroxoprim and sulfadiazine in the proportions, by weight, 2 parts to 5 parts respectively.
Dihydrofolate reductase inhibitor + sulfonamide antibacterial

● **Co-triamterzide** kö-trï·am·ter·zïd
Triamterene and hydrochlorothiazide in the proportions, by weight, 2 parts to 1 part respectively.
Potassium-sparing diuretic + thiazide diuretic

Co-trifamole kö-*tri*·fa·môl
Trimethoprim and sulfamoxole in the proportions, by weight, 1 part to 5 parts respectively.
Dihydrofolate reductase inhibitor + sulfonamide antibacterial

♣ **Co-trimazine** kö-*tri*·ma·zën
Trimethoprim and sulfadiazine in the proportions, by weight; 1 part to 5 parts respectively.
Dihydrofolate reductase inhibitor + sulfonamide antibacterial

● **Co-trimoxazole** kö-tri·*moks*·a·zôl
Trimethoprim and sulfamethoxazole in the proportions, by weight, 1 part to 5 parts respectively.
Dihydrofolate reductase inhibitor + sulfonamide antibacterial

Co-zidocapt kö-*zï*·dö·kapt
Hydrochlorothiazide and captopril in the proportions, by weight, 1 part to 2 parts respectively.
Loop diuretic + angiotensin converting enzyme inhibitor

Names for Ions and Groups

Some substances for which British Approved Names have been established may be used in the form of salts or esters. The ions or groups involved may be of complex composition and it is then inconvenient to refer to them in systematic chemical nomenclature. Shorter nonproprietary names for some such ions and groups have been devised or selected, and they are recommended for use with British Approved Names.

Recommended Name	Recommended Pronunciation	Chemical Name
acetonide	a·*se*·to·nïd	isopropylidene ether of a dihydric alcohol
aceturate	a·*se*·tûr·rät	*N*-acetylglycinate
amsonate	*am*·so·nat	4,4′-diaminostilbene-2,2′-disulfonate
axetil	*aks*·e·til	1-acetoxyethyl
besilate	*be*·si·lät	benzenesulfonate
camsilate	*kam*·si·lät	camphor-10-sulfonate
cilexetil	sï·*leks*·e·til	(*RS*)-1-[(cyclohexyloxy)carbonyloxy]ethyl
cipionate	*si*·pi·o·nät	β-cyclopentylpropionate
closilate	*klö*·si·lät	4-chlorobenzenesulfonate
cromesilate	krö·*mes*·i·lät	6,7-dihydroxycoumarin-4-methanesulfonate
edisilate	e·*di*·si·lät	ethane-1,2-disulfonate
embonate	*em*·bo·nät	4,4′-methylenebis(3-hydroxy-2-naphthoate)
enantate	en·*an*·tät	heptanoate
erbumine	*er*·bü·mën	*tert*-butylamine
esilate	*e*·si·lät	ethanesulfonate
etabonate	e·*ta*·bo·nät	ethoxycarbonyloxy
gluceptate	gloo·*sep*·tät	glucoheptonate
isetionate	ï·se·*tï*·ö·nät	2-hydroxyethanesulfonate
megallate	*me*·ga·lät	3,4,5-trimethoxybenzoate
mesilate	*me*·si·lät	methanesulfonate
metilsulfate	me·til·*sul*·fät	methylsulfate
mofetil	*mö*·fe·til	2-(morpholino)ethyl
napadisilate	na·pa·*di*·si·lät	naphthalene-1,5-disulfonate
napsilate	*nap*·si·lät	naphthalene-2-sulfonate
pivalate	*pi*·va·lät	trimethylacetate
pivoxetil	pi·*voks*·e·til	1-(methoxy-2-methylpropionyloxy)ethyl
pivoxil	pi·*voks*·il	(2,2-dimethyl-1-oxopropoxy)methyl
proxetil	*proks*·e·til	1-[(isopropoxycarbonyl)oxylethyl
soproxil	sö·*proks*·il	[(isopropoxycarbonyl)oxy]methyl
suleptanate	sü·*lep*·ta·nät	sodium 7-[methyl(2-sulfonatomethyl)carbamoyl]heptanoyl
teoclate	*të*·ö·klät	8-chlorotheophyllinate
tosilate	*tö*·si·lät	toluene-4-sulfonate
troxundate	*troks*·un·dät	3,6,9-trioxaundecanoate
xinafoate	zi·*na*·fö·ät	1-hydroxy-2-naphthoate

General information, along with a list of Ions and Groups, utilised by WHO through the international non proprietary name programme can be found at www.who.int/medicines/services/inn/en/

Appendix A:
Structures

These notes are provided as a guide to the semi-systematic chemical nomenclature of certain groups of natural and semi-synthetic products. The following literature should be consulted for further information.

1. The definitive rules of the International Union of Pure and Applied Chemistry (IUPAC) for organic substances are contained in *Nomenclature of Organic Chemistry*, Sections A, B, C, D, E, F and H, Pergamon Press, Oxford, 1979 and modified by means of *A Guide to IUPAC Nomenclature of Organic Chemistry, recommendations 1993*, Blackwell Scientific Publications, 1993.

2. The IUPAC rules for inorganic substances are given in *Nomenclature of Inorganic Chemistry: IUPAC Recommendations 2005*, Royal Society of Chemistry, 2005.

3. *Biochemical Nomenclature and Related Documents*, The Biochemical Society for the International Union of Biochemistry (IUB), 2nd. edn. London, 1992. The following topics are included.

Stereochemistry
> (Nomenclature of Organic Chemistry, Section E)

Natural products and related compounds
> (Nomenclature of Organic Chemistry, Section F)

Abbreviations and Symbols

Amino acids, peptides, peptide hormones and immunoglobulins

Steroids

Tetrapyrroles

Carotenoids and tocopherols

Carbohydrates and cyclitols

Vitamins

A   Aminoglycoside Antibiotics

A.1   The aminoglycoside antibiotics are conveniently named by reference to 2-D-deoxystreptamine, **1**, in which name the configuration and numbering shown are implicit.

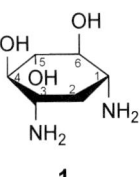

1

A.2   The aminoglycoside antibiotics commonly carry glycosyl radicals on the oxygen atoms attached to C-4 and C-6. The configuration and numbering shown in **1** should be strictly observed if confusion is to be avoided.

A.3   When one glycosyl radical is linked to another the names are separated by two locants which indicate the respective positions involved in this glycosidic union; these locants are enclosed in parentheses and separated by an arrow (pointing from the locant corresponding to the glycosyl carbon atom to the locant corresponding to the hydroxylic carbon atom involved).

B Cephalosporin Antibiotics

B.1 The cephalosporin antibiotics are conveniently named by reference to either cephalosporanic acid (**2**, R = CH$_2$OAc, X = H) or cephem-4-carboxylic acid (**2**, R = X = H).

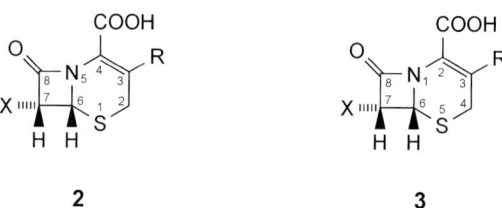

2   **3**

B.2 When names are based on cephalosporanic acid or cephem-4-carboxylic acid the traditional numbering shown in **2** is used.

B.3 Cephalosporanic acid is systematically named as (6R)-3-acetoxymethyl-8-oxo-5-thia-1-azabicyclo[4.2.0]oct-2-ene-2-carboxylic acid. Compounds that are named systematically use the numbering and orientation shown in **3**.

B.4 The cephalosporin antibiotics are ususally 7-acylaminocephalosporanic acid derivatives in which the configuration at position 7 is R.

C Ergot Alkaloids

C.1 Members of the ergoline group of substances are conveniently named by reference to either ergoline itself, **4**, or to (8R)-lysergamide, **5**. When names are so based the traditional numbering shown in **4** is used. In 9,10-dihydro compounds the configuration at position-10 needs to be specified.

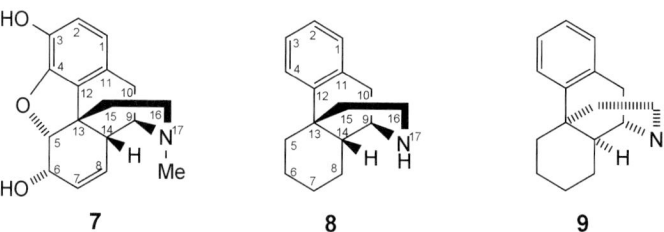

4   **5**   **6**

C.2 Members of the ergotamine group of substances are conveniently named by reference to ergotaman, **6**. Ergotamine itself is (5'R)-5'-benzyl-12'-hydroxy-2'-methyl-18-oxoergotaman-3',6'-dione.

D Morphines

D.1 Members of the morphine and codeine group of substances have traditionally been named with reference to morphine itself, **7**, using the numbering shown. However, names may be based more conveniently on either morphinan, **8**, or *ent*-morphinan, **9**.

7   **8**   **9**

D.2 Morphine, **7**, is (5R,6S)-4,5-epoxy-17-methyl-7,8-didehydromorphinan-3,6-diol.

D.3 In certain morphine derivatives, an etheno or ethano bridge is present joining positions 6 and 14 and a hydroxyalkyl side chain is present at position 7.

E   Penicillin Antibiotics

E.1   The penicillin antibiotics are conveniently named by reference to penicillanic acid (**10**, X = H) when the classical numbering shown is used.

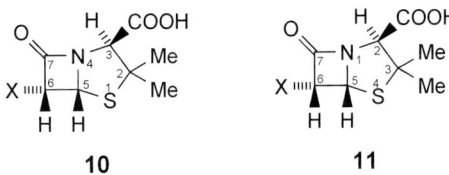

10   **11**

E.2   Penicillanic acid is systematically named as (2S,5R)-3,3-dimethyl-7-oxo-4-thia-1-azabicyclo[3.2.0]heptane-2-carboxylic acid. Compounds that are named systematically use the numbering shown in **11**.

E.3   The penicillin antibiotics are usually 6-acylamino penicillanic acid derivatives in which the configuration at position 6 is *R*.

F   Polypeptides

F.1   The following 3-letter and 1-letter symbols for amino-acids, authorised by the IUPAC-IUB Joint Commission on Biochemical Nomenclature, are used for representing the sequences of polypeptides:

Alanine	Ala	A	*Leucine*	Leu	L
Arginine	Arg	R	*Lysine*	Lys	K
Asparagine	Asn	N	*Methionine*	Met	M
Aspartic Acid	Asp	D	*Phenylalanine*	Phe	F
Cysteine	Cys	C	*Proline*	Pro	P
Glutamine	Gln	Q	*Serine*	Ser	S
Glutamic acid	Glu	E	*Threonine*	Thr	T
Glycine	Gly	G	*Tryptophan*	Trp	W
Histidine	His	H	*Tyrosine*	Tyr	Y
Isoleucine	Ile	I	*Valine*	Val	V

F.2   The following symbols recommended by the Joint Commission are also used:

2-Aminohexanoic acid	Ahx
Sarcosine	Sar
Pyroglyutamic acid	<Glu
tert-Butoxycarbonyl	Boc

F.3   When interpreting 3-letter sequences of amino-acid residues, the hyphen should be considered as part of the symbol. Its use to separate the individual residues or radicals may be illustrated by the following example:

$$Gly \quad = NH_2 \cdot CH_2 \cdot COOH$$
$$Gly- \quad = NH_2 \cdot CH_2 \cdot CO-$$
$$-Gly \quad = -NH \cdot CH_2 \cdot COOH$$
$$-Gly- \quad = -NH \cdot CH_2 \cdot CO-$$

and thus,

$$Gly-Gly-Gly = NH_2 \cdot CH_2 \cdot CO \cdot NH \cdot CH_2 \cdot CO \cdot NH \cdot CH_2 \cdot COOH$$

The residues are conventionally written with the amino group to the left and the carboxyl group to the right. This is implicit in the symbolism.

F.4   Where peptide sequences are shown using 3-letter symbols all amino-acids except glycine have the L-configuration unless otherwise indicated.

G Prostaglandins

G.1 Members of the prostaglandin group of substances are conveniently named by reference to prostanoic acid, **12**, using the numbering shown. Prostanoic acid may be systematically named as 7-[(1*S*,2*S*)-2-octylcyclopentyl]heptanoic acid. Dinoprost, **13**, may therefore be named as (5*Z*,13*E*)-(9*S*,11*R*,15*S*)-9,11,15-trihydroxyprosta-5,13-dienoic acid.

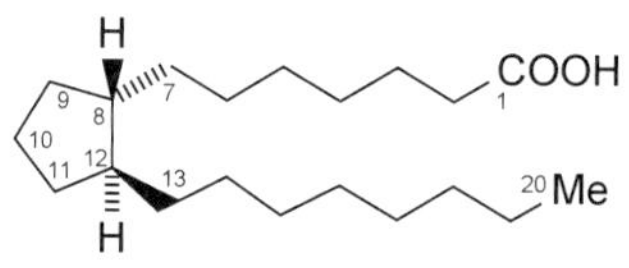

12

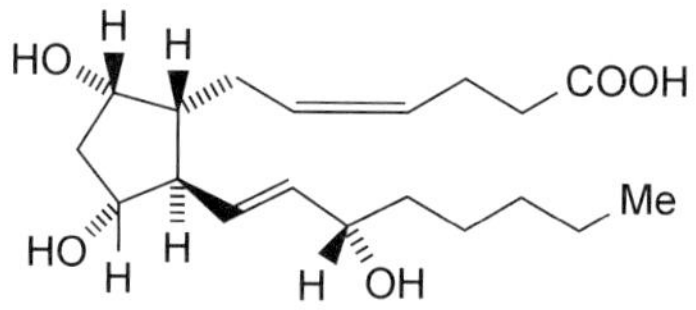

13

G.2 A convenient semi-trivial nomenclature exists by which prostaglandins (PG) are classified into groups **A** to **F** according to the substitution pattern in the cyclopentane ring (shown below). The subscript numerals 1, 2 and 3 refer to the number of double bonds found in the side-chains and subscript α refers to the configuration of the C-9 hydroxy group. Thus, **13** is referred to as PGF$_{2α}$.

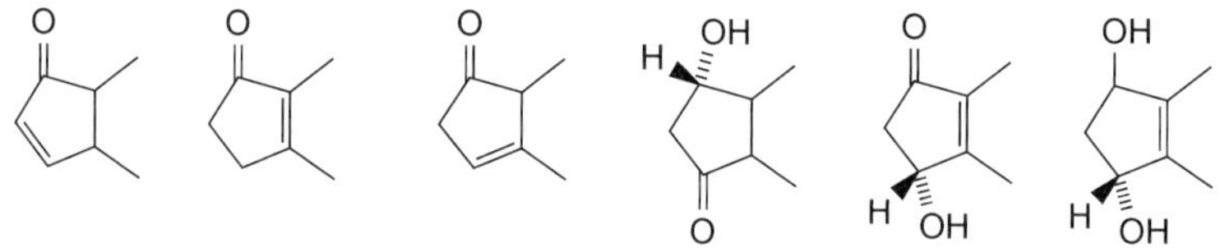

A   **B**   **C**   **D**   **E**   **F**

H Steroids

H.1 Steroids are drawn and numbered, and the rings lettered, as shown in **14**.

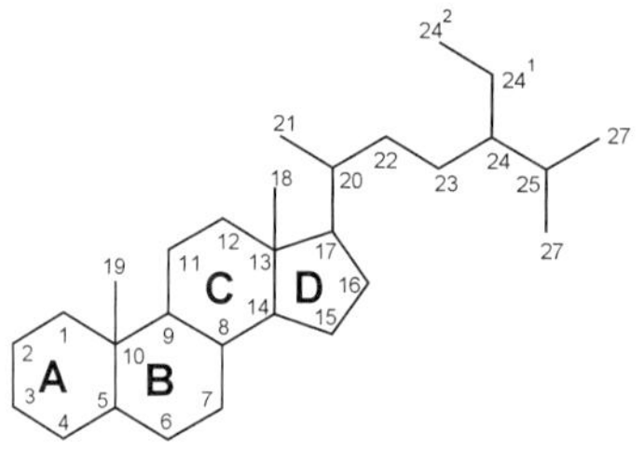

14 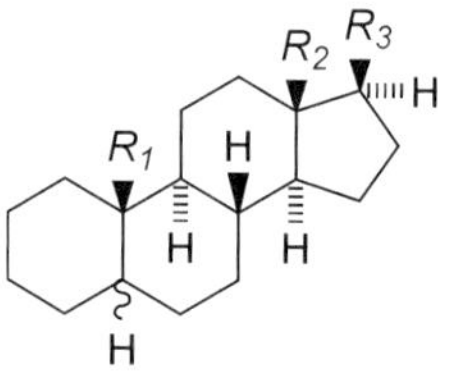   **15**

H.2 Steroids are named with reference to certain basic carbocycles some of which are defined in Table 1. When so drawn, dotted bonds are regarded as lying below the plane of the paper and are designated α, thickened bonds are regarded as lying above the plane of the paper and are designated β and bonds of unknown configuration are shown by a wavy line and are designated ξ.

Table I

	R_1	R_2	R_3
Gonane	H	H	H
Estrane	H	Me	H
Androstane	Me	Me	H
Pregnane	Me	Me	Et

H.3 When the hydrogen atom at C-5 is present, its configuration is always specified, eg 5α-pregnane, 5β-androstane. The configuration at centres, 8,9,10,13,14 and 17 is assumed to be as shown in **15** unless otherwise specified.

H.4 When inversion of the normal configuration occurs, the positions concerned are specified; and thus **16** is named 5β,17α-pregnane.

16

H.5 When inversion occurs at all of the defined asymmetric centres, the original name is preceded by the italicised prefix *ent-*. Racemates are indicated by use of the italicised prefix *rac-*.

H.6 Further fundamental carbocycles are defined in table II:

Table II

Side-chain	Carbon positions present
Cholane	20 - 24
Cholestane	20 - 27
Ergostane	20 - 27, 24'

In addition to retaining the configuration shown in **15**, C-20 has an R-configuration in each carbocycle and C-24 in ergostane has an S-configuration. However, additional substituents at positions C-17, C-20, C-21 may alter the *R* and *S* propriety descriptions without any change at C-20.

H.7 A large number of therapeutically active steroids bear a carbonyl group at position 3 and unsaturation across positions 5 and 5. Ring A is often aromatic in estrogens.

J   Tetracyclines

J.1 The tetracycline antibiotics are conveniently named by reference to tetracycline itself, **17**, (R = H), which may be defined as (4S,4aS,5aS,6S,12aS)-4-dimethylamino-1,4,4a,5,5a,6,11,12-octahydro-3,6,10,12,12a-pentahydroxy-6-methyl-1,11-dioxotetracene-2-carboxamide.

17

J.2 When analogues of tetracycline are named the stereodescriptors R and S may be subject to change even though the steric configuration usually remains unchanged. For example, in oxytetracycline, the hydroxyl group at position 5 imposes assignment inversions at positions 4a and 5a from S to R although the steric configuration at these positions remains unchanged.

J.3 When fully systematic names based on tetracene-2-carboxamide are used, the stereodescriptors given in Table III should be used.

Table III

	Position					
	4	**4a**	**5**	**5a**	**6**	**12a**
Chlortetracycline	*S*	*S*	-	*S*	*S*	*S*
Clomocycline	*S*	*S*	-	*S*	*S*	*S*
Demeclocycline	*S*	*S*	-	*S*	*S*	*S*
Doxycycline	*S*	*R*	*S*	*R*	*R*	*S*
Meclocycline	*S*	*R*	*S*	*R*	-	*S*
Methacycline	*S*	*R*	*S*	*R*	-	*S*
Minocycline	*S*	*S*	-	*R*	-	*S*
Oxytetracycline	*S*	*R*	*S*	*R*	*S*	*S*
Tetracycline	*S*	*S*	-	*S*	*S*	*S*

K   Tropanes

K.1   Members of the tropane group of substances are conveniently named by references to tropane itself, **18**, when the numbering and orientation shown are used. Tropane is defined as *N*-methyl-8-azabicyclo[3.2.1]octane.

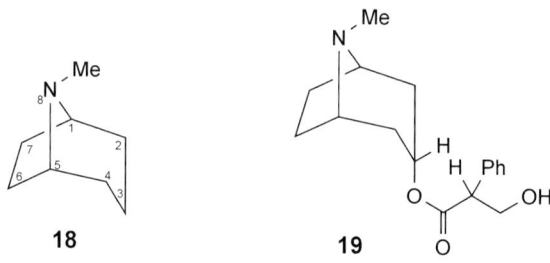

18   **19**

K.2   Atropine, **19**, is (1*R*,3*r*,5*S*,8*r*)-tropan-3-yl (*RS*)-tropate where the term *tropate* represents 3-hydroxy-2-phenylpropionate.

K.3   In the (−) -series the tropoyl side-chain has the (*S*) configuration, **20**.

K.4   In ψ-tropane compounds, **21**, the configuration at position-3 is designated as '3s'.

K.5   In hyoscine and other atropine derivatives bearing a 6,7-epoxy bridge, the configuration is as shown in **22**.

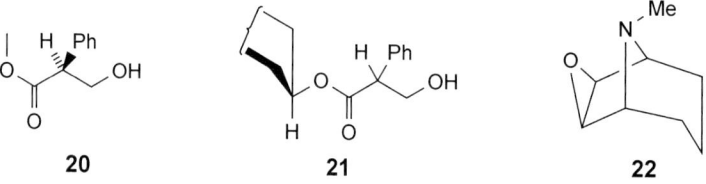

20   **21**   **22**

M   Xanthines

Members of the xanthine group of substances are conveniently named by references to purine, 23, when the non-systematic numbering shown is used.

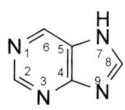

23

Appendix B:

Guidelines for the Construction of Pharmaceutical Trademarks

These guidelines are concerned with the following aspects:

1. Undesirable features in trade marks.
2. The qualification of trade marks by detached words, letters and numerals.
3. The relationship between trade marks and non proprietary names.

Guidelines

1. 1.1 A trade mark should not be liable to confusion in print, in handwriting or in speech with a trade mark of an existing product.

    1.2 A trade mark should not consist wholly of initial letters (other than acronyms) or code numbers.

    1.3 A trade mark should not convey misleading therapeutic or pharmaceutical connotations.

    1.4 Variations of a trade mark consisting of a single word within a range of related products should not be so small as to cause confusion.

    1.5 A trade mark of a discontinued product consisting of a single active ingredient should not be reassigned to a product containing a different single active ingredient.

2. 2.1 Indication of the strength of a product by words such as 'Forte' and 'Strong' in the trade mark should be avoided.

    2.2 Unnecessary qualification of a trade mark by letters should generally be avoided.

    2.3 Qualification of a trade mark by a detached Roman numeral should generally be avoided.

    2.4 Qualification of a trade mark by numbers should be avoided.

    2.5 With the exception of oral contraceptive and insulin products, numbers when used to qualify a trade mark should indicate the strength of the active ingredient.

3. 3.1 A trade mark should not be liable to confusion in handwriting, in print or in speech with an established non-proprietary name.

    3.2 Resolution 46.19 passed at the 1993 World Health Assembly requires that a trade mark should not incorporate a 'common stem' that has been adopted and published by the World Health Organization. The Resolution also discourages the use of trade marks derived from International Nonproprietary Names. These requirements should be observed.

Appendix C:

British Approved Names Assigned to Discontinued or Not Actively Marketed Products.

The following list indicates British Approved Names assigned to compounds that were abandoned during development or are no longer commercially available in the UK.

	Molecular Formula	CAS Number
Acetarsol	$C_8H_{10}AsNO_5$	*97-44-9*
Acetorphine	$C_{27}H_{35}NO_5$	*25333-77-1*
Actaplanin	N/A	*37305-75-2*
Adenosine Phosphate	$C_{10}H_{14}N_5O_7P$	*61-19-8*
Adicillin	$C_{14}H_{21}N_3O_6S$	*525-94-0*
Alletorphine	$C_{27}H_{35}NO_4$	*23758-80-7*
Allyestrenol	$C_{21}H_{32}O$	*432-60-0*
Allylprodine	$C_{18}H_{25}NO_2$	*25384-17-2*
Almasilate	$Al_2O_3 \cdot MgO \cdot 2SiO_2, xH_2O$	*50958-44-6*
Alphaprodine	$C_{16}H_{23}NO_2$	*77-20-3*
Alpidem	$C_{21}H_{23}ClN_3O$	*82626-01-5*
Aminopromazine	$C_{19}H_{25}N_3S$	*58-37-7*
Amodiaquine	$C_{20}H_{22}ClN_3O$	*86-42-0*
Amphomycin	N/A	*1402-82-0*
Amrinone	$C_{10}H_9N_3O$	*60719-84-8*
Angiotensinamide	$C_{49}H_{70}N_{14}O_{11}$	*53-73-6*
Anidoxime	$C_{21}H_{27}N_3O_3$	*34297-34-2*
Anisindione	$C_{16}H_{12}O_3$	*117-37-3*
Anistreplase	N/A	*81669-57-0*
Antilymphocyte Immunoglobulin	N/A	N/A
Arsanilic Acid	$C_6H_8AsNO_3$	*98-50-0*
Ascorbyl Gamolenate	$C_{24}H_{36}O_7$	*109791-32-4*
Azlocillin	$C_{20}H_{23}N_5O_6S$	*37091-66-0*
Benaprizine	$C_{21}H_{27}NO_3$	*22487-42-9*
Benoxaprofen	$C_{16}H_{12}ClNO_3$	*51234-28-7*
Benzethidine	$C_{23}H_{29}NO_3$	*3691-78-9*
Benzoctamine	$C_{18}H_{19}N$	*17243-39-9*
Bile Salts	N/A	N/A
Boldenone	$C_{30}H_{44}O_3$	*846-48-0*
Bovine Fibrin	N/A	N/A
Bromociclen	$C_8H_5BrCl_6$	*1715-40-8*
Buthalital Sodium	N/A	*510-90-7*
Butriptyline	$C_{21}H_{27}N$	*15686-37-0*
Calcium Benzamidosalicylate	$C_{28}H_{20}CaN_2O_8$	*528-96-1*
Canrenoic Acid	$C_{22}H_{30}O_4$	*4138-96-9*
Caproxamine	$C_{15}H_{25}N_3O$	*24047-16-3*
Carbinoxamine	$C_{16}H_{19}ClN_2O$	*486-16-8*
Carfecillin	$C_{23}H_{22}N_2O_6S$	*27025-49-6*
Carteolol	$C_{16}H_{24}N_2O_3$	*51781-06-7*
Cefaloram	$C_{18}H_{18}N_2O_6S$	*859-07-4*
Cefetecol	$C_{20}H_{17}N_5O_9S_2$	*117211-03-7*
Cefodizime	$C_{20}H_{20}N_6O_7S_4$	*69739-16-8*
Cefsulodin	$C_{22}H_{20}N_4O_8S_2$	*62587-73-9*
Ceftizoxime	$C_{13}H_{13}N_5O_5S_2$	*68401-81-0*
Cephalosporin C	$C_{16}H_{21}N_3OS_8$	*61-24-5*
Chloralodol	$C_8H_{15}Cl_3O_3$	*3563-58-4*
Chlormezanone	$C_{11}H_{12}ClNO_3S$	*80-77-3*
Chlormidazole	$C_{15}H_{13}ClN_2$	*3689-76-7*
Chlorothiazide	$C_7H_6ClN_3O_4S_2$	*58-94-6*
Ciclacillin	$C_{15}H_{23}N_3O_4S$	*3485-14-1*
Cicloprolol	$C_{18}H_{29}NO_4$	*63659-12-1*
Cinoxacin	$C_{12}H_{10}N_2O_5$	*28657-80-9*

	Molecular Formula	CAS Number
Cisapride	$C_{23}H_{29}ClFN_3O_4$	81098-60-4
Clamidoxic Acid	$C_{15}H_{11}Cl_2NO_4$	6170-69-0
Clemeprole	$C_{17}H_{20}ClNO$	71827-56-0
Clemizole	$C_{19}H_{20}ClN_3$	442-52-4
Clemizole Penicillin	$C_{19}H_{21}ClN_3 \cdot C_{16}H_{17}N_2O_4S$	6011-39-8
Clofibrate	$C_{12}H_{15}ClO_3$	637-07-0
Clomocycline	$C_{23}H_{25}ClN_2O_9$	1181-54-0
Cloroexolone	$C_{14}H_{17}ClN_2O_3S$	2127-01-7
Cloticasone	$C_{25}H_{31}ClF_2O_5S$	87556-66-9
Colaspase	N/A	9015-68-3
Coumetarol	$C_{21}H_{16}O_7$	4366-18-1
Cyclandelate	$C_{17}H_{24}O_3$	456-59-7
Cyclarbamate	$C_{21}H_{24}N_2O_4$	5779-54-4
Cycloserine	$C_3H_6N_2O_2$	68-41-7
Cycrimine	$C_{19}H_{29}NO$	77-39-4
Cypenamine	$C_{11}H_{15}N$	15302-54-9
Cyprenorphine	$C_{26}H_{33}NO_4$	4406-22-8
Decamethonium Iodide	$C_{16}H_{38}I_2N_2$	541-22-0
Dehydrocholic Acid	$C_{24}H_{34}O_5$	81-23-2
Demecarium Bromide	$C_{32}H_{52}Br_2N_4O_4$	56-94-0
Depramine	$C_{19}H_{22}N_2$	303-54-8
Deslorelin	$C_{64}H_{83}N_{17}O_{12}$	57773-65-6
Desonide	$C_{24}H_{32}O_6$	638-94-8
Dextrothyoxine	$C_{15}H_{10}I_4NO_4$	137-53-1
Diacetamide	$C_{10}H_{11}NO_3$	2623-33-8
Diampromide	$C_{21}H_{28}N_2O$	552-25-0
Diamthazole	$C_{15}H_{23}N_3OS$	95-27-2
Dibenzepin	$C_{18}H_{21}N_3O$	4498-32-2
Dibupyrone	$C_{16}H_{22}N_3NaO_4S$	1046-17-9
Dichloralphenazone	$C_4H_6Cl_6O_4 \cdot C_{11}H_{13}N_2O$	480-30-8
Diclofenamide	$C_6H_6Cl_2N_2O_4S_2$	120-97-8
Dieldrin	$C_{12}H_8Cl_6O$	60-57-1
Diethadione	$C_8H_{13}NO_3$	702-54-5
Dihydroergotamine	$C_{33}H_{37}N_5O_5$	511-12-6
Di-iodohydroxyquinoline	$C_9H_5I_2NO$	83-73-8
Dimefline	$C_{20}H_{21}NO_3$	1165-48-6
Dimetotiazine	$C_{19}H_{25}N_3O_2S_2$	7456-24-8
Diprobutine	$C_{10}H_{23}N$	61822-36-4
Disofenin	$C_{18}H_{26}N_2O_5$	65717-97-7
Disulfamide	$C_7H_9ClN_2O_4S$	671-88-5
Dofamium Chloride	$C_{25}H_{44}ClN_3O_2$	54063-35-3
Droxypropine	$C_{18}H_{27}NO_3$	15599-26-5
Emylcamate	$C_7H_{15}NO_2$	78-28-4
Enbucrilate	$C_8H_{11}NO_2$	6606-65-1
Enpiprazole	$C_{16}H_{21}ClN_4$	31729-24-5
Etafedrine	$C_{12}H_{19}NO$	7681-72-0
Ethotoin	$C_{11}H_{12}N_2O_2$	86-35-1
Ethyl Dibunate	$C_{20}H_{28}O_3S$	5560-69-0
Etidocaine	$C_{17}H_{28}N_2O$	36637-18-0
Etifoxine	$C_{17}H_{17}ClN_2O$	21715-46-8
Etoglucid	$C_{12}H_{22}O_6$	1954-28-5
Etosalamide	$C_{11}H_{15}NO_3$	15302-15-5
Etretinate	$C_{23}H_{30}O_3$	54350-48-0
Famprofazone	$C_{24}H_{31}N_3O$	22811-35-2
Fantridone	$C_{18}H_{20}N_2O$	17692-37-4
Fazadinium Bromide	$C_{28}H_{24}Br_2N_6$	49564-56-9
Fencamfamin	$C_{15}H_{21}N$	1209-98-9
Fenclozic Acid	$C_{11}H_8ClNO_2S$	17969-20-9
Fenetylline	$C_{18}H_{23}N_5O_2$	3736-08-1
Fenimide	$C_{13}H_{15}NO_2$	60-45-7
Fenmetramide	$C_{11}H_{13}NO_2$	5588-29-4
Fenoxypropazine	$C_9H_{14}N_2O$	3818-37-9
Fenpipramide	$C_{21}H_{26}N_2O$	77-01-0
Fenpiprane	$C_{20}H_{25}N$	3540-95-2
Fetoxilate	$C_{36}H_{36}N_2O_3$	54063-45-5
Flazalone	$C_{19}H_{19}F_2NO_2$	21221-18-1

	Molecular Formula	CAS Number
Fluclorolone Acetonide	$C_{24}H_{29}Cl_2FO_5$	*3693-39-8*
Flumedroxone	$C_{22}H_{29}F_3O_3$	*15687-21-5*
Flumethiazide	$C_8H_6F_3N_3O_4S_2$	*148-56-10*
Flurotyl	$C_4H_4F_6O$	*333-36-8*
Fosazepam	$C_{18}H_{18}ClN_2O_2P$	*35322-07-7*
Fosequinan	$C_{11}H_{10}FNO_2S$	*76568-02-0*
Fosquidone	$C_{28}H_{22}NO_6P$	*114517-04-3 (sodium salt)*
Furaltadone	$C_{13}H_{16}N_4O_6$	*139-91-3*
Furethidine	$C_{21}H_{31}NO_4$	*2385-81-10*
Furomine	$C_{20}H_{32}N_2O_4$	*142996-66-5*
Galdansetron	$C_{18}H_{19}N_3O$	*116684-92-5*
Gamolenic Acid	$C_{18}H_{30}O_2$	*506-26-3*
Glucalox	N/A	*12182-48-8*
Glucuronamide	$C_6H_{11}NO_6$	*3574-23-0*
Glysobuzole	$C_{13}H_{17}N_3O_3S_2$	*3567-08-6*
Grepafloxacin	$C_{19}H_{22}FN_3O_3$	*119914-60-2*
Growth Hormone	N/A	N/A
Guanacline	$C_{29}H_{38}N_8O_8$	*16545-11-2*
Hedaquinium Chloride	$C_{34}H_{46}Cl_2N_2$	*4310-89-8*
Heptabarb	$C_{13}H_{18}N_2O_3$	*509-86-4*
Hexoprenaline	$C_{22}H_{32}N_2O_6$	*3215-70-1*
Hydrargaphen	$C_{33}H_{24}Hg_2O_6S_2$	*14235-86-0*
Hydroxytetracaine	$C_{16}H_{16}N_4O$	*495-99-8*
Inproquone	$C_{16}H_{22}N_2O_4$	*436-40-8*
Isamoxole	$C_{12}H_{20}N_2O_2$	*57067-46-6*
Isoetarine	$C_{13}H_{21}NO_3$	*530-08-5*
Isoprazone	$C_{15}H_{18}N_2O$	*56463-68-4*
Isothipendyl	$C_{16}H_{19}N_3S$	*482-15-5*
Isotiquimide	$C_{11}H_{14}N_2S$	*56717-18-1*
Kallidinogenase	N/A	*9001-01-8*
Ketazolam	$C_{20}H_{17}ClN_2O_3$	*27223-35-4*
Lachesine Chloride	$C_{20}H_{26}ClNO_3$	*1164-38-1*
Lanatoside C	$C_{49}H_{76}O_{20}$	*17575-22-3*
Lanproston	$C_{24}H_{31}ClO_7$	*131349-68-3*
Latamoxef	$C_{20}H_{20}N_6O_9S$	*64952-97-2*
Laudexium Metilsulfate	$C_{54}H_{80}N_2O_{16}S_2$	*3253-60-9*
Laurolinium Acetate	$C_{24}H_{38}N_2O_2$	*146-37-2*
Lavoltidine	$C_{19}H_{29}N_5O_2$	*76956-02-0*
Levamfetamine	$C_9H_{13}N$	*156-34-3*
Liver Extract	N/A	N/A
Lorcinadol	$C_{17}H_{19}ClN_4$	*104719-71-3*
Lypressin	$C_{46}H_{65}N_{13}O_{12}S$	*50-57-7*
Lysergide	$C_{20}H_{25}N_3O$	*50-37-3*
Maletamer	N/A	*9006-26-2*
Mazindol	$C_{16}H_{13}ClN_2O$	*22232-71-9*
Mebezonium Iodide	$C_{19}H_{40}I_2N_2$	*7681-78-9*
Mebhydroline	$C_{19}H_{20}N_2$	*524-81-2*
Meclofenoxate	$C_{12}H_{16}ClNO_3$	*51-68-3*
Mepenzolate Bromide	$C_{21}H_{26}BrNO_3$	*76-90-4*
Mephenytoin	$C_{12}H_{14}N_2O_2$	*50-12-4*
Meprotixol	$C_{19}H_{23}NO_2S$	*4295-63-0*
Mestanolone	$C_{20}H_{32}O_2$	*521-11-9*
Metacetamol	$C_8H_9NO_2$	*621-42-1*
Metallibure	$C_7H_{14}N_4S_2$	*926-93-2*
Metamfazone	$C_{11}H_{11}N_3O$	*54063-49-9*
Metetoin	$C_{12}H_{14}N_2O_2$	*5969-06-0*
Methallenestril	$C_{18}H_{22}NO_3$	*517-18-0*
Methandienone	$C_{20}H_{28}O_2$	*72-63-9*
Methoserpride	$C_{33}H_{40}N_2O_9$	*865-04-3*
Methyclothiazide	$C_9H_{11}Cl_2N_3O_4S_2$	*135-07-9*
Methylchromone	$C_{10}H_8O_2$	*85-90-50*
Methylephedrine	$C_{11}H_{17}NO$	*552-79-4*
Metioprim	$C_{14}H_{18}N_4O_2S$	*68902-57-8*
Metisazone	$C_{10}H_{10}N_4OS$	*1910-68-5*
Metofoline	$C_{20}H_{24}ClNO_2$	*2154-02-1*

	Molecular Formula	CAS Number
Metomidate	$C_{13}H_{14}N_2O_2$	5377-20-8
Metoserpate	$C_{24}H_{32}N_2O_5$	1178-28-5
Mezlocillin	$C_{21}H_{25}N_5O_8S_2$	51481-65-3
Mibefradil	$C_{29}H_{38}FN_3O_3$	116644-53-2
Milenperone	$C_{22}H_{23}ClFN_3O_2$	59831-64-0
Minaprine	$C_{17}H_{22}N_4O$	25905-77-5
Minepenate	$C_{18}H_{27}NO_3$	13877-99-1
Mioflazine	$C_{29}H_{30}Cl_2F_2N_4O_2$	79467-23-6
Mitoclomine	$C_{16}H_{19}Cl_2NO$	17692-54-5
Mitotenamine	$C_{13}H_{15}BrClNS$	7696-00-6
Morazone	$C_{23}H_{27}N_3O_2$	6536-18-1
Muzolimine	$C_{11}H_{11}Cl_2N_3O$	55294-15-0
Nafenopin	$C_{20}H_{22}O_3$	3771-19-5
Nanterinone	$C_{15}H_{15}N_3O$	102791-47-9
Neocinchophen	$C_{19}H_{17}NO_2$	485-34-7
Netivudine	$C_{12}H_{14}N_2O_6$	84588-93-0
Nicametate	$C_{12}H_{18}N_2O_2$	3099-52-3
Niclofolan	$C_{12}H_6Cl_2N_2O_6$	10331-57-4
Nicofuranose	$C_{30}H_{24}N_4O_{10}$	15351-13-0
Nilprazole	$C_{26}H_{33}N_5O_2$	60662-19-3
Nimorazole	$C_9H_{14}N_4O_3$	6506-37-2
Noracymethadol	$C_{22}H_{29}NO_2$	50572-73-7
Norethandrolone	$C_{20}H_{30}O_2$	52-78-8
Noretynodrel	$C_{20}H_{26}O_2$	68-23-5
Norgestomet	$C_{23}H_{31}NO_3$	35189-28-7
Norletimol	$C_{14}H_{13}NO$	886-08-8
Octaverine	$C_{23}H_{27}NO_5$	549-68-8
Octoxinol	N/A	N/A
Oletimol	$C_{15}H_{15}NO$	5879-67-4
Ostreogrycin	N/A	11006-76-1
Oxamniquine	$C_{14}H_{21}N_3O_3$	21738-42-1
Oxatomide	$C_{27}H_{30}N_4O$	N/A
Oxycinchophen	$C_{16}H_{11}NO_3$	485-89-2
Oxyphenbutazone	$C_{19}H_{20}N_2O_3$	129-20-4
Pancreozymin	N/A	N/A
Panidazole	$C_{11}H_{12}N_4O_2$	13752-33-5
Papapveroline	$C_{16}H_{13}NO_4$	574-77-6
Paramethadione	$C_7H_{11}NO_3$	115-67-3
Parvaquone	$C_{16}H_{16}O_3$	4042-30-2
Pecazine	$C_{19}H_{22}N_2S$	60-89-9
Pecilocin	$C_{17}H_{25}NO_3$	19504-77-9
Pemoline	$C_9H_8N_2O_2$	2152-34-3
Penamecillin	$C_{19}H_{22}N_2O_6S$	983-85-7
Penicillinase	N/A	9001-74-5
Pendecamaine	$C_{23}H_{46}N_2O_3$	32954-43-1
Pentacosactride	$C_{142}H_{222}N_{42}O_{31}$	17692-62-5
Pentacynium Metilsulfate	$C_{30}H_{48}N_3O_{13}S_3$	77-12-3
Pentaerithrityl Tetranitrate	$C_5H_8N_4O_{12}$	78-11-5
Pentafluranol	$C_{17}H_{15}F_5O_2$	54043-46-8
Pentalamide	$C_{12}H_{17}NO_2$	5579-06-6
Pentamethonium Iodide	$C_{11}H_{28}I_2N_2$	5282-80-4
Penthienate	$C_{17}H_{27}NO_3S$	22064-27-3
Peratizole	$C_{17}H_{26}N_4S_2$	29992-13-4
Perhexiline	$C_{19}H_{35}N$	6621-47-2
Perlapine	$C_{19}H_{21}N_3$	1977-11-3
Phenacemide	$C_9H_{10}N_2O_2$	63-98-9
Phenactropinium Chloride	$C_{24}H_{28}ClNO_4$	3784-89-2
Phenadoxone	$C_{23}H_{29}NO_2$	4467-84-5
Phenazocine	$C_{22}H_{27}NO$	127-35-5
Phenazopyridine	$C_{11}H_{11}N_5$	94-78-0
Phenylcyclidine	$C_{17}H_{25}N$	77-10-1
Pheneticillin	$C_{17}H_{20}N_2O_5S$	147-55-7
Phenformin	$C_{10}H_{15}N_5$	114-86-3
Phenglutarimide	$C_{17}H_{24}N_2O_2$	1156-05-4
Phenmetrazine	$C_{11}H_{15}NO$	134-49-6

	Molecular Formula	CAS Number
Phenoperidine	$C_{23}H_{29}NO_3$	*562-26-5*
Phthalylsulfacetamide	$C_{16}H_{14}N_2O_6S$	*131-69-1*
Picumast	$C_{25}H_{29}ClN_2O_3$	*39577-19-0*
Pifenate	$C_{22}H_{27}NO_2$	*15686-87-0*
Piminodine	$C_{23}H_{30}N_2O_2$	*13495-09-5*
Pimonidazole	$C_{11}H_{18}N_4O_3$	*70132-50-2*
Pipamazine	$C_{21}H_{24}ClN_3OS$	*84-04-8*
Pipenzolate Bromide	$C_{22}H_{28}BrNO_3$	*125-51-9*
Piperoxan	$C_{14}H_{19}NO_2$	*59-39-2*
Pipoxolan	$C_{22}H_{25}NO_3$	*23744-24-3*
Pipradrol	$C_{18}H_{21}NO$	*467-60-7*
Piprinhydrinate	$C_{26}H_{30}ClN_5O_3$	*606-90-6*
Pirbuterol	$C_{12}H_{20}N_2O_3$	*38677-81-5*
Pirenperone	$C_{23}H_{24}FN_3O_2$	*75444-65-4*
Pirenzepine	$C_{19}H_{21}N_5O_2$	*28797-61-7*
Pirquinozol	$C_{11}H_9N_3O_2$	*65950-99-4*
Pivampicillin	$C_{22}H_{29}N_3O_6S$	*33817-20-8*
Pivhydrazine	$C_{12}H_{18}N_2O$	*306-19-4*
Plicamycin	$C_{52}H_{76}O_{24}$	*18378-89-7*
Pituitary Extract	N/A	N/A
Polidexide	N/A	*56227-39-5*
Polyestradiol Phosphate	N/A	*28014-46-2*
Polyvinox	N/A	N/A
Porfimer Sodium	N/A	*87806-31-3*
Porfiromycin	$C_{16}H_{20}N_4O_5$	*801-52-5*
Poskine	$C_{20}H_{25}NO_5$	*585-14-8*
Prampine	$C_{20}H_{27}NO_4$	*7009-65-6*
Prazitone	$C_{16}H_{19}N_3O_3$	*2409-26-9*
Pregnelone	$C_{21}H_{32}O_2$	*145-13-1*
Pretamazium Iodide	$C_{29}H_{29}IN_2S$	*24840-59-3*
Procarbazine	$C_{12}H_{19}N_3O$	*671-16-9*
Proclonol	$C_{16}H_{14}Cl_2O$	*14088-71-2*
Profadol	$C_{14}H_{21}NO$	*428-37-50*
Prolintane	$C_{15}H_{23}N$	*493-92-5*
Promoxolane	$C_{10}H_{20}O_3$	*470-43-9*
Pronetalol	$C_{15}H_{19}NO$	*54-80-8*
Propanidid	$C_{18}H_{27}NO_5$	*1421-14-3*
Properidine	$C_{16}H_{23}NO_2$	*561-76-2*
Propyl Docetrizoate	$C_{14}H_{14}I_3NO_4$	*5579-08-8*
Prothipendyl	$C_{16}H_{19}N_3S$	*303-69-5*
Proxicromil	$C_{17}H_{18}O_5$	*60400-92-2*
Pyrrocaine	$C_{14}H_{20}N_2O$	*2210-77-7*
Pyrvinium Pamoate	$C_{75}H_{70}N_6O_6$	*3546-41-6*
Quadrosilan	$C_{18}H_{28}NO_4Si$	*3546-41-6*
Racemethorphan	$C_{18}H_{25}NO$	*510-53-2*
Razoxane	$C_{11}H_{16}N_4O_4$	*21416-87-1*
Remoxipride	$C_{16}H_{23}BrN_2O_3$	*80125-14-0*
Ribostamycin	$C_{17}H_{34}N_4O_{10}$	*25546-65-0*
Rimiterol	$C_{12}H_{17}NO_3$	*32953-89-2*
Rolgamidine	$C_9H_{16}N_4O$	*66608-04-6*
Rolicyprine	$C_{14}H_{16}N_2O_2$	*2829-19-8*
Rosoxacin	$C_{17}H_{14}N_2O_3$	*40034-42-2*
Rufocrommycin	$C_{25}H_{22}N_4O_8$	*3930-19-6*
Salinazid	$C_{13}H_{11}N_3O_2$	*495-84-1*
Sabeluzole	$C_{22}H_{26}FN_3O_2S$	*104153-38-0*
Salsalate	$C_{14}H_{10}O_5$	*552-94-3*
Secbutabarbital	$C_{10}H_{15}N_2NaO_3$	*125-40-6*
Sodium Glucaspaldrate	$C_{42}H_{54}Al_2Na_8O_{38}$	*12214-50-5*
Spirilene	$C_{24}H_{28}FN_3O$	*357-66-4*
Stirimazole	$C_{14}H_{11}N_3O_4$	*30529-16-9*
Streptoniazid	$C_{27}H_{44}N_{10}O_{12}$	*4480-58-4*
Styramate	$C_9H_{11}NO_3$	*94-35-9*
Sucralox	N/A	*12040-73-2*
Sulfamerazine	$C_{11}H_{12}N_4O_2S$	*127-79-7*
Sulfamoprine	$C_{12}H_{14}N_4O_4S$	*155-91-9*

	Molecular Formula	CAS Number
Sulfapyrazole	$C_{16}H_{16}N_4O_2S$	*852-19-7*
Sulfapyridine	$C_{11}H_{11}N_3O_2S$	*144-83-2*
Sulfasomizole	$C_{10}H_{11}N_3O_2S$	*632-00-8*
Sultamicillin	$C_{25}H_{30}N_4O_9S_2$	*76497-13-7*
Sutilains	N/A	*12211-28-8*
Syrosingopine	$C_{35}H_{42}N_2O_{11}$	*84-36-6*
Talampicillin	$C_{24}H_{23}N_3O_6S$	*47747-56-8*
Taloximine	$C_{12}H_{16}N_4O_2$	*17243-68-4*
Tameridone	$C_{22}H_{26}N_6O_2$	*104269-99-0*
Taurolidine	$C_7H_{16}N_4O_4S_2$	*19388-87-5*
Terodiline	$C_{20}H_{27}N$	*15793-40-5*
Thiethylperazine	$C_{22}H_{29}N_3S_2$	*1420-55-9*
Thiopropazate	$C_{23}H_{28}ClN_3O_2S$	*84-06-0*
Ticarbodine	$C_{15}H_{19}F_3N_2S$	*31932-09-9*
Tigloidine	$C_{13}H_{21}NO_2$	*495-83-0*
Tilidate	$C_{17}H_{23}NO_2$	*20380-58-90*
Tiocarlide	$C_{23}H_{32}N_2O_2S$	*910-86-1*
Tipentosin	$C_{21}H_{25}NO_3S$	*95588-11-7*
Tiprostanide	$C_{33}H_{45}NO_6S$	*67040-53-3*
Tocainide	$C_{11}H_{16}N_2O$	*41708-72-9*
Tofenacin	$C_{17}H_{21}NO$	*15301-93-6*
Tolcapone	$C_{14}H_{11}NO_5$	*134308-13-7*
Tolmetin	$C_{15}H_{15}NO_3$	*426171-23-3*
Tolpropamine	$C_{18}H_{23}N$	*5632-44-0*
Tolpiprazole	$C_{17}H_{24}N_4$	*420326-13-0*
Tretamine	$C_9H_{12}N_6$	*51-18-3*
Trethinium Tosilate	$C_{19}H_{25}NO_3S$	*1748-43-2*
Triamcinolone Hexacetonide	$C_{30}H_{41}FO_7$	*5611-51-8*
Triaziquone	$C_{12}H_{13}N_3O_2$	*68-76-80*
Triazolam	$C_{17}H_{12}Cl_2N_4$	*28911-01-5*
Tricyclamol Chloride	$C_{20}H_{32}ClNO$	*3818-88-0*
Trifluperidol	$C_{22}H_{23}F_4NO_2$	*749-13-3*
Trimetaphan Camsilate	$C_{32}H_{40}N_2O_5S_2$	*68-91-7*
Trimethidinium Methosulphate	$C_{19}H_{42}N_2O_8S_2$	*7009-82-7*
Triparanol	$C_{27}H_{32}ClNO_2$	*78-41-10*
Tripelennamine	$C_{16}H_{21}N_3$	*91-81-6*
Troglitazone	$C_{24}H_{27}NO_5S$	*97322-87-7*
Trolnitrate Phosphate	$C_6H_{12}N_4O_9,2H_3PO_4$	*588-42-1*
Troxonium Tosilate	$C_{25}H_{37}NO_8S$	*391-70-8*
Tuaminoheptane	$C_7H_{17}N$	*123-82-0*
Tulobuterol	$C_{12}H_{18}ClNO$	*41570-61-0*
Urokinase	N/A	*9039-53-6*
Velnacrine	$C_{13}H_{14}N_2O$	*104675-29-8*
Verazide	$C_{15}H_{15}N_3O_3$	*93-47-0*
Vidarabine	$C_{10}H_{13}N_5O_4$	*5536-17-4*
Viloxazine	$C_{13}H_{19}NO_3$	*46817-91-8*
Viomycin	$C_{25}H_{43}N_{13}O_{10}$	*32988-50-4*
Xamoterol	$C_{16}H_{25}N_3O_5$	*81801-12-9*
Xylamide Tosilate	$C_{26}H_{32}N_2O_5S$	*6443-40-9*
Zimeldine	$C_{16}H_{17}BrN_2$	*56775-88-3*
Zolazoxamine	$C_7H_5ClN_2O$	*61-80-3*

information & publishing solutions

Published by TSO (The Stationery Office) and available from:

Online
www.tsoshop.co.uk

Mail, Telephone, Fax & E-mail
TSO
PO Box 29, Norwich, NR3 1GN
Telephone orders/General enquiries: 0870 600 5522
Fax orders: 0870 600 5533
E-mail: customer.services@tso.co.uk
Textphone 0870 240 3701

TSO@Blackwell and other Accredited Agents